ILLUSTRATED
Slovak History

ILLUSTRATED

Slovak History

A STRUGGLE FOR SOVEREIGNTY IN CENTRAL EUROPE

ANTON SPIESZ and DUSAN CAPLOVIC

First English Edition:
Translated and Enhanced with
Notes, Index, Bibliography, and Updates

Editor: Ladislaus J. Bolchazy
et alii

Bolchazy-Carducci Publishers
Wauconda, Illinois, USA

Illustrated Slovak History
A Struggle for Sovereignty in Central Europe
by **Anton Spiesz**
An Afterword
by **Dusan Caplovic**

English Edition
Edited by
Ladislaus J. Bolchazy
in collaboration with
Translators
Joseph J. Palus, Jr.
Albert Devine, David Daniel, Michael Kopanic, and Ivan Reguli
Notes by
Michael Kopanic
Academic Consultants
Martin Votruba, Albert Devine, Milan S. Durica, Frantisek Vnuk,
Ivan Reguli, Charles Sabatos, Patrick Romane, John Karch, Zdenko G. Alexy, et alii
Associate Editors
Joseph J. Palus, Jr., Albert Devine, Patrick Romane and **Richard Wood**
This book was made possible by
Slovak-American International Cultural Foundation (SAICF) and
Donna Schmitz, Dave and Autumn Schmitz, Jeff Schmitz, and Mike Schmitz

Bolchazy-Carducci Publishers, Inc.
1000 Brown Street, Unit 101
Wauconda, Illinois 60084 USA
www.bolchazy.com

ISBN-10 0-86516-500-9, Hardbound   ISBN-10 0-86516-426-6, Paperback
ISBN-13 978-0-86516-500-7   ISBN-13 978-0-86516-426-0

Printed in Slovakia, 2006
Originally published as *Ilustrovane dejiny Slovenska: Na ceste k sebauvedomeniu*,
copyright 1992, 1999, 2002 © Perfekt, a.s., Bratislava, Slovakia

---

Library of Congress Cataloging-in-Publication Data

Špiesz, Anton.
   [Ilustrované dejiny Slovenska. English]
   Illustrated Slovak history : a struggle for sovereignty in Central Europe / Anton Špiesz and Dušan
Čaplovič ; translated and enhanced with notes, index, and bibliography ; editor, Ladislaus J. Bolchazy
et alii.-- 1st English ed.
     p. cm.
   Includes bibliographical references and index.
   ISBN 0-86516-426-6 (pbk.) -- ISBN 0-86516-500-9 (hardbound)
   1. Slovakia--History. I. Title: Slovak history. II.Čaplovič, Dušan. III. Bolchazy, Ladislaus J. IV. Title.

DB2763.S6813 2004
943.73--dc22

2004011379

Table of Contents

Preface to the English Edition by Kopanic. vii

Foreword by Gasparovic 1

Publisher's Statement. 3

1/ Beginnings of History in Slovakia 6

2/ Slavic Arrival: The Founding and Significance of their First State 16

3/ The Arrival of the Magyars: Building of Hungary 26

4/ The Late Medieval Age 40

5/ The First Two Centuries of the Modern Era (1526-1681) 62

6/ A Hunderd Years of Re-Catholicization (1681-1781) 76

7/ Headed towards Revolution (1781-1848) 88

8/ The Revolution of 1848-1849 102

9/ Events Leading to the Austro-Hungarian Compromise (1849-1867) 124

10/ The Era of Dual Monarchy (1867-1918) 142

11/ Between Two World Wars (1918-1939) 188

12/ During the Second World War (1939-1945) 208

13/ Between 1945 and 1960. 234

14/ Socialism: from Rise to Fall (1960-1989). 256

An Afterword by Dusan Caplovic 262

A Decade of Sovereignty (1993-2004). 300

Endnotes 307

Maps 365

Bibliography 372

List of Rulers and Presidents 397

Index 398

ת ת ת ת ת ת ת

List of Maps

Slovak Counties 'zupy' in Hungary*. . . . . vi*

Central Europe, 9th Century**. 365

Central Europe, 1918–1923** 366

Slovakia in the Twentieth Century** 367

Central Europe ca. 1930, with list of districts** 368

Central Europe, 2000, with list of districts** 370

Slovak counties 'zupy' in Hungary

1 Part of Zvolen county until beginning of 14th century
2 Malohont – part of Hont county until 1802
3 Shifting county affiliation in Middle Ages
4 Part of Moson county (Hungary)
5 Part of Győr county (Hungary)

Preface to the English Edition

It is no easy task to catch and hold a reader's attention in a world so full of distractions; it is even harder to nudge him into reading the history of a small nation in the heart of Europe. Nevertheless, such is Anton Spiesz' endeavor in his final work, a survey of Slovak history. Published in the wake of the Velvet Revolution, it is the first such survey attempted after the fall of Communism.

The integrity of such an outstanding Slovak historian as Anton Spiesz, Ph.D., guarantees an interesting read. Dr. Spiesz is known for his tireless search for historical truth, his revisions of older concepts, and his presentation of new views, even in the face of controversy or derision. The timely publication of such a high-quality history is all the more welcome, since its author no longer feels obligated to nod his head to the various 'powers that be', whether smiling thankfully to the left or respectfully to the right.

Spiesz dedicated many years to research at the Historical Institute of the Slovak Academy of Sciences. As an establishment institution with a predetermined methodology, it posited a 'politically correct' Marxist interpretation of Slovakia's past. Eventually dismissed from the Institute over methodological conflicts, Spiesz could not resume his work there until after the political upheaval of 1989. He eagerly welcomed the new historical development that allowed his lungs to once again breathe the bracing air of freedom. Concerns of censorship no longer dimming his thoughts, he was again able to tackle 'unclear issues', no matter their complexity. In that moment of catharsis this book began to take shape.

The monograph is in many ways a consolidation of several basic studies Spiesz had previously published both in Slovakia and abroad: *Manufakturne obdobie na Slovensku* (The Era of Manufacturing in Slovakia), 1961; *Poddani Tekova v 18. storoci* (Serfdom in 18th Century Tekov. A joint study with J. Watzky), 1966; *Remeslo na Slovensku v obdobi cechov* (Slovakian Crafts during the Period of Guilds), 1972; *Statuty bratislavskych cechov* (The By-laws of Bratislava's Guilds), 1978; *Slobodne kralovske mesta na Slovensku v rokoch 1680–1780* (Royally Chartered Towns in Slovakia 1680–1780), 1983; *Remesla, cechy a manufaktury na Slovensku* (Crafts, Guilds and Manufacturing Plants in Slovakia), 1983; and *Bratislava v 18. storoci* (Bratislava in the 18th Century), 1987.

Anton Spiesz also made significant contributions to the following works: *Prehled dejin Ceskoslovenska* (A Survey of Czecho-Slovak History), 2 vol. 1981; and *Dejiny Slovenska* (A History of Slovakia), 1990. He also cooperated with other scholars in compiling the following: *Historicky atlas CSR* (An Historical Atlas of the Czecho-Slovak Republic); *Dejiny ceskoslovenskeho vojenstvi* (An History of the Czecho-Slovak Military); *Hospodarske dejiny*

Ceskoslovenska (An Economic History of Czecho-Slovakia); and finally, *Encyklopedia Slovenska* (An Encyclopedia of Slovakia).

His book is nevertheless something quite exceptional since its scope is the whole sweep of our history rather than isolated epochs. Though it may at times seem so, it is not strictly scholarly, since it lacks the relevant apparatus, such as references, registers, etc. Nor has it any pretensions to being a textbook in modern history. Simply put, it is a retrospective by one of the most scholarly and productive of Slovak historians, the subjective testimony of an erudite, well-rounded individual. This first English edition attempts to correct the deficiencies with copious notes, extensive bibliography, index, and over 300 color illustrations and six maps.

* * *

Slovakia is a small, relatively unknown country, lying inconspicuously among larger neighbors: Austria, the Czech Republic, Poland, Hungary and Ukraine. It is not a trouble-making state, nor does it grab headlines; indeed, few people in the West are even aware of its existence. Many Americans confuse it with Slovenia to the south (beyond Austria and Hungary) or relate it to the former Yugoslavia. It is a very recent addition to the European family of states, but it has a long, eventful history and a rich culture. Anton Spiesz' book helps fill the large gap in works on the subject, while aiming at a reasonably educated readership, not just scholars.

Though not necessarily major players, the inhabitants of Slovakia have been deeply involved in European history. Small in size, Slovakia numbers slightly over 5.3 million inhabitants, predominantly of Slovak ethnicity, but with a sizeable Hungarian component of about 600,000. Smaller minorities include Carpatho-Rusyns, Czechs, Romany (Gypsies), and some Poles and Germans, all of whom reflect the fluidity of migration in past centuries.

Slovakia merits attention as a significant component of the patchwork of European states and ethnicities. Moreover, some 1.8 million Americans trace their ancestry to it, many of whom may be presumed to share an interest in the land of their forebears. In the past, Slovakia has been predominantly rural and agricultural, though it was an important center of Hungarian mining and, in the 16th and 17th Centuries, when the rest of Hungary lay under Turkish occupation, even of industry. Nearly a millennium after the fall of Great Moravia, the Kingdom of Hungary and then the Austrian Habsburg dynasty controlled Slovakia's fortunes. This long period came to a close in 1918 with the devastation of World War I, which reshaped the map of Europe. The Versailles Treaty combined Slovaks with Czechs, Sudeten Germans and Carpatho-Rusyns to form the new state of Czecho-Slovakia. They remained there, except for a brief period of independence as a German satellite (1939–1945), until 1993, when they again achieved independence by democratic process. Through the long period of its history, Slovakia has endured many turbulent times, including Tatar (Tartar) and Turkish incursions, the Reformation, Re-Catholicization, two world wars, and most recently the Warsaw Pact invasion of 1968, subjecting it to the mercy of warring and competing powers. But Slovaks are a good example of a small Slavic people that has survived despite whole centuries of foreign domination. Through it all they have preserved a sense of kinship; but true political self-awareness has been in the process of formation for only about the past century and a half. The author, Anton Spiesz, examines this process of nation-building, as he undertakes the monumental task of surveying Slovak history.

One of the problems this translation faces relates to its intended audience; Spiesz wrote for a home audience. Having composed parts of the work while the Communists still held sway, he rushed to publish it after the Velvet Revolution of 1989. His book first appeared in 1993, but unfortunately Spiesz died on January 1, 1994; had life afforded him time, he might very well have made revisions.

Because Spiesz did not aim his book at an audience unacquainted with Slovak history, he often makes assumptions that can thoroughly confuse a non-Slovak reader. This edition attempts to provide necessary clarifications. Additionally, owing to Spiesz' propensity to revel in details, with lists of people, towns, animals and statistics, the reader may find himself simply overwhelmed. Spiesz also frequently introduces protagonists without adequately preparing the reader, leaving elucidation for later. These are all features of Spiesz' writing style, as well as consequences of his rush to publish.

To make up for these anomalies, explanatory materials in the form of endnotes, arranged by chapter, have been appended to this translation. Also appended is an index and select bibliography, listing major studies in English and some significant Slovak works. Numerous illustrations in color provide a bonus, which will hopefully delight layman and scholar alike.

A consistent problem that hampers understanding of Slovak history and culture is the lack of good, objective surveys. During the 19th Century, when nation-building steadily spread across Europe, the writing of Slovak history became inextricably bound up with the budding national movement, serving to bolster Slovak consciousness and self-image. It was the stuff of romantic poetry rather than factual analysis. Needing precedents, Slovak writers harked back to the early feudal state of Great Moravia, which lasted just over fifty years in the 9th Century, but became an object of veneration as the first Slavic state of Central Europe.

Up to the 19th Century no widely accepted history of the Slovaks and Slovakia had been written, inside or outside Slovakia. It was only during the rise of European nationalisms that Slovaks began seriously exploring their own history. And it was no accident that this Slovak awakening coincided with the Magyar (Hungarian) effort to transform multi-national Hungary into a wholly Magyar kingdom by forcibly assimilating its other, predominantly Slavic constituents. Magyar nationalists advanced the claim that Slovaks did not constitute a distinct nationality and had no history to speak of. For Slovaks, Great Moravia, as an early Slavic state on Slovak territory, provided a forceful rebuttal to that claim, a good springboard for writing a distinctive Slovak history.

The first attempt at such a history came during the 18th Century Enlightenment, with Juraj Papanek's Latin treatise on the Slavs. But not until the national revival in the 19th Century did the first real such history appear in Slovak, written by Frantisek Sasinek (1830–1914), a Catholic priest. His work concentrated on the medieval period, but it was marred by efforts to construe the local power-struggles of feudal magnates, such as Matus Cak, as evidence of inchoate Slovak state-building. While Sasinek dated Slovak history to Great Moravia, he was astute enough to realize that nation-building was a complex, centuries-long process, ongoing even in multi-national Hungary.

The next Slovak historian to enter the field was the teacher and lawyer, Julius Botto (1848–1926). He wrote at the beginning of the 20th Century, covering Slovak history from the earliest times to the middle of the 19th Century, concentrating on Slovak uniqueness in politics and culture. Also dating Slovak origins to Great Moravia, Botto minimized the impact of the Hungarian state on Slovak ethnic development, assigning credit to kindred nations, such as the Czechs. He emphasized the role of culture and language in the rise of Slovak national consciousness.

Between the two world wars, when Slovakia was a constituent part of Czecho-Slovakia, Daniel Rapant (1897–1988) conceived of Slovak history as a combination of the above interpretations. However, he did not downplay the influence of the Hungarian kingdom, but introduced a new treatment in the shape of a total European context, a refinement of the previous views. Rapant's ideas reflect a reaction to efforts to create a 'Czechoslovak history' by merging Slovak and Czech ethnicity, in order to legitimize the new Czecho-Slovak state. In challenging this interpretation, Rapant emphasized the quite different historical experiences of Slovaks and Czechs. Later historians, such as Frantisek Hrusovsky (1907–1956) and Frantisek Bokes (1906–1968), stressed this perspective as Slovak demands for autonomy grew more insistent and at last culminated in the short episode of Slovak independence, beginning in 1939, six months before the outbreak of World War II, and ending in 1945.

With the Communist takeover of Czecho-Slovakia in 1948, historians like Rapant were replaced by Marx-Leninists, who rigidly adhered to theories of class conflict. Nationality was reduced to the status of the handmaiden of class oppression, and Slovaks were seen as a down-trodden peasant people, dominated by an upper class, which happened to be mainly Magyar. Numerous historians, like Ludovit Holotik, Julius Mesaros, Milos Gosiorovsky, Viliam Plevza, Jan Tibensky (in a multi-volume compendium), subservient to the regime, stressed the role of the working class in toppling oppressors. Even Czech/Slovak conflicts were portrayed in terms of class, to wit: Czech bourgeois domination of Slovak markets. Hobbled by this ideology, Slovak historians fell behind world trends in historical research, though they were nevertheless able to achieve some notable success in researching the origins of Slovak folk culture, as well as in exploring socio-economic history, as exemplified by the six-volume study *Dejiny Slovenska* (A History of Slovakia), 1986–1992.

In the English-speaking world, little was known or published about Slovaks until the 20th Century. Much of what was done in the field came from a Czech or 'Czechoslovak' perspective, subsuming 'Slovak' under 'Czech'. Following the 1907 massacre of unarmed civilians at a church dedication in Cernova, R. W. Seton-Watson's *Racial Problems in Hungary* focused world attention on the plight of Slovaks. Later, during World War II, Seton-Watson became the leading scholarly source of information about Slovaks, and even played a role in the creation of the brand-new state of Czecho-Slovakia (the hyphen fell out after 1920). In the inter-war period he continued to sympathize with efforts to promote a 'Czechoslovak' nationality, lamenting the break-up of Czechoslovakia after Munich (1938), when Slovakia became a satellite of Nazi Germany.

After World War II, the Czechoslovak perspective remained in vogue, but came under attack in the writings of Slovak émigré writers, who were mostly dismissed by Western scholars as tainted by supposed Nazi affiliation. Only after the 1968 invasion of Czechoslovakia by the Warsaw Pact nations did Slovak identity begin winning increased recognition in the halls of academia. The studies of Carol Skalnik Leff, James Felak, Stanislav Kirschbaum and others have provided a much better insight into why Slovak national aspirations refused to die in the Czechoslovak state.

Then, shortly after the Velvet Revolution of 1989, Anton Spiesz undertook to write a full survey of Slovak history, the first such work by a single author to come out after the power shift. Its presentation was more consistent and unified than other early post-Communist studies, which were compiled by teams of scholars.

Spiesz' work is special because it provides a first fresh look at Slovak history after forty harrowing years of Communist rule. Shedding the bonds of suppression, Spiesz could express his true thoughts and feelings without the need to hide his disgust with politicians like the former Czechoslovak president, Edvard Benes, and the last Communist president and secretary-general, Gustav Husak, both of whose policies were dismissive of Slovak aspirations. Having shaken off the shackles, Spiesz did not hesitate to tackle controversial topics, some of which exasperate historians to the present day.

In this new-found freedom, a rift has developed between historians of the Historical Institute of the Slovak Academy of Sciences and those affiliated with the Matica Slovenska (Slovak Cultural Institute, a bulwark of Slovak sentiment since its founding in 1863). Many of the Academy members had received their training from Communist mentors which, according to Matica scholars, vitiates their views. On the other hand, members of the Academy accuse Matica historians of extreme nationalism. Spiesz' approach represents a refreshing contrast to both of the above protagonists; though a former academician, he was one of the first to dare to dissent from Communist dogma. His interpretations tend to thread a middle course between the two warring schools, leaving neither of them happy. Perhaps this is his appeal.

Because Spiesz' specialty was Slovak social and economic history during the early modern era, it is here that he makes his greatest contributions. His knowledge of the history of guilds was second to none, and much of his narrative of the period leading up to the 20th Century ranks with the best scholarship.

But controversies continue to proliferate in interpretations of Slovak history. A substantial effort has been made to explore them in endnotes, and suggestions for further reading are provided in my extensive bibliography. Still, the number of studies in English remains limited, and interpretations of Slovak history in Slovakia itself are fluid, gradually evolving as Slovaks seek their rightful place and role in European affairs. General approval of European integration appears to augur an early and assured future with the EU and NATO.

An added historiographical feature of this English edition of Spiesz' history is a review of Slovak archaeological excavations: relevant discoveries and analyses are presented in an afterword by Dusan Caplovic, substantiating and/or qualifying some important assertions made by Spiesz.

Michael J. Kopanic, Jr.
St. Francis University. Loretto, Pennsylvania

Foreword

A Message for the Journey

When on January 1, 1993, the Slovak Republic appeared on the map of Europe as a free, democratic, and independent state, I was convinced that for Slovakia this meant only a beginning of a journey. It is a journey which we Slovaks must undertake so that the world might understand the importance of this historic milestone.

In spite of being one of the oldest European nations, on the first day of our independence we presented ourselves as the newest state of the world. Respected European historians agree that the Slovaks, in their past, were not only passive objects, but also active participants in the march of history. They proved their viability and perseverance by preserving their national culture and identity despite not having their own state.

For a thousand years, Slovakia was a part of the Hungarian State, and for three quarters of a century the Slovaks lived in the Czecho-Slovak Republic. At the start of the 21st century we hope to make it clear that the history of multi-national Hungary is also included in our own history. Having said that, it is my belief that we should not renounce the positive aspects of our life with the Czechs or with the nations that comprised the Hungarian State. We must recognize the continuity of the flow of history.

As I pen this commentary to Anton Spiesz' *Illustrated History of Slovakia* which is designated primarily for American readers, I do wish to express my deep gratitude to the United States of America for embracing several waves of immigrants from Slovakia and allowing them to live in freedom in their newly adopted nation. So many of them found new life and opportunity in America and also found an opportunity to advance their skills and to cultivate their own culture and traditions. Over the years, many individuals of Slovak ancestry became successful and influential in American life and many were able to contribute in great measure to our own movement for independence. Although there were many, I will only mention a few: the inventor, Rev. Jozef Murgas; author and founder of important Slovak American organizations at the turn of 19th and 20th centuries, Rev. Stefan Furdek; the President of the Slovak League of America during the First World War, Albert Mamatey; and more recently the astronaut, Eugene Cernan.

And then, many Slovaks in America demonstrated their gratitude to their adopted country by fighting in the War of Independence in George Washington's Army, in the American Civil War, and during the First and Second World Wars. One of the most outstanding of these was Sergeant Michael (Michal) Strank, born in Jarabina, Slovakia, who was the first in a small group of soldiers raising the American flag on the conquered island of Iwo Jima during

US postal stamp (1945) commemorating the Iwo Jima Monument. Sgt. Michael Strank is third from the left.

1

the Second World War. I would also like to mention John (Jan) Slezak, born in Stara Tura, Slovakia, who became a colonel in the US Army, and a young soldier Janko Jesensky from Krompachy, Slovakia. All three were buried with full military honors in the famous Arlington National Cemetery in Washington, D.C. Also worth noting is Vladimir Stano from Nove Mesto nad Vahom, a Slovak immigrant living in New York who enlisted in the British Royal Air Force. These and many other natives of Slovakia knew what their duty was when either their Slovak or American homeland needed them.

All these acts were expressions of trust and willingness to sacrifice for the cause of freedom, and they occurred during the era when Slovakia was not a free nation. Today, when Slovakia is free and independent, we cooperate even more closely with America. The Slovak Republic is situated in the geographic center of Europe. Through Slovakia one can feel the heartbeat of Europe.

It is my sincere hope that this book by Anton Spiesz will contribute to an even greater familiarity, knowledge, and understanding of the Slovak people and their history by the American public. Friendly relations and cooperation are born of mutual familiarity and knowledge.

Ivan Gašparovič
President of the Slovak Republic, 2004

Publisher's Statement

There are two goals that I as a Slovak publisher have for this Slovak history: (1) to give the general English-reading public a book that is inviting to read; (2) to create an edition of Slovak history in English that displays scholarly integrity.

To begin, I sought guidance among people representing 'Matica Slovenska' and the Slovak Academy of the Sciences. I decided in favor of translating into English the work by Anton Spiesz, published by the Slovak Academy of the Sciences, together with an afterword by Dusan Caplovic, a leading expert in Slovak archeology. Caplovic brings new methodology to the historiography of Spiesz by using archeological evidence to qualify, substantiate, or reject previous statements made by historians like Spiesz and others.

I wanted the book to be a good read. People who have helped in putting this work into English idiom were Dr. Martin Votruba, of the Pittsburgh University Slovak Department; Dr. Albert Devine, Ph.D., J.D.; Mr. Patrick Romane; and Dr. David Daniel. Most of all, Mr. Joseph J. Palus, Jr., MA, of Johnstown, PA, who translated the original texts.

We included over three hundred color illustrations (photographs, documents, maps), in the interest of making this work visually expressive and engaging. The Slovak publisher, Perfekt, a.s. of Bratislava, contributed these rare and beautiful historical illustrations.

Truth is truth if it corresponds to reality. Facts are facts if they can be ascertained. Unfortunately, interpretation and opinion usually reign in historiography. Slovak history is no exception. It has suffered from the biases of many "isms": the bias of the Christian Chronicles: of Magyarism, Teutonicism, Austro-Hungarianism, Czechoslovakism, Nazism, Communism, and Slovak jingoism.

Therefore, copious notes are provided to present scholarly debate on controversial issues and to guide the reader toward a more defensible interpretation. Dr. Michael Kopanic was the primary author of these notes; Dr. Milan S. Durica, Dr. Frantisek Vnuk, Mr. Charles Sabatos, Dr. Albert Devine, Dr. John Karch, Ing. Ivan Reguli, and Dr. Zdenko G. Alexy contributed from their academic specialties.

Michael Kopanic created a comprehensive bibliography that serves as documentation as well as a guide to additional resources, including significant new works, especially that of Florin Curta and Max Domarus.

The index which presents proper names in English, Slovak and Austro-Hungarian spellings is credites to, among many, Richard Wood, Ivan Reguli, and Zdenko G. Alexy.

The final stages of editing were done by Mr. Joseph J. Palus, Dr. Albert Devine, Mr. Patrick Romane, and Mr. Richard Wood.

I am grateful to all these collaborators for their encouragement and for their contribution to Slovak history and historiography. Their efforts have made this work more readable, more eloquent, more comprehensive, and more historically reliable.

Finally, I must express special gratitude to Dr. Magdalena Fazekasova of Perfekt, a. s.

I take full responsibility, however, for any shortcomings, omissions, and oversights.

All of us with roots in Central Europe and an interest in the development of this large part of Western civilization and culture will find this illustrated edition indispensable and visually stimulating.

Ladislaus J. Bolchazy, Ph.D.

ILLUSTRATED
Slovak
History

1. Beginnings of History in Slovakia

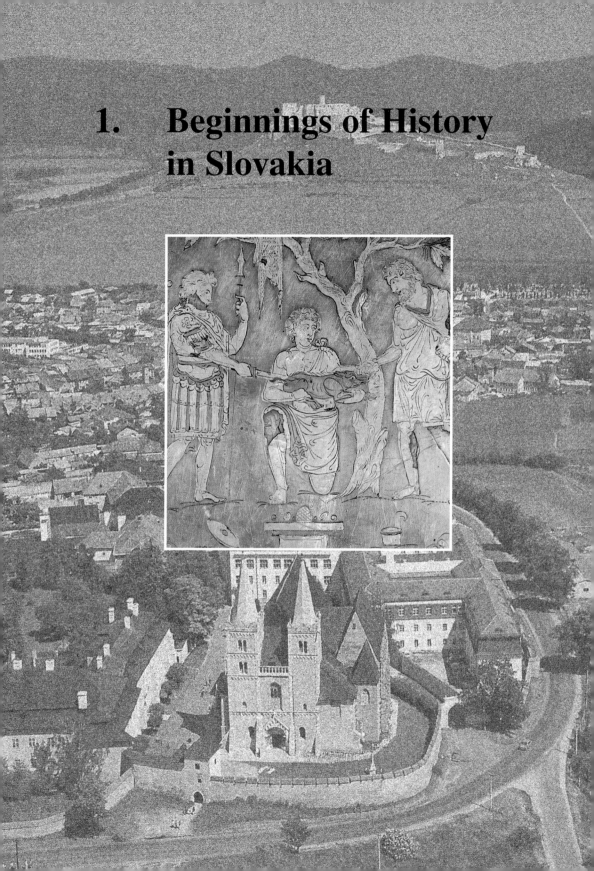

The first evidence of humans on present-day Slovak territory[1] stems from the Early Paleolithic Period, about 200,000 years ago. The climate then in Central Europe[2] was very harsh, inducing people to settle mainly in the vicinity of thermal springs. The best known such spring, showing indisputable signs of human habitation, is Ganovce[3] near Poprad. Archeologists have found the bones of mammoths, rhinoceros, bears, foxes, wolves and beavers layered in native travertines,[4] with indications that people hunted and ate them. Archeologists have found traces of Early Stone Age settlements at Nove Mesto nad Vahom, Sena, Posov, Vysne Ruzbachy, and Drevenik near Spisske Podhradie. Here they have also found a human skull with well-developed brow-ridges.

Skull fragment, Neanderthal man. (Sala nad Vahom, ca. 70,000 years old)

During the Middle Paleolithic Period (100,000–35,000 B.C.), additional settlements are evidenced in Slovakia, located in the vicinity of thermal springs or in caves at present-day Ganovce, Beharovce na Spisi, Bojnice, Banka, Radosina, and in the upper Nitra and Vah valleys. Numerous artifacts confirm the presence of people and disclose their way of life, e.g. awls, chippers, scrapers for leather-working, and other specialized tools for shaping wood and bone.

A great variety of highly specialized chipped-stone implements from the Late Paleolithic Period (35,000–8000 B.C.) has survived (scrapers, bradawls, punches, chisels, gougers, knives, saws, etc.), all of which enabled early man in Slovakia to produce various artifacts from wood, bones, antlers, and mammoth tusks. The most important sites preserving remnants of tools and dwellings from this period are Dzerava Skala near Plavecky Mikulas, Ivanovce, Nove Mesto nad Vahom (in the Mnesice region), Trencin, Vlckovce, Zamarovce, Certova Pec (near Radosina), Banka, Moravany nad Vahom, Zabokreky nad Nitrou, Spisske Podhradie, Velky Saris, Tibava, Barca and Cejkov.

Early Stone Age female sculpture, (Moravany nad Vahom, ca. 23,000 years old)

The earliest art objects discovered on Slovak territory come from this era. Most famous is a 'Venus' found in Moravany nad Vahom and dated by archeologists at a respectable 22,000 years.[5] Workshops had evidently already been built for the production of chipped-stone instruments, as in Sena near Kosice.

At the end of the Late Paleolithic Period (8000–6000 B.C.), the European climate warmed considerably. Cold favoring animals, such as mammoths, moose and reindeer, moved off to the North, while animals preferring warmer weather began appearing in the vacated zone. These movements brought extensive changes in the life-style of people, who nevertheless remained predominantly hunters.

Ceramics and vessel of Bukova Hora Culture, end of 5ᵗʰ Millennium B.C. (Domica Cave)

Sculpture, 'Great Mother', Late Stone Age (Surany-Nitriansky Hradok, ca. 3600 years old)

In the Early New Stone Age or Lower Neolithic Period (6000–2900 B.C.), the inhabitants of Slovakia began cultivating crops, raising domestic animals, and producing polished stone implements. Permanent agricultural settlements replaced the earlier migratory camps. Gradually, people colonized the fertile lowlands of Southwest and East Slovakia, and even moved into upland areas.

The oldest agricultural settlements were occupied by a people that made ceramics featuring ornamentation in fine linear relief. Their homes were multi-chambered structures, six to seven meters wide and as much as sixty meters long, resting on large piles. There were often several such structures to a village. In their vicinity, the dwellers dug pits for storage of grains and legumes. Agriculture became the predominant way of life, hunting providing only supplemental sustenance.

It is from this period that the earliest known burial sites come. The dead were buried in a fetal or flexed position. A burial site uncovered in Nitra is among the largest such finds in Europe. In contrast to preceding periods, males took over leadership in society, as evidenced by the richer assortment of burial gifts in their graves.

The Late New Stone Age or Upper Neolithic Period (2900–1900 B.C.) was characterized by a new technique of tilling soil: the use of wooden plowshares, drawn by livestock. Livestock began to play a larger role in the life of society, which gradually began to diversify on the basis of property ownership. The expression of material culture became more and more varied, as manifested in a proliferation of diverse ceramics.

During the Bronze Age (1900–700 B.C.), cultural development was especially affected by influences from abroad. Cultural currents emanating from Balkan/Anatolian regions enriched both material and spiritual culture. Agriculture continued as the basic way of life, but horses became the main draft animal. People began to build on higher ground, often with fortifications, and some settlements acquired the character of political/economic centers. Bronze became the primary material for weaponry and jewelry, but tools continued to be made of wood and stone. Bronze was imported from various parts of the known world, and trade in northern amber and gold, as well as faience, was carried on.[6] People continued to be buried in a fetal position, with abundant grave goods. About this time, copper was discovered and mined in the region of present-day Slovenske Rudohorie (Slovak Ore Mountains).[7]

Several Bronze-Age cultures emerged and thrived, the most famous being the Unetice culture, which spread to Southwest Slovakia, and the Madarovce culture, whose influence extended not only to pre-historic Slovak territory, but also to all of Central Europe. A relatively high standard of living prevailed in

Anthropomorphic vessel, Mid-4th Millennium B.C. (Svodin)

the fortified settlements (e.g. Nitriansky Hradok), where people produced a great deal of stoneware (pitchers, cups, amphoras, platters, and pots).

The Bronze-Age Otoman culture[8] arose in Eastern Slovakia and extended as far as the foothills of the Tatra Mountains. Its material aspect betrays the influence of Mycenean civilization.[9] Fortifications in Spissky Stvrtok, where stone ramparts have been uncovered, have no equal in the cultural history of contemporary Europe, and certainly not in the Carpathian basin. The material and spiritual content of the Otoman culture is unusually multifaceted, particularly with respect to precision-made ceramics, sculpture, jewelry, tools and weapons, which were some of the mediating commodities of the contacts of North and Central Europe with the Southeast, extending all the way to the Hittite Empire.

During the Middle Bronze Age (after 1500 B.C.), considerable changes occurred in economic/productive methods. Stone was phased out as a material for tool-making and largely replaced by bone, antlers and bronze. Trade in bronze artifacts, mining of ores, and bronze metallurgy expanded considerably. Bronze artifacts were exported to all parts of Europe. Typical of this period was the Carpathian burial-mound culture, which now began to give way to cremation rites. The quality of ceramic production is clearly seen in platters, pot-bellied amphoras, and long-necked pitchers set on hollow legs. Bronze production too, became richer and more diversified.

In the Late Bronze Age (1500–500 B.C.), the presence in Europe of a known ethnic group is documented for the first time, the Greeks, some of whom had

Components of bridle carved from antler, 16th Century A.D, (Surany-Nitriansky Hradok)

9

Amphora depicting funeral cortege, Mid Bronze Age (Velke Raskovce, 15th Century A.D.)

moved northward from the Balkan Peninsula at the beginning of the Second Millennium B.C., and who very likely were acquainted with the territory of Southern Slovakia. Later, two other ethnic offshoots of the Danubian Indo-Europeans, Veneti and Illyrians, appear in historical record.[10]

Progress marched on: the harvesting of grain was sped up by the use of bronze sickles; breeding of sheep (for wool) and horses was expanded; land was cleared for cultivation; carts with wood-rimmed wheels appeared; wooden dwellings were constructed; textile-weaving spread far and wide; the hammer and anvil, as well as solid casting molds, were applied in the working of bronze; various techniques became more sophisticated; rivets were driven, wire drawn and metal beaten into sheets; products from celebrated shops, such as swords, bronze jewelry, and cookware were traded in distant reaches.

Bronze bracelet with ornamental rings and filigree, turn of 3rd to 2nd Century (Chotin)

The Iron Age, which began in the 8th Century B.C., arrived from the Southeast. Its early phase is called the 'Hallstatt';[11] its late phase, 'La Tene'.[12] The new metal came to Central Europe from two centers, the Black Sea and La Tene, which had borrowed from the Greeks. From the Black Sea region came the potter's wheel. Ancient historians familiarize us with the tribal names: Illyrian, Thracian, Scythian, and Kimmerian.

The first ethnic group, whose presence on Slovak territory can be established from written sources, is the Celts. They were one of the most numerous and widespread peoples in all Europe during the second half of the First Millennium B.C. Historical sources mention them at the beginning of the 5th Century B.C., the Hallstatt period. Their original homeland extended from the Alps to Eastern France and Central Germany, as far as the Czech Basin. Troubled by over-population, they spread in all directions, including Slovakia. Their migration considerably altered the ethnic face of Europe. Written records document the advance of Celts to the Mediterranean area, including Italy, Greece and even Asia Minor. The Celts became a part of the ancient civilized world, but remained a restless, barbarian element in our region. They, however, did creatively adopt and adapt production techniques, which they then mediated to the corners of the known world, thus furthering the spread of economic progress. Thanks to trade, the Celts were able to benefit from the prosperity of the Roman Empire.

Facsimile of Celtic belt, (Zemplin County, 1st Century A.D.)

The Celts arrived in the Carpathian Basin in the 4th Century B.C. Their presence in Slovakia is confirmed by burial sites in Stupava and Bucany. Celtic colonization of considerable extent penetrated Slovakia at the end of the 4th Century B.C., with their settling in the lowlands of southeast Slovakia, as well as in south-central regions, finally halting along a line from Nitra to Levice.

A new group of Celtic colonists entered Slovakia after 200 B.C., on the retreat from devastating encounters in Northern Italy. Celtic colonization achieved its greatest density and extent in our region in the middle of the 2nd Century B.C.

Along the Nitra and Hron rivers, Celts lived together with Dacians, whose king, Burebista, was defeated by the Boii and Tauriscans around the middle of the 2nd Century B.C. The Dacian settlements in southeast Slovakia lasted up to the beginning of the Roman era: the ancient sources mention them as neighbors of the Germanic kingdom of Vannius. Northern Slovakia was inhabited by the Celtic Cotini, also mentioned in historical sources. The Roman general Marcus Vinius fought them around 10 B.C.

We know that the Celts, who lived on the territory of present-day Slovakia in the late pre-Christian era, lived in small settlements and scattered homesteads, lying relatively close to each other; their craftsmen possessed well developed and sophisticated skills. The dimensions of a Celtic house were approximately 4 x 3 meters, with a roof constructed like a saddle on a weight bearing beam. They built their settlements on hillocks, close to flowing water. Around the middle of the 2nd Century B.C. the Celts began fortifying settlements that concentrated craftsmen and administrative personnel, who serviced surrounding agricultural areas. The most significant such center was situated on the site of present-day Bratislava,[13] as attested by the many finds of potters'

'Tetradrachma' of Bratislava type, with 'Biatec' inscription.

ovens and numerous caches of Celtic coins of the 'Biatec' and 'Nonnus' type (doubtless, names of tribal chiefs or kings). But some of the Celtic fortifications were built solely to protect cult objects (Liptovska Mara, Zemplin).

Celtic craft production achieved a high level of technique and aesthetics. Iron jewelry and weaponry, as well as ceramics shaped on potter's wheels, and textiles woven of wool and flax, exhibit considerable sophistication. But progress was also achieved in agriculture: farmers used iron plowshares, hoes and spades, cultivating a variety of grains, particularly barley. The rotating millstone played a large role in the preparation of foodstuffs, facilitating faster and finer grinding of flour. Furthermore, the Celts' acquaintance with the

Earring and coin, 1st Century B.C. (Dolny Kubin - Velky Bysterec)

scythe and sickle made it possible for them to gather and store hay for over-wintering livestock. They also raised hogs and poultry, especially chickens and geese. And last but not least, they minted their own coins, a process which required extraordinary technical and artistic know-how, plus access to raw materials, all of which assured the mint-master a privileged status in society.

During the Celtic sojourn on our present-day territory, foreign trade expanded greatly: various products such as metal household vessels, mirrors, amphoras for wine, and amber were imported, mainly from Italy, Germany, and regions around the Baltic and Black seas.

The Celts buried their dead in a prone posture, surrounded by rich furnishings: men with full armor, women in festive garb and ornaments. However, as time passed, cremation rites became more and more common. Celts were familiar with writing, using Roman characters, yet we have found next to no information about their religious beliefs.

At the turn of the millennium a new power-structure emerged on the territory of present-day Slovakia. Germanic tribes, the Marcomanni and Quadi, displaced the Celts, while the Roman Empire began abutting our territory from the South, establishing provinces on the lands of present day Austria and Hungary, Noricum and Pannonia, respectively.

The Quadi (also known as Swabians) came originally from the region between the Main and Neckar rivers and, led by a leader named Turdus, settled along the Morava river in Southwest Slovakia; the Marcomanni came originally from Central Germany, west of the middle reaches of the Danube. Their king, Marobuduus, subdued the Quadi by force of arms.

In order to protect their empire, the Romans built a chain of fortified camps called the 'Limes Romanus', which followed the course of the Danube River and even crossed over into southwest Slovakia. Along this chain they built civilian and military structures, including outposts manned by troops. These camps played a significant role in long distance trade. Archeologists have found their ruins in Iza (Leanyvar) near Komarno, in Milanovce, Cifer-Pac, Devin and Stupava.

Roman helmet, 2nd Century A.D. (Bratislava-Rusovce)

Relations between these two Germanic tribes and the Romans took various forms and passed through several phases. The Romans essentially strove for co-existence, but did not always succeed. In some instances, on campaign, they made deep inroads into Marcomanni territory. Several Roman historians (e.g. Tacitus, Suetonius, and Cassius Dio) have left us detailed reports. In one such instance in 6 A.D., the Romans, under the future emperor Tiberius, mounted an offensive against Marobuduus on what is present-day Slovakia, after enveloping the Germans in a pincer maneuver that advanced from the

13

Scenes on silver plaque,
(Krakovany-Straze)

Figure of comic actor,
2ⁿᵈ– 3ʳᵈ Century (Iza)

Rhine river on one side and the region of Carnuntum[14] (present-day Vienna) on the other. But they were unable to complete the maneuver, because their army was withdrawn to deal with the Great Pannonian Revolt of 6–9 A.D. The Romans later decided to overcome Germanic resistance by appointing a king for them from among the Quadi. Their choice fell on Vannius, who ruled his domain from somewhere in southwest Slovakia.

Eastern Slovakia continued to be inhabited by a Celtic/Dacian populace. Also, an autochthonic people lived in mountainous regions and deep valleys there, but little is known of them. They were bearers of the 'Puchov' culture.[15]

Around 50 A.D. Vannius fell in battle. Then, around the turn of the 1st to 2nd Century, the new Germanic rulers extended their domain to include the valleys of the Nitra, Hron and Ipel rivers, and even the Danube. They then helped the Roman Emperors in a number of internal power struggles. In the years 92 and 97, however, the Roman emperors undertook unsuccessful forays against them. By way of reprisal, the Germans invaded Pannonia.[16] Later, however, they renewed their dependency on Rome, and later still, in the 60s of the 2nd Century, Marcus Aurelius found that he had no choice but to attack them. In the process, he drove deep into the valleys of the Hron, Nitra, Vah and Morava Rivers. It was during this expedition that Marcus Aurelius wrote his famous philosophical discourses, the *Meditations*. The Column of Marcus Aurelius in

14

Rome depicts a miraculous storm which saved his army in our lands, and which, allegedly, Christian believers among his troops called down by their prayers. By the year 179 A.D. Roman troops had reached as far as present-day Trencin (Laugaritio), where they memorialized their presence in stone.[17]

Later, the Romans completely withdrew from Slovakia. However, they continued to maintain the 'Limes Romanus' against possible Germanic incursions and remained in Pannonia until the 4th Century.

The Romans exerted a strong influence on the Quadi and Marcomani, most markedly in the sphere of craftsmanship, especially the designing of fine jewelry. Germanic structures (rectangular in ground-plan) were built at ground-level or on subterranean foundations. They cremated their dead and placed the remains in urns, accompanied by rich grave goods.

During the great migration of peoples in the 5th and 6th Centuries, it was the Huns who ruled over the greater part of present-day Slovakia, and their rule reached its greatest extent under Attila (434–453).[18] The empire of the Huns was very extensive but lacked internal stability. During this period, various Germanic tribes were transient sojourners on Slovak territory, including the Goths, Rugi, Heruli, and lastly the Lombards, who stayed for not quite a century, enroute from their homes in the lower Rhineland to Northern Italy. They left our region in 508, fleeing before the menace of the marauding Avars.

Archeologists have found plentiful relics of Germanic tribes. Because Christianity had already been widely accepted among them, they mostly practised inhumation. The Goths, in particular, left numerous small cemeteries or isolated graves in southern regions of East and Central Slovakia, but mostly in the southwest – in the Hron, Nitra and Vah River valleys. These sites were originally replete with jewelry and other gifts, but in later times they were ransacked by grave robbers. Large metal buckles, smaller cast-iron clasps and various decorative items, mostly designed for horsemen, testify to the movement of Gothic bands from the regions of the Black Sea and the Danube into our lands.

Cache of 108 gold coins, era of migrations, Mid-5th Century A.D. (Bina)

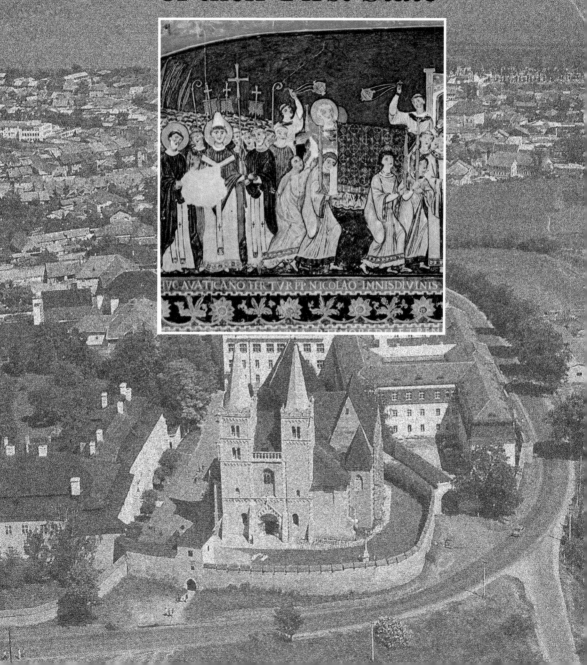

2. Slavic Arrival: The Founding and Significance of their First State

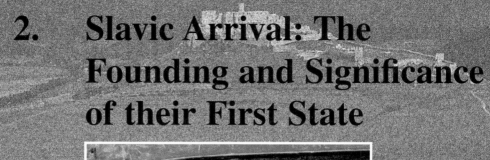

In the middle of the First Millennium the geopolitical situation in Central Europe once again changed. In 476 A.D., under attack by Germanic tribes, the Roman Empire collapsed, leaving a power vacuum. The ancient Germanic tribes abandoned the area, and into the vacated space pressed Slavic[1] tribes from their original homeland between the Oder and Vistula rivers, south of the Pripet marshes and west of the Dniester River.[2] This move did not happen suddenly or with any constancy. The Slavs simply overcame the few remaining inhabitants and gradually assimilated them. This process took place substantially between the end of the 5th and beginning of the 6th Century.

Ceramics from Slavic funeral pyres, 6th Century A.D. (Galanta, Matuskovo)

Shortly thereafter, an alliance of nomadic groups formed on the steppes of Eastern Europe. These nomads began to threaten the life of Slavs in their new homeland. One such group, the Avars,[3] played a leading role in this harassment. Under the leadership of Khagan Bayan, they began to expand into a powerful empire, launching attacks not only against Slavs, but Franks and Lombards in Northern and Central Italy as well. By the mid-Sixth Century even the Byzantine Empire[4] was paying tribute[5] to them. The Avars were warlike, cattle-herding nomads. The state they formed shared no common culture or even a common language; it was held together by brute force. In territory, it extended east to the Byzantine Empire and west to the emerging Frankish realm.[6]

However, in the early 7th Century, when the Avars were defeated at the battlements of Constantinople, the Slavic tribes of the Danubian Basin, whom they had conquered and forced to pay tribute, began to rebel. This resistance began in 623–624, with a Frankish merchant named Samo taking the lead. Samo successfully threw off the yoke of the Avars and established himself as ruler of the Danubian Slavs, his reign lasting for 35 years.[7] After his demise, his principality collapsed,[8] but the Danubian Slavs continued to hold their ground.

From archeological digs we know that Slavs occupied both low-lying land as well as mountain valleys. In addition to working as farmers and herders they mined ore for smelting into various metal artifacts. Slavs constructed homes of logs or thatch, which they plastered with clay, sometimes fired. Near them they dug rounded pits for use as granaries. They cremated their dead and placed the remains in urns or shallow pits, covered over with earth to form burial mounds. Not having yet discovered the potter's wheel, they shaped household vessels by hand, most commonly forming basic slender jars. For tilling the soil they used a wooden plowshare, later replaced by iron. They also raised cattle, sheep and goats, less often pigs, and processed

Golden earrings, 7th Century A.D.

Silver cache,
ca. 670,
(Zemiansky Vrbovok)

animal skins and furs for various uses; they wove textiles, and continued to use stone and bone.

We know that the Avars settled densely in the rich farming region of Zitny Ostrov.[9] They extended their settlements to the Vah, Nitra, and Zitava river basins, then further to the area of the Danubian Gate.[10] Around the turn of the 7th Century they abandoned their nomadic ways, settling down in symbiosis with the local Slavic inhabitants, as evidenced by combined Avar-Slavic burial sites surviving from this period. The Avar burial rites incorporated the deceased's weapons and horses, including saddles embellished with richly ornate metalwork. They built their villages on strategically commanding, elevated terrain and protected them with circular earthen ramparts. Still, our information about the Avars comes mostly from written sources, not from archeological finds.

Harness ornament,
8th Century,
(Cifer-Pac)

By the end of the 7th Century the Franks had defeated the Avars, bringing about the collapse of their empire.[11] The Slavs became free to start expanding political, social and economic relationships of their own, converting to Christianity and building their own state, which came to be known as the Great Moravian Kingdom (in Latin, Magna Moravia).[12] During the time of its greatest extent, this kingdom included not only the greater part of present-day Slovakia and Moravia, but even of Hungary, and in time a significant part of Bohemia and southern Poland.

*Metal spur,
Mid-9th Century,
(Orviste-Basovce)*

The Slavic state in the Danubian river basin found itself at the intersection of the spheres of influence of two major powers: the formally renovated Holy Roman Empire of the 'Germanic nation', and the Byzantine Empire, which since 476 had considered itself to be the rightful successor to the traditions of the original Roman Empire. The newly-founded Frankish (Germanic) Empire, still in its beginnings, was expanding to the East and interfering in the internal affairs of not only the Danubian Slavs but other Slavs as well. In the meantime, the Byzantine Empire was preoccupied with its own internal problems and had to devote its energies to confronting barbarian attacks on various fronts, which limited the influence it could exert on the culture of Danubian Slavs.

From many historic sources, recorded and preserved by monastic scribes as early as the 7th and 8th Centuries in Germany, and especially in nearby Austria, we know that the great Charlemagne subdued Bavaria in 788,[13] then Saxony between 772 and 804, and lastly the Polabian Slavs and Czechs between 789 and 806.[14] The Avars, whom he had vanquished between 791 and 795, he resettled on the borderlands between present day Austria and Hungary in 805, after first forcibly converting them to Christianity. In 811, he also led a military expedition into what is present day Slovakia.

After the death of Charlemagne, when his empire split into several parts, including the East Frankish Kingdom, which abutted Slovakia, the Slavs felt

*Belt buckle,
8th– 9th Century,
(Dolny Kubin-
-Velky Bysterec)*

Sword grip,
2ⁿᵈ Qtr. 9ᵗʰ Century
(Blatnica)

themselves less threatened from the West, and efforts were revived to achieve emancipation on a par with surrounding, more developed nations. Around the third decade of the 9th Century, two Slavic principalities arose here: the Moravian, led by Prince Mojmir, and the Nitrian (Nitra), headed by Prince Pribina. It was for the latter that Adalram, the archbishop of Salzburg, dedicated the first Christian church on the territory of present-day Slovakia, in Nitra (Nitrava). Before long, however, the ruler of Moravia, Prince Mojmir, ejected Pribina and annexed his principality. In this way a new state entity emerged, which received the name 'Great Moravia'. But Mojmir's rule did not last long. In 846, Louis the German, ruler of the East Frankish kingdom, deprived him of his throne and installed Mojmir's nephew, Rastislav, in his stead. Furthermore, Louis the German set up Pribina as his own vassal at Lake Blatno (Balaton) in present-day Hungary.

The significance of Prince Pribina in Slovak history has not yet been sufficiently appreciated. He was the first ruler of Slavic origin to accept baptism and the first to build a Christian church on Slavic territory.[15] Furthermore, his domain fell wholly within the territory of present-day Slovakia.

Rastislav, the successor to Mojmir, became an important ruler of Great Moravia. He put much work into the internal consolidation of his state, although at the beginning of his reign he ostensibly respected his status as vassal to Louis the German. The latter, nevertheless, in 855, mounted an

Partially reconstructed
Great Moravian
courtyard in Ducove

attack on Great Moravia, which failed when Rastislav took refuge in his stronghold.[16] Louis then laid waste the surrounding countryside, but, as he withdrew, the Moravians followed, ravaging Bavarian border areas. A second expedition, planned by Louis for 858, failed to take place, owing to internal disturbances in his own realm. Rastislav was able to take advantage of this situation to consolidate his own power and then later to successfully repel renewed attacks by Louis.

*Hrad Devin
(Stronghold, castle)*

In 870, Rastislav's nephew, Svatopluk, unseated him in turn. He even handed him over to the not so tender mercies of the new East Frankish ruler, Karlman, who had Rastislav blinded and imprisoned for life. Bavarian armies, led by Dukes Wilhelm and Engelschalk, then occupied the western half of Great Moravia, and the latter undertook to enforce political order in the occupied territory. Before long the Germans imprisoned Svatopluk as well.

When news of Svatopluk's imprisonment spread across Great Moravia, the Moravians reacted with a popular uprising, led by Slavomir, his kinsman. In a curious turnabout, the Franks, striving to regain control, turned to Svatopluk for help and released him from prison. The latter, however, quickly struck an accord with Slavomir and fell upon the unsuspecting Franks in their camp, soundly defeating them. Of course, hostilities did not end with this episode: East Frankish forces staged several retaliatory strikes, all of which were fended off by the Moravian armies of Svatopluk.

*Silver jewelry, latter
half of 9th Century,
(Ducove)*

Rastislav

Under Rastislav's rule, Christianity had at last been able to put down solid roots in Great Moravia. Even though his territory had long been the object of Christian missionary efforts, in particular of the bishops of Saltzburg and Passau, as well as those of Byzantium and Italy, it had not been significantly or decisively converted. This was so, partly because of the political tension that existed between Great Moravia and the East Frankish realm, whence came the principal and most persistent attempts at Christianization, but also because those attempts were fraught with political implications. Religion and politics were intimately conjoined, and missionary motives were not always pure.

Rastislav rightly surmised that Christianization would have greater success if it came from Byzantium: on the one hand, because the Eastern Church allowed converts to conduct liturgies in their own languages, while the Western Church tolerated only Latin;[17] on the other, because the Byzantine Empire posed no political threat in the Danubian Basin.

For this reason, in 861, Rastislav turned to Emperor Michael III in Constantinople with a request for teachers of the Christian Faith, who were conversant with the Slavic tongue. Emperor Michael granted the request. He dispatched to Moravia the learned brothers, Constantine (Cyril), a philosopher, and Methodius, a government administrator, natives of Thessalonica.[18] Constantine created a Slavonic alphabet, translated the most important liturgical books,[19] and selected subordinates to fill important clerical posts in the Moravian church structure. Constantine and Methodius arrived in Moravia in 863.

The arrival and success of the Byzantine mission proved to be a thorn in the side of the leaders of the Western Church, who had long devoted themselves to Christianization, but with only middling success. For this reason the

Brothers from Thessalonika, arriving at Papal Court

bishop of Passau attacked the Slavonic liturgy and presented the Pope with a formal accusation against the brothers from Thessalonica.

In 867 Constantine and Methodius had to travel to Rome to thrash out some of the problems of their mission. Pope Hadrian II approved the Slavonic liturgical books and ordained Constantine's pupils, including Methodius, to the priesthood and deaconate. The mission to Rome, therefore, ended successfully. However, Constantine chose to remain in Rome; he entered a monastery, took the monastic name Cyril, and died there on February 14, 869.[20]

Poem by Constantine (Cyril): Proglas *(Introduction/Prologue to New Testament)*

The literary and cultural achievements of Cyril are formidable – truly a pioneering breakthrough for Slavic culture and learning. Constantine, on his own, developed liturgical texts for the Slavonic rite; then in 867, enroute to Rome, he stopped in Venice and successfully defended the use of Slavonic in liturgy; and, lastly, he defended his entire missionary project before the Papal Court in Rome. But it was not long before Latin again became the dominant liturgical language in Great Moravia, and indeed exclusive after 885.[21] Old Church Slavonic[22] went on to become permanently established in the Balkan Slavic nations, as well as in 'Old Rus', where it served as a foundation for their literary languages.[23]

Methodius returned to Great Moravia alone. On his shoulders rested the full weight of the Byzantine mission, with approval from the Holy Father himself. Returning, he stopped in Blatnograd[24] to visit Prince Kocel, Pribina's son, a Frankish vassal and patron of the Slavonic liturgy. One year later, Methodius again traveled to Rome, this time to be ordained a bishop by the Holy Father and to receive his commissions as 'Archbishop of Pannonia' and 'Papal Legate'.

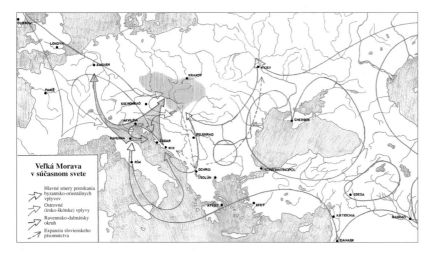

Map of Great Moravia (Jan Dekan)

Legend
→ Main streams of penetrating Byzantine-oriental influence
→ Irish/Scottish influence
→ Ravenna-Dalmatian Circle
→ Expansion of Slavic literature

*Bronze crucifix,
Early 19ᵗʰ Century*

East Frankish ecclesiastical circles were aghast at these developments, because they still considered the Danubian Basin their own territory; after all, they had promoted Christianity there before the arrival of the Byzantine mission. In 870, the Bavarian bishops arranged for the arrest and imprisonment of Methodius.

To resolve this situation, the new pope, John VIII, yet again summoned Methodius to Rome, along with his incarcerators. But Svatopluk, ruler of Great Moravia, had in the meantime intervened on Methodius' behalf and won his release from prison in 870. Still, the German bishops did not relent in their opposition to the Slavonic liturgy, and Svatopluk himself was not a determined defender, being more interested in power politics than liturgy. He was busy expanding his realm, particularly to the North, and in 874 to 877, he annexed the region around the Vistula River (in modern-day Poland).[25]

In 880 Methodius returned to Rome to resolve jurisdictional problems and conflicts with Latin-rite clergy in Great Moravia. It is true that the Pope again confirmed Methodius' ecclesiastical faculties from 870 and his rank as Archbishop and Papal Legate, but he also appointed a German monk, Wiching, Bishop of Nitra. Later, owing to Wiching's continual intrigues, Methodius managed to consign him to missionary work in the Vistula region in Poland. One of the accomplishments of Methodius' last visit to Rome was a compromise by which the Gospel was to be proclaimed in the liturgy first in Latin, and then in Old Church Slavonic; another accomplishment was an agreement by which the Holy See assumed patronage over Svatopluk.[26] Methodius died on April 6ᵗʰ 885. Several months before his death he completed a translation of the Bible into Old Church Slavonic.

In the East Frankish realm, events unfolded which seriously weakened its structure, in effect providing Svatopluk with a significant opportunity to expand his domain. He laid waste to the lands of his political enemies, acted like an equal of Charles the Fat, the Carolingian Emperor, and in 885 signed an advantageous peace pact with Bavaria. Later he annexed Bohemia[27] and Lusatia.[28] He also took pity on Wiching, allowing him to return to Great Moravia, and somehow managed to persuade the Holy See to condemn 'ex post facto' Methodius' missionary work and to outlaw the use of Old Church Slavonic in liturgy. Papal legates shut down the Slavonic seminary and sent its teachers and students into exile with the full endorsement of Svatopluk. The Slavonic exiles subsequently found refuge in Bulgaria, where they were able to carry on.

In the meantime Arnulf consolidated his power in Bavaria, appointing Wiching chancellor, and in 893 he mounted an attack on Great Moravia,

*Foundation of basilica
in Bratislavsky Hrad,
(Turn of 9ᵗʰ–10ᵗʰ
Century)*

roundly devastating it. He began to envisage himself as emperor, an advancement which he eventually did achieve.

After Svatopluk's death in 894, Mojmir, his son, became ruler of Great Moravia. His reign began rather inauspiciously, because the Czech princes succeeded in seceding from Great Moravia, and at the diet in Regensburg, in 895,[29] swore allegiance to Arnulf. Two years later the Lusatian Serbs[30] also seceded.

Mojmir's younger brother, Svatopluk II, also made a bid to take over Great Moravia, and Bavarian feudal lords stepped into the power struggle on his behalf. But by this time, Magyars (Hungarians) had made an appearance in the Danubian Basin,[31] on the move from their original homeland,[32] seeking new locations for permanent settlement. The location they chose was the territory of Great Moravia, which they demolished as a state, and in 907, it was they, not the Moravians, who successfully put up in the vicinity of Bratislava, a military barrier to the Bavarians' farther penetration of the Danubian Basin.

Bronze crucifix with three engraved figures, Turn of 9th–10th Century, (Maca)

Regarding the territory of Great Moravia, it should be noted that its heartland was the area of present-day Nitra, while Zahorie[33] (now in Western Slovakia) was probably part of Moravia, as was Moravske Pole (Marchfeld, in present-day Austria). To its south, Great Moravia was bounded by the Danube River.[34] After Svatopluk's conquests, its borders extended much farther south, even abutting the territory of the Bulgars. Indirectly, it could also make a claim on Trans-Danubia (Pannonia),[35] where Pribina, the exiled former ruler of Nitra, resided with his son Kocel, and where the Byzantine mission had also been active.

Not many relics of Great Moravia have come down to us, and the ones that have do not come from Slovakia, but from Moravia. Of the ecclesiastical structures, the church on Martin's Knoll in Nitra is indubitably of Great Moravian provenance, as is the round chapel near Ducova and the church on the fortified promontory of Devin, as well as the sacral objects found on Bratislava's fort mound.

The weapons, spurs, jewelry and buttons surviving from Great Moravia are made of iron, silver and bronze. Great Moravia did not mint its own coins, nor was it acquainted with the potter's wheel, though many preceding cultures had already possessed that technology. On the other hand, its foundry operations were well developed.

Considerable attention has been paid to socio-economic conditions in Great Moravia, but most of the results have been debatable, including the thesis that Great Moravia was an early feudal formation. Archeological research will no doubt produce many surprising discoveries, which will serve to define in greater detail the size and significance of this state.[36]

3. The Arrival of the Magyars: Building of Hungary

Like other ethnic groups, Magyars did not occupy the whole territory on which they eventually settled in one fell swoop, but gradually with the passage of time. By 881 they had appeared in the vicinity of Vienna, and a year later Methodius had run into them on his way to Byzantium. The main Magyar surge occupied the Danubian Basin in 896, bringing with it an entourage of other ethnic groups, which had their own linguistic and cultural customs: for instance, the Szeklers and Polovtsians, who settled in separate areas but were later assimilated.[1]

The Magyars who invaded Central Europe were nomads. Their warriors moved about on horseback and, finding the level plains of the Central Danube and Tisa River Basins much to their liking, they occupied those areas in the first phase of their incursions, only gradually invading what is present-day Slovakia.

Immediately after their entry into the Central Danube region, the Magyars began making raids into surrounding countries. In 907 the East Frankish kingdom had no alternative but to mount a great campaign against them. The aggressive newcomers, however, easily overcame the Frankish army, which had advanced down both sides of the Danube near Bratislava.

The Magyars made the most of this victory and of the power vacuum that had appeared west of the lands they occupied. For half a century they orga-

Arrival of Magyars in Pannonia

27

Archduke Geza

nized campaigns in all directions, penetrating very deeply into Germany, including its Western, Central and Northern regions, as well as Italy, France, and Spain. The ethnic peoples of these regions, lacking military capacity to resist, were horrified by these plundering raids. Long and hard, they sought a means of effective defense, for the Magyars, coming quickly and unexpectedly, seized their plunder and as quickly galloped off. It was the Emperor Otto I who, in 955, finally brought them to a halt in the Battle of Lechfeld near Augsburg.

This battle proved pivotal. Magyar tribal chieftains were at last forced to recognize that their further existence in the Danubian lowlands could no longer be sustained by raids on neighboring peoples, and that their manner of living had to undergo a change: they needed to progress from simple herding to livestock breeding and a settled agricultural way of life. This fundamental change is evidenced by the large number of Magyar words adapted from Slavic in the fields of government, culture, religion, agriculture, crafts, etc. – all relating to a more settled way of life.[2]

Duke Stephen in initial of illustrated chronicle

The most significant Magyar leader after their defeat in 955, and before they founded their state, was Prince Geza of the Arpad clan. Just before he died in 997, he converted to Christianity and was baptized by the Czech Bishop Adalbert, who at the same time baptized Geza's son, Vajk, giving them both the Christian name Stephen.[3] Vajk (Stephen) shortly thereafter became the first king of Hungary.[4]

Crown of King Stephen

At that time, the Magyars had not yet penetrated the mountains and heavily forested hills of Slovakia, so the Polish King Boleslav the Brave, of the Piast Dynasty, attempted to occupy a considerable portion of Slovakia, mainly in the West, and thus to extend the boundary of his newly-formed state to the Danube. This expansion lasted only to the end of 1018, when the Polish and Hungarian kings reached an accord by which the Polish king surrendered all claims to any land south of the Carpathian range. Thus, a major part of what is Slovakia today was incorporated in the Hungarian state for good. However, for a short time before this event, the Czech duke Boleslav I also occupied part of Slovakia.

The Arpad Dynasty ruled Hungary for three centuries, during which it produced three outstanding statesmen.

The most important of these statesmen was Stephen I, King of Hungary (Saint Stephen), who ruled from 1000 to 1038. He realized the importance of Christianity for his own ethnic group as well as the others over which he ruled, and accepted its western variant, relying on Christian traditions which the Magyars had found already extant when they arrived, and on the Christianizing activities of missionaries in the Danubian Basin from 955 to 1000. Esztergom became the seat of church administration and the residence of the primate of Hungary. Stephen saw to the building of a parochial system and other church institutions, assigning to every ten villages responsibility for building a communal church. He married Gisela, sister of the Bavarian Duke Henry II, thus orienting his country politically to the West and to the Pope, although a strong-Byzantine influence still remained in the southeast regions of his new kingdom.

King Stephen organized his kingdom into counties[5] and appointed counts[6] to administer them. Each county had a central seat (usually fortified), to which were subordinated a given number of villages, of which the male nobility were obligated to present themselves on command, armed and ready for battle. The peasantry were required to give the church a tithe of their crop production, which was earmarked for distribution to various religious institutions.[7]

During Stephen's reign, Old Hungary became a thoroughly feudal state: alongside royal and ecclesiastical land existed huge holdings by nobility. On these lands lived serfs, providing farming services to the lords.

Duel, King Ladislav vs. a Cuman (scene from fresco in church at Velka Lomnica, Early 14th Century)

To this day, Magyars consider Stephen their principal patron saint. Devotion to him spread to Slovakia too, as evidenced by many churches consecrated to him. No wonder, considering that Slovaks lived for nine whole centuries in the state he founded, seven of them free of ethnic strife and misunderstandings – a far-reaching legacy of his high regard for non-Magyar ethnics.[8]

The second outstanding personage of the Arpad Dynasty was King Ladislav I[9] who reigned from 1077 to 1095. He endeavored to strengthen and centralize the ruler's power, which had diminished under weak predecessors. This strengthening is attested by the legal code he composed, which reinforced the internal structure of Hungary by regulating judicial, administrative and economic affairs; and he founded additional bishoprics (e.g. the Nitra diocese in 1083), thus updating the feudal church structure. He excelled in Christian virtue, was a moral exemplar to his subjects in every respect, and was even elevated to sainthood. In foreign policy, Ladislav repelled the Pecheneg incursions[10] and, between the years 1089–1091, annexed Croatia. His nephew Koloman, who ruled from 1095 to 1116, completed the Hungarian state-building process.

Bela IV (1235–1270) also devoted his efforts to firming up royal power, which, thanks to the unhealthy ambitions of the upper nobility, had fallen into

*Supposed crown of
Emperor Constantine
Monomach,
11th Century,
(Ivanka pri Nitre)*

decline. During his reign he reduced the Bosnians, Serbians, Bulgarians and Wallachians to vassalage. But also during this period, the Tatars (Tartars) overran Hungary, wreaking huge material havoc on its inhabitants. When they withdrew, Bela invited settlers, mostly German,[11] to help revive Hungary's economic life, bestowing considerable privileges on them. He arranged for the building of strongholds and fortified towns, thus strengthening the realm's defenses.

The other rulers of the Arpad Dynasty, except for Bela III, made no significant contributions to the realm.[12] They reigned for a relatively short time or suffered untimely deposition, often with help from neighboring German rulers. And, of course, Hungary had to cope with internal power struggles within the royal family.

Andrew I

In its first century Hungary was the target of military assaults from the West mounted by German emperors and kings. As early as 1030, Conrad II marshalled his forces against Bratislava, which had become an important border stronghold of the new Hungarian kingdom, but without success.

Henry II, one of the most notable medieval German emperors, seeking to subjugate Hungary, launched an even more energetic and ambitious offensive. The Hungarian struggle for sovereignty lasted 10 years, interrupted only occasionally by truces.

Romanesque church,
Early 11ᵗʰ Century,
(Drazovce pri Nitre)

In 1043, Henry III launched yet another offensive against Hungary with even greater force. Around the beginning of July 1044, he defeated the Hungarian king, routing him and his army, then replaced him with a protégé, Peter.[13] The latter, however, was soon displaced on the throne by Andrew I, who set about renewing border strongholds and building new ones, at the same time renouncing fealty to the German empire and placing in charge of his army the capable Duke Bela, his brother, a measure which, for a time, discouraged further attacks.

A new war between the German Emperor Henry III and Hungarian King Andrew I broke out in 1050. In August of that year, Henry again marched his forces into Hungary, advancing by both land and the Danube River; the first battles occurred near Hainburg and lasted several weeks. However, the progress of the imperial forces was effectively blocked by the approach of winter.

Andrew made overtures of peace but in 1052, Emperor Henry returned in yet another attempt to subjugate Hungary. Once more he chose to advance down the Danube, which literally swarmed with boats under his personal command. This time, the campaign against Hungary was launched a lot earlier and troops were already at Bratislava's gates by July. The imperial army besieged the town, but its defenders fought heroically, inflicting huge losses on the aggressors.

At this point, Pope Leo IX intervened. Having sought out the emperor for help for his own embattled papal state, he reached him in the midst of the Bratislava seige and was able to dissuade him from the disastrous exercise. The hostile parties halted their confrontation, and not only did Emperor Henry fail to reduce Hungary to vassalage, but soon afterwards, at the Imperial Diet in Goslar, he bethrothed his daughter to King Andrew's son, Solomon.[14]

Bronze Corpus,
12ᵗʰ Century, (Krasno)

A half-century later, during the reign of King Koloman, a later German ruler, Henry V, together with his vassal, the Czech Prince Svatopluk, again unsuccessfully attempted to take Bratislava and to march on the interior of Hungary.

After Hungary subjugated Croatia, the Central European balance of power shifted: the German Empire was reduced to a mere formality, leaving the field to Austria and Bavaria, with a combined military might inferior to that of the Hungarian kingdom. Border conflicts between them petered out, but battles raged all the more fiercely on the southern frontier, where Hungary faced Venice and other powers, mostly on the high seas. These clashes, however, had little to do with Slovakia, except perhaps indirectly.

During the reign of Andrew II, the focus of Hungarian foreign policy shifted to the northeast border (i.e. Slovakia). Andrew II launched about twenty offensives against Galicia[15] in attempts to annex it. In these offensives

Andrew's forces were victorious, but as soon as they withdrew, the local princes and magnates reclaimed their independence. Andrew II also participated in the 1217 Christian Crusade to the Near East, with designs on the imperial crown of Byzantium, which were never realized.

But no serious politico-military conflicts affecting Slovakia occurred until the middle of the 13th Century, when the Babenberger dynasty of Austria died out, and two monarchs began to vie for control: the ambitious Czech King Premysl Otakar II, and the Hungarian King Bela IV. In 1254 they divided the territories of Austria and Styria. But, as it turned out, neither was happy with the result, and in 1260 the clangor of arms once again resounded. The hostile armies met at the Morava River, comprising on the Czech side, contingents from Bohemia, Austria, Moravia, Silesia, Carinthia, Saxony and Brandenburg, and on the Hungarian side, contingents from Hungary, Russia, Poland, Bulgaria, Galicia, Serbia, and even Tartary. On the 12th of July, Hungarian light cavalry crossed the Morava River and attacked, only to incur a crushing defeat, which put the whole Hungarian army to rout in the direction of Bratislava. Happily, the hostilities were finally resolved with a wedding between King Otakar and the niece of King Bela in Bratislava.

In 1271 another clash flared up, between the same Otakar II and Stephen V, the new Hungarian king. Otakar crossed the Morava River and captured Stupava, Devin, and Bratislava, which he ravaged, burning down churches and even individual homes, laying waste to municipal fortifications and destroying

King Bela IV,
fleeing from Tatars

many valuable relics in the city archives and the monastic chapterhouse. Leaving a garrison in the town citadel, he devastated the Vah and Hron river valleys, and turned to Pannonia, to assist his forces against the Hungarians there.

When Stephen V died in 1272 and Ladislav IV the Cuman[16] ascended the throne, strife again erupted between the two neighboring rulers. Premysl Otakar II again captured Bratislava, but when he learned that Rudolph of Habsburg had been chosen Holy Roman Emperor instead of himself, he hurried home to prepare for battle with the 'interloper'. He took the field in 1278.[17] The Hungarian king, siding with Rudolph, sent 70,000 Hungarians and 16,000 Cumans into the fray. A decisive battle took place on August 26, 1278, not far from Bratislava, at Moravske Pole (Marchfeld). Premysl Otakar, defeated, fell on the field of battle, along with 14,000 of his warriors.[18]

But Hungary had endured much worse during the fairly recent Tatar (Tartar) incursions of 1241 and 1242. In March 1241, Tatars under Batu Khan had invaded Hungary through Carpathian mountain passes, and, in a decisive battle on the Slana River, had inflicted a crushing defeat on the Hungarians. King Bela IV had barely escaped by fleeing to Croatia and Dalmatia. In April 1241, a second wave of Tatars, from Moravia, had invaded Slovakia, devastating mainly the western regions. By the end of January 1242 both Tatar armies had combined near Esztergom, subjecting all of Hungary to their ravages.

The Tatars devastated southwest Slovakia, the Vah and Hron river valleys, and probably the County of Spis as well. Only well-fortified strongholds withstood their assaults. But when their great Khan Ughetai died, they departed for home, their commander, Khan Batu, eager to lay claim to the empty throne. And so, as fast as they had come, they were gone.

Ironically, Ladislav IV the Cuman later summoned their help in his struggle with the Hungarian nobility. The Tatars, on this later occasion, wreaked havoc on the counties of Spis, Saris, and Abov. However, they themselves, with their chieftain Nogaj Khan, went down to defeat in 1288 at Podolinec.

What proved to be of lasting significance for Slovakia was the founding of towns, and the royal bestowal of broad privileges on them, like those already enjoyed by the towns of Western and Southern Europe. Trnava received such privileges in 1238; Zvolen and Krupina even before the Tatar incursions; Nitra in 1248; Kosice before 1248; Banska Stiavnica before 1255; Banska Bystrica in 1255; Nemecka Lupca in 1263; Komarno in 1265; Kezmarok in 1269; Gelnica before 1270; and several other towns in the 14th Century. In the County of Spis, German settlements received their collective privileges from King Stephen V in 1271.

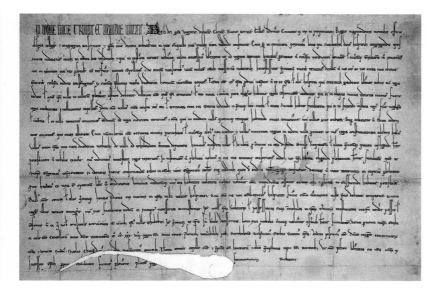

Bela IV, grant of royal privilege to town of Trnava, 1238.

Additionally, in medieval Slovakia many villages sprang up, whose inhabitants held land on the basis of hereditary rights of useage, passed on from parents to children or to close relatives.

Towns settled by Germans became centers of crafts and commerce, and, in some cases, of mining. Farmers from Germany brought new and better methods of tilling the soil. Particularly unique among the privileges of German towns was the right to freely choose their mayors and town councils, an almost unprecedented right in European towns of the time, London being a notable exception. Elsewhere, rich patricians ruled towns, co-opting people from their own midst to fill vacancies in the town council with no input from ordinary townspeople. Following the example of towns, smaller settlements and villages were gradually able to freely elect mayors. In this way Slovakia, as early as the Middle Ages, became an area of communal self-government, another first in Europe.[19]

Thus, the socio-economic relationships that the German settlers introduced became a model that was consciously emulated by local Slovaks. Slovakia became a country in which only Western European forms of social and economic life prevailed; towns, whose citizens were merchants, miners, and free craftsmen, had original charters, unknown elsewhere. In villages, farmers owned their soil individually, by inherited right, with two or three fields each. However, this system did not reach its full development until the following century. Claims that a system of ownership by clan or commune existed, similar to those prevalent among Eastern or Southern Slavs, are totally unfounded.

Golden Bull of Andrew II,
1222 (reverse side)

A huge breakthrough in Hungarian history was King Andrew II's promulgation of the 'Golden Bull' in 1222. What happened in Hungary was substantially the same as had just recently happened in England, where in 1215 the barons forced King John 'Lackland' with the 'Magna Carta' to accept a declaration of the rights of the various classes of his subjects. In Hungary the magnates additionally forced the king to change the royally-controlled system of counties, initiated by King Stephan, to an autonomous system run by the gentry.[20] The Counties henceforth administered the regions entrusted to their care, without interference from the king, and could every year elect their own officials from among a plurality of candidates. This system remained in force up to 1848. It is true that a county commissioner was appointed by the king to head each county, or alternatively the position was held 'ex officio' (for instance, in Nitra County the diocesan bishop was automatically the commissioner), but these commissioners had only a titular function, the real executive power lying in the hands of the vice-commissioner, the sheriff, and the judges elected from among the nobility. Thus the constitution of Old Hungary was, as far back as the middle of the 13th Century, quite unique and not an imitation; all the officials and dignitaries were elected, including the highest political personage, the Palatine.[21] In the Medieval Ages the Hungarian nobility convened for diets and election of a Palatine (the post was for life) in the village of Rakos, near Buda.[22]

Economic conditions in Slovakia from the 10th through to the 12th Century were characterized by settlements of skilled craftsmen in the vicinity of strongholds, where they turned their products over to the feudal lord, or bartered with fellow-townsmen. Thus, there were villages of blacksmiths (Kovace, Kovacova: kovac = blacksmith), potters (Hrnciarovce: hrniec = pot), carpenters (Tesare: tesar = carpenter), plus villages named after shield-makers, fishermen, pitch-makers, bee-keepers, breeders of hounds and falcons, and still other skilled workmen, as reflected in village names to the present day.

Other types of settlements with unique social constituency were villages comprising ordinary slaves (mostly prisoners of war, bought and sold by owners), church slaves (donated to the church in solicitation of prayers for eternal salvation), and freedmen.

The Hungarian kings founded settlements along the Slovak border areas to act as outposts, manned by the ethnics that had accompanied them to Europe, for instance the Szeklers (village of Sekule), Polovtsians (villages of Plavecky Stvrtok and Plavecke Podhradie), or Magyars/Hungarians (villages of Uhorska Ves and Uhorske), which were very quickly assimilated to the Slovak ethnic.

Basilica in Esztergom

The natural world of Slovakia in the 10th through to the 12th Centuries still retained its pristine character. Various animals were still to be found, such as aurochs (European bison), and beavers, which left traces in place names (for instance Tura Luka – Aurochs' Meadow; Zuberec – Bison Field; Bobrovec – Beaver Pond). Woods swarmed with game; streams swam with fish, including pike, sheatfish, and in the North, grayling and trout. But few fish ponds had as yet been built. In the steep mountain valleys, where land was unsuitable for grain, livestock grazed; in the lowlands, however, the more demanding wheat crop flourished. Water mills can be dated to as early as the 12th Century. It is supposed that horses were widely used as draft animals. The major landowners in Slovakia were the king, the upper nobility, and the church (the Archbishopric of Esztergom, the Bishopric of Nitra, monastic chapters and monasteries). In addition, there were petty nobility (whose numbers and economic importance grew after the gentry assumed control of formerly royal counties), and the garrisons of strongholds, who had previously worked the land but now were land-owners (hence, obligated to military service), and who, after the promulgation of the Golden Bull, advanced to privileged status.

Slovak peasants (serfs) turned over to their lords a portion of their natural produce, particularly grain, livestock, chickens and eggs, plus labor if their lords owned estates. The whole economic life of the feudal lord and peasant was directed towards self-sufficiency, i.e. the wresting of their livelihoods from their own resources. Before the arrival of German settlers and the spread of 'privileges', serfs had no rights to the land they worked, and certainly no hereditary rights. The lord could evict them as he pleased and turn his land over to someone else.

Peasants also sold part of their produce at market, which originally operated on Sundays or Saturdays. Later on, market rights were recognized on other days as well, and thus weekdays crept into the names of communities conducting fairs (e, g. Dunajska Streda – Danubian Wednesday; Plavecky Stvrtok – Polovtsian Thursday; Rimavska Sobota – Rimavan Saturday). Merchants even came from foreign lands, though they were required to pay heavy duties and tolls at bridges, fords and other locations. The income from these posts went mainly into royal coffers. The king also taxed coin-minting, controlled by Jews and Ismaelites[23] who had settled in Nitra before 1111. The right to control the quality of coins, however, belonged to the Archbishop of Esztergom.

A major power-broker and cultural arbiter in these times was the medieval church. It is true, a diocesan see (Nitra) existed in Slovakia from very early on, but even so, a majority of Slovak villages and towns belonged to the Archdiocese of Esztergom, while the villages of eastern Slovakia fell under the

Capital of column with relief, First Half of 13th Century, (Bina)

jurisdiction of the bishop of Eger. The most significant medieval monasteries, Benedictine and Cistercian, were at Mt. Zobor near Nitra, Hronsky Benadik, Krasna nad Hornadom, and Bzovik. There were also monasteries in Jasov and Leles, which were founded by Premonstratensian canons.[24] The monastery in Bratislava was a place of worship and a cultural center in one. The monastery in Spis (Spisska Kapitula) was also very influencial. Not far from the border of present-day Slovakia in Vysehrad (Visegrad) lay a monastery of monks of the Byzantine rite.

Monuments of this period are Romanesque: for instance the stone rotundas in Bin, Trencin and Skalica, the circular palace in the Spis stronghold (Spissky Hrad), and the rectangular structure in Kostolany pod Tribecom. One can still make out the remains of original frescos on the interior walls of the churches in Kostolany pod Tribecom (11th Century) and Dechtice (12th Century).

Spis Chapter;
Spis Stronghold
in background

Of the newly founded cities, some (Bratislava, Trnava, Kosice) immediately began building ramparts and thus were incorporated in a network of strongholds defending against invaders.

Great strides were made in 13th Century Slovak mining: prior to the arrival of German settlers, miners primarily worked on the surface (strip-mining); later they dug shafts and headings, drilled ventilation ducts and drained water, all of which demanded considerable financial outlays.

Ducat minted in Kremnica

At the beginning of the 13th Century the most important mining district was Banska Stiavnica, but, starting in the middle of the century, Banska Bystrica moved to the forefront with silver and copper mines. In the vicinity of Kremnica serious mining ventures did not begin until the the 14th Century.

In the middle of the 13th Century, silver mining was launched in Roznava and Gelnica, the latter becoming an important mining town, with mineheads located in the Hnilec and Smolnica river valleys. Spisska Nova Ves became a center for the extraction of copper and iron ore.

At first, most entrepreneurs in mining and metal forging came from the Alpine regions of Europe; later they came from Lower Saxony. Thanks to the development of its towns and its mines and forges, but above all, to the discovery of precious metals, Slovakia began to play an ever larger role in the economic life of Hungary, becoming its most fully-fledged economic region.

At the turn of the 12th Century about 200,000 people lived in Slovakia, with a probable increase to about a quarter of a million by the time of the Tatar (Tartar) incursions. These people lived in more than 1,500 towns and villages. Population density grew in the course of the 13th Century mostly in the vicinity of the Morava River, on the right bank of the Vah River between Pruske and Puchov, on its left bank in the vicinity of Trencin, south of Zilina, and in the Upper Nitra Valley. Unsettled areas remained only in the northernmost regions of Trencin County, the southernmost part of Turiec County, and in the westernmost areas of Liptov County. Population remained sparse in Orava County, in northern Tekov County, in the Upper Hron Valley, in the most southeasterly part of Zvolen County, in northern Gemer County, in northern Saris County, and in Zemplin County, north of the town of Humenne.

4.   The Late Medieval Age

Other kings, whose reigns fell between these great men, or after them, were not particularly memorable. For instance, the two Jagiellonians closing out this period wielded scepters for only short periods.

By the end of the Medieval Ages, the character of Slovakia and its people was set for several subsequent centuries. It can be safely stated that they had become a country and people of Western-European lifestyle and mentality, with western ideas of land ownership. Most Slovaks were Roman Catholic, like the rest of Western Europe, but in the far eastern regions, Byzantine-rite Christianity still held on, intermingling and overlapping with the predominant Roman rite. Rusyns[1] living in the most northeasterly region of Slovakia also professed Byzantine-rite Christianity.

In the political realm, the principles anchored in the Golden Bull of King Andrew II, and confirmed by King Louis I, gelled into definitive form, establishing the dominance of the nobility over the king, as elsewhere in Western Europe. But Hungary, and with it Slovakia, enjoyed a lot of original and positive features in this system not found elsewhere. One such feature was the hierarchy of power in the counties: basically, power was vested in elected dignitaries, chosen from among the petty and middle nobility. Slovakia in the Medieval Ages thus knew only shared political power, at the highest as well as lowest levels, whereas in most other class-based European states including England, control was vested only in the highest level, in the crown and parliament.

The highest legislative power, controlling the conduct of the ruler and having a say in his selection, was not representative in form; indeed, all the nobility (ruling classes) convened 'in toto' for deliberation, i.e. every member of the nobility was eligible to participate in the diet, and decisions had to be unanimous to be valid. The principle of 'majority rule' was still unknown in the Medieval Ages, so that even in county assemblies, resolutions had to be carried unanimously to pass.

This rule was applicable to the election of a palatine as well, though in practice, the crown's preference carried a lot of weight, since king and palatine needed to work in close collaboration.

We know that the rules governing procedures at the highest levels of the body politic (the diet) were also applicable at its lowest levels (the town councils). The mayor and members of the town council were usually elected for terms of one year. Elections took place in each town on an individual date. For instance, in Bratislava, they were held on the feast of St. George; in Pezinok, on the feast of St. Adalbert; in Trencin, on December 30; in Banska Bystrica and Lubietova on New Year's Eve overlapping into the New Year; in Kremnica, Banska Stiavnica and Nova Bana, on Candlemas; and in Kosice, on Epiphany. Some towns, such as Bardejov, Presov, Sabinov, and Levoca, prescribing no precise date, left the decision to the council, which gave notice several weeks in advance.

By the end of the Medieval Ages, settlements had been established over the whole of Slovakia. Villages formed even in the most remote mountain valleys to the North. All told, there were about 3,000 villages and towns, with an aggregate population of perhaps 400,000. By the beginning of the 16th Century that number had grown to about half a million, averaging out to about 23–26 persons per square mile. Western Slovakia was most densely populated, mainly owing to its favorable climate and landscape. Least populated was Central Slovakia, with its heavily forested and mountainous terrain.

Not only did new villages form, but old villages sometimes died out, a common occurrence in the late Medieval Ages, often without ascertainable cause. The Black Death, which devasted the population of most of Europe in the years 1348–1349, struck only a glancing blow at Slovakia and did not claim many lives.

Towns acquired a progressively greater role in the economic life of Slovakia, the most important ones winning privileges as early as the 13th Century, but by the end of the 14th Century other towns had joined them: Zilina (prior to 1312), then Ruzomberok (1318), Bardejov (1320), Pukanec (1321), Smolnik (1327), Kremnica (1328), Stara Lubovna (1379), Brezno (1380), Senica (1396), and still others.

Towns became centers of craft production, maintaining a high level of skills, which guaranteed a steady influx of qualified craftsmen from Germany, Austria and other countries of Central Europe. Indeed, a requirement for a fully-trained German craftsman included wide travel, and thus, often a traveling journeyman came wandering into one of our towns and never again returned to his home.

Slovakian crafts gradually achieved a mastery equal to that of the Germans, though as late as the first half of the 13th Century, they had been nowhere near that level. In medieval Slovak towns there were relatively few master craftsmen, but obviously all the more apprentices: masters' helpers, whose job it was to create demand among villagers, because, judging by evidence, there was no significant craft production in villages.

German craftsmen also founded guilds in their new homeland, but in our towns, guilds played the role of special interest groups, not political organizations seeking representation on town councils. In our towns, craftsmen could be seated on town councils like anybody else, i.e. by individual election, with every townsman eligible to vote. There were none of the bloody battles that played out in the towns of Central and Western Europe in the 13th and 14th Centuries.

Guilds got a relatively late start in Slovakia's towns. The first guild with written bylaws was organized in Podolinec by the town's shoemakers in 1415. By the end of the Medieval Ages, eight guilds had been founded in Kosice, seven in Presov, six in Bratislava, five each in Levoca and Bardejov, three each in Banska Bystrica, Banska Stiavnica and Kremnica, two in Kezmarok, one apiece in Lubica, Komarno, Trnava, Spisska Nova Ves, Krupina and Nemecka Lupca.

In the Medieval Ages there were many towns in Slovakia, distributed over the whole of the country. But they were small, and only a few of them had more than two to three thousand residents. A role no less important than that of the crafts was played in these towns by local as well as foreign merchants.

Weekly market days and annual fairs played a pivotal role in fostering domestic trade. For the most part, agricultural products were sold at town markets, and craft products and livestock at fairs. The most important locations for foreign trade were Kosice, Trnava, Bratislava, Levoca and Bardejov. Eastern Slovak towns took advantage of their vantage-point on the important trade

Water pitcher with green glaze, (Krizovany nad Dudvahom)

43

Tile with green glaze,
(Bratislava)

route between the Black Sea and Baltic ports. When in 1453 the Turks occupied Constantinople and the Black-Sea Coast, this trade route lost its significance.

Very important in the history of medieval Slovak towns was the invitation accorded them, under Emperor Sigismund of Luxembourg, to participate in the Diet as the Fourth Estate, alongside prelates and magnates (First and Second Estates, respectively), and nobility (Third Estate). No law could be passed without their consent, a rule that remained in force to the end of feudalism.

One of the unique phenomena of Slovak history in this period was well-developed mining and forging of copper and iron. These industries were so extensive that they placed Slovakia at the forefront of copper and iron forging in the entire world.

The most significant mining region was Central Slovakia, with operations in Banska Stiavnica, Kremnica, and Banska Bystrica. Ores were also mined in the vicinity of Pukanec and Nova Bana. Another significant mining region was Spis County, with operations in Gelnica, Smolnik, and Spisska Nova Ves, and Gemer County, with operations in Roznava. Liptov County was also known for its ore deposits.

In the middle of the 14th Century, mining for gold in the vicinity of Kremnica yielded 400 kg, but by the end of the 15th Century, the yield had dropped to about 250 kg. In the last two-thirds of the 14th Century, the production of silver in the district of Banska Stiavnica totaled several thousand kilograms annually.

Medieval Bardejov

Between 1410 and 1439 the mines of Smolnik yielded about 182 tons of copper annually; at the beginning of the 16th Century the yield was down to approximately 120 to 150 tons.

Gold and silver coins, Kremnica Mint

Iron ore was extracted in the region of Slovenske Rudohorie (Slovak Ore Mountains), while foundries were located in the vicinities of Gelnica, Krompachy, Richnava, Jasov, Stos, Medzev and the Hron River Basin. Bellows driven by water-wheels were installed in these foundries, as well as forging presses. The first mention of a forge on our territory comes from Stitnik in 1344. Mining regulations were codified by King Charles Robert in 'Banska Sloboda' (Mining Freedoms), in 1327.

The extraction of precious metals was the preserve of the king himself, who established royal mining bureaus to oversee operations, as well as two coin-minting bureaus, in Kremnica and Smolnik. The actual business of extracting and smelting was conducted by mining entrepreneurs and thousands of miners, who were organized into companies for maximum productivity. Jan Thurzo, a member of the gentry from Betlanovce in Spis County, as well as a townsmen of both Levoca in Slovakia, and Cracow in Poland, organized the most important such entrepreneurial company. At the end of the 15th Century, he joined forces with a South German banking house, the Fuggers of Augsburg. The Fugger-Thurzo Company became a giant in the extraction and

Banska Stiavnica

45

Coat-of-Arms, town of Kosice, 1502

processing of copper and other metals, with headquarters in Banska Bystrica, and mines and foundries all over Central Slovakia and even in Poland (near Cracow). In the years between 1494–1526 this company, without parallel in Europe, produced an average of 2,550 tons of copper annually, exporting it to markets in Germany, Poland, the Netherlands and Portugal. It also exported large quantities of silver and lesser quantities of iron.

Not only were Fugger-Thurzo's operations immense, but the standard of living it provided to employees was very high: workers enjoyed an eight-hour day, had health and old-age insurance, and guaranteed pensions for widows and orphans.

A very significant event of this period was the 1330 establishment of a mint in Kremnica, for production of golden ducats. These ducats became one of the most sought-after currencies in Europe. This mint also produced silver 'groshen' (sixteen groshen equaled one ducat, four ducats a silver talent). For small change it produced dinars and half-dinars.

At the end of the Medieval Ages the status of Slovaks in towns markedly improved, though most townsmen were still German. Because many Slovaks had evidently already achieved burgher status, in 1381 King Louis I decided to grant them equal representation on town councils, which usually comprised twelve members.

The demands of Slovaks for equal representation were also accommodated in Trnava, where a struggle for the election of a town pastor pitted Slovaks against Germans. King Mattias (Matthew) Corvinus himself, intervened by

Privilege Grant to Zilina Slovaks, 1381

46

Trnava, ca. 1657

decreeing the instigation of ethnic discord a capital crime. Henceforth, Slovaks were guaranteed equal representation on the town council.

Similarly, in 1517 King Louis II allowed the town court in Krupina to assign the same weight to testimony of a Slovak townsman as to that of a German. Two years later, both Slovaks and Magyars acquired the right to buy houses in town.

In 1518, in Kremnica, the right to buy a house, and thus to acquire property, a typical mark of rights reserved to German settlers, was extended to Slovaks.

Signal evidence of the gradual emancipation of Slovaks vis-à-vis Germans, and of the Slovak language vis-à-vis German, is a 1473 officially mandated translation of the legal code of Zilina into Slovakized Czech.[2]

In summary, it is safe to say that, by the end of the Medieval Ages, Slovak self-awareness in villages and towns had already emerged, although it lacked a political structure on which to lean.[3] Thus, alongside a loose sense of Slovak ethnicity among the common folk, there certainly existed a sense of allegiance to the Hungarian state among the Slovak-speaking nobility, for during the feudal period, this social stratum naturally oriented to the state in which it enjoyed its privileges. (And, it should be remembered that Hungary at this time was a state in which the official language was Latin.)

In Slovakia, the situation of serfs in villages changed with the universal spread of a system, which included heritable rights through purchase, brought in by German settlers. The system was characterized by a division of arable land and pastures into so-called 'sessie' (tenures). Such a system already existed in Bohemia, Moravia, Poland, Silesia, the Baltic region, Transylvania, Western Hungary, and elsewhere. However, in contrast to the above countries, where one 'sessio' comprised 30 jutros (approximately six acres), our 'sessio' varied in size from village to village. When a feudal lord partitioned land for distribution to serfs, it may be assumed that he believed in the mutual rewards of the new arrangement. Such an assumption proved to be accurate in Slovakia. As a consequence, land cultivation by the lord himself lapsed, yielding to a system of monetary payments by serfs to their lords for use of land.

Early on, when settlers from the West took up residence in villages, hereditary magistrates still headed town councils, receiving stipulated fees for services (judging cases, operating water mills, etc.) These villages soon adopted the German system of hereditary property rights and began electing their magistrates. This system spread and gradually became predominant.

Note that it was precisely this system of divided ownership, reserving ultimate ownership to a feudal lord, but assigning practical ownership (rights of use, i.e. tenancy) to the peasant actually working the land, that advanced Western Civilization to the forefront of civilization. For it was precisely this assignment of somewhat limited ownership rights to the masses that motivated hard work and individual initiative, whereas in other civilizations, rights of ownership rested in the hands of the few, with a consequent stifling effect on the masses. It should be noted that, apart from Czechs and Slovaks, other Slav nations acquired such limited rights to land ownership only in isolated instances. In Hungary only Germans and Slovaks enjoyed this unique right. It had no parallel among Rusyns, Romanians, Croats and other ethnics, and among the Magyars the system was common only west of the Danube.

The spread of unique rights of land purchase and bequest meant that Slovak peasants could sell their holdings at any time and move elsewhere, even though in some places the local (county) statutes could limit their application. Of course, even in the Medieval Ages there were more humane and less humane feudal lords, just as there were more and less industrious peasants.

Nitra, 1657

Still, if a peasant failed to carry his weight, the feudal lord was quick to notice, because he was due a portion of the peasant's profits. The claim is unfounded that, after the peasant uprising of 1514, which ran its course outside Slovakia, our peasants were permanently bound to the land, or that a 'new form of servitude' emerged. Indeed, shortly after that event the laws prohibiting free movement of peasants were abolished.

The switch to German-style rights of land purchase and bequest brought about a rearrangement of the residential makeup of villages. A village's land area was henceforth divided into an inner and outer district (intravilan, and extravilan, respectively). The land was surveyed and laid out in regular patterns: homes were built alongside each other in single rows, or facing each other in two rows. But there were also other types of villages, for instance, those with a public square, or with arable land and hayfields behind each house. Even originally multipurpose structures, with courtyards and stables etc. were merged into more regular farming/residential complexes and included in the inner district (intravilan).

Among the most important feudal lords of medieval Slovakia were the Stibors of Stiborice, who ruled over the Vah valley and who held the domains of Beckov, Uhrovec, Cachtice, Holic, Suca, Dobra Voda, Branc, Ostry Kamen, Plavecky Hrad, Korlatka, Koseca, Povazska Bystrica, Smolenice and Ilava. At the beginning of the 14th Century, Stibor II acquired also a domain in Orava County, and controlled several domains in Moravia. He also held the office of Superintendent of Bratislava, Nitra and Trencin Counties.

In Nitra County the largest landowners were the Forgacs; in Tekov County, Peter Cech; in Gemer County, the Bubeks. The Rozgon family owned more property than anyone else in the counties of Bratislava, Komarno and Saris; the Perenis had many peasants in Spis and Abov Counties; the Palocis, in Zemplin and Uz Counties. All of these noble families helped themselves to slices of royal lands, with a resultant drop in the king's block of holdings from 3,000 to about 1,000 villages between the reigns of Louis I and Sigismund.

Under King Mattias (Matthew) some feudal families gained prominence mainly through loyal service to the king. Outstanding among them were the Zapolskys, who came from Croatia and gradually acquired immense estates all over Hungary, including the Slovak counties of Nitra, Trencin, Orava, Liptov and Saris, as well as Spis (1460) and Kezmarok (1461).

The Podmanickys, an old family with roots in Slovakia, acquired a stronghold and estate in Povazska Bystrica and estates in Hricov and Bytca.

The Pongrac family, also with roots in Slovakia, acquired estates named Branc, Strecno and Stary Hrad. King Ladislav V granted the family fortified

*Palatine
Stephen Zapolsky,
(Grave stone –
Spis Chapter)*

estates named Uhrovec, Liptovsky Hradok, Likava and Liptovsky Hrad. The Pongracs also held properties scattered over Northwest Slovakia.

The majority of the nobility in Slovakia, numbering in the hundreds, and even thousands, were members of the middle and lower gentry who often had few serfs or none at all. They were the so-called 'curialists', holding titles of nobility, but subsisting substantially by manual labor. The petty nobility were numerous in Turiec, Liptov, and Orava Counties, as well as Bratislava, Nitra, Tekov, Gemer and Abov Counties, but in the latter they were mostly ethinic Magyars.

In the mid-15th Century the richest Hungarian nobleman was Janos Hunady, the bulk of whose holdings were not in Slovakia. At the beginning of the 16th Century it was the Zapolsky family among Hungarian nobility who climbed highest on the ladder of wealth, with extensive holdings in Slovakia.

A major landowner was the king himself, who owned fortified estates in Orava, Bratislava, Cerveny Kamen, Komarno, Topolcany, Uhrovec and Bojnice, and unfortified estates in the counties of Liptov, Zvolen, Spis, and Saris. In the mid-14th Century he owned approximately 25 to 30 percent of all land; magnates owned somewhat less than that, while the church owned approximately 10 to 15 percent. Most of the rest of the land was owned by middle and petty nobility, among whom the Gorgeis, Berzevicis and Starais stood out.

At this time the towns of Bratislava, Trnava, Kremnica, Kosice and Bardejov were also feudal landowners.

When King Andrew III, the last scion of the Arpad Dynasty, died in 1301, power struggles ignited in which domestic contenders, grown strong, also vied for the throne. The official candidate was Charles Robert, a member of the house of Anjou, still only 12 years old. As a protégé of the pope, he was crowned king soon after arrival in Hungary by the Archbishop of Esztergom. However, Charles Robert failed to gain universal acceptance because another faction of magnates offered the throne to Wenceslaus II, the Czech king or, alternatively, to his son of the same name, whom they crowned Hungarian king Ladislav V.[4] He too was only 12 years old, but when a majority of his supporters defected to Charles Robert, he quickly returned to Bohemia. (Upon the death of his father he became the last monarch in his venerable dynasty.) Charles Robert was recognized as king by the Hungarian Diet in 1307.

At this time the power of the Hungarian magnates was at its peak. One of the most powerful was Matus (Mattias) Cak[5] called 'Trenciansky', who was eventually able to gain control of the greater part of present-day Slovakia, extending all the way to the Spis stronghold (Spissky Hrad), with headquarters in Trencin.

Battle of Rozhanovce: armed confrontation of Hungarian king Charles Robert with Omodej's, East Slovak magnates, 1312

On the territory which he controlled, Cak openly confronted the king, sacking and appropriating properties. Cak had an ally in East Slovakia called Omodej Aba, who gained control of Abov, Saris, and Turiec Counties, behaving much like Matus Cak. Opposing him, the Spis Germans and the town of Kosice, loyal supporters of the king, joined battle and decisively defeated his forces at Rozhanovce in 1312.

But in these wars of attrition with King Charles Robert, Matus Cak steadily lost ground. In March 1321 he died, and, with the capture of Trencin by the king's forces in August of the same year, Matus Cak's domain ceased to exist.

Matus Cak was hardly a Slovak patriot as some 19th Century historians have claimed. He pursued the ordinary goals of a Hungarian magnate and never did establish a sufficiently well-defined territory or political organization to support any Slovak claims to a heritage.

With the collapse of oligarchic rule, the royal power in Hungary began to reassert itself in every direction, relying on a 'banderial' system (i.e. combat units maintained by wealthy magnates, with military obligations to the king), as well as on mercenaries. The king was able to reclaim his usurped properties, but his chief source of income were royal concessions, including mining of precious and base metals, minting of coins, and the collecting of customs and tolls.

The son and successor to Charles Robert, Louis I, who ruled from 1342 to 1382, was called 'the Great' and he really deserved the epithet. He recon-

Coronation of King
Charles Robert

firmed the Golden Bull of King Andrew II and the constitution, which had established aristocratic (county) self-rule. In 1370 he was elected king of Poland, too, but he spent little time there.

The next king of Hungary was Sigismund of Luxembourg, the son of the renowned Czech king and Holy Roman Emperor, Charles IV. His election and ascent to the throne did not transpire without incident, but he was finally able to assume his crown and take possession of the country in 1387.

From the beginning, Sigismund was forced to focus attention mainly on the south of Hungary, where the Turkish threat increased rapidly. After the Battle of Kosovo in 1389, Serbia, which had been a formal vassal of Hungary, fell under Ottoman overlordship. Sigismund himself was defeated in September 1396 and barely escaped with his life.

Sigismund reigned for a relatively long time and stood out as the only medieval Hungarian king to attain the title of Holy Roman Emperor.[6] Besides ruling Italy, he was king of Bohemia, although he was unable for a long time to take his throne in Prague. When he finally did assume that crown, just a year before he died, he intended to make Bratislava or its stronghold, 'Bratislavsky Hrad', his capital, which he had already begun to rebuild for that purpose.

Sigismund of Luxembourg left his mark on Slovak history by pawning a number of Spis County towns and estates to the Polish king, which he was

Louis I

never destined to redeem. These estates were not recovered by Hungary until the partition of Poland near the end of the 18th Century.

The (Czech) Hussites[7] refused to recognize Sigismund as king and invaded various countries that he ruled. As early as 1428 they organized a huge campaign against Slovakia. Advancing through Skalica, Senica and Modra, they reached Bratislava, but then lost momentum and returned to Moravia by way of Senec, Velke Kostolany and Nove Mesto nad Vahom.

In 1430 the Hussites again invaded Slovakia, entering from Moravia by the Czech Road to Trnava, but the Hungarian army, concentrated near Sintava, ambushed the expedition and inflicted huge losses upon it.

Then in 1431, the Hussites invaded once again, this time through the Dunajec Water Gap, reaching Levoca and setting fire to its outskirts before withdrawing.

Unwilling to give up, however, the Hussites came back in the fall of the same year, invading in two prongs, one advancing on Zilina through the Jablunkov Pass, the other up the Vah River valley. Combining forces, they proceeded into Liptov County and overpowered the Likava Fortress, where they stationed a garrison. They then marched through Prievidza and Topolcany to Nitra, which they finally occupied in October. There, unable to agree on a division of spoils, they squabbled and split up. The Taborites (one faction) returned to Moravia by way of Hlohovec and Nove Mesto nad Vahom; the 'Sirotkovia' (Little Orphans) pressed on to southern Slovakia, where they were routed by the Hungarians, and left to straggle home as a mere remnant of their once formidable force.

Sigismund

But these disasters did not discourage the Hussites: the following year they occupied Skalica and captured Trnava, leaving behind garrisons in both towns. They attacked Bratislava as well, but once again failed to take it.

In the spring of 1433 the Hussites, relentless, marched on Spis County by way of Upper Silesia and Southern Poland, capturing Kezmarok. In short order they despoiled this region as far as Spisska Nova Ves, then they assaulted the Cistercian monastery in Spissky Stiavnik and the Carthusian monastery in Lechnica. From there they withdrew to Turiec County, and attacked Kremnica, where they captured the royal mint, before returning to Bohemia by way of the Vlara Pass.

The Hussite garrisons in Trnava, Topolcany, and Zilina pillaged the surrounding countryside and collected 'tribute'. For instance, in June 1434, Blazko of Borotin, captain of the Trnava garrison, embarked on such a 'tribute gathering' expedition through southwest Slovakia, set fire to Svaty Jur, proceeded to Zitny Ostrov, then, turning north, occupied Surany before returning to Trnava.

After suffering defeat at Lipany in 1434, it became obvious to the captains of the Hussite garrisons that they would have to withdraw. However, they did not leave Hungary until May 1435, and then only after pocketing 'fitting compensation'.

In the course of their unrelenting incursions into Slovakia, as in their shameless comportment in Bohemia, Moravia and other countries, the Hussites displayed scant tolerance of enemies; anyone not agreeing with their religious views was eliminated. For instance, they slaughtered monks in monasteries, oblivious in the meantime, that as the good Christians they professed to be, they ought to be mindful of the Fifth Commandment.

Ladislav V, the
Posthumous

King Sigismund had no male heir, hence, pursuant to previously ratified accords, the Hungarian Estates elected his son-in-law, Albrecht of Austria, king. The latter, however, reigned for only two years (1437–1439). The dowager queen, Elizabeth, anxious to preserve her control, summoned assistance from a Czech army captain named Jan Jiskra, who was accustomed to spending most of his time while on missions to Hungary in Slovakia. His help was important to her at this time, when, after her husband's death, she gave birth to a son, Ladislav, who later entered Hungarian history with the surname Posthumous, 'Pohrobok'.[8]

Jiskra recruited about 5,000 mercenaries, most of them former Hussite troops. With this army he succeeded in occupying the Zvolen Fortress and nearby towns, which Elizabeth entrusted to his command. He fashioned a sizeable domain for himself, embracing most of what is today's Slovakia. The formal king of Hungary was Vladislav II[9] whom Elizabeth expected to marry with the understanding that her son, Ladislav the Posthumous, would retain his hereditary right to the throne.

However, in the meantime, the Turkish menace in the Hungarian south continued to grow steadily, requiring immediate and substantial defensive measures. For this reason the Hungarian Diet, meeting in 1443, decided that military action was imperative and, by the end of the year, fielded an army. King Vladislav II[10] took command, aided by Janos Hunady, the wealthiest magnate of Hungary, heady with political ambitions. They conquered some territory in the Balkans, even occupied Sophia, and got as far as the Balkan Highlands, but had to return in the face of winter. The expedition was to be renewed the following year, with foreign reinforcements. These reinforcements, however, failed to materialize, and the following year a relatively weak Hungarian force met defeat at Varna. In the battle, the king himself fell.

After the king's death the Diet elected Janos Hunady ruler of Hungary, with the title of Regent. However, Jan Jiskra, Elizabeth's friend, was still encamped in the country and had to be dealt with. Hunady reached an accord with him on September 13, 1466, allowing Jiskra to retain control of, and income from, the towns of Kremnica, Levoca, Presov, and Bardejov, and from the Spis Stronghold ('Spissky Hrad'), plus 30 percent of the yield from the rest of the territory he held. This accord was substantially confirmed in 1450, but the power struggle with Hunady and the accession of Ladislav V, Posthumous, in 1453, seriously exhausted Jiskra, so that, after twelve years in Hungary, he temporarily departed.

In the meantime there was no respite in the power struggle with the Ottoman Empire, which in 1453 captured Constantinople, the capital of the

Jan Hunady

Byzantine Empire. In 1456, the Turkish army began a siege of Belgrade, where it suffered a devastating defeat. However, Janos Hunady shortly thereafter died of the plague, which also laid waste his army. Not long afterwards, the relatively young Ladislav V died, too; thus it became necessary to elect a new king.

While Jan Jiskra had been active in Slovakia, many former mercenaries had come into the country. Some of them had left military service, refusing to submit to its harsh discipline, or succumbing to injuries or age, and they now tried to make a living by their wits – that is to say, mostly by robbery and plunder. Many of these mercenaries and their hangers-on professed the old Hussite principles and addressed each other as 'Bratrik' (Little Brother, originating the name 'Brethren'). In the years 1447–1449, they stormed and pillaged monasteries in Lechnica, Letanovce, Spissky Stiavnik, Nove Mesto nad Vahom, etc. Mercenaries manning the garrison at Plavecsky Hrad regularly waylaid merchant caravans traveling to and from Poland. Later on, the Brethren were active mainly in the counties of Spis, Saris, Abov and Zemplin.

These former mercenaries of Jiskra set up camp at Zelena Hora near Hrabusice and Haligovce in Spis County, and also at Chmelovo in Saris County. In 1452 there were also Brethren field camps in Medzilaborce, Sabinov, Krnca and Teplica in Spis County, at Vysehrad in Turiec County, at Gajary, Peter pri Hlohovci and Velke Kostolany. In the years 1453 to 1458 the number of Brethren increased to 15 to 16 thousand, some of them coming from Poland, with 36 field camps and fortresses in Slovakia. The authorities became more and more concerned about the aggressive behavior of these armed trouble-makers. In 1454, therefore, they again invited Jiskra to Hungary, this time to remove the Brethren forcibly, putting at his disposal towns in Spis and Saris Counties, and some mining towns, with the income they generated. Jiskra was able to recruit some of his former mercenaries, and with their help he proceeded to mop up the last of the Brethren. In November 1454 he defeated them near Trebisov, but he failed to take Kezmarok. The last of the Brethren camps, located in Velke Kostolany and commanded by Jan Svehla, was not removed until 1467, after King Mattias Corvinus's accession to the throne.

Mattias Corvinus

Mattias Corvinus had been elected king by the Diet in 1458. From the very beginning of his reign he endeavored to create conditions that would bring an end to the anarchy and disorder of the past three decades.

For a time, Jan Jiskra still remained in Slovakia, since he refused to accept the conditions for his departure laid down by the new king. Consequently, having reassembled his scattered mercenaries, he forced the king to renegotiate and grant him the title 'Hungarian Baron', with estates in Southeast Hungary.

Execution of Juraj Doza, 1514

During King Mattias' reign the Turkish menace continued to escalate. The king countered the threat with minor success, but did not undertake a major expedition until 1475–1476. This campaign turned out to be Mattias' only major effort against the Turks, since he was more concerned with campaigns in Bohemia and Austria, where he hoped to become Holy Roman Emperor like his predecessor, Sigismund of Luxembourg. A faction of Czech and Moravian nobility, opposed to the 'Hussite' King Jan of Podebrady,[11] who was in disfavor with the Pope, even elected Mattias king of Bohemia. In the years 1478 to 1479, King Mattias became embroiled in struggles for control of Austria, which he launched from Bratislava, and which lasted for a full decade. In 1485, he succeeded in occupying Vienna, where he died five years later, never having achieved his keenly coveted goal – the imperial crown.

King Mattias introduced major reforms during his reign, including tax increases that served mainly to support the army, which numbered twenty to thirty thousand troops, trained in the tactics of the Hussites. He strove successfully to enhance the power of the state.

After the death of King Mattias, a majority of the nobility elected the Czech King Vladislav Jagiello[12] to the Hungarian throne. During his reign royal power sank to a new low. The weak rule of the monarch was reflected in the caprices of the feudal lords, who often behaved quite recklessly towards underlings, making extraordinary demands on them. Their oppressive behavior eventually produced a backlash in a full-scale peasant uprising in 1514. Juraj Doza, appointed commander of the army, switched sides and took com-

Fateful Battle of Mohac, 29 August, 1526

mand of the aroused mass of about fifty thousand peasants. This uprising, centered in the Tisa River valley, was brutally quashed, its leaders captured and ignominiously executed.

After Vladislav II died, his son Louis II[13] became Hungarian king, although he was still only ten years old. A council of regency was appointed to rule the country during his childhood.

Sultan Suleiman II

At this time, the military-political situation in the south of the state began to deteriorate sharply, as the Turks steadily increased their pressure. Sultan Suleiman gradually conquered Belgrade, Sabac and Zemun. In July 1526 he captured Petrovaradin, and on August 29, in a decisive battle at Mohac, he defeated the Hungarian army. The young Hungarian king himself fell. With the Battle of Mohac, one epoch of Hungary history (and thus, of Slovak history, too) came to a close.

In that epoch Slovakia took its place firmly in the ranks of Western culture. Even its architecture testifies to this alignment, for instance, the precise layout of most Slovak towns. One can see this pattern particularly well in Levoca, Bardejov, Zilina, Prievidza, Kremnica, Smolnik, Roznava, and Rimavska Sobota, although there are also important medieval towns that lack such measured layouts.

Work of Master Paul of Levoca

Master Paul of Levoca

The European features of Slovakia are also accentuated in the Gothic architecture developed mostly after 1300. As surviving churches show, the Gothic style, brought to us by master architects from Western Europe, was characterized by lightly ribbed vaults rising to great heights. In larger towns, basilica-type churches with three aisles were built, while in smaller ones, simpler models with one or two aisles were common.

Many of these churches are decorated with murals, painted in a style developed in the latter half of the 14th Century, especially in Spis County (Levoca). This style flowered in the 15th and 16th Centuries, together with the magnificent late Gothic altars found in Kosice, Bardejov, Sabinov, and elsewhere. It culminated in the statues and altar of Master Paul of Levoca, which were completed in 1517.

During the reign of King Mattias, Renaissance architecture began to spread. One of its first exemplars is the town hall in Bardejov, dating to the years 1505 to 1508. Strongholds and forts were remodeled to withstand artillery bombardments. An outstanding solution of design problems in fortifications is demonstrated by the fortress ('hrad') at Cerveny Kamen, reconstructed by the Fuggers, as the Medieval Ages gave way to the Modern.

During the Medieval Ages a great flowering of education occurred, as reflected in the development of literature, both religious and secular.

In town offices (Bratislava, Banska Stiavnica, Kosice, Trnava, Banska Bystrica, and Zilina) economic data was recorded in the German language. The basic legal handbook was the *Summa Legum Raimundi*, composed by an author of Italian extraction.

Ecclesiastical institutions used only Latin. They compiled handbooks of canon law, legal codices and other handbooks of the most varied kinds. The monastic chapter in Bratislava, in particular, had an extensive library, which was consulted by clergy and students alike. The first expressions of religious literature (prayers in verse and hymns, mostly of West Slovak origin[14]) began to appear, written in Czech or a Slovakized version of Czech. Prayer books, fragments of the Gospels, legends, sermons and baptismal and marriage formulas have also come down to us, written in local dialects of Slovak.

The nobility, as the ruling class in Hungary, formulated its ideology in a legal code known as the *Tripartitum,* whose author was a lawyer named Stephen Werboci. The *Tripartitum* was written as early as the beginning of the 16th Century, and was published even before its approval by the Diet and its ratification by the king. It gradually became the most frequently consulted legal handbook of Old Hungary.

The author recognized various rights of the nobility, based on established custom, including political freedom and the free disposition of property, and defined its chief duty as participation in the defense of the country. He also reserved to the nobility the right to oppose the sovereign. And he recognized even more rights of the nobility vis-à-vis peasants than had already been accorded them in the varying practices of individual counties.

In the sphere of 14th Century education laypersons began to assume a role, having acquired an education mainly in monastic schools, of which the most prominent was in Bratislava. But even town schools achieved a respectable level during the Medieval Ages. Maintained at municipal expense, they taught students coming mostly from among townspeople. The languages of instruction were Latin and German, the latter being the mother tongue of most burghers. We have documentation of prospering municipal schools, e.g. in Banska Bystrica, Banska Stiavnica, Kosice, Kezmarok, and Michalovce (1335).[15] Evidence of

Kosice: aerial view of Cathedral of St. Elizabeth

59

Charter of University of Bratislava, granted by Pope Paul II

village schools can even be found here and there, for instance, in Tekovsky Hradok (1378) and Diviaky nad Nitrou (1342).

Great emphasis was also placed on education in monasteries, especially among the Premonstratensians, Dominicans, and Augustinians, who accepted even lay students. Education at the highest level was attained in universities in Italy (Bologna, Padua). In the 14th Century, universities were founded in Prague (1348), Cracow (1364), and Vienna (1365). Among the students of these new universities, of course, were young men from Slovakia.

In 1465 King Mattias Corvinus founded a university in Bratislava as well, the 'Academia Istropolitana'. Times proved unfavorable, and the university basically did not survive its founder.

This was a time of religious upheavals. The Catholic Church found itself in deep crisis, because the Pope began to succumb more and more to the influence of the major secular powers, so much so that for a time there were simultaneously three popes. This situation led to a relaxation of church discipline, insubordination to hierarchy, and a spread of heretical movements. The papacy found itself targeted by all kinds of criticism, while various sects abounded.

During the second half of the 15th Century, in the halls of the royal court in Buda, Renaissance ideas began to spread, based on philosophical and artistic emulation of classical models. In the realm of thought, rationalism forged to the front, fueled by a desire to understand the world and nature, mixed with admiration for pre-Christian civilization and a loosening of Christian morals.

The ideological springboard of the Renaissance was humanism: a conscious approach to classical learning, with emphasis on the study of Latin and Greek, in an effort to achieve the high quality of classical works.

The ideas of Humanism and the Renaissance penetrated even the ranks of townspeople. In the local school in Bardejov, at the turn of the 15th to the 16th Century, there were several highly educated teachers, and the same was true of schools in Presov and Kosice, as well as in several towns of Spis County. School records from the late Medieval Ages demonstrate a high level of achievement in various towns throughout Slovakia.

Istropolitana Academy, first university on Slovak territory, founded during reign of Mattias Corvinus

In the middle of the 15th Century, Johannes Gutenberg invented the printing press and its use spread rapidly across Europe. No printery was established in Slovakia during the late Medieval Ages, but in Pilsen (Bohemia) there was an active printer of Slovak descent named Mikulas Bakalar Stetina, and another in Venice, named Peter of Bardejov.

At the turn of the 15th to 16th Century, booksellers appeared for the first time in several Slovak towns, for instance, Kosice (1493), Presov, and Levoca. Leading Humanists owned their own libraries.

While in world history the end of the Medieval Ages is identified with the year 1492, i.e. the discovery of America, in Hungarian history (hence Slovak as well) the crucial date is marked by the Turkish defeat of the Hungarian army at Mohac in 1526. Between these two dates there was the Protestant Reformation, which attracted adherents in Slovakia soon after the year 1517.

5. The First Two Centuries of the Modern Era (1526–1681)

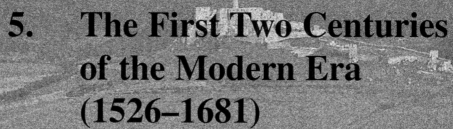

When in 1526, King Vladislav Jagiello, together with many of his leading dignitaries, fell at the battle of Mohac, Jan Zapolsky, the country's wealthiest magnate, sought to mount the empty throne. He was opposed by a powerful rival in the person of Ferdinand Habsburg, a scion of the dynasty that had long ruled the historical core of Austria (Upper and Lower Austria, Styria, Carinthia, Carniola, Tyrol), who also had treaty rights of succession to the Czech and Hungarian thrones.

Ferdinand I of Habsburg

Ferdinand Habsburg was the younger brother of Emperor Charles V, who was king of Spain and ruler of the Neapolitan Kingdom, as well as of Sicily, Sardinia, the Netherlands, and the Spanish colonies of Latin America. After Ferdinand had gained the Czech crown without any major problem and won Croatian backing in his bid for the Hungarian crown, his brother Charles V was willing to come to his aid. But the Habsburg dynasty was constantly at war with its neighbors, so that when Ferdinand did eventually become Hungarian king, he had to send his mercenaries first to one border, then to the other, while his nobles wanted him to avenge the Mohac debacle and expel the Turks.

Another complication in the Habsburgs' attempts to assert their primacy was Europe's post-Reformation split into two camps, Catholic and Protestant. The Habsburgs, as staunch Catholics, took a firm stand in favor of the Pope and the Catholic Church.

Battle of Mohac,
wood engraving by
unknown master,
on contemporary flyer

Jan Zapolsky, contemporary wood engraving by unknown German master

No small problem was posed for the Habsburgs by the Hungarian constitution. That constitution rested on the principle that the power of the ruler was subordinate to the power of the Diet, and the Hungarian Estates vehemently strove to enforce this principle, with basic success. Still, many Hungarian kings had pragmatically seized as much power as they could. Now the Habsburgs, like other European monarchs of the time, began to advocate the principle of absolutism, i.e. concentration of all political power in the hands of a ruler. The most practical way to achieve this goal was to refrain from summoning a diet. Thus the Aragonese estates had last met in 1592, the French in 1614, the estates of Spanish Netherlands in 1632, the Neapolitan in 1642. The Hungarian estates were right to fear the Habsburgs, especially in light of their abrogation of Czech legislative rights after defeating them in the Battle of Biela Hora.[1]

In Seventeeth Century Hungary this situation led to many an armed uprising against the king, but to no avail. A sad corollary of these struggles was that in fighting their emperor or king, these rebels saw fit to join forces with the Turks.

The accession of Ferdinand I of Habsburg did not pass without complications: his rival, Jan Zapolsky, had himself declared king of Hungary, citing a law of 1505 which banned foreigners from the Hungarian kingship. Ferdinand managed to follow suit one month later. But each needed outside help to enforce his claim. Ferdinand, who controlled a lesser part of the country, got help from his elder brother, Charles V, who recruited enough mercenaries to drive Zapolsky's supporters into the hinterlands of East Hungary.

Inasmuch as neither had sufficient strength to prevail, they agreed to a truce in 1538 and divided up the regions of Hungary, free of Turkish occupation. Ferdinand's share included present-day Slovakia and West Hungary, including historic Croatia; Zapolsky's, Transylvania and Northeast Hungary. The latter two regions were merged into a principality named Transylvania, which Zapolsky later ceded to Turkish vassalage. But certain parts of Central Slovakia, for instance Rimavska Sobota, Filakovo, Sahy and its environs, were subsequently occupied by the Turks as well.

The Turkish occupation of Hungary's plains and their raids thence into Slovak territory inflicted immeasurable suffering on the Slovak people. Turks pillaged hundreds of villages, carried off thousands of captives, drove off livestock, looted, and set fire to homes. During their campaign of 1543 they captured Esztergom, and annexed parts of Esztergom, Tekov, Novohrad and Hont Counties, which were predominantly Magyar, converting these lands into the 'Sanjaks' (districts) of Esztergom and Novograd. In 1457 the Turkish Porte signed a five-year truce with Ferdinand I, which proved short-lived, but in the meantime the Turks occupied additional regions of Southern Slovakia. In fact, they captured the Filakovo Stronghold (1554), and created a new 'Sanjak', headquartered in Secany (Szecseny).[2]

The Habsburg administration organized new defensive measures against the Turks and created two new military captaincies, of which the first was successively headquartered in Nitra (1564–1568), Surany (1568–1581), Levice (1581–1589), and the stronghold of Nove Zamky (1589–1663); the second, in Upper Hungary, was permanently headquartered in Kosice from 1564. In spite of all these defensive measures, the Turks succeeded in occupying the strongholds of Modry Kamen and Divin.

The internal life of Slovakia in this century was characterized by the spread of the Reformation, with Slovaks adopting Lutheranism, and Magyars, Calvinism. Only sporadically did a reverse choice occur.[3]

The first manifestations of the Reformation in our country are documented in the Central Slovakian mining towns, where Protestantism was introduced by students attending Wittemberg University. But according to laws passed by the Hungarian Diet at this time, anyone confessing these teachings was subject to burning at the stake. However, when both Hungarian archbishops and five bishops perished at the Battle of Mohac, leaving the Hungarian Catholic Church bereft of practically its entire leadership, the Reformation spread rapidly and consolidated already held positions. After its initial successes in mining towns, Protestantism gained additional adherents in Levoca and Bardejov, mainly among German townspeople, who invited Lutheran preachers and teachers from the Protestant regions of Germany. In Western

Turkish pillaging of South Slovakia, 1543, (wood engraving by unknown master)

Slovak towns, the Reformation was spread by preachers from Bohemia and Moravia who, however, were mostly Neo-Utraquists.[4]

It was not long before the leading families of the nobility joined the Reformation, including the Revais, the Thurzos, the Radvanskys, the Kostkas, the Perenis, the Balas family, and others. A great loss for the Catholic Church was the defection of Francis Thurzo, Bishop of Nitra. Feudal lords found the Reformation particularly appealing, because it proclaimed the secularization of church properties.

At first, the positions of the two Protestant confessions were not clearly differentiated; some of the novelties imported from Germany were not accepted, others were later rejected. However, later adherents of the Lutheran version began to organize their beliefs into distinct confessions, for instance the 'Confessio Pentapolitana' of five Eastern Slovak towns (1549), the 'Confessio Heptapolitana' of seven Central Slovak mining towns (1559), and the 'Confessio Scepusiana' (1569) of the twenty-four Spish towns held in pawn by the Polish king.

Although during the seventies of the 16th Century, adherents of the Reformation constituted the majority of active pastors in Slovakia and the Evangelical Church had organizationally severed its ties with the Catholic Church, they did not formally declare independence until the Synod of Zilina in 1610.

In the middle of the 16th Century, when Mikulas Olah became Archbishop of Esztergom, the Catholic Church began to actively fight back. The new archbishop focused particular attention on the formation of candidates for the priesthood. Therefore, in 1560, in accordance with rules laid down by the Tridentine Council, he founded a seminary to train priests in Trnava. A year later he succeeded in setting up a Jesuit house in Trnava, which had gradually become a center of re-Catholicization.

After a period of relative peace on the southern border of Slovakia, at the end of the 16th Century a new war with the Turks erupted. It lasted almost 15 years. In its first phase, the (Austrian) emperor's armies recaptured Filakovo, Divin, Modry Kamen, and other strongholds and fortresses. In the East, however, the imperial forces lost the town of Rab with its fortress. Then, a year later, in 1595, it was in this region that they achieved signal successes, with the Croatian capture of several fortresses between the Sava and Drava rivers. A year later, the Austrian army occupied Esztergom, Vysehrad and Vacov, but lost an important fortress at Jager.

In the meantime, the efforts of the Habsburgs to establish absolutism in Hungary continued. The going, however, proved to be extraordinarily difficult. It was not enough for the monarch to simply withhold summons to a diet; the

Hungarian estates were able to meet regularly in county sessions, of which there were sixteen in Slovakia alone. Besides, at that time a majority of the nobility was still Protestant and it very much feared forcible proselytizing by the Imperial Court, which was still very Catholic.

These sticking points led to an armed challege to the Habsburgs by Stefan Bocskay, a prince in Transylvania. In the years 1604 and 1605 the prince occupied a substantial part of Eastern and Central Slovakia, with strong Turkish support. In July 1606, the parties finally reached an accord (The Treaty of Vienna), with the emperor making significant concessions: he agreed to an open election of the palatine and to Hungarian officers in Hungarian fortresses, and pledged to uphold religious freedom. (George Thurzo, a major property owner in Slovakia, was subsequently elected palatine.)

Stefan Bocskay

But the ruling Habsburgs, who since 1556 had been flaunting the proud title of Holy Roman Emperor, also notched up some real successes: for instance they imposed a change in the staging of diets, from open-air assemblies (customary in the mid-16th Century) to representational bodies, made up of two deputies per county. Several of these diets met in Slovak towns, for instance, in Krupina in 1605, later in Banska Bystrica, and later still mostly in Bratislava.

The Habsburgs also got their way in the matter of chartering towns and communities as 'free and royal', thus raising them to the fourth estate (with diet participation), and winning valuable political allies for themselves. The most meaningful success in this respect was the inclusion among 'free royal towns' of Modra, Pezinok, and Svaty Jur, whose original lord had been Stefan Ileshazi, one of the richest, most influential feudal lords of Hungary. Even he was bound by this innovation, which forced him to sit in the Hungarian Diet on a par with his former subordinates. But he was appalled by this 'anomaly' and became so enraged that he joined the insurgency, much to his later regret.

On the other hand, the Hungarian estates received a concession from the emperor in the matter of succession: the right was henceforth not to be hereditary (as, for instance, in the Czech Kingdom), but contractual, with a requirement that the new ruler, prior to coronation, sign a commitment to honor the Hungarian constitution, and swear an oath to that effect. The new requirement was entered in the Hungarian Legal Code ('Corpus Juris Hungarici').

While these events were taking place, important economic changes occurred in Slovakia. Between 1550 and 1560 the free royal towns, occupied predominantly by ethnic Germans, lost their leading role in craft production (the trades). The role passed to towns and communities owned by feudal lords,

Financier James Fugger II

Fugger home in Banska Bystrica

of which there were more than one hundred. This change is attested by the fact that, whereas at the end of the Medieval Ages there had existed about 65 to 70 craft guilds (in approximately 25 Slovak towns), just a century and a half later, there were already about 1,000 such guilds (in approximately 150 Slovak towns). And whereas the bylaws of medieval guilds had been printed only in German, the bylaws of the newly founded guilds were printed in Latin, Magyar, and Slovak, in addition to German.

Great changes also occurred in metal forging and mining. Between 1520 and 1540 the Fugger copper enterprise had produced approximately 2,000 tons of copper annually, but in 1545 it had to cease operations for lack of capital. The copper industry was then taken over by the state. During the transition to the early modern era many of our old aristocratic families died out and new ones took their place, among them robber barons. Some of the more notorious of the latter were Jan and Rafael Podmanicky in the Vah Valley, and Frantisek Bubek, Melicher Balasa (proprietor of Bzovik) and Matej Baso (captain of the Muran Stronghold) in Gemer and Novohrad Counties.

During this period, the status of Slovaks in towns underwent impressive improvement, even as members of the Magyar nobility, fleeing Turkish advances, moved in among them. For instance in Trnava, the town council, which had formerly been composed of Germans and Slovaks, seated Magyars as equals in a three-way split.

A regular feature of life in these times was the division of the Lutheran Church in larger towns into separate German and Slovak-Czech parishes, each with its own church, baptismal records, and, most often, cemetery. The Lutherans of native (Slovak) origin used a version of Czech, interspersed with Slovakisms, as their liturgical language. This form of Czech is sometimes called 'the biblical language'. But in fact, some of these Slovak Lutherans actually did consider themselves Czechs and supposed that their Church had been founded by Hussites in the 15th Century.

Latin, however, remained the official language of Hungary: no individual could gain acceptance in any upper level of society without knowledge of Latin. This knowledge was a necessary qualification for positions in church, state and county. Even some 'belles-lettres' were written in Latin, so that determining the precise ethnicity of a given author is sometimes difficult.

An important benchmark in Slovak self-assertion was a law passed by the Hungarian Diet of 1608–1609, which prescribed equal representation of Germans, Magyars and Slovaks on town councils. This law, however, made no mention of the other ethnics of Old Hungary, as for instance Rusyns, Romanies, and South Slavs, because they were without significant town populations.

In this respect, Slovaks were the only ethnic group of Eastern Europe who, though without an independent state structure, nevertheless had social classes above the level of peasant. While it remains problematical to speak of Slovak self-awareness among the nobility, one can safely say that Slovak townspeople of this time played an important role in the history of Slovakia.

The Diet of 1608–1609 passed a law with respect to the freedom of religion, which, however, did not prevent the Catholic Church from pursuing its re-Catholicization campaign. Frantisek Forgach, Archbishop of Esztergom, took the initiative in this direction. He had important allies among the Jesuits, who took up permanent residence in Trnava in 1613. The triumphant advance of the Counter-Reformation and re-Catholicization is most closely linked to the name Peter Pazmany, who became archbishop of Esztergom in 1616 and held the office up to 1637. In this post he accomplished much to revive the Catholic Church in Hungary, working closely with the palatine, Mikulas Eszterhazy.

Peter Pazmany was born into a Magyar Calvinist family, but he converted to Catholicism early on and acquired an outstanding education in Jesuit schools in Cracow, Vienna and Rome. He was an excellent organizer and polemicist, focusing his efforts on winning back to Catholicism leading aris-

Townhall, Levoca,
Early 16th Century

Archbishop Peter Pazmany

tocrats, even making personal visits to their homes. His efforts proved quite successful, and so, by the second half of the 17th Century, there were few Protestants left among the nobility. These 'returned' Catholics then pressured their peasants to abandon Protestantism, too, and achieved results mainly by expropriating churches and installing Catholic priests in them.[5]

In 1635, Pazmany founded a university in Trnava, which became a center of re-Catholicization. It operated continuously on Slovak soil up to the seventies of the 18th Century, when it was relocated in Buda, then later Pest, educating thousands of priests, teachers, and other learned Catholics, and even an occasional Protestant. However, books, pamphlets and other printed matter continued to be published in Czech, with Slovak adaptations.

The political situation in Hungary again heated up, stirring Gabriel Bethlen, a prince of Transylvania, to rebellion against Vienna in 1618. He invaded Eastern Slovakia and, in September 1619, occupied Kosice, where he was declared ruler of Hungary and protector of the non-Catholic faiths.

From Kosice he marched westward and gradually conquered the whole of present-day Slovakia, including Bratislava, which he occupied on October 14, 1619. Here his supporters handed him the Hungarian crown, but he did not ascend the throne until after the 1620 Diet in Banska Bystrica, when the Turks granted him their provisional consent, since he was still their vassal.

After the Battle of Biela Hora in 1620, when the Habsburgs consolidated their position in Central Europe, Bethlen was gradually pushed back to Eastern Slovakia. But the tide of war soon turned again; Bethlen regained control of most of Slovakia and signed a peace treaty (the Peace of Mikolovo, January

Home of Catholic University in Trnava, founded 1635

6, 1622), which served to strengthen his position. All these events took place during the Thirty Years War, which embroiled whole regions of Europe. Bethlen subsequently took part in various campaigns against Vienna, but died suddenly in 1629.

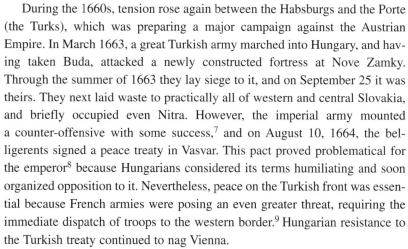

In a final stage of the ongoing struggle between the Habsburgs and Catholic estates on the one hand, and a new Transylvanian insurgent, Prince George I Rakoczi, and the Protestant Estates on the other, the Habsburg side enjoyed intermittent successes. This struggle came to an end in 1645 with the Peace of Linz, and a pledge by the emperor to see to the return of Protestant churches expropriated by Catholics. However, the emperor's people were in no hurry to fulfill this pledge.[6]

Gabriel Bethlen

During the 1660s, tension rose again between the Habsburgs and the Porte (the Turks), which was preparing a major campaign against the Austrian Empire. In March 1663, a great Turkish army marched into Hungary, and having taken Buda, attacked a newly constructed fortress at Nove Zamky. Through the summer of 1663 they lay siege to it, and on September 25 it was theirs. They next laid waste to practically all of western and central Slovakia, and briefly occupied even Nitra. However, the imperial army mounted a counter-offensive with some success,[7] and on August 10, 1664, the belligerents signed a peace treaty in Vasvar. This pact proved problematical for the emperor[8] because Hungarians considered its terms humiliating and soon organized opposition to it. Nevertheless, peace on the Turkish front was essential because French armies were posing an even greater threat, requiring the immediate dispatch of troops to the western border.[9] Hungarian resistance to the Turkish treaty continued to nag Vienna.

The Habsburg compromises prompted the Hungarian lords to once more conspire against Vienna. They were led by the Palatine, Wesselenyi, backed

*Signature of
Gabriel Bethlen*

71

*Palatine Francis
Wesselenyi*

by the archbishop of Esztergom, Lippay, and a judge, Nadasdy, plus numerous magnates, among them members of the Zrinyi clan, who had been spiritedly battling the Turks for decades. The conspirators even solicited allies from abroad. But as the plot was being brewed, many of its leaders died, and the plot came to light, bringing harsh punishments and executions.

Re-Catholicization now began to gain overpowering momentum. Almost all the churches of Lutherans and reformers were expropriated and returned to Catholic hands. During the 1660s–1670s a number of religious orders established houses in Slovakia, enthusiastically joining the re-Catholicization campaign. For instance, the Capuchins took up residence in Pezinok in 1674, and in Bratislava in 1676; the Brothers of Mercy settled in Spisske Podhradie in 1650 and in Bratislava in 1672; the Franciscans founded a monastery in Levoca in 1668; the Piarists established houses in Podolinec in 1642 and Prievidza in 1666, in Brezno in 1673, and in Svaty Jur in 1685. The medieval order of Paulists also built new monasteries: in 1671 in Skalica and a year later in Vranov, and in 1630 they renewed activity in Trebisov. The Ursulines, an order of nuns, came to Bratislava in 1676.

By the reign of Emperor and King Leopold I, the most determined exponents of re-Catholicization, the Jesuits, were already ensconced not only in Trnava, Bratislava and Kosice, but also in Banska Bystrica, Komarno, Levoca, Pezinok, Trencin, Zilina, besides other towns. Their school in Kosice was a university in effect, so that there were actually two Jesuit universities in Slovakia at this time. And we could very well number among institutions of higher learning in Slovakia the lyceum of the Protestant estates, which was active in Presov from 1665 to 1671.

With all these Catholic advances in Hungary, Leopold I, who was also Czech king and ruler of the Holy Roman Empire, supposed that he had scored a huge triumph, finally achieving conditions in Hungary like those long extant in the western half of his realm. But he was soon disillusioned: Hungary could not be ruled like the rest of his empire. Leading Hungarian representatives, including the archbishop of Esztergom, the highest state administrator, gave the emperor to understand that Hungarians were not willing to cooperate with him like his western vassals. A newly armed opposition began forming under the leadership of a nobleman from Kezmarok named Imrich Thokoly.

Leopold I

Thokoly was not a typical leader of opposition to Vienna; in fact, he was not even a Transylvanian prince nor a Calvinist, but a Lutheran. Owing to the rarity of the latter denomination among Magyars, they dubbed him 'the Slovak King', even though he was not Slovak. Compared to the Transylvanian princes, who were vassals of the 'Sublime Porte', his allegiance to the Turks was even

Coronation of Leopold I in Cathedral of St. Martin, Bratislava, 1655

more strongly motivated, for they had formally named him ruler of Hungary, after having once imprisoned him and accorded him far from princely treatment.

The Kurutzi (Kuruci), a group who joined Thokoly in his insurrection, were supported by France, which considered the emperor and the Habsburgs enemies.[10] The French recruited about 3000 mercenaries in Poland and sent them to Hungary, to fight under French command. In 1677 these French mercenaries achieved a major victory, winning control of the Vah, Hron, and Nitra river valleys, including the Central Slovak mining towns.

Even subjects who had no interest in religious and political disputes became quite disturbed, as the Imperial government demanded more and more taxes, took assessments in kind, and required various other sacrifices from the people. These impositions led to a separate uprising in Northern Slovakia led by Gaspar Pika, which in 1672 successfully occupied the Orava Fortress ('Oravsky Hrad'). Many serfs joined this uprising, but it was put down by the imperial army and twenty-five of its leaders were executed.[11]

As Turkish support of Thokoly grew, Leopold I decided that it was time to come to terms with the Hungarian estates. He revoked his offensive impositions, convened a Diet in Sopron, restored the Hungarian constitution, and made a pledge to abide by it.[12]

Imrich Thokoly

Events then moved swiftly. Thokoly refused to honor the decrees of the Sopron Diet and went on fighting. In 1682, with strong Turkish support, he occupied Kosice and, in front of the captured Filakovo Fortress, received a crown from them as 'King of Central Slovakia'. For Turkish services rendered, he pledged to pay 40,000 thalers annually.[13]

Now a major confrontation loomed, because the Ottoman Turks decided to switch their main military focus from their eastern borders (Persia) to their western frontier. They planned to deliver a devastating blow to the Habsburgs by capturing their capital city, Vienna, and subsequently to spread their power and influence over the whole of Hungary.

This period of Slovak history saw the maturation of Renaissance architecture and the birth of the Baroque. Many Renaissance castles were built, of which perhaps the most important was the Bytca residence of the Palatine Thurzo, alongside which stands a magnificent bridal palace, built in 1601, to accommodate the wedding festivities of his daughters, whom he married off one by one to leading magnates. Other such Renaissance structures were the castles in Bethlanovce and Fricovce, the bell towers in Spis County, and many town houses, especially Thurzo's in Levoca and Banska Bystrica. Many Renaissance grave monuments were built during this period, including those in St. Martin's Cathedral in Bratislava and in other Slovak churches (in Trnava, Svaty Jur, Banska Stiavnica, Banska Bystrica, Levoca, and Spisska Kapitula).

Execution of Oravian and Liptovian magistrates, participants in Pika Insurgency, November 24, 1672 (copper engraving in contemporary publication)

74

From the Baroque era, a number of public statues have survived. Good examples can be found in Bratislava: for instance a statue of the Blessed Virgin in front of the Jesuit church, a statue of St. George once displayed in the summer palace of the archbishop but now standing in the courtyard of the primatial palace, and a magnificent statuary depicting Calvary. Bratislava, in fact, became the capital of Hungary at this time, and the residence of the archbishop of Esztergom.

Bratislavsky Hrad (Bratislava Stronghold), Late 16th Century

The beginnings of Baroque architecture are most vividly represented by the university church of St. John the Baptist in Trnava, now the archdiocesan cathedral, built by Jesuits from 1626 to 1637. It became the prototype of Jesuit churches in Slovakia, and of Franciscan churches as well (Trnava, Hlohovec, Nizna Sebastova, and Malacky). Worth mentioning, though of a later date, is the Paulist church in Trnava, the Abbey church in Nove Mesto nad Vahom, churches in Bojnice, Prievidza, Presov, the lower church in Pezinok, and the church in the Fortress of Kezmarok.

Protestants stayed a long time with the Renaissance styles and traditional three aisles, including a spacious main aisle, such as can be found in Bratislava (built from 1636 to 1638), in Svaty Jur (1651–1658), and in Pezinok (1655–1659). Many Lutheran structures were inspired by the Dutch Baroque, as, for instance, in Stitnik (1636), Puchov (1643), and Dolne Strhare (1654).[14]

A dominant role in civil architecture was played by fortresses in Leopoldov (built 1665–1669), and Komarno (1663–1673). Also important was the reconstruction of the Bratislava Fortress, 'Bratislavsky Hrad', (1635–1649), which took on the aspect of a Baroque castle. But the full development of Baroque style was yet to come.

6.   A Hundred Years of Re-Catholicization (1681-1781)

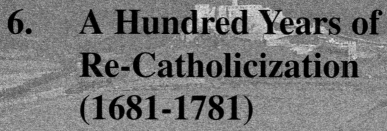

With the Diet of Sopron in 1681, the efforts of Leopold I to establish absolute rule in Hungary, and to suppress Protestantism, came to an end. The Diet renewed the principle, long defended by the estates, that religious freedom was the supreme law of Hungary. This principle, however, was far removed from what we today understand under the concept, because real religious freedom, i.e. free choice of religion, free transfer from church to church, and free co-existence with other religious communities, had not been a self-evident reality in Hungary since at least the time of Peter Pazmany. Nevertheless, the religious complexion of Old Hungary, where, alongside the official (Roman Catholic) church, there were two Protestant denominations, and even an anti-Trinitarian church in Transylvania, was an isolated phenomenon among European states. Elsewhere, non-Catholic religious communities were driven into illegality, forbidden to own churches and cemeteries, or to have their own priests.

The conditions under which the Lutheran Church and, in the Magyar regions, the Calvinist Church, could exist and function after 1681 were oppressive and demeaning. They can be summarized as follows:

A change of religious affiliation was permissible only to Protestants, whereas any attempt by a Catholic to leave his church was punishable by law.

Mixed marriages could be contracted only before a Catholic priest, with offspring to be baptized and brought up as Catholics.

Protestants were allowed churches only in free, royal towns, which were to be built on the outskirts, i.e. outside town walls, without a street entrance or bell-tower, and to be referred to as prayer-halls. Protestants were allowed only two churches per county, of modest, frame construction, to serve only local townspeople. Other Protestants of a given county were not permitted to frequent these churches. All religious rituals (marriages, baptisms, funerals) were to be presided over by Catholic priests, with stipulated stipends. These regulations did not apply in the so-called 'rebellious' counties of northeastern Slovakia, where no Protestant churches had been expropriated. Actually they applied only as far as Gemer County, because there were few Protestants in regions east of there.

The Catholic Church took full advantage of the opportunities served up to it on a silver platter by the Sopron Diet. It concentrated above all on towns where Protestants were a majority, but in doing so overplayed its hand. Although, according to clauses 16 and 18 of the Diet resolutions, a Protestant church was to be allowed in every free royal town, we know that not a single one was ever established in the free royal towns of Trnava, Skalica, Pezinok, Svaty Jur, Pukanec, Brezno, Lubietova, Banska Bela, Zvolen and Nova Bana. Furthermore, a Protestant church that was established in Krupina was soon closed, leaving Protestant churches in only Bratislava, Modra, Trencin, Banska Stiavnica, Kremnica, in five free royal towns in Eastern Slovakia, and in Kosice (one each, Lutheran and Calvinist).

The free royal towns (the Fourth Estate) were actually the only Hungarian locations in which absolutism was fully enforced. Leopold I, revoking the principle of open franchise, restricted the voting rights of the townspeople there to a much smaller circle, the so-called 'external council' which comprised approximately 40 people (100 in Bratislava). A royal bureau even audited the day-to-day 'housekeeping' operations of these towns, and on the occasion of 'restorations,' i.e. town elections, it held them to terms of their original charters and received traditions.

Due to the fact that in the free royal towns only one, or at the most two Protestant pastors, were allowed to function, while Catholics were allowed several chaplains besides a pastor; and since every town had at least one monastery, and the more important ones an active Jesuit house as well, there were more than enough Catholic clergy in every town to account for the relatively rapid change in religious affiliation.

At the time of the Sopron Diet there was a preponderance of Protestants over Catholics in all of these towns, but by the time of the promulgation of the Toleration Edict, the numbers had been reversed[1], with Protestants holding majorities only in Banska Bystrica, Brezno, Krupina, Kezmarok, Lubietova, Modra and Zvolen.

The only wholly Catholic town at this time was Trnava, this thanks to the fact that in the 1730s the town leadership had adopted a resolution granting town rights to Catholics only. By imperial decree, town rights were to be granted to Protestants elsewhere, only if they immigrated from abroad.

It can be stated that, at the time of the Toleration Edict, when Slovakia's population was about a million and a half, the Catholic Church succeeded in changing the religious makeup of Slovakia to a ratio of approximately 3:1, in its own favor. Protestants retained a numerical superiority only in Turiec and Gemer Counties. They also held a slim majority in Hont County, but that county lay only partly in Slovakia. On the other hand, the preponderance of Catholics over Protestants, though slight in Liptov and Zvolen Counties, was very ample in all the other Slovak counties.

The Catholic Church also received a signal boost from the Orthodox Christians of Eastern Slovakia, who accepted the Uzhorod Union (signed in 1646) acknowledging the primacy of the pope, thus becoming Catholics of the Byzantine rite. In 1771 the Byzantine Catholic diocese of Mukacevo was formed, with a separate Vicariate in Kosice. Statistics from 1777 list only 45 schismatic individuals in Uz County, 173 in Zemplin County, and 77 in Abov County, but these individuals could very well have been Orthodox business-men from Balkan countries.

The position of the Catholic Church was also strengthened by the creation of new bishoprics: Spis, Banska Bystrica and Roznava, in 1773; and Kosice in 1804.

To get a true religious picture of Slovakia it is also important to know the number and distribution of Jewish believers,[2] whose population was very uneven: there were no Jews in the counties of Zvolen, Tekov and Gemer, only 6 Jews in Hont, 114 in Orava, 177 in Turiec and 260 in Liptov; but 5,926 in Nitra county, 3,455 in Bratislava, 1,994 in Trencin, 1,063 in Novohrad, 3,390 in Zemplin, 1,293 in Saris, 1,206 in Uz, 1,389 in Abov, and 499 in Spis. The greatest number of Jews, thus lived in the westernmost and easternmost regions of Slovakia. There were no Jews at all in the free royal towns, because the king had barred them at the beginning of the 16th Century, and the mining towns also granted them no entry. Nor were there any Jews in the towns of Spis County.

Altogether there were about 15,000 Jews in Slovakia in 1778, making up less than 1% of the total population. Later on, their numbers grew substantially owing to an influx of Jews from Galicia (Poland), which was annexed by Austria towards the end of Maria Theresa's reign.

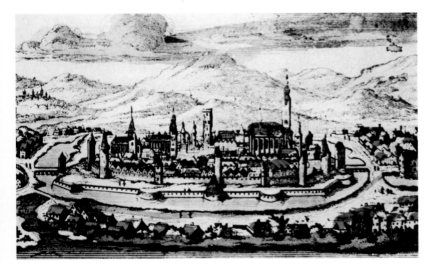

Kosice, ca. 1700

As a result of the strong pressures of re-Catholicization, there was a marked rise in the religiosity of Slovaks. Catholics were introduced to forms of religiosity that reflected a triumphant church, meant to be attractive to Protestants, beckoning them to cross over. The cult of the Virgin Mary expanded enormously, with many pilgrimage sites, such as Sastin, Marianka (near Bratislava), Stare Hory, Gaboltov and Levoca.

But neither did Protestant religiosity flag. For Lutherans and Calvinists there was nothing left but to pray to God all the more fervently to deliver them from a fate like that of so many other Protestants in Europe. It is to this period that we must go to find the roots of Slovak religiosity, which has survived to the present day and has helped Slovaks to overcome the later oppression that rampaging Communism imposed.

As to the great and fundamental change of Slovak religious affiliation, one cannot ignore the reality that it was achieved in a manner that does the Catholic Church little credit. While growing numbers of Catholic priests engaged in re-Catholicization, zealously spearheaded by the Jesuit Order, and while new Catholic churches, monasteries and other objects of religious cult proliferated, the law limited Protestants to a few churches and pastors, whose numbers were not allowed to increase over whole centuries, though the population as a whole steadily expanded. As a result, a Lutheran pastor saw his per capita responsibility always increasing, while a Catholic priest found his per capita load steadily diminishing.

Very demeaning to Protestants was the continuous Catholic probing into whether or not the Lutheran or Calvinist party to a mixed marriage was bringing up offspring in the Catholic faith, sending them to Catholic schools, encouraging them to pray the rosary at home; and, even worse, probing whether or not Lutheran master craftsmen, their families and employees, were taking part in Eucharistic processions, or observing fasts and feast days.[3] In the event that a person neglected these commitments, Catholic institutions appealed to the state to punish their audacity, or even to exile them, though no evidence of such banishment is to be found in the archives.

This great religious turnabout in Slovakia had a nationalistic aspect too, because in Catholic quarters, Slovak identity was considered self-evident, whereas among Lutherans in the 17th and 18th Centuries, some were unsure what their nationality was: Slovak, Czech, or mixed i.e. Czecho-Slovak. For the future development of Slovak national consciousness in the 19th Century and the first half of the 20th, this ambiguity was not without relevance, for it is precisely in Lutheran quarters that the roots of modern Czecho-Slovakism are to be found. This is a problem that has thus far received scant attention,

View of Trencin

though there are many documents (for instance, in Lutheran church registries) which are just waiting to be examined. Indeed, even as far back as 1611, Lutheran Superintendent Abrahamaides was labeling the Lutheran Church in Hlohovec as 'Czech.' In the Lutheran church registry in Trnava, entries recorded during the time of the Rakoczi uprising refer to members, preachers and language as Czech (Bohemian). The registry of the Lutheran church in Modra, during the years 1682 to 1721, refers to that church as Slovak, and its faithful as of Slovak nationality, although earlier on (in the sixties and seventies) it had alternately labeled its Lutheran preacher as Czech or Slovak. Many Lutheran registries were still being labeled Czech as late as Stur's era.

The well-known Lutheran preacher, Daniel Krman, was originally named 'Grman', and many contemporary sources list him in that way, so that it may be assumed that he deliberately changed his name to give it a Czech tone. Furthermore, he labeled his mother-tongue as Czech.[4] Pavol Dolezal speaks in the very title of his Czech-Slovak grammar, published in Bratislava in 1746, of two tongues (dialects) in Hungary, Czech and Slovak, obviously pinning the label 'Czech' on the Slovak Lutherans, of whom he himself was one, though 'real Czechs', for all practical purposes, had not lived in Slovakia for a long time. Post-White Mountain (Biela Hora) exiles had long since been assimilated. In 1783, Ladislav Bartolomeides published a tract in Wittemberg titled *De Bohemis Kishontensibus* (Of the Czechs in Malohont Coun-

Daniel Krman

ty), and even Bernolak counted among the ethnics of Hungary, the Germans, Magyars, Slovaks and Czechs, obviously applying the latter label to Slovak Lutherans.

For this period of Slovak history a very important reality is population expansion, an increase to about one and a half million by the time of the Toleration Edict (1781). In 1713 Slovakia, like other countries, was struck by a plague whose toll, however, was not particularly devastating. Population began to expand rapidly. In our villages, abandoned tracts, so typical of the censuses of the 16th and 17th Centuries, were rapidly disappearing.

The extent of cultivated upland tracts in Tekov County, for example, rose from 958 hectares (2,367 acres) in 1715, to 2,517 hectares (6,219 acres) in 1768, and by 1786 it had reached 9,584 hectares (23,682 acres), i.e. a tenfold increase over 1715; and if the figure for 1715 represented 7.5% of arable land, then in 1786 that figure had risen to 25.4% of all land cultivated by serfs. It was the poorer population strata which improved their productivity, with additional land in upland areas. In Nitra County, upland tracts represented 18.3% of all arable land, of which 38% was in the vicinity of Nove Mesto nad Vahom, and 27.9% in the vicinity of Obdokovce.

The increase in total population was also reflected in an increase in the population of the towns. By European standards our towns continued to be small rather than middle-sized or large: Bratislava, in 1778, had a population of 28,700, with an additional number of about 4,500 in the immediate vicinity of its citadel ('Bratislavsky Hrad'); Komarno had a population of 12,000; Trnava, 7,200; Kosice, 6,000; Presov, 5,700; Skalica, 5,100; Modra, 4,500;

Hospital scene during plague

Levoca, 4,200; Kezmarok, 3,900; Banska Stiavnica, with its mining settlements, more than 20,000, while its town core held only about 2,700 residents.

Statistical data shows that in 1778, the average village had a population of about 400, with approximately 60 homes, each housing 5.5 people. The birth rate at this time was about 52 per thousand, or about three times that of today, but infant mortality was high.

When Emperor Leopold I reached an accord with the Hungarian estates and restored the pre-1670 constitution, he had no inkling of what was about to take place on his eastern borders. In the summer of 1683, the Turks, with their Tatar allies and Thokoly's rebel contingents, laid siege to Vienna and ravaged the whole area around the Habsburg capital, including western Slovakia. The defenders of the city were able to hold out, however, and when reinforcements arrived on September 12, 1683, in the form of the Polish army of Jan Sobieski, they defeated the Turkish army and put it to rout. Emperor Leopold's army then gradually occupied all of Slovakia and defeated Thokoly. In August, it captured Nove Zamky, and later that same year Presov as well. In October 1685 the Turks turned on Tokoli, imprisoning him, and his troops defected to the emperor.

The Turks were subsequently helpless to stop the Austrian advance. On September 2, 1686, Leopold's forces captured Buda and in December, 1687, Eger. The Diet of that year, meeting in Bratislava, gratefully acknowledged the Habsburgs as hereditary kings of Hungary and renounced its right of opposition to the emperor, as granted by the Golden Bull of Andrew II. The regions freed from the Turks soon began to repopulate with peasants, including Slovaks, and in the last decade of the 17th Century, the great task of reconstruction began to remedy the damage wrought by the Turk and Tatar incursions.

This peace, and the work of reconstruction, was rent by a new uprising against Vienna in 1703, led by the wealthiest magnate of Hungary, Francis Rakoczi II. The uprising flared up and ran its course mostly in Slovakia. Rakoczi lured peasants into the uprising by promising alleviation of feudal obligations. At the turn of the year 1704–1705 the rebels occupied al of Hungary, leaving in imperial control only a narrow strip of land in western Slovakia, including Bratislava, the fortresses of Nove Zamky and Leopoldov, and the village of Rakos on the outskirts of Pest. The rebellious Hungarian nobles wanted to hold their diets exclusively in Rakos (as in the Medieval Ages), to show that they meant to restore traditions, not destroy them. They were also dissatisfied about the new limits placed on the conduct of diets, preferring the former open-air sessions, where all noblemen held equal participation rights.

Francis Rakoczi II

Charles III

After lengthy struggles between the emperor and Rakoczi's 'Kurutzi', the tide of war gradually turned in favor of Vienna: in the summer of 1708 the imperial army defeated the rebels near the town of Trencin; in October it gained control of the Central Slovakian mining towns; in the summer of 1709 it occupied Liptov County; in December it overran most of Spis County, then Levoca in the following February, and Kosice in April. On September 30, 1711, in the fields near the town of Satu Mare, the insurgents were forced to sign a definitive surrender (the Peace of Szatmar).[5]

Meanwhile, in 1705, Emperor Leopold I died and Joseph I succeeded him, only to die himself in 1711. His son, Charles VI (King Charles III of Hungary) became emperor and ruled to 1740.

His daughter, Maria Theresa, destined to become the most important imperial personality of the 18th Century, succeeded him in 1740. Her reign did not start without complications, even though her father, to ensure the right of succession to a female Habsburg, had signed the so-called 'Pragmatic Sanction' with surrounding monarchs. Notwithstanding the agreement, when Charles VI died, neighboring monarchs pounced on the Habsburg 'estate', seeking to grasp for themselves as much of it as they could.

In this situation, it was the Hungarian estates that saved Maria Theresa and her rule, although the universal expectation was that it would be precisely they who would administer her 'coup-de-grace'. But those who had entertained this hope were sorely disappointed, since they had failed to understand the political realities of Hungary, where absolutism had never fully taken root and the estates were accustomed to making decisions based on free judgment. When they realized that their legally crowned queen (she was technically 'king', '*rex*', in Hungary) was being badgered from all quarters, the Hungarians rushed to her defense. On the other hand, the Czech estates, which in conditions of absolutism had become accustomed passively to approve various resolutions, did accept the Elector of Bavaria, Charles VII as their king, as well as Holy Roman Emperor.

Maria Theresa

It soon became obvious that the voluntary aid of the Hungarian estates was the deciding factor in Maria Theresa's preservation. The Hungarian forces sent into battle by decision of the Diet expelled the Bavarians, advanced into Germany and part of France, and even stood up to the Prussian king Friedrich II (the Great), who fiercely opposed the new empress and whose army had occupied Silesia, an important economic base of the Habsburg realm.

Maria Theresa was immensely grateful to the 'Magyar nation' for this support, and never forgot the decisive effort made by the Hungarian nobility on

Coronation procession of Maria Theresa

her behalf. She ruled the Western half of her realm as an absolute monarch, but honored the Hungarian estates' conviction that executive power was still subordinate to their legislative power and constitution.

In the late 1750s, however, Hungarian intransigence in this matter led to conflict. Maria Theresa, becoming incensed against the Hungarian estates, stopped convening their diets, and began to rule as absolutely in Hungary as elsewhere. In 1764 she put her son-in-law, Albert of Saxony-Cieszyn, in charge of Hungary, made the city of Bratislava the seat of Hungarian government and the Bratislava Fortress ('Hrad') the residence of Albert, the viceroy. The years 1764 to 1780, when Albert ruled, were a period of great distinction for Bratislava as capital of Hungary.

During the absolutist phase of her reign, Maria Theresa accomplished her most important reforms. For instance, in her plan of scholastic reform, all youngsters were to receive a basic education, including those in villages. The reform and standardization of peasant obligations were very thorough, reducing them by 60% and precisely standardizing conscripted labor throughout her realm.[6]

At this time there were in Slovakia approximately 200,000 peasant farms and 150,000 rural laborers' plots. The average peasant farm was only five to six hectares (approximately twelve to fourteen acres), and in Slovakia there were so many members of the nobility, that the number of peasants averaged out to only about thirty-five each.

In the regulation of 'Urbars' (registries of peasant land), the counties continued to respect and legally guarantee the establishment of self-rule in peasant

A. F. Kollar, Councilor of Maria Theresa

Land Register of Maria Theresa.

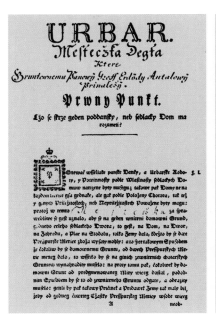

villages and small towns, preserving long-held traditions in most rural communities. The villagers (peasants) elected a village magistrate from among three candidates proposed by the local overlord, but they themselves selected and determined the members of the village council (trustees, aldermen). All the land-owning heads of households (peasants, rural laborers) could actively and passively take part in the elections, which were decided by a simple majority.

Regulation of 'urbar' land was administered by county officials in the relevant ethnic language. But officials were only able to do their job competently in Magyar, German and Slovak villages, because language problems arose in Romanian, Rusyn, Serbian and Croatian villages. Officials were proficient enough in Slovak, even in Eastern Slovak villages, and in fact, even in villages that today lie in Sub-Carpathia, southern Hungary, Vojvodina and Banat, if these locations were occupied by Slovaks who had repopulated them after the Turks left. They did so with the language that educated members of the nobility who implemented the programs had learned in school.[7]

The 18th Century was a period of general economic development in Slovakia. Farm acreage cultivated by peasants expanded, as did the productivity of miners, and the number of craftsmen's shops increased from about 8,000 in 1720, to about 22,500 in 1770. A certain amount of craft production was earmarked for export to southern Hungary and even to the Balkans. The production and export of linen cloth, which was mostly designated for export to Balkan markets, showed a marked increase.

New forms of production began to appear in Slovakia, in manufacturing plants. The first of these was founded by a local businessman in 1725 in Banska Bystrica. It manufactured whole cloth, mostly for miners. Of the new plants, the most important was a calico plant in Sastin, founded by Frantisek Stefan Lotrinsky. At the height of its operations, this plant employed thousands of weavers in western Slovakia, Lower Austria and in Vienna.[8] In the 1760s additional important textile plants were established in Halic near Lucenec, Teplicka nad Vahom, and Ceklis (Bernolakovo), all on the basis of privileges granted by Maria Theresa.

In Central Slovakia, in the vicinity of Banska Stiavnica, mining of silver expanded explosively, eventually employing approximately 20,000 miners.

The period from 1681 to 1781 is also marked by a consolidation of Slovak status in towns. Not only did their numbers increase, but Slovaks also began to demonstrate substantial ethnic awareness.

Titular page,
An Apologia,
by J. B. Magin,
first political defense
of Slovak nation

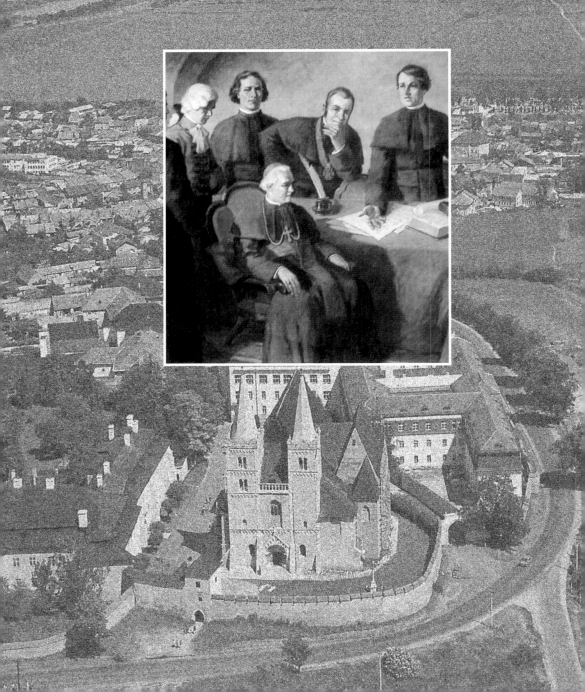

7. Headed towards Revolution (1781–1848)

After the death of Maria Theresa, her son Joseph II ascended the throne. The new emperor and king, realizing the need for many substantive changes, put off his coronation as king of Hungary. He was thus able to avoid taking the oath to uphold the Hungarian constitution and hoped to be able to accomplish fundamental, progressive changes in existing conditions there. His decision had only one drawback: the time was not yet ripe for some of his changes, and so, ten years later, on his deathbed, he had to retract them. In making decisions, he had not relied on capable advisors, and had often not even consulted any advisers, but, convinced of his sovereign superiority, had acted substantially alone.[1]

Joseph II

His first reform was issuance in October 1781 of the *Toleration Patent*, effective in both halves of his realm. The practical impact of this decree was far-reaching and positive, but its relevance to the two parts of his empire was quite different. After all, Bohemia, Moravia and Silesia were almost wholly Catholic, but in Hungary, Protestants constituted a sizeable part of the population, because in spite of hostility, they had been able to legally profess their faith, under specific circumstances and in well-defined spheres. After the issuance of the Toleration Patent, Protestants could build their own churches, own cemeteries, organize pastorates and associations, and engage in various religious activities.[2]

This new tolerance, however, did not apply to Jews. Their situation did improve slightly too, but they were still not permitted to settle in towns, attend Christian schools, acquire burgher rights, practice a craft, or hold office, and in the case of individuals who had somehow won these rights, they were immediately stripped of them after Joseph's death.

Another very important reform of Joseph II was the abolition of serfdom, which in Hungary took effect in 1785, four years later than in the Czech Kingdom and Austria, where the Patent had already been published in 1781. The effect of this decision was not as far-reaching as its issuer had assumed it would be, although it did mean a lot to serfs. With it, the emperor had in fact not totally abolished serfdom, but had removed only the aspect of hereditary servitude.[3]

Toleration Patent

The emperor made some major changes in the religious sphere, too. His intention was to create a compliant instrument of the churches (especially Catholic), ready to perform state-assigned tasks. This apparently was his goal when he supressed monasteries (all told, over 600, housing about 20,000 monks).[4] He sent the ordained monks to work in parishes, many of which were

89

Pope Pius VI visits Emperor Joseph II

gaping with pastoral vacancies at the time. He removed priestly formation from episcopal control and concentrated it in general seminaries, where future priests were educated under state supervision in the spirit of the Enlightenment.

However, the main burden of Emperor Joseph's reforms in Hungary rested on the liquidation of self-rule (dating from the Medieval Ages) and its replacement by state officials at all lower echelons; it also included the displacement of administrative Latin by German, already official in his western possessions.

Joseph II also eliminated issuance of guild charters in favor of freer forms of craft production. Although he strongly approved of manufacturing, he granted no privileges to manufacturers, leaving them to their own devices.

These reforms, unfortunately, were put in effect at a time when several lean years followed one upon another, raising mortality rates, especially among children, and devastating livestock. The superstitious and poorly educated populace interpreted these visitations as obvious punishment from God, and refused to be enthusiastic about the emperor's reforms.

An unusually important reality of Slovak history in these times was the decision of Catholic clerics in the general seminary at Bratislava, under the leadership of a professor, Anton Bernolak, to standardize the Slovak language for use in print publication.

Slovak was already then a relatively mature language, in which even the Viennese government published such legal documents as guild bylaws. Many personages, later to become highly placed dignitaries, had already been acquiring this language and had, in fact, even translated (though not yet published) Sacred Scripture, and had been proficient in its use even outside specifically Slovak areas. The *Presburske noviny* (Bratislava News) was at this time coming out in Czech, but many of its readers complained that they could not quite understand it, though its language was riddled with Slovak words and phrases.

Under the leadership of Bernolak, Bratislava seminarians banded together in the 'Societas excolendae linguae Slavicae' (Society for the Cultivation of the Slovak Language) and worked up a philological treatise, *Dissertatio Philologico-Critica de Literis Slavorum* (A Philologico-Critical Dissertation on the Slovak Language), published in 1787. In 1790, Bernolak published the first normative grammar of Slovak, *Grammatica Slavica*. In 1791 he published his final work, *Etymologia Vocabulorum Slavicorum* (An Etymology of Slovak Words). He completed his Slovak studies with a huge work, *Slovak-Czech-Latin-German-Hungarian Dictionary*, published posthumously.

Anton Bernolak

Fading echoes of a wide-spread belief can still be heard among us that Bernolak elevated a West-Slovak dialect to literary status, but in reality, he only normalized a cultural Slovak already widely current, much like what was done in the codification processes of other Central European languages.

When Joseph II abrogated many of his reforms and died, a very explosive situation arose in Hungary.[5] Generalized dissatisfaction with the conditions brought on by his reign prevailed, for his reforms had adversely affected the Church, nobility and townspeople, taking away old privileges and subordinating towns to counties and counties to central government. Even farmers were not particularly elated by his decrees, because they included some burdensome impositions, not placed on them by his predecessors.

The new emperor, Leopold II, was hard put to hold off the impending explosion: he naturally had to proceed with his coronation, take an oath on the Hungarian constitution, and convene a traditional diet.

This Diet confirmed the reforms that Joseph II had not abrogated, specifically the abolition of serfdom and the Toleration Patent. As to official language, Hungary returned to Latin, with the expectation of its early replacement by Magyar.

The deliberations of the Diet sent forth a signal promoting Magyarization, i.e. the conversion of multi-national Hungary into a Magyar state. This promotion assumed various guises. For instance, the middle nobility and townspeople began to 'Magyarize' in imitation of Magyar aristocracy. The proponents of the Magyar language succeeded in creating an atmosphere in which the ways of the nobility and the Magyar language were viewed as the wave of the future, an assumption that Magyar ought to be cultivated at least as much as Latin, and a belief that all the other languages of Hungary were merely ethnic dialects with no future. In some towns, pastors stopped preaching in Slovak, and guilds no longer published Slovak bylaws, using only Magyar, German, or Latin.

Tensions between the emperor and the Hungarian estates, which had heated up in 1790, gradually abated under the influence of revolutionary events in

France. There, the whole absolutist system had been overthrown, and with the king and queen executed, nobility deprived of privileges, feudalism was consigned to the dustbin.

By November 1790, when Leopold II was crowned Hungarian king, Hungary was already at peace and the Diet consented to bypass election of a palatine from the ranks of its domestic magnates in favor of a candidate from prominent members of the imperial family. The first to be so chosen was a younger brother of the emperor, Alexander Leopold, and, following him, his brother Joseph.[6]

Leopold II ruled for only two years. After his death, Francis II ascended the throne, destined to rule for almost 40 years. He returned to conservative policies and practices. His agents spied on politically suspicious members of the nobility, liberal politicians, and intellectuals, and they infiltrated oppositional associations. Francis II banned Masonic lodges. He was struck by fear when a conspi-

Coronation of Leopold II, Cathedral of St. Martin, Bratislava, 11 November 1790

racy was uncovered in Hungary, organized by a former Franciscan friar, Ignac Martinovics, who had become a confirmed atheist and informant. Francis ordered the execution of Martinovics's co-conspirators, though they were isolated individuals, incapable of posing a threat without extraordinary circumstances.

When, out of the chaos of the French Revolution, Napoleon Bonaparte emerged triumphant, the focus of political life in the Habsburg Empire shifted to wars with France.

In 1796, the Hungarian Diet willingly came to the aid of its king and emperor, sending him 50,000 recruits and considerable material. This conflict ended unsuccessfully for Emperor Francis, and in the terms of a peace treaty signed in 1797, he was forced to give up present-day Belgium and Luxemburg, receiving in return Venice, as well as Istria and Dalmatia.

In 1799, new hostilities erupted with France, who again emerged victorious. The peace signed in 1801 confirmed and renewed the terms of 1797.

In 1805 Vienna allowed itself to be drawn into a third war with France, this time as an ally of Britain and Russia. Again France prevailed: Napoleon occupied Vienna and a part of western Slovakia. At Slavkov (Austerlitz) he routed the combined armies of Austria and Russia.

In the ensuing peace, signed in Bratislava on December 26, 1805, Austria lost a considerable part of its territory. A year later, after defeating Prussia, Napoleon declared a so-called continental blockade, meant to bring Britain to its knees.

Execution of participants in Martinovic Conspiracy, 'Bloody Field', Budin

In 1809, Austria engaged in yet another war with France, losing again and once more incurring occupation of Vienna by Napoleon.

After this last defeat, the Habsburg monarchy changed sides, becoming an ally of France and Napoleon, who by this time had conquered most of Europe. In 1812, buoyed by his military successes, Napoleon undertook an invasion of Russia. There the arrogant French emperor finally met defeat.

After Napoleon's debacle in Russia, the Habsburg Empire regained its original territories and even expanded, assuming an important place among European superpowers in a newly constituted Holy Alliance. The alliance's principal role was to prevent revolutions and to nip in the bud all movements that could lead to revolution. The Viennese imperial government leaned mainly on Russia and Prussia, the two other great powers in the alliance, for support; Britain and France were not in complete accord with some of Vienna's policies. After all, in Britain, parliamentarianism was the norm and conditions were freer, while in France a new revolution in 1830 had dethroned the House of Bourbon.

Chancellor Metternich of Austria used his troops to intervene in various rebellions and uprisings; he persecuted progressive movements in Germany, especially in the universities, and muffled the press if it wrote the least bit liberally. However, he could not help but notice the July revolution in France and the Polish uprising of 1830–1831. Also disquieting were the bourgeoning national unification movements in Germany and Italy, and the decline of Viennese influence in German principalities, as well as Prussia's drive to

Emperor Francis I
meets Napoleon

leadership after the creation of a German customs union in 1834. Vienna found itself orienting to St. Petersburg rather than to Berlin.

In this situation, the Viennese imperial government again encountered serious problems in Hungary. There the political infra-structure was still divided into counties, founded on the principle of aristocratic self-rule and a diet open to all members of the nobility (the four estates), convening every three years and passing laws which were supposed to be binding, even on the king. Nevertheless, imperial power did not become toothless: Vienna continued to intervene in internal affairs.

After a deterioration of relations between Vienna and the Hungarian estates following the Diet of 1811–1812, Francis II stopped summoning diets and began directing Hungarian affairs by cabinet decree. At this time, Vienna was able to push through a requirement for Hungarian participation in amortizing debts arising from currency devaluation, and it was also able to get its way in many matters on the level of county and town. For instance, the Imperial Court prevented the regular annual elections of magistrates in the free royal towns. Elections were only allowed when a specific royal decree authorized them.

Chancellor Metternich

In the end, however, Vienna did have to relent in 1825 and convene a diet, to thrash out intractable problems. This diet's deliberations lasted whole years, as did subsequent diets (1832–1836, 1839–1840, 1843–1844), except for the 1830 diet, which was quickly adjourned owing to a cholera epidemic.

These diets and the whole population of Hungary faced a myriad of insoluble problems in the second quarter of the 19th Century. Indeed, after the revolutionary events in France, it had become obvious to everyone that the feudal system in Hungary no longer had a future. The basic problem was the aristocracy's powerful hold on Hungarian society, even while it faced the same fate that had befallen the aristocracy in Poland, where excessive attachment to privileges had destroyed the state.[7]

The Hungarian nobility continued to lead its tax-free existence, which it rationalized as a fair offset for the obligation of defending the country. After the establishment of a standing army and its subsequent defeat by Napoleon in 1809, the Hungarian nobility no longer had a leg to stand on. In the meantime, no commoner was eligible for county office, no matter how well–educated, since only aristocrats could participate in assemblies which elected county officials. There was a whole list of problems in Hungary, and no one had solutions. Matters were further complicated by the fact that participants in the diets, for the most part, felt themselves Magyar, rather than Hungarian, and as such, wanted to accomplish something for their own developing nationality, in spite of the fact that Magyars in no way represented a majority of Hungary's residents.

The Diet of 1840 passed laws which replaced Latin with Magyar, signaling a new wave of Magyarization and new attempts to have the leading role of Magyar culture and language accepted as a 'fait accompli'. The guiding father of these strivings was the great Magyar patriot, Count Istvan Szechenyi, who contributed a considerable sum of money towards the founding of a Magyar Academy of Sciences, which, he supposed, would provide leadership in this cause.[8]

But another proposal was made by a deputy named Louis Kossuth, who favored using forcible means to achieve the goal.[9] He advocated the principle of 'Every nobleman a Magyar'. Kossuth perceived Hungary as a Magyar state, and was explicitly scornful of non-Magyar nationalities. This attitude was totally unacceptable to Slovaks and other nationalities.

A law passed by the Diet in 1840, providing serfs the right to buy their way out of feudal obligations, was essentially a shot in the dark, since it generated no appreciable response.[10] (On the other hand, in the Czech and Alpine regions of Austria, serfs could buy their way out of conscripted labor without legal sanction.) Just as worthless was a law on promissory notes, stock companies, and the fostering of industries, since Hungarian nobility, receiving ample income from the sale of agricultural produce, felt no need to found industries. By contrast, Czech, Moravian and Austrian nobility had no comparable resource to fall back on.

With wool sheared in Hungary, a strong and prosperous cloth industry arose in Moravia and elsewhere in Austrian lands, and this industry in turn sold its products mainly to Hungarian markets. Kossuth and other Magyar politicians strove to organize a protectionist movement, boycotting industrial products from Austrian regions, but in vain, since there were few comparable domestic products, and what did exist was more expensive and inferior. When the calico plant in Sastin closed (1840), there was not a single cotton-cloth manufacturer left in all of Hungary; all calico and other cotton products were imported from Lower Austria or the Czech lands.

It was precisely in this quarter-century that the economic dichotomy of the Habsburg Empire reached its culmination: the Czech Lands, Moravia, Silesia, Austria and its North Italian provinces took over the role of industrial base, while Hungary, together with Galicia, became both agricultural hinterland and consumer market. Contemporary Magyar radicals and deputies to the Diet, and Magyar historians later on, blamed Vienna for this unfavorable balance, but, in reality, its cause lay in a lack of entrepreneurship and the unwillingness of Hungarian propertied classes (i.e. the nobility) to invest in industry.

Since the total value of Hungarian agricultural exports exceeded the total value of industrial imports, a demand for a customs barrier between the two parts of the empire was well-founded. Still, the Imperial government continuously derived a relatively smaller income from Hungary than it received from its Austrian regions, and to make matters worse, the Hungarian Diet continued to pursue its own tax policies.

During the war-time economic boom of the turn of the 18th to 19th Century, the price of grain in Hungary had risen steeply and exports to western parts of the empire soared, but when the Napoleonic wars ended, grain prices dropped precipitously and outlets evaporated.[11]

In the early 1820's, a bull market in wool replaced the collapsed grain market. Hungarian wool was sold not only in Austria and the Czech lands, but in Britain, Holland and Germany as well. This boom lasted three decades, peaking in the 1840s, when wool production reached a volume of 20,000 tons annually. Of this amount, 20% was used internally, not by industry but in private homes.

Measurable progress in agricultural production was made on landed estates rather than on small farms. The increase came mainly from expanded use of threshing and sowing machines. In the 1830s and 40s, the cultivation of potatoes spread among peasants, particularly in mountainous areas and adjacent valleys. There is no doubt that the potato saved a lot of people from starvation, but used in the distillation of alcohol, it also created many social problems. Famine was a visitor in Slovak villages in 1817 and 1818, causing 44,000 deaths in five eastern Slovak counties. In the years 1846 and 1848, 3,200 people died of starvation in Orava County, and 32,000 in Saris County, a quarter of its population.

In 1831, a 'cholera uprising' broke out in eastern Slovakia, when peasants and others imagined that the nobility was poisoning them with powders distributed as medicine. The villagers, in their delusion, killed several members of the nobility but mostly Jewish tavern keepers and lenders, for which actions the courts condemned and hung up to 100 people.[12]

Between the years 1785 and 1850 the population of Slovakia rose to about 2,300,000. Actually, many of the residents of Slovakia had moved away and many had succumbed to cholera or starvation, so that the relative population increase in Slovakia was less than that in the rest of Hungary. There was, however, a sizeable influx of Jews from Polish Galicia. Their share of the population of Slovakia in 1846 represented as much as 4.3%. Most of these Jews lived in eastern Slovakia, making a living chiefly by tavern-keeping.[13]

In 1846, in all of Hungary, there were 1,722,500 Slovaks; of these, 1,238,000 lived on the territory of present-day Slovakia. In the south of Hungary, in regions liberated from Turkish occupation, there lived more than 170,000 Slovaks, 24,000 of them in Bekescaba, 17,500 in Sarvas, and 38,000 in Pest County.

The Slovak nation-building process, which had begun in the 18th Century, ran its course through some very unfavorable circumstances, because it was concurrent with an analogous Magyar process, whose aim, however, was to change the Old Hungarian Kingdom into a Magyar national state. The Magyars did achieve some successes. German and Magyar townspeople of Old Hungary, as well as the nobility who lived outside compact Magyar areas, began to behave and dress in Magyar fashion; they began taking an interest in Magyar language and culture, attended church services with Magyar sermons and hymns. Slovaks were particularly sensitive to these developments, because, thanks to losses by assimilation to German and Magyar ethnics in towns, they were becoming a predominantly rural people, like other ethnics in Old Hungary. The more well-to-do nobility began to lose their Slovak identity, or were already well on their way to assimilation. The petty nobility, who spoke Slovak and continued to relate to Slovak ethnicity, were basically small farmers, or even less. Many owned nothing but their coat-of-arms, and made a living by physically tilling their own soil.

The national revival, or wake-up process, of Slovaks began rather more auspiciously than did that of other Hungarian ethnics, and even earlier.

However, the relatively successful process put in motion by Anton Bernolak and his supporters did not continue to evolve; it led to no flowering of Slovak letters and culture. Many negative factors influenced this failure. For instance, Slovak Lutherans rejected the newly codified language of Bernolak and continued to use biblical Czech. Furthermore, the ideological wave of Enlightenment in which Bernolak and his supporters had grown up, petered out when Francis II mounted the throne. Then, at the turn of the 18th to 19th Century, a strong wave of anti-clericalism and anti-Catholicism swept across Europe. The suppression of the Jesuit order by the pope in 1773 severely hurt the Catholic cause, while the order's reinstatement in 1814 did little to recoup its influence. The issuance of the Toleration Patent and the leveling of rights between Protestants and Catholics enabled Protestants to increase their activity and rebuild their self-esteem. Its effect on Catholics, including Bernolak and his followers, was not at all the same; conditions at the beginning of the 19th Century were no longer blatantly favorable to Catholics.

Lutheran Lyceum, Bratislava

Anton Bernolak, having finished his theological studies in the general seminary at Bratislava, was ordained and first worked as a chaplain in Ceklis; then, from 1791 to 1797, he worked as a secretary in the archdiocesan vicariate in Trnava; from 1797 to his death in 1813 he served as a pastor and dean in Nove Zamky. At this last station he completed his linguistic work with a five-part dictionary, Slovak-Czech-Latin-German-Magyar. One of his closest co-workers was Juraj Fandly, a pastor in Nahac, who used Bernolak's literary norm in his works of enlightenment, aimed at the common man.

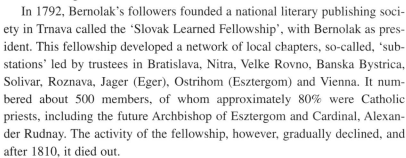

Juraj Fandly

In 1792, Bernolak's followers founded a national literary publishing society in Trnava called the 'Slovak Learned Fellowship', with Bernolak as president. This fellowship developed a network of local chapters, so-called, 'substations' led by trustees in Bratislava, Nitra, Velke Rovno, Banska Bystrica, Solivar, Roznava, Jager (Eger), Ostrihom (Esztergom) and Vienna. It numbered about 500 members, of whom approximately 80% were Catholic priests, including the future Archbishop of Esztergom and Cardinal, Alexander Rudnay. The activity of the fellowship, however, gradually declined, and after 1810, it died out.

The Lutheran intelligentsia working in Slovakia and elsewhere in Hungary, who remained loyal to biblical Czech, joined forces with Czech revivalists, among whom the most prominent was Josef Dobrovsky. It was he who, with his scholarly work, exerted an immediate influence on Juraj Rybay, a Lutheran pastor in southern Hungary. And it was thanks to his influence that Lutherans continued to support the idea of literary-linguistic unity between Slovaks and Czechs. For the Czech revivalists, orientation towards Slovakia

Slovak Learned Fellowship

Juraj Palkovic

Pavol Jozef Safarik

Jan Kollar

served as an escape gap from near total encirclement by the Germans, who many assumed would one day engulf the Czechs. This idea of Czech-Slovak unity was based on impulses originating with Slovak Lutherans, among whom the unsubstantiated thesis had taken root and grown that they were descendants of Czech Hussites, who had supposedly founded their Church in Gemer and Malohont Counties.

In the twenties and thirties of the 19th Century, a new generation of Slovak revivalists grew up and became active in both Catholic and Lutheran camps. It went through formation at a time when Magyarization was gaining momentum, but also at a time when a Czech revival was enjoying success and acceptance on the territory of Bohemia and Moravia, rebutting predictions of German assimilation. A new element of this revival was the rapid growth of Russian political influence after 1812; Russians were viewed by Czechs and Slovaks as a bulwark of their ethnicity, providing a bright outlook for the future of the great family of Slavic nationalities.

The Czech revivalists of this period did not shy away from fabricating documents to enhance national pride and to prove the ancient origins and uniqueness of Czech culture.[14] Subsequent research has disclosed that these documents actually originated in the years 1812 to 1816. In spite of the well-founded and unconcealed skepticism of Josef Dobrovsky, these documents were put forward as genuinely historic works, comparable to medieval German epics. Using them as a basis, many literary, artistic and musical works, considered jewels of Czech culture today, were composed. In 1820, the Czech National Museum was founded, and new Czech scientific, literary and popular/instructional magazines began appearing, spreading the Czech national revival ever more widely.[15]

In the Slovak Lutheran camp, personalities of such broad erudition as Pavol Jozef Safarik and Jan Kollar appeared, destined to become pillars of a new phase of the Czech national revival. Safarik wrote scholarly literature in the field of Slavistics, while Kollar wrote masterful poetry and created the concept of Slavic reciprocity.

In the Catholic camp, Juraj Palkovic, a contemporary of Anton Bernolak, forged his way to the forefront. He translated the Sacred Scriptures into Slovak, and published them in Buda, which, with Pest, was becoming a center of Bernolak's followers. The genial poet, Jan Holly, who created an extraordinary poetic oeuvre using Bernolak's norm of literary Slovak, was a tremendous force for unity among Slovaks.[16]

In the meantime, a new generation of revivalists was maturing. Lutherans became ever more aware that biblical Czech, as used in Slovakia, was barely understandable to ordinary Slovaks, and that identification of themselves as Czechs had no basis in fact. Even the oeuvre of Jan Holly nudged them closer to the Slovak language, as opposed to Czech.

Ludovit Stur, born in 1815, took the lead in this generation. It was he who won over the students of the Lutheran Lyceum in Bratislava for Slovak as a literary medium and an awareness of the national distinctiveness of Slovaks. This idea of ethnic distinctiveness and uniqueness of tongue found expression and reinforcement in a visit by Ludovit Stur, Jozef Miloslav Hurban and Michal Miloslav Hodza to the Bernolakian poet, Jan Holly, at Dobra Voda in 1843. They later reached an accord at Hurban's parish house in Hlboke, after discussions that lasted from the 11th to the 16th of July, 1843, to codify Central Slovak, with various adaptations to East and West Slovak, as the standard Slovak literary language.[17]

Jan Holly

Even before this meeting they had made an attempt to put up a defense against the growing pressures of Magyarization. On June 2, 1842, they submitted a petition to the emperor (*A Slovak Petition to the Throne*), requesting protection from Magyarization, which however, only provoked intensified attacks from Magyars.

The first book published in Stur's codification of Slovak was an almanac, *Nitra*, which came out in the summer of 1844. Stur wrote a defense of his norms in *The Slovak Dialect or the Need to Write in Slovak,* published at the beginning of 1846, together with a grammar, *Lessons in the Slovak Language.*

8.   The Revolution of 1848–1849

When the Hungarian estates convened at the king's summons for their regular diet in Bratislava in November 1847, they had no inkling that the session would be so brief. Under the strong influence of the revolution in France, whence a spark had jumped to Vienna, a revolution exploded on March 13, 1848.[1] A day later, the Hungarian estates proclaimed laws ending feudalism, ceding land to serfs (based on local land registries), abolishing the privileges of nobility, and extending equal rights before the law to all residents of the country.

Lajos Kossuth

These were the ideals raised to the heights by the French Revolution at the end of the 18th Century, for the realization of which, the people of Hungary, like others, were fervently longing. Had Old Hungary been troubled by no other problems than economic and social, the delegates could well have peacefully disbanded and gone home. But a big problem still remained, the problem of Hungary finding its place in the Habsburg realm, of working up a new constitution, and of defining the place of Magyars and their language in the Hungarian state, vis-à-vis a majority of non-Magyar residents.

In the 1840s, radical currents on the Magyar scene grew ever stronger. Magyars were not satisfied that their language had achieved a high level of development and enrichment, or that it had successfully replaced Latin in public life, nor even that these achievements were also appreciated by non-Magyar nationalities, including Slovaks. Under the slogan 'One country – one language – one nation' the Magyars launched a fanatical campaign to Magyarize all spheres of public life.

The outstanding protagonists of this campaign were the middle nobility, which had considerable political privileges at their disposal but no great wealth, particularly no great number of serfs. Its political orientation was liberal and its leader was Lajos Kossuth, the editor of *Pesti Hirlap*, a newspaper that had begun circulating in January 1841. Kossuth had a very low esteem for non-Magyar Hungarian nationalities: he demanded a renunciation of all ethnic aspirations and a willing submission to Magyarization. The ideas of Istvan Szechenyi, who represented the conservative wing of the Magyar national revival, and who would have liked to gain Magyar converts by milder means, were dismissed.

Istvan Szechenyi

The drive to Magyarize invaded not only the socio-political but the religio-ecclesiastical sphere as well, and in the Protestant camp its most important spokesman was Count Karoly Zay, Inspector General of the Lutheran Church, who energetically strove for a union of Lutherans and Calvinists. Zay went so far as to accuse Slovak Lutherans of treasonous intentions.[2]

What course did events take in those dramatic days of revolution in March 1848?

March 14, 1848, the day of the proclamation of the laws mentioned above, was not a particularly conspicuous day in Bratislava.[3] The *Pressburger Zeitung* (Pressburg News) carried reports of the events of the 13th, followed by an announcement on the 17th that press censorship had been abolished.

Before noon on March 16, all the most radical deputies of the diet departed by steamboat for Vienna to file a petition of Hungarian demands. The Viennese populace hailed them enthusiastically, and Kossuth, in particular, received heady ovations. The crowd cheered long into the night, and he responded by emerging to make several brief addresses. On the following day, the Magyar delegation rather quickly reached an agreement and returned to Bratislava with a report that the emperor had acquiesced to their demands.

More celebrations followed as events unfolded, especially when Hungarian independence was proclaimed in the capital city of Pest. Buda and Pest had not as yet been merged administratively, but they had already been joined by

Hungarian Diet announces March Laws, giving wings to Magyar Revolution

104

a sturdy bridge, built on the initiative of Count Istvan Szechenyi. This bridge was the first and only one in all of Hungary that did not require a toll.

Both cities, in particular the dynamically growing Pest, with its prosperous craft-shops and businesses, its huge fairs (of statewide import), were the industrial and commercial centers of Hungary, full of young men studying at a university wholly suffused with Magyar sentiment. Here was where Kossuth worked, disseminating his opinions, and here too, was where he published his radically oriented daily, *Pesti Hirlap*.

March 15, 1848, was a great day in Pest, still celebrated as a Hungarian state holiday.[4] Close examination will reveal that Hungary as compared, for instance, with the Czech Kingdom, had enjoyed relative independence even before 1848, and could hardly have been described as completely subordinated to Vienna in economy and politics. But the fall of absolutism, the shamefaced flight of Metternich, the termination of the police state, of censorship, of political oppression, and the release of political prisoners, were all causes for jubilation, whether they happened in the whole of the empire or just in Hungary. Hopes for creation of independent relations with Vienna were justifiably great.

Ignominious flight of Chancellor Metternich from Vienna, in period caricature

According to the March laws, the future government of Hungary was to be subordinated to its Diet, which was to meet annually, no longer in Bratislava but in Pest. The Diet was still to be composed of two chambers, in the upper of which were to sit magnates and prelates, as in the past (i.e. the wealthiest nobles and the highest clergy), while members of the lower chamber were to be elected; but the right to vote was to be tied to property or level of education, so that the leading role in political life would continue to fall to the middle nobility, which had filled this important role since the Medieval Ages. A condition of the right to vote, however, was to be an active command of the Magyar language.

In April, a compendium of laws passed by the Diet received the sanction of the king in the primatial palace in Bratislava. In accordance with the constitution, the king formally appointed a new Hungarian administration (cabinet ministers), with Lajos Batthany at its head. Among the eight appointees were Lajos Kossuth and Count Istvan Szechenyi, two protagonists, who in the pre-March days had occupied sharply contrasting political positions.

Although the government was headed by Count Lajos Batthany, a rich magnate, the leading and most influential personage of Hungary after March was Lajos Kossuth, an attorney in his forties, of Calvinist faith, from a region of Hungary in which altogether different socio-economic conditions from those in Slovakia or Trans-Danubia had long prevailed. That area had

Primacial Palace, Bratislava, site of ratification of March Laws, in presence of Ferdinand V

been a bastion of opposition to Vienna and the Habsburgs for centuries, as well as of pugnacious adherents of the Reformation and anti-Catholicism. Kossuth had been educated in the Protestant schools of eastern Hungary (Satoraljaujhely, Sarospatak, and Presov). In the years 1823 to 1832, he practiced law in Zemplin County; from 1832 he was a deputy to the Hungarian Diet, including its longest ever session (1832–1836), during which he published *The Diet Reporter;* in 1837 he was sentenced to four years in prison for politically incorrect views, serving almost the full term of his sentence. This imprisonment brought him great popularity, not only in Hungarian oppositional circles, but among revolutionaries of the entire Habsburg realm. In the Diet of 1847–1848, he was one of the most radical of its deputies and one of the framers of the March laws.

As Minister of Finance in the newly constituted Magyar government, Kossuth actively backed a proposal to create an independent Hungarian army and currency, with a covert goal of eventually seceding from the Habsburg realm.[5] He climbed ever higher on his career ladder and, after Prime Minister Batthany resigned in August 1848, Kossuth became president of the Committee for the Defense of the Homeland, thus formally the leading spokesman for the Magyar opposition to Vienna.

In April and May 1848, the Hungarian government, which permanently settled in Pest, organized country-wide demonstrations, at which it proclaimed laws abolishing serfdom and church tithes. Of course, the representatives of the government had to present themselves as adherents of a social class that had voluntarily renounced its privileges, and now wanted to recruit former serfs to fight for Hungarian independence. But a problem arose: how do you satisfy farmers who had tilled other than registered lands ('urbarska poda') – i.e. upland fields ('kopaniciarska poda') – and were not designated to receive any rights to land unless they paid full price? This situation was quite critical in the vicinity of Nove Mesto nad Vahom, Myjava, Prievidza, and in the counties of Hont and Gemer.

Before the outbreak of revolution, Slovak activists had to concentrate on press rebuttals of Magyar attacks, which they published mainly in German for the sake of wider circulation. Meanwhile, several representatives of the Czech National Movement rallied to the defense of Slovaks. At this time, most Czechs supported Austro-Slavism, i.e. conversion of Austria into a government representing all nationalities, including Slavs. After all, Slavs constituted a substantial part of the Austrian empire's population.[6]

Under the pressure of Magyar attacks, the two religious confessions of Slovaks were becoming more mutually amicable, striving to present a united front. August 26–28, 1844, in a meeting of leading Slovak activists in Liptovsky Svaty Martin, the home base of Miloslav Hodza, an association of nonsectarian character was formed under the name *Tatrin*, to unite various Slovak factions in one national bloc. At first Catholics hung back, but at a meeting held on March 10, 1847, with fifteen participants, they opted to accept the grammatical and syntactic norms of the Slovak language in Ludovit Stur's formulation.

Front page of first issue of Slovak National News

107

A very important event for the Slovak movement was the decision of governmental authorities to allow publication of *The Slovak National News,* a newspaper edited by Ludovit Stur. The first issue came off the press on August 1, 1845. Stur, who became the universally acknowledged political leader of the Slovaks, considered this event to be symbolic 'of a higher national life'.

The Slovak National News came out in Bratislava twice a week on four pages, in a run of 400 and occasionally as high as 800 copies. A supplement, *The Tatra Eagle*, came out bi-weekly on eight pages. These publications were printed in Roman characters, which were somewhat of a novelty compared to the usual Gothic. Of course, they were censored, a fact that Stur needed to always keep in mind if he wanted his paper to reach the public.

In 1846, Jozef Miloslav Hurban began publishing *Slovak Views on the Sciences, Arts and Literature*, but only two issues had come out by the 1848 revolution. Later, Hurban proved himself an outstanding organizer of Slovak military operations, and a personality who instilled a fighting spirit in the Slovak Volunteer Corps.

The leading representatives of the Slovak National Movement in the 1840s devoted themselves to work among people at the grassroots level, promoting the moral, social and cultural edification of the common Slovak man and woman, making them aware of the need to fight actively for social betterment.[7] They advocated organization of so-called Sunday schools. Stur proposed the establishment of libraries and reading rooms, and backed amateur theater, to be followed by social entertainments in a Slovak spirit. He also res-

Session of Lower House of Diet, Bratislava

olutely fought alcoholism. These proposals and initiatives caught on in large part and brought positive results.

In 1848, Daniel Lichard, a Lutheran pastor in Skalica, began publishing a newspaper for farming/husbandry, crafts and domestic life. In 1845, Samuel Jurkovic founded a credit cooperative in Sobotiste, called the Farmers' Association, which was the first of its kind in Europe and a model for similar groups in Vrbovce, Brezova, Myjava and elsewhere.

Thanks to the efforts of the followers of Stur, contributors to the *Slovak National News* began coming forward, even before the revolution. Stur's supporters also organized amateur theater, farmers' associations, temperance societies and Sunday schools in Slovakia and in Slovak enclaves elsewhere, except in the easternmost Slovak regions, where people were not yet fully 'awakened'. Slovak students of various Lutheran middle schools came together in 1846 to form a *Union of Slovak Youth*, which had six branches, headquartered in Levoca, then Bratislava.

The Slovak National Movement, led by Ludovit Stur, was from the very beginning consistently popular and democratic, in contrast to the analogous Magyar movement, which was led by members of the nobility with their arrogant attitude towards the common man, full of themselves as molders of the national character. This Magyar self-absorption lasted at least to 1918 and was still in evidence in 1945.

Stur grasped the need for a principled approach to Slovak problems, the need to back his fellow Slovaks in their anti-feudal struggle and the need to terminate serfdom with its economic dependency as quickly as possible. He broached these issues on the pages of *The Slovak National News*, and Stur's co-editor, Peter Kellner Hostinsky, spelled them out in a series of articles run from January to August 1846. Stur and his newspaper had not yet called for an obligatory state buy-out of serfs, as had Kossuth. Hostinsky argued that buy-outs should be made by individual contract between the feudal lord and serf. In July 1846, Stur himself addressed the problem and went beyond the demands of Hostinsky, winning approval even from Kossuth.

Ludovit Stur

Stur was also in favor of building industry and railroads, and developing new technology. He opposed the nobility's exemption from taxation, decried the unavailability of credit, demanded court reform and favored extension of voting rights to non-gentry, as well as expansion of the intelligentsia's role in public life. In an article titled, *What are the Root Causes of our Poverty?*, Stur expressed the conviction that nothing would stop Slovaks on the road to property, enlightenment and freedom, and that one day all the misery of Slovaks would come to an end.

In November 1847, Stur took part in the Hungarian Diet as a deputy for the town of Zvolen. He summed up his program in the following platform:

1. To proclaim through the Diet the legal, universal and permanent abolition of serfdom, achieved through a buy-out with state funds and a minimum imposition on the resources of the common man.

2. To abolish the patrimonial court (the county system), and to free the common man from gentry control.

3. To make secure the political rights of commoners, allowing them to protect their own interests through representation in counties and the Diet.

4. To free privileged towns from county jurisdiction, to reorganize the administration of royally chartered towns on the principle of representation, and to strengthen their voting rights in the Diet in a way that would match their importance in the economic and social life of the country.

5. To abolish the privileges of the nobility and make all persons equal before the courts; to abolish tax exemption of nobility and the principle of inheritance; to ensure commoners the right to serve in all public offices; and to insure freedom of the press.

6. To reorganize the educational system in a way to best serve the needs of the people and to ensure a better livelihood for teachers.

Of course, he did not forget about the use of Slovak in government or cultivation of ethnic languages in general, or about curbing the forcible insinuation of Magyar into all spheres of life, including religious.

Stur addressed the Diet several times and, together with supporters of reforms among the Magyar gentry, mainly Lajos Kossuth, appealed for the earliest possible abolition of serfdom and the liberation of serfs, all to be put into practice in the manner most acceptable to the serfs themselves. In view

L. Stur, addressing Hungarian Diet

of the fact that the official language of the Diet was Magyar, he, like other deputies, made his appeals in that language, but even in this forum he defended the rights of members of other nationalities to use their own languages. His defense fell on deaf ears.

The enthusiasm that prevailed in the whole country and, above all, in the capital city after the liberation of serfs, and especially after the proclamation of Hungarian independence from Vienna, soon began to subside. Many of the expectations of poor farmers were not realized, since the southern regions of Hungary, inhabited predominantly by Magyars, were full of individuals who had already long enjoyed personal freedom but owned no land, occupying their tracts by very unfavorable leases instead. This group gained nothing from the events of March 1848.

In the various non-Magyar ethnic regions discontent with Magyarization spread, even though these other ethnics, like the Slovaks, were still far from fully conscious of their national identities.

For ordinary people the idea of a completely independent Hungary seceding from the Habsburg Empire and creating an independent Magyar state, as favored by Lajos Kossuth, must have seemed very precarious. After all, the Austrian regime had not been all that bad, and it really had not oppressed Hungarians as horribly as some claimed. Would not oppression by Kossuth be even worse?[8] The emperor and king had a strong army; he could very well find Magyar behavior repugnant. Also, he had potential allies on all sides, ready to come to his aid. Could the hastily recruited Magyar army and the various local militias successfully counter such a force? Meanwhile, the Magyar leaders did not give a hoot for the other nationalities; they fundamentally rejected even a helping hand, and scornfully dismissed the 'plebeian' leaders of other ethnics.

Since March 1848, the Pest regime had been conducting a campaign to suppress the unrest of non-Magyar ethnic groups. It was well aware that, in Slovakia, activists had taken over the leadership of disgruntled farmers. In Hont County, it was Janko Kral and his friend, a village notary named Jan Rotarides, who demanded a systematic liquidation of serfdom and recognition of the Slovak language in government offices and public schools. These demands landed them in jail. In Liptovsky Svaty Mikulas, Slovak leaders took advantage of an assembly of former serfs convened by Liptov County on March 28, 1848, to present demands for a more systematic implementation of the new freedoms, with rights extended to Hungarian nationalities, particularly Slovaks. The Liptovian public enthusiastically hailed these demands. And in Central Slovakia, miners boisterously demonstrated, compelling the regime to send a special commissioner to quiet them.

Jozef Miloslav Hurban

At the beginning of April 1848, Stur and Hurban departed for Vienna to contact representatives of the various nationalities of the realm. There they agreed to convene a Slavic congress in Prague, which would develop a common strategy for all Austro-Hungarian Slavs. Jozef Miloslav Hurban, returning home and campaigning in the vicinity of Myjava, organized a large public rally in Brezova on April 28, which reviewed newly passed legislation. He next tried to call another such rally in Nitra, but county authorities banned it.

On May 10, 1848, twenty Slovak activists gathered in Liptovsky Svaty Mikulas and jointly prepared a document entitled *Demands of the Slovak Nationality*. It listed 14 points, setting forth the national, as well as social, demands of the Slovak movement. Owing to the faintheartedness of M. M. Hodza, these demands were not publicly announced until later, in the presence of a rather modest gathering at Ondrasova.

When the demands were publicly announced, the government responded by declaring martial law. It labeled them 'Pan-Slav rabble-rousing' and issued arrest warrants for Stur, Hurban and Hodza. The regime made the same kind

Mikulas Demands of Slovak Nationality

of response to demands by Romanians and the Serbs of Vojvodina, against whom it organized a punitive expedition in mid-June. In the face of such rebuffs, all attempts by Hungarian ethnic groups to come to peaceful terms with the regime ceased; their next recourse was to arms.

The first to resort to arms were the Serbs in the southern regions of Hungary, where for a long time there had existed a so-called 'military border', whose inhabitants were simultaneously farmers and soldiers, obligated to fight at the threat of war.[9] Their military preparedness put Hungarian officialdom in a bind. On May 13, a congress in Karlovac proclaimed an independent Serbian province of Vojvodina and elected a commander and patriarch. On June 16, the Serbs of Vojvodina repulsed a Magyar attack and declared an alliance between Serbs and Croatians.[10]

Numerous Slovak participants in Prague Slavic Congress (Stur standing at left)

In Croatia, which had long been a legally self-governing entity within Hungary, the national revival had been so successful that its governor was no longer chosen from among Hungarian nobility, but from among staunch Croatians, and at this time he was a Croatian nobleman named Josip Jelacic. On June 5, Jelacic convened a Croatian diet in Zagreb.[11] This diet declared in favor of a Croatian constitution and freedom for all South Slavs. The declaration, however, turned out to be a little much for Magyars and prompted them to prevail on the emperor to dismiss Jelacic from office. But then, just a few days later, the emperor received Jelacic at the Imperial Court and revoked the dismissal. It appears that Vienna had suddenly become aware of the governor's usefulness against the Magyars, should such leverage prove necessary.

Hurban, too, saw fit to go to Zagreb. Addressing the Croatian Diet on the plight of Hungarian Slovaks, he gained the support of the Croatians. As a result, Slovakian demands were incorporated in a joint program with the Serbs and Croatians, and presented in this form to the Magyars, who immediately rejected them. Still, Hurban was able to obtain considerable material support from the Serbs and a promise of arms in the case of armed conflict.

Talk of Austria being swallowed up in some sort of unified German political structure, which was cropping up in various circles, could not have been an attractive prospect for Czechs, who in the course of their on-going national revival had become distinctly emancipated. To pacify its nationalities, the Viennese Court hurriedly published a new constitution; the date of publication was April 25, 1848. To the Czechs and other nationalities in Cisleithania, it promised the inviolability of national character and language, participation in an All-Austrian Imperial Diet, plus regional diets, promises that fired up expectations in Hungary, too, especially among Slovaks.[12]

113

In the meantime, in Prague at the beginning of June 1848, a Slavic Congress convened which, among other things, meant to resolve the question of Slovak status in a future reorganization of Central Europe.[13] At this time talk spread far and wide of the creation of a Greater Germany, embracing all the original components of the medieval Holy Roman Empire, which had devolved into a multitude of greater or lesser states and principalities. Both Bohemia and Moravia had once belonged to this medieval empire. Indeed, there was not only talk, but serious debate: on May 18, 1848, a German National Assembly was convened for this very purpose in Frankfurt am Main.

Slovaks showed up at the Prague Slavic Congress in considerable numbers. Stur came, as did Hurban and Hodza, plus many others. They were received in Prague with warm sympathy. At the opening session, Michal Miloslav Hodza spoke, as did Pavol Jozef Safarik. The Slovak delegation was represented on the executive committee and on two lesser committees.

In discussions of separate Slovak incorporation in the Habsburg Empire, the question of continuing or liquidating the Hungarian kingdom received prominent attention, as did the possibility of a union of Slovaks, Czechs and Moravians, or of a separate Slovak political entity within the framework of Austria or Hungary.

During the course of the congress, the Slovaks secured the cooperation of two former Austrian army officers of Czech extraction, Bedrich Bloudek and Frantisek Zach, as a contingency for armed conflict with the Magyars, and these two men did, in fact, later become commanders of a Slovak volunteer corps.

Uprising in Prague, 12 June 1848, bloodily suppressed by Field Marshall Windischgratz

But when an armed uprising broke out in Prague, the Slavic Congress came to an abrupt end, and the uprising itself was brutally put down by Austrian troops. Stur, Hurban and Hodza joined the insurgents on the barricades. The Hungarian regime had earlier requested that Vienna disperse the congress, but the Austrian regime had refused to take a stand, either pro or con, because the congress endorsed the preservation of the Empire.

Flag of Slovak Volunteer Corps

After the forced adjournment of the Congress, the Slovak participants faced a dilemma: what next? In Hungary, elections to the Diet had already taken place in accordance with a new election law, which allowed sufficiently propertied peasants to vote. Seventy percent of the deputies elected in Slovakia were recruited from among the nobility and higher office holders, but only a negligible number from the intelligentsia, among them not a single Slovak.

In this situation, Stur, Hurban and Hodza, along with the rest of the Slovak leaders, decided to cooperate with the Croats, who had started taking an active role in politics. The relationship between them and the Magyars had become so exacerbated that the Croats fielded an armed force. The Ban (Governor) Jelacic, a political conservative, was a friend of the Slovaks and an enemy of the Magyars. He leaned ever more strongly towards the Viennese side, especially after the Magyar Diet of August 11, 1848, approved a law providing for a standing Hungarian (Magyar) army and a separate Magyar currency, unsupported by gold bullion.

When the Viennese authorities authorized Ban Jelacic to proceed against the Pest regime, which had defied an order of the sovereign, Slovak leaders decided to join Jelacic with a volunteer corps in Slovakia. The organization of the corps had been begun at the turn of August to September 1848, after Slovak leaders returned to Vienna from their visit to the South Slavs. They chose to confront the Magyars in a region of Slovakia where Hurban had actively campaigned, while Jelacic was to attack through Trans-Danubia in a northerly direction.[14]

Seal of Slovak National Council

The Viennese regime placed no obstacles in the way of the Slovak preparations for armed intervention, nor did it offer any tangible support; in fact, at the very time when the Slovaks were laying their plans with Jelacic, Vienna had turned over to Magyar disposition several units of the imperial army for preservation of internal order.

To lead the Slovak armed contingent, a Slovak National Council was organized, comprising Stur, Hurban and Hodza; Bloudek was appointed commander, Zach, chief-of-staff. But the overall plan for the corps' activity was quite fuzzy. A decision was made on September 16 to advance through

Slovakia up the Vah valley into Turiec and Liptov Counties. About 600 of the corps' members assembled in Vienna's Prater district, then moved on to Bre-clava in Moravia, and from there to the Slovak border on foot.

The Hungarian regime, preparing for Jelacic's attack, recruited a force of national guardsmen, which was gradually converted to a regular army. Martial law was tightened. In its anti-Slovak agitation, the regime enlisted the support of the highest representatives of the Lutheran Church who, like Count Zay, had long been pro-Magyar.

The volunteer corps reached the Slovak border on September 18, where they joined a group of about 500 men who had come from Prague and Brno. At the border they received arms and swore an oath on the Slovak flag. When they encountered imperial army troops on the road to Myjava, they were regarded with glares of annoyance and distrust, since regular troops had received scant information about them.

After the arrival of the corps in Myjava, the first ever national assembly of Slovaks took place there, with Hurban presiding. This assembly renounced obedience to the Magyar regime and charged people not to pay any more taxes or provide any more recruits to Magyar army units.

Slovak Volunteers, 1848

The commander of the imperial army called on the Slovak National Council to leave Myjava. The Council ignored the call, and instead issued an order for its troops to attack. The Slovak volunteers thrashed the Imperial unit and confiscated its supplies.

Arriving in Brezova from Myjava, the corps ran into some imperial cuirassiers sent against them by Hungarian authorities, who were well aware of Hurban's considerable influence there and the growing number of his adherents.[15] However, the Slovaks were possessed much more of high spirits than of arms. The Slovak National Council halted its advance at this point, because the imperial troops had received orders to preserve the peace and were preparing, together with Hungarians, to take stiff measures against Slovak volunteers. In anticipation of further engagements, it was necessary to improve the organization and discipline of the volunteers, beginning with close-order drill and the rebuttal of Magyar agitation. The Slovak National Council made an effort everywhere to replace hostile local officials, and thus to lay the groundwork for Slovak administration.

When the Slovak Volunteer Corps later tried to push through to Senica, its advance was not only blocked, but forced back. It then veered in the direction of Stara Tura, where Magyarone (Slovak renegade) officials and the commander of the local militia rejected Hurban's invitation to join the insurgents.[16] The Slovaks troops then successfully stormed the town. However, in retreat, the Magyars torched and reduced it to ashes, leaving the dismayed Slovaks with a Pyrrhic victory. The Slovak corps then turned towards Myjava, but after it had skirmished with several Magyar units, the Slovak National Council decided to pull it back to Moravia. Although several regions of Slovakia were heated to a boil, and people should have been happy to join the insurgents, in fact they did not. Magyar representatives in Slovakia (for instance, Ludovit Benicky), entrusted by the regime to organize support in Central Slovakia, were nevertheless quite wary of the ferment.

Thus the first Slovak armed episode in history ended unsuccessfully. This lack of success was due in part to the imperial army's siding with the Magyars. Vienna even abandoned Jelacic to his own resources, so that his campaign, too, wound up futile. Vienna was totally preoccupied with its own machinations, and on September 25, it named Count Lamberg supreme commander of imperial forces in Hungary. Lamberg was charged with restoring order in, among other places, northern Hungary and hence Slovakia.

But three days after his arrival in Pest, the city residents brutally murdered Lamberg, thus definitively shutting down any negotiations between Vienna and Pest. The battlers for Slovak rights found themselves facing a new conundrum: who was really in charge of Hungary?

After Lamberg's murder, the Viennese Court named Jelacic chief commissioner and commander of its armies in Hungary. It dissolved the Hungarian Diet, declared martial law and ordered its armies to join battle.

This order, however, had unforeseen consequences in Vienna, where the populace became restive, in fact, rebellious. Some army units even refused to carry out the order, and so, the very next day, the Minister of War, Latour,[17] ordered army and artillery units to put down the dissenters. His efforts proved unsuccessful, his forces were defeated, and he, himself, hanged. This latest uprising was carried out in the name of a Greater Germany. The emperor fled Vienna and, with some of the members of the Imperial Diet, took refuge in Olomouc (Olmutz),[18] Bohemia. But on about October 20, imperial troops under the command of Prince Windischgratz surrounded Vienna and succeeded in restoring order. The Magyars, who must have felt that the uprising was playing right into their hands, were in no hurry to come to the aid of the Viennese; apparently they arrived too late, and were repulsed and put to flight. In Hungary, a new reign of terror was unleashed against non-Magyar nationalities, and tens of Slovak patriots were summoned before courts martial, sentenced to prison, and even executed. The leaders of the Slovak National Council were stripped of Hungarian citizenship.

This Magyar terror only served to drive the Slovaks more solidly into the arms of the Viennese Court. The leaders and commanders of the Slovak Volunteer Corps once more met in Vienna and began organizing a new campaign,

Sláva šlechetním. *)

Kdo za pravdu horí V svatej obeti, Kdo za ludstva právo Život posväti, Kdo nad krivdou bjednich Slzu viroňi: Tomu moja pjeseň Slávu zazvoňí.

2. Keď zahrmja delá, Orol zaveje, Za slobodu milú Kdo krú vileje, Pred ohňivím drakom Kdo vlasť zasloňí: Tomu moja pjeseň Slávou zazvoňí.

3. Kdo si stojí slovu, Čo prjam shrkňe svet, Komu nad statočnosť Venca v ňebi ňjet, Koho dar ňezvedje, Hrozba ňeskloňí: Tomu moja pjeseň Slávou zazvoňí.

4. Pan Boh šlechetnosti Ňebo vistaviu, Večnuo on pre podlosť Peklo podpáliu; Kdo ctí pravdi božskej Božskje zákoni: Tomu moja pjeseň Slávou zazvoňí.   K. Kuzmány.

Text of a Slovak hymn: 'He Who Burns for Truth'

this time working in close concert with the Austrian military. The Austrian Commander-in Chief, Prince Windischgratz, however, was very conservative and regarded the Slovaks with suspicion, but he did finally agree to the creation of a relatively small mixed Slovak volunteer unit.

18 year old Franz Josef I, Austro-Hungarian Emperor, after Ferdinand V abdicates

The volunteers were to advance into Slovakia through Tesin, and from there, through the Jablunka Pass into northern Trencin and Turiec Counties. Windischgratz assigned Bloudek to lead them. Another military detachment, coming from Galicia, was to meet up with Bloudek. The Slovak National Council and Bloudek failed to present as many troops at the starting point as had been originally planned, but they marched out on December 4.

Meanwhile, at the end of November, a second Slovak Volunteer Corps began organizing in western Slovakia to cooperate with the Austrian army, which was at that very time making its way from eastern Galicia to western Slovakia. This army was instructed to cooperate with Jelacic's forces. On November 1, it occupied Trnava and got as far as Pezinok before turning northeast and advancing upstream through the Vah River valley. There they were supposed to make contact with units already in Slovakia, but failed to reach the rendezvous point.

At this time, some very important events were occurring in the Empire. On November 22, 1848, the Imperial Diet met in Kromeriz and debated the possibility of converting the realm into a constitutional monarchy. This diet remained in session until March 7, 1849, but failed to reach a consensus on a new constitution. Meanwhile, by the beginning of December 1848, Ferdinand V had abdicated, and the 18-year-old Franz Josef mounted the throne.

In Slovakia, the war between the Austrians and the Magyars continued to rage, with success intermittently changing sides. The Magyars and Magyarones succeeded in gaining the support of the petty nobility and some of the common folk of Trencin, Nitra and Orava Counties, and were thus able to stall occupation by the Slovak Volunteers, but in Cadca, which the Magyars had emptied of inhabitants, the Volunteers set up a provisional ruling council to manage local affairs and recruit new members. On December 9, the Volunteers were instrumental in the victory of the imperial forces at Budatin and the subsequent rout of the Magyar contingents.

After the Austrian army, together with Slovak Volunteers, had penetrated Turiec County, and in January 1849, occupied Turciansky Svaty Martin, the Slovaks staged a mass rally on January 13, linked with the installation of a county administration led by the local pastor named Horwath[19]. On this occasion, many new volunteers signed up.

Later, the Austrian army, again together with Slovak Volunteers, occupied Kremnica where changes were also made in the local governing body. The Magyar commissioner for Central Slovakia, L. Benicky, worked hard to attract as many recruits as possible to the Magyar militia, and to gain the sympathy of the local Slovak gentry, hoping for timely help from Pest. When it became evident that the Magyar commander, Gorgei, was preparing an attack on Turiec County, the Austrian commander called a second mass rally in Turciansky Svaty Martin, from which approximately a thousand recruits enlisted in the Slovak corps immediately, and a thousand more later. This rally was called to emphasize the goals of the uprising in anticipation of the imminent defeat of Kossuth.

Among the new recruits were such outstanding individuals as Juraj Langfeld, a teacher from Turciansky Svaty Martin, originally from Sucany, who was commissioned lieutenant in the volunteer corps. In May 1849, under his leadership, a platoon of the corps fell upon a detachment of Magyar troops and scattered it. Sometime later, however, the Magyar Honved (the Home Guard) captured, tried and executed him.

Austrian units, together with Slovak volunteers, next occupied Orava and Liptov Counties, where the volunteers acquainted residents with their program. As they were advancing towards Spis County, Stur, Hurban, Bloudek and Zach agitated for the Slovak cause, addressing crowds in Banska Bystrica, Brezno and Zvolen. On February 26, Bloudek, marching his troops from Levoca through Branisko, occupied Presov, whence he proceeded, on March 2, to Kosice, where Stur had already established a presence. In the meantime, on February 26, another detachment of Slovak volunteers clashed with the Magyar army near Muran and took a beating.

However, much to the dismay of the Slovaks, the new administration installed in Central Slovakia under Austrian supervision included many Mag-

Slovak deputies, presenting petition to Emperor, 20 March 1849

yars and Magyarones. To make matters worse, clashes broke out between Czech and Slovak officers in the corps.

A prime goal of Slovaks at this time was the conversion of Slovakia into a separate crown territory. Activists agitated for this cause in numerous rallies called in regions under Austrian control, but, owing to resistance from the Austrian military, were unsuccessful in efforts to convene a grand rally of all Slovakian regions. In March 1849, Stur and Hurban continued their agitation in rallies held at Presov and Turciansky Svaty Martin.

On March 13, 1849, the Slovaks sent a delegation of 24 men to the emperor in Olomouc (Olmutz), petitioning for an autonomous territory, free of Hungary, to be incorporated directly into the Austrian empire as a grand duchy and entitling Slovakia to share in the constitution governing the nations of Cisleithania, with proportionate representation in the imperial diet. As to local affairs, their petition requested a Slovak provincial diet. Obviously the official language in Slovakia was to be Slovak. However, the Constitution of March 4, 1849, drawn up not by the Diet of Kromeriz, but by the Imperial Court, splashed a cold shower on the nations of Cisleithania and the Slovaks, presenting them with a done deal. The petition needed to be reworked. The idea of a grand duchy was abandoned. An audience with the young emperor produced no constructive results, just more promises. Still, Viennese officialdom, led by Count Stadion, conceded that Slovaks needed protection from forcible Magyarization.

However, events on the battlefield proved decisive: the Austrian army suffered a reversal as the Magyars counterattacked in the spring of 1849. Kossuth's 'Honved', buoyed up by visions of Hungarian independence, swept along huge masses of Magyars, along with non-Magyars who were ethnically oblivious. They began winning. In Slovakia, things got so bad that armed gangs began to terrorize Slovak activists, many of whom had to flee to Moravia. Local Magyar administrations were renewed.

These changes were reflected in the morale of the Slovak Volunteer Corps. After a battle at Muran, the troops commanded by Bloudek moved camp from Kosice to Presov. Squabbles broke out between officers, many wanting to leave. The corps next moved to Orava County, and at Jablunkov a decision was made to disband. Indeed, even before that decision, many men had simply got up and gone home.

Jan Francisci, Captain of Slovak Volunteers

Command of the troops was now taken over by Jan Francisci. He moved them to the vicinity of Komarno, where the contingent participated in the siege of the stronghold there. Then it was transferred to Bratislava and Skalica.

On April 14, 1849, when the Hungarian Diet in Debrecin declared the Habsburgs deposed, the Russian Czar decided to go to his aid. A Russian army crossed the Carpathian mountain passes and, together with the Austrians, gradually eliminated all Magyar resistance. Baron Haynau, the Austrian general, and his officers now became lords of Hungary,[20] and Baron Geringer became Chief Imperial Commissioner.

In the closing phases of the war, the Slovak Volunteer Corps, commanded by Major Lewartovsky, was transferred to Central Slovakia, where it participated in the mopping-up of the scattered Magyar remnants. However, the Austrian authorities, failing to realize that what Slovaks cared about most was an ethnically just Austrian realm and autonomy, remained suspicious of Slovak enthusiasm and the supposed Pan-Slavism, especially of Stur and Hurban. They remained, therefore, oblivious to their repeated petitions.

On August 13, 1849, at Vilagos, the Magyar armed forces capitulated. Kossuth fled Hungary as Austrian and Russian troops captured his fellow insurgents and restored order in the land.

On October 9, 1849, the Austrian regime dispensed with the services of the Slovak Volunteer Corps; it transferred the remaining volunteers from Central Slovakia to Bratislava, to be disbanded at the end of November 1849. Thus the Slovak armed struggle came to an end.

This recounting of the bare facts of the events of 1848 and 1849 can hardly satisfy the curiosity of interested readers. These events need to be evaluated, because even historians differ widely in their views on them.

Many Magyar historians have presented a positive evaluation of Kossuth and the Magyar revolution. On the other hand, they have branded the activi-

Capitulation of Magyars at Vilagos

ties of Stur and the Slovak volunteers and their cooperation with the Viennese Court and the Imperial army as counter-revolutionary.

In truth, Stur and the Slovak leaders, by their conduct during the revolution of 1848–49, demonstrated that they well understood the diseased nature of Magyar nationalism, which refused to even acknowledge Slovak existence. The Viennese Court had accommodated the demands of the Magyar political leaders by granting them autonomy at the very beginning of the revolution, including control over Hungarian internal affairs. But that was not enough for Kossuth: his efforts were directed at complete secession. His contention that the Viennese Court was oppressing Hungary economically and politically cannot be accepted without significant reservations. After all, Hungary had enjoyed a permanent credit balance in trade with the nations of Cisleithania; more money had flown into the Hungarian treasury from those nations than vice versa. Indeed, even the measure of political freedom enjoyed by Hungary had been greater than that of the Czech Kingdom, or even of Austria 'proper' and the other ethnic groups of Cisleithania.

It is possible, however, to sympathize with Kossuth and the Magyar leaders in their fear of various political combinations under active contemplation in Central Europe at the time; for instance, German unification, embracing the entirety of the Habsburg realm, or a complete restructuring of the Austrian Empire on an ethnic basis. In either of these constructs, the Magyars would have found themselves in the minority. Czech political leaders had similar fears: after all, the Czech Kingdom had historically been a component of the medieval German Empire (the Holy Roman Empire). These various considerations may help clarify, but they certainly do not justify, the total suppression of non-Magyar nationalities in Hungary.

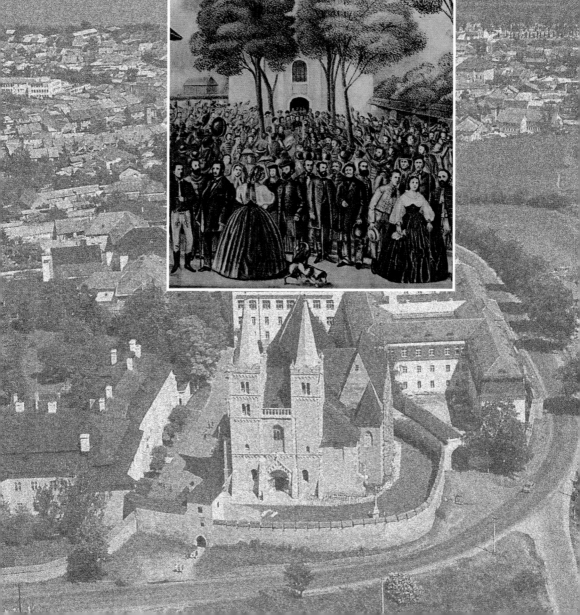

9. Events Leading to the Austro-Hungarian Compromise (1849 to 1867)

When the events of 1848–49 closed with the military capitulation of the Magyars, the Viennese Court and Emperor Franz Josef I brutally settled accounts with the defeated Magyar leaders. Those who had not fled abroad were tried before military tribunals and sentenced to stiff punishments, including execution. Even Count Lajos Batthany was executed, though the harshness of his punishment hardly fit the seriousness of his crime. Gorgey, who had signed the terms of capitulation at Vilagos, was imprisoned and not released until 1867.

Young Franz Josef

The Magyar revolution of 1848–49, in which the major segment of the Magyar nation was involved, and its suppression, brought on hard years of subordination to Vienna, liquidation of Magyar administration in all of Hungary (including the Magyar ethnic regions), reimposition of censorship, and further measures associated with military occupation and control.

On November 1, 1849, the Viennese Court, having abolished the Hungarian constitution, the Hungarian diet and county self-rule, incorporated Hungary into the united Habsburg monarchy as a crown territory. Any dreams or figments of a Slovak grandduchy became irrelevant. A new era had begun, named after Alexander Bach, the Austrian Prime Minister. On September 14, 1851, a Hungarian governorship was installed, with Grand Duke Albrecht at its head.

A bureaucratic, absolutist network was ingeniously built up to rule the state, with huge governing structures, distinct for the two halves of the realm. Hungary was divided into five provinces, two headquartered in Bratislava and Kosice, respectively. County structures were retained, but without their traditional open elections. An important prop of the absolutist system was a newly built network of gendarmes and police, and the organization of police bureaus in Bratislava and Kosice, with branch offices, to keep close watch over political and public life.

The political life of the state was controlled by imperial decree, with the force of law. Throughout the empire, official business was conducted in German, for the enforcement of which the Habsburg regime commissioned a large number of bureaucrats from the western half of the empire, among whom were Czechs and Germans from Bohemia and Moravia. If these 'Bach hussars' understood Czech, they were able to communicate with parties in Slovak ethnic areas; elsewhere they had to use interpreters.

After the quelling of the Hungarian Revolution, the leading representatives of Slovaks were again confronted with the dilemma of which Slovak language to use, be it in official business, in print, or even in personal correspondence.

As it turned out, the language dilemma was rife with possibilities: literary

Slovak as codified by Stur; the Bernolak norm; so-called western cultural Slovak, in use since the 16th Century and most widely distributed of all; biblical Czech; and standard Czech (which had acquired literary status in the first half of the 19th Century, thanks to the intensive efforts of Czech revivalists). This multiplicity of choice did not help the Slovak cause, since debunkers could claim that Slovaks themselves did not know what they really wanted.[1]

Individual Slovak writers and speakers in Slovakia and in Vienna, where Slovak matters were largely decided, chose among available Slovak variants as follows:

• Jan Kollar who, opposing the Bernolak and Stur versions, used pre-Bernolak cultural Slovak in publications of the Viennese Court;

• Jan Palarik who, with the help of Andrej Radlinsky, published a magazine entitled *Cyril and Methodius,* using the same older form of cultural Slovak as Kollar, with the conviction that it was best understood by ordinary Slovaks. However, after Stur's codification of Central Slovak, he adopted that norm.

• Stefan Klempa who, publishing *The Catholic News*, at first used the Bernolak norm, then later switched to the more modern Stur codification.

• Stefan Moyses who, having revived the magazine *Cyril and Methodius* in 1852 and installed Michal Chrastek, then Juraj Slota, as editors, consistently used the Stur norm, as amended by Hodza and Hattala, but later also returned to cultural West Slovak.

• Jozef Hurban, who with Stur had developed the Central Slovak Codification, consistently used that form in his publications. Although under police surveillance, he renewed publication of *Slovak Views* in 1851, working to preserve the Stur norm, at least for literary purposes.

• Lastly, modern Czech was occasionally used in official government documents, in secondary schools after 1852,[2] and in *The Slovak News*, edited by Daniel Lichard in Vienna.

Martin Hattala

In view of this Slovak linguistic chaos, a group of leading Slovaks met in Bratislava in October 1851 to definitively resolve the question of a standard for literary use. The participants were Stur, Hurban and Hodza, as well as Jan Palarik, Andrej Radlinsky, Stefan Zavodnik and Martin Hattala. They reached agreement on changes to Stur's orthography and other adjustments. Also, they chose an etymological system of spelling as opposed to phonetic, in an effort to stay as close as possible to Czech and its orthographic usages. Martin Hattala, a teacher of Slovak at the secondary school of natural sciences in Bratislava, was charged with working out the details of the new orthography.

A momentous social occasion for all Slovak patriots was the unveiling at Dobra Voda of a bust of the Bernolakian poet, Jan Holly, who had died in

Martin Hattala.

126

1849. The ceremony took place on May 11, 1854, in the town where Holly had been Catholic pastor. Ludovit Stur, under police surveillance in Modra, where he had moved to care for the children of his brother Karol after the latter's death, also came to the affair. In 1853, Stur published in Bohemia a work on Slovak oral traditions plus a collection of poetry titled *Singing and Songs;* he died in 1856 in a tragic hunting accident.[3]

Stur's final work was a dissertation, *Slavs and the World of the Future,* first published posthumously in German. He had written it in a pessimistic, very depressed mood, after the failure of the revolution for which he had held such high hopes. He, nevertheless, still believed in Herder's thesis that the Slavs would one day take the lead in Europe, and that the Habsburg monarchy was doomed to collapse. However, he envisioned the future role of Russia in a way that today can only evoke a bitter smile. Stur, in his fantasy, idealized autocracy; he imagined the Czar as a benevolent protector of Slavic nations and a just ruler. In the Russian patriarchal commune he saw a solution to the social problems of the modern world.

Martin Hattala, with his Slovak grammar

At this time another Slovak activist, Andrej Radlinsky, accomplished an enormous amount of work for ethnic betterment. In August and September 1850, he made the rounds of the villages in eastern Slovakia to ascertain whether or not the people there could handily grasp the written and spoken form of Stur's redaction of Slovak. When he was convinced that they did understand, he was able to persuade the bureaucracy to establish Slovak as the official language of the district of Kosice. He consistently promoted the new standard literary language, and in this way contributed markedly to the national unification of Slovaks.

In his work as a publisher, Radlinsky strove to achieve independence from the Magyar Society of St. Stephen, which looked askance at Slovak initiatives, and in 1857, he proposed the organization of a new association to be named The Society of St. Adalbert, but the Catholic authorities failed to approve its bylaws. Starting in 1859, Radlinsky made considerable contributions to the Slovak linguistic cause by publishing *A Friend of School and Literature* as a supplement to the periodical *Cyril and Methodius.*

Andrej Radlinsky was a native of Orava County. He studied at the Pazmaneum in Vienna, where he received a degree in theology. As an assistant pastor, he organized temperance societies, amateur theater, was a charter member of Tatrin (a cultural society), and after the suppression of the revolution, one of the foremost organizers of Slovak affairs. In 1849, he began publishing *Treasures of the Art of Preaching* and became editor of *The Legal Landbook* (sic). In 1854, he began publishing *The Catholic News.* He also authored an

127

Jan Palarik

important prayerbook entitled *Religious Effusions*, which made its way into many Slovak Catholic homes, achieving a distribution unmatched by any Slovak publication up to 1918.

Radlinsky was just one in a long line of Slovak priests who spread religion and culture among common people. Through his activity and his attitude toward life he continued the educational work of Anton Bernolak, Jan Holly and other revivalists.

Jan Palarik was not an exemplary priest like Radlinsky. He was a good Slovak, but because of his relatively liberal views, he clashed with his archbishop. He criticized the dictatorial methods of the church hierarchy, demanded establishment of a Slovak archbishopric, propagated the idea of a union of western and eastern Christians, pilloried Slovak priests who were renegades from their own nationality, and demanded democratization of church administration with an improvement in the material situation of priests. In the 1860s he strove for an orientation of Slovak politics towards Budapest and the Magyars, but with little success.

Use of the Slovak language in secondary schools after 1849 took off rather promisingly. The number of preparatory schools (gymnasia), both Catholic and Lutheran, that used Slovak as the language of instruction or included it in their curricula, was considerable. In the preparatory school in Bratislava, Martin Hattala was an instructor in Slovak. As time went on, this promising situ-

'Fish Square' in Bratislava, ca. 1860

128

ation deteriorated, with linguistic squabbles among Slovaks not a little to blame. Kollar was able to introduce the use of so-called 'cultural' West Slovak in these schools, but, starting in 1852, literary Czech displaced it.

In the end, the only preparatory school using Slovak as the language of instruction was the school in Banska Bystrica, which enjoyed the patronage of the local bishop, Stefan Moyses. Together with Jozef Kozacek, a school official, Moyses succeeded in attracting such outstanding Slovak pedagogues as Culen, Geronetto and Slota, as well as a number of erudite and ethnically conscious Czech teachers.

Starting in 1854, the Viennese regime supported the Germanization of secondary schools in an effort to create a pool of qualified officials for state administrative posts, so much so that, by 1857, there was no longer a single exclusively Slovak preparatory school in all of Slovakia.

Of course, it should be understood that not all residents of Slovakia were Slovak, and that not all families that did speak Slovak were interested in a Slovak education for their children. In a state with German as its official language, there were obvious benefits accrued to a student graduating from the German polytechnical institutes of Vienna and Prague; Slovak education offered only minimal advantages. There was also a new factor at play: after 1848, when Jews were granted equal rights, children from Jewish families in which Slovak was not spoken, also began to pursue an education.

At that time, not a few Slovaks were able to get government jobs. For instance, in Zvolen County almost all government positions were filled by Slovaks, and the same was true to a lesser extent of Gemer County, and elsewhere. But these Slovak officials were required to do official business in German. J. Kozacek achieved the office of school inspector in the Bratislava district, and Gustav Zechenter became official physician of the Central Slovak Mining District. Janko Kral, the Slovak poetic firebrand, was an official in Balasske Darmoty, starting in 1849; he was transferred to Cadca in 1854 where he served in the sheriff's office; then, in 1858, he served as an official in Turciansky Svaty Martin; in 1860 and 1861 he was deputy sheriff in Klastor pod Znievom; finally, he served as assessor in Tekov County. Slovaks also occupied official posts in regions outside of Slovakia.

Stefan Moyses

Furthermore, from 1850, Stefan Moyses, an outspoken Slovak patriot, occupied the bishop's throne in Banska Bystrica. The bishops of Spis and Roznava (Gemer County) were also Slovak, but they were not assertive in Slovak matters. Jan Scitovsky, a native of Kosicka Bela and archbishop of Esztergom, who staunchly opposed the Magyar revolution, was branded by Kossuth insurgents as a traitor to Magyar national interests. In the 1850s he supported publication of Slovak religious literature, but opposed introduction of Slovak in schools, as well as other Slovak initiatives.

But not even in this changed situation did Viennese officialdom sever contacts with Magyar conservatives, whom they found politically more congenial than Slovak activists, who were of plebeian origin. After 1849, in addition to highly placed Magyar nobility in Vienna, members of Magyar middle nobility, who made no secret of their anti-Slovak sentiments, filled administrative posts all over Slovakia. These new officials not only boycotted Slovak efforts, but actively sought to 'uncover' Pan-Slav and Communist features in the Slovak movement and its representatives.

The repressive system built by the Viennese Court banked heavily on approval in international circles and on support from neighboring states.

In the early years, after the Russian intervention in the Hungarian revolution, cooperation between Austria and Russia, where serfdom still existed, rested on a mutually satisfactory base, and thus Russia came to Austria's aid in its battle for German hegemony. But when the Crimean War broke out, Austria declined to support Russia, even massing a large military force in Transylvania, which could be interpreted as a gesture hostile to Russia. In this way, Austria lost an ally while antagonizing France, which went on with Britain to defeat Russia.

Consequently, in 1859 when war broke out in Northern Italy, Austria found herself isolated. The Italian national liberation army, in fact the army of the Kingdom of Piedmont-Sardinia, supported by Napoleon III, delivered a defeat to the Austrian forces at Solferino, which brought about the fall of the Bach regime.[4]

Austrian defeat at Solferino, weakening realm and awakening Hungarian hopes

In Hungary, this defeat evoked huge political turmoil. It became clear to everyone that great changes were in store. The liberal middle nobility and gentry expected a re-instatement of the Hungarian Constitution of 1848, but made no attempt to exploit the situation. After all, Hungary was full of unfulfilled social yearnings, and the nobility had reason to fear a social explosion in Magyar regions which could well turn against the rich. The Emperor and King, Franz Josef I did nothing but promise that he would convene a regional diet, that he would make Magyar an official language along with German, and at the same time allow use of ethnic languages locally. But Hungarian autonomy was not immediately renewed; it was to be drafted later by an expanded Imperial Council, in which representatives of individual regions would also be assigned a place.[5]

October Diploma, renewing Austrian constitution

On October 20, 1860, the emperor issued the 'October Diploma', the main purpose of which was to pacify opponents of Viennese centralism, especially the Magyars and Czechs, who were to have their separate regional diets, but who were also to send representatives to an Imperial Diet. At the same time, the emperor made a pledge that he would never renew absolutism, which he was destined to keep.

In Hungary, election of county officials was restored; also, an imperial bureau was installed, along with a regional governorship, headed by two Hungarian magnates, Anton Forgach and Moric Palffy. Still, Hungary was to be integrated into the empire, its military, financial, commercial, and foreign affairs to be managed from Vienna. As might be expected, the Magyars wanted no part of such arrangements. The Edict of February 22, 1861, did nothing to allay their fears, though it acknowledged the historical rights of the Hungarian Kingdom, the hegemony of the Magyar ruling classes, and made Magyar the official language of Hungary, thus curtailing the erstwhile reign of German.

When on April 2, 1861, the newly elected Hungarian Diet convened without a single Slovak deputy (all Slovak candidates had failed to secure election, even those in Slovak ethnic districts), it demanded a renewal of the terms approved in 1848, as well as a renewal of total political sovereignty, free of Viennese meddling. In view of the fact that the Diet and the emperor were completely at odds, unable to agree on a single issue, on August 22, 1861, the emperor dissolved the Diet.

The situation following the collapse of the Bach system nudged Slovak political leaders into trying to reconcile their accumulated differences. When the Imperial Council met to make statewide decisions without inviting a single Slovak, the position of the conservative Magyar nobility became so much

Budapest Intelligencer

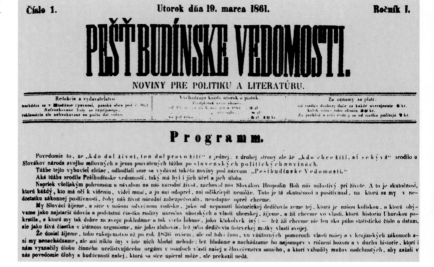

stronger. A group of Slovak leaders in Pest led by Andrej Radlinsky, consequently, turned to a Croatian bishop named Strossmayer to represent Slovak interests in that forum. Strossmayer willingly took on the task, and received backing from a Romanian Orthodox bishop named Sagun.

After the issuance of the October Diploma, Jan Palarik was particularly active among Slovaks pressing for the orientation of Slovak politics to the Magyar liberal nobility and its political party. He spurned orientation to Vienna and Emperor Franz Josef. On the other hand, Jozef Hurban, the leader of the unsuccessful Slovak insurgency, argued that the Magyars were not trustworthy, while Vienna had more to offer. Hurban himself worked up a *Memorandum of Slovak Demands*, which he submitted to the Ministry of the Interior in Vienna at the beginning of February 1861. He requested that Slovakia be sectioned off from the rest of Hungary, and that it be granted its own diet and executive, a university, and an independent Lutheran Church.

The time was now ripe for publication of Slovak newspapers, and so on March 19, 1861, the *Budapest Intelligencer* made its first appearance. This newspaper was printed in Stur's Slovak. With its publication, the vexing question of Slovak literary language was settled once and for all. Slovaks rallied around the paper. They decided to organize a campaign for an all-Slovak rally to debate, formulate and approve a Slovak national program. This rally took place on June 6, 1861, in Turciansky Svaty Martin.

About 5,000 people showed up, including the commissioners of Turiec and Liptov Counties, Barons Revay and Svatojansky respectively, as well as the newly elected deputy to the Hungarian Diet, Jozef Just, all three scions of noble lines, longtime Slovak residents, fluent in Slovak but not Slovak in perception.

The rally lasted two days. Debates took place under open skies, as well as indoors in small committees. The main discussions, moderated by Janko Francisci, were very lively. Stefan Marko Daxner, a lawyer, drafted and presented the main address. Results were summarized in eight items, which were given the title *A Memorandum of the Slovak Nationality*. This document requested:

1. That Slovak be designated the official language in Slovak regions, and that offices, courts and schools in these regions be turned over to Slovaks.

2. That Magyar be retained as the official language, but without detriment to the language rights of other nationalities.

3. That all laws heretofore denying the equality of nationalities be abrogated.

4. That all laws be published in an official Slovak transcript.

5. That a Slovak school of law and a chair of Slovak language and literature be founded in the University of Pest, and other Slovak literary institutions elsewhere, all to be funded by the state.

6. That Slovaks be allowed to freely found literary and educational societies and to collect contributions.

7. That Slovaks be permitted to use their mother tongue freely in public life and schools outside the Slovak regions, and that non-Slovaks be granted analogous rights in predominantly Slovak regions.

Stefan Marko Daxner

Memorandum assembly in Turciansky Svaty Martin

8. That Slovaks be granted proportional representation in future reorganizations of the upper chamber of the Diet.

The conclusion of the *Memorandum* declares that, in the struggle for civil rights, Slovaks wish to stand side by side with the other nationalities of Hungary, in solidarity with Rusyns, Romanians, Serbs and Croats; they demand in the territory they inhabit 'exactly the same rights as their brother Magyars already actually enjoy'.

The *Memorandum* takes the position that the Slovaks of Hungary inhabit a compact territory, which it calls the Slovak Region, which should be sectioned off from the rest of Hungary and granted a form of autonomy. Some of those present objected to this position, among them Palarik and the three above-mentioned leading Hungarian noblemen. Still open was the question of whether the *Memorandum* was to be presented to the Hungarian Diet, which happened to be in session, or to the emperor, or possibly to both. The idea of presenting it to the Diet won out. A special delegation was created to do the presenting, which for added weight was to include the three above-

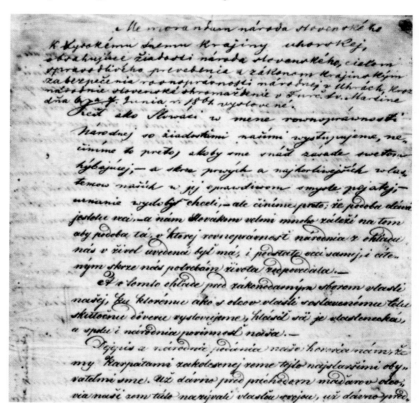

*Manuscript of draft of
'Memorandum of Slovak
Nation' (detail)*

134

mentioned dignitaries of Slovak extraction, but they unfortunately demurred. On June 26, 1861, the *Memorandum* was delivered by a delegation including Daxner, Hurban, Francisci, and Palarik. Meanwhile, a counter campaign was waged in the Slovak counties to demonstrate that Slovaks and their various local representatives did not concur with the document's demands, and that they were satisfied with the status quo. In truth, at least as many Slovaks rejected the *Memorandum*, or were ambivalent towards its contents, as embraced it. The Slovak political leaders who composed the *Memorandum* used the designation, 'nation', though Slovaks did not fully meet the criteria of the definition, since not all those who spoke Slovak felt themselves to be part of such a nation.

The hopes placed in this document proved delusive. Tisza put the *Memorandum* to the Nationalities Committee of the Diet, which was willing to grant Slovaks only certain minor linguistic concessions at most. In response, the Magyar press unleashed a campaign of hate against Slovak 'Separatism', and accused Slovak leaders of anti-Hungarianism.

The assembly that created the *Memorandum* elected a twenty-three member standing committee headed by Janko Francisci to make an accurate Magyar translation, to work for implementation, and to conduct negotiations with appropriate political offices. This committee was also charged with developing a set of bylaws for a Slovak cultural institute, to be named the Matica Slovenska, and with developing plans for a Slovak school system as well as Slovak publications. However, it had no permanent address or financial resources, and its members were scattered over the whole of Slovakia, some even abroad. Janko Francisci himself worked in Pest, where he edited the *Budapest Intelligencer.*

When the Slovak leaders received no positive response from the Diet, they turned to the emperor, who had in the meantime, dissolved the Hungarian Diet and had in fact, even abolished county elections, the pillar of Magyar opposition. Counties had become mere lower-level organs of state executive and judiciary administration. Gradually the idea of presenting the *Memorandum* to the emperor had found acceptance among a majority of the committee, including Janko Francisci. In November, the latter met with Bishop Moyses in Buda, who agreed to head a delegation to the emperor.

The members of the planned delegation and the rest of the National Committee met in Vienna at the beginning of December. They chose eight delegates from among themselves to approach the emperor. On December 12, 1861, this select delegation presented the Slovak demands, essentially the same as those of the *Memorandum*, except that they placed added emphasis on the demand for a Slovak Region. This Region was to have its own separate diet, with a permanent seat in Banska Bystrica. Its official language was to be, of course, Slovak.

The emperor, receiving the demands, passed them on to the Imperial Council for debate, which submitted them in turn to the Hungarian Royal Chancery, which forwarded them to the Hungarian Governorship. In the meantime, the Magyar press, learning of the initiative, again unleashed a broad hate campaign against the Slovak demands.

Still, in the 1860s, the Slovaks did achieve some partial successes in the matter of schools. On the basis of directives from the Imperial Chancellory dated December 27, 1861, Slovak was to be the language of instruction in Catholic preparatory schools in Trnava, Trencin, Skalica and Levice, and, together with German, in preparatory schools in Banska Bystrica, Levoca, Nitra, Banska Stiavnica and Presov. All the same, Slovak gradually began to disappear from middle schools, holding on exceptionally well only in Banska Bystrica, where the school principal, Martin Culen, had attracted a highly qualified staff of teachers.

Lutherans, in the meantime, successfully organized a high quality Slovak middle school in Velka Revuca. On September 16, 1862, they had opened a preparatory school there and had gradually expanded it to eight grades. Its principal was Augustin Horislav Skultety, while the president of its sponsoring committee was Stefan Marko Daxner.

The greatest triumph of the Slovak movement in this period of relaxed political tensions, before Magyars gained complete control of Hungary, was the founding of 'Matica Slovenska' (The Slovak Cultural Institute).

The idea of Matica was not original to Slovaks: Serbs, Czechs (since 1831) and Moravians (since 1849) already had such institutes, and Kollar, Kuzmany, Lichard, Zaborsky and Radlinsky, having worked up a set of bylaws prior to 1850, presented them for approval to the Hungarian regime. But despite the fact that Jan Kollar, thanks to his connections, had intervened on its behalf at the highest levels, the project failed. Kollar had conceived Matica Slovenska as an institute for the publication of literature, as well as for the laying of foundations for a national museum, archive and library. Slovaks in Vienna had also been thinking of founding a Slovak literary association, but had also seen their plans come to naught.

Cover of bylaws of Matica Slovenska

After the fall of Bach absolutism, the idea of creating Matica Slovenska revived. An ad hoc committee presented bylaws to the Hungarian Governorship for approval on August 1, 1861. The seat of the institute was originally to have been Brezno, but, since the pro-Magyar leadership there turned it down, the choice went to Turciansky Svaty Martin. The authorities gave definitive approval to its bylaws on May 31, 1863, and the emperor donated a welcome one thousand florins to the cause.

The approval of Matica Slovenska occurred precisely in the year that Slovaks planned to commemorate the millennium of the arrival of Cyril and Methodius in Great Moravia. The idea of this jubilee was zealously promoted by Andrej Radlinsky and Bishop Stefan Moyses, who took the lead in preparations. But the highest church dignitary of Hungary, the pro-Magyar Archbishop Scitovsky of Esztergom, opposed it, as did the bishop of Nitra, where the celebration was to be staged. Bishop Zabojsky of the Spis diocese supported the project and expressed willingness to stage the jubilee celebration in his diocese as well.

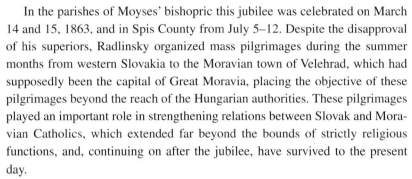

Karol Kuzmany

In the parishes of Moyses' bishopric this jubilee was celebrated on March 14 and 15, 1863, and in Spis County from July 5–12. Despite the disapproval of his superiors, Radlinsky organized mass pilgrimages during the summer months from western Slovakia to the Moravian town of Velehrad, which had supposedly been the capital of Great Moravia, placing the objective of these pilgrimages beyond the reach of the Hungarian authorities. These pilgrimages played an important role in strengthening relations between Slovak and Moravian Catholics, which extended far beyond the bounds of strictly religious functions, and, continuing on after the jubilee, have survived to the present day.

Even the charter assembly of Matica Slovenska was connected to this great jubilee. It took place in Turciansky Svaty Martin on August 4, 1863, and even surpassed the *Memorandum* rally in number and enthusiasm. Moyses' journey from his summer residence in Kriz nad Hronom through the vil-

*First home of
Matica Slovenska*

lages of Tekov and Turiec Counties by coach was a triumphal event. Two thousand new members joined the Matica and financial contributions exceeded all expectations.

This meeting elected Bishop Stefan Moyses to the presidency of Matica Slovenska, and Jan Orsag and Karol Kuzmany, a Catholic and Lutheran respectively, to joint vice-presidency. In the very first year of its existence, Matica began publishing *The Annals of Matica Slovenska,* which were edited by the erudite Slovak historian, Frantisek Sasinek.

After 1865, the European political situation steadily deteriorated; political rivalry between Austria and Prussia for hegemony in German affairs intensified. Because the threat of a military confrontation between these two powers became more acute, Austria hurriedly attempted to put its internal affairs in order. It therefore began negotiations with Magyar representatives. The Viennese Court finally agreed in 1865 to re-establish local elections of county administrations, and announced new elections to the Hungarian Diet. Although the Slovaks took pains to prepare for these elections, none was elected. Only one Rusyn candidate, Adolph Dobriansky, won a parliamentary

Coat of arms of Austro-Hungarian Empire

mandate in Slovakia, and it was he who later defended Slovak interests in the Diet, with help from Svetozar Miletic, a Serbian deputy.

Soon a full-scale war between Prussia and Austria did in fact break out. The Prussians marched into Bohemia, and after a victory near Hradec Kralove (Konigsgratz), they pushed farther into the Habsburg heartland, occupying a large part of Moravia and Zahorie,[6] right up to Bratislava. After signing a peace treaty in Prague, the vanquished Viennese Court could no longer avoid ceding power in Hungary to the Magyars, which it did in 1867. The old Magyar dream of full hegemony came true. The Austrian Empire became 'Austria-Hungary'. The ideas of Kossuth triumphed: his people took complete control of Hungary, though he himself remained in exile and never again set foot in his homeland.[7]

These fast-moving events had a great social and economic impact on Hungarian society, but the central problem, the relationship between masters and their erstwhile subjects, still remained unresolved. The March Laws of 1848 served only as an outline in this respect, as the details had been left to be worked out in the emperor's *Urbarial Edict* of March 2, 1853. This edict granted farmers only the land which they had held on the basis of the *Urbar* (Land Register), established during Maria Theresa's reign. Other land, for instance, upland farms and lands held in freehold, had to be acquired by direct purchase. As far as the reverse process, i.e. confiscation of upland farms by a former landlord, was concerned, it was banned if the land in question could be proved to be the main source of a farmer's family income, who, nevertheless, still had to pay to hold on to it.

When permanent ownership of land passed to a farmer on the basis of the *Urbarial Edict*, the state paid the former landlord in installments of 300 to 700 florins for a one family farm, and 50 florins for a tenant farm. Since there were approximately 70,000 family farms in Slovakia, and more than 200,000 tenant farms, the former feudal lords received payments totaling approximately 45 million florins. The individual payments were enormous and, with wise investment, could have produced immense profits. Of course, not every formerly privileged individual owned a great estate.

At this time, large estates were relatively quick to introduce mechanization, for instance, steam-powered threshing machines, harvesters, mowers, and planters.

The average size of a family farm was very small and, with population growth, it became even smaller,[8] so much so that most family farms were necessarily of a subsistence kind, leaving little for the market. What is more, farmers were required to pay increased taxes into a fund used to amortize the value of the land they had received, so that they now had even less to invest in equipment and structures. Hunger was a frequent guest in Slovak villages. This was the reason so many Slovak families moved to the flatlands of South Hungary, where many had been accustomed to go in summer months as migrant farm-hands.

The conditions arising from abolition of serfdom and the passage of land ownership to farmers could scarcely be called capitalism. It is true that by this time the first savings banks were already in existence, but not a single credit institution or genuine bank had yet been founded, the number of modern industrial enterprises was dismally small, and machinery very inefficient.

The headstart enjoyed by Austrian and Czech-Moravian industry, compared to that of Hungary, was not only great, but its advantages kept multiplying. This situation was somewhat alleviated for Hungarians on August 1, 1850, by the abolition of customs barriers; Hungary was able to export its agricultural products to Austria at a lower price, while receiving cheaper imports of industrial products in exchange. Hungary's network of railroads, however, continued to be inadequate. Up to the time of Austro-Hungarian equalization its trackage had grown to 2,342 kilometers, but only 160 of these were in Slovakia, the most important line being Kosice – Miskovec – Budapest.

For business to function well, an expansion of the rail network was imperative, which in its turn was dependent on increased iron production. The latter did increase sharply in Slovakia, representing, in 1860, seventy-five percent of the total iron production of Hungary. Fifty-four of Hungary's sixty blast furnaces were located in Slovakia.

New ironworks emerged, as for instance in Podbrezova (1854), which specialized in rail manufacture. In 1852, the Rimava Coalition, the Muran Union,

Ironworks in Podbrezova

140

and the Association of Gemer Ironworkers merged to form the Rimamuran Iron Company. Also, by 1863, the number of steam-operated ironworks had risen to fourteen, a steep rise from four in 1852.

At this time, machinery manufacturing plants emerged in Krompachy and Vyhne, turning out equipment for alcohol distilleries and sugar mills, for flour mills, breweries and saw mills, for blast-furnaces, and for finishing mills that produced nails, anvils, vices, pliers and hammers of all kinds. Other forms of industry included, first of all, food-processing plants, which were the most important economic enterprises in Hungary, dictated by topography. Of these, grain mills were most prominent. Modern mills were concentrated mostly in the vicinity of large towns, above all, Budapest. In villages, grain was still ground the old-fashioned way, by waterwheel. Czech capital played a part in the building of modern sugar mills; a sugar mill was built in Surany in 1854 by a Czech entrepreneur named Frey. It was one of the most modern in all Hungary. In 1858, an entrepreneur named Bauer founded a sugar mill in Gabcikovo, which employed about 300 workers.

Of the various enterprises that started up at this time, a large tobacco plant in Kosice deserves mention, as does also a furniture factory in Uherce, founded in 1865 with about 300 workers; also, a leather processing plant in Velke Bosany with 150 workers, which sold mostly to the military; and a steam-operated sawmill, founded in Velka Bytca in the 1860s, the first of its kind.

The productivity of towns and cities continued to be based on skilled craftsmen in traditional shops. There were in Bratislava, before 1867, 2,372 craft shops, employing 5,293 journeymen and apprentices, and in Kosice, 1,324 shops, employing a total of 5,367 workers, or an average of 4 workers per shop, while Bratislava's average was only 2.2 workers per shop.

10. The Era of Dual Monarchy (1867–1918)

The political equalization (compromise) of Austria and Hungary was negotiated for the Hungarian side by Ferenc Deak and Count Gyula Andrassy. They announced the results of negotiations to the Hungarian Diet on February 18, 1867. Equalization became a reality with the ratification of Article XII of the Constitution, and the coronation of Franz Josef I as Hungarian king; a totally new constitution took effect in December 1867. The unity of the monarchy was secured in the person of the monarch and joint ministries of the army, foreign policy, and finance. Negotiation of mutual affairs and control of the activities of joint ministries were assigned to so-called delegations, which were made up of sixty members from each side. A new state appeared on the map of Europe, named Austria-Hungary, simultaneously an empire and a kingdom.

Franz Josef I

On the surface, the Hungarian kingdom was a liberal, parliamentary state within the dual monarchy, in which the role of legislature was greater than in its counterpart, Cisleithania, but which nevertheless continued to be basically bureaucratic. The role of the parliament in Hungary was control over the activities of government; the king was obliged to respect the laws passed by the Diet, though they had no force until he signed them. The Hungarian Diet had about 400 deputies, elected in precincts by simple majority.[1] To cast his vote, an eligible subject was required to pronounce the name of his choice before an electoral commission. Elections to the Diet were scheduled every two to three years. The prime minister was appointed by the king from a list of nominees presented to him by the diet, as were other members of government.

The historic county structure of Hungary was retained, along with its substantial powers. At the head of the counties were commissioners appointed by the king from a list of nominees recommended by the respective county governments. The county executive board was elective, but the number of electees was equal to the number of 'virilists', i.e. the wealthiest taxpayers in a given county, who sat with elected officials. Municipal committees managed internal affairs of counties, appointing officers, issuing ordinances, making motions to the county executive board for various political and economic regulations, and electing a vice-commissioner, the chief executive officer of a county.

Counties were divided into districts, at the head of which were sheriffs, named by the county executive board. Notaries played an important role in large villages, and also in smaller villages, which were merged into notary districts. County executive and also judicial powers were separated: royal judiciary boards sat in the county courts, lower judiciary boards in the district courts.

The right to vote in elections to the diet or to county offices was tied to a property census; ownership of a home with at least three rooms, or of a business or factory, was a requisite for qualification. A tradesman could acquire the franchise if he employed at least one journeyman; a farmer, if he owned at least a quarter of a traditional family farm, which in practice amounted to five to eight acres of plowed fields or hayfields. People with advanced education, including pastors and chaplains in villages, and teachers and notaries, also had the right to vote, but women never enjoyed the franchise in Austria-Hungary. In practice, only five to six percent of the adult population was enfranchised.

The Hungarian Diet had two chambers, of which the lower, comprising elected deputies, was supreme. In 1896, it consisted of 379 Liberal Party deputies and 97 oppositional deputies. In the upper chamber sat 17 archdukes, 29 Catholic and 8 Orthodox or Byzantine bishops, 10 high Protestant clergy, 7 dukes, 143 counts and 41 barons, all from among the Hungarian nobility, and lastly, 75 life-time appointees of the king.

Ferenc Deak, the head of the Liberal Party and erstwhile member of the 1848 regime which had included Kossuth and Batthany, became the first prime minister after Equalization. The Liberal Party remained the leading political force in Hungary for the entire duration of the dual monarchy, though undergoing some significant internal changes. A certain importance and political power was enjoyed by the Party of 1848 (called the Party of Independence), which had set its sights on secession. Its strength was centered in the Calvinist southeast, while the Catholic and Lutheran northwest voted mostly for Liberal Party candidates.

The newly transformed state sought a new international orientation. Bismarck, who at that time controlled Prussian policy, had dictated extremely mild peace terms to the Austrian emperor in 1866, clearly signaling a desire to make him an ally. The Magyars sensed this intention, particularly Count Gyula Andrassy, who was the minister of foreign affairs in the dual state. Austria-Hungary was no longer the most powerful Central European state; Prussia had taken over that role.

Gyula Andrassy, Sr., native of Trebisov

Count Gyula Andrassy was particularly concerned about possible Russian aggression in the Balkans and the expulsion of the Turks, two eventualities that could very well serve to buoy up the hopes of subject nationalities in Hungary. But in no time at all, a new European war broke out, in which Prussia defeated France and then united all of Germany into one powerful state.

The newly created German Empire (the second in German history, counting the medieval Holy Roman Empire) preferred an alliance with Russia to one with Austria-Hungary. Nevertheless, it drafted a treaty with Austria-Hungary in 1872 to combine forces against the bourgeoning labor movement. After a meeting of emperors in 1873, the three conservative monarchies of Central and Eastern

Europe formed an alliance, but an alliance based on mutual fear of the others' growing power. Military expenditures grew rapidly and universal military service was introduced.

A general feature of this period was the economic growth of a united Germany, which was building a strong industrial base and gaining rapidly in this respect on Britain and France. Berlin and Vienna endeavored to buttress their power in the Balkans, signing treaties of alliance with Serbia in 1881, and later, with Bulgaria. Russia, in this situation, began orienting itself to France, signing a pact to open its industry to French capital and its markets to French products. In 1893, a Russo-French military pact was contracted to create a balance of power, later taking in Britain as well. Now it was Germany that posed the threat.

After Equalization, the policy of the Magyar government was characterized by minor tactical concessions to nationalities. In April 1868, the Diet appointed a thirty-member nationalities committee of Serbian, Romanian and Rusyn deputies to prepare a draft for a nationalities bill, but without a single Slovak representative.

This Diet eventually approved such a bill on December 6, 1868, but non-Magyar deputies voted against it, since the new law, though confirming the equality of all citizens of Hungary, subsumed all nationalities in the definition of a united Hungarian political nation. Magyar was declared the official language of the state; the use of nationality languages was conceded in courts and church schools, in county committees, in local communities and churches. The language of instruction in state schools was to be determined by the minister of education. The cultivation of nationality languages was to be guaranteed, and chairs of the various

Opposition (nationalities) deputies in Hungarian Diet, 1868

145

Front page of
Slovak News

languages and literatures were to be set up in universities. Nationalities were to be permitted to organize associations and fraternities fostering the development of their languages, arts, sciences, economies, businesses and industries. Certainly, there was much to the good, but this law was destined never to be enforced.

At this time, the Magyars came to terms with the Croats, who had long since had their own formal regency, under the scepter of the Hungarian king. The Magyars had been forced to respect this arrangement, which was anchored in Article XXX/1868 of the legal code, which declared Croatia, Slavonia and Dalmatia to be distinct components of the united Hungarian state. This separate regency had its own diet, with Croatian the official language, and 29 deputies in the all-Hungarian Diet.

Slovak politics at this time split into two wings: alongside the old political constellation, which continued to invoke the *Memorandum*, emerged a 'New School', headed by Jan Bobula, a building contractor from Pest. The latter oriented themselves towards cooperation with the Magyars; their base was Pest. Bobula and his associates counted Palarik as one of them, but the latter soon died. They entertained a hope that, through cooperation with the Magyars, they could achieve a certain degree of progress in Slovak matters. In 1868 in Pest, they began publishing *The Slovak News*. Abandoning the demand for a Slovak region, they emphasized preservation of Hungarian state integrity.

But the majority of Slovak politicians continued to stand by the program of the *Memorandum*. At the end of 1869, they decided to relocate the editorial offices and publishing facilities of the *Budapest Intelligencer* to Turciansky Svaty Martin, determined to make this town a center of Slovak national life. They changed the title of their periodical to *The National News*, after which its supporters began calling themselves 'Narodniari' (Nationalists).

That same year, in this small, unimpressive, provincial town of Turciansky Svaty Martin, a mutual stock company was formed with a capital investment of 45 thousand florins, to publish Slovak print material. Meanwhile, Francisci, Pauliny-Toth and Lichard encouraged people to found mutual savings banks, economic clubs, and share-holding companies, not without some success.

Towards the end of the 1860s, Viliam Pauliny-Toth became a leading figure in Slovak affairs. He had joined the Slovak movement back in the *Memorandum* years, and after Austro-Hungarian Equalization he increased his efforts, encouraging petty Slovak burghers to become entrepreneurs in the capitalist mode, through economic clubs, credit unions, and savings institutions. He even approached Slovak Jews to recruit them to the Slovak cause, but without success. Prior to 1848, the Jews had been forced to live under the patronage of various feudal lords, but having acquired equal rights, they dispersed over Slovakia. Since they rarely

146

engaged in any artisan or agricultural pursuits, but had mainly made their livelihood in commerce, they maintained the same lifestyle by opening up shops in towns, trading in agricultural produce, making loans, and founding factories. They also began to acquire an education and became lawyers and doctors. Meanwhile, in their new pursuits, with the exception of the doctors, they were perceived as behaving quite unscrupulously, particularly as tavern-keepers, businessmen and usurers. In this manner, they aroused considerable animosity, and so anti-Semitism put down strong roots, which lasted well into the middle of the 20th Century.[2]

Viliam Pauliny-Toth

The Jews affected Slovak politics negatively in another way: their relative wealth and economic independence gave them access to voting rights. Magyar was not their familiar tongue, but during enforced Magyarization, they became its staunch devotees. They could not send their children to any but Magyar schools, for the simple reason that there were none[3], and as a consequence, they became props of Magyarization. They cast their votes for deputies of the ruling party, thus, in a sense, shrinking the pool of available votes for Slovak deputies, not to mention the fact that many Slovaks themselves, possibly even a majority, were not politically mature enough to vote in their own interests.

Three Slovak candidates were elected to the diet of 1869: Viliam Pauliny-Toth, from a district in Lower Hungary, where Slovaks and Serbs lived in harmony, and two representatives from the New School who, however, worked hand in hand with the government.

This time, Slovaks did achieve some successes. For instance, they were able to ensure the education of Slovak school teachers in a preparatory school in

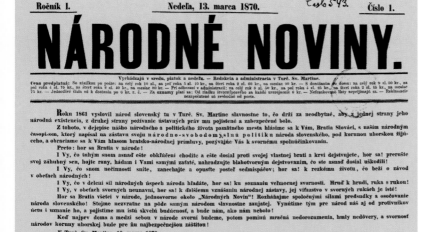

Front page of
National News

147

*Facsimile of report card
of Revuca prep school*

*Anna Pivkova, first
president of Zivena
(women's association)*

Revuca, and to organize a Catholic preparatory school in Klastor pod Znievom. On July 4, 1869, they founded a women's association named 'Zivena' (Nurture), and intensified efforts to found training schools for girls, child-care centers, and various educational courses for women. In 1869, an association called 'Slovenska Omladina' (Slovak Youth) was founded in Turciansky Svaty Martin, which welcomed Slovak students from all over Hungary.

In 1870, Andrej Radlinsky, a native of Orava County and pastor in Kuty, founded the Society of St. Adalbert and became its honorary president.[4] This society had three divisions: one for translating the bible into Slovak, another for preparing a universal hymnbook, and the last for publishing Slovak textbooks. Its permanent base was Trnava. It published mass editions of Slovak prayer-books, songbooks and elementary textbooks, plus *The Catholic News*, *The St. Adalbert Pilgrim* (an almanac), and a variety of books. It was able to garner considerable support. Membership grew from 5,275 in 1886, to 26,189 by the First World War.

Nor were Slovak Lutherans without a publishing society, though theirs did not get started until 1896,[5] after the General Convention of the Lutheran Church had rejected a proposal for a Slovak publications society, on the grounds that the function was being adequately performed by a Magyar Lutheran Association. The Slovak Lutheran publishing house was named 'Tranoscius' and its base was Liptovsky Svaty Mikulas.

In the political life of these times, the Hungarian Slovaks gained an unexpected ally in the person of a deputy of the Independent Party, Lajos Mocsary, who began to speak out in the diet against Magyar chauvinism and ruthless Magyarization. He joined forces with a Serbian deputy, Miletic, and two Romanian deputies, in support of Slovak interests. Recruiting the support of three other deputies of his own party, Mocsary also made a joint appeal with them for equal nationality rights and the use of nationality languages in county offices and schools. He served a relatively long term as deputy, backed numerous Slovak causes, and never betrayed his convictions or principles.

In the 1870s, Magyars began to publish a Slovak periodical in Banska Bystrica called *Svornost* (Solidarity), whose ideologist was Bela Grunwald, the vice-commissioner of Zvolen County. The periodical's chief thrust was opposition to Slovak schools. It organized a petition against them, solicited from unsophisticated voters in Slovak communities. He also circulated a petition against Slovak prep schools, and was able to obtain signatures in all the Slovak counties except Trencin.

These anti-Slovak campaigns were joined by the churches too, and thus, on August 20, 1874, the Catholic hierarchy shut down the preparatory school in Revuca, on December 30, the preparatory school in Klastor pod Znievom, and on January 5, 1875, the preparatory school in Turciansky Svaty Martin. Each of these had taught 100 to 150 students. Meanwhile, the preparatory school in Banska Bystrica, over which Bishop Moyses had held a protective hand, was converted into a Magyar facility.

Another target of Magyar attacks was Matica Slovenska which, in 1874, had approximately 1,200 members, some of them group memberships. It was not, by any means, a mass organization, but all over Hungary, and even abroad, it established a network of subscribers, who were the driving force behind Slovak educational and cultural activities.

In the course of its publication, it focused above all on scientific, cultural and educational works. A major role in the development of Slovak science was played by its periodical, *Letopis* (Annals), of which twelve volumes appeared prior to 1875. It also published 41 book titles. It sparked the founding of choral groups in Turciansky Svaty Martin, Trnava, Dolny Kubin and Tisovec. Each year in August it sponsored a festival. Its library held more than ten thousand volumes of books and manuscripts, plus archeological finds, coins and nature specimens.

Matica Slovenska was founded on contributions from ordinary Slovaks and it was they who kept it alive. Its capital fund amounted to a respectable ten thousand florins. Matica was banned by an edict of the Ministry of Interior dated April 6, 1875. Its library and collections were confiscated, along with the capital fund. Miletic protested on the floor of the diet, but to no avail; no one joined him. The new Prime Minister, Count Koloman Tisza, who had just assumed office, announced that he knew of no such entity as the Slovak nationality, and this pronouncement continued to be the policy of his cohorts up to the collapse of multi-national Hungary.

Fifteen years of Tisza rule inflicted on Slovaks not only the closure of Matica Slovenska, but many additional blows, which seriously impaired their ability to keep pace with the progress of other European nations.

In the diet elections of 1875, Slovaks once again failed to achieve a mandate. In this desperate situation, even such old warriors as Jozef Miloslav Hurban, who together with Samuel Stefanovic had sought support (mainly financial) in Prague, wavered and began to lose hope; the Czechs turned them down, and Frantisek Ladislav Rieger, a leading Czech politician of the time, declared that, since Slovaks preferred a kind of 'coachman's jargon' to the Czech language and wanted their own way, they could expect no financial support from Czechs.[6]

In 1878, Hurban tried to get some relief at the Imperial Court, but the emperor refused to receive him and returned Hurban's memorandum.

At this time, death took Hodza, Palarik, Kral and Pauliny-Toth. Pavol Mudron, a lawyer in Turciansky Svaty Martin,[7] and his brother Michal, a lawyer in Bratislava, took over the reins of the Slovak Movement. They courageously defended the rights of Slovak farmers in so-called 'Urbarial' cases. Pavol also filed

Announcement banning Matica Slovenska

Svetozar Hurban Vajansky

a lawsuit for return of the property of Matica Slovenska, and later defended Slovak and other political activists against political prosecution. Another leading figure of the Slovak Movement in the 1870s and 1880s was Svetozar Hurban Vajansky, the son of Jozef Miloslav, who was not only a prolific poet and author, but a publicist and ideologist of the Slovak struggle at the turn of the 19th and 20th Centuries. Very prominent with him in this struggle was another outstanding author, Pavol Orsagh Hviezdoslav, Slovakia's pre-eminent poet of the time.[8]

Chauvinist persecution of the Slovaks culminated during the Russo-Turkish war, which resulted in the liberation of the Bulgars from Turkish rule, an outcome naturally welcomed sympathetically in Slovakia. Meanwhile, the Viennese Court and Magyar politicians did everything they could to weaken the role and influence of Russia in the Balkans. They staged a show trial against Svetozar Miletic and imprisoned him for five years. Bela Grunwald also intensified his anti-Slovak activities. He wrote a work *Felvidek* (The Uplands), and in 1879, presented a bill to the diet to make Magyar a mandatory subject even in non-Magyar schools. This bill was ratified.

A campaign was unleashed against Slovak student organizations. Many, including seminarians, were expelled from middle schools for 'Pan-Slav' agitation. During his studies in Spis seminary, Andrej Hlinka, the great Slovak leader to be, narrowly escaped this fate.

Chauvinism embroiled even church hierarchies, both Catholic and Lutheran. Bishops assigned Magyar and pro-Magyar priests to Slovak parishes, and promoted Magyar sermons in Slovak churches. Even rank and file clergy actively Magyarized. The general synod of the Lutheran Church, whose believers were basically Slovak, resolved to take energetic measures against the 'Pan-Slavism' of some of its pastors. They were not to be allowed to serve in any official capacities, or conversely, were to be removed from any official positions they might already hold.

In 1882, Magyars founded The Upper-Hungarian Educational Association, known by the acronym 'FEMKE'. Its goal was to convert every person in Hungary to Magyar affiliation, focusing primarily on youth, who were to be influenced at a tender age. The association organized abductions of Slovak children for rearing in Magyar families in the Hungarian plains. In the school year 1887–1888, five hundred children were thus carried off, of whom about three hundred managed to escape and return home, mostly on foot, through harrowing circumstances. These abductions aroused a storm of protest at home and abroad, particularly in Bohemia and Moravia.

Another Magyar tactic was the sowing of discord among Slovaks. With this intent they spread the theory that the inhabitants of eastern Slovakia were not

150

genuine Slovaks, and based their theory on textbooks in the Saris dialect, for use in the schools of Saris, Spis and Zemplin Counties. In this truly desperate situation, Svetozar Hurban Vajansky sought to orient Slovak politics to Russia. Russian orientation was essentially nothing new; it was an accommodation to conditions, built on a firm faith in the future of the Slavs, particularly of Russia. Vajansky's conviction that the Romance and Germanic nations of the West had succumbed to materialism, atheism and capitalism, while the Slavs had remained morally incorrupt, sounds amusing in the light of present-day circumstances.[9]

At this time, relations between Czechs and Slovaks enjoyed a revival, manifested, for instance, by members of the suppressed Matica Slovenska joining Matica Ceska (an analogous Czech cultural institute), by lively contacts between Czech and Slovak cultural workers; and by mutual interest in national affairs. A Slovakophile movement sprang up in Bohemia, represented chiefly by the poets Adolf Heyduk and Rudolf Pokorny, by the painters Jaroslav Vesin and Mikulas Ales, and by the author of *A History of Slovak Literature,* Jaroslav Vlcek, the son of a teacher who had once taught in the Banska Bystrica preparatory school.

In 1882 in Prague, a Slovak student association was founded under the name 'Detvan' (The Detvaner).[10] At that time, the Czech language had achieved parity with German, numerous Czech middle schools sprang up, and separate universities and technical colleges were founded in each language. Czech print media began to take a much greater interest in Slovak affairs.

Slovak politics turned passive in the latter years of the 1880s. In the elections of 1884, 1887, and even later, Slovaks did not field even one candidate. *The Catholic News* ran a broad campaign to spread the Great Moravian and Cyril-Methodian traditions, and in 1863 drew upwards of 5,000 Slovaks to Velehrad, Moravia, to celebrate the millennium of that historic period. Commemorative celebrations of the *Memorandum* were also planned for this time, but they were banned by authorities

(Turciansky Svaty) Martin, provincial town, hub of Slovak national life in latter half of 19th Century

151

*Members of Slovak
student association,
'Detvan' in Prague*

at the last minute. Meanwhile, in 1887, the women's association, 'Zivena' (Nurture), opened an exhibit of Slovak embroidery in Turciansky Svaty Martin.

Turciansky Svaty Martin, a provincial town in Turiec County, became a center where Slovak political leaders, publicists, writers, and lawyers took up residence. It had a Slovak publishing association, six Slovak periodicals, a Slovak museum and, every August, a national festival. It also had an active choral group and, starting in 1889, a National Home housing a large theater. The Tatrabanka (a bank, the most important Slovak financial institution up to 1918), was also

*Home of Tatrabanka
in Turciansky Svaty
Martin*

152

located there, as was the Slovak Museum Association, founded by Andrej Kmet in 1895, with 350 members.

For Slovak Catholics, the town of Trnava, where the Society of St. Adalbert had set up headquarters, was especially important. Following Radlinsky, Martin Kollar, a pastor in nearby Hadas (Trstina), became the leading personality of Slovak Catholic life. He took care to extend the activity of the Society of St. Adalbert to eastern Slovakia, and he reached out to emigrant communities in America, with support for their national organizations.

It was mostly thanks to Radlinsky's efforts that western Slovakia became the most ethnically sophisticated part of Slovakia, where even the broad masses engaged in nationalistic activities. Since here the Slovaks had long been predominantly Catholic, they were able to establish contacts with their counterparts in Moravia. Here also, Slovaks found an important ally in the person of Dr. Alois Kolisek, a Catholic publicist, who was a teacher at the technical preparatory school in Hodonin. Dr. Kolisek eagerly propagated Slovak and Moravian songs, which he personally performed not only in Bohemia and Moravia, but even as far away as England, Paris and Vienna. He took part in the August festivals in Turciansky Svaty Martin, Czecho-Slovak meetings in Luchacovice, and in similar undertakings.

After the fall of Kolomon Tisza, who ruled for fifteen years, there followed an era of short-term prime ministers, including Count Gyula Szapari (1890–1892), Sandor Wekerle (1892–1895), Dezso Banffy (1895–1899), and Kolomon Szell (1899–1902). None of them made any substantial concessions to the nationalities. There was no let-up in ethnic oppression, even if some sporadic minor relaxation occurred. But it was not just the nationalities that created problems for Pest; historic Hungary, especially in the south, was full of social problems. The government paid little attention to agricultural and industrial workers; its policies explicitly ignored the masses. In Hungary, feudal anachronisms abounded at all levels, politics was 'upper-class rascality'. Well-born gentlemen strove energetically to get the common people to fear them and to show 'proper respect'.

A novelty in Hungarian politics was the rise of new parties. As early as 1890, the Social Democratic Party was founded, but with no hope of making it into parliament, because the workers who founded it were economically dependent, thus ineligible to vote. In 1892, the National Party was founded, with Albert Apponyi at its head.

Szapari's administration had passed a law setting up health insurance and disability funds, but his rule soon gave way to the government of Wekerle, who was not of noble birth, a decided novelty in Hungarian politics. He succeeded in getting the diet to pass a law enacting state registries of vital statistics, obligatory civil marriages, and freedom of religious confession, the latter achieved in spite of marked clashes with the Catholic Church. The Liberals of the end of the 19th Century were quite hostile to religion and the church, proud of representing 'progress' and leading the charge against religious 'backwardness'. Wekerle also enacted a law making knowledge of Magyar mandatory for non-Magyar teachers, and extending state inspections to religious schools.

This period saw preparations for the commemoration of the millennium of Magyar arrival in Europe,[11] which was to be celebrated with great pomp, and during which Hungary was to present itself to the world as a state with a constitution going back to the 13th Century, just like the English model. For this occasion, Magyar political leaders agreed to bring a halt to all controversies and misunderstandings among themselves.

On the other hand, a trend began to develop in Slovakia towards closer cooperation between non-Magyar nationalities, and an increase in contacts with the Czech nation.

As early as 1891, the Slovaks had established close contacts with the Romanians, and had taken part in a conference held in Sibio in July 1892. The Slovak delegation made a pact agreeing to cooperation in political struggles. In January, 1893, a meeting of leading politicians from both sides took place, with participation by Hungarian Serbs as well. An invitation to cooperation was also to be extended to the Rusyns, Croats and Germans. The parties resolved to prepare for a congress of the non-Magyar nationalities of Hungary, which aroused great consternation in Magyar circles.

The political mosaic of Hungary changed in 1895, when a Catholic political party appeared on the scene, the People's Party ('Neppart', in Magyar), with Count Ferdinand Zichy taking the lead. It planned to get involved in nationality affairs and to press for enforcement of the nationalities law of 1868. But before long, its leading aristocratic members jumped ship.

The first congress of Hungarian nationalities took place in Budapest on August 10, 1895. Two hundred Slovak delegates participated. The three-member

Farmers' homes
in Sumiac

presidium included Pavol Mudron, a Slovak. It was an event which attracted the attention of even the foreign press. The government succeeded in dissuading Rusyns and Germans from participating, since the latter two ethnic groups manifested considerable openness to Magyarization, or at least willingness to be led by Magyarophiles from among their own people.[12]

The congress resulted in a twenty-two item compilation of demands, and the creation of a twelve-member committee, which was to coordinate future undertakings, inform domestic and foreign publics of the nationalities problem in Hungary, and work up a memorandum for presentation to the king.

Spurred on by its victory in the elections of 1896, the government infensified Magyarization efforts in schools, mandated Magyarization of place and family names, and tightened censorship of nationality presses. Worse still, it began throwing up blocks to economic ventures by non-Magyar ethnic individuals and groups.

The government felt compelled to intervene with police against protest demonstrations by farmers and workers, inflicting considerable harm on the demonstrators, including even death. Prime Minister Banffy made it quite clear that he meant to protect the interests of Magyar estate owners and capitalists. The latter two segments of Hungarian society organized into two camps, agrarian and mercantile respectively, with each camp striving to gain as many adherents as possible.

In the last decade of the 19th Century, Slovak politics remained passive. Neither Slovaks, nor even Serbs or Rusyns, fielded a single candidate in elections, but this did not mean the Slovak People's Party was totally inactive. On the contrary, it strove to make use of the religiosity of its Catholic adherents, though unfortunately only a few of them could vote. As to the Jews, they were scattered among the Slovak and Magyar populations, and, though they did enjoy the vote, as did also many officials and state employees, they were unlikely to vote with Catholics: their votes went to candidates of the ruling party. In pre-election rallies, it was not unusual to see crowds of ten, even fifteen thousand participants. The Slovak People's Party was able to take some advantage of these rallies by joining them and cheering opposition candidates.

In time, the Slovak national movement began to differentiate. In major cities of the monarchy – Prague, Vienna, Budapest – a new generation of Slovak intelligentsia matured, with a desire to make its mark on the political life of Hungary and to give it a new face. Onto this political scene stepped a new personality – Andrej Hlinka, a Catholic pastor from Sliace in Liptov County. He had joined the Zichy People's Party without, however, cutting ties to the Slovak National Party. His efforts on behalf of the Slovak movement began in the trenches, so to speak, attempting to gain the goodwill of people and to help them as much as possible

Andrej Hlinka,
with Moravian friend
Alois Kolisek

materially. He was especially successful in countering the activities of Jewish lenders and tavern-keepers, who had gained control of many villages. He founded cooperatives for the sale of mixed goods, and Slovak hostelries meant to drive unscrupulous businessmen from villages. In addition to credit unions and consumer cooperatives, he also founded temperance societies and reading circles.

Hlinka's path to the priesthood, chaplaincy and pastorate, had not been easy. The staff of the seminary in Spisske Podhradie had wanted to expel him as a 'Pan-Slavist'. In 1898, he campaigned in the Ruzomberok district as a candidate of the Zichy's People's Party, but he lost and parted company with Zichy. He then began to organize an independent Slovak populist and Catholic movement, but still maintained ties to the leadership of the Slovak National Party in Turciansky Svaty Martin.

Hlinka published his views in *The National News*, *The Catholic News*, and *The People's News*, the last of which had started up at the end of 1897 under the editorship of Hlinka himself and a journalist named Anton Bielik. He also expressed support for the idea of Czecho-Slovak reciprocity but, of course, under the banner of Catholicism, which was the religious affiliation of the majority of Czechs and Slovaks. His models were the national revivalists among Catholic priests in both camps. Gradually, towards the end of the 19th Century, Hlinka worked his way up to political leadership in Slovak Catholic circles.

Slovak youth at this time banded together in three main organizations: Tatran (The Tatraner, Vienna), Detvan (The Detvaner, Prague) and Slovensky Spolok (The Slovak Society, Pest). They leaned to the Slovak National Center in Turciansky Svaty Martin and were at first unreserved in their support. They also supported growing cooperation with non-Magyar ethnic groups, and strove to build ethnic self-esteem. These young people came, for the most part, from middle-class families in towns, from wealthier farm families, and from the intelligentsia. During the course of their studies, they had broadened their outlook and were well aware that the Slovak movement was lagging behind others. After all, Romanians and Serbs already had independent national states, on which their Hungarian brethren could lean.

Gradually opposition to the Martin Center evolved within this new Slovak generation. This opposition was strongest in Prague, where a group of Czech Slovakophiles had emerged, who realized that Slovaks could be an important source of strength to Czechs. For, after the unification of Germany, Czechs felt themselves squeezed in a German vise externally, while being commingled with Germans internally. It should be borne in mind that Germany at that time was already in control of Silesia, eastern Prussia and Pomerania. Slovakia could provide a bridge out of this encirclement to that most powerful of Slavic nations, Russia. Magyarization of Slovakia would break this opening, and leave the Czechs completely surrounded by non-Slav Germans and Magyars.

On May 7, an organization called 'Ceskoslovenska Jednota' (Czechslovak Unity) was founded in Prague, dedicated to the cultural and economic advancement of Slovakia.[13] S. H. Vajansky, the Slovak publicist and author, personally took part in its activities, as did Matus Dula, another figure in the Slovak national camp of this time. But Tomas G. Masaryk, who was the ideological leader of this cooperation, began broaching the idea of a national union between Czechs and Slovaks; he began to revive efforts to win the Slovaks over to the Czech literary language; and he developed a philosophy of Czecho-Slovakism, which naturally met resistance in Turciansky Svaty Martin. But the Prague political circle did find supporters in Slovakia, among them Karol Salva, who in his newspaper, *Slovak Letters*, espoused the ideas of Masaryk, finding inspiration in close cooperation with Czechs, especially in economics and education.

Tomas G. Masaryk

This opposition, emanating from Prague, remained completely under the spell of Tomas G. Masaryk, and gained a very important political representative in Slovakia in the person of Vavro Srobar. Srobar established contacts with Slovak students in Vienna, one of whom was Pavol Blaho. He encouraged Blaho to get together with other Slovak young people and organize an association like the Czech 'Omladina' (Youth).

In 1898, students who were studying in Prague and Vienna, or who had returned to Slovakia from those cities imbued with the idea of Czecho-Slovak

First issue of Hlas
(The Voice),
monthly publication

cooperation, decided to publish a periodical called *Hlas* (The Voice). Students from Budapest joined them, as did some graduates – Hodza, Medvecky, Jesensky and Zaturecky.

Tomas G. Masaryk regularly spent his summer vacations in Slovakia. There, in a meeting with Vavro Srobar, the two decided on ideological policies for the periodical *Hlas*: it was to be expressly directed against the Slovak group centered in Turciansky Svaty Martin, and it would promote universal voting rights, a progressive tax structure, reform of the Hungarian judiciary, free public education, Slovak schools and a university, and freedom of the press; instead of Stur and Hurban, it would play up Kollar and Safarik and thus undermine the ideological pillars of Slovak ethnic and linguistic distinctiveness, deriding the Slovak language which, in Masaryk's view was not at all suitable for publishing academic texts. Electoral passivity was to be abandoned, as was the struggle for a Slovak 'region' and opposition to Magyar as official language.

In this periodical, Blaho and Srobar began to criticize the Martin Center, accusing it of apathy, of being out of touch with the people, of aristocratic airs, and Russophilism.

The most important critic of *Hlas* was the Slovak poet Jan Donoval (penname, Tichomir Milkin), a Catholic pastor in various towns of Zahorie, who opposed Czecho-Slovakism on principle, and considered it an obstacle to fraternal relations between the two nations, citing the relationship between Slovak and Moravian Catholics as a model of cooperation.

The Hlasists (as the *Hlas* people came to be known) failed to grow into a broadly popular movement because they were considerably splintered in their thinking. But with their efforts, they contributed to an activization and renaissance of political and social thought in Slovakia on the threshold of the 20th Century.

In the 1890s, a new political force appeared – American Slovaks. Starting with the seventies of the 19th Century, thousands, and even tens of thousands of Slovaks emigrated to the United States, which was enjoying a sustained economic boom after the Civil War. In conditions that were substantially better than those in Hungary, with much improved material comfort, they began to become ethnically aware.

In America, Slovaks began to organize. On photographs of members of Slovak fraternal societies of the time, we also begin to see women interspersed among the men, for in the United States, women were beginning to achieve equality and voting rights, something unheard of in Hungary. An important leader of these organizational activities was Peter Vitazoslav Rovnianek. Born in Dolny Hricov, Rovnianek moved to the United States in 1868, after being expelled from theological studies for his ethnic convictions. In his new homeland, Rovnianek began to work on his fellow Slovaks to arouse their ethnic awareness. He became a publisher of Slovak newsprint. In 1890, he founded the National Slovak Fraternal Society and became its first president. In 1893, he and Stefan Furdek, a Catholic priest and fellow Slovak immigrant, founded 'Matica Slovenska v Amerike' (The Slovak Cultural Institute of America); in 1894 he helped with the founding of Zivena[14] (a women's society); and in 1907 he was one of the founders of the Slovak League of America. In 1900, Rovnianek was instrumental in getting the U.S. Census Bureau to record immigrants from Hungary by their mother tongue. He fought the spread of socialist ideas among Slovak immigrants, founded financial institutions, and a Slovak settlement in Arkansas called Slovaktown. In 1901, Rovnianek founded the *Slovensky Dennik* (The Slovak Daily News), and published the first American Slovak almanac, *Americky Slovak* (The American Slovak).

Stefan Furdek, president of Slovak League of America

Stefan Furdek, a native of Trstena, who was forced to finish his theological studies in America and was the first president of The Slovak Cultural Institute of America, was at first pastor of a Czech Catholic parish in Cleveland, Ohio. In 1890, he founded The First Catholic Slovak Union (Jednota, a fraternal society) in Cleveland and became editor of its periodical, *Jednota (*Unity).[15] He was also one of the founders of the Slovak League of America.[16]

Socialistically oriented Slovaks formed a fraternal society in Chicago called 'Rovnost' (Equality), which strove to organize Slovak workers under the aegis of Socialism or, at least, to get Slovak and Czech workers to join in common causes. Out of these efforts sprang the Czecho-Slovak Workers' Party in 1902. The leading figure in this movement was Stefan Martincek who had migrated to the United States at the beginning of the century after having been a prominent socialist in Hungary.[17]

Meanwhile, in 1901 in Slovakia, the Slovak National Council abandoned its electoral passivity and began to prepare for activism. It entrusted the job of working up a campaign to Ambro Pietor, the editor of *The Slovak National News.[18]* The council decided to field only thirteen candidates, although there were eighty-four electoral districts, of which forty-seven had Slovak majorities. All told, there were about 200,000 qualified voters in Slovakia, of whom 87,000 were Slovak. There were also two predominantly Slovak electoral districts in Lower Hungary.

Membership badge of Slovak League of America

Three candidates of the Slovak National party were victorious in the elections, one each in the electoral districts of Liptovsky Svaty Mikulas, Vrbove, and Senica. In addition, Martin Kollar, a Catholic priest and administrator of the Society of St. Adalbert, campaigned and won the election in the district of Trnava. Against two of the elected Slovak deputies, F. Veselovsky and J. Valasek, the authorities filed charges of anti-Magyar agitation, persuading the Diet to revoke their immunity. The two were then convicted, and each sentenced to a year in prison.

At the beginning of the 20th Century, Slovak politicians faced the quandary of whether or not to continue cooperating with the non-Magyar nationalities of Hungary. The matter was brought to a head by Milan Hodza, who in *The Slovak Weekly News*, which he had been publishing since 1903, called for the subject to be brought up on the floor of the Hungarian Diet. This was a totally new ploy, demonstrating great political foresight. As elections drew near in 1905, Hodza decided to make a run for office himself, but in an electoral district of Lower Hungary.

The Pest government began noticing a growing self-esteem in the working class, among whom only isolated members enjoyed the franchise. Workers expressed this new-found self-esteem by staging strikes, as for instance in 1897 in Budapest, when several thousand bricklayers and construction workers went on strike, among them many Slovaks. At this time, even social-democratic farm workers began forming labor organizations.

At the turn of the century, Hungarian socio-democratic elements united in a mass party, which was actually trade-unionist rather than party-cell in nature.[19] This party began falling away from the principles of the Second International, as had other similar parties,[20] and in its platform for 1903 it adopted, as a primary objective, the achievement of universal, secret and equal voting rights. It also called for abolition of capitalism and the socialization of production facilities, the seizure of power by class struggle, and even freedom of press and assembly, as well as equality among nations and disbanding of standing armies.

Market scene in Pest, with Slovak vendors

From 1903 to 1905, the prime minister of the Hungarian government was Count Istvan Tisza, son of Koloman Tisza, and an admirer of his policies. As the new elections drew near, all the Hungarian political parties united against the Liberal Party and its dirty electoral practices.[21] The combined forces won a total of 231 seats against the Liberal Party's 156. Of the Slovaks, only Milan Hodza and Frantisek Skycak were elected, Hodza in a predominantly Slovak district of Lower Hungary, Skycak in Orava County, as a candidate of the People's party.

Young Milan Hodza

Milan Hodza helped to organize newly elected diet deputies into a nationalities party, and became its secretary; a Romanian became its president. As a deputy of the diet, Hodza proceeded to press for democratic reforms in public life, and at a public demonstration staged in Hodonin in 1905, he proposed interim cooperation with Social Democrats, who, despite all their ideological shortcomings and immersion in Marxism, were at least basically opposed to ethnic oppression.

After the election, a caretaker regime led by Gejza Fejervari took over the reins of government. However, the combined opposition forces expressed a lack of confidence in his regime and forced new elections.[22] Even the Slovak National Party split into two wings at this time, with strong opposition to Hodza, who insisted that the party orient itself not only to ethnic demands, but to economic interests of the Slovak middle class as well.

Dissatisfaction also developed in Catholic political circles too. Members of the Slovak People's Party were unhappy with the attitude of Magyar and pro-Magyar clergy, and called for the creation of an independent Slovak-Catholic People's Party. They pointed out that Skycak had had to face another Catholic candidate in his district, a pro-Magyar member of the gentry from Orava County named Zoltan Zmeskal, while Martin Kollar, another Slovak candidate, had found himself facing an interdict by the archbishop of Esztergom, forbidding Catholic priests to back Slovak candidates and wrecking his bid for office. Thus the Magyar Liberal Party, though defeated in Hungary as a whole, was nevertheless able to elect 65 of its 84 candidates in Slovakia.

The creation of a Slovak Catholic party received strong support from the wise politician and strategist Milan Hodza, who at this time was campaigning for universal suffrage. As for Frantisek Skycak, he left the Magyar People's Party in favor of a new Slovak Catholic party, and was joined by F. Juriga, F. Jehlicka, M. Kollar, F. R. Osvald, A. Kmet and J. Buday, plus some opposition politicians who were not necessarily practising Catholics. Hlinka meanwhile, from 1906 to 1909, was serving a three-year sentence in a Magyar prison.

This new Slovak party was organized on March 18, 1906, but it did not immediately make a formal break from the Slovak National Party. Its platform included universal suffrage and enforcement of the Nationalities Act of 1868. Its ethnic goals were identical with those of the Slovak National Party, and the two made a pact to conduct a common campaign as 'The Slovak Party'.

Working as one, the two parties reached out, even to the four electoral districts of Saris County, where the sense of Slovak identity was still weak, though steadily expanding under the influence of 'American' returnees. Also, an American organization, the Central Slovak National Committee, organized in New York in 1905, contributed considerable financial support to this campaign. In all, the Slovak National Party fielded five candidates, and the Slovak People's Party thirteen, of whom five were former Hlasists.

Slovaks chalked up unprecedented successes in this election. Seven deputies were elected to the diet: People's Party candidates P. Blaho, F. Jedlicka, F. Juriga, M. Kollar, F. Skycak, and M. Hodza; and National Party candidate M. M. Bella. Additionally, four Serbs were elected, and an impressive total of fourteen Romanians, bringing the number of nationalities deputies in the diet to twenty five, an unprecedented and by no means negligible bloc of votes.

The extraordinary success of the Slovak People's Party infuriated the Magyar and pro-Magyar church authorities; they retracted permission to use the name 'Catholic' in the party's newspaper masthead, prompting the Slovak People's Party to rename its paper simply *The People's News*. The situation became so fraught that the newspaper's editor-in-chief fled to America. Pavol Blaho and Anton Stefanek then took over its management. Because of its open animosity towards Magyar clergy, in 1907 the archbishop of Esztergom and the other diocesan bishops put it on the church index of prohibited publications. Nevertheless, the newspaper's influence spread to eastern Slovakia and to Protestants as well, propagating the idea of Czech/Slovak cooperation and even, in fact, of a Czecho-Slovak nation, clashing in this respect with the Slovak National Party.

Meanwhile, a tragic event occurred at a church consecration in a suburb of Ruzomberok called Cernova. Parishioners had requested Father Andrej Hlinka, who was a fellow townsman and initiator of the construction, to preside. When pro-Magyar clergy attempted to take over the ceremony, the parishoners, who had funded the project, intervened and were fired upon by Magyar gendarmes, and fifteen parishoners died.[23] Though political shootings had become quite common in Hungary, especially under Prime Minister Banffy, shooting people at a simple church service was certainly unusual. The act outraged decent people everywhere, and Bjornstjerne Bjornson, a Nobel Prize winner, spoke out on behalf of the Slovaks and sought to inform the world of Magyar oppression of nationalities.

Bjornstjerne Bjornson

Under Prime Minister Wekerle's rule (1906–1910), Albert Apponyi, the minister of education, strove to completely Magyarize the primary school system. In 1890, Slovak had still been the language of instruction in 1,115 church primary schools; by 1905 this number had dropped to 241, the remnant to be eliminated in the near future.

In the last decade of existence of the Kingdom of Hungary, Slovak politics crystallized around two leading personalities, Andrej Hlinka and Milan Hodza.

Andrej Hlinka was a Catholic priest who, after finishing seminary studies in Spisske Podhradie, was not sent to round out his theological grounding in Esztergom or Vienna (the Pazmaneum), as was customary, but was assigned straightaway to pastoral work in Ruzomberok. He undertook his pastoral mission with a sense that only people content in their material circumstances could be truly receptive to the Word. As a conscientious Slovak patriot, he was prepared to make the greatest sacrifices for his nation, while faithfully adhering to Catholic doctrine. He rejected Marxism on principle, as well as other ideological currents of the modern era, like social democracy, free-thinking, freemasonry and Masaryk's Czecho-Slovakism. He was never absent from Liptov County for any extended period except when serving time in Magyar prisons. In 1906, he founded a People's bank in Ruzomberok; in 1910 a publishing association in Bratislava; and in 1917, with other dedicated Slovaks, a printery named 'Lev' (Lion) in Ruzomberok.

Milan Hodza, on the other hand, was a Lutheran, born in 1878. He finished his study of law in Budapest and Cluj (Romania), and philosophy in Vienna,

Gendarmes arresting Andrej Hlinka

where he earned a doctorate. His goal was to build a political movement devoted to the betterment of the lot of farmers, favoring easy credit and redistribution of landed estates. But Hodza never much personally associated with farmers; he spent his time primarily in big cities: Vienna, Budapest and Prague. Still, he made political allies among Czech Agrarians, and supported Crown Prince Franz Ferdinand in his efforts to transform the Habsburg Empire from the ground up. Hodza took part in the founding of the Slovak Catholic People's Party, but never became a member. In 1906, he did become the vice-president of the Slovak National Party, with plans to convert it into a party of the agrarian type.

The events of Cernova significantly strengthened solidarity between Czechs and Slovaks, as reflected even in the flow of Czech financial contributions into Slovak political coffers. Hodza and Blaho at this time strove to expand economic cooperation between the two nationalities. Blaho also made an attempt to establish a presence in the Czech lands, and in 1906, opened a cultural center in Luhacovice, under the name 'Slovacka Bouda' (The Slovak Booth), which became a center for staging various Slovak activities. These activities took place on a regular basis and were presented in a broad-based folk-style. In 1907 in Prague, a review began appearing under the name *Nase Slovensko* (Our Slovakia), while in Slovakia, *National News* began printing a regular column titled *Cesko, Morava, Sliezko* (Bohemia, Moravia, Silesia).

Starting in 1908, Luhacovice became the site of an annual seminar called 'Czecho-Slovak Unity', attended regularly by activists of the Slovak national movement. These seminars dealt with cultural, economic and political problems, and were closed to the public. Other seminars aimed at Slovak activists were also held there. They were initiated by Pavol Blaho, who in 1906 began organizing farmers' conventions in Skalica, and helped spread practical Czech innovations among farmers of the Zahorie region of western Slovakia.

In 1909, Czecho-Slovak Unity decided to devote itself exclusively to cooperation with Slovaks, emphasizing support for Slovak students attending Czech schools, and for cultural, literary and economic contacts between Czechs and Slovaks. In this way, the idea of Czecho-Slovak cooperation in the era before the First World War received very concrete expression. 'Unity' had many affiliations in Czech and Moravian towns, and a network of devotees who stayed in contact with the Prague scene.

A very effective program for acquainting Czechs with Slovak problems were lecture tours conducted by Blaho, Hodza, Stefanek and Hlinka. Andrej Hlinka, in particular, as the person around whom the events of Cernova had swirled, gained extraordinary popularity in Bohemia and Moravia. In 1907, when the idea of universal suffrage triumphed in Cisleithania, Czech deputies in the Imperial Parliament became bold enough to call for Viennese intervention against the murder 'of our brother Slovaks' in Hungary.

Abroad, in addition to Bjornson, there was a (Scottish) publicist named Seton-Watson, writing under the pen-name 'Scotus Viator', who published English studies about Magyar oppression of Slovaks and other nationalities in Hungary, informing the world of real conditions there.

But even democratically inclined Magyars were disturbed. Oszkar Jaszi was interested in the plight of the Slovaks, and advocated resolution of the nationalities question on the basis of cultural autonomy, within the framework of the ratified, but not yet enforced Nationalities Act of 1868.[24]

Nor did cooperation slacken between Slovaks, Serbs and Romanians on the diet floor. In their addresses to that body, the deputies of the three nationalities called for enforcement of national equality and recognition of various nationality rights; they also demanded democratic reforms, such as universal suffrage. Hodza strove to get the diet to approve his agrarian ideas and sought allies among Magyar opposition parties (for instance, Independent Socialists).

In 1910, Karol Khuen-Hedervary, who had been intensively promoting universal suffrage, became prime minister of Hungary, but he failed to win acceptance for the idea. Nevertheless, the cooperative parliamentary efforts of Slovaks, Romanians, and Serbs from 1906 to 1910 played an important role in internal Hungarian politics during this period.

In 1909, the periodical *Prudy* (Currents) began appearing in Budapest, and around it a new political constellation began to form, made up mostly of young Slovaks. It harked back to the traditions of *Hlas* (The Voice) and took a stand in favor of the concept of a single Czecho-Slovak nation. It also opposed the leadership of the Slovak National Party in Turciansky Svaty Martin, while emphasizing the need for the democratization of public life. Vavro Srobar, in particular, exercised considerable influence on this new group. Their periodical criticized Hodza and his close relationship with the Habsburg crown prince, and additionally focused attention on the Slovak labor movement.

In the elections of 1910, Slovaks fielded eight candidates, of whom only three won election, namely Pavol Blaho, Frantisek Juriga and Frano Skycak. Even Milan Hodza failed in his election bid. After this defeat, the Slovak National Party began seriously considering Hodza's suggestion that they restructure along the lines of an agrarian organization.

First issue of Slovak People's News, *1910*

In 1910, Slovak populists (the People's Party) transferred their official organ, *The People's News*, from Skalica to Bratislava and changed its name to *The Slovak People's News*. Their dissatisfaction with the Slovak National Party, which

165

was supposedly being overrun by liberals and Lutherans, grew deeper. Sharp polemics began firing back and forth between the *Slovak People's News* and the *National News*. The *Slovak People's News* also attacked *Labor News* and socialist ideas in general, and criticized Czech-Slovak cooperation, adopting a firm stance in favor of the idea of a distinct and autonomous Slovak nation.

These antagonisms eventually led to the dissolution of the political ties between the adherents of the Slovak National Party and the Slovak People's Party, and the proclamation of an 'independent' Slovak People's Party. This took place in Zilina, on July 29, 1913. Andrej Hlinka became its leader with Ferdis Juriga and Frantisek Skycak, his closest collaborators.

In 1911, official ties were established between the Slovak National Party and Czecho-Slovak Unity. Starting in 1912, the meetings in Luhacovice began dealing mainly with economic matters. A national economic committee was organized, with the mission of attracting Czech capital to Slovakia. In 1913, there was also talk of founding a special Slovak preparatory school in a city of Bohemia or Moravia. But in spite of all the positive effects of the Luhacovice meetings, it should be remembered that the Czech assistance to Slovakia stemming from these meetings was given in the name of a single Czecho-Slovak nation, and that this idea was favored by many Slovak intellectuals.[25]

In view of the fact that from 1913 on, there were two nationally oriented parties in Slovakia, plus the Social Democrats, Matus Dula, who became leader of the National Party after the death of Pavol Mudron in the summer of 1914, proposed the establishment of a Slovak National Council – a coordinating body for Slovak policy. The Nationalists discussed this proposal with the Social Democrats, but People's Party members had no intention of cooperating with socialists, and in August 1914, the First World War broke out, side-tracking any substantial moves in this direction.

Austria-Hungary declared war on Serbia because Serbia was unwilling to allow investigation into the circumstances of the assassination of the Crown Prince and Archduke Franz Ferdinand in Sarajevo. But Germany was eager to fight to settle old scores with France and Russia. Hungary, too, like the other countries which became belligerents, was caught up in this war fever, while in Slovak villages fanatics ran about crying out in Magyar, "Eljen a haboru!" (Long live war!). All parties were convinced that the war would last only a few weeks; in fact it lasted four long years. Millions died, among them thousands of Slovaks.[26]

During the war, political activity on the home front subsided: the last diet elections were held in 1910. With the outbreak of hostilities martial law was declared, press censorship tightened, suspect politicians placed under surveillance, some newspapers shut down completely, others reduced to limited edi-

Emperor Franz Josef, announcing outbreak of war (WWI)

tions, while 3.8 million Hungarians enlisted in the military, and twenty three billion Hungarian crowns were spent on war. Labor shortages occurred, grain production fell off, inflation set in, consumer goods disappeared from the shelves, material and equipment of all kinds was requisitioned for the front. Northeast Slovakia was immediately occupied by Russian troops, who in the winter of 1914–15 took Humenne, Michalovce and Stropkov. The war steadily expanded and in 1917, the United States entered the fray as well.

At the end of May 1917, Czech deputies in the Viennese Imperial Council submitted a declaration proposing a union of the Czechs and Slovaks in a federated Habsburg Monarchy. Meanwhile, plans for the future of the Czechs and Slovaks were being laid outside the Monarchy; in the midst of hostilities, Tomas Garrigue Masaryk, a Czech professor and author, had moved abroad and begun a struggle for a joint state. In 1916, together with a Slovak, Milan Rastislav Stefanik (a French citizen and leading scholar) and a Czech, Edward Benes (a prominent politician), Masaryk created a Czech National Council in Paris, which was shortly renamed the Czecho-Slovak National Council. Furthermore, in Russia after the February 1917 Bolshevik revolution, the so-called Provisional Government there approved formation of a Czecho-Slovak military force of prisoners of war, who numbered approximately 350,000, including about 20,000 Slovaks.[27]

Shortly after its founding, the Czecho-Slovak National Council in Paris established contact with the American Slovak League, which in turn proceeded to work up a joint cooperative program with its American counterpart, the Czech

167

National Association. Out of this cooperation sprang the Cleveland Pact, in which both parties agreed to work for a future federative union of Czechs and Slovaks, with full autonomy for Slovakia.[28]

Having briefly described the first fraternal societies of the American Slovaks and introduced their first leaders, we have paid them scant attention. However, to give them their due, they were not indifferent observers of events in Hungary. Among other things, they sent the Hungarian Government a memorandum protesting persecution of Slovak leaders. And on May 26, 1907, at the initiative of a Slovak emigre named Anton Bielik, they formed an umbrella organization, the Slovak League of America, of which the first presidents were prominent Slovak immigrants Furdek, Rovnianek and Mamatey, respectively.

The Magyars were well aware of the danger posed by organized and well-heeled American Slovaks, but it was beyond their reach to affect.[29] Indeed, Slovaks prepared very unpleasant receptions for Magyar politicians who visited the United States, particularly for leading Magyar politician A. Apponyi in the years 1904 and 1911.[30]

Many American Slovaks achieved substantial success in their new homeland, for instance Michal Bosak, a native of Okruhle in Saris County, who worked his way up from mine laborer to owner of three prosperous banks. Indeed, before the war there were nine Slovak banks in the United States, seven of them in Pennsylvania,[31] holding savings of Slovak immigrants. And American Slovaks, printing

M. R. Stefanik,
with representatives
of Slovaks and Czechs
in America

their own periodicals and literature, were able to disseminate them in Slovakia over government censorship.

As the end of the war drew near, France and Britain became reconciled to the idea that the Austro-Hungarian Monarchy was doomed. The American president Woodrow Wilson concurred, declaring a policy of self-determination for the

Manifest of Czecho-Slovak National Council, by M. R. Stefanik

nations of that monarchy. Indeed, even the Bolshevik regime in Russia proclaimed the right of self-determination for nations. The concept of a Czecho-Slovak state became more and more plausible. Slovak politicians, in May Day festivities in Liptovsky Svaty Mikulas, declared common cause with the Czechs through their spokesman, Vavro Srobar. In an ad hoc meeting of Slovak politi-

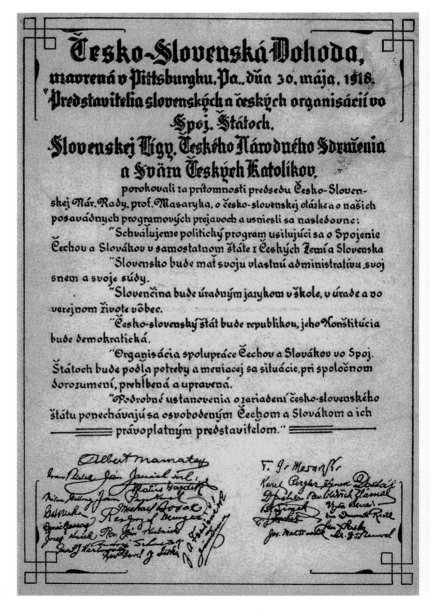

Text of Pittsburgh Pact

170

cians on May 24, 1918, Andrej Hlinka, as leader of the Slovak People's Party, spoke in favor of such a state, though Milan Hodza still clung to the hope of salvaging the Hungarian state.

In the meantime, Tomas G. Masaryk, as representative of the Czecho-Slovak National Council, signed the well-known Pittsburgh Pact, an accord with Slovak activists in the United States, which ratified the previous such agreement between American Czech and Slovak organizations signed in Cleveland in 1915.[32] The Czecho-Slovak National Council was recognized as representative of the projected state by France on June 29, 1918, by Britain on August 9, by the United States on September 3, and by Italy on October 3. On November 3, 1918, as Austro-Hungary was capitulating after suffering defeat at Piava, Italy, the independent state of Czecho-Slovakia was already several days old.

The population of Slovakia continued to be predominantly rural, living from the land on relatively small family farms. According to official statistics in 1869, farmers with less than five acres in Slovak counties represented as much as 58.2% of all farm owners. These were the people who under feudalism had been called 'zeliari', cultivators of small home gardens; of the rest, 26.4% owned 5 to 15 acres; 9.5% owned 15 to 30 acres, and only 1.27%, with holdings of 30 to 100 acres, could be considered rich farmers or estate owners. The first group comprized a total of 103,793 homesteads, the second 132,609, while the third and fourth groups combined, numbered 47,665. Only the last group owned sizeable or extensive estates.

At the end of the 19th Century (1896), statistics listed 9.44% of the population as landless, 11.53 % with less than 1.5 acres, 31.1% with 1.5 to 5 acres, 21.26% with 5 to 10 acres, 16.9% with 10 to 20 acres, and 7.6% with 20 to 50 acres. There were 1,529 estate owners with 100 to 200 acres, 768 with 200 to 500 acres, and 806 with more than 1,000 acres.

The division of land in Slovakia was extremely uneven: there were relatively few rich estate owners, compared to the many poor farmers who needed to supplement their farm yield by labor for hire.

In 1890, there were 275,603 farms in Slovakia, but as many as 108,588 indentured servants (obligated for one year), and 200,645 agricultural day laborers. There were, of course, considerable variations in this respect in the individual counties, but agricultural land constituted everywhere about 60% of all land. Slovakia was therefore essentially a country of small farms and large landed estates. The problem of farmers who had permanently leased their land from former feudal lords remained unresolved for fifty long years, to be finally addressed in 1896 by a law which required a farmer to pay a purchase price equal to twenty times his annual obligation for title to his land. But this buy-out could only be achieved if the former serf could prove that his forefathers had occupied the land in question, and had worked it prior to the year 1848, and that their lease had been permanent. Assistance from the state was available in the form of loans over a 20 year time-span at 5% interest. This plan had already helped former vineyard workers to acquire land.

Owing to the poor quality of most of their land, Slovak farmers had difficulty cultivating grains, particularly wheat, but they successfully raised livestock, particularly cattle. And in the second half of the 19th Century, they were able to clear additional acreage for plowing.

This land-clearing process occurred mainly in Southern Slovakia at the expense of pasture and hayfields. On the whole, there was an increase in the planting of wheat, fodder, barley, sugar beets, and potatoes. Lesser amounts of rye, mixed fodder, and flax were sown. Acreage of grain crops totaled 74% of all arable acreage in 1870, and 67% in 1900.

The number of cattle raised in Slovakia increased between 1870 and 1890 from 885,000 to 1,057,000 head, but the number of horses declined from 255,000 to 249,000, while the number of hogs rose from 425,000 to 640,000 and the number of sheep dropped from 1,730,000 to 301,000.

As to machinery, between 1870 and 1900, the number of steam-powered plows increased from none to 41, steam-powered threshing machines from 360 to 1,346, horse-drawn threshing machines from 666 to 13,192, mechanized hay

Though Slovak countryside at turn of century showed evidence of capitalist development, appearance of Slovak villages hardly changed.

mowers from 358 to 1,417, and sowing machines from 1,230 to 7,938. Of course, the bulk of this machinery was to be found in the southern regions of Slovakia; the northern regions experienced only a limited increase.

The evolution of capitalist conditions in agriculture widened the gap between large estates and small farms ever more. Large estates surpassed small farms in every respect: they responded quickly to market conditions and expanded mechanization as necessary, consolidating their advantages still more. Only the richest individual farmers could keep pace with them, and such individuals were rare.

Thanks to the founding of savings banks, use of credit and loans steadily gained acceptance. Between the years 1894 and 1909, the overall number of mortgages grew by about 165%, most markedly in Liptov County, by a whopping 330% and in Gemer County, by 280%. Lending at high interest rates, mostly by Jewish lenders, was driven off to the far Eastern regions of Slovakia. Land area encumbered by mortgages increased fourfold between 1894 and 1909. In 1895, Slovak credit unions alone issued loans totaling about 30 million Crowns, climbing to 70 million Crowns just fourteen years later, or approximately 20% of all loans extended in Slovakia. Farmers used credit to buy fields, livestock, fertilizers and machinery, and they began building brick homes instead of the traditional wooden ones.

Statistics for the year 1910, as displayed in the following table, give an overview of the size in 'jutros' (about one acre) and the number of agricultural enterprises, as well as the ethnic makeup of their proprietors.

Groups by Size	Slovaks	Magyars	Germans	Other
Owners of 1000 Jutros or more	1.7	84.8	13.8	0.4
Owners of 100 Jutros or more	22.3	54.3	10.5	13.0
Employees: 100 to 1000 Jutros	5.3	64.4	27.0	1.3
Owners and Employees: 50 to 100 Jutros	48.8	42.6	5.9	1.7
Owners and Employees: 10 to 50 Jutros	63.1	23.9	3.9	9.2
Owners and Employees: 5 to 10 Jutros	65.9	20.9	3.4	9.9
Owners and Employees: less than 5 Jutros	71.2	19.4	4.1	5.3

In Slovakia, approximately one third of all land was heavily forested and belonged to old established families of the upper nobility (the Palffys, the Andrassys, the Erdodys, the Karolys, and the Coburgs), as well as to Prince Hohenlohe and others. The royal family also owned a lot of forested land, as did the church and the cities of Kosice, Levoca, Brezno and Kremnica.

The birth rate in Slovakia averaged about 42 per thousand, but in the whole of Hungary, only 39 per thousand, in spite of the extensive migration of Slovaks to Lower Hungary, to Budapest, as well as the United States of America. People were also moving into cities, causing a jump in population in the years 1869 to 1890; in Bratislava, for instance, from 46,500 to 61,500, in Kosice from 21,740 to 35,580, and in Banska Bystrica, from 5,550 to 8,680.

In 1869, Old Hungary had a Slovak population of 1,817,228 (approximately 1,570,000 in Slovakia); by 1900 it had grown to 2,008,744 (about 1,750,000 in Slovakia). Statistics show a Slovak growth rate of 10.5%, while the Magyar rate is given as a whopping 40.9%. By 1890, the official number of Magyars had reached a total of 8,679,014, a majority of the total Hungarian population. These figures reflect the practical results of Magyarization, since the country-wide growth rate over this period was only 13%.

The effects of Magyarization could also be seen in the largest cities of present-day Slovakia: Bratislava and Kosice. If in 1880 the ratio of Slovaks to Magyars was practically even, by 1900 the balance had shifted against Slovaks: in Bratislava 1:2, and in Kosice, 1:3. The proportion of Slovaks fell in other cities as well. In actual numbers, the largest population of urban Slovaks lived in Budapest.[33]

In terms of employment, in 1898, 80% of Slovaks were engaged in agriculture, 2% in mining, 12% in crafts, 2% in commercial pursuits, 3.2% in white-collar and the free professions. By 1900, the ratios had changed to 68.3% in agriculture, a combined 25% in railroads, mines, crafts, and manual labor, 3.4% in commerce and 3.3% in white collar work and the free professions.

By 1910, Hungarian statistics listed 9,944,627 Magyars but only 1,946,357 Slovaks. In Slovakia, 1,684,681 persons (57.5%) claimed Slovak as their mother tongue, 885,397 (30.3%) claimed Magyar, 198,755 (6.8%) German, and 96,528 (3.4%) Carpatho-Rusyn. Jews named Magyar as their mother tongue. Magyarization made particular inroads in cities where manufacturing and railroad shops were located.

Emigration to the United States also played a role in the shrinking number of Slovaks: between 1899 and 1913 a total of 394,713 Slovaks left Hungary, averaging about 20,000 annually, but 116,099 of them later returned. Between 1905 and 1907, the annual average topped 40,000, many of whom, perhaps over 15,000, returned home in 1907 and 1908. And, as before, the greatest number emigrated from Eastern Slovakia. Before the outbreak of the First World War, Slovaks in the United States numbered about 600,000, or approximately a quarter of all Slovaks.

To a certain extent, this emigration precipitated a change in the religious complexion of Slovakia: in the United States, some Greek Catholics learned that their rite stemmed from a break with the Eastern Orthodox Church, causing many of them to gradually return to what they came to consider their original confession;[34] indeed, a feeling of Russian ethnicity spread among them. In Slovakia this movement began in the village of Becherov in 1901, but its major momentum was in Sub-Carpathia. Magyarization had enjoyed greater success there than in Slovakia, because the Rusyns had not yet codified their literary language and vacillated between their own dialect, Ukrainian and Russian.

On the whole, the situation in Slovakia was characterized by illiteracy because in 1880, only 35% of the population knew how to read and write; by the end of the century, the average still hovered around 50%. The average life span of an individual ranged between forty and fifty years. In 1873, a cholera epidemic killed about 170,000 people in Slovakia. Various forms of typhus, small-pox and diphtheria were common, tuberculosis was rampant, and rickets afflict-ed children. Medical care was concentrated in cities: in the country there was only one doctor for every 75,000 inhabitants, one trained midwife for every fifty thousand persons, and one pharmacy for every 150,000 people. After the cholera epidemic, Hungarian authorities were forced to pay greater attention to public health; they succeeded in lowering infant mortality by 30%, but it still remained very high. Indeed, between 1900 and 1914, every fifth newborn child died, and in 1910, infectious disease accounted for one quarter of all deaths. At the turn of the century there were 48 hospitals in Slovakia with 3,450 beds, the largest being in Bratislava and Trnava.

In spite of the fact that after the Compromise, political power in Hungary remained in the hands of the landed gentry, capitalism began to make inroads in the country's economy, as evidenced mainly by the building of railroads and establishment of financial institutions (banks).

*Kosice-Bohumin
rail line*

175

By the end of 1873, 4,091 kilometers of railroad track had been laid in the whole of Hungary, of which only 891 were in Slovakia. The pace of construction greatly accelerated in the 1890s so that by 1900, the rail network had increased to 14,153 kilometers, 2600 of them in Slovakia. At this point, the rail network was essentially complete. Originally, railroads had been privately owned, but gradually the state bought them out, and by the turn of the century the state owned 92%.

As concerns financial institutions, by the end of 1872, five new major banks had sprung up as well as 117 smaller banks and 206 savings banks, all with the help of foreign capital. And by 1873, fifty new credit bureaus had been established, but the financial crisis of that year closed many of them.

Slovak political activists encouraged their countrymen to establish credit bureaus and credit unions. Particularly agile in this respect was Viliam Pauliny-Toth. By the mid-seventies, twenty-four credit bureaus had been established, the most important ones in Tisovec, Brezno, Skalica, Klastor pod Znievom, and Mosovce. Of the Slovak savings banks the most important and soundest in terms of capital were in Turciansky Svaty Martin, Dolny Kubin, Prievidza, Zilina, Krupina. The same could be said of a credit bank in Ruzomberok.

In 1884, Tatrabanka was founded in Turciansky Svaty Martin and gradually evolved into a relatively sound financial institution, turning a clear profit of

Bratislava rail tunnel,
Vienna-Bratislava
rail line

50,000 Gold Florins (the rough equivalent of 5,000 Gold Dollars) in 1890. Other banks were soon starting up: the Myjava Bank in 1893, the Zilina Financial Aid Association in 1894, and the Tisovec Credit Cooperative and Savings Bank in 1896. In 1897, Slovak financial institutions started up in Nove Mesto nad Vahom, Necpaly, Trnava and Revuce, and a year later in Pukanec. Tatrabanka opened branches in Dolny Kubin, Senica, and Velka Bytca. As can be seen, in the course of the last third of the 19th Century, Slovak capital undoubtedly gained strength and was able to participate, though modestly, in the founding of industries.

In the 80s and 90s of the 19th Century, industrial and financial capital began to play a role in Slovakia, creating significant new investment capital. By 1873, one hundred and twenty four such new industrial stock companies had started up in Hungary, with individual capital stock value of at least 100,000 Gold Florins each. All told, these capital investments came to 65,000,000 Gold Florins, but people of Slovak ethnic origin played no role in establishing these institutions. In 1900, there existed 312 industrial stock companies in all of Hungary, with capital investment of 325,000,000 Gold Florins. Of these enterprises about fifty were located in Slovakia, with combined capital of 74,000,000 Gold Florins. Of this amount, 16,500,000 was in railroads, 16,000,000 in the Rimamuran-Salgotariany Ironworks, and 6,000,000 in the Pohornad Ironworks. Of the industrial companies with Slovak capital, the most well-known was the Cellulose and Paper Works in Ruzomberok, worth more than 600,000 Gold Florins. But the total capital investment of Slovak entrepreneurs could hardly have exceeded 1,000,000 Gold Florins.

After 1900, however, the number of industrial companies with Slovak or Slovak/Czech capital rose. They included a cement works in Lietavska Luka, a cement/lime works in Zilina, a sand, lime and cement works in Kralovany, a modern cellulose plant in Turciansky Svaty Martin, the Hungarian Paperworks in Ruzomberok, a cellulose plant in Zilina, and a plant for the manufacture of technical glass in Teplicka nad Vahom. The cooperation of Czech and Slovak capital was being forged on the basis of Czecho-Slovak solidarity, and was most explicitly demonstrated in the area of double loan discounts granted to Slovak banks in the amount of 11,000,000 Crowns by the Central Bank, founded mainly with Czech capital in Budapest in 1908, and the Central Cooperative for Agriculture and Business, founded also in Budapest in 1912. In Trnava, the Czech Agrarian Bank founded an enterprise for the sale of Czech agricultural machinery, and in 1913, the Consumer Bank was planning to found a Czecho-Slovak Business Company, plans that went awry with the outbreak of the First World War.

The Hungarian government did not lend support to industrial development. Except for the abolition of guilds and a declaration of free consumer enterprise, it was very slow to come to the aid of industry. And though it did play a major role in the construction of railroads, it was the interests of agribusiness and the large estate owners that dictated its policies.

Not until 1881 was a law generally supportive of industry passed; it provided fifteen years tax relief to newly founded enterprises. Legislation in 1890 extended this tax abatement to all types of industry, and freed banks from taxes on profits from loans to industry. A Hungarian industrial and business bank was established to promote exclusively the development of industry and the creation of new enterprises. In the 1880s, the government also began paying attention to schooling for industry.

The most significant industries in Slovakia during the latter half of the nineteenth century were mining and iron forging, which had acquired importance in connection with the laying of railroads. In the 1890s, about a million tons of iron ore were extracted in Slovakia. Slovakia's share in the production of iron was about 60% and it continued to expand during the first half of the 1880s. By 1899, production had increased to 270,000 tons of iron. Sixty blast furnaces were constructed in Slovakia in 1875, but only forty-three of them became functional. In 1881, with the merger of the Rimamuran Iron Company and the Salgotariany Iron-Ore Refinery, three new iron foundries were constructed, making the new company the largest industrial concern in all Hungary.

March 1881, Rimamuransko--Salgotarjan Stock Company founded, with numerous forging and mining plants in Slovakia

Industrial machinery was originally manufactured in plants in Vyhne, Kosice, and Bratislava, but none of them had more than 150 workers. More extensive machine shops for the manufacture of rail equipment were to be found in Bratislava, Nove Zamky, Zvolen, Kosice, and especially Vrutky, where a plant was founded in 1893 with 800 employees.

Mining for precious metals in Slovakia produced 375 kilograms of gold annually, dropping to 340 in 1900. Silver production reached 16,865 kilograms in 1868, but also fell to 12,790 kilograms in 1900. As earlier, extraction of precious metals was concentrated mainly in Kremnica (750 workers) and Banska Stiavnica (3,000 workers). Among the other industries that reached modern levels at this time were sawmills, of which 186 were powered by steam by the end of the century, employing approximately 4,000 people, but only two of them had more than 200 employees. Their proprietors were mainly Jewish.

In the woodworking industry, the most important was a furniture factory in Turciansky Svaty Martin, funded in part by Tatrabanka; founded in the 1890s, it employed 300 workers. All told, at the turn of the century there were 35 woodworking factories in Slovakia, employing more than 2,000 workers.

In the glass working industry, only two new plants were added to the 15 in existence prior to 1898, but the older plants greatly expanded production. By the end of the century the glass industry employed 2,100 workers.

In 1871, there were 47 steam-powered flour-mills in Slovakia, but 4,186 were still operated by water, which was the exclusive power source in the counties of Orava, Liptov, Zvolen, Trencin, Nitra and Gemer. By 1895, there were 33 large and 99 smaller steam-powered mills in Slovakia, but in four counties, water continued to power their mills. The most important mill was in Velky Saris, milling 30,000 thousand tons of grain annually, with a gross income of 3,000,000 Florins and 180 employees.

After the Austro-Hungarian Compromise of 1867, sugar refineries started up in Trnava, Sladkovicovo, Zlate Moravce, and Tovarniky. In 1890, a new refinery sprang up in Zahorska Ves, and another in Sastin in 1882, only to shut down after brief runs, while another new refinery was built in Pohronsky Ruskov in 1893. At the end of the century, six of the existing sugar refineries in Southern Slovakia merged to form a cartel, which produced 30% of all of Hungary's sugar and employed 3,000 workers.

Owing to Austrian and Czech-Moravian competition, for a long time only one significant textile factory existed in Slovakia, a plant in Halic, near Lucenec. It worked exclusively for the army and employed 400 workers. In 1868, an additional cloth factory opened in Lucenec, with 250 workers, in 1871 another one in Bratislava with 150 workers, and in 1884, yet another in Banska Bystrica with

*Thread factory
in Bratislava*

130 workers. At the beginning of the 1890s, a cloth manufacturer started operations in Zilina, producing woolen fabrics for the army and the public as well; it employed 800 workers right from the start.

In 1889, a Czech entrepreneur named Klinger opened a plant in Bratislava for producing wax cloth and finishing linen, and jute fabrics, employing 450 internal and 250 external workers. In Rybarpole, a suburb of Ruzomberok, a factory for finishing cotton fabrics was founded in the mid-1890s, with about 1,000 employees. It was the first such modern plant in Hungary.

Slovak entrepreneurs at this time enjoyed their greatest success in Liptovsky Svaty Mikulas, where six factories grew out of the local tanning shops, employing about 500 workers. In 1910, there were 199,157 people working in the industries of Slovakia, which was 35,000 more that had been employed in 1900, representing a growth rate of 21.6%. Of these, 111,860 were employed in light industry, 65,448 in heavy industry, and 21,849 in construction. Of the individual branches of industry, the production of clothes and footwear was the most developed, with 43,440 employees, though this number represented mainly master tailors and shoemakers, since only 4.1% of such enterprises employed more than twenty workers. Mining, iron forging, and other metal-processing plants employed 39,376 people, and food processing concerns, 28,205.

Heavy industry, including mining and forging of ores, stagnated at the beginning of the 20th Century, but metal processing, production of chemicals, machinery and building material, enjoyed a rapid development. In light industry, food processing maintained its importance, while the number of employees in the milling industry dropped off; but at the same time, the pace of development in textiles, paper, cellulose, and footwear quickened. After the

*Ironworks
in Krompachy*

economic crisis at the beginning of the century, modernization of industry accelerated and productivity increased.

In 1910, more than a thousand persons were employed in each of the following eight companies: an ironworks in Podbrezova (3,350); a textile factory in Ruzomberok (2,469); an ironworks in Krompachy (1,907); gold and silver mines in Banska Stiavnica (1,161); a clothing factory in Zilina (1,160); a tobacco factory in Kosice (1,123); railroad shops in Vrutky (1,089); and a sugar refinery in Surany (1,073).

There were thirty-two enterprises with more than 500 employees in Slovakia, of which seven were in Bratislava and three in other towns of Bratislava County; there were five each in Zvolen and Spis Counties, two each in the Counties of Trencin, Hont, Novohrad and Liptove, and one each in the Counties of Nitra, Turiec, Gemer and Abov-Turna. Of the 73,496 businesses dealing in consumer goods in Slovakia, 59.9% were owner operated, but only 1,161 or 1.6% had more than eleven employees. The working class, which was then in the process of forming, was divided into various sub-groups.

Miners of iron ore or precious metals continued to be considered members of a privileged class, whose mark of distinction was no longer just personal freedom, but the fact that they enjoyed various privileges (e.g. an eight-hour workday, plus health, retirement, and life insurance benefits from a Fraternal Fund). Their wages were certainly not exceptional, but they did provide a relatively decent livelihood, especially if the miner's family could supplement its income with cottage work. The Miners' Bureau continued to provide them, as before, with grain, legumes and other foods. Miners had a health plan, could not be arbitrarily fired, were exempt from military service, and, if they were home-owners,

181

they enjoyed voting rights. But it must be borne in mind that the well being of miners depended on the prosperity of mines; if ore seams gave out, miners had to look elsewhere for work.

As workers who acquired specialized work skills, they enjoyed benefits similar to those of journeymen in the trades, without a master craftsman's independence. They worked at least 14 hours a day, with an hour off for breakfast, plus another for dinner. The old craft traditions managed to survive for a long time.

The men with the worst work conditions were the railroad trackmen of the last third of the 19th Century. A relatively large number of men found employment in rail projects (for instance, as many as 12,000 in the Kosice-Bohumin tract). They were usually ordinary men from surrounding villages, but also miners experienced in the handling of explosives. Enjoying no social benefits, they worked long hours for low wages, without provision for housing, meals or sickness.

Laws governing industry, passed in 1872 and 1884, defined a workday as 16 hours, including, of course, lengthy breaks for breakfast and dinner; not until the 1890s was a reduction achieved in some industries to 12 hours, and even 10 in some cases. In July, 1891, Sunday was declared a legal holiday in all jobs except transport, iron work and work requiring around the clock operation.

Workers continually pressed for the betterment of their lot, especially in the form of legislated health insurance. The Hungarian Diet finally did pass health insurance for factory workers. Deductions for this purpose were not to exceed three percent of gross wages, towards which the employer was to contribute a third. Workers in all branches of industry began to form organizations to promote their demands and interests, seeking mainly improvement of work conditions, disability and retirement benefits, universal suffrage, the dissolution of the army, abolition of military conscription, and expanded political rights, to all of which they felt entitled. In my opinion, however, the call for class struggle and

Paperworks in Slavosovce

the abolition of capitalism, including the take-over of factories and other productive facilities, in fact, total socialist revolution, must be considered misguided; the
adoption of such measures as a political program by any society is regrettable.[35]

Still, it must be acknowledged that contemporary social conditions were
intolerable: wealth was concentrated in the hands of a few, with little left for the
poor; industry and agriculture had at last succeeded in producing a sufficiency
of goods, yet most people suffered hunger; the poor had few rights, and only the
rich and well-educated could vote. Yet surely the means of betterment were not
to be found in ethnic hatred, proletarian dictatorship and a one-sided approach
to the problems of a new era.

It was this latter approach that a segment of the working class adopted, following the ideology and program formulated by Karl Marx, a philosopher, and
his friend Friedrich Engels, an industrial entrepreneur. At the same time, other
thinkers came forward with differing options and solutions, some of whom may
be listed as follows:

Ferdinand Lassalle was the organizer of a Universal German Workers' Association in Leipzig founded in 1863, the first of its kind in Germany. He worked
for the creation of workers' cooperatives and voting rights, by means of which
a 'people's state' could be created and a transition to socialism accomplished
without revolution. He rejected the idea of a proletarian dictatorship linking
industrial workers and farmers.

Franz Hermann Schulze-Delitzsch was an economist, who advocated
a cooperative movement and harmony between industrial workers and the
bourgeoisie. He felt that private property ought to be preserved and the darker
aspects of capitalism eliminated by reforms. Cooperatives were to serve to protect small businesses from unfair competition by giant entrepreneurs. But in his
opinion, nevertheless, entrepreneurs needed to retain a right to exert political
influence on workers.

As early as the end of the 19th Century, Christian socialist ideas and a Christian socialist movement began spreading through Hungary, and consequently
Slovakia, but no extensive evidence of them is to be found.

According to *Encyklopedia Slovenska* (Slovak Encyclopedia, 1979) the first
association of Christian Socialists in Slovakia was founded in 1885, a regional
federation of Christian Socialist Unions in Budapest in 1904, and a Regional
Christian-Socialist Party in 1906. The latter had affiliates in Slovakia in the
cities of Kosice, Banska Bystrica, Nitra, Levice, Komarno, Trnava, and Zilina.

The first workers to make an attempt to found self-help organizations in Slovakia were qualified tradesmen. Up to 1872, the latter had had guilds to help
them in crises. With the demise of the guilds, they organized self-help groups,

to which they contributed dues as a hedge against sickness, incapacity, old age and the like. Typographers in Bratislava founded such a self-help society in 1867, followed by typographers in Kosice a year later, and by their counterparts in Turciansky Svaty Martin in 1870. Such associations are documented in other trades as well. In 1867, the numerous journeymen in Kosice and Komarno, and later those in Roznava also founded their own burial societies; retail business-men created a similar association in Bratislava in 1868, then in 1870 in Kosice and Dunajska Streda.

In 1869, journeymen in Kosice, irrespective of trade, founded a Self-Study Association of Trade-Union Youth, supported by membership dues to provide for education and sickness-benefits, as well as to assist traveling journeymen coming to the city, since the era of traveling journeymen had not yet come to an end. It is true that this association fell apart within a year, but its very existence demonstrates the desire to confront their problems.

In 1864, the First International was founded with the aim of uniting workers of the world, or at least those who believed in the principles of 'Scientific Socia-lism'. Its ideas penetrated the borders of Hungary, which at that time was not nearly as developed a country as England, France or Northern Italy, or even the German Ruhr Valley and Saxony, and thus did not yet have much of a working class to speak of. But even so, the first socialist association with contacts in the International appeared in Budapest as early as 1868. Its members included Slo-

Chorus of Bratislava typesetters

vak journeymen and others who were working in Budapest. Basically, they declared themselves 'Lasallists'.

In Bratislava journeymen tailors (actually garment workers), working for the garment firm of Mandl, plus several typographers, founded a self-study association called 'Vpred' (Forward), which subscribed to socialist ideas. Its focus was member welfare, but it engaged in political activity as well. On March 29, 1869, it called a mass rally of Bratislava workers, which included participation by labor leaders from Budapest and Vienna. The spread of internationalism was in conflict with the ideas of nationalism touted by ruling nations as positive values, but workers strove to unite the proletariats of all lands, regardless of nationality.

The Socialist movement became the object of increasing police interest. The situation came to a head with the rise of the Paris Commune in 1871 and its subsequent domination by leftist elements. The government in Pest, led at the time by Count Andrassy, called for a meeting of the Interior Ministers of Austro-Hungary and Germany, which subsequently took place in Berlin in 1872; the two governments agreed on the surveillance and persecution of the workers' movement.

But it was not only workers' organizations of socialist bent that came under suspicion; any associations that created self-help funds in the spirit of cooperation between employers and workers were suspect. A case in point was a company called 'Union' in Zvolen, in which workers contributed 4% of their wages to a sickness benefit fund, supplemented by 1% from the employer. There were similar associations in a sugar mill in Surany, a tannery in Velke Bosany, state-owned iron-works in Hronec and the Coburg ironworks in Pohorela.

At the end of the 1860s, the first labor strikes occurred in Slovakia, a not wholly unknown phenomenon in our history. After all, miners had rebelled more than once when they were not paid on time. But this time it was railroad workers, certainly the most exploited and oppressed of all, who resorted to this tactic. We have written evidence of strikes in the laying of the Zvolen-Lucenec rail line (1870–1871), as well as Kosice to Michalany (1871), which incurred army intervention in response to owner appeals. Striking typesetters were able to hold out from April to September 1873, thanks to material support from their organization.

1878 saw the founding of the first trade union in Hungary, which was organized by typesetters, and which included members from Bratislava, Nitra and Kosice. Rail workers, for whom the Transport Ministry drafted a decent benefit and pension system by the standards of the time, formed the First Hungarian Self-help and Advisory Association of Railroad Employees in 1876.

The first attempts to found a workers' organization associated with the names of Leo Frankel and Victor Kufoldy, occurred in the late 1870s. Frankel, who had played a role in the First International, was a friend of Karl Marx, as well as a former Commissar of the Paris Commune. Frankel founded a party of the disenfranchised; Kulfoldy founded the Hungarian Workers' Party. The two groups merged in May 1880 under the name 'The Universal Workers' Party'. This party's platform advocated the communalization of land and means of production.

But this was a time of economic prosperity, expanding productivity and the founding of various organizations of workers and qualified craftsmen, as well as of company sickness-benefit funds. In some cases, membership mounted into the hundreds. The center of the workers' movement on the territory of present-day Slovakia continued to be Bratislava. Vpred (Forward) published a newspaper called *Die Wahrheit* (German for 'Truth'), and its leader, Karol Hanzlicek, maintained contacts with foreign counterparts.

The labor movement grew stronger by the day, as did its socialist tendencies. On the July 14, 1889, the founding congress of the Second International convened in Paris. Trade unionism also developed rapidly, particularly in the latter months of that year. A number of trade union affiliations arose, with a broader regional reach.

A chartering convention of the Social-Democratic Party of Hungary met in Budapest in December 1890. Delegates from Bratislava and Vrutky were among its participants. The Party ratified a platform defending the interests of the proletariat and promoting education, "…in order that it might be competent to save all of human civilization from the imminent collapse of capitalism." The party was to strive to bring the means of production into the hands of society as whole.

At the end of the century, the Social-Democratic Party of Hungary was restructured into a mass party. Its strength lay mainly in trade unions, which had the right to send delegates to congresses. Its chief goal was the enfranchisement of all citizens aged twenty years or over. Party congresses were held quite frequently. By 1904, the party was holding its XI congress, with 665 delegates from 276 cities and communities, many of them non-Magyars. Besides Magyar and German, Slovak, Serbian and Rumanian were accorded official standing. Resolutions were recorded in all of these languages. In 1909, *Slovak Labor News* began publication in Bratislava with editions running to 2,000, but appearing somewhat irregularly. During the 1905 revolution in Russia, the labor movement and trade unionism steadily gained ground. On October 10, 1907, about 100,000 people demonstrated in front of the Hungarian Parliament in Budapest, and about 12,000 in Bratislava.

Slovak Labor News

186

Out of this atmosphere came the idea of founding an independent Slovak Social Democratic party. Its charter session took place in Bratislava on June 10, 1905, with 44 delegates in attendance from Western and Central Slovakia, as well as from Vienna and Budapest. Czech Social Democrats promised and, indeed, delivered considerable material support. The leading figure among the Slovak Social Democrats was E. Lehocky. Hungarian Social Democrats had little sympathy with their independent approach, the central leadership in Budapest vowing that it would accord them no recognition.

Social Democrats of Central and Eastern Slovakia met in Spisska Nova Ves on November 5, 1905, and founded the Social Democratic Party of Upper Hungary, which opposed the Slovak Social Democratic Party, labeling it Pan-Slavic.

By mid-1913, the Slovak Social Democratic Party had gained a foothold in thirty industrial centers of Slovakia and in their trade unions.

In 1909, the Social Democrats succeeded in scraping together funds to begin publishing the *Slovak Labor News* as a weekly, with considerable aid from Czech Socialists in posting the required bond. Ideologically, this movement was directed against clericalism, devoting its energies to opposing cooperation between Christian workers and their employers.

But the Christian workers did not allow themselves to be outdone by the Social Democrats. In October 1904, they convened a congress of Christian-Socialist associations, which were active in various Slovak cities. Their activities were directed in particular against the Social Democrats. But the new Christian Socialist Party was a country-wide Hungarian organization, in which, of course, the Magyars held the upper hand. In 1902, the most important Slovak Christian Socialist organization emerged in Budapest; it was an expressly Slovak organization, with Slovak as the language of debate. It is a fact, though, that the Christian Socialists, Populists ('Ludaci'), Socialists and Marxists never deigned to sit together around a single table to debate any of their common problems, whether before 1918 or after.

The leadership of the Hungarian Social Democrat Party was wholly Magyar, and the Party's Slovak adherents, in particular, strongly objected to being exclusively represented abroad by Magyars. To be sure, these party leaders were not as unfriendly towards Slovaks as was the common run of Hungarian politicians, but they simply did not believe that Slovaks could long withstand the process of assimilation.

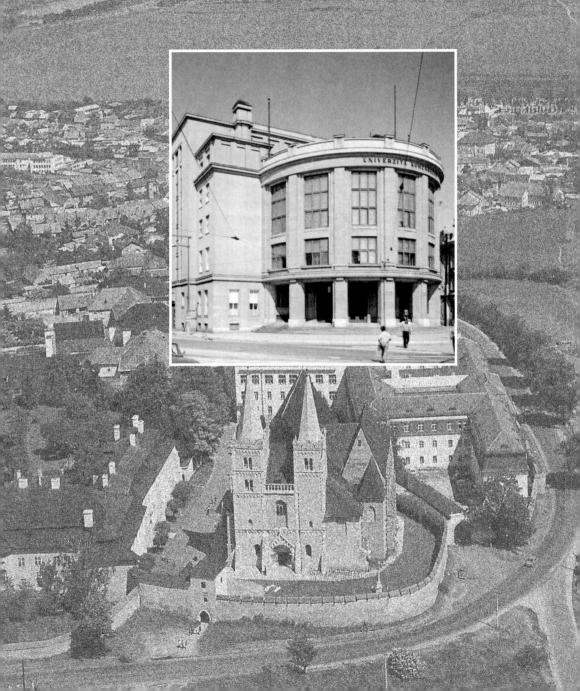

11. Between Two World Wars (1918–1939)

On October 28, 1918, the Czecho-Slovak National Committee proclaimed the Czecho-Slovak Republic to jubilant crowds of Czech citizenry in Prague.[1] The crowds tore down the symbols of the old monarchy and Austrian flags, and put up in their place the flag and symbols of the new republic. Two days later, the Slovak National Council and Slovak national politicians, meeting in Turciansky Svaty Martin, declared Slovak allegiance to the new state.[2]

Let us take a look at how these events unfolded and what they brought.

After Russia capitulated and Woodrow Wilson's Fourteen Points were universally broadcast, political life in Hungary began to revive. The Social Democrats organized a May Day demonstration in Liptovsky Svaty Mikulas which drew about 3,000 people. Vavro Srobar gave the triumphal address. Citing President Wilson's demands, he called for the right of self-determination for all of Austria-Hungary's nations, including the Hungarian branch of the Czecho-Slovak race. The 'Mikulas Resolution' became widely known in the Czech lands and beyond, and was cited by Slovak representatives of the struggle living abroad.

Ferdinand Juriga

This initiative also stirred activity in local political circles. In May 1918, Milan Hodza succeeded in renewing publication of his lapsed *Slovak Weekly*; likewise, *The Slovak People's News* (the organ of the Slovak People's Party) again appeared on news-stands, carrying the lively columns of Ferdis Juriga, a parliamentary deputy. These newspapers called for a revival of political activity in Slovakia. Only the Martin Center demurred to declare itself for the time being, though its affiliate in Budapest, led by Emil Stodola reacted somewhat more forcefully and pressed for a meeting of Slovak leaders.

A confidential meeting did take place in Martin on May 24, 1918. Neither Hodza nor Juriga, hesitant to commit, was present, but Hlinka, the leader of the Populists did attend and expressed the opinion that, "the Slovak match with the Magyars had failed; the time had come for a divorce and a new match with the Czechs". The meeting passed a resolution backing the unconditional and unreserved right of self-determination for the Slovak nation, and invoking on this basis its right to participate in the establishment of an independent state comprising Slovakia, Bohemia, Moravia and Silesia. The position of the Slovak National Party went further than that formulated in the spirit of Czecho-Slovakism by Vavro Srobar in the Mayday demonstration at Liptovsky Svaty Mikulas. What it amounted to was an unequivocal orientation of Slovak politics to a common state with the Czechs, a move impatiently anticipated at the time in Prague, from which Slovak politicians did not later renege.

Vavro Srobar

On July 13, Czech politicians, including Social Democrats, created the Czecho-Slovak National Committee, which was to include Slovaks, though they were not formally incorporated, since the Magyar government was keeping close watch over people who might transgress Hungary's territorial integrity. It was on this very charge that Vavro Srobar received two months imprisonment for his participation in the demonstration at Liptovsky Svaty Mikulas. The Slovaks were represented on the Czecho-Slovak National Committee by the Slovakophile, Rotnagl, who, together with Slovak politicians, set up a committee to act as liaison between the two groups.

A Slovak National Council was created at a meeting of Slovak activists in Budapest with twenty-five members, among them Andrej Hlinka, Matus Dula, Pavol Blaha, Ferdis Juriga and the Social Democrat, Emil Lehocky. Members of the Slovak National Party clearly predominated. The Council's character was secretive and conspiratorial.

With the middle of October 1918 events gained considerable momentum. On October 16, the Emperor Charles I issued a manifesto declaring the federalization of Cisleithania, which would become four separate state entities: German-Austrian, Czech, South Slav and Ukrainian. But as to the Hungarian component of his empire, he was non-committal.

On October 19, Ferdis Juriga, the only active deputy in the Hungarian Diet (Skycak had resigned in 1914, and Blaha was incapacitated by illness), announced that the Slovaks would invoke their right of self-determination and part with Hungary. His remarks provoked a storm of protest from Magyar deputies.

On October 24, the emperor named a new minister of foreign affairs, whose assignment was to renounce alliance with the Germans, and request a cease-fire from the Allies. The Allies accepted the overture and the Habsburg Empire capitulated, in effect exiting from history.

On October 23, the Wekerle government in Budapest fell, and the Magyar Democrat M. Karolyi created a Magyar National Council on which he welcomed Social Democrats as well. He called for elections based on a universal secret ballot and accepted the fourteen points of President Wilson; but at the same time he demanded respect for the territorial integrity of Hungary. On October 29, ten days after the capitulation, the Emperor named a new Hungarian government, with Count Hadik at its head.

Karolyi, who had become a leading figure in Hungarian politics, tried to salvage what he still could in negotiations in Prague, while calling for a complete break with Vienna. He also met with nationalities spokesmen, inviting Milan Hodza to Budapest and offering to create a Slovak Ministry. But he also played with the idea of a plebiscite in Slovakia, to be conducted, of course, by Hungarian authorities.

At this time, Matus Dula, the president of the Slovak National Council, called a session of the committee of the Slovak National Party in Turciansky Svaty Martin to confer official status on the Slovak National Council, as well as to elect an executive committee and issue a national declaration. The session was held on the morning of October 30 in the Tatra Bank building, which was surrounded by Hungarian troops. More than two hundred delegates came. Unaware of what was going on in Prague, the session made a decision to join the Slovak nation to the Czechs in a Czecho-Slovak state.[3]

In the afternoon, after the Slovak National Council had been officially constituted, it issued a Declaration of the Slovak Nation. It was mainly members of the Slovak National Party that were represented on the Slovak National Council, with Matus Dula as president, and K. A. Medvecky as secretary. Additional members were A. Hlinka and F. Juriga of the People's Party, V. Srobar and P. Blaho, and three Social Democrats, of whom E. Lehocky was named to the Council's steering committee.

Srobar had meanwhile secretly departed for Prague, where he arrived in time to add his signature, in the name of the Slovaks, to the declaration of the Czecho-Slovak state.

The Martin Declaration named the Slovak National Council the sole representative of the Slovaks, and demanded the right of self-determination on

Signatories to Declaration of Slovak Nation

the basis of full independence, as well as an immediate peace agreement. The Declaration had the character of a legal state document, officially dissolving the union of the Slovak nation with Hungary, and establishing a new union with the Czechs. It was officially delivered to Prague. In it occurred the term 'Czecho-Slovak nation', with which a significant number of the participants could not have been in agreement, but they offered no dissent. Why this was so is not clear; it might have been from the euphoria of the moment, or from a reluctance to complicate the matter in the court of world opinion. Other sources claim the expression did not exist in the original text. During negotiations with representatives of the Czech National Committee, and in a session of the Slovak National Council in Turciansky Svaty Martin on October 31,

OHLAS

Slovenskej Národnej Rady.

Bratia Slováci!

Public notice of Slovak National Council, 8 November 1918

Slovenská Národná Rada:

Matúš Dula v. r.,
predseda.

Karol A. Medvecký v. r.,
tajomník.

some representatives demanded autonomy for Slovakia, including a deliberative body of its own.[4]

In the new republic, such a deliberative body and autonomy proved illusory, not only for Slovaks, but for Moravians as well,[5]since the Czecho-Slovak government emerged as strictly centralistic, with all important decision-making vested exclusively in Prague. Czecho-Slovakia, it is said, was a marriage of convenience. But if so, the convenience was mutual: the Czechs benefited, too, by gaining coveted egress from German encirclement, there being as yet no Polish state in 1918, so that the path to the other Slavic nations led through Slovakia. At the turn of the century, the Czechs were totally obsessed by the idea of Slavdom. One of the most well-known Czech politicians of this era – Karel Kramar – even entertained the notion that a scion of the Russian Romanov dynasty might one day sit on a Czech throne.

In the Czech lands, Czechs and Germans did not live side by side very amicably, and so, when the Czecho-Slovak Republic became a 'fait accompli', the Germans assigned to the new state also decided to take advantage of the right to self-determination, and declared their own independent state (Deutsch-Bohmen). But before their state could begin functioning, the Czecho-Slovak army, arriving from Italy and France, occupied the German regions and annexed them to the new republic. Masaryk and Benes supposed that they had thus resolved the German question in Bohemia, only to have the flouting of German rights of self-determination in Bohemia and Moravia explode violently twenty years later as one of the proximate causes of the collapse of Czecho-Slovakia.

For the Slovaks, the union with the Czechs was an immensely important and progressive move, resulting in conditions that were people-oriented and democratic. Compared to the semi-feudal conditions that had prevailed in

Welcoming of provisional Slovak government in Skalica, November 1918

193

*Commenius University
in Bratislava,
founded 1919*

Hungary, they were a giant leap forward. The Republic introduced universal suffrage, including women, and extended compulsory schooling from six to eight years, with strict enforcement. It established an eight-hour workday, freedom of association and the press, independent courts, regulation of police powers and, of course, schools in the national language, from primary to university level. In 1919 a university had been established in Bratislava with faculties of law, philosophy, and medicine, and now access was extended even to women. A Slovak National Theater was founded, albeit with exclusively Czech casting in its first seasons.

The establishment of the Czecho-Slovak Republic brought with it a great renaissance even for ethnic Germans living in Slovakia. Before the demise of the Kingdom of Hungary, there had been only seven German primary schools and seven mixed German-Magyar schools in what is present day Slovakia, but by 1931, Slovak Germans already had 111 primary schools, 6 middle schools, 2 technical high schools, 2 business schools, and 22 vocational schools.

At the same time, the union of the Czech lands and Slovakia served to highlight the huge gaps that existed between the two parts of the country and the relative disadvantages they posed for Slovaks.

In the field of agriculture, individual Czech and Moravian farmers had long possessed three to four times the land acerage owned by the average Slovak. The breakup of large landed estates did little to alleviate this disparity, which was patently evident in the use of fertilizers, mechanization, the productivity of the land and the standard of living, all lasting up to 1938. In comparison with the

194

Bratislava, 1918

Czech lands, Slovakia lagged a century behind in yield per hectare and in profitability of animal husbandry.

Though Slovakia held 37% of the Republic's total agricultural acreage and 32–33% of its arable acreage, its share of the gross agricultural product in 1936 amounted to only 23%, and its market share was only 18%.

There was also a very great difference in development between the two parts of the country in the field of industry. The Czech lands and Moravia had at their disposal a mature industrial plant, having been the industrial base of the Habsburg Empire. Though in a Hungarian perspective, Slovakia had been relatively mature, its industrial level was nowhere near that of the western half of the dual monarchy. During the 1920s, 184 industrial enterprises sprang up in Slovakia, providing 7,003 jobs, but meanwhile 167 crashed, eliminating 13,386 jobs.[6] Competition from the more advanced Czech industries led to the dismantling of plants in Slovakia, with consequent increases in unemployment and emigration.[7] Vast differences loomed in the ideological realm as well. Slovaks professed a Christian worldview. And though birth registers listed the religion of most Czechs, Moravians and Sudeten Germans as Catholic, after 1918 these ethnics defected by the thousands, even tens of thousands, from a church they viewed as pro-Austrian (which in fact, it was).[8] In particular, Czechs who came to work in Slovakia after the change were often flagrant in their animosity towards the Catholicism, which more than 70% of Slovaks professed and indeed, towards religion in general. They were free-thinkers, admirers of Jan Hus, and atheists. The cream of Czech society, concentrated in large cities, belonged to

Jan Vojtassak

195

Milan Hodza

Masonic lodges which the Church condemned as hotbeds of anti-Catholicism. All this offended the religious sensibilities of the ordinary Slovak and deepened the already deep furrow of alienation between the two nations.[9]

The Prague regime, recognizing the religiosity of Slovaks, took care to get the Pope to appoint Slovak bishops as soon as possible and to dismiss Magyar prelates. The first new Slovak bishops, Vojtasak, Kmetko and Blaho, were consecrated in 1921, initiating a gradual conversion of the whole episcopal corps in Slovakia to Slovak.

Czech culture, schools, literature, sports, physical education and other aspects of life became models for Slovaks, who zealously strove to emulate them.[10] In spite of the fact that in 1919 and 1920 certain people from the Catholic camp, meeting in Poland, tried to split the Slovaks from the Czechs in favor of an independent Slovakia, the new state was accepted by Slovaks as their own homeland, with which they had a positive, steadily deepening relationship. Of course, a significant number of Slovaks ever more vociferously demanded that Prague grant Slovakia autonomy. Spearheading these advocates of autonomy was the Slovak People's Party, later renamed Hlinka's Slovak People's Party.[11]

But Hlinka's party failed to win over a majority of Slovak voters to its platform of autonomy,[12] because many Slovaks were attracted to the strong agrarian movement of Milan Hodza and impressed by the positive things the Prague regime did for farmers, thus gaining their support.[13]

A majority of Slovak Lutherans also opposed autonomy. Prague politicians, perceiving Slovak Lutherans as allies against the Catholic majority, gave them preferential treatment in state employment.[14] Meanwhile, the continued use of Biblical Czech in the liturgy sustained the Slovak Lutherans' sense of fellowship with the Czechs.

It remains a matter of dispute whether the Slovaks were, together with the Czechs, the joint ruling nation of the Czecho-Slovak Republic, or just another nationality ruled by the Czechs, along with Germans, Magyars, Poles, and Carpatho-Rusyns. Prague policy maintained that there was a Czecho-Slovak nation and that the Slovaks were an integral part of it. It strove to advance this thesis in the court of world opinion as well. Even the first population census in 1920 recognized only the Czecho-Slovak nation. A factual ethnic picture of Slovakia in 1930 looked like this:

Slovaks ⟶	2,337,816 ⟶	70.4 %
Magyars ⟶	571,952 ⟶	17.2 %
Germans ⟶	148,214 ⟶	4.5 %
Rusyns (Ukr.and Rus.) ⟶	90,824 ⟶	2.7 %
Others, and unspecified ⟶	173,228 ⟶	5.2 %

No number is assigned to Czechs in the above statistics, but as early as 1921 there were some 71,733 Czechs in Slovakia, a significant increase from 7,949 in 1910. By 1938 their number had grown to 200,000.

Of all the Slovak politicians involved in the founding of the new state, it was Vavro Srobar who played the most active role. He returned to Slovakia from Prague as Minister-plenipotentiary for Slovakia affairs, first setting up headquarters in Skalica, then Zilina, and, after its occupation by the Czecho-Slovak and Italian armies on March 4, 1919, in Bratislava. In 1920, Srobar's commission expired and he was appointed Minister of Education and National Information (1921–22), after which his political career came to an end.

Milan R. Stefanik

The most significant Slovak politician and statesman in Czecho-Slovakia between 1918 and 1938 was Milan Hodza, who in 1919–20, and again in 1922–27, was Minister of Legislation; in the years 1922–26, and again in 1932–35, Minister of Agriculture;[15] and, lastly, in 1935–38 Prime Minister. For a short period in 1936 he was also Minister for Foreign Affairs.

After 1918, Hodza achieved his dream to become head of the agrarian movement in Slovakia. By 1920, he had become vice-president of the National Committee of the Agrarian Party, and was, for its whole duration, a parliamentary deputy of the party officially named The Republican Party of Agriculture and Small Farmers. He was also a member of the International Agrarian Bureau.

As Prime Minister, Hodza was well aware that Czecho-Slovakia's fate was sealed by President Benes's reluctance to grant certain rights to the Sudeten Germans, leaving no alternative but capitulation to Hitler.[16]

After the 1938 Munich betrayal, Hodza exiled himself to France, where he founded the Slovak National Council and became its first president. But he parted company with the exiled Czecho-Slovak government in London, turning down the post of vice-president of the National Council, which Benes offered to him. When France fell, he moved to the United States, where he advanced the idea of a federation of Danubian nations. By this time he had grasped the significance of an independent Slovak state for Slovakia's future, but did not live to see the end of the war.

Immediately after the founding of Czecho-Slovakia, Benes commissioned Hodza as Czecho-Slovak plenipotentiary in Budapest, charged with the demarcation of the Southern border of Slovakia. In negotiations with the Magyar representatives, Hodza recommended that the border follow the course of the Little Danube, thus excluding the cities of Bratislava and Kosice. But Benes, as Minister for Foreign Affairs, intervened and was able to push through the border in its eventual form.

The first year of Czecho-Slovakia was marred by the tragic death of Milan Rastislav Stefanik, when his aircraft crashed near Bratislava on May 4, 1919.

*Monument at grave of
M. R. Stefanik, Bradlo*

The circumstances of the crash were suspect, since by some reports, the airplane was fired upon. Stefanik at the time was already a very sick man. Furthermore, in the weeks preceding his death, he had seriously clashed with Benes. Suddenly there was no room for him in the new government; for many, his French citizenship all at once became a huge stumbling block.[17]

In the meantime, Hungary was unhappy with the obligatory evacuation of Slovak territory: its army and officials had to be forcibly expelled by the Czecho-Slovak armed forces. Though the peace treaty required Hungary to leave by December 25, 1918, it was not until the end of January 1919 that all Magyar military units were expelled.

However, as soon as the Hungarian Prime Minister Karolyi resigned and turned power over to a Bolshevik regime, the latter made the re-annexation of Slovakia its primary goal. It succeeded in occupying a considerable portion of Slovakia and on June 16, 1919, occupied Presov, then declared a Slovak Soviet Republic, headed by a Czech Communist, Antonin Janousek. This Slovak Soviet Republic issued decrees nationalizing land, industry, banks and savings institutions, but it did not quite succeed in implementing them. Heading northeast, the Bolsheviks occupied Slovak territory all the way to the Polish border, but the Czecho-Slovak army counter-attacked, and drove them back into Hungary.

On June 24, 1919, a cease-fire was arranged and the Magyars definitively withdrew from Slovak territory. With that, the Slovak Soviet Republic ceased to exist.[18]

In December 1920, a general strike was called in Czecho-Slovakia, when the left wing of the Social Democratic Party attempted to seize power. In Slovakia, about 50,000 industrial and agricultural workers from forty-two districts joined the strike. In Vrable, on December 17, gendarmes shot dead three striking workers and a girl, but the authorities regained control and restored order by Christmas.

How did the evolution of power politics in Slovakia look in the years 1918–38? What results did parliamentary elections produce?

In the first elections, held on April 18, 1920, the Social Democrats won a resounding victory, achieving 50% of the votes, including 38.1% for the Slovak Social Democrats, and 12% for their German and Magyar counterparts, so that the 'Reds' at this time received more votes and parliamentary members than any other party in Slovakia. The Slovak People's Party, campaigning in cooperation with their Czech counterparts, received only 17%, and the Slovak National Party, together with the Agrarians, received a total of 8.9% of the votes.

Martin Razus

Five years later, after Hlinka, who had sat out the 1920 elections in prison, announced that 'Red' Slovakia must change and proceeded to expend an enormous amount of energy to that purpose; the Slovak People's Party (renamed Hlinka's Slovak People's Party in 1925) succeeded in winning 34.3% of the total votes cast, while the Social Democrats netted only 4.3% and the newly formed Communist Party of Czecho-Slovakia 13.9% – a combined Marxist total of only 18.2%. Meanwhile, the Agrarians won 17.4% of the votes, but the Slovak National Party did not even get enough votes for a single member. The National Socialists won 2.6% of the votes, mainly from Czech bureaucrats; the German-Magyar Social Democrats disintegrated. A total of twenty-nine parties fielded candidates in this election, and almost as many in subsequent elections.

In the elections of October 27, 1929, Hlinka's party received 28.27% of the votes, while Social Democrats markedly improved their tally to 13.7%; Communists fell to 10.5% and Agrarians to 13%, but National Socialists jumped to 4.4%.

In the last elections held before the war May 15, 1935, the autonomist block (Hlinka's Party and the Slovak Nationalist Party led by Martin Razus) won 30.12% of the votes; the Communists regained some ground with 12.95%, surpassing the 11.4% total of the Social Democrats. Agrarians made the biggest gain with 20.62% of the Slovak vote.

Andrej Hlinka

Magyar parties won about 3.5% of the total votes cast in the last two parliamentary elections.

Just as in the latter years of Austria-Hungary's existence, political life in the new republic was stamped by two extraordinarily strong and forceful personalities, Milan Hodza and Andrej Hlinka.

When Hlinka became pastor in Ruzomberok in 1905, he could hardly have foreseen that this relatively small town was soon to become an important industrial center. After the founding of the Rybarpole textile plant, which in 1920 was

the second largest industrial concern in Slovakia, and shortly after the establishment of additional textile enterprises there, its population increased sharply, growing from 6,878 inhabitants in 1890, to 14,220 in 1921. Thus Ruzomberok became the largest city in Central Slovakia.

Thanks to the efforts of Andrej Hlinka, Ruzomberok with its relatively large number of inhabitants became the most 'Slovak' city of Slovakia. Also, thanks to Hlinka's efforts, it did not become a 'Red' city. The Communists had originally earmarked Ruzomberok as their operational base in Central Slovakia; it was here that the Marxist Leftists wound up their congress when the police dispersed them in Lubochna on January 17, 1921.[19] From that day to the founding of the Czecho-Slovak Communist Party, Ruzomberok housed the secretariat of the Marxist Leftists; then up to October 1, 1922, it was the seat of the Czecho-Slovak Party's regional executive committee and secretariat in Slovakia; from 1919 to 1928, it was the center of operations for Slovak trade unions; and from 1920 to 1923, it was the publishing site of the official organ of the Czecho-Slovak Communist Party in Slovakia, *Pravda Chudoby* (The Poor Man's Truth).

The Communists, however, soon realized that they had no chance of winning the battle with the ascetic pastor of Ruzomberok, who knew how to stir up the masses and was unequivocally anti-Communist, so they moved their headquarters for Central Slovakia to Vrutky. There, in a city of railroaders and railroad shops, which was substantially smaller (only 6,807 inhabitants in 1921) and less important economically, they built their printery, Bratstvo (Brotherhood), published *The Poor Man's Truth*, and maintained their Slovak headquarters.

As leader of the Slovak People's Party, Hlinka worked out of Ruzomberok and fought vigorously for Slovak autonomy, which continued to be denied to Slovakia. His party included Christian trade unions which it organized in Zilina in 1920. These trade unions, which went through a number of official name changes, were made up of various federations, of which the strongest was the Federation of Slovak Rail Workers. In 1937, the Christian trade unions in Slovakia numbered 45,401 members.[20]

The Social Democrats also had their trade unions, as did the Communists and the Agrarians. In 1937, the 'Red' trade unions had a membership of 29,764, the Social Democrats 23,505, and the Czecho-Slovak Trade-Union Association, the strongest centralized organization of trade unions in Slovakia, 77,301.[21] The Republican Employment Center, strongly influenced by the Agrarians, had 59,192 members. In 1937, there were in Slovakia altogether 289,891 individuals organized in trade unions, i.e. 40.8% of all employees.[22]

The Hlinka party had its Christian Farmers' Association, which originated in 1922. At first, the association's headquarters were in Trnava, then in Bratislava. Agrarian associations of this type, however, were stronger than the Christian Farmers' Association. Still Hlinka's position in his party was unshakeable, and no challenger was able to make much headway against him. In 1929, Ferdis Juriga was forced to face this fact when he was expelled from the party, as were others later.

Even though Hlinka undoubtedly made substantial contributions to the Slovak nation, it needs to be acknowledged that there were also negative aspects to his political career. For instance, in 1919 he used a Polish passport to get to the peace conference in Paris, to fight for Slovak rights. But the diplomatic arena was much too slippery a place for a simple country pastor. Although some participants politely heard him out, it was Benes who prevailed, while Hlinka netted only several months imprisonment for his efforts. Even his choice of company for this trip was disastrous: F. Jedlicka turned out to be an agent of Magyar irredentism, who never again returned to Slovakia.[23]

Ivan Derer, co-author of Martin Declaration, Minister of Schools and Justice in Czecho-Slovakian government

No less unfortunate was Hlinka's association with Dr. Vojtech Tuka, who was sentenced to fifteen years imprisonment for high treason in 1929 by the Czecho-Slovak regime. Hlinka backed him fully, visited him in prison, and hailed him as a Slovak martyr. In the 1950s, though, when Magyar institutions allowed our historians access to their archives, documents surfaced which exposed Tuka as a Magyar agent.

Czecho-Slovakia's social democracy, the source of its prestige in international circles, was centrally organized from the start and dominated by the idea of Czecho-Slovakism. One of its leading functionaries was the Slovak intellectual Ivan Derer, who occupied a ministerial post in several administrations. Another leading functionary was Ivan Markovic, the editor-in-chief of the periodical *Prudy* (Currents) and, from 1926, a practising lawyer in Bratislava.

The Communist Party of Czecho-Slovakia got off to a relatively late start in 1921.[24] It took little interest in nationalistic ideas and recruited revolutionaries throughout the country, regardless of nationality. Among its leading functionaries in Slovakia were Czechs, Magyars, Germans and Jews. A leading personality among ethnically Slovak Communists was Julius Vercik, but he dropped out of the Party in 1930. Like all Communist parties, it was a branch of the III International and had to follow its directives.

Following the ideology of Lenin, the Communist Party was preparing to seize power by force. It energetically promoted this ideology, especially during the period of the party's Bolshevization after 1929, under the leadership of Klement Gottwald, who had been active in Slovakia.[25] The party stood on a platform of class warfare and was particularly active instigating labor strikes, of which there were 30 to 40 a year, with participation by an average of 10,000 people.

Typical wooden homes, village of Hrustina

Political and economic conditions gradually stabilized with emigration; there was no inflation in Czecho-Slovakia such as that which plagued neighboring defeated countries, and in 1927, production surpassed pre-war levels by more than 40%. But in Slovakia, industrial production stagnated and failed to rise to pre-war levels. For instance, Slovak iron production, which at the end of 1918 had represented as much as 10 to 12% of the total iron production in the country, dropped to 2.7% by the end of 1926. As many as two hundred enterprises in this industry in Slovakia failed. Industrial workers represented 56.7% of all wage earners at the end of the 1920s, but the overwhelming majority of Slovaks continued to subsist on farming.

The social problems of Slovakia were alleviated mainly by emigration. Between 1920 and 1924, a total of 50,000 people left Slovakia looking for work; in 1925–29 an additional 10,000 left. This time their destination was not just the United States, which had put limits on immigration, but Argentina, Canada, Belgium, and France.[26] Of the 324,000 people who emigrated between 1920 and 1938, about 104,000 headed overseas. Additionally seasonal migration was the fate of almost 222,000 agricultural workers from 1919 to 1938.

Adolph Hitler, German Reich Chancellor, January 30, 1933, with President Paul Von Hindenburg

The economic crisis of 1929 to 1934 hit Slovakia particularly hard, with industrial production falling by more than 40%. In 1930, there were in Slovakia 1,136 businesses with more than twenty employees each, totaling 255,364 in the aggregate, 90,247 of them in factories; but by 1932, 150,000 of them were unemployed. Additionally, the wages of those still employed fell by more than a third. Unemployment benefits totaled millions of Crowns, but were still grossly inadequate.

In the middle of the world economic crises Hitler rose to power in Germany. Like Mussolini in Italy, he took as a model 'a new type of party' and based his

202

power on a totalitarian one party state. He began by banning the Communist and Social Democratic parties, then proceeded to ban all the rest. He announced a platform uniting all Germans in a single state, a new German 'Reich'.

This announcement most immediately affected Germans in Bohemia and Moravia, since they had, after all, been annexed to Czecho-Slovakia in 1918 against their will. The situation in Europe was rapidly radicalizing as Fascists strove for power, for instance in Spain, with both Hitler and Mussolini intervening in the civil war that broke out there. The Soviet Union and Communists (including those in Czecho-Slovakia) rushed to the defense of the Republic, which increasingly veered into the Communist camp.

Radicalization afflicted Slovakia as well, which continued to be run by Czechs occupying all the most important official posts. Meanwhile, schools were graduating people who had never experienced Hungarian rule and had attended only Slovak institutions. By 1938, the first class-year born before October 28, 1918, had taken their matriculation examinations, but Czech officials in Slovakia were still running their offices exclusively in the Czech language.

The growth of Slovak self-awareness is reflected even in the rise in the membership of the Society of St. Adalbert: in 1921 it numbered 31,311 members, by 1935 its numbers had passed the 100,000 mark, and by the end of the Second World War, its membership totaled about 150,000. Membership in the restored Matica Slovenska (Slovak cultural institution) also rose.

Benes, who after Masaryk's resignation became the second President of Czecho-Slovakia, reacted in his own inimitable fashion to Hitler's courting of the Sudeten Germans:[27] he built strong border fortifications, put the army on ready-alert, extended military service, and forged an alliance with the USSR, although Czecho-Slovakia had been one of the last to grant it diplomatic recognition. Benes was convinced that, if he had on his side such world powers as France (and, through it, Britain) and the Soviet Union, he was immune to serious harm. Besides, he had the Little Entente to protect him against Hungary.[28]

Benes was unwilling to grant the Sudeten Germans anything, but he did promise Hlinka's Slovak People's Party to resolve the problem of autonomy, if it backed him in his bid for re-election. And so it happened that the second president of the Republic misled the Slovaks, as had the first.[29]

In Slovakia, the Magyars and Germans became more radical too. In 1936, the Magyar parties merged in the Magyar United Party and lent their support to the idea of Slovak autonomy. Together with representatives of the 'Karpatendeutsche Partei' (Carpathian-German Party), they annouced their decision to the aged Hlinka. The Carpathian-German Party had been founded in 1927 or 1928 and drew its support mainly from the Germans of Spis County. The latter were enjoy-

Principals of
Munich Pact

ing a period of national renaissance, but had not yet sufficiently overcome Magyarization to do without Sudeten German help.

At the head of their party was Franz Karmasin, a native of Olomouc.

In September 1935, a meeting of minority nationality parties took place in Prague, where Tiso and Hassik represented Hlinka's Slovak People's Party. These parties formed a coalition against Prague centralism though with little prospect of success at that particular moment, since the German Agrarians and Social Democrats were then entrenched in the central governing coalition.[30]

Benes drove the Sudeten Germans into the embrace of Henlein, whose party was an offshoot of Hitler's National Socialist German Workers' Party (the Nazis). Their leader was not wrong when he warned his supporters that they would never get any concessions from the Czechs. In the parliamentary elections of 1935 his party received two-thirds of all German votes cast, and in the regional elections of 1938, an estimated 90%, making it the strongest party in the Prague Parliament.

By the end of summer 1938, the situation in Czecho-Slovakia had deteriorated so much that in border areas armed skirmishes broke out between German insurgents and Czecho-Slovak troops. Hundreds, even thousands of Sudeten Germans were fleeing to Germany; German soldiers and officers were deserting from the recently mobilized Czecho-Slovak units. Hitler demanded that the Czechs resolve the Sudeten situation or face war. Benes, however, was at least as much a Czech chauvinist as Kossuth and other Hungarian politicians of the time had been Hungarian chauvinists; he was unwilling to budge and had no intention of giving up the presidency.[31]

*First autonomous
government of Slovakia*

As the situation became critical at the end of September, 1938, a four-power conference met in Munich, including France, Britain, Italy and Germany. Hitler, who held all the trump cards, played the leading role. In view of Prague's unwillingness to yield, Hitler demanded that the Sudetenland, in which more than 3.5 million Germans lived, be ceded to the German Reich. Such is the historical truth. That, too, was how Milan Hodza, the Prime Minister, viewed the situation, as his 'defeatist' government resigned under pressure from the Czech public. That public was guided, after all, by the philosophical legacy of the 'father of the Czech nation', Frantisek Palacky, which held that the main theme of Czech history was the struggle against Germans. Now, however, the time had come to fight with weapon in hand against a well-armed, well-trained and substantially stronger German army, which was, furthermore, guided by a more modern military doctrine than that of the French or its derivative Czecho-Slovak model.

To the general public of Czecho-Slovakia, abandonment by France and England in such a crisis came as a shock, catching the Slovaks completely off guard. After all, they had shown their willingness to live with the Czechs and reported for duty in the mobilized army, seeing Hitler for the gigantic menace he was as he led Germany and the world to ruin. They appreciated democracy and stood ready to rally to its support. But a considerable number of Slovaks, by now perhaps a majority, were no longer happy with Benes' intrigues, or his broken promises, or the concept of governance that he represented.

After the shock to Czecho-Slovakia, the leading Slovak politicians were no longer willing to wait on the will of Prague, and on October 6, 1938, in Zilina, they took it upon themselves to declare independence.[32] That was two days after Benes had abdicated and flown the country. Abroad, Benes portrayed himself as a victim of Hitler, totally suppressing any mention of his many political foibles and deficiencies;[33] Milan Hodza, on the other hand, recounted them diligently. But the world had its own worries and little understanding for the problems of Czecho-Slovakia.

The next day, the Prague government officially recognized Slovakia's autonomy and accepted a hyphenated spelling of the state name. On November 22, 1938, the Prague Parliament approved a law granting autonomy to Slovakia and to Carpatho-Ukraine as well.[34]

In Slovakia delegates of Hlinka's Slovak People's Party, the Agrarian Party, the Consumers' Party, the National Socialist Party, the Fascist Party, and the Slovak National Party, all signed the act of autonomy. The Social Democrats also offered to sign, but the People's Party rebuffed them, as it apparently also did Clementis and the Communists. But Slovaks were not fated to peacefully build the country in which they were now masters, because the foreign ministers of Germany and Italy had already signed a resolution in Vienna on November 2, 1938, requiring Slovakia to cede to Hungary 10,390 square kilometers, with 854,217 inhabitants (270,000 of them Slovak), including the cities of Komarno, Nove Zamky, Levice, Lucenec, Rimavska Sobota, Roznava and Kosice, with their environs.

Subsequent conditions in Slovakia could no longer be labeled democratic. All the existing parties merged into only one, which assumed the name Hlinka's Slovak People's Party. The Communist and Social-Democratic Parties were banned. A paramilitary organization called the Hlinka Guard was created, modeled on

Map of Slovakia after Viennese Arbitration

—— *border of Slovakia after Viennese Arbitration in 1938*

- - - *southern border of Slovakia till 1938*

······· *southern border of Slovakia claimed by Czecho-Slovak delegation in Paris in 1918*

▨ *territory surrendered to Poland after Munich and regained in 1939*

▧ *territory occupied by Magyars on the basis of Viennese Arbitration*

▤ *territory of Eastern Slovakia surrendered to Magyar state in 1939*

▥ *territory gained by Slovakia after the defeat of Poland in September*

■ *territory surrendered to Germany in 1938*

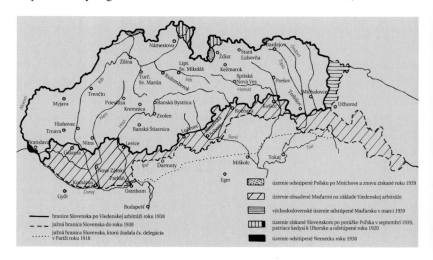

hranica Slovenska po Viedenskej arbitráži roku 1938
južná hranica Slovenska do roku 1938
južná hranica Slovenska, ktorú žiadala čs. delegácia v Paríži roku 1918

územie odstúpené Poľsku po Mníchove a znovu získané roku 1939
územie obsadené Maďarmi na základe Viedenskej arbitráže
východoslovenské územie odstúpené Maďarsku v marci 1939
územie získané Slovenskom po porážke Poľska v septembri 1939, patriace kedysi k Uhorsku a odstúpené roku 1920
územie odstúpené Nemecku roku 1938

analogous fascist party militias, with Karol Sidor as commander. Elections to the newly formed Slovak parliament in December 1938 were conducted with only a single slate of candidates, returning only sixty-three delegates.

When the Prime Minister of Britain, upon his return from Munich, waved a supposed copy of the Munich Agreement at the camera, he claimed he had preserved the peace, and though nodding approval, Hitler was already planning his next aggression. On October 21, 1938, the Nazis approved a plan to annex the rump state of Czecho-Slovakia, but even Hitler did not quite know how to assimilate the Czechs: the best solution would be for Czecho-Slovakia to simply vanish from the earth and with it, its complications.[35]

At the beginning of March 1939, jurisdictional disputes arose between the Prague government and the autonomous government of Slovakia. The Germans goaded each side on, urging them both to stick to their guns. When a putsch of Czech generals commanding military units in Slovakia erupted under the leadership of General Homola, the Nazis saw their chance. Hitler yearned to annex Bohemia and Moravia (both historical components of the medieval German empire). He fantasized about having the event occur on the first anniversary of the annexation of Austria on March 12, to make himself appear a far-sighted leader. But his wish came true just three days late.

Prodded by the Germans, President Emil Hacha dismissed the autonomous Slovak government, proclaiming martial law in Slovakia. Hacha replaced Slovak president Jozef Tiso with Karol Sidor. But when the latter refused to negotiate a resolution of the crisis with Hitler, the German dictator turned to the ousted Tiso, who had returned to his duties as pastor in Banovce.[36] Tiso accepted an invitation to a meeting in Berlin on March 13, 1939. During discussions, Hitler confronted Tiso with a dilemma: either declare an independent Slovak state, or see Slovakia partitioned between Germany, Poland and Hungary. Hitler left no alternative, but, when he announced his desire to create a protected German military zone in Slovakia, encompassing the whole Vah River Valley, Tiso got up from his chair and prepared to leave. The Fuhrer, however, challenged him to stay put, and the two finally agreed on a protective zone just a bit larger than the Malacky Administrative District. Tiso then rejected Hitler's suggestion that he declare Slovakia's independence directly from the chancery in Berlin. Instead, he telephoned President Hacha and requested that the Slovak Parliament be convened on the following day, after which he returned to Bratislava.[37]

The following day Tiso relayed Hitler's demands to the assembled parliament. Left without a meaningful choice, the parliament resolved in favor of an independent Slovak state, which it declared on March 14, l939.[38]

12. During the Second World War (1939–1945)

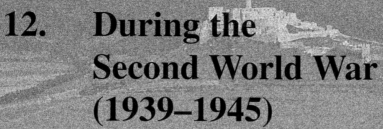

Hitler also had plans to destroy a third republic in Germany's vicinity, to wit, Poland. He was careful to secure his attack by signing a non-aggression pact with the Soviet Union. Finally the scythe struck stone. Britain, which for centuries had striven for a balance of power on the European continent, declared war on Germany. France immediately followed suit, and thus, what started out as a regional conflict, quickly grew into a world war, longer and more destructive than the First World War. Slovakia, in view of its geopolitical location, could hardly avoid getting involved.

As part of its planned attack on Poland, the German high command used the territory of Slovakia to station part of the southern German army group. The Slovak army on its part took to the field to recover those regions of Slovakia which had been ceded to Poland by the Treaty of Versailles in 1918 (thirteen villages in Spis and twelve in Orava County), as well as regions which had been annexed by Poland after the Munich Pact.

It makes no sense to try to deny that the wartime Slovak Republic was anything but a fascist state.[4] Political science knows only three types of modern state: democratic, fascist, and communist.[5] Democracy means free elections from a plurality of parties; fascism and communism exist in various permutations.[6] Furthermore, it is no use objecting to the characterization of the Slovak type of fascism as 'clerical fascism', though the term is of Communist provenance.[7] After all, the role played by priests in the Slovak Republic's politics was considerable, and at times, so inappropriate that even the Pope and Slovak bishops found occasion to censure it. In fact, the influence of the Catholic Church, and even the Lutheran Church, was so strong on public life that failure to have a child baptized, marriage outside the church, or a non-religious burial, were causes for social ostracism. The state even turned over to churches the schools which it had built during the First Czecho-Slovak Republic, and made religion a required subject in elementary and middle schools. What is more, the civil authorities persecuted unrecognized sects and their members; the state was to be run wholly on Christian principles.

Despite all of these negatives, the Slovak Republic did carry over a number of positive traditions from the former republic, for instance, an apolitical army: no career officer, commissioned or non-commissioned (or police officer), was eligible for party membership; no executive power was exercised through party channels or party organs; and even the uniformed branch of Hlinka's Slovak People's Party, the Hlinka Guard, was unarmed – weapons were held exclu-

Jozef Tiso

sively by the army and police. Furthermore, there were no instances of interference in court verdicts or the independence of the judiciary, nor were there any new arrangements for political prisoners, whether held without trial or subsequent to trial.

The Slovak Republic occupied an area of 38,000 square kilometers and had 2,600,000 inhabitants, 85% of them ethnic Slovaks, the balance being German (140,000), Magyar (65,000), and Rusyn (70,000). Administratively, it was divided into six counties and sixty-one districts, with administrators appointed by the government.

On the basis of official statistics dated December 31, 1938, hence, during the period of Slovak autonomy, its religious affiliation broke down as follows: 73% Roman Catholic, 6.9% Byzantine Catholic, 14.6% Lutheran, 0.6% Calvinist, 3.2% Jewish, 0.2% Eastern Orthodox, 0.37% unaffiliated, and 0.47% other. This census tallied a total population of 2,656,427.

The origin, existence and demise of Slovak statehood, i.e. the Slovak Republic, is closely tied to the name of Dr. Jozef Tiso.[8]

Jozef Tiso was a generation younger than his great role model, Andrej Hlinka, and like him, a country pastor. His parish, however, was in the town of Banovce nad Bebravou, which was much smaller than Ruzomberok, with 3,008 inhabitants in 1921, and 3,656 in 1940. There was, for all practical purposes, no industry in the town, therefore no industrial laborers. Unlike Hlinka, Tiso was not permanently settled in his parish house, because Slovak politics, in which he became heavily involved, required his presence in the capital city. Tiso was moderate and well-balanced in temperament, and suitably energetic, and he lacked Hlinka's explosiveness. But just like Hlinka, he was an excellent public speaker.

The Church hierarchy saw him as a talented clergyman with a promising career, and therefore sent him to the Pazmaneum in Vienna to round out his theological studies. There is no substance to the allegation that as a theology student he was suspected of Pan-Slavism,[9] nor to converse allegations that he was pro-Magyar in sympathies on the basis of articles he wrote as a young priest for Magyar Catholic periodicals.[10]

Prior to 1918, therefore, he was not yet a full-blown Slovak nationalist like Hlinka. As a young priest, he stepped immediately into a pastorate (1910), but as soon as war broke out he enlisted in the army as a military chaplain.[11] In 1915, he took a job as spiritual director in the seminary in Nitra, and at the same time taught religion in the local preparatory school in the Magyar language. From 1918 to 1920 he was a professor of moral and pastoral theology, and from 1920 to 1923 the bishop's personal secretary in Nitra. Then in 1924, he took up his pastorate in Banovce, but between 1927 and 1929, when Hlinka's Slovak People's Party joined the governing coalition in Prague, he was Minister of Health and Physical Education.[12] It was not long before he became parliamentary spokesman of his party, then party vice-president and after Hlinka's death in 1938, its president.[13]

For the duration of Slovak autonomy Tiso was Prime Minister, but, when it became the Slovak Republic in July 1939, he was elected President by the Slovak Parliament. Dr. Vojtech Tuka then succeeded him as Prime Minister.

Tiso considered his elevation to head the political embodiment of the Slovak nation as an act of divine providence, which is able to use ignoble people for noble purposes. It was in this light that he viewed Adolf Hitler from whose head the idea of an independent Slovak state had sprung at this precise time.

Since circumstances had shown that the Slovaks could not build their state within the framework of autonomy, but instead thrust independence upon them, albeit as a satellite of the German Reich, President Tiso decided not to gamble with the nation's fate by gratuitously provoking Hitler. He strove to avoid furnishing any pretext for gross interference in Slovakia's internal affairs, and up to August 1944, his efforts proved successful. The one exception occurred in July 1940 at a meeting in Salzburg when Hitler pressured him into dismissing Prime Minister Ferdinand Durcansky.[14]

On the whole it can be said that Hitler was satisfied with Tiso, and Tiso with Hitler. In 1943, Tiso received from the Fuhrer the Gold Cross of the Order of the German Eagle, but was unable to reciprocate with an equivalent Slovak award.[15] Hitler respected Tiso and trusted him, possibly because he was the only politician who ever stood up to him, as in their meeting in the Reich Chancery in Berlin on March 13, 1939.[16]

Jozef Tiso, meeting with Hitler, 13 March 1939, in Berlin

During the Second World War, relationships between small states and their powerful imperial neighbors were sometimes resolved in strange ways, as in the case of Finland and the Soviet Union. When the Finns realized that Stalin meant to annex Finland to restore the traditional Russian border, they declared war, without much chance of winning. Although, to everyone's surprise, things went well for the Finns in its early stages, the war ended as expected with a Soviet victory. But the Soviet Union then found itself forced into peace negotiations and a subsequent guarantee of Finnish independence.[17] Meanwhile it was able to annex the other Baltic states, Lithuania, Estonia and Latvia, without further ado.

The Slovak Republic had no need to resort to such desperate measures. The German Reich posed no threat; in fact, as early as March 1939, it signed a treaty of alliance with the Slovak Republic, guaranteeing its borders for twenty-five years.[18] This fact has to be considered a triumph of Slovak diplomacy, surely no consolation to Budapest. On March 14, 1939, the Magyars annexed Carpatho-Ukraine and, a year later, Transylvania (Romania) or rather its ethnically Magyar portion.

Hitler did not impose his political system, or even his theories of National Socialism on Slovakia. Though in the German Reich Christianity was repressed, in Slovakia it served as the underpinning of the state ideology. Hitler was satisfied to have Slovak representatives assure him of peaceful conditions on Slovak territory.[19] He apparently had fears, as reflected in German documents from early 1939, that, if provoked, the Slovaks might mount a resistance from their mountain fastnesses.

Jozef Tiso, swearing in as president of Slovak Republic

Tiso meanwhile did not trouble to reconcile German and Slovak National Socialism; that was the preoccupation of Vojtech Tuka, who was a sincere admirer of Hitler. Tuka let Hitler know, directly and indirectly, that he would certainly be able to do a better job of building National Socialism than Tiso, particularly after the new German ambassador, Ludin, was installed in Bratislava in 1941. Ludin and Hitler, however, were well aware that it was Tiso who enjoyed the confidence of the Slovak people, not Tuka.

Tiso adopted the title of 'Vodca' (leader) and now and then made an appearance in a Hlinka Guard uniform;[20] he used the fascist salute to greet members of the Hlinka Guard and Hlinka Youth as well as others who liked it. And though Tiso accepted German advisors in Slovakia, in reality he did things his own way.[21]

The Nazi leaders got the impression (and rightly so) that Tiso and the people around him were dissembling. Thus, for instance, in October 1943, the 'Sicherheitsdienst' (the German Security Police) in Vienna reported that Tiso was playing a two-faced role, enabling, through personnel policy, the exclusive hiring of people who were at the very least unsympathetic to the Reich, and filling top posts in his administration with individuals of an anti-German mind-set.

After the outbreak of the Slovak National Uprising against Germany, Karl Herman Frank voiced the opinion that the Hlinka Guard, the standard bearer of Slovak independence, had been shunted aside and weakened, and that Slovakia was being dominated by people lukewarm towards the German Reich.

The Slovak public was generally satisfied with Tiso's presidency and its handling of relations with the German Reich. He was not only a titular but also a genuine 'Vodca' (Leader) of his nation, a worthy successor to Andrej Hlinka. Thanks to his wisdom and discretion, the Slovak nation survived the war period with a minimum of material and spiritual loss.

No reliable exposition of Slovak National Socialism is available in official word or writing, or even in Tiso's public utterances, because all of those were vetted in the German Embassy. Views to the right of Tiso were expounded by the Hlinka Guard which published its own blustering newspaper *Gardista*, edited by the popular Slovak author Milo Urban. Also to Tiso's right were, of course, the Slovak Germans who were, for instance, unhappy that the Slovak Jewish Code defined Jews by religion rather than race.

Jozef Tiso was fortunate in that his two main opponents from among radicals made complete fools of themselves in the eyes of the Slovak public. Tuka, who barely weighed 132 lbs., presented a grotesque picture in his Hlinka Guard uniform and knee-boots, thick glasses, long white hair streaming down his neck, and garbled Slovak speech. The Slovak public was not convinced that he was a 'Slovak martyr' as portrayed in official propaganda. Rightly, it considered him a former Magyar agent, who justly deserved the long sentence he received on that charge from the Czecho-Slovak courts.

Alexander Mach, on the other hand, was a normal person and the good father of a large family, but foreign propaganda broadcasts, mainly from London, portrayed him as a bon vivant, who drank a bit much, kept mistresses, and had built himself a luxuriously furnished home on Jewish money. He was the frequent butt of witty jabs by the Slovak satirical paper *Kocur* (The Tomcat). [22]

Tiso and his supporters curtailed the Hlinka Guard by rescinding, after only two months, a regulation of September, 1939, that had prescribed compulsory membership in the Hlinka Guard for the age-groups 18 to 60, and in the Hlinka Youth for ages 6 to 18, and authorized the Hlinka Guard to run its own intelligence service, with input in security matters. This reversal substantially limited the activity of the Guard, making its membership voluntary and subjecting it to supervision by the Interior or Defense Ministry. In spite of these restrictions, the Hlinka Guard did its best to meddle in the internal affairs of the state. It was particularly active in the regulation of Jewish affairs and the transport of Jews to Poland.

The really major decisions in this small state were made in 'religious retreats', to which Tiso regularly summoned the Catholic clergy. Not a single lay person other than Tiso's personal secretary, Dr. Karol Murin,[23] participated, no minutes or written records were kept, and no priests known to lean towards Benes' Czecho-Slovak government in exile in London or Moscow were invited. It was at these meetings that Tiso's clerical supporters received their instructions on how to influence the public.

The German ethnic minority in Slovakia posed a particular problem.[24] Well aware that they dare not give the Germans any pretext for complaint, the Slovak leadership catered to their every demand regarding ethnic schools, publi-

Presidential palace

cations, and representation in government (not excluding parliament), etc. The Slovak leadership readily acquiesced in Slovak-German demands for the authorization of SS units, since these units would help to channel the excess energies of their most radical young bloods. The Slovak Germans had their own party, the 'Deutsche Partei' (DP), led by Franz Karmasin, which contained about 60,000 members – in effect, the entire German adult population of Slovakia. If a German failed to join the DP or enrol his children in the 'Hitlerjugend' (Hitler Youth), the default was taken to be an expression of opposition to Germany. The 'assault troops' of the DP, the 'Freiwillige Schutzstaffel', or FS (The Volunteer Guard Unit), wore brown shirts like their role models in Germany. They created street disturbances, terrorized Jews and, again like their role models in Germany, conducted themselves with the utmost arrogance, demanding the annexation of Slovakia, or at least of Bratislava and a so-called 'buffer zone', to the German Reich. Their actions succeeded in provoking a Slovak antipathy to Germans that had not existed in Slovakia prior to 1938.

But not all Slovak-Germans were Nazi sympathizers. The Christian-oriented ethnic Germans of Bratislava marveled at the Slovaks' success in building their own state and were supportive of them. On the other hand, German Communist sympathizers in the upper Nitra valley became involved in illegal activities and, when the Slovak National Uprising erupted, formed their own partisan units.

The Slovak government solved the problem of how to deal with Karmasin, the leader of the Slovak German minority, by appointing him head of the State Secretariat for German Minority Affairs, thus putting him in charge of all business relating to Slovak-Germans. Karmasin was authorized to participate in deliberations of the Slovak Government and to sit in the Slovak Parliament.

Janos Esterhazy (1901–1957), a scion of a well-known aristocratic Magyar family, represented the Magyar minority. As their leader and deputy in the Slovak Parliament, he criticized conditions in Slovakia, abstained from voting on the Jewish Code, and now and again directed scornful and haughty aristocratic remarks at it. His personal attitude and role in Slovak history are currently the subject of historical research.[25]

Janos Eszterhazy

As far as the Magyar minority in Slovakia was concerned, the Slovak government accorded it the same rights accorded the Slovak minority in Hungary. Both minorities were approximately the same size, at least on paper.[26]

The Slovaks who now found themselves in Hungary were no longer subject to the mercies of the Magyar authorities, as they had been prior to 1918. They felt that at least the Slovak government was ready to back them up, which lessened any sense of oppression they might have felt, and was an advantage their compatriots of Carpatho-Rusyn extraction, in a similar plight, lacked.

The Magyars and Slovaks living in the southern regions of Slovakia, annexed by Hungary before the outbreak of the Second World War, enjoyed a higher level of development than did the general population of Hungary, not only from the standpoint of economics, but of civil rights as well. Annexation to Hungary meant regression to the semi-feudal conditions prevalent there, to which they adjusted very reluctantly.

The fate of Slovak Jews, numbering about 85,000 after the loss of the southern regions, was extremely tragic. Responding to hoary anti-Semitic traditions [27] and to pressures exerted by representatives of the German Reich as well as domestic Germans, the Slovak government passed an ordinance early on 'aryanizing' Jewish property, pursuant to which every Jewish business owner was required to take on an, 'Aryan', partner. The latter was supposed to buy a 51% share in the business, but whether or not such an investment was actually made in every instance is highly doubtful. Though the Jewish owner of a business was permitted to pick and choose amongst 'aryanizers', it can be assumed that all kinds of pressures were brought into play in the process. Despite the fact that Jews were perceived as a foreign element in Slovakia, this means of strengthening the Slovak share in the economy can only be condemned as patently immoral.[28]

In the years 1939 and 1940, it was still possible for Jews to emigrate from Slovakia, obviously on government permit granted largely on a self-serving basis.

Beginning in September 1940, however, under German pressure from Salzburg, the Slovak Parliament conferred full powers on the government to completely exclude Jews from economic and other aspects of public life. Jews were stripped of all political and civil rights, their property confiscated, bank accounts frozen, and they were dismissed from government and private employment; Jewish children were banned from all but elementary schools, the public movement of Jews was drastically restricted, the wearing of a yellow star was prescribed and a labor camp was created for them in Novaky. On September 19, 1941, the Slovak government promulgated the so-called 'Jewish Code', Slovak Law no. 198/1941, which was thereafter followed.[29]

In 1942, German officials informed the Slovak government that Hitler had decided to create a special state for Jews on occupied Polish territory. (Coincidentally, Russians had already created such a special state for Jews in the Soviet Union.)[30] Jews were supposedly to manage it themselves and perform agricultural, trade, and other physical work there. This concept, with which the German authorities deceived other governments as well, suited the Slovak authorities well;[31] after all, Slovaks were accustomed to viewing the Jews as professionals, tavern-keepers, and businessmen:[32] the reversal seemed only

216

*Deportation of Jews
from Slovak Republic*

fair. In arranging this special treatment of Jews the Slovak government signed a pact pursuant to which it was to pay the German Government a resettlement fee of 500 Deutsche Marks per Slovak Jew transported to this 'special state' created for them. Of course, it did not pay in hard currency; the fee was deducted from Germany's huge Slovak trade deficit.[33]

In reality, and contrary to pretences, the Germans were building gas chambers and gigantic crematoria in the 'special Jewish state', located in Oswiecim (Auschwitz), Poland. When the Slovak government became aware of this horrendous reality, it immediately halted the transportations, but it was too late; thousands of Slovak Jews had already perished.

Meanwhile, President Tiso granted numerous exemptions from the Jewish Code, making it possible for some Jews to live a more relaxed life. We do not know the number of those who were spared in this way; reports vary from a thousand to 35,000 persons.[34]

It is true that after the Germans occupied Slovakia in August 1944, the Slovak Jewish Code no longer applied, because the Nazis did not recognize religion as determinative of race. Many Jews, however, did find refuge among Slovaks, who provided hiding places for them (in monasteries, convents, parish houses, in the mountains, in private homes, and all kinds of other places), where the Germans did not or could not find them. Motivation for this kind of protective concern was varied, including self interest: some Jews were able to pay, and besides, the war was winding down – a good deed could pay off once the front had passed.

In a public address in Holic in August 1942, Tiso made some very harsh references to Jews, labeling them immemorial enemies, of whom the nation wanted to be rid; and he made the assertion that they were being deported into a state of their own, granted by Hitler. At that time, he had no idea that the Germans would liquidate them.

The Slovak bishops, however, took a diametrically opposite position regarding Jews. They submitted five memoranda to the government in this matter, and issued two pastoral letters to the faithful, one dated April 15, 1942, and the other March 21, 1943, in which they demanded humane treatment of Jews, respect for their property, and regard for their family ties. They invoked the constitution of the Slovak Republic, which spoke of the right of every citizen to protection by the state, without regard to ethnicity or religion. And on November 21, 1939, the Association of Lutheran Pastors also addressed a letter of protest to the President and the parliament.

Bishop Vojtassak, whose diocese included Spis County with its many German faithful, led the fight for Jewish citizens.[35] He was courageous enough to admit to his seminary a Jewish student who did not convert to Catholicism until after his graduation in 1939. Meanwhile, relations between the Vatican and the Slovak Republic were unusually cool. Though the two states maintained normal diplomatic ties, the Holy Father considered Tiso's functioning as the head of state very problematic. [36] He was justifiably afraid of possible repercussions for the Church were Tiso's presidency to fail in some way. In fact, even before the war ended and the Soviets occupied Slovakia, Pope Pius XII severed relations with the Slovak Republic. Up to the time of this rupture, Karol Sidor had been the Slovak ambassador to the Holy See. [37]

The Slovak state, which originated so unexpectedly, neither through natural evolution nor by the will of the Slovak people, was recognized 'de facto' and 'de jure' by the overwhelming majority of European and Latin American states, but not the United States. [38] Its first government included only members of Hlinka's Slovak People's Party, not admitting even the prominent Agrarians Lichner and Teplansky, or National Party leader Vanco, but making an exception for General Catlos, who as a military officer was ineligible for membership in any party. The Ministries for Foreign Affairs and the Interior were both occupied by F. Durcansky, Financial Affairs by M. Pruzinsky, Economic Affairs by G. Medricky, Transport and Public Works by J. Stano, Justice by G. Fritz, and Education by J. Sivak. A. Mach was Chief of Propaganda.

A constitution for the new state was drafted and ratified by Parliament in July 1939, changing the name from Slovak State to Slovak Republic, and establishing the principle of primacy of legislative branch over executive, however

Karol Sidor

the former never very zealously pressed its prerogative, while Prime Minister Tuka took no pains to honor it. Confident of German support, Tuka arbitrarily pushed through the infamous Jewish Code, declared war against the USSR, and saw to the passage of other legislation, all of which were outside the competency of the executive branch, and were rightfully the domain of the legislature.

Alongside the executive branch and parliament there existed a State Council, invested with oversight and advisory powers. Its membership comprised the Prime Minister, the Speaker of Parliament, leading representatives of professions, ten nominees of Hlinka's Slovak People's Party, and leading representatives of the German and Magyar minorities. Additionally, the President had six nominees at his disposal. The State Council's term of office was three years, and its members enjoyed the same immunity from prosecution as did members of Parliament. Its competency included criminal prosecution of the President, Prime Minister and other members of cabinet, and it was empowered to propose legislation. In 1943, however, these powers were significantly curtailed. [39]

Alexander Mach, Commander of Hlinka Guard and Minister of Interior of Slovak government

One of the first tasks facing the new state was the creation of an army, which suffered from a serious shortage of officers, because up to 1938, the Prague government had been careful to fill the officer corps with their own (ethnic Czech) people. This shortcoming was solved in part by the activation of Slovak reserve officers, most of whom were teachers, which were in oversupply at the time.

As an authoritarian state, the Slovak Republic encountered considerable political opposition, especially from supporters of Benes on the one hand and Moscow on the other. To house recreants from these camps, it converted the old Ilava prison into a concentration camp, through which passed 2,800 prisoners up to the summer of 1944. This old prison was a far cry from the Nazi or Communist internment camps.

A Center for State Security kept track of political opponents of the regime, spies and the like. Its agents did not distinguish themselves by any significant originality; their target was by and large Communists. Hlinka's Slovak People's Party, as the only legitimate state party,[40] was able to achieve a remarkable increase in membership, growing from 50,000 in 1939 to 280,000 in 1943. Although the reasons for such an influx no doubt varied, it can be reasonably assumed that a good number of new members joined from admiration for the party's contributions to the successful process of state building that was taking place. In September 1939, Hlinka's Slovak People's Party held a convention, destined to be its last, as war intruded on the normal processes of political life.

The ideological foundation of the Slovak Republic was an emphatic struggle against Communist ideas, in spite of the fact that, judging by pre-1938 elections, a considerable number of Slovaks espoused those ideas. This support was sharply shaken by the Soviet-German pact of August 23, 1939, when the two powers curtailed their hostile propaganda against each other, and Slovakia, as a political satellite of Germany, had to follow suit.

The USSR quickly accorded diplomatic recognition to the Slovak Republic and built an embassy in Bratislava, staffing it with relatively numerous employees preoccupied mainly with gathering information about Slovakia as well as surrounding countries. Propaganda from Benes' London government-in-exile reached Slovakia, but the Bratislava government was not overly troubled by it; the number of people who still believed in a single Czecho-Slovak nation was steadily declining. On the other hand, the Slovak public appreciated the relatively good, objective information broadcast by the BBC.

In January 1942, after enacting various anti-Jewish measures, the Slovak government, unable to deliver its negotiated quota of 20,000 Slovak workers to Germany, offered to supplement them with Jewish workers. The Slovak authorities could hardly have guessed how readily the Germans would snap up this offer – not for the sake of the workers, but for the sake of additional fodder for their gas chambers.

Working in concert, the Hlinka Guard and the German-Slovak Volunteer Guard ('Schutzstaffel') quickly assembled a transport of young, able-bodied Jews, which left for Poland in late March 1942. The whole operation, involving 17,000 victims, was directed by the German advisor Wisliczeny, one of Adolf Eichmann's closest collaborators.

These transportations, however, soon came to a halt, because the hasty deportation of Jews aroused strong opposition from the Slovak public, the Catholic and Lutheran Church, members of Parliament, the regime itself, the State Council, and even the Holy See. The stipulated goal of 20,000 able-bodied persons aged 16 to 35 was simply not met.

To get the transports back on track, the Chief of the Reich Security Office, Reinhard Heydrich himself came to Bratislava on April 10, 1942. He assured Tuka that the transport operation was European in scope, already encompassing cooperation by occupied France, Holland and Belgium, and that after Slovakia, Hungary and Romania would also join. Heydrich promised that the Jews would be treated humanely, that they would be permanently resettled in the vicinity of Lublin, Poland [41] and that baptized Jews would be resettled separately, with freedom to worship as they pleased.

On the basis of these assurances, the Slovak government gave its consent for family members to join the transports. In this way 25,000 additional individuals of Jewish ancestry gradually left Slovakia for liquidation.

Meanwhile, however, the excessive zeal of Tuka and Mach in this matter provoked the resistance of the Slovak public, which triggered a constitutional amendment, no. 68, dated May 15, 1942, limiting the scope of Government Directive no. 198/1941. This amendment excluded persons baptized prior to March 14, 1939, from designation as Jews, as well as every Jewish person living in a valid marriage with a non-Jew contracted before September 10, 1941, and persons who had received or would receive in the future an exemption from the President or a member of his Cabinet.

Vojtech Tuka,
Prime Minister of
Slovak government

Some six weeks later, Adolf Eichmann, visiting Bratislava, also promised Tuka that Slovak Jews would be treated with utmost humanity. But despite the German assurances, the deportation of Jews from Slovakia was definitively halted. It is an historical fact that, from the fall of 1942 to September 1944, not one additional Jew was deported from Slovakia, and this despite repeated pressure from German authorities. The Slovaks demanded that they be allowed to visit deported Slovak Jews, and since the Germans found it impossible to accommodate this demand, the Slovak government found sufficient cause to cancel the program. The Nazi-prescribed solution of the Jewish question was not only discontinued, it in fact provoked a reverse development, which the German Embassy duly noted and reported to Berlin: additional work camps for Jews were constructed in Slovakia, holding approximately 4,500 people, while the remaining Jews went on running their 'Aryanized' businesses, mainly industrial concerns, or making their living in the professions.

In the spring or summer of 1943, when reports leaked out about the true fate of deportees, Jews in the Protectorate (Bohemia and Moravia) and in Poland received secret instructions to try to get to Slovakia. The main proponents of this course of action were Rabbi Weismandel and his eight co-workers, who did their best to influence Slovak authorities in the search for a solution to the Jewish question in Slovakia.

In the summer of 1943,[42] after the arrival in Slovakia of two escapees from Auschwitz, the Jewish Council in Bratislava did what it could to inform influential individuals around the world, for instance, Pope Pius XII, about this death camp. And after German occupation of Hungary on March 14, 1944, when deportation of Jews was commenced there, many Jews took refuge in Slovakia (as previously they had fled from Slovakia to Hungary). Indeed, it was from Bratislava that information was forwarded to organizations in Bern, London and Istanbul, which in their turn provided the Jewish 'shadow government' in Bratislava with the financial where-with-all to conduct rescue operations.

President Tiso was in no small measure personally involved in efforts to save Slovak Jews from the fall of 1942 to the fall of 1944. He put at risk the

221

very existence of Slovak statehood and his own personal safety by resisting pressures from Germany and from Slovak Germans, as well as from Tuka, Mach and their cohorts. His skillful maneuvering in these matters was crowned with success. But in the eyes of many, he was seen as guilty of the entire tragedy of the Slovak Jews.[43]

In the economic sphere, the Slovak government assumed a sad legacy of 60,000 unemployed. In an effort to come to their aid it signed labor agreements with Germany (December 8, 1939, and June 19, 1941). Slovaks continued to travel to Germany for work as late as 1942 and 1943, but because of deteriorating living conditions there and the bombing of industrial plants, as well as the increased availability of work in Slovakia, interest in German labor opportunities waned, except for farm work.[44]

Inasmuch as the Slovak National Bank had not received a single gram from the gold reserves of the now defunct Czecho-Slovakia, and gold reserves being essential for the stabilization of the Slovak Crown, the government appealed to the public for gold, with very gratifying results. I well remember how, when I was a boy, donors of wedding rings, like my parents, received in return a steel wedding ring, with the inscription, 'The Slovak State thanks you'. A part, however, of the gold reserve of the Slovak Republic came from Slovak gold mines extracted in 1939.

From its very beginnings the Slovak Republic faced hard times. The rupture of political ties with the Czechs resulted in shortages of capital, raw materials and semi-finished goods.

Since the Slovak Republic was a political satellite of Germany its economy was necessarily oriented to that country, with concomitant advantages and disadvantages. As early as May 1939, a fact-finding delegation from German industry visited Slovakia in order to make an analysis of the Slovak economy and venture suggestions on how it might be better integrated with their own, to the Reich's benefit. As much as 75% of Slovakia's exports went to Germany, Austria and the Protectorate of Bohemia and Moravia. The exchange rate of the German Mark to the Slovak Crown was set at 1:11.62, which was hardly fair to the Crown.

Unable to meet its import debt to Slovakia, or pay the mounting transit fees for moving materiel across Slovak territory to the Eastern Front and the Balkans in cold cash or goods, Germany accumulated a huge negative trade balance with Slovakia, amounting to about eight billion Crowns by the end of the war. This debt has never been settled, and the account remains open to the present day.

Not surprisingly, Slovakia was plagued by inflation as the total currency in circulation rose from 1.22 billion Crowns in March, 1939, to 11.64 billion in

March, 1945. Nonetheless, the Slovak Crown remained the strongest currency among the countries occupied by Germany and its allies.

Germany was particularly interested in Slovak raw materials, and in pursuit of these interests, I.G. Farben and Hermann Goering Werke took over many Slovak enterprises, while Deutsche Bank and Dresdner Bank made deep financial inroads in Slovakia's economy, replacing Czech capital, which had previously been dominant.

In 1942, the German share in Slovak stock-holding companies had already risen above 51%, while its share in metallurgical companies was 60%, in chemical companies 76%, and in mining and steel forging almost 100%.

In March 1939, the German Wehrmacht seized as spoils of war Czecho-Slovak weaponry and military supplies in Slovakia valued at several billion Crowns. Some enterprises and their stock were seized in the process of Aryanization. Germans also wanted to take over a munitions plant in Dubnica nad Vahom and Povazska Bystrica, but the Slovak government blocked their intentions. In January 1940, the Slovak government signed a pact with Germany on the war-time economy which affected twenty-five of the most important industrial enterprises, including the Apollo Refinery, the Dynamit-Nobel Chemical Works, various machine shops, foundries, and blast furnaces, as well as the two above mentioned munitions plants. German officials were to be given free access to these enterprises, with authorization to audit the filling of German orders and to arrange the transfer of work forces.[45]

The Slovak public was well aware that economic conditions in Slovakia were better than elsewhere and referred to their country as 'another Switzerland'. I doubt that the Slovak government had anything to do with concocting this nickname. German soldiers on leave in Slovakia, including Slovak Germans stationed in Petrzalka and Devin (annexed by the Reich) called Slovakia a 'Schlaraffenland', which translates as 'a fairytale land'. German diplomats from Berlin and elsewhere, who were permitted to exchange Marks for Crowns, made such frequent shopping trips to Bratislava that the Foreign Minister Ribbentropp found it necessary to remind them of due diplomatic propriety.

Official Slovak historians have explained the economic prosperity of the Slovak Republic as a war-time boom. But were not the same conditions of war prevalent in Hungary, Romania, Bulgaria, and Italy, as well as in the Protectorate of Bohemia and Moravia, without creating conditions of prosperity?

Slovakia joined the war alongside Germany immediately after achieving independence, not by parliamentary declaration as required by the Slovak Constitution, but by executive decree, at the insistence of Prime Minister Vojtech Tuka. Two Slovak divisions numbering more than 40,000 men were sent to the

Slovak soldiers departing for front

223

Eastern Front, where from the very first days of combat they came across murdered and often unburied corpses of Bolshevik victims, including civilians, and other such scenes of mind shattering intensity. They were able to compare Communist propaganda with reality. But neither did German claims that the war was about saving European civilization impress Slovak soldiers. They wrote home about what they had seen in letters that got past military censors, some of which found their way into hometown newspapers. They learned quickly that German troops were no better than their Soviet counterparts. Being able to interact more easily with civilians than German troops, Slovak soldiers often shared their food rations and made contact with partisan forces. Eventually, in 1943, a relatively large Slovak military unit defected and opened up its sector of the front to Soviets. That was the beginning of the end of Slovak deployment on the Eastern Front where more than 1,200 Slovak soldiers perished.

Towards the end of the war, the German Command transferred Slovaks to the Italian front, where they were no longer consigned to front-line duty but put to work building fortifications. There, too, many Slovaks defected to partisan units, joining the fight against the Germans.

While the Slovak Republic lasted, unprecedented advances were made in education, the sciences, and culture in general. As early as 1939, a Slovak Technical University was founded in Bratislava, having originally been planned for Kosice which subsequently fell to Hungarian occupation. In 1940 this university inaugurated schools of civil engineering, specialized research, forestry, and agriculture, and in 1942, schools of mechanical, electrical and chemical engineering. The first chancellor of the university was the well-known mathematician Jur Hronec, followed in 1943 and 1944 by the well-known hydrologist Stefan Vladimir Bella.

In 1940 a Slovak Business College was founded. Meanwhile, Comenius University (named Slovak University up to 1955) increased its enrollment from approximately 2,000 to 5,000 students, and in the academic year 1939–1940 it added a faculty of natural sciences.

In 1940 a Slovak Learned Society was founded, to be followed in 1942 by the Slovak Academy of Arts and Sciences with its various scholarly institutes and journals, modeled on the Soviet Academy of Sciences.

The theatrical entertainment sphere was expanded by the founding of new theaters in Presov and Turciansky Svaty Martin. Film-making saw the founding of a company called 'Nastup' (Forward), which produced weekly newsreels and made topical and documentary films. Movie-houses showed not only German, but Czech films as well, both old and new, including some from the Protectorate of Bohemia.

In classical music, composers Alexander Moyzes, Eugen Suchon and Jan Cikker excelled; in operetta and popular song, composer Gejza Dusik and vocalist Frantisek Kristof Vesely enjoyed huge success.

Painting was represented by some of the best compositions of Martin Benka and Ludovit Fulla, sculpture by the monumental creations of Jan Koniarik, and portraiture by the masterful characterizations of Frano Stefunka. The younger generation of artists (some only beginners, others already well-established), included Jan Mudroch, Peter Matejka, Vincent Hloznik, Jozef Kostka, Rudolf Pribis, Stefan Bednar, and many others. And Slovak architects displayed their mettle in the buildings of the International Danube Fair on the Bratislava riverfront.[46]

Many artists, like the painters Cyprian Majernik and Jan Zelibsky, opposed the regime of the Slovak Republic from the very beginning. In literature Janko Jesensky, whose poetry was disseminated in what would later become known as 'samizdat', was a dissenter. The poet Emil Boleslav Lukac continued to write, as did the prose authors Margita Figuli, Dobroslav Chrobak, and Frantisek Svantner without restriction. The poet Jan Smrek affronted the wary eye of the 'Ludaks' (Hlinka's Slovak People's Party), and, after the outbreak of the Slovak National Uprising, succeeded in bringing out his literary journal *Elan,* to which poet Laco Novomesky, a dissenter under state surveillance, had been a contributor.

The most notable author of the war period was Jozef Ciger Hronsky, who continued to support the Ludak cause but fled the country ahead of the front

The Unconsolable,
oil painting by Vincent Hloznik, 1945

and continued his writing in exile. The extraordinarily prolific poet Rudolf Dilong did likewise, and the painter and graphic artist Koloman Sokol, who had won international acclaim in Mexico, stayed there for the duration. [47]

As the end of the war drew near and Nazi defeat became a certainty, opposition to the Slovak government as an ally of Germany grew.[48] People tried to distance themselves from Hlinka's Slovak People's Party because broadcasts from the Benes government in exile in London and Moscow warned of the consequences for collaboration. The situation got so bad that every shoemaker who had ever repaired boots for the Hlinka Guard feared arrest and punishment. Officials began performing duties lackadaisically; local police stopped locking up people suspected of anti-state activities; agents of State Security, instead of arresting people attending illegal meetings, provided protective services; prison guards helped prisoners escape; and courts gave only mild or probationary sentences.

As a result, the activities of opposition groups expanded, becoming so widespread that the government intervened to suppress them, and in this respect, Slovakia ceased being another Switzerland. Cells of the Communist Party also revived, increasing their activities. (It helps to remember that before the war, the Slovak Communist Party had less than 300 cells enjoying support from only about 13% of the electorate.). As early as 1942, the Communists attempted to organize a partisan group in Eastern Slovakia with twenty-five members, eighteen of them Jewish. In 1943, a reserve officer, Viliam Zingor, refused an order to report for duty on the Eastern Front and had soon acquired an armed following, though without ostensible enemy, since as of then there were no German forces in Slovakia.

In London the Czecho-Slovak government-in-exile of Edvard Benes who, oblivious of abdication, was acting presidential again and becoming increasingly assertive. Ignoring a warning from Winston Churchill, on December 12, 1943, Benes signed an Agreement of Friendship, Mutual Assistance and Post-War Cooperation between Czecho-Slovakia and the USSR, the only great power of the anti-Hitler coalition that had recognized both the Slovak Republic and the Munich Pact.[49]

There was not a single Slovak in Benes' London exile government, since Milan Hodza who had also fled into exile, refused to work with Benes. Outstanding among Slovaks in London was the Communist Vlado Clementis. Benes continued to stand firm on his advocacy of a unitary Czecho-Slovak nation and made no secret of it. Supporters in Slovakia sent him reports that appeared to confirm the belief that Slovaks were yearning for his return. He was no longer of any interest to Slovak Communists and his political sup-

226

porters in Slovakia constituted only a minuscule fraction of the Slovak population. Besides, by this time, the younger generation of Agrarians, Nationalists, and adherents of other parties, including the strongly Czecho-Slovak Social Democrats, had been converted to the notion of an independent Slovak nation.

By this time, the Communists were into their fifth illegal leadership conference (the first four having been dispersed by police)[50] with Karol Smidke and Karol Bacilek, sent by Moscow, presiding. The democratically oriented opposition was led by the old Agrarian signatory to the Zilina Agreement, J. Ursiny, the much younger and staunchly Slovak J. Lettrich, and the relatively unknown M. Josko. Also aligned in opposition were a resistance group called Flora and the seventy-seven year old Vavro Srobar. In December, 1943, after prolonged negotiations in Matej Josko's Bratislava apartment, a Slovak National Council was illegally created, including Peter Zatko, General Secretary and Vice-President of the Central Association of Slovak Industries and later on, representatives of Social Democrats and Agrarians as well. Thus united they began to organize an armed uprising against the Germans and Tiso's regime.

Karol Smidke

By this time, all of Germany's allies were considering ways of crossing over to the enemy camp. Among them were elements of the Slovak army led by the Slovak Minister of Defense, General Ferdinand Catlos, who used his official capacity to mobilize two strong divisions and position them in Carpathian Mountains, nominally to guard the Dukla Pass. Placing in command of them the best and most popular Slovak general, Augustin Malar, Catlos planned to allow free passage to the rapidly approaching Red Army and thus facilitate penetration through Slovak territory to the very heart of Europe. He also planned to marshal Slovak troops against Hungarian forces.

Originally a volunteer in the Czecho-Slovak Legion in Russia during the First World War, Catlos was not popular with his officers, and, worse, he was compromised as a German collaborator. Consequently, Slovak officers bent on resistance and in collusion with Edvard Benes, worked up a plan of their own along the same lines as that of Catlos, but with reliance on committed officers planted in advance in command of Slovak garrisons and military units. However, Catlos' plan envisaged preservation of Slovak independence and was objectively better, because it expected the entire Slovak army to rise up on command, without internal disruption or change of command. Catlos sent a courier to the Red Army Command to inform it of his plan, but by a fateful coincidence his courier (Karol Smidke) was also carrying the plans of the army conspirators, as well as plans of the Slovak National Council.

General
Ferdinand Catlos,
Minister of Defense
of Slovak government

In the meantime, however, the situation in Slovakia underwent a fundamental change: the Soviets ordered a diversionary parachute drop of guerrillas from partisan headquarters in Kiev into Slovak territory, targeting Turiec County because its population was mostly Lutheran and consequently much more likely to be ill-disposed to the regime. These guerilla parachutists recruited partisan supporters from among the local people, many of whom readily joined their ranks, as did Soviet POWs who feared retaliation for having been captured and thus hoped to redeem themselves.[51]

The plans of the army conspirators took partisan activity into consideration, but the partisans were essentially undisciplined, and, not facing an armed German presence in Slovakia, wanted at least to sabotage German transports to the front, block tunnels and blow up railroad tracks, all of which conflicted with the plans of the Slovak rebel leadership and General Catlos. After all, it was along these tracks that the Red Army transports were soon to be rolling westward.

Indeed, the partisans were very arbitrary in their behavior, in many cases summarily murdering people without any form of trial. For instance, even before the occupation of Slovakia by the German army, partisans killed about thirty civilians in Turiec County, mostly Germans. Part of the problem was the fact that anybody could pose as a partisan, since they wore no uniform or distinctive garb. In this situation, people had no way of telling a genuine partisan from a pretender. In the fall of 1944 and the following winter 'Partisans' who peeled off from their units murdered Jews hiding out in the woods as well as other people in the vicinity of Povazska Bystrica, Ladci, and Ilava.

To add to the confusion, the Germans sent agent-provocateurs into Slovak villages, pretending to be partisans and thus testing people to see if they were willing to cooperate with partisans. After all, without civilian support a partisan war is impossible. As mementos of these tests, German provocateurs left behind the devasted communities of Tokajik, Klak, and Ostry Grun.

When a garrison commander in Turciansky Svaty Martin allowed partisans to shoot down a whole German military mission returning from Romania,[52] the Germans at last lost all semblance of restraint. Finally realizing that the Slovak army no longer heeded its officers and was unwilling to confront partisans, they sprang into action. This was a time when allied forces were successfully advancing in France and Italy, and the Red Army, rapidly advancing on the Prussian border, had already crushed the German Army Group Center in Belarus and Ukraine; a time, in fact, when even Yugoslav partisans were enjoying substantial success. In Slovakia, anti-German sentiment was on the rise: the Slovak army would have been glad to take up arms, but primarily against Germans rather than Hungarians. However, for that to happen it needed an order from the top.

Any historian acquainted with this bewildering array of events will find it very hard to judge whether those who took up arms against the government in Bratislava were combating fascism, settling personal scores, or fighting for a better Slovakia.

When German troops stormed into Slovakia at the end of August 1944, the Slovak military command in Banska Bystrica, spurred on by the precipitate actions in Turciansky Svaty Martin, had no choice but to call upon the army to fight back. The Slovak troops were told that Germans had abducted President Tiso to Germany. However, when Tiso made a public address by radio, the troops lost their zest for battle. Still, they could hardly have avoided firing on the Germans, since the latter had already launched an attack on them. At this point, realizing that the Slovak army was no longer willing to submit to his command, General Catlos decided to cross over to the partisans, but they rebuffed the overtures he made to them.

In some states allied with the Germans, uprisings succeeded if the head of state and army worked in concert, as in the case of Romania, Bulgaria and Finland. In instances such as Italy and Slovakia, where the revolt took the form of a conspiracy by only part of the army, it failed. But it is also true that at the end of 1944, Tiso consented to deployment of German troops in Slovakia, or at least, granted his grudging approval after the massacre of the German military mission to Romania by rebel troops at the Turciansky Svaty Martin barracks. Even at this early stage the Slovak army proved as incapable of dealing with the undisciplined partisans as later on, after it had been renamed the First Czecho-Slovak Army.

On September 20, 1944, in Sklene partisans shot and killed 190 males aged 16 to 60; a little later, in Ruzomberok they shot and killed a German factory owner with twelve workmen; and in nearby Biely Potok they murdered 164 German civilians, as well as one or two people at random in various predominantly German villages of Turiec and Upper Nitra counties. On August 30 in Vyhne they leveled a camp full of children from bombed-out families of the German Ruhr region and their house-mothers. On September 23, well into the Slovak National Uprising, 83 Germans were murdered in Banska Stiavnica, 60 of them originally from the town of Velke Pole.

Can any discerning and responsible historian call the Slovak National Uprising that followed such a prelude, without reservation, the most glorious chapter of Slovak history?

The Germans disarmed the divisions of General A. Malar deployed in Eastern Slovakia[53] and took the officers and men prisoner, though some of the higher-ranking officers succeeded in crossing over to the other side. Mean-

Announcement of Mobilization, Turciansky Svaty Martin, 30 August 1944

Rudolf Viest

Jan Golian

while, garrisons in the Vah valley dispersed and headed for home, while the garrison in Trnava was relocated to Central Slovakia, as originally planned. Major J. Smigovsky, the commander in Nitra, maintained good order in the garrison and city, refusing to turn over command to the officer designated by the rebel troops. His garrison, remaining loyal to the Bratislava government, escaped disarmament by the Germans. Thus it happened that the only garrisons to turn against the Germans were those within reach of the Command of the Ground Army, whose chief of staff, Jan Golian, had taken over leadership of the Uprising. The latter remained at his post up to the collapse of the revolt, enduring endless friction with partisans, who made up about 20% of the men under his command and included deserters from among his former troops. Benes, in the meantime, promoted Golian to general and sent him assistance in the person of R. Viest, who had once served in the Slovak army.

The Germans tried to free up the railway track running from Zilina to the Eastern Front as quickly as they could, occupying other sectors in Slovakia only to the extent that their diminishing strength and the resisting Slovak army allowed. But the fighting spirit of the Slovak army was not particularly high: inasmuch as Slovak sentiment at this time was very anti-German, the troops had an opponent and ideology against which to fight, but nothing to fight for; the ideology of Benes and the Communists drew support from only a minority of the Slovak population.

The fact that they allowed no say in their affairs to Benes, or to a delegation he sent to Slovakia, reflects well on the leadership of the Uprising. In this sense, the Uprising was truly a Slovak, not Czecho-Slovak, affair. The idea of restoring Czecho-Slovakia no longer held any appeal. The citizenry, having experienced self-rule, realized that having one's own state was a great boon.[54] Old Czecho-Slovakism, which had enjoyed considerable Slovak support before the war, was dying out. The Slovaks, by the end of the Second World War, had become a mature and self-confident nation, with justifiable national pride.

On October 27, 1944, Germans occupied Banska Bystrica, which tolled the end of the Slovak National Uprising. The claim that the rebels had just been driven back into the mountains is mere Communist windowdressing to mask the fact of defeat.[55]

Communist historians have accumulated mountains of half-truths and outright lies about the events that occurred in Slovakia from August through October 1944 and thereafter.[56] My own personal sense is that it will take a whole new generation of historians to draw an objective picture of the Slovak National Uprising, a picture no longer beholden to the Communist Party.

In September 1944, Heinrich Himmler, the Reich Leader of the SS and Chief of Police, who had long despised Tiso and the conditions that prevailed under his leadership, visited Slovakia. He roundly upbraided Slovak representatives and declared that, had they disposed of Jews in a timely and thorough fashion instead of coddling them, they might have spared themselves the unpleasantness that had now befallen them. The new situation that Slovaks faced was wholly orchestrated by the Germans, with Slovak authorities in a totally subservient position.

The Jews were the ones who felt the consequences of this new situation most acutely: as SS units, in the process of occupying Slovakia, discovered Jews in hiding or fighting alongside partisans, they killed many on the spot, herding the rest into former work camps and thence to extermination. Thus it happened that on September 30, 1944, after a two-year hiatus, a transport of Jews once again left Slovakia, now under exclusive SS control. The final such transport departed on March 31, 1945, headed for Terezin in the Czech Protectorate. Altogether, approximately 12,000 Jews were deported in this second wave of transports from Slovakia. By this time Auschwitz was already in the hands of the Red Army, a fact that served to spare the lives of many.

After the outbreak of the Uprising and arrival of German occupiers, the Jozef Tiso administration stepped down and a new administration took over. Dr. Stefan Tiso,[57] heretofore presiding judge of the Supreme Court, assumed

Headquarters of Slovak National Council during Slovak National Uprising, Banska Bystrica

231

Flyer against Nazism

the dual function of Prime Minister and Minister for Foreign Affairs. (By this time Tuka's health had deteriorated so badly that he was no long capable of functioning as Prime Minister.) Stefan Hassik, originally a career soldier and most recently Superintendent of Nitra County, stepped into the vacancy left by the Minister of Defense, Catlos. The rest of the cabinet stayed on.

The Slovak army fought the Germans to the end of October 1944. It suffered many casualties on the Eastern Front and many men simply decamped for home, while others became prisoners-of-war or deserted to the partisans. The administration converted the Nitra garrison into a home defense force, and outfitted the Hlinka Guard with regular army uniforms and arms, renaming it the Hlinka Guard Emergency Force. All told, there were seventeen such units, deployed mainly against partisans.

Inasmuch as the Germans had now gained complete mastery of Slovakia, it was a matter of considerable concern how they would relate to the Slovak authorities, who had resumed functioning. At stake was whether Slovakia could formally and legally remain independent, or whether it was to become a protectorate or even an integral part of the German Reich. Had Tiso been an opportunist, he could simply have stepped down from the office of President and let events run their course.

Nazi criminal activities in Slovakia left behind a legacy of bloodshed: whole Jewish families rounded up and shot on the spot, people burnt alive in the Kremnicka lime-kilns, mass graves, etc.

The newly formed Hlinka Guard Emergency Force was deployed in the campaign against the partisans under the leadership of Otomar Kubala, who was sentenced to death as soon as the war ended. But other members of these units were not brought to trial until ten or more years later in the Communist campaign against Slovak Bourgeois Nationalism.

Official propaganda of the Slovak Republic labeled what happened in Slovakia in the fall of 1944 a 'putsch', while organizers and participants in the fight against fascism labeled it the 'Slovak National Uprising'. The truth lies somewhere in between.[58] The label 'Slovak National Uprising', in my opinion, is unacceptable, if for no other reason than that the whole nation did not participate in it, as for instance, in Yugoslavia. Hlinka's Slovak People's Party and many other Slovaks had nothing to do with it, being quite content with Tiso, while Communists, partisans, and Benes supporters represented no sizeable constituency of the Slovak nation. In any case, Tiso at the time was such a commanding figure on the Slovak scene that neither the Communists, nor Benes' London cohorts, nor, least of all, the conspirators in Banska Bystrica, could hold a candle to him.[59]

232

The Tiso administration bid farewell to the Slovak citizenry in early 1945 by distributing rations from the whole year's stock of flour, sugar and other imperishable food stuffs.[60]

On September 21, 1944, the Red Army occupied its first village in Slovakia. On October 6 the Soviets and accompanying units of the Czecho-Slovak army crossed the Slovak-Polish border at Dukla Pass. The Red Army gradually drove the German occupiers out of Slovakia, but not without a horrendous cost in casualties. It occupied Kosice on January 19, 1945, Banska Bystrica on March 25, Bratislava on April 4, and Zilina on April 30, as it advanced towards Silesia. Units of the Romanian army arrived with help from the South, and units of the Czecho-Slovak army contributed aid as well. Both sides suffered heavy casualties, leaving behind numerous military graveyards.

The occupation of Slovakia and expulsion of the Germans was executed in strict accordance with the plans and wishes of Secretary-General Stalin. Behind the Red Army, like a second wave of invasion, came the minions of the NKVD. The Communists set up National Revolutionary Committees in towns and villages, as they had demanded in broadcasts from abroad, admitting 'pro forma' a few non-Communists, but retaining complete power on the local level.

One way or another the revolutionary committees placed 'collaborators' on the rack, and it is likely that they also had a hand in the illegal deportation of fellow citizens to the USSR. We now have partial knowledge of the tens of thousands of individuals who met such a fate, many dying on the way or on arrival, from hunger and even simply thirst. They were abducted, then had to live and work in extremely inhuman conditions. There is little to distinguish the fate of these people from the fate of the Slovak Jews.

The passage of the front left Slovakia in a state of desolation. Highways were destroyed, railroads and bridges blown up, factories leveled, machine tools disappeared, people's homes and other buildings were riddled with bullets and bombed out. There was nothing left to do but dig in and start rebuilding from scratch. People were elated that, after so much travail, the anxiously anticipated peace had come at last. They looked forward to a better life and hoped to see a renewal of democratic conditions, cooperating with the Communists in the meantime to make it happen. Ironically, though, not only Hitler and the Fascists were enemies of democracy, but Stalin and the Communists were as well.

Certainly, it is not right to exaggerate or minimize what happened in Slovakia at the end of the war; it behooves us, rather, to seek an objective perspective on those events.

13. Between 1945 and 1960

With the approach of the end of the war and the occupation of the greater part of Slovakia by the Red Army, Benes and his government left London in March 1945 and moved to Moscow. There, together with the Czech Communists and representatives of Slovak political factions, they reached an agreement on the principles that were to guide them in the building of their new state. Two important parties that had existed in pre-1938 Czecho-Slovakia were excluded from negotiations: the Agrarian Party, and Hlinka's Slovak People's Party (the HSPP). The latter party was banned because it had been a principal in the founding and governance of the Slovak Republic; the Agrarians because they had cooperated in the governance of the Protectorate of Bohemia and Moravia, and were, besides, old political foes of Benes and the Communists. Thus they were excluded from the Czecho-Slovak political spectrum its principal conservative elements. It is true that in the Czech lands and Moravia the Catholic People's Party was able to continue its activities, but in Slovakia the absence of any party or parties of conservative orientation was sorely felt. After all, the autonomist block and the Agrarians together had won more than 50% of the vote in the last free elections in 1935. In the Czech lands, the conservative political parties had always been weaker than in Slovakia. [1]

During this transitional period, political power in Slovakia was held by the Communist Party allied with the Social Democrats. In addition there was a so-called Citizens' Block, which in April 1945 in Kosice changed its name to the Democratic Party. In this political constellation, which lacked any politicians of clearly defined profile, Lutherans predominated. Its outstanding personalities were Jan Ursiny and Jozef Lettrich.

Ursiny was an estate-owner and functionary of the Agrarian Party, which in October 1938 had signed the Zilina Pact (for Slovak autonomy). Later on he had parted company with the Ludaks (HSPP) and even landed in prison. Later still he favored cooperation with the Communists, but continued to maintain ties with the factions of Karol Sidor and Vavro Srobar. Lettrich, who was Ursiny's junior by almost ten years, was an attorney-at-law. He had begun his career in the judiciary, became a functionary of various Agrarian institutions and editor of their periodicals, and from 1941 practiced law. Losing faith in Czecho-Slovakism, he became a supporter of Slovakia's right to independence. Twice he served time in prison. [2]

After the war, the Communist Party formally split in two: the Czech Communist Party, active only in the Bohemia and Moravia, and the Slovak Communist Party, which was formally independent. The split was initiated by the Slovak Communists, whose self-esteem had swelled to the point that they were no longer

Jan Ursiny

willing to accept, or take seriously, party leadership from Prague. The Slovaks had become convinced that they were capable of building and running their own state, but unfortunately time ran out on them: the victorious powers had irrevocably decided to reconstitute Czecho-Slovakia.

The leading personalities among Slovak Communists were Karol Smidke, Viliam Siroky and Gustav Husak.

V. Siroky, a Bratislava native, was a charter member of the Communist Party and a party official from 1938 on, in both the Czech lands and Slovakia.[3] He moved to the Soviet Union after the dismemberment of the Czecho-Slovak Republic but returned in 1941, with instructions to engage in illegal Communist activities. Within a month, he had been arrested and jailed, but in January 1945 he managed to escape to Soviet controlled territory.

Karol Smidke was born in Vitkovice, but early on, in 1919, his family settled permanently in Banska Stiavnica. A trained craftsman, he worked at various locations. During the First Republic he had held various Communist posts, mostly in Slovakia, but in August 1939, he fled to the Soviet Union and did not return until June 1943 (in the company of Karol Bacilek), at which time he resumed contact with the Communist leadership. At the end of 1944, by a coincidence described above in our coverage of the war years, Smidke flew to Moscow with the insurrectionary plans of both the Slovak National Council and General Catlos. He then returned to Slovakia and helped organize partisan activity, becoming partisan chief-of-staff, but only nominally, since their real leadership was headquartered in Kiev, Ukraine. Smidke survived the winter of 1944–45, not in the mountains like his fellow partisans, but in a Bratislava apartment. Elected president of the Communist Party of Slovakia, he held the post into the summer of 1945.

Gustav Husak was considerably younger than his two Communist colleagues just described. He was born into a Catholic family in Dubavka near Bratislava and received a Catholic upbringing. While studying law, he lived with friends who were members of a Communist cell. His first employment after finishing school was as a law clerk, followed by a job in the offices of a dispatchers union. Though a known member of left-wing student organizations, he escaped significant imprisonment during the war years. In August 1944, Husak helped organize a demonstration against Hlinka's Slovak People's Party (HSPP) in Banska Bystrica and, after its dispersal by the police, hid out in a Central Slovakian village. When Soviet troops arrived just before Christmas, they arranged for him to be flown to the Soviet Union.

Gustav Husak

Decisive negotiations about the new government and policies of the restored Czecho-Slovak Republic took place in Moscow on March 22–29, 1945. A delegation of the Slovak National Council arrived on March 12, five days before the Czechs, who were led by Edvard Benes. These discussions were dominated by the

Communists, who had already achieved political control of the Slovak areas occupied by the Red Army, for the simple reason that they had no serious competition.

The Foreign Affairs Bureau of the Czecho-Slovak Communist Party prepared the draft of a platform for the restored state, which the delegates approved as the agenda for negotiations. Since three of the four Czech parties in attendance were socialist, while the Slovak bloc was without clear political profile, the Marxists (the socialist parties) overpowered the non-Marxists under the leadership of spokesman Klement Gottwald, who had been elected president of the National Front of Czechs and Slovaks. The platform they approved at these negotiations was destined to rule political life in Czecho-Slovakia for decades up to the collapse of Communism in 1990, categorically ruling out political opposition and banning any party that was not a member of the National Front. This arrangement was the ingenious invention of Moscow's Communist Central, analogous to arrangements in all the other countries occupied by the Red Army, where Communists were well on their way to taking over government.[4]

The one controversial point of the platform approved at the Moscow negotiations was Chapter VI, which dealt with the relationship between Czechs and Slovaks. The Slovak Communists had proposed equal standing for the two nations, to be achieved by a federal arrangement, in which the Slovak National Council and the Czech Parliament would be co-equal. That was the kind of arrangement Husak had argued for at a working session of the Slovak Communists in Kosice in late February and early March 1945. But Gottwald somehow managed to dissuade his colleagues from adopting the concept, which would have meant complete political defeat for Benes and his cronies, still in thrall to the idea of a unitary Czecho-Slovak nationality and making no bones about it. Gottwald and some other Czech Communists ostensibly backed the idea of a distinct Slovak nationality, but in their hearts they were just die-hard Czecho-Slovaks.[5]

That in brief was the manner in which the asymmetric model of the Czecho-Slovak state, which was to last up to 1968, came about.[6] It is to the credit of the Slovak Communists that neither during the Slovak National Uprising when they were in control, nor after liberation by the Soviets, did they grant any say in Slovak matters to representatives of Benes' government-in-exile.

Klement Gottwald

The newly created Prague government had twenty-five members, nine of them Slovak. Zdenek Fierlinger, a Social Democrat, was appointed chairman, the heads of the other political parties, Klement Gottwald, Viliam Siroky and Jan Ursiny, his deputies. There were also several independents in the administration, namely Ludvik Svoboda, Zdenek Nejedly and Jan Masaryk.

The new government arrived in Kosice by train on April 3, 1945. The following day, the members took their oath of office, and on April 5 they present-

President E. Benes and representatives of Slovak National Council

ed their program to the public. Imbedded in it were the chief features sponsored by the Communists.[7]

That same day, in a meeting with the Slovak National Council, the new government declared the program legally binding, and Gottwald, waxing historical, declared it the 'Magna Carta' of the Slovak nation. Such was the official inauguration of the Czecho-Slovak Socialist System, dubbed the 'People's Democracy' even as its minions went about consolidating absolute control.

As the new system was being installed, the citizenship of ethnic Magyars and Germans was nullified. State policies were oriented explicitly to the Soviet Union, not surprisingly, in view of the treaty of friendship and alliance signed by Benes in December 1943. The Socialist and Communist maneuvers were crowned by decrees nationalizing industrial enterprises, banks and insurance companies, which President Benes signed in October 1945. The Communists and National Front members, including Benes, considered these decrees so important that they thereafter celebrated the day of their signing, October 28, as Nationalization Day.

Building in which Kosice Government Program was signed

At a rally in Prague in October 1945 celebrating nationalization, Klement Gottwald declared: "We are now undoing an internal Munich in the economic sphere. In this sense, the process of state take-over is deeply national and deeply democratic, a logical extension of our national liberation struggle, waged at home and abroad against both occupiers and domestic traitors."

On April 7, 1945, a presidium of the Slovak National Council was formed, with Smidke and Lettrich as joint chairman and six deputies, three each from the

238

ranks of the Communists and the Democrats respectively, with the latter serving additionally as commissioners (trustees) on the council. Ironically, neither in the course of the Slovak National Uprising nor later in Kosice and other liberated Slovak territories, was executive power divorced from legislative, though in the 'fascist' Slovak Republic such a divorce had been mandated by constitution and observed in practice – in spite of war-time conditions.

Not until after the transfer of government headquarters to Bratislava on April 11, 1945, was a formal separation of these powers established: Lettrich became chairman of the Slovak National Council, Smidke chairman of the Board of Commissioners (trustees), with the remaining seats divided equally between the two parties (Communist and Democratic).

The leading power-block in Slovakia after 1945, i.e. the Slovak Communists, negotiating with representatives of the Foreign Affairs Bureau of the Czecho-Slovak Communist Party in Kosice on April 8, 1945, reached an agreement with them to henceforth act as two distinct parties, each with its own chairman, executive secretary, and other office-holders. The Czecho-Slovak Communist Party agreed to operate only in Bohemia and Moravia, while keeping its name intact, since, after all, even the Slovak Communists looked to Klement Gottwald (Chairman of the Czecho-Slovak Communist Party) as their leader. In the meantime, political ideology in the Czech lands naturally remained unchanged.

On the other hand, in Slovakia, political ideology had experienced a sea change: a majority of Slovaks had come to perceive themselves as constituting an independent nationality, and Czecho-Slovakism was drawing its last breaths. Although it claimed internationalism, and in large part admitted Magyars, Germans and Jews, whose mother-tongue was not normally Slovak, the Slovak Communist Party attempted to win the goodwill of fellow Slovaks by expelling from its ranks true Magyars and Germans, including a deserving revolutionary like Stefan Major.[8] At their Zilina congress in the summer of 1945, the Slovak Communists replaced Chairman Smidke with Siroky, thus aping in a sense the Democrats, who at their Turciansky Svaty Martin congress had dropped the somewhat older Agrarian, Ursiny, for the younger Lettrich.

The Democratic Party was from the start in tow to the Communists, habitually following their lead. Its leadership was Lutheran, a small minority among Slovaks.[9] However, it gradually began to formulate its own policies, demanding a slowing down of the hasty pace of nationalization, tolerance for private ownership in small business, even if German or Magyar, and the conversion of the new state to plain democracy rather than People's Democracy.

In April 1946, to attract Catholic votes in the upcoming elections, the leaders of the Democratic Party decided to free up some leadership positions to

Jozef Lettrich

Catholics. Of the new members thus accepted, the only one with any real public exposure was the Nitra canon, Cvincek, sixty-five years old at the time and an erstwhile official in the Czecho-Slovak People's Party. Among the new officials were two executive secretaries added to the existent executive secretary, Fedor Hodza, a son of Milan Hodza and a member of the State Council in London during the war. The power of Slovak Catholicism, which had increased greatly during the war, was beginning to command respect.

Even Communists had become aware of Catholic strength: they could count votes and knew that they had no prospect of winning Catholic votes directly. This knowledge was the real reason the Communist newspaper *Pravda* carried so much invective at this time against 'reactionaries' and 'the Populist (Ludak) underground'. As early as the fall of 1944, a dispatch from Jan Sverma in Communist controlled territory to Klement Gottwald had stated that Catholics were holding their tongues and biding their time. He warned that, enjoying undeniable influence especially in the villages, they posed a problem of the first magnitude.

On July 19, 1945, after having demanded on July 13 that the landed estates of the Church be divided up for distribution to farmers, the Slovak Communist Party condemned anti-state and anti-social activities hiding behind cover of church authority and religion, thus hoping to drive a wedge between the church hierarchy and the laity.[10]

By December 1945, the Slovak Communist Party had grown to 197,363 members, 12,000 of them carry-overs from pre-war times, and another 20,000 former

Vladimir Clementis, addressing Slavic festival in Devin

240

Social Democrats. Approaching the May 1946 elections, the Party had achieved a firm grip on power, because, in the wake of the front, it had taken almost complete control of local affairs through revolutionary national committees, set up by presidential decree. These committees also controlled the Young People's League, the Women's League, the Farmers' League, and, most importantly, the newly created Revolutionary Trade Union Movement. The Communists in these organizations were told to hide their party affiliation, and to represent their opinions as non-partisan. But having achieved total power in 1948, they threw off their cover and declared their organizations to be 'levers' for Communist initiatives.

Even the League of Slovak Partisans was a Communist organization, its members being mostly Communist or strongly left-leaning. Many of them had done things during the war which can only be described as war crimes, and as a result, had lost credibility with the majority of decent people. By arrangement with their chairman, Smidke, and his executive secretary, Zingor, they exerted constant pressure on behalf of Communist causes. From April 16–18, 1947, the Slovak Communists in Bratislava (and obviously elsewhere as well) were on continuous alert for 'reactionaries' who might act up in the days leading up to the execution of former President Tiso. Then, after the February 1948 Communist coup, they allowed themselves to be manipulated into demanding strict punishment for their former comrades-in-arms who were being tried for 'crimes', namely Zingor and his associates.

Indeed, the restored 'democratic' conditions were hardly improved by the fact that there were in Slovakia, as early as September 1945, 63 internment camps holding more than 26,000 inmates, most of them 'collaborators', plus Germans and Hungarians. The largest such camps were in Petrzalka and Novaky.

A serious problem in the post-war period was how to accomplish a deportation of Germans and Hungarians from Czecho-Slovak territory, the former naturally posing a major dilemma in the Sudetenland. A conference of the victorious powers in Potsdam had consented to a transfer of approximately 3,000,000 people. The execution of the complicated process lasted until the end of 1946, and generated horrendous incidents in the Czech and Moravian borderlands. Sudeten German organizations have registered 242,000 lives lost, mainly of women, children and the elderly. Of course, Germans were deported from Slovakia as well, but there, the deportations were accomplished without such wretched hatefulness. Only Slovak Germans who had taken up arms against the German army, and their families were granted leave to stay, a boon many eligible candidates never got to enjoy, since they had already fled in advance of Soviet occupation.[11]

The Slovaks had originally given equal priority to the resolution of the Hungarian question, but that problem never made the agenda of the victorious powers.

241

Only the deportation of the Hungarians who had settled on Slovak territory after the pre-war Horthy annexation of southern Slovakia was carried out without a hitch.[12] International organizations, the United Nations in particular, and the Hungarian government, objected to the deportation of Hungarians from Slovakia. In the event, after long negotiations, a treaty was signed in Budapest on February 27, 1946, providing for a mutual exchange of populations, based on the principle that only those persons would be relocated who asked to be. The question came down to how many Slovaks would want to move from Hungary to Slovakia.[13]

There still remained approximately 400,000 Hungarians in Slovakia who, by Presidential Decree No. 33/1945, became the target of harsh repression. They were stripped of their rights, lost their citizenship and schools, were denied use of Magyar in official matters, and their businesses (even small family-run operations) put under state management. Hungarian villages lost their elective offices to state-appointed managers; 44,000 Slovak Hungarians were resettled in Bohemia and Moravia,[14] and the remainder subjected to re-Slovakization, on the premise that they were, after all, Magyarized Slovaks. Almost all of them did request 're-Slovakization', but by the end of 1947, only about 200,000 had gained certification. After the Communist takeover, oppression of Hungarians ceased: they regained their citizenship and schools, and got to participate in the May 1948 elections. In the last phase of re-Slovakization, in early 1948, many villages and towns in southern Slovakia were renamed after Slovak historical personages. In truth, the application of the principle of collective guilt to the Hungarians (Magyars) remains a stain on the Slovak conscience. The Czecho-Slovak Communist Party accepted full responsibility for this aberration, and in 1963, admitted the culpability of Czecho-Slovak as well as Slovak Communists in failing to do more

Free elections in Slovakia, 1946

to prevent the oppression of Hungarians. Still, the objective truth is that blame must also fall on the Democratic Party since it shared power during this period.

Before the elections of 1946, two new parties sprang up in Slovakia. The first of the two was the Freedom Party, which had originally wanted to be called the Christian Republican Party but had failed to get National Front approval. Potential voters could not but question its Christian credentials, since the party's leader happened to be Vavro Srobar. True, Srobar had been a close co-worker of Andrej Hlinka in old Hungary, having campaigned so vigorously on his behalf that he landed in jail. Later on, however, he turned to Masaryk and Czecho-Slovakism, and became a confirmed freethinker. At the war's end, it was to Srobar and his creation, the National Front, that ex-President Benes turned in his search for Slovak support, rather than the Slovak National Council. The other new party in Slovakia was the Workers' Party, organized by Social Democrats. After the elections of September, 1946, it had changed its name to the Social Democratic Party in Slovakia; then in November it merged with the Czecho-Slovak Social Democrats, and up to the state's demise, operated under the name Czecho-Slovak Social Democrats in Slovakia. Its honorary chairman was Ivan Derer, a staunch Czecho-Slovak of the old school.

The Slovak elections of 1946 brought the Democratic Party a convincing victory with a huge total of almost one million votes, despite exclusion of 'collaborators', Hungarians, and Germans, and despite blank ballots cast by dissenters. The Democratic Party, with 62% of the vote, won forty-three seats in Parliament; the Communist Party with 30.3%, twenty-one seats; the Freedom Party with 4.2%, three seats; and the Social Democratic Party with 3.1%, two seats. The

The new Board of Commissioners (Trustees), after 1946 elections, with Jozef Lettrich, Chairman of Slovak National Council

243

Czecho-Slovak Communist Party made its strongest showing in Bohemia and Moravia and won the right to name a prime minister, placing its chairman, Klement Gottwald in that post.[15] In Slovakia, Gustav Husak, the most radical Slovak Communist and great admirer of both Stalin and Gottwald, replaced Smidke as president of the Board of Commissioners (Trustees). This change resulted in nullification of the *Magna Carta* of the Slovak nation, so headily proclaimed by Klement Gottwald in Kosice in April 1945, because thereafter, every Slovak commissioner was subordinated to an analogous Czecho-Slovak cabinet minister in Prague. Husak never did look after the interests of Slovakia and the Slovaks, but as a fanatical Communist, concerned himself first and foremost with the interests of the movement, inside Slovakia and beyond. His fondest fantasy was Communist rule over the entire world.[16]

The economic picture of Czecho-Slovakia in this period was dictated by the relative inequality of development in its two parts. Nationalized industries employed roughly 60% of all workers in the two parts, but while in the Czech lands the share of the public sector in nationalized industries, based on number of employees, was 35.4%, in Slovakia it was only 16.7%. The private sector in Slovakia employed more than 28% of all workers.

In 1946, wage earners and their families represented 45 to 46% of Slovakia's population, of which 1,230,000 (nearly 37%) were workers of all types, including domestics, handymen and the like, and their families. In June, 1945, only 63,936 of this work force had been employed by industry, 43,222 of them directly in production. By the end of 1947, these numbers had increased to 177,936, which, together with family members, comprised approximately 10 to 11% of the total population. In 1946, there were more than 130,000 workers engaged in agricultural activities.

Small-scale manufacturers comprised 35.8% of the population, with 30.3% of their number concurrently engaged in farming. Almost one half of the population of Slovakia (48.1%) depended on agriculture for their livelihood. The metal workers of Slovakia, approximately 80,000 to 100,000 in number, also worked small family farms.

At the end of 1947, there were 45,000 artisan workshops in Slovakia, 43,819 consumer-oriented businesses, such as retail stores and restaurants, 1,948 transportation companies, and 7,924 service operations. The sum total of family businesses in Slovakia was 99,345 with 92,960 owners, supporting 200,000 people. White-collar workers made up only about 7% of the population, entrepreneurs-industrialists, bankers, businessmen of all types, estate-owners and others approximately 5%. At that time, only about 1,500 people had the highest technical qualification, i.e. a diploma in engineering.

In Bohemia and Moravia, wage earners constituted 67.4% of the population, almost 50% of them workers and handymen in manufacturing. More than 900,000 workers were employed in Czech and Moravian industry in May 1946, i.e. approximately one half of all workers there. Small scale manufacturers made up only about 25% of the population.

In the second half of 1946, the Communists and the National Front (Communist controlled) decided to inaugurate another jewel from the treasure-trove of socialist ideas, to wit a 'centrally planned economy'. For the years 1947–48 they drafted a two-year plan of 'reconstruction and renewal of the national economy'. The Czecho-Slovak Communist Party had announced the necessity of such a program at its Eighth National Congress in 1946, with the goal of achieving pre-war levels of production and, in key industries, even to surpass it by as much as 50%. A program of industrialization was to be put into effect in Slovakia, with a 31.6% allocation of total state investment there. In the two years of the plan, over-all employment in Slovakia increased by 45,000 workers, even though agriculture lost 88,437. Substantial growth was achieved in the production of electricity, which recorded an increase in consumption as compared to 1937, from 104 kWh to 228 kWh. The manufacturing sector began producing refrigerators, motorcycles, machine tools and woodworking machines. Agricultural production was drastically affected by a great drought in 1947, causing it to reach only 75% of its pre-war yield. Midway into this two-year period, the Communist Party seized

Jozef Tiso, on trial, before death sentence in 1947

245

total control of the government and declared the goals of the campaign met, in clear conflict with reality.

In the first half of 1947, the trial of Slovak President Dr. Jozef Tiso held the public spellbound. Communists and former partisans were determined to get him a death sentence, while the Democratic Party feared the dangers of conviction and execution.[17] Alexander Mach and Ferdinand Durcansky were charged as co-defendants before trial judge Dr. Igor Daxner, a former Agrarian and Czecho-Slo-vak. Tiso presented his defense with telling spontaneity, and held up well under interrogation; expressing no regrets, he plainly scored a moral victory.[18] In the meantime, alarmed by the public's intense interest, the government quickly took the unusual step of suspending radio coverage of the trial. Indeed, most Slovaks considered Tiso innocent, since they were quite cognizant of his accomplish-ments and of his success in guiding the nation through the perils of war-time.[19] A noteworthy fact of Tiso's rule is that it managed to get by without a single exe-cution. For these reasons, the Slovak public was confident that he would escape the death penalty. On April 15, 1947, however, the court found him guilty and sentenced him to death. Meanwhile, Mach was sentenced to thirty years impris-onment, and Durcansky to death, but 'in contumatiam' (i.e. 'in absentia'), since he was living abroad by this time.

Husak, who controlled the predominantly Democratic Board of Commis-sioners, took charge of carrying out the sentence, while keeping his associates in the dark. He rightly calculated that the majority Marxists and National Socialists would favor execution, and only the minority Czech Populists and Slovak Democrats would favor clemency. Benes deferred to the decision of his govern-ment. Thus, within three days, with court-martial swiftness, on the morning of April 18, 1947, Tiso died by hanging, spiritually composed and in his own mind a victim of worldwide Communist conspiracy.

This lightning-quick execution of Dr. Jozef Tiso was not the only example of justice beholden to the powers that be; Dr. Vojtech Tuka, too, in a wheelchair, with death written on his face after a second stroke, was sentenced to death and hanged.

Mourning settled upon Slovakia after the execution of Dr. Tiso, since many more Slovaks were conservative than were leftist.

After the 1946 elections, the Czecho-Slovak political atmosphere became highly charged. The Democratic Party, recognizing the Communist drive to Sovi-et-type dictatorship, gradually evolved into an opposition party, and strove to expose the Communists' deceitful tactics and manipulation of mass organiza-tions. It sought to preserve the largest possible sphere for free enterprise and favored acceptance of the American Marshall Plan for economic aid to Europe. At first, Czecho-Slovak Communists also favored the Marshall Plan, but at a critical moment, the Soviet Union warned that acceptance of the plan would constitute violation of the 1943 Pact of Alliance with the USSR, since the intent of the plan was clearly hostile to Soviet interests.[20] Consequently, the Czecho-Slovak government rejected Marshall Plan aid.

Under the direction of Gottwald from Prague (and Stalin from Moscow), Husak and the Communist Party of Slovakia responded to criticism by raising the stakes and actively seeking confrontation with Democrats. Turning to the Soviet Union for aid in the lean year of 1947, they received a promise, but whether the promise was kept, lies deeply hidden in the archives. Out in the open, railroad cars labeled 'Grain from the USSR' were seen moving about here and there, but how was one to tell whether they were full or empty? Official propaganda touted Soviet aid, while opposition periodicals dared not challenge the Soviet Union.

In 1947, the Communists demanded passage of a so-called 'millionaires tax', which they claimed would bring several billion crowns into the state treasury. Rejecting the idea at first, the government ended up approving it.[21]

In Slovakia at this time, the Communists began to make a fuss about cleansing the government of people compromised by cooperation with the war-time regime of the Ludaks (Hlinka's Slovak People's Party). In September 1946, they 'uncovered' an anti-state conspiracy, operating from three centers, and filed charges against six hundred individuals, including the two executive secretaries of the Democratic Party, Jan Kempny and Milos Bugar, plus a personal secretary of Jan Ursiny, Vice-Premier of the Slovak administration. At the same time, the Party, pandering to the mass organizations to which it was beholden, demanded their admission to the National Front.

A welcome diversion for the Communists occurred in the form of an incursion of Ukrainian partisans (the so-called 'Benderovci'), who were attempting to get through Czecho-Slovakia to reach the American forces in Bavaria. Having cooperated with the Germans during the war, these Ukrainian nationalists were

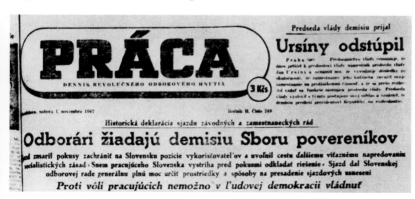

Period press reporting negotiations between industry and employee councils

now striving to create some sort of satellite state which could procure arms and act on their behalf. Against these 'Benderovci' the Communists of Czecho-Slovakia deployed the army, the national security police (in which they were firmly entrenched), and former partisans. At their insistence, a congress of industrial and employee councils convened on October 30, 1947, to generate pressure for the satisfaction of Communist demands. To reinforce this pressure, Communist members of the Board of Commissioners and the chairman himself tendered their resignations, with support from partisans, union leaders, and Communist run organizations. In the aftermath, the Democratic Party felt compelled to grant major concessions. On November 27, 1947, a new Board of Commissioners was named, comprising only six Democrats but five Communists, plus one representative from each of the minor parties and two independents. Behind this whole affair, pulling the strings, was Klement Gottwald, to whom the newly named Commissioners swore their oath of office. This Communist success in Slovakia served only to heighten political tensions. In January 1948, the Communists pressed their demand for complete nationalization of wholesale businesses, foreign and domestic. A plenary session of the Central Committee of the Communist Party of Slovakia in December 1947, approved a declaration that they would never allow themselves to be deflected from Socialism by anybody or anything, an intimation of the complete Communist takeover in the offing.

For Benes and the non-Communist parties, the writing was on the wall. The situation came to a head at the end of February 1948, when Communists strove

People's Militia in Bratislava

once more to strengthen their grip on the Ministry of Interior in Prague. Benes, by now quite ill, suggested to the democratic parties of the National Front, i.e. the Slovak Democrats, the National Socialists and the Czech People's Party, that they advise their ministers to tender their resignations, which he would turn down and thus pressure Klement Gottwald and the Communist ministers into resigning. The suggested tactic was defensive and passive at best; much more sensible would have been a Parliamentary vote of no confidence in the Communist ministers, since, with the replacement of Fierlinger by Lausman in the Social Democratic Party, the non-Communists had gained a voting majority.[22]

After this maneuver, however, the Communists mobilized their forces and persuaded industrial concerns, for the most part in Prague, to create People's Militias, which they could arm through the Ministry of Interior; they also organized Action Committees to combat 'reaction'. These moves applied such powerful pressure on Benes that, after a few days of hesitation, he caved in.[23]

Thus it came about that on February 25, 1948, President Benes accepted the resignations of the 'reactionary' ministers and named a new government made up of Gottwald nominees: ten Communist ministers, two non-aligned (but actually Communist), and only nine 'others'.

Gustav Husak cleaned house in Bratislava, almost literally throwing out the Democrats from the Board of Commissioners, and arguing that since the Democrats had resigned their ministries in Prague, they had in essence abrogated their counterparts' right to sit on the Board of Commissioners as well. On the new board the Communists took seven seats, the Democrats (who changed their party name to the Party of Revival) only two.

This tactical success of the Communist Party marked the onset of a dark age in Slovak history, as well as in Czecho-Slovak history as a whole. Benes, for whom these events precipitated a second career collapse (totally unprecedented in modern European history) remained president into May 1948, then stepped aside for the victor. Shortly thereafter, in September, he died.[24]

Like his mentor, T. G. Masaryk, Benes had remained a staunch proponent of the theory of a single Czecho-Slovak nation, never recognizing Slovak national distinctiveness, and planting obstacle after obstacle in the path of Slovak emancipation. He persisted in denying that only a fraction of Slovaks espoused his ideology. In his foreign policy, he looked to the Soviet Union as an ally against Germany and German aggression, dropping reliance on France.

Integrity was a stranger to Benes' political agenda, which was built on behind-the-scenes intrigue. In his mind, German and French reconciliation was inconceivable. Having given assent to, and personally witnessing the murder of Sudeten Germans, Benes must surely have felt some twinge of conscience before he died,

Caricature of so-called 'bourgeois nationalists'

since the deportation of the Germans was hardly a moral achievement. Additionally, he surely must have been aware of his country's inexorable drift to Communism, especially after the Soviets blindsided his compatriots by barring participation in the Marshall plan: Stalin was plainly working towards a Communist coup and the destruction of the democracy that he (Benes) had so ardently proclaimed.

It is important to remember that the Communist struggle for total control in Czecho-Slovakia as a whole continued to be orchestrated by Klement Gottwald, and regionally in Slovakia by the same Gustav Husak who, as Chairman of the Slovak Board of Commissioners, had consented to subordination of its members to their counterparts in Prague ministries. Husak, a dyed-in-the-wool Communist, worked in total concert with his two chiefs, Gottwald and Stalin; the very idea of cooperation with Slovak Democrats and the opponents of Prague centralism was anathema to him as he pursued the goal of stamping out 'reaction' wherever and whenever it might rear its head.

Thus, only fifteen months after Gottwald's April 1945 'Magna Carta' speech in Kosice, centralization of all power in Prague became hard reality, with Slovaks practically excluded from a say in state affairs. Shortly thereafter, a deadly power struggle erupted between the Slovak Communists, Husak and Siroky. Viliam Siroky donned the mantle of a battler against bourgeois nationalism, joined by Klement Gottwald, who abandoned his erstwhile protégée in Bratislava, Husak. Yet the latter never lost his admiration for his great mentor; restored to power in 1969 after long years of imprisonment and torture, Husak went so far as to revive the cult of Klement Gottwald, the standard-bearer of Marxism-Leninism and Bolshevization.[25]

The Communist victory in Czecho-Slovakia, destroying democracy and expanding Soviet power, posed a threat to the rest of Europe, and indeed the world. Consequently, the USA, Canada and Western Europe created a mutual defense organization called the North Atlantic Treaty Organization (NATO). Yugoslavia, however, quickly dropped its candidacy, as J. B. Tito succumbed to Moscow inducement. The cold war took on an increasingly ominous mien, exploding into armed conflict in Korea in June 1950. In the meantime, Germany split into separate halves, forming first, in September 1949, the Federal Republic of Germany under Western occupation, then a month later, the German Democratic Republic, under Soviet occupation.

Following the Czecho-Slovak coup, membership in the Communist Party increased spectacularly, reaching 407,150 by July 1948. At that point, the Communists themselves put a lid on growth, calling for background checks in November 1948, and introducing a probatory period on the Soviet model as well. On January 31, 1949, on completion of background checks, they reduced the membership to 267,560, including 79,488 new applicants, 41.7% of them blue-collar workers. In the meantime, on July 27, 1948, the Czecho-Slovak Communist Party and the Slovak Communist Party had formally reunited, under Prague control, chaired by Klement Gottwald. In this asymmetrical arrangement the Communist Party of Slovakia retained some degree of autonomy, identifying itself variously as Czecho-Slovak or Slovak, to fit the case.

After the February coup, the Communists were firmly in the saddle. In spite of everything, they proceeded through the formality of enacting a new constitution, which went into effect in May 1948. It became obvious that the constituent assembly elected in 1946 had done its job well. The new constitution recognized the existence of a distinctive Slovak nation, but only on paper, and power remained vested in Prague, as prior to 1938.

The May 1948 elections fielded only a single slate of candidates. Meanwhile the ethnic Hungarians (Magyars) of Czecho-Slovakia had regained full citizenship, including revival of their schools and press rights, and on March 5, 1949, creation of a cultural organization, *Csemadok* (The Cultural Association of Magyar Workers in Czecho-Slovakia).

In the economic sphere, the Communists confiscated 418,740 hectares (one hectare = roughly 2.5 acres) of mostly landed estates, of which they granted 41% to 90,000 landless people and small farmers. In 1948 the sector comprising small farmers, consumer businesses and artisans (skilled craftsmen) employed 64.5% of all manual laborers, while the socialist sector employed 25.3% of all wage earners. All told in 1948, of economically active persons in Slovakia, 61.8% worked in agriculture and forestry, 21.2% in industry and construction, and 17% in other occupations.

When the Communists seized power, they faced the problem of adapting the dictatorship of the proletariat (i.e. of their own party) to the Soviet model, in which there existed only one party and no body analogous to the National Front. They therefore settled for a compromise, agreeing to retain a system of plural parties, but on the condition that the other parties would operate on Communist guidelines. The compromise posed no serious threat because the other parties were willing to collaborate, being long accustomed to viewing the ideas of socialism as their own.

A very major economic innovation was introduced at a session of the Central Committee of the Communist Party of Czecho-Slovakia on November 17–18, 1948, in which the Committee approved a system of collectivization, bringing to a halt the parceling out of large estates, and in fact ordaining its reverse, the consolidation of individual farms into cooperatives.

On February 23, 1949, the National Assembly passed "a law establishing uniform farm cooperatives." As early as the fall of 1948, the Communists had begun liquidating independent retail businesses in favor of communal enterprises. By this maneuver, some artisans (craftsmen) were to be incorporated into national enterprises, and thus deprived of their independent earning capacity.

On October 27, 1948, the Party approved a five-year economic plan, to run from 1949 to 1953, and in May 1959 the Ninth Czecho-Slovak Communist Congress passed "general guidelines for the building of Socialism."

It would be a waste of time to dwell on all that the Communists planned to do, as opposed to what they were actually able to accomplish; or to recount how they went about presenting their case; or to guess at how firmly they believed that Communist productivity was destined to overtake Capitalism's; or to marvel at how feverishly they worked to build industry, particularly heavy industry. From the standpoint of this history, the only point of interest is how the plan to industrialize Slovakia was implemented, and how close Slovakia came to achieving equal footing with the Czech lands, because this was the one objective the Communists actually were able to attain. After all, sincere Slovaks could hardly be indifferent to the condition of their own nation. Were they simply marching in place? Had Slovakia ever been in the past, or was it in the present, a modern developed country?[26]

At the end of 1948, the leadership of the Czecho-Slovak Communist Party leveled serious charges against leading functionaries of the Central Committee of the Slovak Communist Party, namely Vladimir Clementis, Gustav Husak and Laco Novomesky, all three being accused of taking a non-Marxist approach to solving the problems of Slovak nationalism, as well as insubordination to central leadership. These charges, which can be summed up neatly as 'Bourgeois Nationalism', were upheld at a session of the Central Committee of the Slovak Communist Party, and were later also directed at Karol Smidke at the Ninth Congress of the Slovak Communist Party in Bratislava on May 24–25, 1950. Husak, dismissed as chairman of the Board of Commissioners, was replaced by Karol Bacilek, to be replaced in turn by Julius Duris in November 1951, followed in his turn by Rudolf Strechaj in January 1953. In the meantime, Frantisek Kubac succeeded to the chair of the Slovak National Council. Of the original trio of defendants, Clementis was sentenced to death and executed, while Husak and Novomesky were given long prison sentences.[27]

Between 1950 and 1952, a veritable hell of Communist oppression engulfed Slovakia as the Communist regime dropped the mask from its criminal face, as it had long since done in the Soviet Union. It went about prosecuting, imprisoning, and executing friend and foe alike. Between October and the end of 1952, the regime passed 233 death sentences, 178 of which it actually carried out. The number of people beaten to death without trial is unknown to this date, and may never be known.

In April 1950, the Greek Catholic (Byzantine rite) Church was formally abolished. The campaign to enforce the ban got underway during the night of April 14, as the People's Militia broke into monasteries and abducted monks to concentration camps. It soon shut down nuns' convents too, though more gradually, and dispersed their inmates to civilian life.[28] Bishops Gojdic, Buzalka and Vojtassak were imprisoned and tried, and after brutal interrogation, sentenced to long-term imprisonment, during which Bishop Gojdic eventually died. That same year, even former partisan leaders were thrown into prison and executed, incredibly at the behest, and to the satisfaction of their former comrades-in-arms. Hundreds of Catholic priests and ministers of various denominations found themselves in prison, too.[29]

In villages, meanwhile, all hell broke loose over collectivization, which cost many lives to establish. Furthermore, abandoning all pretense of religious tolerance, the Communists began indiscriminately spreading atheist propaganda. Many people lost their jobs, especially teachers and white-collar workers. Both the Catholic and the Lutheran Church, however, were ready for the onslaught, since they had been carefully preparing their faithful for just such an eventuality since 1945.

In March 1953, in quick succession, both Stalin and Gottwald died, and the criminal practices of Communism went through a period of gradual abatement.

During 1950s, Slovak agriculture undergoes drastic change

At the beginning of 1956, the Twentieth Congress of the Communist Party meeting in Moscow provided the occasion for Khrushchev's now legendary revelations of Stalinist crimes, perpetrated largely on fellow Communists. In October, 1956, the Hungarian masses, reacting to those terrible disclosures, rose in revolt, only to be brutally put down by the Soviet army. In Slovakia, these events precipitated an endless round of political screening, costing thousands of additional people their jobs and forcing many professionally qualified people into manual labor, with unqualified Communists stepping into their posts.

If the statistical data of the socio-economic changes that took place in Slovakia from 1945 to 1960 are to believed, industrial productivity in Slovakia increased annually by 10% after 1950: it was 500% higher in 1960 than in 1948, and an astounding 1000% higher in 1960 than in the immediate pre-war years. In 1961, workers in industry represented 37.7% of all workers, while in 1937, the total had been only 17.8%. Dozens of new industrial enterprises started up and older firms expanded.

A starting point for the analysis of agricultural development is the fact that in 1948, there were 12,000,000 parcels of land in Slovakia averaging 0.25 hectares (1 hectare = roughly 2.5 acres), or 32 parcels per farmer. Gross agricultural pro-

Construction of Slovak Ironworks, end of 1950s, to speed up industrialization

ductivity per hectare was 37.7% lower than in the Czech lands, production for market 56.4% lower, and livestock production 70.5% lower. By 1957, the socialist sector (cooperatives, state-run properties) held 54.4% of all arable land under cultivation, rising to 66.6% in 1958, and 78.7% in 1960. Of the arable land cultivated privately, 22.8% lay in upland regions and on lower mountain slopes that the government never planned to (nor ever did) collectivize. Between 1949 and 1960, agricultural production in Slovakia grew by 47%. By then, only 27% of all workers were in agriculture, as compared to 1950, when the ratio had still been as high as 41.9% and further back in 1930 when it had been an even higher 56.7%.

Living standards in general jumped, as did the availability of beds in health-care facilities, which increased from 9,169 in 1937 to 19,836 in 1955, along with a rise in the number of physicians from 1,878 to 6,159 (1960), while the number of patients per physician dropped from 1,893 to 675 (1960), and the rate of infant mortality from 159.8 per thousand in 1937 to 44.3 in 1955.

New state emblem of Czechoslovak Socialist Republic

Individual consumption of meat rose from 21.2 kg in 1937 to 47.1 kg in 1960, of wheat flour from 101 to 130.3 kg, of sugar from 15.2 to 30.0 kg, and of shortening and oil from 9.3 to 5.4 kg. Human life expectancy during this period rose too: for men, from 48.8 years (1929–32) to 68.3, for women from 50.8 years to 72.7. The number of universities increased from one to sixteen, and the number of university students rose from 2,784 to 20,298.

But socio-economic growth was not the only feature of this period, which was marked by the prosecution of 'Slovak Bourgeois Nationalism' under the leadership of uneducated Czech Communist, Karol Bacilek, First Secretary of the Central Committee of the Slovak Communist Party. Other Czechs took over strategic posts in Slovakia as well, many of them holdovers from the interwar period. Furthermore, whereas the percentage of Czech managers in Slovak enterprises was unusually high, practically no Slovaks worked in the central government offices in Prague.

Of course, Slovak art, culture, education, literature and science all enjoyed an expansion during this period, but only time will tell how much of it was worthwhile.

In July 1960, the Central Committee of the Czecho-Slovak Communist Party declared the building phase of Socialism successfully completed. Parliament passed a resolution changing the official name of the state to the Czecho-Slovak Socialist Republic, and dropping the Slovak double cross atop three hills from the state seal, replacing it with a 'campfire roast at the foot of Krivan Mountain' (Husak's words). Slovak jurisdictional reach shrank to a minimum. The Slovak Board of Commissioners, with its Chair, became a thing of the past and, just as during the Slovak National Uprising and the months following German expulsion, the only representation left to Slovaks was the Slovak National Council, which was neither fish nor fowl, being neither fully legislative nor fully executive.

14. Socialism: from Rise to Fall (1960–1989)

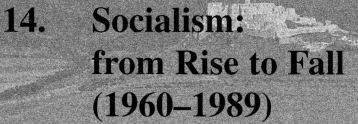

In the summer of 1960, when the Czecho-Slovak Communists announced that the build-up phase of socialism, longingly anticipated, was complete at last, there was no outburst of enthusiasm as one might have expected: after all, socialist ideas had been around for a long time, especially in the Czech lands; indeed, even prior to 1918, the Social Democrats had been preaching Marxist ideas, claiming that when economic exploitation ceased, paradise would descend to earth, since capitalism was the root of all of man's evils. Lenin had built on this idea, and Communists have since pursued it with fierce fanaticism, in Czecho-Slovakia as well as in Russia. But what happened in 1960 was the reverse of the socialist ideal, and it became more and more apparent that the West, united in fear of Communism and relying on the capitalist principles of economics, was enjoying ever more prosperity. The 'economic miracle' of the German Federal Republic, which had been a heap of rubble at the war's end, was particularly fascinating. It became apparent that the slogan 'No Experimentation!', coined by Adenauer, was the true path to economic, social, and other kinds of progress. Communist Socialism, staggering from crisis to crisis, from unsuccessful reform to unsuccessful reform, from pursuit of scapegoats to solutions that were faulty from the start, was a system at odds with human nature and the laws of economics.[1]

People began to look more and more for an escape from this 'paradise', leaving behind belongings, and even exposing relatives to certain persecution. As international tensions eased and tourism expanded, escape became increasingly possible, no longer requiring hazardous passage through barbed wire fields and roadblocks.

I can still remember how years ago, when I was a student of history, professors used to caution students to allow at least thirty years to elapse before attempting to write historical analyses of any given events. Wishing to abide by the advice of those conservative mentors of mine, I intend, in this last chapter, to present only a tentative sketch of the events of 1960 to 1989, through which I have lived.

An important feature of this latter period was the 1963 resolution of the Prague Central Committee winding up the campaign against bourgeois nationalism (Slovak, of course), which was by then labeled fabrication and fiction. A logical result of the resolution was the political downfall of the Prime Minister, Viliam Siroky, and the First Secretary of the Slovak Communist Party, Karol Bacilek. A storm of indignation and dismay erupted among the members of the Slovak Communist Party, who sought someone to blame for having been so grossly deceived and made a laughing stock for Czech Communists. However, their arguments for an extension of focus to the Czech milieu as well proved ineffectual, since the Czech Communists were simply uninterested.[2]

257

Ladislav Novomesky

In the fall of 1964, however, an earnest discussion did arise, not only in Slovakia but in the Czech lands as well, when Khrushchev's fall from power sparked fears that his successor, Brezhnev, would revive Stalinism. The Communist Party created various commissions to scour its past, it admitted mistakes, rehabilitated victims of the 1950s show trials and their survivors (including Vlado Clementis). Of course, Husak and Novomesky were released and again admitted into the Party, even awarded honors on the 20th Anniversary of the Slovak National Uprising. It became increasingly apparent that behind much of the mischief of those times was Antonin Novotny, who, after Gottwald's death, had succeeded to the office of First Secretary of the Czecho-Slovak Communist Party and, later, to the Presidency as well.[3]

In the latter months of 1967, there had been persistent calls for Novotny's resignation, but the balance of power in the Communist Party at that time was very close, causing all votes in the matter to be inconclusive. Finally, however, at the beginning of January 1968, he was forced to resign as First Secretary, while still temporarily retaining the post of President. Alexander Dubcek, a Slovak, succeeded to the office of First Secretary of the Central Committee of the Czecho-Slovak Communists Party, and 'ipso facto' became the most powerful man in the country – the first Slovak to climb so high. Vasil Bilak, who helped unseat Novotny, succeeded to Dubcek's vacated post in Bratislava.[4]

Alexander Dubcek had grown up in a Communist milieu. His father, a founding member of the Slovak Communist Party, was a staunch Socialist, both in the United States, where he lived for a while, and in Slovakia.[5] In 1925, as part of the international Communist drive, 'Interhelp', he moved to the USSR, where he remained with his family until 1938. The young Alexander naturally had to join 'Komsomol', the Soviet youth organization. Although some of the Communists who had come to the Soviet Union in this drive to build Socialism were liquidated by Stalin, the Dubceks remained true believers. Back in Slovakia, the young Alexander joined the war-time partisans and was wounded in action.[6]

Alexander Dubcek

After the end of the war in 1945, Alexander Dubcek launched a career as professional party bureaucrat. By 1950, when monasteries were being abolished, he had become the Secretary of the Central Committee of the Slovak Communist Party in Trencin and was, of course, in charge of the People's Militia during that operation. It was his job, after all. He continued to advance through the ranks and, in his various posts, must have at least consented to everything that was going on at the time. He made it to the top in 1962, becoming First Secretary of the Central Committee of the Czecho-Slovak Communist Party, while also serving as First Secretary in Bratislava as well (1963–68).[7]

*Bratislava streets
in August 1968*

In the Prague milieu he decided to promote a reform of socialism, to give it back its 'human face'. During his tenure, conditions underwent a sea change, easing up drastically. However, before anything really concrete could be accomplished, just a few weeks before a Party congress scheduled to resolve all problems definitively, the armies of five Warsaw Pact countries (the USSR, the German Democratic Republic, Poland, Hungary and Bulgaria) invaded Czecho-Slovakia.[8]

Top Czecho-Slovak Party officials were abducted to the Soviet Union. When the Czecho-Slovak citizenry stood up to the occupying troops, in effect, morally defeating them, Brezhnev was left with no choice but to negotiate with the abducted party leaders. President Svoboda flew in from Prague to join his compatriots, but his role in the negotiations was not particularly effective. Dubcek, facing Brezhnev manfully, held out to the very edge of physical and psychic collapse, but, caving in at last, signed a protocol which, among various demeaning conditions, imposed Soviet troops on Czecho-Slovakia, "on a temporary basis." During this crisis, Husak, then Deputy Prime Minister and newly elected First Secretary of the Central Committee of the Slovak Communist Party, succeeded in getting close to Brezhnev.[9]

Solemn signing of constitutional amendment establishing Czecho-Slovak Federative Republic, in Bratislavsky Hrad, October 30, 1968

Lessons to be learned from critical evolution of Party and society, after 13th Congress of Czechoslovak Communist Party

POUČENIE
z krízového vývoja
v strane a spoločnosti
po XIII. zjazde KSČ

*Schválené na plenárnom zasadaní
ÚV KSČ v decembri 1970*

Dubcek remained formally in power up to April 1969, when he yielded to Gustav Husak. Taking over in Prague, the latter revealed his true colors of resolute friendship to the Soviet Union, and to Brezhnev, by stamping his approval on the 1968 Warsaw Pact intervention, as well as by expressing thanks for the help against 'counter-revolution' and by re-evaluating Party membership lists, precipitating the expulsion of roughly half a million people, with attendant professional ruin for most of them.[10]

To make matters worse, Husak began to use the Czech language at public appearances in Prague, in the process alienating many Czechs, as well as Slovaks. Vasil Bilak, a prominent turncoat in the events of 1968, became one of Husak's closest associates, moving to second place in the party ranks. People's hopes were rudely shattered as life went back to the way it was: the Party resumed its dominance in government and society, terrorizing it as never before.

First Secretary Husak reshaped the Party in strict keeping with the tenets of Leninism: all passivity was severely punished, including non-participation in meetings and non-payment of dues, in this respect trumping both Gottwald and Novotny. Not even his long imprisonment, owed mainly to Gottwald, disrupted or shattered Husak's faith in the Party. Amazingly, he went on to resurrect the cult of Gottwald, particularly as the author of Bolshevization in 1929 to 1933. Gottwald's portrait again began to appear on speakers' daises (on May Day, for instance), though beneath Dubcek's, to be sure, and this in spite of the fact that he had practically dropped out of the public mind, remembered at most for the many crimes committed on his watch. Husak even took on the additional office of President, though in 1968, the Party had expressly prohibited the vesting of the offices of First Secretary and President in one person.

Once again, people withdrew into passivity, not stirring again until the beginning of 1977, when dissidents in Prague, most of them expelled party members, composed *Charter 77*.[11]

Gustav Husak, General Secretary of Central Committee of Czechoslovak Communist Party and President of Czecho-Slovak Federative Republic

But life went on. The head-start of the capitalist West became progressively more evident, the miseries of Socialism more obvious. More and more people, mostly the young, defected each year, the planned economy continued to produce more and more shortages, and incompetent Communist leaders went on denying that the cause lay in faulty theory. But for all that, the standard of living remained higher in Czecho-Slovakia than in other Communist countries, with the exception of the German Democratic Republic. Consequently, people just put up with the bad, while holding their tongues.

However, when the young, energetic Gorbachev came to power in the USSR and called for 'perestroika' (restructuring), hope for improvement began to sprout in Czecho-Slovakia as well. After all, as a satellite of the Soviet Union, Czecho-Slovakia could not ignore what was happening in Moscow. Czech and Slovak Communists began to announce the beginnings of a process of economic transformation and democratization, if only for effect.

In 1989, pressures for change in the Communist world were coming to a head, but it seemed that those pressures were brewing everywhere except in Czecho-Slovakia. When the Prague police brutally put down a peaceful demonstration of students celebrating the 50th anniversary of November 17, 'Students' Day', events took a dramatic turn: day after day, in protest, theaters stopped performing, evening after evening people assembled for demonstrations in Prague and in Bratislava, and a general strike shut down the economy.

These various pressures brought to bear by the people against the Communists soon began to yield fruit; a gentle revolution spread across the land. Without the application of violence, the government collapsed: Chairman Husak and General Secretary Jakes stepped down; the People's Militia disbanded; Parliament rescinded Party primacy; Party organizations withdrew from factories, businesses, and other institutions. National reconciliation became the order of the day. The era of Socialism was over as the Communist system collapsed like a house of cards. New goals were set, including democratic elections, transition to a pluralistic political system, and creation of a free market economy. But individual Communists managed to hold on to leading positions, especially in industrial enterprises.

Mikhail S. Gorbachev

One stage of Slovak history was over, another about to begin.

An Afterword

History is 'the evidence of the ages, the light of truth, the soul of memory, the guide of life and the messenger of antiquity' *(testis temporum, lux veritatis, vita memoriae, magistra vitae, nuntia vetustatis).* Thus wrote the great Roman statesman, philosopher, author and preeminent orator of his age, Marcus Tullius Cicero more than two millennia ago.

As I leaf through the first post-November synthesis of Slovak history by the leading Slovak historian Anton Spiesz (whose doctoral dissertation [Dr.Sc.] was blocked until his political rehabilitation in 1991), it is altogether natural for me to recall the above thought of Cicero. Because, despite the fact that this work was written 'a little too hastily', it was written in a sincere effort to capture in brief the rich history of this territory and its inhabitants, from times preceding the emergence of today's nations to the recent past, when nation building had been substantially completed. At the same time, it emphasizes the relevance of historical events to the genesis of the Slovak nation. Spiesz strives to interpret this process, not in isolation, but with a view to its interconnectedness, on a regional/ethnic scale, as well as on a continental/European scale. At the same time, he also strives to capture the many ethnic interactions and the accompanying acculturational processes. He views the development of these processes with a great deal of empathy for its actors and creators, rejecting a historical mythologization of Slovakia and its inhabitants, while presenting in an accessible way its long and tortuous journey to self-awareness, emancipation, and at last, independent, democratic statehood, which he himself unfortunately never lived to see.

Despite any reservations one may feel, the work retains its relevance for today; it speaks to the reader, and gives him access to times long past, as well as times quite recent, in all their historical consistency as well as in their many contradictions. It is the statement of a renowned historian, portraying what past times have witnessed, while shedding light on the many aspects of historical truth. In a pluralistic democracy, every historian has a right to his own view of his nation's history, of its moments of grief and joy, shame and pride, cowardice and courage, as well as its moments of supreme heroism and achievement. For that is the way of history: people themselves willy-nilly create it, with their characters and from their experiences and inherited wisdoms; and some very exceptional people have the unique ability to see far into the future. This work presents its dominant notes in individually gradated chapters, which deserve to be expanded and deepened on the basis of the most recent scholarly findings and developments, particularly in archaeology and medieval studies. Special attention needs to be given to eras preceding nation formation, and to the shaping of the earliest inchoate features of our nationality, as well as its later vicissitudes in multi-ethnic Hungary and in Czecho-Slovakia. We have, however, also felt the need to supplement the presentation with information about the post-November 1989 period, and the foundation of the present modern, internationally recognized Slovak state (January 1, 1993). That is what this supplement is about.

In the period preceding nation formation, our territory, too, witnessed the complicated development of mankind, its struggles with surrounding nature, through and between ice-ages, and particularly after the recession of the last ice cover. Without question, we can date the beginnings of prehistoric Slovakia more than a quarter of a million years back. The significance of this region has been confirmed by the 1993–1994 finds of two pieces of bone from the skull of a Neanderthal man (a left parietal bone and the left half of a forehead bone) on the left bank of the Vah River near Sala, dated back over 80,000 years. These bones have an extraordinary scientific value for Europe and the rest of the world, throwing light on the anthropological development of modern man's immediate predecessor – homo sapiens. New discoveries have been made in archaeological analyses of the late Paleolithic Age (40,000–8000 years B.C.) on the outskirts of the town of Moravany and Banka near Piestany. The territory of Slovakia was resettled after the retreat of the glaciers from north central Europe, i.e. during the Middle Stone Age (Mesolithic), 8000 to 6000 B.C. Primitive man lived not only on the territory of Southwest Slovakia, but in the region of the High Tatra Mountains as well (Velky Slavkov), in fact, even in Eastern Slovakia (Medvedia jaskyna near Ruzin and Kosice-Barca).

Gradually the unproductive way of life (hunting-gathering), which had existed for hundreds of thousands of years, came to an end. Man began increasingly to work free of his simple dependence on nature by actively manipulating his environment. The presence of farming communities on the territory of Slovakia, as elsewhere in Central Europe, is documented from as early as the first half of the Fifth Millennium B.C. These communities were agents of revolutionary change, engaged in the process of creating a new civilization. Settlements like the one in Sturovo were unique, covering an area of several dozen hectares, with dwellings twenty to thirty meters long, built on poles running laterally from a central carrying beam (Muzla-Cenkov, Blatne, Patince). (Contacts with well-developed civilizations to the Southeast are evident.) Also unique are extensive, centrally oriented communities with architecturally well-developed dwellings, surrounded by so-called 'rondels', fortified walls averaging 70 to 150 meters in diameter, dated to the 4th Millennium B.C. in Svodin, Bucany, Zlkovce, Borova. These forts are a particularly dominant feature along the central course of the Danube.

Ground-plan of home of Lengyel Culture, in Zlkovce, end of 4th Millennium B.C.

During the Late Stone Age (end of 4th millennium to 1900 B.C.) the first golden ornaments begin appearing (Tibava, Male Raskovce), as do copper ax-heads (Tibava, Handlova). Mass graves in Nitriansky Hradok call attention to dramatic changes occurring from the middle of the 3rd millennium B.C. A significant part of these changes is the expansion of 'artistic' activities. In the sculptures of this period, in the ornamentation and modeling of ceramics characteristic of the individual stages of the Middle and Late Stone Age, we see vivid expressions of artistic sense in a primitive society. It gradually appears depicting ancient shepherds living in the higher elevations of the Carpathians.

Pestles for ore-crushing, Spana Dolina, 2nd Millennium B.C.

But the truly dominant age of these early times was the Bronze Age (1900 to 700 B.C.), which left its indelible mark on development all over Europe. The lands on the middle Danube, in the shadow of the Carpathian Mountain peaks, and on the upper and middle reaches of the Tisa River, became a central receiving area for influences from the Southeast and Southwest, as well as from the North. Growing sophistication in architecture (similarly fortified settlements can be found throughout the Carpathian basin, the Balkans and the Eastern Mediterranean), expansion of surface mining for non-ferrous ores (particularly copper), and development of bronze metallurgy, all these, plus lively commercial activity, rich religious cults, and splendid art, were characteristic of precisely this region. These developments are documented by pestles for grinding ores found in Spana Dolina (Second Millennium B.C.), and decorated bone and antler items (ca. 1600 B.C.) found in Nitriansky Hradok, Kosice-Barca, Spissky Stvrtok, as well as bronze artifacts, bronze and gold jewelry, and ceramics throughout the region. Proof of well-developed building arts is to be found in the already mentioned fortified communities (we could call them early towns), surrounded by extensive suburbs (Nitriansky Hradok, Vesele, Ivanovce, Barca, Nizna Mysla, Rozhanovce, Spissky Stvrtok, Vcelince). The mature level of civilization of the Bronze Age has left its mark on all subsequent developments. Evidence has also been found of the use of iron in this region (Ganovce-Studna). In art and architecture, it is possible to trace contacts with the Mycenaean and Hittite realms, and it is even possible that they reflect a mutual exchange of ideas, as reflected in their unique artistic and architectural sensibility.

Cult mask from Majda Hraskova Cavern, Silica, 11th Century B.C.

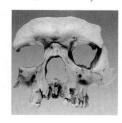

In more recent pre-history, burial mound cultures begin appearing on the European scene (including our own), and they originated precisely in the regions of the middle Danube. They take the form of mound burial, and bi-ritualism (interment and cremation). This culture spread outward to the West, as well as to the South; it was accompanied by an astonishing development of bronze metallurgy, mass production of weaponry (long and short swords, daggers and arrowheads), reflecting a sophisticated arms technology. The copious and varied

Moon idol,
Chrovatsky Grob,
turn of 7th to 6th
Century B.C.

findings of bronze jewelry (pins, pendants, rings) are evidence of the aforementioned esthetic sensibility of their creators and lenders. Quite unique is the bronze waistband discovered in Chotin.

The expansion of that culture identified with ash-urn fields belongs to the period of the great migrations of bronze-age man. The well-known activities of so many nations, which at the turn of the 13th to 12th Century B.C., attacked contemporary states and cities in the Eastern Mediterranean region, evidently were spurred by impulses from Central Europe. In our area, the unique burial mounds of tribal chiefs, with their special construction and lavish accoutrements (garments and armaments) pointing to influences from the Near East and the Homeric world (Ockov, Dedinka, Kolta, Caka), were quite extraordinary. Our territory continued to be an important crossroads of economic, cultural and artistic movements between East and West, North and South. This period, the Bronze Age, was a veritable golden age of European pre-history.

A culmination or fruition, in a sense, of the heretofore autochthonic development on our territory, was the early Iron Age (700–400 B.C.). In the context of

Vessel from
Dunajska Luzna

ongoing ethnic differentiation, three substantially independent, cultural/historical regions evolved in Slovakia: Southwestern, Northern and Eastern. The early Iron Age was a final chapter, a kind of epilogue to the pre-history of the whole Central European scene. Thracian tribes came into our territory, with their version of the cultural/historical values of Hellenic civilization. Princely citadels sprang up (Smolenice), along with burial mounds with rich accoutrements, where 'princes' were buried (Reca, Dunajska Luzna-Nove Kosariska). Our territory, as well as better known historical regions, found itself on the threshold of a 'new' era of European civilization. Iron became an important factor in further social and economic development. Unique centers of commerce evolved, and with them, new methods of production, administration and religious worship. Beside the contacts with the Southeast, we can trace active links to the Etruscan/Italian culture. We find its influence in art, metal sculptures, and household vessels. The incursions of Southeastern nomadic tribes (the Sigynnians and Kimerians) also left their mark on the cultural/historical life of man in the Carpathian basin. Through Thracian mediation, and outright invasion by Thracian/Scythian tribes, Scythian artifacts found their way onto our territory (Chotin arrows, metal quivers, women's jewelry, and mirrors). Indeed, it was the incursion of mounted nomadic groups that caused the disappearance of many splendidly constructed and well-fortified bastions at the end of the pre-historic period.

Detail of clasp, Nitrianske Pravno, 4th Century B.C.

Towards the end of the early Iron Age, Celts coming from the West spread across our region. This early historical nation, mature and aggressive, influenced evolution through the latter centuries of our pre-history, and left its mark on the cultural/social processes of the late Iron Age (4th Century B.C. to the end of the millennium). Occupying southern Slovakia at first, the Celts gradually dispersed from there to the North and East. They brought with them ancient Etruscan production methods and contemporary artistic styles. New, heretofore unknown, techniques in pottery (for instance decorative ceramics, turned on a potter's wheel) came as a revelation, as did also innovations in metal casting and forging, building of fortified 'oppida' (early urban settlements), coin-minting, jewelry crafting (the mask-like buckle in Nitrianske Pravno) and, of course, practices in 'international' trade. Definitely unique are the 'oppida' in Bratislava and Zemplin counties, and the mint in Bratislava, which produced a Celtic coin stamped with the image of Biatec (a Celtic prince?). Gold, silver and especially bronze artifacts from this period are quite impressive, as are ornate swords of iron and their partially preserved scabbards. We get a good glimpse of life in Celtic society through the finds in grave sites at Izkovce, Drna, Dubnik, Palarikovo, Mana, and Male Kosihy. Numerous finds provide valuable insight into how the Celts penetrated into new areas (invasion of the Celtic Cotini), and how they were at first influ-

Stylish clasp from grave of prince, Krakovany-Straze, 3rd. Century A.D.

enced by the Illyrians, then later by the Dacians (around the turn of the millennium). Towards the end of the last century, before the birth of Christ, we can discern signs of a symbiosis of Celts and Dacians. Gradually, however, Celtic traditions taper off and Germanic influences become predominant.

Around the start of the Christian era, the geopolitical situation in Central Europe began to change drastically, responding, above all, to expansive pressures from the South, the regions of Roman civilization. Adjacent to Slovakia, immediately south of the Roman 'limes' (border) on the Danube, two Roman provinces were created – Pannonia and Noricum. Between the 1st and 4th Century A.D., Germanic tribes became the dominant element on the territory of Slovakia. A period of interaction between so-called 'barbarian' regions and the Roman provinces arose. Incursions of the Marcomani and Quadi tribes seriously impacted our area, as well as others, and Germanic tribes reacted by forming an alliance under a chieftain named Marobuduus. This alliance expanded under Marobuduus' successor and became known as the Kingdom of Vannius, which established ties to Roman power, including rich trade in beautiful, and even luxurious goods, as attested by finds in Kostolna pri Dunaji, Abraham, Sladkovicovo. New military outposts for the Roman legions were constructed on the left bank of the Danube (Iza-Leanyvar, Devin, Stupava, Bratislava) facilitating steadily deeper penetration of Roman armies into the Germanic hinterlands. Starting with the end of the 1st Century, rapacious raids by 'barbaric' Marcomani, Quadi and Sarmatians troubled the province of Pannonia in particular, and it was these raids, plus possibly those of other 'barbarians', that touched off the Marcomanian wars, starting in 166. At this point, the Roman emperor, Marcus Aurelius, enters the pre-history of Slovakia, encamping on the lower reaches of the Hron River, where he wrote the introductory chapter of his *Meditations*. An inscription at the base of the stronghold in Trencin (179 A.D.) is a tangible memento of these events. The death of Marcus Aurelius (180 A.D.), and the peace initiated by his son Commodus, subsequently created conditions for a relatively peaceful Roman-Germanic co-existence. But the power of the Quadi was growing, settlements became more concentrated, including an important agglomeration of settlements on the middle reaches of the Vah River (the crematory burial site in Ockovo, the princely graves in Kralovany-Straze), and on the left bank of the Morava River (Vysoka pri Morave, Zohor, and Cacov). This 'peaceful co-existence' is reflected in the deep penetration of Roman building techniques into Germanic territory (Milanovce, Cifer-Pac, Stupava, the remains of baths in Bratislava-Dubravka). In the southern areas of Eastern Slovakia, and even to their north, can be seen influences of the Dacian and Sarmatian peoples (Jazygos). From the latter half of the 2nd Century on, we can trace the expansion of the Hazdings, one of various tribes of Vandals (Zemplin, Kvakovce) who settled mainly in areas north of the Carpathians. It is quite possible that, together with them, came Slavic tribes, living in a kind of natural symbiosis. From the end of the 2nd and beginning of the 3rd Century we can trace cultural growth in this region, extensive economic changes, and social differentiation, as evidenced, for instance, by the graves of a princely class in Cejkov and Ostrovany. Gradual colonization continued through the 4th Century, though around mid-century, Roman influence began gradually to decline. Nevertheless, under the Emperor Valentian I, new fortifications were built on the Roman 'limes' and old army posts reconstructed.

Helmet, with silver and gold ornamentation, Dolne Semerovce, ca. 500 A.D.

At this point, our territory found itself on the threshold of a 'new' historical era, which separated Antiquity from the Middle Ages. The decline of ancient Rome and the rise of new 'barbarian' states on its ruins, exerted considerable influence on the historical and cultural/social evolution of our territory. Our southern regions, above all, became the scene of an ongoing chain-reaction of ethnic migrations. In northern and central Slovakia, and to a large extent, even on the territory of Eastern Slovakia, a more or less autochthonic evolution continued. An era arose which received the name 'the great migration of nations'. The Huns, the Goths, the Heruls, the Lombards, and other ethnics living on horseback, built short-lived empires on the rich remains of the crumbling Roman Empire. Indisputably, Slavic tribes enjoyed an important vantage point as this process ran its course. The time of our Slavic adolescence had arrived.

On the basis of archaeological findings, V. Budinsky-Kricka has long since expressed the hypothesis that the middle reaches of the Torysa River were one of the crystallizing 'centers' of Slavic ethnogenesis in the Carpathian region, as early as the 3rd to 6th Century A.D.[1]

This hypothesis is supported by some broadly based premises, one of which is the fact that the Gepids respected a 'solid border' in the North, defined by the remains of former Sarmatian ramparts. Another is an inscription on the gravestone of St. Martin of Tours (died 397), a native of Pannonian Sabaria, who participated in 4th Century missionary activity in Pannonia, where Slavic tribes were among the recipients of the covenant of Christ. The baton of history was passed on in the multi-ethnic Central European milieu between the 4th and 6th Century, and Slavic elements indisputably played a significant role in the passing, above all in the pristine mountain valleys of the Carpathian escarpment. The importance of the Slavic tribes is attested by the Byzantine historian, Procopius of Caesarea. Procopius also describes Hildigis, a pretender to the Lombard throne, who took refuge from Lombard King Wach (527–536) among Slavs who were quite capable of putting together an army, and made an alliance with them. Recent research points to a likelihood that the Slavs mentioned here were from the middle

Danube. The existence of a strong Slavic community is suggested by the fact that, as the Lombards migrated southward, they bypassed present-day Slovakia, making only tentative forays against the Devin Gate. These events took place before the arrival of the Avars, and not quite a full century before the rise of Samo's Slavic kingdom.

Samo's kingdom (623–658) represents an attempt to effectively withstand the unrelenting pressures of the Merovingian realm of the Franks. Samo's rule bolstered the self-confidence of the Slavs of the middle Danube, where the core of his domain lay in present-day Slovakia. After the death of Samo (658), it was the proximity to the Avars and commercial contacts with the Byzantine and Frankish empires that created qualitatively better conditions for further development. Settlements were concentrated along important arteries of communication between the Slavs and Western European regions north of the Danube, and the strategic points where army units were stationed (Devinska Nova Ves at the confluence of the Danube and Morava rivers, Komarno at the confluence of the Danube and the Vah, and Zelovce near the Ipel). Two veritable treasure troves of artifacts found in these areas call attention to important transregional commercial relations, and trade routes running through them: one is in the vicinity of Halic in Novohrad County, the other near Zemiansky Vrbovok.

After 670 we can speak of a kind of cultural and ethnic symbiosis of two distinct ethnic groups, with contrasting mentalities and ways of life – the Slavs and the Avars. Gradually, in the course of the 8th Century, the more resilient Slavic group went through a period of territorial consolidation during which regional princes/chieftains created military retinues, adopting Western-European as well as Northern-European styles of armament. The Avars ended up being assimilat-

Fortified Avar settlement

ed by Frankish and Slavic societies after their definitive defeat at the hands of Charlemagne and the Franks (796).

At the turn of the 8th to 9th Century, a new and important center of economic and cultural/political power sprang up along the middle flow of the Nitra River from which it took the name the 'Nitranian Principality'. It was in this period, too, that Nitra became a fortified town. Christianity played an important role in the process, particularly through the activities of Scottish, Irish, Frankish and Italian missionaries. Citadels sprang up on the middle Nitra River in Turiec County, on the middle Vah River, and in lower Orava, Spis and Zemplin Counties. The existence of 'magnates' is attested by rich burial sites in Blatnica and Maly Cepcin in Turiec County. It is quite obvious that, as early as the turn of the 8th to 9th Century, the prerequisites for state formation were already in place among the Slavs north of the Danube and in the vicinity of the fortified town of Nitra.

Gilded bronze buckle, Brodziany, early 9th Century

Prince Pribina founded the principality of Nitra, taking advantage of the collapse of the Avar Kingdom (aptly described by M. Kucera as 'a monarchy of the steppes'). Towards the end of the 9th Century, at the latest, conditions became favorable for a political emancipation of western Slavs. At this time a new epoch of early Slovak history was beginning to take shape. An important manifestation of the process was the dedication of a Christian church in Nitra (Nitrava) by the archbishop of Saltzburg, Adalram (ca. 828). During the course of the 9th Century, the social structure of the Slavs living north of the Danube was undergoing additional integrative processes. The rise of Great Moravia was presaged in 833 by the military expansion of Mojmir I, the ruler of a Moravian Principality, at the expense of the Nitran Principality. A battle between these opposing forces took place, most likely somewhere near the Vah River, which brought down Pribina's fortress at Pobedim. Mojmir's Moravian kingdom, however, never succeeded in completely erasing the territorial independence and, in a sense, the autonomy of the Nitran Principality. What had begun as a kind of dualism was preserved, a fact attested by Nitra's continuance as the seat of a feudal duke or prince, a member of the Mojmir dynasty. The first such duke to achieve prominence was Svatopluk I, King Rastislav's nephew. Under Rastislav, an extensive program of reconstructing old citadels and building new ones took place at various locations: Nitra, Ducovo, Bratislava, Devin (Dowina), Muzla-Cenkovo, Stary Tekov, Divinka near Zilina, Vysehrad in Turiec County, Detva-Kalamarka, Zvolen-Motova, Spisske Tomasovce-Cingov, Zehra-Drevenik, Sarisske Sokolovce, Kusin, and Zemplin County. The Nitra Principality as a vassal state of Great Moravia, which from its beginning had been an early, politically/administratively dualistic ('Moravian-Slovak') medieval state, represented an important phenomenon in the development of Slovak ethnic individuality and in the delineation of its territorial base.

Detail of Spur, Vysny Kubin (first half 9th Century)

'Politicians and statesmen' of great foresight, Mojmir, Rastislav, and Svatopluk I, and, in no lesser measure, the Christian missionaries Constantine (Cyril) the Philosopher, and his brother Methodius, both from Byzantine Salonika (and both later canonized), as well as their pupils, St. Gorazd,[2] Naum, Clement, and the ecclesiastical retinue of Bishop Wiching of Nitra – all of these men lifted Great Moravian statehood to the level of the surrounding European civilization. It was this territory that became the first beneficiary of the mutual enrichment of Rome and Byzantium that resulted from their activities. The arrival in Great Moravia of the Byzantine mission (863), led by the brothers Constantine and Methodius, at King Rastislav's invitation, became a significant factor in a bi-polarization of intellectual and political interests that evolved at this time. By their defense of the Old Slavonic liturgical language in Venice and in Rome (867), the Byzantine brothers raised it, both liturgically and literarily, to the level of the then leading languages of Europe, Greek and Latin. They created an alphabet and literature on a par with the best in Europe; and on this Central European line of demarcation between the two substantially supra-national cultures, Latin and Byzantine, a unique Slavonic culture, literature and written legal code emerged (*A Prologue, An Admonition to Rulers, A Great-Moravian Legal Code, The Order of Confession, Great Moravian Legal Procedures, Life of Constantine, Life of Methodius, Notes on Letters by the Monk Chrabr,* and a *Life of Naum).* Education flourished in church schools (e.g. at Devin and Nitra), and churches and basilicas were built

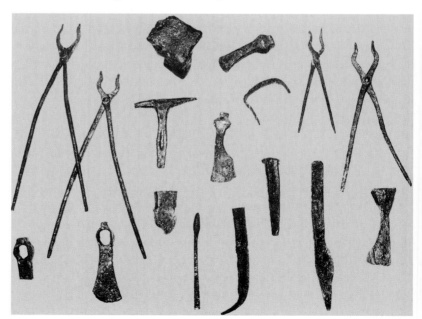

Collection of blacksmith, farmer, and woodworker tools, Vrsatecke Podhradie, late 9ᵗʰ Century

in Nitra, Bratislava, Devin, Ducovo, Nitrianska Blatnica, and possibly even at Kostolany pod Tribecom. With the death of Methodius (April 6, 885), and after the short-lived (one year) activity of Gorazd, a gradual dying out or liquidation of the unique Slavonic liturgy and culture in Slovakia ensued. This sad demise took place with the tacit approval of Svatopluk I, influenced by Wiching, the German Bishop of Nitra. With the departure of the brothers' disciples, to which Svatopluk I gave tacit consent, Slavonic church schools, a wellspring of culture and identity, were discontinued. After 886, Svatopluk accorded priority to military expansion over the dissemination of culture, and thus lost the important domestic support of Slavic clergy.

Indisputably, Great Moravia was, in the latter half of the 9th Century, a completely crystallized state, with full executive, military, administrative, judicial, ecclesiastical, and, lastly, international functions. We find echoes of its existence even in King Alfred's England with the Anglo-Saxon translation (ca. 874) of Orosius' *Historia Mundi* (A History of the World), in which the author construes Great Moravia as a point of orientation for the Danube basin.

The assault of multi-ethnic nomads from the East (the precursors of the later Magyars) towards the end of the 9th Century, was directed mainly against the eastern regions of the Nitran Principality, where the vassal prince Svatopluk II, the younger son of Svatopluk, resided. Later, the onslaught of these nomadic marauders (one of their seven tribes was called Megyer – Magyar) took aim at the very center of Great Moravia, and in July 907 at Bratislava (Brezalauspurc, or Predslav's bastion), and with the help of the Slovaks and Moravians, it succeeded in defeating the armies of the Bavarians. The course of these intrusions of nomadic tribes (the 'Ougri', 'Ungari', 'Uhri') and of later multi-ethnic farming/herding societies into Central Europe, can be traced on the basis of present-day archaeological evidence. However, during two periods (between 920 and 925 and between 930 to 940) they left untouched the regions north of a line running easterly through Trnava – Nitra – Levice – Krupina – Lucenec – Rimavska Sobota, thus allowing the process of Slav settlement there to go on uninterrupted. South of this line, a natural symbiosis of local Slavs and the newly arriving nomadic peoples (including farmers/herders) occurred, as attested by the distinctive 'Belobrd' culture uncovered by archaeological diggings.

After the defeat of nomadic invading tribes at the Lech River near Augsburg by the German King Otto I the Great on August 10, 955, a new situation emerged in the Central European region. The defeated marauders withdrew to their 'new homeland', more specifically, to land already occupied by our ancestors for several centuries. On arrival, they found people with a mature economic, socio-political, Christian and cultural life-style already there. Neither the previous nomadic incursions, nor those of the later Czech Premysl dynasty had substantially disrupted the inhabitants' development. The first to recognize the importance of the local culture and traditions was Gejza, a duke from the Nitra area and a scion of the strongest of the nomadic tribes, the Megyers (later Magyars). Around 970, he united other chieftains, and founded a Magyar principality south of the Danube. Having invited Bavarian missionaries, and later a Bohemian mission led by St. Adalbert, he received baptism in 995 together with his son Vajk, who was later to become King Stephen I of Hungary. It was probably around this time that a church was built in the Nitra bastion, and consecrated to St. Emeram, a German saint from Regensburg.

We learn of the existence of Great Moravia, and of developments after its demise, from a work by the Byzantine emperor, Constantine VII Porphyrogenitus, *De administrando imperio* (About Managing an Empire), which describes 'he megale Morabia' (Greek for Great Moravia). We also gain valuable information from a more recent source, which cites Magyar marauders captured in Spain in 942 speaking of a country called 'Morabia'. Constantine VII Porphyrogenitus, uses the names 'Huns' and 'Avars' for the Turkish and Onogur tribes (probably on the basis of oral traditions in which the lifestyle of these people was preserved). Contemporary sources call these tribes 'Ongri' and 'Ungari'. Apparently the Magyar ethnic evolved in the latter half of the 10th and the beginning of the 11th Century, during the same period that the multi-ethnic state of Hungary was taking shape. In this period, the latter half of the 10th Century, the ethnogenetic process of the Nitran Slovene/Slovaks was also nearing completion. The Slovaks along with the Magyars were indisputably an important constitutive element in the founding of the Kingdom of Hungary.

Slovaks, Magyars, Germans and other medieval ethnic groups were all constitutive elements in the building of the Hungarian kingdom. Prince Gejza laid the foundation for a centrally ruled state in the latter third of the 10th Century. Later, Gejza's son Vajk (the future King Stephen) became vassal duke in Nitra; then in 997 he became Grand Duke, and on December 25, 1000, he was crowned first king of Hungary by legates of Pope Sylvester II. Thus, early Hungarian statecraft preserved the continuity of the Great Moravian system of governance, which was not simply an imitation of the practices of the Ottonian dynasty of Germany. The predominant organizational foundation of the Moravian king's dominion had been the royal court and a network of citadels. There is no doubt that these organizational elements remained after Great Moravia was gone. Our history thus became an important part of Hungarian history, and the Slovenes/Slovaks of Nitra undoubtedly made many contributions to the economy and culture of Hungarian life, to contemporary movements and changes in

Coin minted during reign of St. Stephen

the early medieval environment. The principality of Nitra and the kingdom of Great Moravia created values and shaped foundations for the historical evolution and preservation of Slovaks for an entire millennium. In fact, the roots of the Slovenes/Slovaks were firmly anchored in this region, even back beyond the Great Moravian era. It was precisely because of these facts that Slovaks were able to survive through the whole subsequent millennium, even without their own statehood. Slovak history became an important component of Hungarian history: Slovaks never disappeared in the leveling processes of European feudalism, but continued to exist, after their own fashion, as a distinctive people.

Execution of Kopan, leader of insurrection against Stephen I

Grand Duke Gejza, and later his son Stephen I (1000–1038), incorporated many values adopted from the Slovenes/Slovaks in the formative processes of the multi-ethnic Hungarian kingdom. A grasp of the principle of 'multi-ethnicity' in the building of an early-medieval state, was formulated by King Stephen in an instruction to his son Emerich: "*…a kingdom built on one language and one tradition is weak and fragile…*" Taking advantage of the older administrative structure, its system of agriculture, crafts and metal-working, the Hungarian feudal state was able to take shape and grow steadily stronger. King Stephen I was eventually able to defeat his rebellious pagan tribal chiefs, leaning on the Slovene/Slovak governing families north of the Danube. He was able thus to defeat Koppanyi in the southern Danube region, as well as Ajtonyi, the ruler of Transylvania and the Lower Tisa River region. Of course, King Stephen I appreciated the important support he received from the Slovene/Slovak families, the Hunt-Poznans (the Diviaks), and the Bogat-Radvans. Archaeological and historical sources (charters, letters), as well as medieval chronicles and legends in Slovakia, and finally, historical linguistics (for instance, the craft-based names of towns), historical geography, and iconographic sources, all of these inform us of the oldest 'Hungarian' history of our territory and its inhabitants.

Nitra was one of three ducal seats of the Arpad dynasty. The oldest known Hungarian diocese north of the Danube was later merged into the archdiocese of Esztergom. King Andrew I (1046–1060) turned over administration of a third of his kingdom to his brother Bela. This third included not only the early medieval principality of Nitra, but all of Northern Hungary (present-day Slovakia), and the eastern territories of Hungary (headquartered in Bihar, on the border of modern Romania and Hungary). This huge expanse of territory embraced fifteen counties, which tied it to the territorial/legal structures inherited from the times of Great Moravia. The original symbol of the duchy was a double cross, which was later horizontally incorporated in the town of Nitra's coat-of-arms. In the latter half of the 10th Century, the bishopric of Nitra was renewed and a bishop's castle was built on the site of the 9th Century Great Moravian fortress. The impor-

Gilded bronze sculpture,
Velky Kamenec,
12ᵗʰ Century

tance of the principality of Nitra in this period is highlighted by the fact that it was precisely this territory that bore the brunt of almost all the contemporary Germanic assaults on Hungary. In the course of the 12th Century, this principality lost its erstwhile standing, partly because, after the personal union of Hungary with Croatia, the focus of many Hungarian activities moved to its southern border regions. The ethnic makeup on our territory underwent a gradual change during the transition from the 11th to 12th Century, with the influx of German settlers (mostly in Spis County and Central Slovakia) and of Italian master masons (in Spisske Vlachy). These settlers came with the consent of King Geza II. In the meantime, after losing a battle with the Czech Premysls in 1116, King Stephen II ceded to the Czech ruler land bounded by the White Carpathians, the Olsava and Morava Rivers and Velicka Creek. The mining industry continued to expand, particularly the mining of silver for the Hungarian Mint, and favorable conditions arose for the granting of royal charters to certain towns (Bratislava, Trnava, Kosice, Levoca), as well as the construction of royal fortresses, including borders bastions, for instance on the Devin heights, in Bratislava, in Trencin, in Pusty Hrad nad Zvolenom, as well as of castles in Gemer, Spis, Turna and Saris Counties. The territory of Slovakia became an important economic and cultural region of medieval Hungary.

The process of state consolidation went hand in hand with the construction of churches, founding of monasteries and building of elaborate feudal residences. An epoch-making event was the reinforcement of nobility rights by Andrew II's proclamation of the Golden Bull in 1222. However, progress was rudely interrupted by the Tartar invasions of 1242. After the departure of the Tartar hordes, a period of rebuilding ensued: Slovak castles were restored under King Bela IV (1235–1270), new residences were erected by middle and petty nobility, and new towns were constructed. During this rebuilding period, which included the granting of royal charters (privileges) to various towns, the flow of German immigration went on unabated. The territory that is Slovakia today was the most urbanized part of the Hungarian Kingdom. By end of the 13th Century, under King Andrew III (1290–1301), there were twenty royally chartered towns on our territory. The mining industry also began a huge program of expansion in the latter half of the 13th Century. Following the mining district of Banska Stiavnica in

Excerpt from Golden
Bull of Andrew II

Central Slovakia, the mining district of Banska Bystrica emerged; then the region of Spis and Gemer Counties, centered on the town of Gelnica, emerged as still another mining district, producing copper and silver ore. The extraction of gold and silver created conditions necessary for the founding of a royal mint in Kremnica, where Hungarian golden florins and ducats were minted, beginning in the last third of the 14th Century.

Battle of Rozhanovce

When various contenders vied for the Hungarian throne after the demise of the Arpad dynasty in 1301, the greater part of the territory of Slovakia was taken over by ambitious magnates. Best known among them was Matus (Matthew) Cak, who ruled from Trencin, and the Omodejov (Amadeus) family, which dominated Eastern Slovakia and built the well-known fortress overlooking the city of Kosice, at that time a growing town. Up to his death in 1321, Matus Cak controlled almost two-thirds of the territory of Slovakia. The battle of Rozhanovce on June 15, 1312, between the Omodejovs, supported by Matus Cak, and the royal army of Charles Robert supported by Kosice and various Spis towns, bolstered Charles Robert's royal power. Matus Cak's sway gradually waned, falling off from a peak when he controlled approximately fifty fortresses or castles, together with their surrounding estates.

Slovak townspeople began playing an important role in the governance of towns, as attested, for instance, by King Louis' grant of parity to the Zilina Slovaks with Germans on the town council. Slovaks did not die out during the course of the Medieval Ages but, quite the contrary, played an important role not only in medieval villages, but in settings involving nobility and townspeople, and no doubt in the royal court as well. They were actively engaged in the extraction of minerals and ores, and in the development of medieval crafts, occupying an important place on the Hungarian scene, and indisputably playing an important role in the building, maintaining and changing of church structures and church institutions. They held respectable positions in the archdiocese of Esztergom, the diocese of Eger, in archdiaconates, in chapters and monasteries, and in the oldest schools. The nobility of Upper Hungary, particularly the lesser nobility, was of Slovak origin, and without a doubt enjoyed a good command of the Slovak language. Of course, in the highest circles the official language of debate was the medieval 'Esperanto', – Latin, which erased potential linguistic barriers and ethnic tensions in Central Europe. The official Hungarian state structure was a mosaic of emerging nationalities: Slovaks, Magyars, Germans, Croatians, Romanians, and, later on, Rusyns (Carpatho-Ruthenians). In the Carpathian mountain regions, even people of Romanian origin were represented, but to a lesser extent. The territory of Slovakia also played a progressively more important role through the 14th Century and right up the battle of Mohac in 1526. The status of Slovakia received an additional boost after the Habsburg ascension and the Ottoman Turkish control of large parts of Hungary, and later still, during the period of social and religious conflicts accompanying the Protestant Reformation and Re-Catholicization.

In Slovakia, the Reformation was spread mainly by Lutherans of the Augsburg Confession. Germans and Slovaks converted mainly to Lutheranism, while Magyars converted to Calvinism, though some Slovaks in Lower Zemplin County also became Calvinists. During the period of Turkish ascendancy, as well as during the periods of fierce internal conflicts, it was Slovakia that comprised the most important compact mass of Hungarian territory under Habsburg rule. In the years 1534 to 1544, the Ottoman Empire reached the southern border of Central Slovakia, a region rich in mineral resources; the inhabitants of Slovakia, including Hungarian nobility, lived for a century and a half under pressures of Turkish proximity. Into this perilous space-time setting thrust the political and military strife of anti-Habsburg uprisings. These revolts were precipitated by the Habsburg imposed re-Catholicization of Slovakia, at this time predominantly Protestant. Our territory thus became not only the site of splendidly equipped anti-Turkish fortifications, but also the stage of numerous military conflicts, of violations of religious freedom, and later of progressively more intensive re-Catholicization efforts. The University of Trnava was founded in 1635 to promote the conversion of Protestants, as was a later Jesuit university founded in Kosice in 1660. These efforts adversely affected the predominantly Protestant schools in 17th Century Slovakia, including the best-known Lutheran lyceum (later college) in Presov. A conspiracy of the Hungarian nobility, supported mainly by Slovaks, was not only treacherously exposed and harshly suppressed, but also used as justification for an unprecedented persecution of Protestant clergy and Slovak and German intellectuals, and the near extermination of Lutherans on the part of the emperor's court.[3] These persecutions, unfortunately, were carried out with effective help from the Inquisition, administered mainly by priests of the Jesuit order. They included court trials, sentencing to the gallows, executions (for instance, of the magistrates in Orava and Liptov Counties, for complicity in the Pika uprising of 1672), and the infamous Presov butchery of 1687. The persecutions were intensified after a meeting of Catholic dignitaries in Trnava (1658) during which a decision was reached to pursue the measures of the counter-reformation even more vigorously. A short-lived episode of this period was the unsuccessful uprising of Imrich Thokoly (1678–1683), dubbed 'the Slovak King', because during his heyday he was able to conquer and control a large portion of Slovak territory. Then a definitively new era of socio-cultural development was heralded by the Turkish defeat at Vienna on September 12, 1683.

First Slovak Catholic hymnbook (Cantus Catholici), *1655*

278

*Defeat of Turks
at Vienna*

Up to the end of the 17th Century, Slovaks constituted somewhat more than 50% of the population of Hungary. The nobility – except for its lesser, impoverished members – was obviously of Magyar origin. Gradually, after the expulsion of Turks and the end of Ottoman rule, Magyars surpassed Slovaks in numbers. At the beginning of the 18th Century, Habsburg meddling in the governance of free royal towns, a sharp increase in taxes, and unrelenting military pressure provoked an uprising by Francis II Rakoczi (1703). For practically five years (to 1708), the territory of Slovakia (with the exception of Bratislava and Trnava) was controlled by Rakoczi, or more precisely, occupied by his insurgents. Hence it follows that most of the military confrontations of the time took place there, causing much pain and hardship to the local populace. After the uprising was put down (1711), a period of relative peace ensued, allowing for undisrupted development in the country. Unfortunately, it was accompanied by a progressively harsher repression of Slovaks. The official ideology of the ruling Magyar nobility was built on medieval legends and chronicles (for instance, the *Anonymous Chronicle* from the 12th Century), which were finely tuned to the interests of the ruling Magyar classes, justifying immemorial rights to 'their ancient homeland'. The Slovaks, who lacked even regional autonomy, were considered a subjugated people without political rights. Jan Baltazar Magin, a Catholic priest from Dubnica, took up the Slovak defense in a work titled *Apologia Slovakov* (An Apology for Slovaks, 1728), with support from the sundry estates (classes) of Trencin County. In it he offered proofs that Slovaks (Sloveni) were descendents of the original Slavic population of the country, and that the Magyars had not subjugated them, but had jointly founded the Kingdom of Hungary with them. It is astonishing how closely this author's national defense of Slovaks parallels present-

279

Matthias Belius,
apud Euangelicas Posonienses, V.D.M.
et Regiæ Societatis Scientiarum

Matej Bel

day historical/ cultural theses about the genesis of the Slovak nation and the rise of early medieval Hungary. Many of his theses about Slovak rights to equality have become staples of the ideology of Slovaks, in their national defense during the Slovak national revival, and later in the course of struggles for recognition as a modern nation. Two other important protagonists of the Slovak cause in these times were Matej (Matthew) Bel and Samuel Timon. In the first half of the 18th Century re-Catholicization gradually intensified on the principle of 'Koho panstvo, toho nabozenstvo' (Ruler's religion – subjects' religion). The lesser nobility and the more affluent classes in the free royal towns resisted these pressures. Still, the privileged status of the Catholic Church was not officially proclaimed until 1738.

In 1735, a Mining Academy was founded in Banska Stiavnica under the auspices of the Habsburg Monarchy.

Maria Theresa, influenced by the Enlightenment, introduced various economic and cultural reforms during her reign. For instance: she standardized obligations of serfs with her 'Urbar' (Land Register, 1767–1769); she established a uniform system of schools (1777); she authorized the carving out of three new bishoprics from the archdiocese of Esztergom – in Spis county, Banska Bystrica, and Roznava (1776), as well as an additional bishopric in Kosice (1804) and a Byzantine Catholic bishopric in Presov (1816); for the first time ever, she circulated paper money, which carried even a Slovak inscription (1748 and 1749).

Joseph II, Maria Theresa's successor, issued a Toleration Patent (1781), granting Protestants (Lutherans and Calvinists) equal social and civil status with Catholics. Joseph II also abolished serfdom (1785), thus restricting the intrusion of estate owners on the individual rights of peasants. He also left his mark on

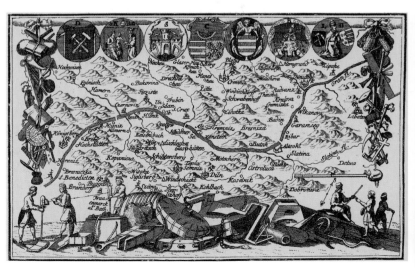

Map of Central Slovak Region, with coats of arms of seven mining towns, 1766

ecclesiastical affairs, abolishing many contemplative monasteries. After the death of Joseph II (1790), the Magyar nobility attempted to establish Magyar as the official language in public life and in parliamentary deliberations. This attempt, however, provoked wide-spread protests in multinational Hungary, where a majority of the citizens were non-Magyar. Inspired by the French Revolution, a movement of Hungarian Jacobins sprang up (1794), engaging active participation from Slovaks. This movement pursued long-standing goals: civic reform, federalization of government, freedom from Habsburg tyranny, and autonomy of the Slovaks and the other nationalities. Unfortunately, it was unsuccessful, its five leaders were hanged in Buda in 1795 (among them were Slovaks, Hajnoci and Martinovic).

Portrait of Ignac Martinovic, leader of Hungarian Jacobins

Harassment of nationalities eased off during the Napoleonic wars, only to be resumed more vigorously under Metternich's absolutist policies, when Magyar activists strove to reinforce dominance; taking advantage of a parliamentary majority, they promoted Magyar hegemony, fostering Magyar culture, language and science. Pan-Hungarianism put down progressively deeper roots in official policy, rebuffing Slovak demands for recognition, along with those of the other nationalities. At this time, a Slovak national revival emerged and flowered, only to be followed by renewed and intensified Magyar repression. In the midst of these social conflicts, Slovak strategies were also clarifying and maturing, under the leadership of new protagonists: Adam Frantisek Kollar, a legal historian, Jan Severini, a Lutheran minister, historian and philosopher, and two Catholic priests, Anton Bernolak and Juraj Fandly. Both of the latter – Bernolak, a philologist, the codifier of the first Slovak literary language and pioneer of the Slovak National Revival, and Fandly, a writer and national enlightener – were co-founders of the *Slovak Learned Fellowship* (1792), which disseminated books written in Bernolak's new 'literary language'. A Slovak freedom movement, with ties to the above leaders, was initiated by Jan Baltazar Magin. The Archbishop of Esztergom, Cardinal Alexander Rudnay (1760–1831), a native of Povazany near Nove Mesto nad Vahom, was also an important spokesman for Slovak Catholics, avowing his national convictions with the affirmation that he was Slovak and would continue to be, even if raised to the Chair of St. Peter ('Slavus sum, et si in cathedra Petri forem, Slavus ero', as recorded by the historian Jozef Skultety).

The Lutheran Superintendant of Nitra, Daniel Krman, a writer, translator and publisher, also contributed to this national movement, as did the writer Bohuslav Tablic and the Lutheran pedagogue Juraj Palkovic. Palkovic taught at the Lutheran lyceum in Bratislava, which reared the cultural activists of Ludovit Stur's generation. All these illustrious personalities endeavored to bring about legal equality for Slovaks. Despite the fact that their paths were not always the same, their goals were similar, in fact, identical. While one branch of the movement pursued

NAUKA
REČI SLOVENSKEJ.

VISTAVENÁ

LUDEVITA STÚRA.

NÁKLADOM TATRÍNA ČÍSLO I.

V PREŠPORKU 1846.

Stur:
Lessons in Slovak
Language, *1848*

recognition of Slovaks as an autonomous nationality with its own literary language within the context of the Hungarian state, another branch sought support from their closest racial kin in the Austrian realm, i.e. the Czechs and Moravians. The leading spokesmen of the latter arm were Jan Kollar, and Pavol Jozef Safarik. The latter, writing influential scholarly works, considered the Slovaks a separate Slavic nationality. This fashioning of Slovak/Czech and Slovak/Moravian reciprocity was indisputably a positive development. Both branches of the Slovak movement eventually converged regarding the basis of a common Slovak literary language, derived from the Central Slovakian dialect. A meeting of minds took place between July 11 and 16, 1843, in Jozef Hurban's Lutheran parish house in Hlboke, with the blessing of Jan Holly, a Catholic priest and major poet of Bernolak's version of Slovak. The accord was achieved mainly through the efforts of Ludovit Stur, abetted by Joseph Miloslav Hurban and Michael Miloslav Hodza. In 1851, on the basis of this accord, the linguist Martin Hatalla prepared *A Short Grammar of the Slovak Language.*

But before these events happened, an important phase of the Slovak emancipatory process had become history. Ludovit Stur was elected by the Slovak town of Zvolen to sit in the Hungarian Parliament, where he became one of the most radical proponents of the abolition of serfdom and introduction of civic reforms (1848). But the time was coming when not only he as an individual, but all Slovaks, as scions of a modern evolving nation, would get a chance to demonstrate their political will. In the revolutionary years of 1848 and 1849, Slovaks stepped forward to achieve national liberation, presenting themselves as a modern nation with sights set on progressive revolutionary goals – the ideals of social equality, freedom and autonomy. On May 10, 1848, at a mass gathering in Liptovsky Svaty Mikulas, they worked up a set of demands for presentation to the Hungarian parliament, including a common parliament for all nationalities, where deputies could use their mother tongues, separate national parliaments, recognition of Slovak as an official language in Slovak regions, Slovak as a language of instruction in schools, banishment from public office in Slovak regions of renegades who reviled their mother-tongue, rights to Slovak publication and lastly, freedom of association and assembly. The Hungarian government refused to negotiate with the Slovak deputies; on the contrary, it continued to suppress and quash Slovak initiatives. The Slovaks sought protection from these oppressions in the Viennese imperial court, requesting the release of Slovakia from Hungarian jurisdiction.

One of the most dedicated and determined Slovaks, Jozef M. Hurban, a Lutheran pastor from Hlboke near Senica, expressed his compatriots' sentiments most forcefully, declaring: "Must we decent Slovaks be the only ones forced to stand by listening, while others are singing songs of freedom? Hey, brothers, no, no, and again no! Indeed, we dare not keep our peace while others are singing, or humbly serve, while others are ruling from on high, or grovel on the ground while others are lifting their heads, or sink in despair while others are celebrating triumphs! For us too, for us decent Slovaks, the bell is finally pealing". For the first time, Slovaks took up arms. Volunteer units, abetted by the Emperor, began an uneven campaign against overwhelming Magyar forces. Despite eventual defeat, the Slovak national uprising of 1848 and 1849 has been recorded with golden letters in the history of Slovakia and the Slovaks. Equally important was the convening of the Slovak National Council in Myjava on September 19, 1848, which, as the highest Slovak revolutionary tribunal, renounced submission to the Magyar government, espoused secession from Hungary, and summoned all Slovaks to the struggle for national rights. But owing to the Viennese Court's reluctance to heed the revolutionary demands of the nationalities of Hungary, disappointment soon prevailed. A campaign of Germanization in the form of the absolutism of Austrian minister Bach subsequently permeated Slovakia, and incongruously, hand in hand with it, came an intensification of Magyar and pan-Hungarian activism.

The disillusionment of Slovak political leaders was soon replaced by new activities, especially in the 1860s, when Bach's absolutist regime collapsed. Even after the emperor authorized a special session of the Hungarian parliament, Slovaks were simply without representation. Once again their political program needed to be revitalized. The new boost took the form of *A Memorandum of the Slovak Nation* (Turciansky Svaty Martin, 1861), containing a salient demand for

Period tableau of outstanding Slovak personalities, 1860–1870

283

the creation of an independent political entity within the framework of Hungary to be called the 'Slovak Precincts' (*okolia*). Slovak intellectuals realized that, without national publications, institutions and schools, national life could not flourish; the lesser Slovak nobility, in particular, faced forcible Magyar assimilation, which eroded the ranks of the ethnically enlightened intelligentsia. Thanks to ecumenical rapprochement between Catholics and Lutherans, representative churchmen, headed by the Catholic Bishop Stefan Moyses and the Lutheran Superintendent Karol Kuzmany, met in Turciansky Svaty Martin on August 4, 1863 and founded the Matica Slovenska, a Slovak cultural institution. This institution soon commanded immense respect. Shortly thereafter, three Slovak gymnasia (prep schools) sprang up: a senior gymnasium in Revuca, and two junior gymnasia in Turciansky Svaty Martin and Klastor pod Znievom, respectively. But a time was again drawing nigh, when after a short-lived stir of activity, Slovak progress would again be bogged down by even more drastic measures of repression.

Shortly after the Austro-Hungarian Equalization (Compromise) of 1867 the Matica Slovenska was banned, and the three Slovak gymnasia closed (1874–1875). These newest liquidations were a harbinger of the Nationalities Code adopted by the Hungarian Parliament in 1868, which enshrined the imaginary concept of 'one, single Hungarian (i.e. Magyar) nation'. Gradually the restrictive measures of the Magyar government, endured before the First World War mainly by the beleaguered Slovak nation and its bravely struggling leaders, were brought to bear on all non-Magyar nationalities. Except for a few village priests, the state ideology of *Pan-Magyarism* had a mesmerizing effect on Catholic clergy, particularly the hierarchy: Catholic schools were controlled by people completely under the spell of that ideology. In contrast, Lutheran intellectuals, particularly priests and teachers, were able to preserve their 'Slovakness' through Biblical Czech, their liturgical language, and through systematic contacts with their Czech and Austro-German co-religionists in Prague, Vienna, and Halle. Some impoverished Catholic priests in village parishes, e.g. Andrej Kmet and Andrej Hlinka, also maintained intensive contacts with their Czech and Moravian counterparts. The harshness of this period and the arrogance of the Magyar government are best exemplified by the bald assertion of Prime Minister Koloman Tisza that, "there is no such creature as the Slovak nation". The government was wholly engaged in an effort to transform Hungary into a state of one nation and one language and thus, in effect, to wipe out the ethnic distinctiveness of the Romanians, Rusyns, Serbs, Croats, Germans, and particularly the Slovaks, the largest compact non-Magyar linguistic entity. A further well-aimed blow was the so-called Apponyi laws (1907), prescribing complete Magyarization of ele-

Svetozar Miletic

284

mentary schools, supplemented by a government order to teach religion exclusively in the Magyar language (1909). The slogan 'Tot nem ember' ('A Slovak is not a human being') spread across the Hungarian land. A bitter reaction culminated in the forcible repression of a Slovak Lutheran worship service in Kovacica, Southern Hungary, and then in a bloody police massacre at the consecration of a Catholic church in Cernova near Ruzomberok, which left fifteen dead and many more wounded. Both incidents occurred in 1907, and were followed by boisterous trials. The Cernova tragedy, in particular, stirred public opinion throughout Europe. Demands for democratization of conditions in Hungary multiplied, accompanied by strong protests against the government's Magyarization policies. In the meantime, wide-spread poverty in Slovak regions spurred heavy waves of emigration, mainly to the United States.

At the end of the 19th and beginning of the 20th Century the principal political parties in Slovakia were the Slovak National Party and the Slovak People's Party. The main plank in their platforms was the defense of basic Slovak rights in pursuit of eventual independence. A group that called itself 'Hlasists', after their periodical *Hlas* (The Voice), was strongly influenced by the ideas of a Czech professor named Tomas G. Masaryk, including his concept of Czecho-Slovak unity. Additionally, prior to the First World War some extremely competent politicians grew up and stepped onto the Slovak political scene, including Vavro Srobar, Andrej Hlinka, Pavol Blaho, Ferdinand Juriga, Milan Hodza, Emanuel Lehocky and Matus Dula.

Slovakia and the Slovaks had at last arrived at a time when they could do something to assure national survival. The First World War, despite the suffering it caused, created the conditions for the national liberation of Slovaks who faced

Site of Cernova tragedy

cultural extinction[4] from a state policy of pan-Hungarianism, for, aside from domestic Slovak politicians and a handful of Slovak-oriented intelligentsia in Hungary, there were numerous Slovak activists abroad destined to play an important role in this struggle, especially in the United States of America. From among many available alternative solutions to the Slovaks' dilemma, eventually the idea of a joint state with the cognate Czech nation gained ascendancy. Ivan Daxner, the executive secretary of the Slovak League of America, declared: "Away from the Magyars, but not into Czech subservience; we want to join Czechs as equals". The Cleveland Accord (1915) between American Slovak and Czech fraternal associations unambiguously proposed a federative arrangement, with complete autonomy and equality for Slovaks and Czechs in a joint state.

Towards the end of the war, T. G. Masaryk, the leading representative of the Czecho-Slovakia resistance abroad, signed an accord with Slovak fraternal organizations in the United States, commonly known as the Pittsburgh Pact (1918). This accord guaranteed Slovaks separate governmental instrumentalities in the future Czecho-Slovak State, with full legislative and executive powers. It specifically set forth: "We demand complete autonomy and freedom of self-determination for the Slovak nation, as much in the political as in the cultural and economic spheres". By this time, a splendid scientist, soldier, and politician, Milan Rastislav Stefanik, the son of a Lutheran minister from Kosariska near Brezova, was playing an important role in international political circles on behalf of the Slovak cause, winning access to European political salons for the other two leading representatives of the 'Czecho-Slovak National Council', T. G. Masaryk and E. Benes. His efforts were also directed towards a common democratic state, to be known as the Czecho-Slovak Republic, a state composed of two legally equal Central Europeans nations, built on the rubble of the Austro-Hungarian Monarchy. His earthly star shone briefly, maybe only to shine all the more brightly for eternity in the distant heavens, which had been the object of his scientific investigation for so many years. Not yet fully appreciated in domestic political circles, he died on May 4, 1919, under mysterious circumstances: while returning to his native Slovakia as the newly named Czecho-Slovak Minister for War, a principal of the new state to which he had so selflessly devoted his life, his plane crashed.

Karol Anton Medvecky

There is yet another important reality that was happening on the home scene that should not be overlooked: starting in the spring of 1918, while much was happening elsewhere, politics in Slovakia came alive, too, auguring new, qualitatively better times for Slovaks. The Resolution of Turciansky Svaty Mikulas, prepared by Vavro Srobar on May 1, 1918, called for the right of self-determination and the right of Slovaks to manage their own affairs in union with the Czechs. Later the

Slovak National Council was formed (Turciansky Svaty Martin, October 30, 1918) as the highest representative of Slovaks, marshalling Slovak individual talents and national resources. Its members became known as the 'men of October 1918'. With a *Declaration of the Slovak Nation* they pledged their allegiance to the new state, to a union of Slovakia and the Czech lands in the state of Czecho-Slovakia, emphasizing thereby that only the Slovak National Council (not the Hungarian government) was authorized to speak and act in the name of the Slovak nation. In the spirit of this declaration, Ferdis Juriga, a parliamentary deputy, spoke out in the Hungarian parliament, stressing that "other than a Slovak national assembly, or instrumentalities authorized by such a body, nobody has the right to conduct debates affecting the political predicament of the Slovak nation, or to make decisions for it, or without it, and least of all against it".

*Samuel Zoch,
author of Declaration
of Slovak Nation*

The need for a definitive parting of the ways with Magyars and a coupling with Czechs was also pointed out by Andrej Hlinka, one of the signatories to the Martin Declaration: "Let us state frankly that we stand for a Czecho-Slovak orientation. The thousand-year marriage with the Magyars has failed. We must get a divorce". With tremendous help from the victorious powers (France, USA and Great Britain), the Czecho-Slovak Republic was successfully established and, in its early years, defended. With its establishment, Slovaks were able to close the chapters of their history linked to Hungary. Obviously getting Czecho-Slovakia internationally recognized within clearly defined boundaries required, at its beginnings, the union of two constitutive nations, particularly in view of the large German and Magyar ethnic minorities the new state incorporated. Unfortunately, the proclamation of a single Czecho-Slovak nation in the constitution

*Declaration
of Slovak Nation*

of 1920, ratified by parliamentary appointees, rather than by duly elected representatives, was just a rubber stamp on a 'fait accompli'. It was at fundamental cross-purposes with Slovak goals of constitutional recognition of their national distinctiveness and the implementation of the Pittsburgh Pact. It presaged not only ethnic and social conflict, but fragility at the heart of Czecho-Slovak statehood as well. These flaws were inherent in the state structure, though the situation of Slovaks had indeed improved, particularly in the spheres of schools and culture. Close administrative control from Prague created avoidable tensions in the new state, in the economic sphere as well as in sphere of local administration. Not until the mid-1930s was a state-aided program of munitions factories initiated in Slovakia. And it is true that this latter positive step was taken in response to the rapidly disintegrating political situation in Central Europe, when our democracy was threatened by developments in Nazi Germany and nationalistic Hungary. Unfortunately, deepening internal crises, directly and indirectly abetted by neighboring states, progressively weakened the little island of democracy in the Central European milieu.

At this time, two currents in Slovak politics were radically at odds. A centrist current defended the thesis that there were not two nations in the new state, but only one – a Czecho-Slovak nation. This current was represented by centrist parties controlled from Prague, namely the Agrarian and the Social-Democratic parties led by Vavro Srobar, Milan Hodza and Ivan Derer. An autonomist current, espousing the notion of a distinctive Slovak nation and demanding autonomy for Slovakia, was represented by the Slovak People's Party (after 1925, Hlinka's Slovak People's Party), and the Slovak National Party, led by Andrej Hlinka and

Workers' homes in Bratislava

Martin Razus, respectively. An autonomist program was also favored by a majority of other ethnic political leaders, particularly the Magyars (J. Esterhazy, M. Szentivanyi, and A. Jarros). Ethnic politics in Central Europe at this time were extremely sensitive, never having been resolved to everybody's satisfaction. The words of Ekes Kormendy, a Magyar deputy to the National Assembly in Prague (1920) still echo with timely truth, as if just spoken: "In the name of the deputies of the Magyar and German parties, I state flatly, that in the matter of state affiliation, neither the Magyar nor German nation has been asked for an opinion; they have therefore been unable to express their will. The truth is that the territory of Upper Hungary has been occupied by a Czech army, and that in a politics of revenge, Magyar citizenry has been forcibly transferred into the Czecho-Slovak State, like pawns on a chess-board". Lastly, there was a third, though not very powerful current, the Communist Party, whose goal was social revolution, under direction of the International in Moscow. Unfortunately, it was the 'Czecho-Slovak' concept, springing from Czech/Slovak ethnic kinship and mutual regard, magnified into the full-blown thesis of a single Czecho-Slovak nation – legally, economically, culturally and even linguistically – which, in the final analysis was a major source of the state's weakness internationally, as well as the 'well-intentioned' digger of its grave. Both economic crises and ethnic tensions weakened Czecho-Slovak democracy. Slovakia was particularly hard hit by these conditions, in which poverty 'bloomed', emigration swelled, 'hunger pockets' proliferated, unemployment spread, causing widespread social unrest, including so-called 'hunger marches', demonstrations, strikes and even police strafing of luckless masses in Slovakia. During the year 1933, every third adult was unemployed. A weak economic upturn in the latter half of the decade was too late to solve the country's basic problems.

Czecho-Slovakia, and Slovakia as a component, felt threatened. Germany was intensively building armaments, Hungary unceasingly dreaming (and continuing to dream) of complete or partial renewal of 'Greater Hungary'. What is more, even neighboring Poland evinced claims to part of the republic's territory. Events were inexorably drifting towards an occupation of parts of Bohemia, Moravia, Silesia, Slovakia and Sub-Carpathian Russia, while many Slovak intellectuals were crying out in verse with Janko Jesensky: "I open up my atlas. Whence will a pair of conjoined hands beckon me, without threatening calamity, fire, or flood? What has happened to the map of Europe?"

At this particular time, as if in anticipation of doom to come, T. G. Masaryk (September 1937) and A. Hlinka (August 1938) passed away, both politicians and statesmen who made significant contributions to the founding of the Czecho-Slovak Republic. Numerous Slovak politicians were among those who

Children
of Slovak workers

Original manuscript, first piece of legislation, 1ˢᵗ Slovak Republic, March 14, 1939

rose to defend the republic against Nazism and Fascism, and gradually achieved, international recognition, among them Milan Hodza, Stefan Osusky, and Vladimir Clementis. The Munich dictate of September 29, 1938, and the subsequent declaration of Slovak autonomy on October 6, 1938 (ratified by the Czecho-Slovak parliament in November), the Viennese Arbitration authorizing Hungary's prompt annexation of a fifth of Slovak territory with several hundred thousand Slovaks living alongside Magyars, all these momentous events continued to augur sad times, the hulking apocalypse of war. To the front of the Slovak stage stepped Karol Sidor, Jozef Tiso, Vojtech Tuka, Alexander Mach, and Ferdinand Durcansky. The time had come, or at least was on the way, when basic civil rights would be violated – gone would be freedom of the press, speech and assembly. One political entity was on the way to assuming all political power and constructing a single state party, and in the process abusing the name of A. Hlinka – the Hlinka's Slovak People's Party.

The character of this party is best expressed in the text of a speech by Jozef Tiso, its president: "The party must lead, it must organize the whole of social and public life. The party is the nation and the nation is the party. The nation speaks through the party. The party thinks for the nation. What harms the nation, the party bans and vilifies. The party will never err, as long as it keeps its eye solely on the interests of the nation". In March 1939, the actual demise of truncated Czecho-Slovakia arrived. Pressured by Adolf Hitler, Jozef Tiso asked Emil Hacha, President of the Czecho-Slovak Republic, to summon a session of the Slovak parliament. On March 14, 1939, the Slovak parliament declared Slovak independence, after Karol Sidor, President of the autonomous government, had rejected a demand by German political leaders that he personally make the declaration. On July 21, 1939, the parliament ratified the Constitution of the first Slovak Republic whereby, under the patronage and by guarantee of Nazi Germany, it became a reality, creating a new geopolitical situation in Central Europe. The majority of Slovak citizens, who had not experienced the ruthless pressures of the Nazis and who had been denied the autonomy promised in interwar Czecho-Slovakia, welcomed the independent state, even with its limitations in sovereignty affecting primarily foreign affairs and waging of war. Internal conflicts arose in the Hlinka's Slovak People's Party between a conservative wing, headed by President and Party Chairman J. Tiso, and a radical pro-Nazi wing, headed by the Prime Minister-cum-Foreign Minister V. Tuka, and Minister of the Interior and Commander of the Hlinka Guard, A. Mach. Through the direct intervention of Hitler, many of the more important political and state functions were gradually occupied by the devotees of Nazism. Whereas the moderate wing, led by Tiso, advocated a cautious political regimen, 'without foreign models' and a degree of independence from Germany, the devotees of Nazism (V. Tuka, A. Mach) strove to imitate Nazi techniques, and wanted to install the ideology and usages of National Socialism. Only too well known is the public address of A. Mach, in which he demanded: "Every member of the Guard should designate two to three people in his area, for that matter, anyone who is an enemy of the state, for elimination". A declaration of V. Tuka was in the same vein: "…Slovakia is entering the ranks of those cultured nations who want to arrange their lives in keeping with the principles of National Socialism".

Emblem and flag of 1ˢᵗ Slovak Republic

Many Catholic clergymen got involved in politics, and the official state policy espoused Christian values, but the Holy See remained cautious in the face of these various developments, following the extensive political involvement of Catholic clergy in a state allied to the anti-Christian Nazi regime with great uneasiness. It reacted to the promulgation of an ordinance on the legal status of Jews (The Jewish Code of September 9, 1941) with a diplomatic note: 'The Holy See has learned with intense pain that even in Slovakia, where almost the whole population has cherished the most beautiful Catholic traditions, a government ordinance has been issued on September 9, 1941, which establishes detailed racial procedures in obvious conflict with principles of Catholicism'. The note leaves no doubt that these provisions had given rise to the basest discriminatory actions against Jews. The authorities gradually stripped Jews of basic political, civil and finally even human rights: confiscation of Jewish property was followed by emigration, aryanization of businesses, exclusion from schools and jobs, concentration in detention camps, and finally deportation 'en masse' to Nazi death camps in Poland. All of this in a state that officially touted the highest Christian values.

The gradual branding of all Jewish citizens with the six-pointed yellow star added a humiliating coloration to the background of these times. Thousands of grants of presidential exemptions and conversions to Christianity attest to official awareness of these shattering life-realities and efforts to alleviate some of the rampant injustices, but without putting a complete halt them.[5] In 1942, 58,000 Jews were forcibly deported to 'death camps' and, after the German occupation of Slovakia in the fall of 1944, 13,000 more. The disgraceful anti-Semitic mind-set common at this time is reflected in a flyer disseminated by the Hlinka Guard in 1940: 'Nobody is going to bamboozle us with the stupid phrase that a Jew is a human being. Jews are the representatives and agents of the devil. A Jew is not a divine creation, but satanic, and therefore not a human being; he just looks like one. Anyone who supports or aids Jews in any way – will not escape the judgment of God'. Slovak Catholic bishops actively protested the Jewish Code and the practical measures taken by the government to enforce it. Nevertheless, in 1942 President

Image of President Tiso, on Slovak coin

Tiso was accorded the title 'Leader' ('Vodca'). An active parish pastor, J. Tiso did not always conduct himself in politics as a priest, though he did want to tone down many of the injustices being perpetrated. Pope Pius XII, faced with the dilemma of two evils, kept quiet and thus enabled the genocide of Jews in Europe.[6] Throughout this period of time photographs of Hitler, Tiso and Pope Pius XII alternated daily on the pages of Slovak newspapers. Vain were the pleas of genuine Christians, Catholics and Lutherans, priests and bishops, who argued that since God was the author of life, no one on earth had the right to take it away; all of us had come from the same roots, Christianity and Judaism.

The Slovak Republic was a German satellite, but the rule of one party (Hlinka's Slovak People's Party) had its idiosyncrasies. Among other things, it was dubbed 'totalitarianism riddled with holes'. Evidence supporting this description is the fact that not a single death verdict was carried out during the life of the Slovak Republic. Gradually, forces expressing dissatisfaction with the political regime emerged and grew stronger. These forces were not directed against Slovak statehood as such, but against government by a totalitarian-party and against economic and political dependency on Nazi Germany. On the front lines of the Second World War a resistance movement was building, while in Slovakia, armed partisan units began organizing. Two opposing political constellations arose: a democratic and civil resistance aiming at renewal of pre-war Czecho-Slovakia, and a Communist resistance, oriented at first to the creation of a Soviet Slovakia merged into the Soviet Union. Later, as a result of a change in leadership, the Communist resistance, too, espoused a renewal of the Czecho-Slovak Republic, but as a state of two sovereign nations. Still later, a fusion of the two constellations occurred under a joint leadership – the Slovak National Council. Its members were J. Ursiny, J. Lettrich, M. Josko, K. Smidke, G. Husak, L. Novomesky, I Horvath, and P. Zatko. In December 1943, this Council developed a political program titled 'The Christmas Pact' that called in substance for a renewal of a democratic Czecho-Slovakia, in which the distinctiveness of the Slovak nation would be recognized, as well as legal equality with the Czech nation. Taking into consideration the anticipated clout of the future victorious powers, which favored the reestablishment of Czecho-Slovakia in its pre-Munich form, the resistance movement abroad decided that its goals could be achieved only through an armed uprising, accompanied by a declaration against Fascism and Nazism, and membership in an anti-Fascist coalition. Such an uprising actually did erupt on August 29, 1944, when 60,000 Slovak soldiers led by Generals R. Viest and J. Golian revolted, with collaboration from approximately 18,000 partisans, among them several thousand foreign nationals. Called the Slovak National Uprising, the revolt was fully national in character, supported by the citizenry as a whole,

Entrance to home on Gajova Ulica (Street) in Bratislava, site of Christmas Agreement, 1943

including many professionals, priests, teachers, cultural workers, journalists and students. Unfortunately, some of the insurgents took advantage of the turmoil to rob civilians and to commit self-serving murders, even after the uprising had been suppressed. The anti-Fascist uprising created pre-conditions for the incorporation of Slovakia into post-war Europe on the side of the victorious powers [communism]. The government of Tiso did not want such a way out of its predicament. In an award ceremony in Banska Bystrica after the suppression of the Uprising, President Tiso decorated German soldiers. Worse, the emergency units of the Hlinka Guard, together with special German police commandos, took part in a brutal persecution of soldiers, partisans and civilians, involving murders and arson. The Slovak Government finally found itself at a dead end. This dilemma might explain why Tiso sent a telegram of loyalty to the Nazis after Hitler's death.[7]

After liberation, political life began reawakening. Two political protagonists stepped onto the stage – the Democratic Party, and the Communist Party. In the clashes and confrontations that took place in post-war, democratic Czecho-Slovakia, the growing influence of the Soviet Union and its Communist ideology became progressively more blatant. Thousands of Slovak citizens were unaccountably deported to Russian camps for forced labor. The great majority of Slovaks wanted change but, after their experiences during the war, they rejected Sovietization with one-party rule, this time by a Communist state party and ideology. They declared in favor of Christian and democratic values. In the first and last post-war free democratic elections in Slovakia prior to 1990, it was the citizen-oriented Democratic Party that won, with 62% of the votes cast, compared to the Communists' approximately 30%. (By contrast, in the Czech lands, it was the Communists who were victorious.) There followed a period of gradual dismantling of the agreements couched in the 'Kosice Government Program'. In Slovakia, the Board of Commissioners stopped clearing its activities with the Slovak National Council, finding itself organizationally subjected to the analogous departmental ministries in Prague, a change initiated by the Communist Party and supported by centrists. The Communists were in the process of planning a coup, under Moscow's stage direction. They began their critical assault in the fall of 1947 with mass demonstrations backed by National Front parties. Using coercion and populist pressure they prevailed on the Democratic Party and its representatives, J. Lettrich, J. Ursiny, J. Kempny, M. Bugar, J. Stasko, L. Obtulovic and others, to give up the control of the Board of Commissioners which they had won by free election in 1946. Last-ditch efforts in February 1948 by non-Communist parties in the Czech lands and Slovakia to stop the dismantling of democratic institutions failed. With promises, threats and mass demonstrations, the Communists installed a one-party regime, taking with them only

*Jozef Urvalek,
prosecutor,
representative
of Communist justice*

their flunkies, the petty satellite parties of the National Front. They next installed a dictatorship of the proletariat, so named after its Soviet prototype, a dictatorship in reality of one party, incorporating an armed militia, state security and political action committees. There followed a period of persecutions and purges of non-Communist parties, churches and lastly, even of fellow party members accused of betrayal of homeland and social class. The victims of these persecutions and purges were branded class enemies, imperialist agents, Zionists, Titoists, with Slovaks bearing the additional particularly foul stigma of bourgeois nationalism. The Bolshevik party-mill, aided by Soviet advisors, ground relentlessly on, crushing even its own adherents and devoted fellow-warriors of the anti-Nazi and anti-Fascist resistance. In the years 1948 to 1952 alone, 233 death sentences were read, 178 of them carried out. 'Personae non gratae' were sent to forced-labor camps; students were expelled from schools and assigned to 'Auxiliary Technical (Work) Brigades'; people were evicted from apartments in a campaign labeled 'Action B'; religious houses were dissolved and monks and nuns interned, all of which led to a grand culmination in show trials charging 'anti-state conspiracies' by representatives and functionaries of the Democratic Party, and in fabricated prosecutions of the Roman Catholic bishops J. Vojtassak and M. Buzalka, and the Greek Catholic Bishop P. Gojdic, as well as of 'bourgeois nationalists' V. Clementis, G. Husak, and L. Novomesky. In conjunction with these trials, Prago-Centrism was steadily expanded, concentrating more functions in the central government and progressively reducing the reach of Slovak offices. The centralist model of power and one-party 'government' was fortified by a 1960 update of the constitution. Abolishing what little power was left to the Slovak National Council and the Board of Commissioners, the revised constitution promoted the principle of 'Czech and Slovak state polity' (practically replicating the inter-war 'Czecho-Slovak nation') and confirmed the leading role of the Communist Party. The aping of the Soviet Union went on apace. At this point, Party leadership succumbed to an illusion of success, and publicly declared that the building phase of socialism had finally reached completion. In the meantime, however, many of the concrete accomplishments of the pre-1968 and post-1969 years had nothing in common with the actual ideals and practices of socialism, dubbed democratic socialism by the regime.

Despite all these ploys, there came a time when attempts at reform began to resurface: science and the arts in particular made an attempt, in the interest of simple growth, to break out of the existing political strait-jacket; members of the intelligentsia became steadily bolder in pointing out the undemocratic and inhuman nature of the existing system; dissatisfaction with the status quo in Czech-Slovak relations was fed by a failure to solve economic, as well as political problems. The opposition in Slovakia coalesced around the person of Alexander Dubcek, an advocate of reform Communism, with the slogan: 'Socialism with a Human Face'. Indeed, the well-known 'Prague Spring' of 1968 had its seeds in Slovakia; it was in fact a 'Dubcek Spring' since it was, after all, Dubcek who had been and continued to be the symbol of the unrealized experiment to reform Communism, of its constriction by dogmatic forces at home, and of its suppression by the Warsaw Pact invasion from abroad. Despite the forcible crushing of this reform movement and subsequent occupation by Soviet armed forces, the memory of the movement's enthusiastic support by a majority of citizens lived on, as did the memory of the joy at the lifting of censorship, at the rise of new organizations and associations (destined to become new political parties), at the new freedom of speech, at the open criticism of Bolshevik brutality and the injustice of recent years, at the partial relaxation of religious controls, and finally, at the completion of the process of converting Czecho-Slovakia into a federation (Czecho-Slovakia). For on October 30, 1968, in Bratislava Castle, President L. Svoboda had signed into law a federative restructuring of the Republic into two autonomous parts. But the memory of the sadness and resentment of the violence of August 1968 did not go away; many memories were quietly stored away and covered over, only to burst forth more robustly 21 years later in the new, deeply rooted qualities of democracy, plurality, freedom and justice.

But before these latter days could arrive, it was necessary to survive years of 'normalization' and stagnation. The disappointment, and then the fear that came with those years were all too great. Gradually, the federative model of two state-forming nations living in harmony began to be squeezed in a vise-like grip, as asymmetrical practices of state government again began to proliferate. The Communist 'Nomenklatura' in Prague continued to rule the state in the spirit of the old centralism. Rigid dogmatism, modeled on Soviet totalitarianism, finally reduced federation to a legal formality, a mere scrap of paper. Czecho-Slovakia was once more a servile satellite of the Soviet Union. The reforms of 1968 were progressively dismantled, public purges begun anew, 'anti-Socialist elements' hunted down, civil and human rights violated. Political trials resumed, the 'all powerful head of the powerless' perceived any expression of dissatisfaction or independent thinking as inimical to the state. A new wave of emigration ensued. In a mindboggling coincidence, at the end of 1977 when this new witch-hunt was at its height, Pope Paul VI authorized the creation of an independent Slovak ecclesiastical province, unwittingly presaging the national independence to come. In Prague in 1977, under the influence of the Helsinki Conference on Human Rights, a citizens' initiative called *Charter 77* sprang up to call attention to violations of civil and human rights. In Slovakia resistance grew, particularly among Christians and Catholic believers who began to demand respect for religious rights and freedoms as guaranteed in the Constitution. This resistance culminated in a quiet public protest in Bratislava on Good Friday 1988, which was forcibly dispersed by police. Resistance was also mounting within unofficial associations of environmental protectionists, and among independent intellectuals. Samizdat literature was reaching a wide audience. Meanwhile, in the Soviet Union Chairman Mikhail S. Gorbachev introduced his policy of 'perestroika' (restructuring, 1985), which was followed by a period of 'glasnost' (open government), and which was supported by many Communists coalesced around their courageous Chairman. The conservative leadership of Czech and Slovak Communists, the so-called 'Nomenklatura', which stood to be a loser in any reform process, naturally defended its prerogatives fiercely. They intensified the persecution of various independent groups as they sensed the onset of their political demise. A definitive collapse of those in power, by now powerless to resist, was drawing near. After the memorable mass demonstrations of November 17, 1989, in Prague, which were preceded the day before in Bratislava by a student demonstration, not even police violence and persecution could halt the collapse.

In the Czech lands a movement sprang up called 'The Citizens' Forum', which was complemented in Slovakia by a movement called 'The Public against Violence'. The leaders of the Slovak movement were F. Gal, J. Budaj, M. Knazko, J. Carnogursky, F. Miklosko and M. Kusy. Millions of citizens took to the streets to demonstrate for the movement. Communists scrambled to salvage their positions by replacing many functionaries, but it was too late. A repeat of

Mass demonstration in Hviezdoslav Square, Bratislava, November 11, 1989

*Alexander Dubcek with
Bratislava residents*

1968 was impossible for the simple reason that all society was in upheaval, totally heedless of the dogmatic, fossilized Communist Party line. Alexander Dubcek
returned to political life as chairman of the Federal Assembly, and with him came
the protagonists of the reform process of 1968, many of them also signatories of
Charter 77. After the abdication of G. Husak on December 10, 1989, and after
elections to the Federal Assembly, Vaclav Havel, the leading activist of *Charter
77* and of the Citizens' Forum, took up residence in Hradcany Castle, the seat of
the Czecho-Slovak Government. Even before this event, the predominantly Communist Federal Assembly had ratified a law abolishing the leading role of the
Communist Party in government and society. A paradox of historical evolution
is the fact that the very people who had persecuted and imprisoned V. Havel for
the preceding two decades were among the deputies of the National Assembly
that almost unanimously elected him president. Subsequently, up to the first free
elections since 1946, the country was administered by the federal government
and separate national governments of reconciliation, with restructured parliaments. After a forty-year gap, Czecho-Slovak parliamentary democracy had
finally been renewed with free elections in June 1990. In Slovakia 'the Public
against Violence' emerged victorious; in the Czech lands, it was 'the Citizens'
Forum' that came out on top.

*Pope John Paul II,
in Slovakia, 1990*

Not until after the elections, however, did it become apparent that 'the Public
against Violence' was satisfied with the federative status quo, despite the fact that,
in view of the ongoing processes of radical change, a time had come to re-evalu-
ate Slovak and Czech co-habitation. In Slovakia, various citizens' initiatives and

297

Joint meeting of National Council of Slovak Republic and Slovak regime

associations arose that contributed to a new awareness of Slovak identity as it had evolved through whole centuries of history. These initiatives highlighted the importance of sovereignty, reflecting a Slovak reaction similar to that of other nations escaping the East-Central European jail of nations. New associations sprang up: 'Sixty-one Steps to Slovak Identity', 'The Independent Association of Economists in Slovakia', 'Roots', 'The Congress of Slovak Intelligentsia', 'The Association of Slovak Journalists', and 'The Society of Slovak Writers'. These new organizations were some of the reasons why 'The Public against Violence' split in two, giving rise to 'The Movement for a Democratic Slovakia'. The same kind of evolution took place inside 'The Christian Democratic Movement', where a separate 'Slovak Christian Democratic Movement' spun off. Alongside 'The Slovak National Party', a relatively conservative defender of Slovak interests, new protagonists stepped onto the political scene, with even more pointed programs supporting Slovak interests in the Federated Czecho-Slovak Republic. Almost three whole years of clashes in the National Parliaments and in the Federal Assembly were spent on the 'hyphen debate' over the legalization of the hyphen in the name 'Czecho-Slovak Federative Republic' (1990). At the same time, a proposed Pact between the Czech National Council and the Slovak National Council to fine-tune relations between the two nations was hotly debated, only to be eventually rejected by the Presidium of the Slovak National Council at Milovy.[8] This matter was finally resolved by a second round of free elections held in June 1992. The victory of The Movement for a Democratic Slovakia in the Slovak elections and of The Citizens' Democratic Party in the Czech elections, created the conditions for a definitive resolution of the relationship between Slovaks and Czechs.

Michal Kovac, president of Slovak Republic, swearing in

298

Prime-minister Jozef Moravcik, receiving congratulations from C. Lalumier, after signing Statutes of European Council

As a result of various such internal developments including the positive political contribution of a round-table discussion organized by Matica Slovenska (the Slovak Cultural Institute), as well as of a relatively favorable international situation (disrupted only by civil war in the Balkans), the time was ripe for a mutual agreement, free of intervention, establishing two separate republics. Just as the men of September 19, 1848, and October 30, 1918, have inscribed their names indelibly in Slovak history, so have the modern deputies who voted for a Declaration of Slovak Independence on July 17, 1992, and the subsequent ratification of a constitution on September 1. Equally deserving of commemoration are the delegates who shortly thereafter, on November 25, voted in the Federal Assembly in Prague to split the country into two independent states, Slovakia and the Czech Republic. Those deputies were members of The Movement for a Democratic Slovakia, The Slovak National Party, and The Party of the Democratic Left. Thus, on January 1, 1993, The Slovak Republic was also able to join the world family of independent states. It was gradually accorded official recognition by all the countries of the world, as well as by many international organizations and associations, until at last, in February 1993, the white, blue and red flag of Slovakia, with its historic Cyrillo-Methodian cross above three peaks, could fly over the headquarters of the United Nations in New York City. People throughout the world were particularly appreciative of the fact that the demise of the Czecho-Slovak Federative Republic, and the subsequent establishment of two independent states were accomplished without chaos or reciprocal killings.

Dusan Caplovic

A Decade of Sovereignty (1993–2004)

Michal Kovac

January 1, 1993

The Slovak National Council, the parliament of Slovakia, renamed itself, the National Council of the Slovak Republic (NRSR) and declared the independence of the Slovak Republic (SR). The same day, 91 countries recognized the SR as an independent state. By the end of 1993, 107 countries officially recognized Slovakia as an independent state.

January 19, 1993

The SR was admitted to the United Nations Organization as the 180th member state.

January 22, 1993

The Slovak Republic was accepted as a special observer at the Council of Europe.

February 8, 1993

After the currency separation with the Czech Republic, the Slovak Crown ('Slovenská koruna', Sk, SKK) became the official currency of the SR.

February 9, 1993

The Slovak Republic became a member of UNESCO.

February 15 – March 2, 1993

In the third round of presidential elections in the NRSR, Michal Kovac, the candidate of HZDS, was elected by 106 votes (out of 150), on March 2, 1993, as the first president of the second Slovak Republic.

April 2, 1993

In Bratislava an options and futures exchange, the first in central or eastern Europe, began to function.

June 30, 1993

The Slovak Republic became the 31st member of the Council of Europe.

July 10, 1993

The National Bank of the Slovak Republic devalued the Slovak crown by 10 percent.

August 9, 1993

The trade balance of the Slovak Republic concluded with a surplus of 2.9 billion Sk.

August 17, 1993

The government of the Slovak Republic accepted an agreement of association with the European Community. The agreement was signed in the Kirchberg European Center in Luxemburg on October 4, 1993. The European parliament ratified it on October 27, 1993, and the National Council of the Slovak Republic ratified it on October 15, 1993.

February 9, 1994

The Prime Minister of the SR, Vladimir Meciar, signed the 'Partnership for Peace' in Brussels. The SR thus became the third state of the 'Visegrad Four' and the seventh central/east-European country to officially declare cooperation with NATO.

March 11, 1994

Members of parliament (NRSR) including the former members of HZDS gave a vote of no confidence to V. Meciar's cabinet.

March 16, 1994

President M. Kovac designated new government led by Jozef Moravcik.

May 25, 1994

NRSR moved to its new quarters on 'Hradny vrch' (Castle Hill – renamed later as the Alexander Dubcek Square).

October 1, 1994

Early parliamentary elections took place with 18 political parties participating. HZDS (Movement for Democratic Slovakia) in coalition with Workers' Party of Slovakia was the winner.

November 3, 1994

The new parliament (NRSR) elected Ivan Gasparovic again as its Speaker of the Parliament.

December 13, 1994

President of the SR Michael Kovac designated Vladimir Meciar the head of the HZDS for the position of the Prime Minister. For the third time, V. Meciar became the Prime Minister of the SR.

June 27, 1995

Prime Minister V. Meciar submitted membership application on behalf of the SR to the European Union (EU) in Cannes.

June 29 – July 3, 1995

Pope John Paul II was on his second pastoral visit to Slovakia. Over five days, he visited Bratislava, Nitra, Sastin, Presov, Levoca, and the High Tatras.

August – September 1995

President Michael Kovac received criticism about the democratization process in Slovakia during a visit to the United States. This resulted in an open conflict between Kovac and Meciar. It culminated in the abduction of President's son to Austria and in an appeal by the government for President's resignation.

March 27, 1996

After long negotiations, the NRSR passed Act 125/1996 on *Immorality and Lawlessnes of the Communist regime*.

June 26, 1996

Premier of the SR V. Meciar declared the interest of the SR to join NATO in an address to the European Parliament in Strasbourg.

September 29, 1996

After extensive renovations, the Grassalkovich Palace became the official seat of the President of the SR for the second time in Slovakia's history.

October 10, 1997

NRSR approved the *Declaration of Intention* of the SR to join the EU by 131 votes (out of 150).

January 23 – 24, 1998

A working conference of ten presidents of Central European countries, sponsored by Slovak President M. Kovac, took place in the historic city of Levoca. The theme of the conference was *Civil Society – Hope for a United Europe*.

March 3, 1998

After the expiration of President Kovac term of office, the government of the SR empowered Premier V. Meciar to assume a part of constitutional functions of the head of state.

March 12, 1998

The European Parliament, concerned about excessive concentration of power by V. Meciar, appealed to the Slovak government to declare a referendum for popular (direct) elections of President of the country.

September 29, 1998

Although HZDS became the winner in Parliamentary elections, the party was unable to form a government which would have support of parliamentary majority.

October 29, 1998

The new parliament (NRSR) elected Jozef Migas as its new Speaker of the Parliament.

October 30, 1998

Since the office of the President was vacant, Jozef Migas, Speaker of the Parliament, recalled the government of V. Meciar and subsequently approved a new government headed by Mikulas Dzurinda.

Rudolf Schuster

January 11, 1999

Jan Ducky, former Minister of Economy in V. Meciar's cabinet, a member of NRSR, and general director of Slovak Gas Works, became a victim of the first political murder in the SR.

May 29, 1999

Rudolf Schuster was the winner in the second round of popular presidential elections, defeating the chairman of HZDS and former premier V. Meciar.

December 10 – 11, 1999

The EU summit held in Helsinki decided to start official negotiations with the SR as a prerequisite of joining the EU. Premier M. Dzurinda represented the SR at the summit.

January 22, 2000

Judge Jan Mazak became the new Chairman of the Constitutional Court.

June 15, 2000

President Rudolf Schuster underwent a serious operation in Bratislava. In critical condition, he was transfered to a hospital in Innsbruck, Austria.

February 2001

NRSR approved far reaching changes to Slovakia's Constitution, a key step towards gaining membership in the EU and NATO. The amended Constitution decentralized political and administrative power in the SR, increased the authority of the State Audit Office, strengthened the power of the judiciary, and provided greater recognition to minorities.

March 19, 2002

Pavel Kandrac became the first ombudsman of the SR.

President Rudolf Schuster and Cardinal Jan Chryzostom Korec, S.J. exchange good will (Bratislava, December 12, 2002)

June 2002

During session of the *Permanent Conference of Slovaks Living Abroad*, The World Association of Slovaks Abroad (WASA) was established. Dusan Klimo of Germany became its first President.

September 21, 2002

LS-HZDS (recently renamed HZDS) was again the winner in parliamentary elections, but was unable to find coalition parties to form a government which would have support of parliamentary majority.

November 16, 2002

President R. Schuster appointed the new government again headed by M. Dzurinda.

November 21, 2002

EU summit in Prague formally invited Slovakia to join in 2004.

May 16 – 17, 2003

Citizens of Slovakia approved Slovakia's entry into the EU in a referendum.

December 2003

NRSR reformed Slovakia's tax system, enacting a 19% flat tax. Presidential veto was overriden and the new Tax Law became effective on January 1, 2004.

February 2004

Unconformable communities of Romany population plundered shops selling alcohol and food in several villages in eastern Slovakia, protesting against the proposed changes reducing various welfare programs. Police and army units were engaged to control the riots.

March 29, 2004

Premiers of Slovakia, Slovenia, Estonia, Latvia, Lithuania, Rumania and Bulgaria signed ratification documents during a celebration in Washington, D.C. Premier M. Dzurinda led the Slovak delegation. With these new seven countries NATO was expanded to 26 countries, including the United States and Canada.

April 16 – June 15, 2004

Ivan Gasparovic was elected the new President of the SR, winning in the second round of popular elections over his political rival V. Meciar. He began his term of office on June 15, 2004.

May 1, 2004

The Slovak Republic together with Cyprus, the Czech Republic, Estonia, Lithuania, Latvia, the Magyar Republic (Hungary), Malta, Poland, and Slovenia became members of the EU. With this expansion the EU now includes 25 countries with a population of 455 million.

Ivan Gasparovic

Ivan Reguli

305

Prime Minister Mikulas Dzurinda and President George W. Bush (Bratislava, February 24, 2005) (©TIO UV SR, 2005)

February 24, 2005

U.S. President George W. Bush and Russian President Vladimir Putin met in Bratislava Castle. Despite some disagreement over the course of democracy in Russia, the two world leaders affirmed their common commitment to cooperation in the struggle against terrorism and the spread of nuclear weapons. They stressed the need to work closely together as statesmen on the big issues that matter most in the effort to secure world peace.

President Bush marked a milestone – the first visit by a U.S. president to Slovakia. He spoke to an enthusiastic crowd of thousands in Hviezdoslav Square, where he stated that Slovakia has chosen freedom, the country had the opportunity to help "spread liberty around the world".

The Bratislava Summit put Slovakia in the limelight of the world for a day, and symbolized the progress which the country has made in building a democratic society with an expanding market economy.

Michael J. Kopanic, Jr., 'Slovakia in the Limelight', *Jednota*,
March 2, 2005

Endnotes

Chapter 1.

Summary: During the pre-historic era, peoples other than Slavs inhabited the territory of present-day Slovakia. About 200,000 years ago its first inhabitants lived in a cold climate and settled mostly around thermal springs. Their culture resembled that of other Stone-Age peoples around the world and was based on hunting and gathering. The first evidence of polished tools and primitive art comes from the end of the Middle Stone Age. The best-known artifact is a figurine of 'Venus', found in Moravany nad Vahom, dating to more than 22,000 years ago.

[1] To simplify reference, the text sometimes uses the names of contemporary countries (Slovakia, Austria, Hungary, Poland, Germany, etc.) as a shorthand for the territory occupied by these countries today.

[2] Central Europe is a geographic concept, comparable to that of the Midwest in the US. It is usually understood to include the territories of present day Switzerland, Germany, Poland, the Czech Republic, Austria, Slovakia, Hungary, Ukraine, and often Slovenia as well.

[3] This translation consistently uses present-day place names and spellings or their customary English versions (e.g. Venice, Vienna), thus enabling the reader to find them on contemporary maps. Many Central European towns and villages have appeared under several names or spellings in documents and treatises, depending on the language of the writer, and in Latin versions as well. Some English histories of Central Europe impose one or another language on all the place names, usually German or Hungarian (Magyar).

[4] Travertines are composed of layers of stone that form around organic remains through the interaction of minerals and waters in hot springs. According to the Slovak archaeologist, Dusan Caplovic, stone can even form inside a body fallen in water. Such a process can provide researchers with an exact copy of a Neanderthal skull, as is the case in the remains of a prehistoric man found at Ganovce. A summary of Dr. Caplovic' display at the Cleveland Museum of Art can be found in 'The Treasures of Ancient and Modern Slovakia', *The Slovak Catholic Falcon* (July 9, 1997), p.7.

[5] The Venus of Moravany is a figure of a woman, carved from mammoth tusk, found at the hot springs in Piestany. It is currently on display at the Slovak National Museum in Bratislava Castle. Generally considered to be one of the finest examples of Upper Paleolithic Art in Europe, it is unquestionably the greatest piece found in Slovakia to date.

[6] Faience is glazed earthenware pottery or wall tile. It originated in Italy and thence spread across the Mediterranean region and the rest of Europe.

[7] *Rudohorie,* the Slovak Ore Mountains, lie to the South of present-day Spis-

ska Nova Ves and North of Roznava.

8 There is no link between this ancient Otoman culture and the Ottoman Empire which expanded to Central Europe in the 16th Century A.D. The Otoman culture derives its name from a site in the Transylvanian region of Romania, where it was first discovered. From there it spread to Hungary, Ruthenia, and Southeast Slovakia.

9 Mycenaean refers to an ancient Greek civilization, which peaked between 1400 and 1200 B.C., known for elaborate palaces, fortifications, and extensive trade in the Eastern Mediterranean and Aegean regions. (Thomas F.X. Noble, *Western Civilization: The Continuing Experiment.* Boston: Houghton Mifflin Co., 1998, pp. 7–68.)

10 Indo-Europeans were the ancient linguistic ancestors of the present-day Slovaks, English, Germans, French, Italians, Greeks, Hindus, Iranians, and other European and Asiatic nations, excluding Magyars, Finns, and Turks.

11 The Hallstatt Age is named after an archaeological site in Austria.

12 The La Tene era occurred at the end of the Late Iron Age and is named after an archaeological site in Switzerland.

13 The capital of Slovakia was officially named Bratislava in 1920. Before that it was also called Presporok by Slovaks, Pressburg by Germans, and Pozsony by Magyars. Its first recorded form was 'Brezalauspurc', in the 9th Century, possibly derived from Predslav, a son of Svatopluk.

14 Modern-day Hainburg, Austria.

15 The Puchov culture is named for its discovery site at Puchov-Skalka in Northwestern Slovakia. It dates to the 2nd Century B.C. to the 1st Century A. D. Evidence from archaeological digs shows it spread mainly across North and Central Slovakia, into South Poland and Northwest Moravia. Scholars believe it originated in the Lusatian culture, with influences from Illyria and the Adriatic region. The people there, who scholars believe were Celts, built fortified hill sites with local stone. They traded extensively with the Romans and other Celts, and evidence points to the practice of a form of human sacrifice. The culture gradually disappeared as its bearers were assimilated into Dacian and other migrating tribes. (*Slovaks: A Concise Encyclopedia,* p. 489.)

16 This was the name of a province of the Roman Empire, which extended to the Western bank of the Danube River in today's Hungary. The name was still in use centuries after the fall of Rome, often referring to the whole Danubian basin.

17 A victory over the Quadi was recorded with the following inscription: "In memory of the victory of the Emperor's army, encamped at Laugaricio, 855 soldiers of the Second Legion. Inscription by Constans, Commander of the Second Auxiliary Legion." (Gilbert L. Oddo, *Slovakia and its People.* New York: Robert Speller & Sons, 1960, p. 4.)

18 While the English name of Hungary derives from the Huns, there is no link between them and the present-day Hungarians (called *Magyarok* in their own language), whose Ugric ancestors arrived in Central Europe about 400 years after the invasion of the Huns.

Chapter 2.

Summary: In the late 5th and early 6th Centuries A.D., as the Roman Empire weakened and ultimately collapsed, the Slavic ancestors of the Slovaks first migrated as tribes into the Danubian Basin. Since the Slavs lacked any central organization, nomadic Avars from the steppes of present-day Ukraine were able to subjugate and rule them for several centuries. Frankish troops finally defeated the Avars in the 8th Century. With the exception of a short-lived state run by a Frankish merchant named Samo in the 7th Century, the early Slavs of Slovakia lacked any semblance of self-rule.

By the early 9th Century, two Slavic states emerged, one in Nitra, the other in Moravia (straddling the Morava River). In the former, Prince Pribina allowed German clerics to consecrate the first known Christian church on Slovak territory in 828. Five years later, the Moravian Prince Mojmir (833–846) annexed Nitra to his kingdom and founded the first large Slavic state in Central Europe, which came to be known as Great Moravia. Over the next seven decades this state expanded to include most of what was to become 20th Century Czecho-Slovakia, as well as parts of South Poland, western Hungary, and eastern Austria. Fearing the power of the neighboring Frankish kingdom, the next Moravian ruler, named Rastislav, besought Byzantine emperor, Michael, to send Slavic speaking missionaries to his kingdom. His plea was answered in the persons of Constantine (later Cyril) and Methodius. This mission antagonized the German clergy and led to a series of political and religious intrigues to keep Moravia under the jurisdiction of the Latin rite and the Germanic hierarchy. In the meantime, Great Moravia succumbed to incursions by Magyar marauders, and faded from the historical record.

[1] As opposed to *Slovak*, which refers to the inhabitants of Slovakia and their ancestors, *Slavic* embraces over a dozen contemporary nations, including Slovaks, Poles, Czechs, Russians, Croats, Slovenes and others. The common name for their ancestors in the first millennium A.D. is *Slavs,* the adjective *Slavic*. It can be compared with the term *Germanic*, which includes Germans, Norwegians, English, etc., and *Romance,* which includes Italians, French and Spanish, among others. Slovaks, Czechs, Poles and Lusatian Serbs are classified as West Slavs; Serbs, Croats, Slovenes, Bulgarians and Macedonians, all settled in the Balkans, are South Slavs; Russians, Ukrainians and Belo-Russians are East Slavs. The Rusyns (Ruthenians) present a special dilemma, since they lie on the borderlands between East and West Slavs, and scholars have placed them in either group.

[2] Most historians agree on this as the ancestral location of the Slavs, only a few proposing that they may have lived in Central Europe, too, perhaps since the beginning of the Indo-European period. See: F. Curta.

[3] The Avars migrated to Central Europe from the steppes of what is now Ukraine. They occupied the central plain of what was to become Hungary, between the latter third of the 6th Century and the end of the 8th Century.

⁴ After the Western Roman Empire, centered in Rome, declined, its Eastern part, known as the Byzantine Empire, centered in Constantinople (today Istanbul), continued to thrive.

⁵ Paying tribute was a convenient way to avoid costly war. Since the Byzantines were so fabulously wealthy, they often paid off their foes rather than fight them.

⁶ Central Europe fell within the sphere of influence of the Eastern Frankish Empire, which became an independent, mostly Germanic entity. Later it became a conglomerate of feudal countries under the name 'Holy Roman Empire', though it did not actually include Rome.

⁷ Other historians place the territory ruled by Samo elsewhere in Central Europe, or say there is not enough evidence to determine its location.

⁸ There is a great deal of controversy surrounding Samo and the location of his realm. Czech historians put its center somewhere in Bohemia; the 19ᵗʰ Century Czech historian F. Palacky surmised that Samo was indeed of Slavic origin. (Jaroslav Purs, and Miroslav Kropilak (Eds.), *Prehled dejin Ceskoslovenska, do roku 1526.* Prague, 1980, pp. 57–58.) Slovenian historians claim Samo as the founder of their first tribal state. According to Matus Kucera, one of the foremost Slovak historians of the Early Middle Ages, Samo was an ordinary merchant from an 'ancient minority', and 'his name clearly betrays his Celtic origin'. The state organized by Samo warded off an attack by the Frankish Dagobert I in 631. (Robert B. Pynsent, *Questions of Identity: Czech and Slovak Ideas of Nationality and Personality.* Budapest: Central European University Press, 1994, pp. 158–159). Pynsent cites Kucera's *Postavy velkomoravskej historie.* Martin: 1986, p. 19.

Pynsent, an English scholar, questions Kucera's theory positing Wogatisburg as the site of present-day Bratislava. In fact, he challenged the interpretation of many Slovak historians who have looked to Samo's state and the later Great Moravian Empire as precursors of the modern Slovak state. Pysent compares such interpretations to the myth making of Greeks, used even by Homer, to provide a sense of continuity to Greek history (Robert B. Pynsent, *Ibid.,* 157).

Research on Samo remains difficult because of the scarcity of sources. Only three exist, and the *Fredegar Chronicle* (c. 660 A.D.) is the only one close to Samo's time. The two other sources, the *Gesta Dagoberti Regis* (c. 835 A.D.) and the *Conversio Bagoariorum et Carantanorum* (c. 871 A.D.), contradict many of the assertions of the *Fredegar Chronicle*. See: Frano Tiso, 'The Empire of Samo', in *Slovak Studies* 1. (1961) pp. 1–24.

An émigré publicist in the United States, Dominik Hudec, disagrees with historians of the Slovak Academy of Sciences, who have traditionally assumed Samo to be of Frankish origin. His theory has generated fierce debate in contemporary Slovakia, between the Matica Slovenska (The Slovak Cultural Institute) and the Historical Institute of the Slovak Academy of Sciences. Hudec quotes a Slovak translation of the *Fredegar Chronicle* in *Pramene k dejinam Velkej Moravy*. Bratislava: 1964: "In the fortieth year of the rule of Clovis, a man named Samo, of Frankish descent…" led the Slavic peoples. Hudec argues that a poor translation of the original sources has misled past historians. Hudec goes on to claim that Samo was of Slavic descent, whose place of birth was the Frankish state, and citing the description 'natione Francus', relates it to three other uses of the term 'natione' in the text, which clearly refer to state membership. Hudec additionally notes that Slovenian historians consider Samo a prince of Carinthia, based on the Bavarian cleric's work *De Conversione*, while others still have placed his domain in the region of Salzburg, Austria. Hudec quotes the *Gesta Dagoberti*, dating from the 9th Century: "In that year the Sloveni (Slavs), also known as Vinidi (Wends), whose king was Samo…" as indicating that the Franks themselves considered Samo a Slav. Hudec claims that the Slavs were a self-aware people who stubbornly refused to be ruled by a foreigner. (Dominik Hudec, *Velky omyl, Velka Morava*, Martin: Matica Slovenska, 1994, pp. 31–32.)

9 In English 'Wheat Island', not really an island, but a large area in Southwest Slovakia between the Danube and the Little Danube ('Csallokoz' in Hungarian). Having formed from sediments of the Danube, with abundant ground water, it is the most productive agricultural area in Slovakia. (M. Strhan, and. D. Daniel, (Eds.), *Slovakia and the Slovaks*. Bratislava: Slovak Academy of Sciences, 1994, p. 721.)

10 This is the area west of Bratislava, where the Danube flows between the Carpathians and the hills of Lower Austria, long used as a trade route. See F. Curta.

11 Charlemagne decisively defeated the Avars in 796.

12 Great Moravia describes a geographical more than political entity, for the Slavic components were only loosely bound together. (Stanislav J. Kirschbaum, *A History of Slovakia: The Struggle for Survival*. New York: St. Martin's Press, 1995, pp. 23–24). The name is a literal translation of the Greek, occurring only once in a work by Byzantine Emperor, Constantine VII Porphyrogenitus (905–959 A.D.). Slovak, Czech, Polish and other archaeologists and historians use the name Great Moravia to refer to the artifacts and political structures that Anton Spiesz describes here as found on the territory of present-day Moravia, West Slovakia, and neighboring areas. Except for the name given by Porphyrogenitus, we have no clue as to what the inhabitants themselves might have called their country. A few researchers have suggested that this name may have referred to an entirely different area. See P. R. Magocsi, *Historical Atlas*.

13 Many of our historical sources are writings by monks in various German monasteries. They recorded and protected the data for future generations. Many of the references to Slovakian events come from the East German Mark, which today is Austria.

14 Just as the Slovaks were not a clearly defined ethnic group at that time, neither were the Czechs.

15 Pribina did not immediately convert to Christianity, but recognizing his

geopolitical situation, he permitted his subjects to convert and thus strengthen ties with the community of European nations and culture. Later, in exile, he became a zealous Christian and received a fiefdom from Louis the German.

[16] Historians are still not sure of the location of Rastislav's castle, at the center of Great Moravia. Among suggested locations are Devin, Bratislava, Velehrad, Stare Mesto, Mikulcice, Pohansko, Nitra, Vysegrad, and Komarno. In light of archaeological finds, the most likely location seems to be the fortified castle Valy, near Mikulcice, on the West bank of the Morava River. Excavations have uncovered ten churches, administrative buildings, and various 9th Century relics. (Michal Lacko, S.J., *Saints Cyril and Methodius*. Rome: 1969, pp. 64–65).

[17] The Papacy at the time recognized Greek and several oriental languages, besides Latin, as liturgical languages, but they were not normally used in the Western Rite.

[18] Thesalonike, on Greek maps.

[19] Located in Northern Greece, Salonica had a sizeable Slavic population, which traded and interacted with the Greeks.

[20] The late Michal Lacko, S.J., the foremost authority on SS. Cyril and Methodius, provides abundant details about the lives of these two missionaries to Central Europe. (See his: *Saints Cyril and Methodius*. Rome: Praeses Pontifici Instituti Orientalis, 1969.) Also useful is the work of the eminent historian Francis Dvornik, *Byzantine Missions among the Slavs: SS. Constantine-Cyril and Methodius*. New Brunswick, N.J., (1970.)

[21] The Slovak original gives the year 865, which is probably erroneous.

[22] It is customary to use the term 'Slavonic' rather than Slavic in references to the Old Slavic liturgical language.

[23] Old Rus refers to the early medieval state of Kievan Rus, located in the Ukraine and ruled by Vikings, who worked the trade routes to the Near East. The name Russia derives from this term, and Russian historians generally claim this political entity as their first state. Ukrainian historians dispute the claim and posit their own counterclaim. Kievan Rus was destroyed by the Mongol invasions of the 13th Century.

[24] This old place-name, as well as the name of Lake Balaton nearby, is derived from the Slavic word for 'clay, mud'.

[25] Vislansko, or Vistula Land, refers to the area of the Upper Vistula River in modern Poland. During the 9th Century a Slavic tribe known as the Vislany occupied this area.

[26] That is, Svatopluk would be under the jurisdiction of the Papacy.

[27] That is, the Western part of the modern Czech Republic.

[28] These were Slavic areas in what today is South-East Germany.

[29] The diet was simply an assembly of nobles that met periodically to advise the emperor and to assure him of support.

[30] These were West Slavic tribes, whose descendents still live in South-East Germany, not the South-Slavic Serbs of modern Yugoslavia. The Lusatian Serbs are the smallest group of Slavs in present-day Europe. Those who

have escaped German assimilation live in rural areas.

[31] This ethnic group is commonly called 'Hungarian' in English. The author and other historians use 'Magyar' (pronounced *maawd-yar*, which is the Hungarians' own name for their ethnic identity. They reserve the names 'Hungary' and 'Hungarian' for use in reference to the multi-ethnic Kingdom of Hungary, which included Magyars, Slovaks, Romanians, Germans, Croats, and others. The present-day Hungarian name for their state is 'Magyarorszag', meaning the land of the Magyars.

[32] The Magyars were a group of Ugric herders and warriors, who roamed the steppes north of the Black Sea on horseback before they moved into Central Europe in the late 8th and early 9th Century, on the run from devastating attacks by the Pechenegs. Their earlier homeland was north-east of the Ural Mountains. Their name derives from the Megyeri tribe, the dominant among seven tribes of varying ethnicity and language. For sixty years Magyar raids penetrated deep into Western Europe, but finally they suffered defeat by the Germans in 955 near Lechfeld, not far from Augsburg. The language of the Magyars belongs to the Finno-Ugric family, along with Turkish and Finnish, and is not related to Indo-European languages. However, it has assimilated many words from Slavic and German.

[33] That is, the area northwest of Bratislava, west of the Carpathians.

[34] There is no universal agreement among scholars about the location of Great Moravia. Some Czech archaeologists, such as J. Poulik, argue that Mikulcice may have been its center. The fortified settlement there contained the foundations of ten separate churches. Church foundations have also been discovered in Sady, near Stare Mesto, and at Modra. (See F. Dvornik, *Byzantine Missions*. pp. 81–89.) While Slovak historians tend to claim their own land as central, Imre Boba, a Hungarian historian, argued that it was farther to the South, near Lake Balaton, in modern-day Hungary. (See his *Nomads, Northmen, and Slavs: Eastern Europe in the 9th Century*. The Hague: Mouton, 1967.)

[35] That is, the area west of the Danube in modern Hungary.

Chapter 3.

Summary: The Magyar arrival in Central Europe marked a new phase in the history of the Slavic ancestors of the Slovaks. When Svatopluk died in 894, his sons vied for control of Great Moravia, with no lack of outside 'help', and the Magyar incursion simply overwhelmed their weakened forces. By 907, the Magyars were in control. With the baptism of Stephen I of the Arpad Dynasty in 997, Hungary took its place alongside established European states. Then, by taking a Bavarian wife, King Stephen I oriented Hungary, and thus Slovakia, to Western Europe, and adopted Germanic models of government and church organization.

Hungarian monarchs spent the next several centuries consolidating their rule and expanding their borders, in the process clashing with neighboring powers, particularly the Holy Roman Empire and the Kingdom of Bohemia.

In the 13th Century, to strengthen his country and its economy, King Bela IV invited German settlers. In exchange for socio-economic privileges and the right of self-government in towns, the Germans brought skills and habits to their new homeland which stimulated crafts, increased trade, and introduced new methods of mining.

In the meantime important political changes limited the power of Hungarian kings and upheld the rights of the nobility. Hungary was reorganized into a system of counties, which gave powerful magnates a great deal of local autonomy. A manorial system evolved which obligated the peasantry to deliver part of its produce and to provide manual services to a manor lord. The medieval church also expanded, as evidenced by many Romanesque churches and monasteries and a proliferation of monastic orders. By the end of the Medieval Ages most of Slovakia had been settled and developed; only some heavily forested, mountainous areas remained pristine.

[1] The Szeklers were an ethnic group with a distinct identity, who spoke Magyar and settled mainly in Transylvania. The Plavci were the advance guard of the nomadic Asian Polovci, who settled near a Polish pass in the 12th Century. Some of them also settled in Slovakia, as indicated by place names there, such as Plavec, in North-East Slovakia. (*Slovakia and the Slovaks: A Concise Encyclopedia.* p. 464.)

[2] Magyars borrowed many common words from Slavic, including words for 'window, cup, butcher, smith, horseshoe, straw, hay, furrow, harrow, Thursday, Friday'. (Scotus Viator, *Racial Problems in Hungary.* London: 1908, p. 21.)

[3] Acceptance of Christianity was seen as a prerequisite for recognition by the Papacy and Christian Europe.

[4] In Spiesz' history the term 'Hungary' usually refers to the former multi-ethnic Kingdom of Hungary, which included parts or all of Slovakia, Hungary, Romania, Croatia, Austria, Ukraine and Serbia. Present-day Hungary is only a rump of that former kingdom. For further reading on the frequent raids by the seven tribal chieftains (Arpad, Szabolz, Gyula, Ors, Kund, Lel, and Bulcsu) see the work of the 13th century chronicler Simon of Keza, *Gesta Hungarorum* (The Deeds of the Hungarians), translated by L. Veszpremy, et al., Budapest: Central European University Press, 1999.

[5] That is, 'zupa' or 'stolica', in Slovak, and 'comitatus' in Latin. The Latin language was retained as the language of administration through the late 18th and early 19th Centuries.

[6] 'Comes' (companion) in Latin.

[7] One must keep in mind that the medieval church was independently wealthy and that, in addition to its own upkeep, it also ran institutions for the care of the poor and assumed many responsibilities which are carried

by governments today. Europeans thus came to look at church-state relationships quite differently from Americans. For instance, even today in
Europe a part of tax revenue goes to support one's church affiliation.

8   In the Middle Ages, one's faith and loyalty to lord and sovereign were of
primary importance; ethnic identity was still relatively weak. Modern
nationalism did not emerge until the 19th Century.

9   Also spelled Ladislaus.

10   The Pechenegs were nomads from Central Asia; they entered Hungary after
being driven out of Ukraine.

11   Of course, this was not Germany in the modern sense. It was the eastern
part of the Holy Roman Empire, an entity established by Charlemagne in
the 9th Century.

12   Educated at the court of the Byzantine emperor, Bela III (1173–1196)
mounted the throne with a promise of non-interference from Byzantium.
He pursued an independent foreign and domestic policy. His second wife,
a French princess, influenced both the political and cultural life of the royal
court. A permanent bureaucracy was established at this time. In religious
matters, the Cluniac reform movement of France exerted a profound influence on the church in Hungary. (Julius Bartl, et alii, *Lexikon slovenskych
dejin.* Bratislava: 1997, pp. 24–25. *Slovak History: Chronology & Lexicon.*
Wauconda, IL: Bolchazy-Carducci Publishers, 2002.)

13   King Stephen originally selected Peter to be his successor when his only
son Imre died. The son of Stephen's sister and the Doge of Venice, Peter
fled to the emperor when the Hungarian nobles refused to recognize his
succession, selecting Stephen's brother-in-law, the Palatine Samuel Aba,
instead. Although Peter regained the throne with the help of the emperor,
he later fell victim to a pagan revolt led by Vata, a tribal chief. (Laszlo
Makkai, 'Hungarians' Prehistory, Their Conquest of Hungary and Their
Raids to the West to 955'. in *History of Hungary.* Peter F. Sugar, Ed.,
Bloomington: Indiana University Press, 1990, p. 18.)

14   His father, King Andrew, lost his life in a power struggle with his brother,
Bela. Bela I ruled for a short time before being replaced by his nephew,
Solomon.

15   This was not Spanish Galicia, but the Galicia in South-Eastern Poland and
Western Ukraine.

16   The Cumans were a tribe from Southern Russia, who fled west after being
attacked by Tatars. They begged Bela IV of Hungary for sanctuary. The king
acquiesced, counting on their aid in coming battles with the Tatars. About
40,000 Cuman families settled in Hungary and were assimilated to the Magyars. (Gilbert, Oddo, *Slovakia and its People.* New York: 1960, p. 28.)

17   The Czechs were defeated because the Bohemian nobility, abandoning him,
backed Rudolf. (Francis Dvornik, *Slavs in European History and Civilization.* New Brunswick: 1962, p. 30.)

18   Details may be found in Jaroslav Purs, and Miroslav Kropilak, (Eds.),
Prehled dejin Ceskoslovenska. Praha: 1980, pp. 261–262.

[19] The granting of special privileges was not an exclusively Hungarian phenomenon. Polish kings also granted royal charters of self-government, to encourage German settlement during the Middle Ages. (Jean Sedlar, *East Central Europe in the Middle Ages, 1000–1500*. Seattle: University of Washington Press, pp. 134–135.)

[20] Because Andrew II was a relatively weak ruler, powerful nobles began expropriating royal property and taking over administrative powers in the early 13th Century. They objected to foreign settlers who were creating a separate power base in towns, with little loyalty to the local nobility. The Golden Bull essentially increased the power of the landed class at the expense of the Crown. See Oddo, p. 28.

[21] The Palatine was usually an elected member of the royal family.

[22] Budapest, the capital of present-day Hungary, is a consolidation of the earlier towns of Buda and Pest.

[23] Ismaelites were members of a Moslem Shiite sect; they were Arabs, experienced in minting coins.

[24] The Premonstratensians, also called Norbertines, are an order of Augustinian canons founded by St. Norbert in 1120. They practised a life of austerity but, unlike monks, worked and preached among people. In Eastern Europe they played an important role in the conversion of the surviving pagans. (*Encyclopedia Britannica*, Vol. 21. London: 1926, p. 279.)

Chapter 4.

Summary: In the last two centuries of the the Medieval Ages (14th and 15th Centuries) Slovakia experienced one of its greatest periods of progress and development, no little thanks to four great personalities who ascended the Hungarian throne and conducted themselves in their 'divinely' conferred office with the utmost responsibility. Each of them ruled for a relatively long time: Charles Robert of Anjou for 34 years; his son Louis I (the Great) for 40 years; Sig(is)mund of Luxembourg for 50 years; and Mattias (Matthew) Corvinus for 32 years. Of course, Slovakia's ascent to, and permanent inclusion in, Western Civilization, owed most to the industriousness and perseverance of its people, including non-Slovak ethnics, particularly Germans, to whom Slovaks purposefully adapted themselves.

[1] This ethnic group has usually been referred to as 'Ruthenians'; their leaders in the United States prefer 'Rusyn'.

[2] The written standard used by Slovaks was modeled after Czech, which differed from the various Slovak dialects but was still understandable.

[3] About a dozen and a half of the Northwestern counties of the Kingdom of Hungary were inhabited predominantly, or almost exclusively, by Slovaks,

but these counties did not form any special links among themselves – each was integrated in the kingdom like any of the other counties.

4   Spiesz calls him Ladislav V, which must be erroneous: Ladislav V ruled more than a hundred years later.

5   'Csak' in Hungarian sources; full name, Matyas Csak.

6   That is to say, he was also elected ruler of the conglomerate of German feudal states west of Hungary.

7   Named after the Czech religious reformer Jan Hus, who was partly inspired by John Wycliffe, the Hussite rebellions started after the Church condemned Hus for heresy and burned him at the stake in 1415. The Hussite movement preceded the Protestant Reformation of Martin Luther by approximately 100 years, and was acknowledged by Luther as one of his inspirations.

8   That is, Ladislas/Ladislav/Laszlo, who was born on February 22, 1440, in Komarno. Elizabeth had him crowned as Ladislav V, King of Hungary, in Szekesfehervar, on May 5, 1440.

9   That is, Wladislas/Wladyslaw III, Jagiello of Poland (1424–1444), who was elected by the Diet and crowned Wladislas/Wladyslaw/Laszlo I of Hungary, in Buda, in July 1440. Spiesz misidentifies him as Wladislas II – who ruled Hungary, 1490–1516.

10   See previous note.

11   Spiesz misidentifies him as Jan of Podebrady; he was Jiri (George) of Podebrady.

12   He became Vladislav/Ulaszlo II, of Hungary in 1490, having been previously crowned King of Bohemia in 1471. (He lived from 1456 to 1516.)

13   Born 1506; crowned King of Hungary 1508, but did not take power until his father's (Vladislav II) death in 1516; died in 1526.

14   The oldest preserved religious text comes from Eastern Slovakia and is full of Eastern Slovak dialect features.

15   Ferdinand Ulicny, *Dejiny osidlenia zemplinskej zupy*. Michalovce: Zemplinska Spolocnost, 2001, pp. 323–337.

Chapter 5.

Summary: The Ottoman Turkish victory at Mohac in 1526 marked a significant turning point in Hungarian and Slovak history. The death of the king left a power vacuum. Austria's Habsburg rulers inherited the Hungarian throne and were destined to dominate the country's politics for the next four centuries, serving as its kings and attempting to establish absolute rule. A continuous struggle ensued, as the Hungarian nobility jealously guarded its constitution and traditions of self-government, while the Habsburgs remained intent on concentrating power in the imperial capital, Vienna.

The spread of Protestantism and the continual incursions of the Ottoman Turks intensified and complicated the power struggle between crown and nobility. And since many members of the Catholic hierarchy had perished at Mohac, a religious vacuum occurred, enabling Lutherans and Reformed Calvinists from German and Czech lands to make significant inroads among German and Slovak townspeople and among Hungary's population in general. Some of the refractory nobles joined the Turks in their quest to control northern and eastern Hungary. Much of Hungary fell into Turkish occupation, causing many nobles to take refuge in Slovakia, which then became the center of Hungarian culture and politics until well after 1683, when the Turks were finally rolled back.

The Catholic Counter-Reformation went on the offensive in the late 16th Century. By the end of the next century it had succeeded in reconverting much of the population, including the nobility. During the 17th Century the Jesuits turned Trnava into a center for a reinvigorated and triumphant Catholicism. One can still see its achievements in the abundance of magnificent baroque churches across Slovakia. Although many Protestants retained their faith, the Catholic Habsburgs introduced new laws that tightly restricted their freedom of worship.

Spiesz maps the gradual advance of Slovak self-awareness during this period. Of course, no Slovak nationalism in the modern sense existed until after the French Revolution in 1789. He is nevertheless able to show how proportional quotas of Slovak, German, and Magyar representatives on town councils, in guilds, and in Lutheran churches reflect the beginnings of ethnic differentiation. People were clearly aware of ethnic diversity and expected their own group to have a say in important decisions.

The 16th and 17th Centuries were a time of economic decline in Slovakia. Many mines closed or substantially reduced production. Turkish raids, wars, rebellions, and banditry interfered with trade and economic growth.

Despite the religious travails and Turkish wars, Slovakia enjoyed an artistic and cultural efflorescence during this era. Renaissance architecture peaked, and the Catholic Counter-Reformation led to a flurry of baroque construction, ecclesiastic and civil. The perceived need to foster Catholic education led to the founding of new institutions of learning, the most famous in Trnava. Thus for Slovakia turbulent times unleashed fresh energy to create.

[1]   In 1620, at the battle of the White Mountain near Prague, the Emperor Ferdinand II's Bavarian army routed a rebellious Czech army. Over the next decade, both Bohemia and Moravia lost all semblance of self-government as the Crown emasculated the Bohemian estates. By 1627, Protestantism was banned in the Czech lands, something that never happened in Slovakia. The Czechs consider the White Mountain a defining event in their history, humiliating them and subordinating them to foreign absolutist rule. (Richard S. Dunn, 'The Age of Religious Wars, 1559–1689', Part II, in *The Norton History of Modern Europe*. Felix Gilbert, Ed., New York: W.W. Norton & Co., 1971, p. 251. Also: Robert A. Kann, and Zdenek, David, *Peoples of the Eastern Habsburg Lands 1526–1718*. Seattle: University of Washington Press, 1984, pp. 103–4.)

[2]   The Slovak territory occupied by the Turks was ruled by the Pasalik in Buda, and was divided into districts called 'Sanjaks', each headed by a Beg.

The Sahy region fell within the Sanjak of Estergom, while Filakovo was the center of a separate Sanjak. (See Kann and David, *Ibid.* p. 76.)

3 David P. Daniel, 'The Protestant Reformation and Slovak Ethnic Consciousness', *Slovakia.* (1978–1979), pp. 49–65. Daniel shows that an ecclesiastical leadership vacuum allowed a newly educated Lutheran clergy to emerge within existing Catholic institutions. Most Slovaks and Germans embraced Lutheranism, while Magyars leaned to Calvinism.

4 'Utraquists' and 'Neo-Utraquists', variant names for Hussites in the 16th Century. They had gained the right to receive Communion in both forms, bread and wine, as part of the Compacts of Prague of 1485. Many Lutherans also called themselves 'Neo-Utraquists' to avoid persecution.

5 Peter Pazmany was a truly fine Jesuit priest and preacher, renowned throughout Europe. He believed in peaceful conversion, but his suggestions were not always followed by the nobility. He also believed that Hungary's future lay with the Habsburgs and orientation to the West. (Carl J. Friedrich, *Age of the Baroque, 1610–1660*. New York: Harper and Row, 1952, p. 267.)

6. In fact, the terms of the Peace of Linz were never fully carried out. Of the approximately 400 churches seized by the Catholics, only 90 were ever restored. However, in Hungary, the Diet of 1646–47 did pass legislation protecting religious liberty. (Kann and David, *Ibid.* pp. 136–137.)

7 Though outnumbered by the Turks, the Imperial army resisted fiercely near the Convent of St. Gotthard, at a Raab River crossing. Using superior tactics, the Imperial forces inflicted a 'swift and humiliating defeat' on the invading Turks. The Austrian cavalry, led by 'the dashing Prince Charles of Lorraine', split their foe and drove them back across the river. 30,000 Turks fled in terror, leaving 10,000 dead. This was the first major setback of the Ottoman Turks since their original victory at Mohacs in 1526, and it left 'the glory of the day to the Christians'. (Lord Kinross, *Ottoman Centuries.* New York: Morrow Quill, 1977, p. 335. Also: Noel Barber, *Sultans.* New York: Simon and Schuster, 1973, p.102.)

8 The twenty-year truce concluded at Vasvar cost the Turks no territory, but they did have to agree to the election of the prince of Transylvania by the local estates. (William, L. Langer, Ed., *Encyclopedia of World History.* Boston: Houghton Mifflin Co., 1948, p. 483.)

9 The Hungarian nobility interpreted the humiliating terms of the treaty as a form of bribery to allow the Emperor a free hand in dealing with the opposition. (*Ibid.* p. 137–138. Also: Peter Katalin 'Later Ottoman Period and Royal Hungary, 1606–1711', *History of Hungary.* Sugar, Ed. p.115.)

10 King Louis XIV had plans to expand his French kingdom to its 'natural' border, the Rhine River, putting additional pressure on the Habsburgs from the West.

11 Hungarian deserters in Transylvania began the rebellion. Pika, himself, was from Zemplin County. Before entering Orava County, they invaded eastern Slovakia and captured many towns. As the movement gained momentum in Orava and Liptov Counties, attracting peasants to their cause, the Emperor

intervened. (*Slovakia and the Slovaks: A Concise Encyclopedia.* p. 461.)

[12] The Sopron Compromise indicated that political realities trumped religious concerns. With the Turks once again threatening to penetrate deeply in the Habsburg Empire, Leopold I was forced to concede traditional rights and privileges to the Hungarian nobility. Protestants were allowed to keep their churches, but, oddly, churches confiscated during the 1670s were allowed to remain Catholic. But religious liberty, allowed to nobility and towns, was denied to peasants. (Kann and David, *Ibid.* pp.139–140.)

[13] The 'thaler' ('toliar', in Slovak), a silver coin minted from a silver mine in Joachimsthal (Jachymov), Bohemia, from 1516, and introduced in Hungary in 1553. It remained one of the principal currencies of the Habsburg Empire until 1892, when the crown was introduced. The thaler, which originally contained 25.78 grams of pure silver, declined over the centuries. Incidentally, the term 'dollar', adopted by the U.S., derives from this name. (*Slovakia and the Slovaks: A Concise Encyclopedia.* p. 646.)

[14] The Lutherans were not allowed to use metal nails in the construction of their churches; they consequently developed a unique technique of building with wooden nails.

Chapter 6.

Summary: During the century following 1681, Catholicism firmly reasserted itself in Slovakia. Although Protestants were allowed to practise their faith, numerous new laws strictly regulated the number of non-Catholic priests and churches, and restricted their locations to free royal towns. Catholicism was officially promoted in schools, and by 1804 four new dioceses had been established. Spiesz contends that the intense religious feelings many Slovaks harbor derive from this era of re-Catholicization, as do Protestant feelings of resentment over the violation of their religious freedom.

The 18th Century also witnessed a tremendous growth in the population of Slovakia, despite the migration of many Slovaks to southern regions of Hungary in the wake of the Turkish departure. Newly cultivated lands and improved farming methods helped substantially to increase population in towns and villages.

The Habsburg emperor Leopold I attempted to introduce absolutism in Hungary, but experienced only moderate success. The Rakoczi rebellion (1703–1711) challenged imperial authority. After Leopold I died, his successor, Joseph I, also soon died, and was succeeded in turn by Charles VI, who spent much of his time working to secure the 'Pragmatic Sanction', to ensure the right of succession for his daughter. When the daughter, Maria Theresa, began her reign, she was at first preoccupied with foreign invasions. She struck a deal with the Hungarian nobility, gaining their support in exchange for assurances of greater self-government. Having secured her position, Maria

Theresa pursued reforms which enforced state Catholicism, reduced and regularized peasant obligations, and promoted nascent industries. Her reign was marked by a flourishing cultural life in Bratislava, which at the time was the capital of Hungary.

[1] Influenced by the European Enlightenment, which placed a high value on religious toleration, Emperor Joseph II issued a Toleration Patent in 1781.

[2] There were Jews living in Slovakia as early as the 10th Century, but they were periodically expelled from Hungary, or persecuted for political, religious, or economic reasons. Typically, when the Jews returned, they settled in separate quarters of towns and villages (ghettos). In the Middle Ages they comprised the lowest social stratum, and were prohibited from interacting with the other citizens, except in financial matters. (*Slovakia and the Slovaks*: *A Concise Encyclopedia.* pp. 297–298.)

[3] Either carrying the crucifix in procession, or benediction with the Eucharist. Protestants, especially Calvinists, deplored the representation of Christ in this manner, and considered it idolatrous.

[4] Daniel Krman was one of the most famous Lutheran pastors and a gifted writer in Slovakia during the late 17th and early 18th Centuries. He studied theology in Germany, at Leipzig and Wittenberg, then returned home to serve as pastor in a number of Slovak parishes. A skilled linguist who knew both Hebrew and Greek, he researched the Slovak language for ten years and then wrote a Slovak grammar (really Czech, with Slovak adaptations). He also began work on a new translation of the Bible from the original languages, but there is no indication he ever completed the project. Krman's most famous work was his history of the Christian Church, with emphasis on the story of the Evangelical (Lutheran) Church in Hungary: *Hungaria Evangelica, sive Historia Evangelii Jezu Christi in Hungaria et Provinciis eius.*

Several attempts were made on Krman's life. Also, he served time in prison for his beliefs and was exiled on three different occasions. In his last brush with the law in 1731, a trap was set for him at the instigation of the Emperor himself, and Krman was arrested to serve the last ten years of his life in prison, where he died in 1740. (August Skodacek, *Lutherans in Slovakia.* Pittsburgh: Slavia Printing Co., 1982, pp. 88–111.)

[5] The story of Juraj Janosik, the legendary Slovak Robin Hood, dates from this period of rebellion. He is said to have robbed the rich and given to the poor. He was finally betrayed, put on trial, and sentenced to death by hanging. After his execution in 1713, peasants recounted his heroism and defiance of authority in folk tales and songs which have endured to the present day.

[6] Maria Theresa pushed for reforms, not from sympathy for the peasants, but from a realization that a happy peasant is a more productive peasant. This attitude is most subtly expressed in her bon mot that "sheep should be well fed so that they might yield more wool and more milk". (Piotr S. Wandycz, *Price of Freedom: A History of East Europe from the Middle Ages to*

the Present. London: Routledge, 1992, p. 118.)
7 After the removal of the Turkish yoke, many Slovaks and Germans were settled in Central and Southern Hungary to repopulate the areas. Serb and Romanian immigrants, too, moved into regions that had previously been predominantly Magyar. Later Magyar historians decried these migrations as deliberate attempts to 'denationalize' Hungary. Actually, national issues loomed far less importantly in these policies than did the simple need to restore a Christian population to the southeast corner of the Empire. (Sir George Clark, *The Seventeenth Century*. New York: Oxford University Press, 1961, p. 370.)
8 In the middle of the 18th Century this business employed as many as 20,000 domestic spinners. (*Slovakia and the Slovaks: A Concise Encyclopedia* p. 528.)

Chapter 7.

Summary: Two themes are dominant in this chapter: the failure of imperial attempts at reform before 1848, and the codification and establishment of a Slovak literary language.

When Joseph II became emperor of Austria in 1780, he sought to impose the ideas of the Enlightenment by simple fiat. His rash behavior and disregard of Catholic and Hungarian sensibilities alienated the nobility, the clergy, and even the peasantry, whom he had aimed to free from serfdom. The imposition of German as the language of administration backfired, producing a surge of Hungarian opposition and sparking an intense Magyar nationalism. By trying to do too much too quickly, Joseph II isolated himself from most of the populace, and when he died in 1790 most of his reforms died with him.

Over the next half century, as disease and famine wracked the country, repeated rebellions erupted. These outbreaks underlined the need of significant reforms, if Hungary hoped to compete in the modern world. Because of its unwillingness to change and invest in new industries, the Hungarian nobility relegated the country to the status of a supplier of semi-finished and agricultural products. In the meantime, Austria and the Czech lands became the industrial hub of the Habsburg Empire.

The rise of Magyar nationalism and the outbreak of the French Revolution, two very disparate processes, stimulated Slovaks to strive for their own niche in the world, and one of the first steps in this direction was the codification of their own literary language. Spiesz highlights the reality that Slovak had, in fact, been widely used in times past, but with no definitive codification, there had been no consensus on a literary medium acceptable to all Slovaks. Slovak Protestants had used Czech, while Slovak Catholics published in Latin, cultured West Slovak, and local dialects. At the end of the 18th Century Anton Bernolak, a Catholic priest, codified a version of Slovak based on a western dialect, but Protestant clergy in Central and Eastern Slovakia refused to adopt this standard, considering it difficult to understand. By the 1840s, the various factions reached a compromise, which was based on a Central Slovak dialect, with some adaptations to East and West dialects. It proved to be mutually acceptable to both Catholics and Protestants, and both eastern and western Slovaks. Ludovit Stur played a pivotal role in establishing the Central Slovak dialect as normative, and thus laid the foundation for modern literary Slovak.

[1] Interestingly, the pragmatic Maria Theresa rightly feared what her reckless son Joseph would do when he ascended the throne, so she tried to keep him out of power as long as she could. Joseph II's 'impatient tolerance' extended even to those who agreed with him. His attempt to ram the Enlightenment down his people's throats left his empire in a state of rebellion. For a colorful, though somewhat dated, picture of the emperor, see: S. K. Padover, *Joseph II.* 1928.

[2] The Patent of Toleration even extended to conversion to Protestantism, though only to individuals, not whole communities. (Robert Kann, *History of the Habsburg Empire 1526–1918.* Berkeley: University of California Press, 1974, p.191.)

[3] The Patent altered the status of peasants by granting them freedom of movement and choice of occupation. It also recognized their legal claim to land. Joseph II did not abolish obligatory service to one's lord, but he did alter tax payment from kind to cash. Since the rural economy in Slovakia had functioned largely by barter, the new laws sparked indignant resistance from peasant and noble, alike. (Kann and David, *Ibid.* pp. 198, and 246–247.)

[4] Joseph II dissolved two-thirds of the monasteries in his land, but only those of contemplative orders, i.e. those that performed no 'useful work'. The law did not apply to institutions and orders engaged in charitable work, education and agriculture. (Kann and David, cited above, p. 224.)

[5] Owing to the outbreak of the French Revolution and Austria's defeat by the Turks, Joseph rescinded most of his reforms, except those affecting the peasants, and his Patent of Toleration. (Wandycz, *Ibid.,* p. 121.)

[6] Alexander was not the 'younger brother' of Leopold II, but in fact the son of the king and emperor. (Kann and David, *Ibid.* p. 227.)

[7] The Polish nobility was so wary of any strong central authority that it elected foreigners to the throne, with the expectation that they would be weak rulers. Poland consequently became so weak that its neighbors, Austria, Prussia, and Russia, partitioned it among themselves on three separate occasions in the 18th Century. The independent Polish state ceased to exist in 1795.

[8] An excellent book on Szechenyi is George Barany's *Stephen Szechenyi and the Awakening of Hungarian Nationalism 1791–1841.* Princeton: 1968.

[9] Some historians have claimed Slovak ethnicity for Kossuth. His parents were born on what is today Slovak territory. On the other hand, Istvan Deak of Columbia University disputes this claim. (Istvan Deak, *Lawful Revolution: Louis Kossuth and the Hungarians 1848–49.* New York: Columbia University Press, 1979.)

[10] This new urbarial law allowed individual serfs or even whole communities to purchase their freedom and become full-fledged landowners. (George Barany, 'The Age of Royal Absolutism, 1790–1848', in *History of Hungary*. Sugar, Ed., p.198.) However, since few peasants could afford to purchase manumission, the law had limited impact.

[11] Between 1818 and 1824, prices for grain dipped to 30 percent of their value during the Napoleonic wars. (Kann and David, *Ibid.* p. 255.)

[12] A poor harvest and the spread of Asian cholera triggered an uprising in 1830–31, but inequitable socio-economic conditions lay at its root. The uprising peaked in July 1831, when about 130 villages and 40,000 discontented peasants, tenants, and even miners, went on a rampage in Abov, Zemplin, Saris, and Spis Counties. The events and the trials were subsequently described by A. Corba, a Lutheran pastor who had been condemned by the rebels, in his book *Hrozne a strasne rozpravky o chorobe cholera* (Horrible and Frightening Stories about the Disease of Cholera). See also *Slovakia and the Slovaks*. p. 103, and Geri Harris, 'The Scourge of Cholera', *Slovakia*, Summer 1998, p. 2. Harris' article describes the origins and character of the disease, and shows that even many nobles succumbed to it.

[13] Many Slovaks came to resent Jews because of their role as tavern owners. They were seen as taking advantage of the poor. This attitude was especially prevalent among wives who were trying to stop their husbands drinking.

[14] For instance, Thomas Garrigue Masaryk, who later became president of the First Czechoslovak Republic, researched works by the early 19th Century Czech national revivalists and found deliberate falsifications and forgeries, meant to boost Czech pride. Though disinclined, Masaryk did expose the falsifications and suffered bitter personal attacks. Some detractors accused Masaryk of betraying his nation and accepting German bribes. (Arthur J. May, *The Habsburg Monarchy 1867–1914*. Cambridge, MA: Harvard University Press, 1968, p. 206.)

[15] Peter Brock has recently published a fine study titled *The Czech National Awakening*. Toronto: University of Toronto Press, 1994.

[16] Holly is most noted for his epic poems, which glorify the deeds of Great Moravia and claim the medieval state to be a prime example of Slavic and Slovak greatness. Holly, using the Bernolak orthography, translated many of the great classics of ancient literature.

[17] The best English treatment of Stur and his codification of literary Slovak can be found in Peter Brock's *Slovak National Awakening: An Essay in the Intellectual History of East Central Europe*. Toronto: University of Toronto Press, 1976.

Chapter 8.

Summary: In 1848, the revolution that broke out in France spread like wildfire and soon ignited Austria and Hungary. In Vienna, the revolution ousted the reactionary government of Count von Metternich and sounded the death knell of feudalism. Characteristically, it spun out of control and moved in unforeseen directions: in Hungary it took a giant step beyond unlocking the shackles of serfdom. Magyar leaders transformed their revolt from a drive for autonomy in 1848 into a struggle for a totally independent Magyar state in April 1849, when an assembly in Debreczen severed ties with the Habsburg monarchy and declared Hungary a republic. The new eighteen-year old emperor, Franz Jozef, who had succeeded his uncle, the Emperor Ferdinand, had not as yet been crowned king of Hungary.

While on its surface the Hungarian revolution appeared liberal, it proved to be quite conservative in its chauvinistic denial of any rights to nationalities other than Magyar. Louis Kossuth, a prominent orator and leading personality of this revolution, had little tolerance for these other nationalities; he called for nothing less than the Magyarization of the whole Hungarian population. This chauvinism alienated the Slavic peoples of Hungary and led them to seek assistance from Vienna.

Inflamed by revolutionary fervor and nationalistic emotion, Slavic leaders met for the first time ever, to air their grievances and aspirations. This meeting, the Prague Slavic Congress, was held in Prague in 1848. Initially some type of union was contemplated by Slovaks and Czechs, but after the Austrian army occupied Prague, the congress was disbanded, leaving Slovaks to seek their fate on their own. They organized a military unit of Slovak volunteers and created a Slovak National Council to provide leadership. The Slovak volunteers were somewhat successful, as long as the imperial army cooperated with them. Buoyed up by Austrian support, Slovak leaders called for the creation of an autonomous Slovak district ('okolie') within the framework of the Habsburg Empire. However, Kossuth created a new Hungarian army (the Honved), which recovered much of Slovakia and drove back the Austrians. The new Hungarian government then persecuted and even executed many Slovaks who had fought for the Slovak cause.

But the Hungarian revolution was cut short when Russian troops intervened and saved the Habsburg Monarchy. Ironically, Slovaks received nothing for their support of the empire. Vienna dissolved the Slovak Volunteer Corps and imposed a centralist administration on Hungary.

Interpreting the events of 1848–1849, Spiesz dismisses the arguments of Magyar historians, who maintain that the Slovaks, in finding common cause with the Austrians, were reactionary counter-revolutionaries. In truth, he says, they joined forces with Vienna only in self-defense against the intransigent, intolerant nationalism of the Magyar revolutionaries.

[1] For a more thorough English analysis of the Slovak Revolution of 1848, see Vladimir Baumgarten, 'Slovakia in the Revolution of 1848' (unpublished dissertation). University of Florida, 1982. The most scholarly Slovak study is Daniel Rapant's five volume work, published between 1937 and 1973. Some of its findings are summarized in English in Daniel Rapant, 'Slovak

Politics in 1848–1849'. *Slavonic and East European Review*, 1948, pp. 70–83.

[2] Zay made this accusation because such a large proportion of Lutheran pastors were in the forefront of the Slovak national movement. On the other hand, the overwhelming majority of Calvinists were Magyars, concentrated in Central Hungary and Transylvania. Many Magyar nationalists were Calvinist, including Louis Kossuth. Only half a percent of Slovaks followed that creed, many of them living in the easternmost county of Zemplin.

[3] The city of Bratislava did not officially receive that name until 1919–1920, though Slovaks had previously called it both Presporok and Bratislava. It had a sizeable German population (about 40%), and was commonly called Pressburg by them. Magyars called it Pozsony.

[4] Independence from the Habsburg monarchy was not declared until more than a year later, in April 1849. March 15, 1848, really marks just the beginning of the Hungarian Revolution, which resulted in more Hungarian autonomy and a new government approved by the emperor. Ultimately the revolution led to a short-lived independence in 1849. Of course, this independence evaporated when the Austrians and Russians defeated the Magyar army at the end of summer, 1849.

[5] One might notice that Spiesz here uses 'Magyar state' rather than 'Hungary', then reverses course. He is trying to emphasize the fact that the radical Magyar nationalists changed their concept of Hungary from that of the medieval Hungarian kingdom which included diverse peoples with equal standing, to a Magyar nation-state with Magyar accorded a privileged standing. In such a state, only those professing Magyar nationality would have full rights of citizenship.

[6] The Austro-Slav movement, led by moderate Czech nationalists, such as Karel Havlicek and the noted historian, Frantisek Palacky, hoped to protect the interests of Slavic peoples by achieving political autonomy within the Habsburg Empire. The Slavic peoples would become a third constituent element, besides the Germans and Magyars. (Kann and David, *Ibid.* p. 202.)

[7] The word 'praca', itself, usually implies non-physical work, as opposed to 'robota', which peasants and laborers commonly used for their work. 'Drobna praca' means grassroots work, reaching out to common folk, to bring people without any sense of ethnic awareness into the Slovak national fold.

[8] The 19th Century Magyar drive to found a national state must be viewed in the general context of European history. Since the time of the French Revolution and Napoleon, nationalism had grown in intensity, and many groups within multi-national empires began to pursue a state of their own, or at least an autonomous status within a larger entity. Those peoples who had had their own traditional states during a previous era, such as the Czechs and Magyars during the Middle Ages, were among the first to demand greater autonomy and, eventually, outright independence. Smaller nationality groups such as the Slovaks lacked such a previous history. This was

one of the reasons so many Slovak revivalists looked to Great Moravia, which might provide the missing history for them.

[9] The military border refers to the Viennese administered regions in Croatia, Transylvania, and Serbia that bordered the Turkish Empire. Especially after the Habsburg victories over the Turks in the late 17th and early 18th centuries, many Slovaks moved into the vacated zones and formed agricultural communities, with a military organization. Hungary disliked the fact that Vienna continued to administer these military border zones long after the Turkish threat had receded.

[10] A revolutionary government had formed in Vojvodina, which included several counties, the Croatian region of Srijem, and all the neighboring military borders. Vienna did not recognize this government and mobilized to bring it down. (Kann and David, *Ibid.* pp. 25–26).

[11] The Croat Diet wished to transform the Habsburg Monarchy into a federation of autonomous lands. The central Viennese government would concern itself with only common matters, such as defense and foreign affairs. (Kann and David, *Ibid.* pp. 392–393.)

[12] Cisleithania refers to the traditional Habsburg lands, which lie to the West of the Leitha River, the historic boundary with Hungary. Cisleithania included Austria, Bohemia, Austrian Silesia, Austrian Poland, and Slovenia. 'Cis' derives from Latin, and means 'within, on this side of', thus betraying the terms of Austrian perspective. Transleithania refers to 'across, on the other side of', i.e. the historic Hungarian lands, which included Burgenland, modern Hungary, as well as Slovakia, Transylvania, Ruthenia, and Banat.

[13] For the best overview of the Prague Congress, as well as information about the Slovak participants, see Stanley Z. Pech, *Czech Revolution of 1848*. Chapel Hill: University of North Carolina Press, 1968.

[14] Hurban spoke to the Croatian National Assembly (Sabor) on July 2, 1848, requesting help against the Magyars. Stur did obtain financial support for the Slovak cause from the Serb prince, Michal Obrenovic. (M. S. Durica, *Dejiny Slovenska a Slovakaov*, p. 203.)

[15] 'Cuirassiers' were heavy cavalrymen who wore metal breastplates.

[16] 'Magyarones' were ethnic Slovaks who assimilated Magyar language and culture, considered renegades by loyal Slovaks.

[17] Spiesz spells his name 'Letour', Robert Kann, 'Latour' (pp. 306 and 635).

[18] Actually, the Emperor and Reichstag set up their headquarters in Kromeriz ('Kremsier', in German), which served as the summer residence of the Archbishop of Olomouc. (Kann, *Ibid.,* p. 308,)

[19] Spiesz is here referring to Jozef Horvath (1819–1906), who studied at the Lutheran Lyceum in Bratislava and at the University of Halle in Germany before accepting parish duties in Turciansky Svaty Martin in 1847. A Slovak activist, he was imprisoned for his support of the Slovak volunteers, but went on to play a leading role in Slovak literary and political circles for over the next half century. (*Slovak Biographical Dictionary*. Martin: Matica Slovenska; Wauconda, IL: Bolchazy-Carducci, 2002, p. 392.)

[20] Haynau became military governor of Hungary and brutally suppressed all revolutionaries. He had already established a ruthless reputation as a hangman in 1848 when he crushed uprisings in Brescia, Italy. He had no qualms about hanging revolutionaries and flogging women. Critics referred to him as the 'Hyena of Brescia'.

Chapter 9.

Summary: After the unsuccessful Hungarian Revolution of 1848, Austria severely punished its leaders and subordinated all Hungarian political institutions to Viennese control. In 1851, Alexander Bach, the interior minister, ruled the empire with an iron fist. Historians associate the Bach era with the police state which he created and oversaw. German became the official language of the empire, including Hungary and thus, of course, Slovakia. Austria dispatched its own officials, including some Czechs, to run the government in Slovakia.

In this political climate, Slovak leaders could hardly hope to achieve their dreams of an autonomous region. However, on the positive side, Slovaks were somewhat freer to develop their language and culture, to start up newspapers and journals, and able to open new schools. During the 1850s, the new Slovak literary language codified by Stur gained general acceptance among the 'literati', made up mostly of Catholic and Lutheran clergymen. It is important to remember, nonetheless, that not all Slovaks supported the linguistic and political objectives of the activists, and that the bulk of the population remained unaware or unconcerned.

As Austria's international situation changed, the repressive Bach regime began to unravel. By refusing to support Russia during the Crimean War, Austria lost an ally that had helped suppress the Hungarian rebellion. Taking advantage of Austria's subsequent isolation, its Italian provinces revolted in 1859, seeking independence. In its weakened condition Austria made some concessions to the Magyars in the October Diploma of 1860, which ultimately failed to satisfy them, and, after further weakening at the hands of the Prussians in 1866, Vienna granted the Magyars full autonomy in the Austro-Hungarian Compromise of 1867.

During the political bargaining over Hungary's future, Slovak appeals for an autonomous region, first to Budapest and then to Vienna, went unheeded. However, the Slovaks did manage a giant step forward culturally in 1863 with the founding in Turciansky Svaty Martin of the Matica Slovenska, a cultural institution promoting literature, education and communication among Slovaks in Slovakia proper, as well as those scattered through other parts of Hungary.

In the sphere of socio-economic affairs, the post-1848 era saw the abolition of serfdom in Slovakia. However, the results of abolition were not all positive. Former serfs were now free, but they lived at a subsistence level and were forced to pay high taxes by way of compensation to their former feudal lords. The peasants, who had formerly leased or rented, were forced to buy their land, and thereby fell even deeper into poverty. The expansion of railroads, iron works, food processing and other forms of industry created new jobs, but not nearly enough to keep pace with population growth. In search of work, Slovaks increasingly migrated to the agricultural lowlands and the larger cities of the empire. Still, there were not enough jobs to go around. Migration in search of employment would become a central theme of Slovak history in the next half-century, as many Slovaks opted to go even farther, crossing the ocean to America.

[1] Czech scholars, who wanted Slovaks to adopt Czech as their literary language, bitterly opposed efforts to codify Slovak; Czech-Slovak relations deteriorated after the 1848 revolution. (Albert Prazak, 'Czechs and Slovaks after the Revolution of 1848', *Slavonic Review* 6, 1933. pp. 131–141).

[2] Such secondary schools called 'Gymnasia' are roughly equivalent to college preparatory schools in the United States.

[3] Stur accidentally shot himself while hunting and died after days of excruciating pain. (Michael J. Kopanic, Jr. "Changing Faces of Ludovit Stur', *Jednota Furdek Annual,* 1982, pp. 207–219).

[4] Interestingly, Louis Kossuth and a Hungarian government in exile (Hungarian National Directory, founded in Paris) helped organize an anti-Austrian alliance. Napoleon III received Kossuth in the Tuilleries and promised to send troops to Hungary to aid the Hungarian revolt. The Hungarians pledged to make constitutional reforms, according recognition to the nationalities. The plan fell through when the Austrians suffered a quick and devastating defeat at Solferino, Italy. (Eva Somogyi, 'The Age of Neo-Absolutism 1849–1867', *History of Hungary.* Sugar, Ed., Bloomington: Indiana University Press, 1990, pp. 242–243).

[5] In referring to the Imperial Council, Spiesz means an advisory body that was added to the Reichsrat. It comprised 38 members, representing various regions. It had no real power. Most of its members were landed aristocrats, who feared any sort of social change. Selected by the Emperor from a list prepared by the Diet, they served for six years. This council was made up of six Magyars, two Croats, Two Serbs, but no Slovaks since Slovakia was not a separate administrative region. (Kann, *Ibid.* p. 326.)

[6] Zahorie is a lowland region of Slovakia, lying west of the Low Carpathian range, north of Bratislava.

[7] In exile, Kossuth continued to call for nothing less than an armed rebellion and complete Hungarian independence. He particularly feared the formation of a common army, which could be used, as in the past, to enforce Habsburg absolutism. (Eva Somogyi, 'The Age of Neo-Absolutism 1849–1867', *History of Hungary.* Sugar, Ed., p. 250.)

[8] The shrinking size of the average farm plot was also due to the Slovak practice of partitioning estates among all the sons of a family.

Chapter 10.

Summary: The Austro-Hungarian Compromise of 1867 resulted in a re-organization of Hungary and gave the Magyars a virtual blank check to rule as they pleased. The political system, which facilitated the manipulation of elections, favored the Magyar propertied classes, granting the vote to only about 5% of the population. Although it was the liberals, in charge after 1867, who pressed most strongly for Magyarization, actually all the Magyar parties supported the official policy of forcible assimilation.

Thus the era of the Dual Monarchy became, for Slovaks, a struggle for survival. The old school of Slovak activists, based in Turciansky Svaty Martin, publicly opposed the official Hungarian policy, but the new school pursued a policy of accommodation and compromise. Both approaches failed to stop the ruthless onslaught of Magyarization, which, in these years, steadily whittled away at the Slovak population. Slovak intellectuals and ethnically aware clergymen worked to keep the national idea alive, but found the going hard, as the government took the drastic steps of shutting down the Matica Slovenska and closing all secondary schools where Slovak was the language of instruction. The pervasive pressure even interfered with the use of Slovak in church-run elementary schools, and induced people to adapt their Slovak names to Magyar. In the meantime, most Slovaks were peasants who had little awareness of ethnic identity and whose main concern was physical survival.

It is important to keep in mind that Slovaks themselves were divided in their view of what was to be done. A sizeable number of erstwhile activists lapsed into passivity. Some, like Svetozar Hurban Vajansky, Jozef Hurban's son, would look to Russia for salvation. Pan-Slavism and the idea of cooperation among Moravians, Czechs and other Slavs revived in the late 19th Century. In a sense, this search for other partners laid the groundwork for creation of a Czecho-Slovak state after World War I. At the same time Slovak intellectuals became increasingly divided in their concern about strong Czech influences and the relationship between Czechs and Slovaks. Many of the Slovaks centered in Turciansky Svaty Martin began to fear a new form of ethnic aggression – Czechization.

At the turn of the century Slovak political movements began to differentiate in various ways, responding to the tremendous social and economic changes brought on by an expansive capitalism. In the latter half of this chapter Spiesz expands on the increasing economic pressures felt by subsistence-level farmers (a majority of Slovaks) and on their migration to other parts of Hungary, Austria, the Czech lands, and especially America.

As the working class grew, it sought to improve its lot by organizing mutual aid societies, trade unions, and a Social Democratic Party, which would provide workers with a political voice. Christian Socialism emerged to provide an alternative to the ideas of class struggle propagated by socialists. As these political movements matured and attracted Slovak members, they eventually split into separate Slovak wings, which in the case of the Christian Socialists evolved into the Slovak People's Party, led by a populist priest named Andrej Hlinka.

Finally, as a result of efforts by Czech intellectual and publicist Tomas Garrigue Masaryk, the Czech politician Edvard Benes, and the Slovak astronomer and soldier Milan R. Stefanik, with support from the Czech and Slovak communities in the United States, after World War I an independent Czecho-Slovakia appeared on the map of Europe. Many Slovaks, particularly those from the more remote eastern counties of Slovakia, had first acquired a sense of national identity in the United States. American Slovaks served both as a source of financial aid and of moral support when Magyarization was at its most oppressive in the early 20th Century. And since as many as a quarter of all emigrants returned to their native Slovakia, they invigorated the Slovak national movement with fresh energy. The creation of a democratic Czecho-Slovakia appeared to offer hope for a more promising future.

[1] The number of Diet members varied. During the 1870s, there were 413 members. (Tibor Frank, 'Hungary and the Dual Monarchy 1867–1890', *History of Hungary*. Sugar, Ed., p.263). But the size of the Lower House kept changing and eventually it reached 453 members, which included 40 delegates from Croatia. (Jorg K. Hoensch, *History of Modern Hungary 1867–1986*. London: Longman, 1988, p. 27).

[2] Here Spiesz refers to the roots of anti-Semitism, which were strong in Slovakia, as elsewhere in East Central Europe. He uses the strong word 'hatred' of Jews, but this hatred was by no means universal, and Jews enjoyed considerable tolerance in Slovakia. One should not confuse 19th Century anti-Semitism with the racism of the 20th Century. No doubt some anti-Semitism had existed in Slovakia since the Middle Ages, but not to such an intense degree as in Germany or many other places. In Bratislava a synagogue was built next door to St. Martin's Cathedral, a rarity in the Habsburg Empire. Anti-Semitism increased during the late 19th and early 20th Century, and Jews increasingly became scapegoats for many of the economic problems of early industrialization. In Slovak villages, Jews were commonly tavern-keepers and were seen as enablers of alcoholism.

[3] Although Jews generally accepted Magyarization, particularly before the 1867 Austro-Hungarian Compromise, some were quite sympathetic to the Slovak national movement and even helped found the Matica Slovenska. (Jozef Lettrich, *History of Modern Slovakia*. New York: Frederick A. Praeger, Publishers, 1955, p. 174).

[4] Sources list conflicting dates for the founding of the St. Adalbert Society. S. Kirschbaum dates it to 1869 (p.138), as does a collective history compiled in Slovakia: Jan Tibensky, Ed., *Slovensko: Dejiny*. Bratislava: Obzor, 1978, p. 553. But Oddo very specifically mentions that its by-laws had to wait thirteen years for final approval with an initial meeting taking place on

September 14, 1870 in Trnava (p. 131).

5   Spiesz dates Tranoscius' founding in 1896, but Slovakia and the Slovaks lists the date as 1898 (p.660). *Lexikon slovenskych dejin* also shows the latter date (p.120). J. Janoska was the first president of this publishing and bookselling association.

6   Rieger was showing his appreciation to Vienna and Budapest for the gradual expansion of Czech political rights in Cisleithania. Under the government of Count Taaffe (1879–93), the franchise was expanded to include many Czechs, while the Czech parliament was able to pass legislation to protect Czech language rights. A conservative member of the Old Czech faction, Rieger believed that Czech autonomy could eventually be achieved through compromise and concession. He refrained from public criticism of Magyar treatment of Slavs. However, Rieger represented only his own Old Czech Faction. Young Czechs were much more aggressive vis-a-vis the imperial government and after 1890 supported the Slovak and Slavic quest for national rights. (Kann and David, *Ibid.* pp. 297–310.)

7   Spiesz is referring to Pavol Mudron's defense of peasants' property rights against landlords. Mudron also defended Slovaks and non-Magyars in political trials. His brother Michal was also active in defending peasants and non-Magyars, as well as workers in the labor movement (*Slovakia and the Slovaks*, p. 403).

8   Hviezdoslav was the pen name of Pavol Orszagh (1849–1921), who is considered by many as the greatest poet in Slovak literature. He was born in Dolny Kubin, Orava County, and is well known for his linguistic originality and his translations of Shakespeare.

9   Writing just after the revolution of 1989, Spiesz makes an ironic gibe at Communism.

10 For details about Detvan see Edita Bosak, 'Czech-Slovak Relations and the Student Organization Detvan 1882–1914', *Slovak Politics*. Stanislav J. Kirschbaum, Ed., Cleveland: Slovak Institute, 1983, pp. 6–41.

11 Many of the architectural monuments of Hungary date from this era, e.g. Heroes' Square in Budapest, when Hungarian nationalism bourgeoned with glorification of Hungary's past. Since the celebration was exclusively Magyar and fanned hubristic passions, it rankled other nationalities, deepening alienation. (Geza Jeszenszky, 'Hungary through World War I and the End of the Dual Monarchy', *History of Hungary*, Sugar, Ed., p. 270.)

12 While Rusyns did not attend the Budapest Congress of 1895, it is simplistic to dismiss all Rusyns as Magyarizers. Such a description certainly did not apply to the uneducated Rusyn masses, which still lacked all ethnic awareness. But it could be applied to many educated Rusyns, particularly those in Budapest. The Magyars had seized control of the Greek Catholic Church in Hungary, in the same way they had gained control of Catholic and Lutheran hierarchies. The Rusyns had even tried to change the Slavonic liturgy to Magyar, but the Vatican rebuffed their efforts. The Magyars realistically feared the heightened influence of the Russian Orthodox

Church, which was sending books, newspapers, and even priests to support Orthodoxy and Russophilism. Besides, Rusyn emigrants to America were undergoing a genuine national awakening through contacts with Slovaks, Russians and Ukrainians from Galicia. Thus Rusyn-American feedback contributed strongly to a national awakening in the old homeland. (Paul Robert Magocsi, *The Shaping of a National Identity: Subcarpathian Rus 1848–1948.* Cambridge, MA: Harvard University Press, 1978, pp. 63–72).

[13] Though Spiesz writes 'Ceskoslovenska Jednota', early documents feature the name 'CzeskoSlovanska Jednota', an indication that the organization meant to appeal to all Slavs, not just Slovaks.

[14] Spiesz gives 1884 as the founding year of Zivena, though it was founded in 1891, one year after its sister organization, the National Slovak Society. (R. Vladimir Baumgarten, and Joseph Stefka, *National Slovak Society: 100 Year History 1890–1990.* Pittsburgh: 1990, p. 20.)

[15] Jednota became the largest American-Slovak fraternal, with over 100,000 members at its peak. Spiesz here confuses it with the First Catholic Slovak Ladies Union ('Zenska Jednota'), which was founded in 1892, by Anna Hurban following Furdek's example, in a Cleveland Catholic parish. Women felt their concerns needed more attention than they got from the male fraternals. (Anthony X. Southerland, 'Slovak Ladies' Fraternals', *Jednota,* February 21, 1990.)

[16] Cleveland became a center of Slovak-American life and by the First World War had more Slovaks than any city in Slovakia itself. (Michael J. Kopanic, Jr., *Slovaks, Identity, Conflict and Cooperation: Central Europeans in Cleveland 1850–1930.* Cleveland: Kent State University and Western Reserve Historical Society, 2002, 65 pp.)

[17] Stefan Martincek (1874–1959) was born into a working class family in Budatin, near Zilina. Trained as a locksmith, he moved to Budapest where he became involved in the Socialist Workers' movement. He irregularly published a short Slovak monthly, *Nova Doba* (The New Era), from May 1897 to May 1899. Lack of funding and support from even the Hungarian Social Democrats led to its collapse. (E. Kabos and A. Zsilak, Eds., *Studies in the History of the Hungarian Trade Union Movement.* Budapest: 1977, pp. 46–47 and 824–825.) In 1902 he emigrated to the U.S. and was one of the founders of 'Rovnost' (Equality), a workers' educational society. In May 1911, he was among the founders of the Slovak Socialist Party and became the first president of its central committee. (Frantisek Bielik, et alii, *Slovaci vo svete,* 2. Martin: Matica Slovenska, 1980, pp. 185–186.) Although these sources, published under the Communists, give great weight to the socialist movement among Slovaks in the United States, it never had more than a handful of followers. Most American Slovaks shunned it, preferring to join religious fraternals, and, upon becoming citizens, voted for mainstream American political candidates.

[18] Ambro Pietor (1843–1906) edited *Narodnie noviny* from 1870–1898, and was well known for his articles on a variety of social, economic and polit-

ical problems in Slovakia. (*Slovakia and the Slovaks: A Concise Encyclopedia* p. 460.)

[19] In Hungary and Slovakia there was virtually no difference between the Social Democratic Party and the Socialist trade unions. Workers joined the unions without understanding that the two could have different spheres of interest. The Social Democratic Party used the popularity of the trade unions to expand its constituency. See Michael J. Kopanic, Jr., 'Industrial Trade Unions in Slovakia 1918–1928' (unpublished dissertation). Ann Arbor: University Microfilms Intl., 1987, pp. 67–98.)

[20] The Second International was founded in 1889, but its methods engendered sharp dissent. In 1896, at its London congress, delegates rejected the anarchist minority view, which opposed any state-sponsored legislation. The International would support a gradualist approach as long as it served the goal of changing capitalism to socialism. At its second congress in Paris in 1900, the Second International formed an administrative bureaucracy to coordinate its various member parties. (Wolfgang Abendroth, *Short History of the European Working Class*. New York: Monthly Review Press, 1972, pp. 67–98.)

A split developed in the world Communist movement over whether the expected revolution would occur by violent overthrow of the existing order or through evolutionary processes. The opponents of violence were dubbed 'reformists'. During this era, there were many social democratic parties in Europe, particularly Germany, where social democracy was the strongest. German Social Democrats enjoyed active input in government. (Warren Lerner, *History of Socialism and Communism in Modern Times*. Englewood Cliffs: Prentice-Hall, 1994, pp. 57–77.)

[21] Fraud, bribery, gerrymandering, intimidation, and fixed elections were regular features of the government in Hungary. (Tibor Frank, *Ibid.* p.263; and Kann and David, *Ibid.* pp. 354–355.)

[22] Kann, *Ibid.* p. 456; and Kann and David, *Ibid.* pp. 358–359.

[23] According to R. W. Seton-Watson, there were more than sixty people wounded, in addition to those killed. His account was (at the time) the most detailed description of these momentous events, which shocked the world. (*Racial Problems in Hungary*. New York: Howard Fertig, 1972, p. 342.)

[24] After the First World War, Jaszi moved to the United States, where he lectured at Columbia University and wrote of the strengths and weaknesses of the Habsburg monarchy. He firmly believed that the power vacuum left by the monarchy's disappearance would haunt Europe and that the Magyars had wasted the opportunity to keep their state intact by maltreating the nationalities. (*The Dissolution of the Habsburg Monarchy*. Chicago: University of Chicago Press, 1929.)

[25] This was particularly true of the Slovak Lutheran leadership, which had always felt a close affinity to the Czech Slavic brethren.

[26] Estimates cite 69,700 Slovak soldiers killed in World War I, with 61,680 wounded. (Elena Mannova, Ed. *Concise History of Slovakia*. Bratislava:

Historicky ustav SAV, 2000, p. 239.)

[27] Spiesz assigns 350,000 troops to the Czecho-Slovak Legion, which appears to be a very excessive figure. There were about 70,000 troops in Russia, 20,000 in Italy, and 10,000 in France. Some of these volunteers came from Slovak and Czech families in America, but not as many as Stefanik anticipated, and their number was further reduced by U. S. entry into the war in 1917. (*Slovakia and the Slovaks: A Concise Encyclopedia* p. 133.)

[28] Marian Mark Stolarik emphasizes the fact that American Slovaks insisted on autonomy because Czechs outnumbered Slovaks two-to-one. Slovak Americans remembered the sad experience of Slovaks under the Magyars and did not want a repetition. ('Slovak Migration from Europe to North America 1870–1918'. *Slovak Studies.* Cleveland – Rome: Slovak Institute, 1980, pp. 116–117.)

[29] The Hungarian government tried to interfere with Slovak-American publications in the United States, but failed. In the United States, some Slovaks, particularly those from Eastern Slovakia, gained a first sense of ethnic identity. (Stolarik, Marian Mark, *Ibid.* pp.79–80.)

[30] For details, see the *Cleveland Plain Dealer*, February 17, 1911. Some had even planned to break up Apponyi's talk, but a cool-headed Father Furdek prevailed and got them to take a more peaceable approach. See *Cleveland Plain Dealer*, February 14, 1911. Apponyi was less fortunate in Chicago, where angry demonstrators pelted him with eggs.

[31] Slovaks did much better in the United States than in their homeland; some even began their own businesses, most commonly saloons. But most began as lowly laborers, who saved first to buy a house, then gradually improved their lot. When they did go into business, it was in small, family shops. (*Jednota*, July 18, 1906; and Jan Pankuch, *Dejiny clevelandskych a lakewoodskych Slovakov.* Cleveland: Pankuch Printing, 1930, 286 pp.)

[32] The Pittsburgh Agreement would become a political hot potato in the First Czecho-Slovak Republic, because Slovaks favoring autonomy pointed to it as an example of broken Czech promises. The pact followed the spirit of the Cleveland Agreement in promising Slovaks a separate and autonomous region, with its own Slovak administration. Masaryk signed the agreement with American Slovaks knowing full well that he needed their support. He later reneged, claiming the document had no validity: it was only a 'scrap of paper' that he had signed in order to mollify American Slovaks. (Victor S. Mamatey, 'Czecho-Slovak Agreement of Pittsburgh, May 30, 1918, Revisited'. *Kosmas: Journal of Czecho-Slovak and Central European Studies*, Winter 1983, pp. 41–48.)

Later, in his *Making of a State* (New York, 1927), Masaryk wrote that he had signed 'the Czecho-Slovak Convention' in Pittsburgh as merely a local understanding and that details would follow. He claimed the document 'was concluded in order to appease a small Slovak faction that was dreaming of God knows what sort of independence for Slovakia, since the ideas of some Russian Slavophils, and of Stur and Hurban-Vajansky, had taken root even among the American Slovaks'. (Joseph A. Mikus, *Slovakia. A Political Histo-*

ry: 1918–1950. Milwaukee: Marquette University Press, 1963, Note 9, p. 7.)

[33] Part of the problem of obtaining statistics about the number of Slovaks in Budapest derives from the fact that many were seasonal workers. Slovaks worked in the Budapest construction industry, which was booming at the time, and scholars have estimated that between 50,000 and 100,000 lived in pre-war Budapest. The forcible assimilation of Slovaks in the Hungarian capital also makes statistics difficult to come by. (Kopanic, 'Industrial Trade Unions in Slovakia'. Notes 42–45, pp. 544–545.)

[34] Many Rusyns adopted Orthodoxy in America, because the Irish-dominated Roman Catholic Church refused to accept married priests in the Greek Catholic (Byzantine) Rite clergy.

[35] Spiesz is extremely critical of Communists because of the ideological constraints they placed on his professional career. The Communist regime had recently collapsed when this book was first published.

Chapter 11.

Summary: As the First World War came to a close, Slovak representatives met in Turciansky Svaty Martin and decided to join the Czechs in forming a new state, named the Czecho-Slovak Republic. It marked the beginning of a new chapter in Slovak History, one in which Slovaks became freer to develop to their fullest potential.

Life in the new democratic state brought tremendous social progress to Slovakia. In it Slovaks obtained an array of national and civil rights, including educational opportunities not available before 1918. Slovak national self-awareness increased as more and more people acquired an education. Even Germans benefited culturally, as more German schools opened. But the Magyar minority in Southern Slovakia resented separation from Hungary.

However, economically the picture was not as rosy. Joined to a more developed Bohemia and Moravia, Slovak industry and agriculture suffered from competition. In the post-war years, many workers lost their jobs as a difficult transition took place. Some of the more radical parties, such as the Communists, looked for alternative solutions to economic and political problems.

There were other factors, too, that served to divide the Slovaks and Czechs. The greater religiosity of Slovaks tended to clash with Czech secularism. Catholic Slovaks resented the preference shown to Protestants and Czechs in government jobs. The ideology of Czechoslovakism, which many Czechs and some Slovaks espoused, increasingly polarized Slovak political life. These clashes led to a strong movement towards Slovak autonomy under the leadership of a nationalist Catholic priest, Father Andrej Hlinka. His Slovak People's Party and the Agrarian Party, led by Milan Hodza, were the two largest and most successful political parties in interwar Slovakia.

Despite the turmoil of the post-war years, Slovakia's economy began recovering by the mid–1920s and democratic practices settled in. Even the right-wing Slovak People's Party of Hlinka won a role in the Czecho-Slovak government between 1925 and 1929.

The Great Depression and international developments changed all that. Unemployment skyrocketed. The new Nazi regime in Germany encouraged separatism among the Czecho-Slovak Germans and Slovaks. Slovakia gained autonomy after the Munich Pact forced Czech concessions to Germany. Dissatisfied, Hitler wanted nothing less than the destruction of Czecho-Slovakia. Ultimately he nudged Slovaks into declaring their independence. Had the Slovaks refused, they would have faced the alternative of being swallowed up by Poland, Hungary and Germany. (For an 'indispensable' collection of sources and commentary, see Max Domarus.)

[1] At the Versailles Peace Conference, and during the early years of the First Republic, the state was always referred to as Czecho-Slovakia: hyphenated and with a capital 'S' for Slovakia. As the state gradually became more centralist, the hyphen disappeared. The 1920 Constitution, not discussed here by Spiesz, adopted the name 'Czecho-Slovakia' and the adjective Czecho-Slovak. 'Czecho-Slovak' was named the official language, though no such language actually existed. (Jozef Anderle, 'First Republic 1918–1938', *Czechoslovakia: The Heritage of Ages Past*. Hans Brisch and Ivan Volgyes, Boulder: 1979, p. 91.) The hyphen came back in 1938 when Slovakia became autonomous, then left again in 1945 when Slovakia was annexed to Czecho-Slovakia. But the issue was still not ready to rest; the hyphen re-emerged in 1989 when Communism collapsed.

[2] One of the best books on the First Czecho-Slovak Republic is the anthology *History of the Czechoslovak Republic*. Victor Mamatey, and Radomir Luza, Eds. Princeton: 1973. The first chapter, 'Establishment of the Republic', pp. 3–38, by Victor S. Mamatey, gives more details than does Spiesz. Other useful political analyses are: Joseph Rothschild's chapter 'Czechoslovakia' in *East Central Europe between the Two World Wars*. Seattle: University of Washington Press, 1974, pp. 73–136, as well as chapters IV and V; and Peter A. Toma, and Dusan, Kovac, *Slovakia from Samo to Dzurinda*. Stanford: Hoover Institution Press, 2001. Future references to this book will not include Kovac's contribution, because he has strongly objected to Toma's editing and watering down his original.

[3] Carol Skalnik Leff mentions that 'more than a hundred' people attended the Turciansky Svaty Martin meeting. This group, self-appointed, had little contact with the outside world or Slovak leaders in Budapest, Prague or Vienna. The document was a last ditch effort to protect Slovak interests amidst the confusion of war. (Carol Skalnik Leff, *National Conflict in Czechoslovakia: Making and Remaking of a State 1918–1987*. Princeton, 1988, pp. 39–41.)

[4] Spiesz stresses the disagreement at the Martin meeting with the idea of a 'Czecho-Slovak nation'. But Czech authors consistently used the spelling

'Czecho-Slovak', agreeing with Jozef Korbel, who simply states that all the delegates supported the Martin Declaration's assertion that the 'Slovak nation' was 'linguistically, culturally, historically, a part of a united Czecho-Slovak nation'. (*Twentieth Century Czechoslovakia: Meaning of its History*. New York: 1977, p. 94.)

The full text of the Martin Declaration can be found in: *Dejiny Slovenska slovom i obrazom,* 2 (History of Slovakia in Word and Picture). Bratislava: Osveta, 1982, pp. 140. This original document includes the hyphen, as do others; and in fact, the negotiators at the Paris Peace Conference in 1919 referred to the new state as 'Czecho-Slovakia'. This issue became politicized and symbolized Slovak self-rule.

5   In fact, there never was a strong movement for autonomy in Moravia. The Slovak leaders themselves were divided: Hlinka and the Populists vigorously pursued autonomy, but for others autonomy was a less pressing issue than the break with Hungary.

6   The best book on economic conditions in this era is Milan Strhan, *Kriza priemyslu na Slovensku v rokoch 1921–1923* (Crisis of Industry in Slovakia, 1921–1923), Bratislava: SAV, 1960). Strhan shows unemployment in Slovakia rising from 78,857 at the end of 1921 to 473,841 by the end of 1922 (p. 30). From this low point, it gradually rose to 369,520 by March 1923. The renowned Slovak labor historian Jan Mlynarik characterized unemployment as the most critical issue of Slovak history. (*Nezamestnanost na Slovensku 1918–1938* [Unemployment in Slovakia, 1918–1938]. Bratislava: 1964.) An English summary can be found in Prior, Zora P., 'Czechoslovak Economic Development in the Interwar Period', *History of the Czechoslovak Republic*. Victor Mamatey and Radomir Luza, Eds. Princeton: 1973, pp. 205–208.

7   There are no precise figures for unemployment just after World War I, but it was quite high, as might be expected in the aftermath of a major war. Between 1921 and 1923, industries laid off large numbers of workers, and many factories closed their doors for good. Slovak historians have labeled this the period of 'deindustrialization'. (M. Kopanic, 'Industrial Trade Unions in Slovakia 1918–1929', pp. 44–60.)

8   In the early days of the First Republic, devout Slovaks were alienated by Czech attitudes towards religion.

9   Many Slovak Catholics were outraged by the anti-Catholic and anti-clerical behavior of some Czech activists. For example, a Czech mob in Prague tore down a Marian statue in Old Town Square, which they considered to be a symbol of Habsburg rule. To Slovak Catholics, the act was sacrilegious. Many Czechs seemed to be insensitive to the feelings and beliefs of Slovaks. Slovak clergy, the most respected members of Slovak society, were particularly resentful of such behavior and what they felt were Prague's attempts to curtail the power of church authorities.

10   Owen Johnson believes that Czech educational help had the paradoxical effect of enabling the development of a strong Slovak national movement

between the wars. (*Slovakia 1918–1938: Education and the Making of a Nation*. New York: Columbia University Press, 1985.)

[11] For a good overview of the first two years of the Republic see Benes, Vaclav L. 'Czechoslovak Democracy and its Problems', *History of the Czechoslovak Republic*. Victor S. Mamatey and Radomir Luza, Eds. Princeton: 1973, pp. 39–98. For the interwar years, see Mamatey, Victor S. 'Development of Czechoslovak Democracy 1920–1938'. *Ibid.* pp. 99–126.

[12] The People's Party's best showing was in the 1925 parliamentary elections, with 34.29% of votes cast. (Dusan Caplovic, et al., *Dejiny Slovenska*. Bratislava: AEP, 2000.)

[13] Hodza was a political opportunist and realist, who worked in close cooperation with Anton Svehla's moderate, well-organized Agrarian Party. Svehla was a master at building coalitions, while Hodza was a man with whom one could make deals. The Agrarian Party was second only to the Slovak People's Party in attracting followers. (Daniel Miller, *Forging Political Compromise: Antonin Svehla and the Czechoslovak Republican Party 1918–1923*. Pittsburgh: 1999.)

[14] Prague's favoritism towards Slovak Protestants can be seen in the make-up of the first Slovak administration, which had only one Catholic minister, Martin Micura, the Minister for the Administration of Slovakia. (Oddo, *Ibid.* p. 210.)

[15] The Ministry of Agriculture was very important, since two-thirds of Slovaks worked in farming.

[16] There can be little doubt that Benes' intransigence vis-à-vis the Sudeten Germans was short-sighted, but in hindsight Czechoslovakia's doom. It was Czecho-Slovakia which might have survived if the Slovaks had the hypen.

[17] Here Spiesz has drawn his own conclusion. Stefanik, who served as Minister of War in the Exile Government, died along with three Italian officers, when his plane crashed on the approach to Vajnory airport on May 4, 1919. Controversy over the cause has raged ever since. Some witnesses claimed they heard shots, which led to speculation in some quarters that Benes had ordered Stefanik's assassination as a dangerous rival. But the evidence has been inconclusive. (Jozef Ihnat, et alii, *General Milan R. Stefanik 1880–1980: Historical Profile*. New York: 1981.) Particularly interesting in ruling out possibilities is an article by Milan S. Durica, 'Milan R. Stefanik and His Tragic Death in the Light of Italian Military Documents', pp. 3–32. Stefanik backed Czechoslovak unity, but he seems to have had some problems with Benes and Masaryk, since he failed to be appointed Minister of Defense in the new government; it went to a man named Klofac. Some have speculated that the Czecho-Slovak air defense mistook his plane for Magyar. Durica dismisses the latter possibility, since the plane was clearly marked as Italian and arrived as per schedule. Thus the mystery remains,.

[18] The best study in English is Peter A. Toma, 'The Slovak Soviet Republic of 1919', in *American Slavic and East European Review*. 1958, pp. 203–215.

[19] Slovak Communists founded their own party even before the Czecho-Slovak

Communist Party was formed at its congress in Prague, May 14–16, 1921. The Czecho-Slovak Communist Party always used the unhyphenated spelling to minimize the concept of nationality. The Party was truly multinational. (Zdenek Suda, *Zealots and Rebels: History of the Ruling Communist Party of Czecho-Slovakia*. Stanford: Hoover Institution Press, 1880.)

[20] For the times, Czecho-Slovakia had some of the most progressive labor legislation in Europe, including an eight-hour day, unemployment benefits, old age pensions and, after 1925, guaranteed paid holidays. (Kopanic, 'Industrial Trade Unions', Chap. 12.)

[21] The Czecho-Slovak Trade Union Association (OSC) was always affiliated with the Social Democratic Party. Spiesz errs in stating that the Social Democrats had 23,505 members. That figure belongs to the National Socialist trade unions, whose members were mainly Czech civil service employees working in Slovakia. Furthermore, these statistics do not show the tremendous instability and fluctuation of members among the various trade unions. (Kopanic, *Ibid.,* and *Slovakia and the Slovaks: A Concise Encyclopedia.*)

[22] One of the reasons for the rise in trade union membership was a 1921 law, which introduced the 'Ghent System' of unemployment compensation. This law required the state to match the unemployment contributions of unions, but without exceeding, in total, two-thirds of an employee's average wage (Gustav, Habrmann, 'Social Legislation in Czecho-Slovakia'. *International Trade Union Movement*. Amsterdam: 1926, pp. 109–110.)

[23] Leaving the country on a Polish visa was technically illegal, but Benes had aroused the ire of the Slovaks, especially Catholics, by his lack of respect for Hlinka. Benes portrayed Hlinka as an extremist, and the 'Big Four' at the Versailles Peace Conference paid little attention to Hlinka's demands for Slovak autonomy. To make matters worse, Benes caused Hlinka to be arrested on his return to Slovakia, an act that permanently alienated many Slovaks.

[24] The Communists used the spelling 'Czechoslovakia'.

[25] Stalin personally picked leaders for the various national Communist parties. Their most valued quality was unquestioning loyalty.

[26] In 1924 the United States limited immigration from Slovakia to 2000 per year. This limitation was meant to keep out 'undesirables' from Southern and Eastern Europe.

[27] Obviously, Spiesz had a low opinion of Edvard Benes. Several books have chronicled the life of this controversial foreign minister and president, who played such an important role in the history of Czecho-Slovakia. (Zeman, Zbynek, and Antonin Klimek, *Life of Edvard Benes: Czechoslovakia in Peace and War*. Oxford: 1997.) Also useful for understanding Benes' policy toward the Soviet Union in the 1930's is Igor Lukes, *Czechoslovakia between Stalin and Hitler: Diplomacy of Edvard Benes in the 1930s*. New York: Oxford University Press, 1996. Interestingly, Slovakia receives little mention in the latter book, except in discussion of border negotiations after

World War I (pp. 5–6). Slovakia simply did not much matter to Benes, and Lukes' book implies as much.

28 What the Little Entente feared most was Magyar revanchism, but it was also wary of Bulgaria. Attack by a great power was not considered. France initially held back, but later granted the Entente its full support. The members had also hoped for economic benefits, which, however, never materialized.

29 According to James Ramon Felak, three explanations account for the HSPP's decision to vote for Benes: 1. The Vatican maintained good relations with Benes and pressured Hlinka; 2. According to Ivan Derer, Milan Hodza influenced Hlinka to back Benes, hoping thus to gain points with Benes; 3. According to Tiso's biographer, Konstantin Culen, Tiso and Benes made a deal, based on a promise of 'broad autonomy' for Slovakia and a share of positions in the Prague government, after the elections. Since nothing came of the latter promise, HSPP supporters considered the failure just another example of Czech perfidy. Furthermore, no record exists of the Benes-Tiso talks, making any historical judgment moot. Even Felak believes that Tiso would never have trusted Benes to fulfill an unwritten promise. As to the Vatican's influence, Culen thought it important enough to mention, while also citing Tiso's fear of the opposition candidate, the Agrarian Nemec, as more of a threat than Benes. (James Ramon Felak, *At the Price of the Republic: Hlinka's Slovak People's Party 1929–1938*. Pittsburgh: 1994, pp. 153–154.)

30 In the 1935 parliamentary elections, Hlinka's Slovak People's Party formed an autonomist bloc with the largely Lutheran Slovak National party.

31 Spiesz may be assigning too much blame to Benes for failing to resolve the problems of the German minority. Hitler had made his intentions clear in a meeting in the Reich Chancellery on November 5, 1937. He intended to bring all Germans under his aegis and to create more living space (Lebensraum) for the expanding German population. Whatever stood in the way was to be crushed. ('Hossback Memorandum: A Strategy Conference?', *World War II: Roots and Causes*. Keith Eubank, Ed., Lexington: D.C. Heath & Co., 1992, pp. 115–120.) See Domarus, p. 959 ff.

32 For additional details on Slovakia's achievement of autonomy, see Joseph Anderle, 'Establishment of Slovak Autonomy in 1938', *Czechoslovakia Past and Present*, Miloslav Rechcigl, Jr., Ed., The Hague: 1964, pp. 76–97. Useful, too, is: Dorothea H. Mallak, *Slovak Autonomy Movement 1935–1939*. Boulder: 1979.

33 Curiously, Spiesz terms Benes' resignation an abdication, like a flustered monarch giving up his throne.

34 For a summary of Slovakia's six months of autonomy, see F. Vnuk, 'Slovakia's Eventful Six Months', *Slovak Studies,* 4, 1964, pp. 7–164.

35 For a summary of Germany's policy towards autonomous Slovakia, see Ladislav Susko, 'German Foreign Policy towards Slovakia and Carpatho-Ukraine in the Period from the September Crisis in 1938 to the Splitting of Czecho-Slovakia in March 1939', *Studia Historica Slovaca*, 8, 1975, pp.

111–155. One of the most complete works in any Western language is Jorg K., Hoensch, *Die Slowakei und Hitlers Ostpolitik: Hlinkas Slowakische Volkspartei zwischen Autonomie und Separation 1938–1939*. Koln: 1965.

[36] Karol Sidor wrote of his 1939 experiences in *Moje poznamky k historickym dnom*. (My Comments on Historic Days.) Middletown: Jednota Press, 1971.

[37] Official German records of Hitler's meeting with Tiso can be found in *Documents on German Foreign Policy 1918–1945, Series D*. pp. 243–245. See Domarus (note 38).

[38] The war-time Slovak Republic has provoked much controversy. Critics write it off as an ill-begotten satellite of Nazi Germany, while defenders praise it for its skillful maneuvering through perilous times, i.e. making the best of a bad situation. Critics who anathemize Tiso or those who would canonize him can find defensible evidence only for the middle ground in Max Domarus, *Hitler: Speeches and Proclamations 1932–1945* (4 vols.). Wauconda, IL: Bolchazy-Carducci, 1990–2004. The four-volume work, now translated into English from the original German (*Hitler. Reden 1932 bis 1945: Kommentiert von einem Deutschen zeitgenossen,* 1963, fourth edition 1988), contains the most comprehensive collection of Hitler's speeches, proclamations, and correspondences, with extensive commentary and copious notes by Max Domarus. The work is hailed as 'indispensable' by scholars like J. Mikus (*Jednota*), Alan Rosenberg (*Dimensions*), Hugh Trevor-Roper, Joachim C. Fest, and Alan Bullock. See index in Domarus, s.v. Benes, Chamberlain, Mach, Munich Conference, Tiso, and Tuka.

Re Generals' Conspiracy of 1938: Many senior staff officers became increasingly dissatisfied with Hitler's policies, particularly what they saw as a rush to war for which Germany was not ready. During the build up to the Sudetenland crisis of 1938, many officers of the German army joined to convince chief of staff Brauchitsch to remove Hitler. They feared the open front facing France, which would happen when most of Germany's forces moved against Czechoslovakia. United with civilian opponents of Hitler, these officers sent spokesmen to London to request a firm stance against Hitler's demands. As a result, the planned military coup collapsed when Chamberlain and Deladier gave into Hitler's demands at the Munich Conference. Clearly, as Winston Churchill said, if the French and British had presented a strong opposition backed up by military force, Hitler's Germany would have dissolved into chaos, and World War II would not have happened. See: Walter Gorlitz, *Der deutsche Generalstab: Geschite und Gestalt 1657-1945*. Frank-a-m: 1950: (ET History of German General Staff 1657-1945. New York: 1957. pp. 323-339.) J. W. Wheeler-Bennett, *The Nemesis of Power: The German Army in Politics 1918-1945*. New York: 1964. pp. 438-445. Winston S. Churchill. *The Gathering Storm.* Boston: 1948. pp. 298-321.

Chapter 12.

Summary: During the Second World War, the new Slovak government faced an unenviable dilemma. As it strove to establish its independence, the war that raged on all sides placed it in increasing peril. Hitler's war machine clearly subordinated the interests of all satellite states, including Slovakia, to that of Germany. Slovak soldiers were forced to fight on the Eastern Front. The entire Slovak economy was reorganized to serve German needs for raw materials, labor, foodstuffs, and military supplies.

Spiesz paints a picture of Slovakia's president, Tiso, as a genuinely devout priest, entrusted with the difficult task of protecting his flock. Be that as it may, Slovakia was clearly an authoritarian state, dominated by the Slovak People's Party, with characteristics which Communist historians derisively termed 'clerico-fascist'. Other Slovak historians have objected to the charge of fascism, and compare the Slovak state to Austria and its clerical authoritarianism. Though it is true that free elections never took place in the Slovak state, it must be acknowledged that the Slovak Parliament that opted for independence had been elected in strict accordance with Czecho-Slovak law. German and Magyar parties did exist, too, though both the Communist and Social Democratic parties were outlawed. The state had certain important democratic features, such as an independent judiciary and a government administration separate from the People's Party. President Tiso tried to walk a balancing wire, countering the more extreme elements of his party as well as the 'Deutsche Partei', the German party in Slovakia, which continuously clamored for a more Nazi orientation, and even the outright incorporation of Slovakia into the Reich. His intentions were quite evident to German diplomats in Slovakia, but it appears that Hitler thought best to countenance them for the sake of stability in the war effort, since Tiso was immensely popular among his own people.

German intervention continually hovered over Slovak affairs, especially when the Soviets took the offensive on the Eastern Front. But once the Slovak Uprising of August 1944 broke out, German troops moved onto Slovak soil, and the German military presence removed any semblance of Slovak self-rule.

But well before the uprising, pressure for anti-Jewish measures was strong, coming from both the German government and an anti-Semitic faction in the Slovak People's Party. The Slovak Republic passed laws which singled out the over 80,000 Slovak Jews for discrimination in public life: Jews lost property to aryanization, and were denied many of their civil rights. Tiso spoke out against Jews, and, in doing so, provided ammunition to radically anti-Semitic elements in the Hlinka Guard. Whether he meant what he said or was merely attempting to placate the Germans and radical Slovaks remains controversial.

As early as 1941, Germany had exerted pressures on Slovaks to resolve 'the Jewish question', and had even made a secret agreement to this effect with the Slovak radical prime minister, Vojtech Tuka.[1] The Government agreed to the transportation of Jews from Slovakia to 'work camps' in a special zone in Poland, but it is unlikely that they had any idea of the horrible fate awaiting them. Some Jews who were essential to the economy got to stay in Slovakia.[2] However, by October 1942, when escapees showed up in Slovakia, with reports of the true fate of deportees, and after protests by the Slovak bishops and the Vatican, President Tiso halted the transportations. Over the next two years Slovakia became a safe-haven for Jews, but in 1944, after the Slovak uprising and the resultant German occupation of Slovakia, transportation resumed.

Historians like Milan Durica contend that, given the war and a Europe dominated by Nazi Germany, Tiso was hard put to resolve the Jewish situation in a spirit of Christian justice but he did try. Another school, headed by Dusan Kovac and the Slovak Historical Institute, argues that Tiso collaborated with the Nazis in persecuting Slovak Jews and was therefore guilty of war crimes.

Conditions in Slovakia sharply deteriorated when the Slovak Uprising of 1944 triggered a full-scale German occupation. Attacks on German soldiers and ethnic Germans increased, and many Slovak soldiers refused to fight for Germany. Spiesz notes that partisan guerillas committed atrocities against Slovaks and Slovak Germans.[3] The resistance consisted of many groups, hardly coordinated, pursuing a variety of political aims, from the introduction of Communism to restoration of the Czechoslovak state. Benes' government-in-exile in London lacked strong Slovak support. Spiesz plainly states that the Germans soundly defeated an uprising in which most Slovaks did not participate, ignoring the fact that a sizeable minority did and that many of them supported a resurrection of the Czechoslovak state. Also, many top Slovak military officers did take part in what has come to be called the Slovak National Uprising.

Despite its disadvantages as a 'country under German protection', the Slovak Republic brought many positive changes to Slovak life. Culture and education flourished. The exit or removal of many Czechs and Jews from political and business positions opened up numerous opportunities to a new generation of educated Slovaks. The Slovak economy prospered far more than did those of most European states. The experience of independence left Slovaks with a sense of being capable of independence, thus accelerating their momentum on the path of self-awareness and bolstering the belief in their right to sovereignty. That is its lasting legacy. Still, it remains tainted by the alliance with Nazi Germany. And it remains a controversial issue to this day, ideology, politics and emotion often hindering a genuinely objective historical picture of the Slovak Republic and its president, Jozef Tiso.

[1] Durica, Milan S. 'Dr. Jozef Tiso'. *Zbornik z vedeckeho seminara.* Bratislava, 22. September 2001. Bratislava: SAH, 2001: and Milan S. Durica, 'Dr. Jozef Tiso a problem Zidov na Slovensku', *Jednota*. Nos. 3420–3426, April–May 1957.

² According to German documents, only President Tiso and his economic ministers could grant exemptions from Jewish deportation. During the summer of 1942, a German official reported to Berlin that approximately 35,000 Jews had received such exemptions. Durica cites this figure as trustworthy, but a number of historians have considered it far too high.

³ Durica writes that two-thirds of the partisans committed atrocities against German civilians in Slovakia.

⁴ This assertion puts Spiesz at odds with historians arguing that the Slovak Republic was more Christian authoritarian than fascist. Rigid labeling can confuse rather than clarify historical phenomena. (Roland Schoenfeld, *Slowakei*. Regensburg: F. Pustent, 2000, pp. 104)

⁵ Here Spiesz's categorization is an oversimplification, applicable only to Europe in the 1930s. Many Islamic states and more traditional societies have had and continue to have governments which defy categorization into his three systems.

⁶ For a good summary of the Slovak variant of fascism, see Peter F. Sugar, Ed., *Native Fascism in the Successor States 1918–1945*. Santa Barbara, 1971, pp. 51–61.

⁷ The term 'Farska republika' (A Republic Run like a Parish) was coined by Dominik Tatarka (1913–1989) in his 1948 novel, critical of the Slovak Republic. The novel was published during an intensely anti-Catholic campaign waged by triumphant Czechoslovak Communists. Tatarka himself incurred Communist persecution after the 1968 Warsaw Pact invasion of Czechoslovakia. Yeshayahu Jelinek borrowed the phrase for the title of his monograph on the wartime Slovak state, *The Parish Republic: Hlinka's Slovak People's Party 1939–1945*. Boulder, 1976. (the only English book-length treatment of this subject).

Slovak exiles, sympathetic towards the wartime state, published a compilation about it under the editorship of Mikulas Sprinc, *Slovenska republika 1939–1945* (The Slovak Republic). Scranton: Obrana Press, 1949. The book contains a series of reflections by people who had had close ties to President Jozef Tiso. A more critical treatment of the subject can be found in a pamphlet by Ivan Kamenec: *Slovensky stat* (The Slovak State). Praha: Anomal, 1992. Milan Durica has written that the pamphlet was published in Prague because Kamenec could not find a willing publisher in Slovakia. (Correspondence, August 2002.) The most detailed study to date is Karin Schmid, *Die Slowakische Republik 1939–1945*, 2 vols. Berlin: 1982.

⁸ Jozef Tiso is probably the most controversial leader in Slovak history. To those holding independence as the supreme value of Slovak history, as well as to his former People's Party fellows, Tiso was a virtual saint, doing everything he could to help Slovakia achieve independence, as well as to avoid German or Hungarian occupation. The earliest biography of Tiso was written in exile by Konstantin Culen: *Po Svatoplukovi druha nasa hlava* (Our Second Head of State after Svatopluk). 2 vols. Cleveland: 1947. Slovak exiles have published an assortment of articles, books and pamphlets,

which are virtual hagiographies of Tiso.

On the other hand, Marxist historians have vilified Tiso. In fact, no Marxist historian has composed a scholarly biography of him, though other controversial figures such as Hlinka, Stefanik, and Hodza have had such treatment. Lubomir Liptak, in a historiographical essay writes that 'no order ever came down to undertake such a project'. Valerian Bystricky, Ed., *Pokus a polititicky a osobny profil Jozefa Tiso* (An Essay of the Personal and Political Profile of Joseph Tiso). The latter volume contains useful portraits of Tiso by forty scholars, who participated in a 1992 symposium, written with considerable objectivity.

Communist historians may have considered Tiso too hot to handle: favorable remarks would have been taboo.

After the Velvet Revolution, there was a surge in Tiso's popularity. Ivan Kamenec reacted to this public sympathy by calling for an unemotional review, based on facts: *Tragedia politika, knaza a cloveka 1887–1947* (The Tragedy of a Politician, Priest and Man). Bratislava; Archa, 1998.

Milan S. Durica adopts a more positive view of President Tiso in: *Jozef Tiso: Slovensky knaz a statnik* (Joseph Tiso: Slovak Priest and Statesman). Abano Terme, 1989. Durica's study is the most comprehensive work by a single author to date. Durica has also published excerpts from secret German documents about Tiso in: *Katolicka cirkev na Slovensku 1938–1945 v hodnoteni nemeckych diplomatov a tajnych agentov* (The Catholic Church in Slovakia 1938–1945, as Evaluated by German Diplomats and Secret Agents). Trnava: Spolok svateho Vojtecha, 2001. The Italian historian Lis Guarda Nardini has also published a more positive assessment of Tiso in: *The Political Program of President Tiso*. Padova-Trieste, 1984. A German, Franz Schneider, has written: *Jozef Tiso, Katholisher Priester und Staatsprasident der Slowakei* (Joseph Tiso, Catholic Priest and President of Slovakia). Cleveland-Rome: Slovak Institute, 1970.

Only time and distancing from persons and events will allow for a completely even-handed evaluation of Tiso's life and presidency. As the historian Ivo Samson has pointed out, we need to look at what Tiso actually said and did to get a truly objective perspective. (Ivo Samson, 'Tiso' in Domino Forum on-line *www.dofo.sk/10.html.*)

[9] During this period of heightened ethnic tensions, Slovaks and other Slavs were often suspected of Pan-Slavism. Spiesz finds no evidence of such suspicions about Tiso during his theological studies, but Milan Durica provides photocopies of a document that does confirm them. (*Jozef Tiso: Slovensky knaz a statnik*. Abano-Terme, 1989, pp. 52–58.)

[10] There appears to be little basis to suspect Tiso of having been a Magyarone (a defector to Magyar nationalism). Born of humble peasant stock in the small town of Velka Bytca, he studied Slovak, Magyar, and German in a trilingual grammar school. During his studies in Vienna, he clashed with secular and liberal minded Hlasists, defending his conservative Catholic world-view. Returning to Bytca as curate to Father Teselsky, an outspoken

Magyarone, he was accused by Doctor Minarik, of being a poor Slovak, because he worked so well with the pastor, though there is no evidence that he supported any of his political views. (Anthony X. Sutherland, *Dr. Jozef Tiso and Modern Slovakia.* Cleveland: First Catholic Slovak Union, 1978, pp. 29–31.)

[11] Tiso was drafted in the Hungarian army as a chaplain in August 1914, and served with his regiment in Galicia (in present-day Ukraine). He became ill and was sent to Slovenia for recuperation. (Milan Durica, *Correspondence*, August 2002.)

[12] Having delivered a fiery Slovak speech in Nitra, Tiso was arrested and imprisoned for six weeks on the charge of incitement to riot. At the time, he was serving as personal secretary to Bishop Kmetko of Nitra, who disapproved of such activity and asked for his resignation. Tiso then returned to parish work in Bánovce.

[13] Tiso was not immediately chosen chairman of the Hlinka Slovak People's Party; he advanced gradually, assuming the duties and responsibilities of the office.

[14] Durcansky, as Slovak Minister of Foreign Affairs, angered the Germans with his independent attitude. The German Foreign Minister Ribbentrop threatened to exert pressure on Tiso if he refused to fire Durcansky and replace him with Tuka, a Nazi fawner. Tiso, left with little choice, reluctantly agreed. (*D.G.F.P.*, D. X.:284, no. 2; also, Jelinek, *Parish Republic*, pp. 41–44.)

[15] Hitler did not accept awards even from his allies, Japan and Italy. He was too proud to accept honors from inferiors. (Milan Durica, *Correspondence*, August 2002.)

[16] Tiso refused to declare independence on his own; he insisted that such a declaration required parliamentary approval. (*D.G.F.P.*, D. X: 284, no. 2.) See Domarus, *Ibid,* pages 1486–1487.

[17] The Soviet Union annexed some strategic border areas of Finland. For an account of the Russo-Finnish war, see: David M. Glantz, and Jonathan House, *When Titans Clashed: How the Red Army Stopped Hitler.* Lawrence: University Press of Kansas, 1995, pp. 16–23.

[18] Spiesz calls the Treaty of Protection a success, but it clearly subordinated Slovak foreign policy to the Reich: no important military decision could be made without 'close consultation' with the German Wehrmacht. The March 1939 treaty lacked specifics, leaving the Germans free to interpret it as they pleased. (*D.G.F.P.*, D VI: 43; Mikus, pp. 344–345.)

[19] Hitler also wanted to use Slovakia as a model, to show how cooperation with him could benefit his allies.

[20] Milan Durica wrote that, though he had frequently seen Tiso at public events, he had never seen him in a Hlinka Guard uniform. The same was true of the many archival photographs of Tiso that he had examined. (*Correspondence*, August 2002.)

[21] Tiso's executive powers were limited to parameters set by the Germans, and

he was well aware of them. Spiesz overstates the reach of Tiso's powers, since German advisers clearly curtailed his political options, particularly in foreign affairs.

[22] Milan Durica points out that the Slovak press was relatively free during the war. The satirical review *Kocur* took jabs at many politicians, but it continued to publish. Curiously, it never attacked Tiso. (*Correspondence*, August 2002.)

[23] The memoirs of Karol Murin, Tiso's personal secretary, are available in an English translation which, though poor, gives a good overview of what went on in President Tiso's inner circle and provides clues to Tiso's motivations. Murin argues that Tiso wanted to create a Christian state, but was constrained by factors beyond his control to yield to Hitler's demands in the hope of preventing even greater evils. When the Germans forced Durcansky to resign, Tiso, too, was on the verge of resigning, but was persuaded by moderates to stay, rather than concede the presidency to Tuka. (Dr. Charles Murin, *Remembrances and Testimony*. Translated by Vladimir J. Cincik. Montreal: Real Time Publishing Reg., 1992.)

[24] For more details on the German minority in Slovakia, see Lubomir Liptak, 'Role of the German Minority in Slovakia in the Years of the Second World War', *Studia Historica Slovaca* 1 (1963) pp. 150–178.

[25] An opponent of Czechoslovak independence, Janos Eszterhazy was the leading ideologue of the irredentist Magyar Christian Socialist Party and cooperated closely with Budapest between the wars. After 1936, he headed a Magyar coalition and was one of the few Magyars to remain in Slovakia's parliament after 1939. His goal was annexation of Slovakia by Hungary. He was condemned to death by the National Courts after World War II, but his sentence was commuted to life imprisonment in 1950.

[26] It is especially difficult to find objective writings about Slovaks in Hungary, or Magyars in Slovakia, during the Second World War: national emotions ran high. English language publications generally ignored the subject. One such rare work was Jan Sveton, *Slovaci v Madarsku* (Slovaks in Hungary). Bratislava: 1942. The deportation of Magyars after the war has received several treatments, including a recent book by Jan Bobak: *Madarska otazka v Cesko-Slovensku 1944–1948* (The Magyar Question in Czecho-Slovakia 1944–1948). Martin: 1996. Even more recent is Ladislav Deak: *Slovensko v politike Madarska v rokoch 1938–1939* (Slovakia in Hungarian Politics in 1938–1939). Bratislava: Veda, 1990. However, the latter work covers the war years only superficially, and lacks source references.

Before he died in 1990, Emanuel Bohm wrote in exile about the subject. He had lost his job as a grammar school teacher in Magyar occupied Southern Slovakia because of his pro-Slovak leanings. Under the Hungarian occupation he edited *Slovenska jednota* (Slovak Unity) and chaired the Party of Slovak National Unity. Later, in Canada, he was a founding member of the Slovak World Congress and published the pamphlet *The Arbitration of Vienna* (Toronto, 1975), and *The Slovak Minority in Mag-*

yarorszag: A Memorandum of 1942 (1983).

[27] Hlinka's Populist Party had always been anti-Semitic, but not in the Nazi racial sense. Besides being different religiously, Jews were disproportionately more educated and held more professional positions; in the days of the monarchy they had been ardent Magyarizers, and were viewed by Slovaks as inimical to the Slovak National movement.

[28] Shortly after the Velvet Revolution an anthology of writings about Slovak Jews appeared. (Dezider Toth, et alii, *Tragedy of Slovak Jews*. Banska Bystrica: DATEI, 1992.) A Slovak documentary appeared soon after: Gabriel and Ladislav Hoffman, *Katolicka Cirkev a tragedia slovenskych zidov v dokumentoch* (The Catholic Church and the Tragedy of Slovak Jews in Documents). Partizanske: Vydavatelstvo G-print, 1994.)

[29] The Slovak Jewish Code used Germany's Nuremburg Laws as a model. According to Milan Durica, several thousand businesses, generating an income of 1,184,196,000 crowns annually, were shut down; another 1,888 businesses, with annual income of 1,465,261,000, were Aryanized. (To compare, the entire annual budget of the Slovak Republic in 1940 was 2,758,876,000 crowns.) (Milan Durica, *Dejiny Slovenska a Slovakov*. 156 pp.)

[30] A document from the Wannsee Conference, where the Final Solution of the Jewish Problem was formulated, makes the Slovaks appear much more cooperative than Spiesz represents them. It reads: 'In Slovakia and Croatia the matter is no longer difficult, as the most essential, central problems in this respect have already been brought to a solution there. (Protocol of the Wannsee Conference, January 20, 1942. A Holocaust Reader. From Ideology to Annihilation. Rita Steinhardt Botwinick, Upper Saddle River: Prentice Hall, 1998, p. 168.)

[31] A rather sweeping and controversial statement, which Spiesz does not support, implying that Slovaks were more pleased to be rid of Jews than were other nationalities. In truth, anti-Semitism was rife among nearly all the peoples of East Central Europe and elsewhere.

[32] This is a stereotype of Jews in Slovakia. Jews did not engage in physical work, which was reason enough for many Slovaks to dislike them. Slovaks, coming largely from working-class and peasant stock, placed a high value on physical labor, and usually were more sympathetic to blue collar than to white collar workers. This contrasting view of work constituted a fundamental cultural difference between Jews and Slovaks. Spiesz seems to be implying that many Slovaks were glad to see Jews forced to perform physical labor.

[33] Slovakia made only one payment on this account. Besides, it began negotiations to lower the payment for each deported Jew. The actual amount was about 160 Deutsche Marks per person. (Milan Durica, *Correspondence*, August 2002.)

[34] Jelinek argues that Tiso protected only those Jews who either paid huge bribes or who were indispensable to the economy, but without documentation.

[35] This is a subject of considerable controversy in recent debate, especially in view of the fact that the Vatican is considering Jan Vojtassak for beatification, on the basis of his persecution, imprisonment and eventual death at the hands of Communists. Some historians, such as Milan Durica, have argued that Vojtassak did undertake considerable action on behalf of Jews.

[36] Milan Durica disputes this statement. He writes that the Holy See never broke off diplomatic ties with the Slovak Republic while it still legally existed. Mutual ties were severed only after the Slovak government had fled to Kremsmuenster, Austria and unconditionally surrendered to American General Walton H. Walker on May 8, 1945. When the Vatican Secretary of State Tardini informed Karol Sidor, the Slovak Ambassador, that the Slovak government had ceased to exist, formal diplomatic ties were no longer necessary. And that occurred on May 30, 1945, or over three weeks after the above-mentioned surrender. (Karol Sidor, *Sest rokov pri Vatikane* (Six Years at the Vatican). Scranton: Obrana Press, 1947, pp. 263–280.)

[37] Karol Sidor's memoirs of his Vatican experiences were published under the title *Sest rokov pri Vatikane* (cited above). He later wrote some reflections on his experiences in 1939, titled *Moje poznamky k historickym dnom* (My Notes on Historic Days). Middletown: Jednota Press, 1971. Before the war, Hlinka had designated Sidor as his successor. A staunch nationalist, Sidor disagreed sharply with the government's pro-German policy and favored closer ties with Poland. Assigning him to the Vatican was a polite way of sidelining him.

[38] Thirty two states on various continents, Europe, Africa, Asia and South America, extended diplomatic recognition to the Slovak Republic. (Milan Durica, *Slovenska republika 1939–1945: Vznik a trvanie prveho slovenskeho statu 20. storocia* (The Genesis and Duration of the First Slovak State of the Twentieth Century). Bratislava: Luc, 1999, pp. 22–23.)

[39] According to Statutes 105/1943 and 106/1943, the State Council was reduced from 21 members to 12, and the position became honorary, i.e. unsalaried. (Milan Durica, *Correspondence*, August 2002.)

[40] Spiesz incorrectly states that the Slovak People's Party was the only legal party in the state.

[41] Reinhard Heydrich had a reputation as the most ruthless of Nazi butchers. He is infamous as the architect of the 'final solution', which sent millions of Jews to the gas chambers. Calm and collected, Heydrich had no moral qualms about executing mass victims. Even his fellows branded him 'the blond beast'. He served as Reich Protector of Bohemia and Moravia until May 27, 1942, when he was assassinated by a team of Czechs and a Slovak, Jozef Gabcik, sent on this mission from England.

[42] Spiesz should have said 1944, that is a year later, not 1943.

[43] Tiso had the authority to stop deportations of Jews, but resisted using it until pressured by the Vatican and Slovak bishops. He knew he would risk his presidency if he ignored German orders.

[44] Spiesz's picture of Slovak laborers in Germany is too rosy. The Reich negotiated for Slovak labor to relieve shortages; not all migrant Slovak laborers

went voluntarily. (J. K. Hoensch, 'The Slovak Republic 1939–1945', *History of the Czechoslovak Republic 1918–1948.* pp. 288–289.)

Durica writes that many young men did volunteer for work in Germany because of the higher wages there. When they visited home they often brought bicycles, cameras, and other items 'that people in Slovak villages could only dream about'. (Milan Durica, *Correspondence*, August 2002.)

[45] Spiesz does not have much to say about Slovak labor and labor organizations during the war years. The Slovak People's Party consolidated trade unions into one big Christian Socialist Trade Union Association, and outlawed unions controlled by Communists and Social Democrats.

On the whole, Slovak unions were relatively freer than those in the Protectorate of Bohemia and Moravia, and workers enjoyed relatively high wages, but union membership was compulsory, and unions lost much of their power. (M. J. Kopanic, Jr., 'Czech and Slovak Federal Republic', *European Labor Unions*. Joan Campbell, Ed., Westport: Greenwood Press, 1992.)

[46] For samples of Slovak ethnic art, see: *Slovak Tales for Young and Old: Dobsinsky in English and Slovak*. Wauconda, IL, Bolchazy-Carducci Publishers, 2001.

[47] Sokol worked as a professor of graphic arts at La Escuela de las Artes del Libro and at the National University in Mexico City from 1937 to 1941. After several years in New York, he returned to Slovakia in 1946 to teach at the Technical University. As the Communists were seizing control of Czecho-Slovakia in 1948, he again fled the country, never to return. (*Slovakia and the Slovaks*, p. 605.) Samples of Sokol's art can he found in: *Milan Rufus: And That's the Truth*. Wauconda, IL, Bolchazy-Carducci Publishers, 2005.

[48] For a review of Slovak events during the last two years of the war, covering topics such as the resistance movement, the economy, diplomatic activities, and societal turmoil as German defeat seemed imminent, see *Slovensko na konci druhej svetovej vojny – stav, vychodiska a perspectivy*. (Slovakia at the End of World War II – Conditions, Alternatives and Perspectives.) Bratislava: Historicky ustav SAV, 1994.

[49] It is difficult to assess the reasons for Benes' turn to the Soviet Union. The obvious rationalization is that he no longer trusted the Western Powers after the Munich sell-out. Apparently, owing to Czechoslovakia's geopolitical location, he believed that Soviet cooperation would be of paramount importance to the country in the post-war world. (Korbel, 175–178.)

[50] The new party leadership brought a new party line from Moscow. Stalin, preoccupied with winning the war, instructed Slovak party leaders to soft-pedal the primacy of class-struggle in their public pronouncements. Smidke was of Silesian Czech and German origin, and had worked in Slovakia between the wars. He received his ideological training in Moscow during the war, then returned to Slovakia (Yeshayahu A. Jelinek, *The Lust for Power: Nationalism, Slovakia, and the Communists 1918–1948*. Boulder: East European Monographs, 1983.)

[51] Stalin instructed his commanders to fight to the death and resist capture.

Repatriated prisoners of war were considered untrustworthy and were frequently deported to labor camps in Siberia.

52 Ukrainian partisans dropped Lt. Peter A. Velicko by parachute in Slovakia during the night of July 25–26, 1944. His mission was to train Slovak partisans for an uprising. On August 27, in Turciansky Svaty Martin, a Slovak unit under Velicko's command captured a German military mission returning by train from Rumania and shot all twenty-eight Germans, including their families. This action precipitated an immediate German occupation of Slovakia. (Anna Josko, 'Slovak Resistance Movement', *History of the Czechoslovak republic 1918–1948.* pp. 362–384.) Milan S. Durica adds that the German soldiers were first imprisoned and then killed on Lt. Velicko's orders. (Milan Durica, *Correspondence*, August 2002.)

53 General Malar, disregarding the partisan command's order to attack, flew to Bratislava instead and broadcast a message discouraging insurrection. Josko incorrectly notes (p. 379) that he warned against 'premature' action. In fact, the warning against 'premature' action occurred in a telephone conversation with his cousin, Captain Jan Malar, the commander of a resistance unit in Topolcany, which the Germans apparently tapped. Suspecting General Malar of complicity in the insurrection, the Germans arrested and executed him. (Jozef Jablonicky, *Zbornik o Slovenskom narodnom povstani,* 2. Toronto: 1980, pp. 168–169 and 178–179.)

54 Slovaks were not of one mind regarding the restoration of Czechoslovakia. No doubt many preferred an independent Slovakia, but a sizeable number would have settled for more autonomy in a reconstituted Czecho-Slovak Republic. In general, Communists and people outside the Slovak People's Party, such as Social Democrats, would have preferred restoration.

54 The captured insurgency leaders were sent for interrogation, first to Bratislava, then to Berlin. According to John O. Crane and Sylvia Crane, they were subsequently executed at Mauthausen: *Czechoslovakia: Anvil of the Cold War*. New York: Praeger, 1991, p. 223. John Crane's father was a personal friend of the Masaryk family, and wrote favorably about Benes' actions during and after the Second World War.

Durica has cited recent testimony out of Russia that the Germans merely interned Slovak generals and did not execute them. However, it should be remembered that the Soviet Union itself routinely executed German prisoners-of-war.

About 13,500 partisans in Slovakia carried on after the uprising was put down. In the meantime, deportations were renewed and 11,532 additional Jews were transported to the death camps. In this last phase of deportations, Czech nationals who lived in Slovakia were also rounded up and deported. (Stanislav Kirschbaum, *History of Slovakia*, p. 218.)

56 A partial list of Communist historians includes Samo Faltan, Imrich Stanek, Ivan Kamenec, Ludovit Holotik, Ladislav Hubenak, Miroslav Kropilak, Ladislav Lipscher, Bohuslav Graca, Milos Gosiorovsky, Dusan Kovac,

Miro Hysko, Viliam Plevza, and Lubomir Liptak. All of them compromised the truth in the interests of the regime.

[57] Stefan Tiso sat on the Council of State, a kind of upper house of Parliament. The Germans seemed to favor him for the prestige of his name.

[58] On the whole, Western historians have paid scant attention to wartime Slovak resistance and the Slovak National Uprising. On the other hand, domestic historians have had a lot to say, but most of it has been tainted by politics. One of the most balanced short studies in English is Anna Josko, *Ibid.* pp. 362–384. Among the few Western studies are: Wolfgang Venohr, *Aufstand fur die Tschechoslowakei: Der Slowakische Freiheitskampf von 1944* (The Uprising for Czechoslovakia: The Slovak 1944 Struggle for Freedom). Hamburg: 1969; and the same author's *Aufstand in der Tatra: der Kampf um die Slowakei 1939–1944* (An Uprising in the Tatra Mountains: The Struggle for Slovakia 1939–1944). Konigstein: Athenaeum, 1979.

A great deal is available in Slovak, including a self-serving account by Gustav Husak, Czecho-Slovak Communist President: *Svedectvo o Slovenskom narodnom povstani* (Testimony to the Slovak National Uprising). Bratislava: 1964. Mention must also be made of the huge collection of documents assembled and edited by Vilem Precan: *Slovenske narodne povstanie: documenty* (The Slovak National Uprising: Documents). Bratislava, 1965.

In the West, a three-volume work has been published through the efforts of the late Dr. Martin Kvetko, a Democratic Party leader who fled into exile after the Second World War. It includes: *Zbornik o uvah a osobnych spomienok o Slovenskom narodnom povstani* (A Collection of Reflections and Recollections about the Slovak National Uprising), Martin Kvetko and Miroslav Jan Licko, Eds., Toronto: Novy domov, 1976; and Jozef Jablonicky, *Zbornik o Slovenskom povstani,* 2–3. (A Collection on the Slovak National Uprising, Volumes II–III). Toronto: Nase snahy, 1980, 1983, originally written as a 'samizdat' in 1978. Volume III includes reflections on American participation by Miroslav Licko.

Also worth mention is Nikolaj Sinevirsky, *Partisan Revolt in Slovakia.* New York: H. Holt, 1950; and Vnuk, Frantisek *Neuveritelne sprisahanie* (An Incredible Conspiracy). Middletown: Jednota Press, 1964.

[59] Dr. Durica sent us a manuscript where this paragraph has the follwing alternate reading:

"The post-war accounts of events of the last months of WW II, as presented by various authors in their works, are full of lies, half-truths and misinformations. The crowning piece of this mythology is Husak's *The Testimony concerning the Slovak National Uprising* [see note 58]. The presentation and evaluation of these events passed through several phases, and each version reflected the attitudes of those who were in power at the time. In fact, the episode was neither Slovak nor a national uprising. It was not supported by the majority of Slovak citizens, but only by a minority which consisted of Communists, the so-called Czechoslovaks and misguided Benes sympathizers. The mass of the Slovak population remained loyal to the Slovak Government and President Dr. J. Tiso.

[60] Apparently Spiesz makes this statement to indicate that Slovak officials wanted to leave with the good will of the Slovak public. This behavior contrasts sharply with the rapacious behavior of the Soviet occupiers.

Chapter 13.

Summary: In this chapter, Spiesz summarizes how the Communists seized power in the revived Czechoslovakia after the Second World War. As in other countries of Eastern and Central Europe, a national front government was formed with the backing of the Soviet Union and the consent of President Benes, who distrusted the West after the Munich debacle in 1938. The national front government excluded all former collaborationist parties and gave the left a decided advantage. More organized and determined than any of the other parties, the Communists seized the initiative and occupied many of the important government posts and used its influence to gain leadership in the newly formed mass organizations, especially the unified trade unions, the People's Militia, and the Union of Partisans.

One important point, which Spiesz fails to mention, is the fact that the Red Army eventually withdrew from Czechoslovakia after the war. Obviously Stalin felt confident that the Communists could seize power without the direct intervention of the Soviet Union.

In the so-called People's democracy (the term applied to the transitional national front governments that preceded total Communist takeover), the administration pushed the notion of a centrally planned economy. The plan included the nationalization of large businesses to serve the interests of the people. Across Europe the mobilization of business by governments had acquired respectability after the total governmental organization of the war economies. The fragility of the post-war economy and a terrible drought, on which Spiesz does not elaborate, furnished the Communists with ready-made issues. Of course, the Communists, occupying pivotal government posts, were well placed to move into control of important business positions.

Spiesz does not neglect to mention that many Germans and Hungarians were deported from both parts of the Republic. These deportations were enacted on the basis of the 'Benes decrees'. Unless they actively opposed German occupation, or were Communists, over three million of such people were driven from their homes. We might also add that their properties were assigned to influential Communists, particularly in the Czech lands and the Magyar-speaking areas of Southern Slovakia.

The Communists were much stronger in Bohemia and Moravia, than they were in Slovakia. The parliamentary elections of 1946 clearly demonstrated this fact, when the Communists, allied with the left-leaning Social Democrats, obtained a clear majority of votes in the Czech lands but not in Slovakia, where they received only 30.3%, compared to the 62% of the unified Democratic Party. Thus, in order to seize power with some semblance of legality, the Communists fiercely attacked the 'reactionaries' of Slovakia.

In the immediate post-war years the renewed Czechoslovak government tried and sentenced members of the former Slovak government, including the president of the war-time Slovak state, Jozef Tiso, who was hanged for treason against Czecho-Slovakia. The hanging was hardly a popular move among Slovaks and evoked much resentment. When President Benes refused to commute the death sentence, many Slovaks, including Spiesz, attributed his refusal to vengefulness. With Tiso and the collaborators out of the way, the Communists turned on the Democratic Party in Slovakia. Obtaining support from mass organizations, the Communists accused hundreds of Democratic Party leaders of collaboration during the war and called for their removal from government positions. Then, having neutralized Slovakia, they went to work preparing for the Spring parliamentary elections. Non-Communist ministers in the central government in Prague protested the increasing abuse of power by the Ministry of the Interior and offered their resignations in an attempt to bring down the government. The Communists, in response, mobilized a massive protest by the trade unions and the armed People's Militia. In a controversial move, President Benes, instead of calling for new elections, caved into pressure and accepted the resignations of the non-Communist ministers. From that point on, the Communists were in control, and the May 1948 elections in their pockets. The Communist tactics of intimidation and illegality had won the day without a shot being fired.

Once in power, the Communists proceeded to eliminate opposition and extend their control over all aspects of society. They persecuted church leaders and forced the Greek Catholic Church to merge with the Russian Orthodox Church. They then moved against their own, attacking fellow party members who had displayed the least inkling of sympathy for Slovak national rights. Prague re-emerged, but now under a Communist command.

[1] For discussions of the post-war era, leading up to the Communist seizure of power, see the following works: M. R. Myant, *Socialism and Democracy in Czechoslovakia 1945–1948*. Cambridge: 1981; Karel Kaplan, *Short March: Communist Takeover in Czechoslovakia 1945–1948*. New York, 1987; Josef Korbel, *The Communist Subversion of Czechoslovakia 1938–1948*. Princeton: 1959; Zdenek Suda, *Zealots and Rebels: History of the Ruling Communist Party of Czechoslovakia*. Stanford: Hoover Institution, 1980; Hubert Ripka, *Czechoslovakia Enslaved. The Story of the Communist Coup d'etat*. London: Victor Gollanz Ltd., 1950. (An older work, but still useful.)

[2] Lettrich (1905–1969) became a confirmed opponent of both the Slovak People's Party and the Communists. He moved to the United States after the Communist takeover, and later wrote: *History of Modern Slovakia*. New

York: Praeger, 1955. In the latter work he portrays both of his opponents as ruthless totalitarians, presenting photographs of President Tiso in the company of Nazis, giving the Nazi salute.

[3] According to Stanislav Kirschbaum, Siroky was a Communist of Hungarian origin. Upon becoming chairman of the Communist Party of Slovakia, he moved its headquarters to Prague. (Stanislav Kirschbaum. *Ibid.* p. 227.)

[4] For a summary of Communist strategies, see Ivo Duchacek, *The Strategy of Communist Infiltration: the Case of Czechoslovakia.* New Haven: Yale University Press, 1949. The pattern of the Communist takeover in Czecho-Slovakia closely resembled that used by Stalin in other countries, except that the Red Army did not remain in the country as it had done elsewhere. (*Anatomy of Communist Takeovers.* New Haven: Yale University Press, 1975.)

[5] Stalin insisted that the Slovaks remain tightly aligned with the Czechs. He dismissed the idea of Slovak annexation to the Soviet Union, which some Slovak Communists had favored since the beginning of the war. But Ruthenia was annexed, giving the Soviet Union a common border with Czecho-Slovakia.

[6] The asymmetrical model refers to the unequal power structure in the state. The Slovak National Council was invested with legislative powers, the Board of Trustees with executive powers. These bodies had no counterparts in Czech lands.

The Kosice Agreement of 1945 set up a provisional government to rule until elections could be held. Slovakia turned over to Prague authority to handle foreign policy, defense and foreign trade. The agreement mollified Slovak concerns for regional control, but many Czech Communists, and even some Slovaks, considered it a temporary measure, meant to win over Slovak support. It was vague enough to allow for various interpretations: Declaring the Slovaks to be an 'independent nation ethnically', and affirming the 'principle of equality in Czech-Slovak relations', it left the actual division of powers to be decided by the 'legitimate representatives of the Czech and Slovak nations'. (See document in Lettrich, *Ibid.*, pp. 317–318.)

[7] A reference to Communist demands for nationalization of major industries, finance, banking, insurance, and mining, as well as for extensive land reforms. Small enterprises were allowed to operate until their assets were used up.

[8] Stefan Major (1887–1963) was a leading Magyar Communist in Slovakia and former secretary of the powerful Metalworkers' Union in Bratislava. In the 30s he was an effective strike organizer among agricultural laborers. He served on the Central Committee of the Czechoslovak Communist Party while editing Magyar-language newspapers. Though, as a Hungarian, he was temporarily denied Czechoslovak citizenship, after the Communist takeover he resumed his top-level functions in the party. (*Slovensky biograficky slovnik,* 4. pp. 35–36.)

[9] Although Lutherans comprised only about 15% of the Slovak population,

they wielded a disproportionate amount of political influence.

[10] The Communists, being quite sensitive to Catholic influence, made it a point to emphasize that good Catholicism could co-exist with good Communism. (Conversations with James Felak, June 2002.)

[11] The expulsion of three million Sudeten Germans was a very traumatic event, and is quite controversial to the present day. An early work favorable to the Czech perpetrators is Radomir Luza, *Transfer of the Sudeten Germans: A Study of German-Czech Relations 1933–1962*. New York, 1964. More recently, Jan Mlynarik has publicized the plight of many German families who suffered great harm, though they had not necessarily been Nazi sympathizers.

[12] Most of the Magyars who came with the Hungarian occupation in 1938 left quite quickly after the war, to escape possible persecution. They numbered approximately 30,000.

[13] The deportation of Magyars was supposed to be part of a mutual population exchange, but 70,000 Slovaks left Hungary, since so many of them had been forcibly Magyarized over the years. To this day, officially about 30,000 Slovaks still live in Hungary, but Slovak sources estimate the actual figure to be much closer to 90,000 or 100,000.

[14] Peter Toma estimates that 60,000 Magyars were forcibly moved to the Czech lands (compared to Spiesz' 44,000). They settled on farms and in the coal-mining regions of the Sudetenland, where deportation of Germans created a labor shortage. (Peter Toma, *Slovakia from Samo to Dzurinda*, pp. 125–126.)

[15] In the Czech elections, the Communists won 40.1% of the vote, the National Socialists 23.5%, the Populists 20.2%, and the Social Democrats 15.6%. Thus, when combined with the left-leaning Social Democrats, the Communist total constituted a majority in Bohemia and Moravia. Thus Slovakia stood in their way to total victory.

[16] Spiesz is harsh in his assessment of Husak because of his association with 'normalization' after the 1968 Warsaw Pact invasion of Czecho-Slovakia, in effect holding him accountable for the failure of reforming Communism.

[17] The execution of Tiso was likely to create a martyr for the cause of Slovak independence, and alienate Catholics, a major part of the population.

It has been amply demonstrated by recent archival research that the Tiso trial had been an act of political revenge. Neither the legal traditions nor the procedural norms were respected. Long before its opening the President of Czecho-Slovakia, Dr. E. Benes declared: "Tiso must be hanged", and ordered the prosecuting judge, Dr. I. Daxner, to conduct court proceedings accordingly.

[18] Tiso maintained that he acted in defense of the Slovak nation. Though he considered Hitler and Nazism to be evil, he nevertheless saw them as God's instruments in the attainment of Slovak independence. During the court proceedings, Dr. Tiso pointed out that his trial was 'one-sided' and demanded to be judged by the whole nation by means of a plebiscite (an easy procedure in a small nation). For an evaluation of the Tiso trial, see: Brad

Abrams, 'Politics of Retribution: Trial of Jozef Tiso', *East European Politics and Society*, 1996.

[19] This was also true of most Slovak-Americans, who to this day consider Tiso to have been a martyr and defender of the Slovak nation. The Slovak League of America and most Slovak fraternals backed the Slovak Republic. The National Slovak Society was an exception in this respect and withdrew from the Slovak League of America, until the 70s.

When the death sentence was pronounced, the majority of Slovaks expected that President Benes would pardon Tiso and thus spare his life. Such an act of mercy was requested not only by the Conference of Slovak bishops, but also by the Westminster Archbishop Griffin, by the diplomatic representatives of the Vatican and Great Britain and by 135 public personalities and organizations from Slovakia and twenty-nine foreign courntries. But Dr. Benes refused to grant pardon.

[20] The Czechoslovak delegation to Paris had originally accepted participation in the Marshall Plan, and rescinded its approval only under pressure from the Soviet Union. Many observers at the time saw this rescission as proof of Soviet control of Czechoslovakia.

[21] The 'millionaires' tax' was a psychological ploy, sheer propaganda. There never had been many millionaires in Czechoslovakia, and their number was diminished by the war. The success of the Communists with this non-issue caused the Social Democrats to join them in support of it. (Lubomir Luza, 'Czechoslovakia between Democracy and Communism 1945–1948', *History of the Czechoslovak Republic 1918–1948*, pp. 409–410.)

[22] Bohumil Lausman was a center-leaning Social Democrat. A former leader of the Social Democrats, Zdenek Fierlinger was a 'fellow-traveler', supporting the Communists in everything. Fierlinger was instrumental in convincing fellow party members not to join the twelve non-Communists who submitted their resignations in protest of the 1948 Communist takeover.

[23] The Communists ordered organized workers to stage mass protests, thus to give the appearance of nationwide acceptance of the resignations tendered by the non-Communist ministers. This 'revolution' was orchestrated by the Communists from above, with the working class acting as 'a largely willing accomplice'. (Jon Bloomfield, *Passive Revolution: Politics and the Czecho-Slovak Working Class 1945–1948*. London: Allison and Busby, 1979.) The trade-union leaders who opposed Communist policies lost their positions shortly after the coup.

[24] Benes essentially opted out of the political picture after the February coup, retiring to his country estate in Sezimovo Usti.

[25] Husak, along with several other Slovak Communists was tried in 1954 on charges of 'bourgeois nationalism'. The trial was similar to the 'purge' trials in other Communist states. It was a ploy to rid Czechoslovakia of its 'Slovak problem'. In combination with accelerated industrialization, it was meant to solve the Slovak question for good. But, in fact, the issue remained a 'hot potato' throughout the Communist period. (Gustav Husak, *Speeches*

and Writings. New York: 1986.)

[26] One could argue that this was the one positive achievement of Communist rule in Slovakia. Between the wars Slovakia had remained largely agricultural. Industrial investment in Slovakia was meant to wipe out socio-economic differences between the two parts of the country, and increase the size of the working class, thus of the party as well. A fringe benefit was to be the eradication of Slovak nationalism, but this benefit failed to materialize. (Jaroslav Krejci, *Social Change and Stratification in Post-War Czechoslovakia*. New York: Columbia University Press, 1972.)

[27] Another part of the plan was the elimination of Jewish elements in the Party. (Jiri Pelikan, Ed., *Czechoslovak Political Trials 1950–1954: Suppressed Report of the Dubcek Government's Commission of Inquiry 1968*. Stanford: Stanford University Press, 1971.)

[28] Many nuns and priests were hauled off to work in Czech mines. One nun told this writer (Kopanic) that nuns were required to work daily at hard labor, but that they baulked at Sunday work. Threatened with death, the sisters responded: 'Go ahead, kill us, but we will not work on Sunday, our day of prayer'. Taken aback by such faith, the Communists relented and left the nuns to their Sunday prayers.

[29] Repression of the Catholic Church has been the subject of recent historical scholarship in Slovakia. Failing to negotiate a deal with Slovak bishops, the Communists initiated their own version of Catholic Action with a schismatic Slovak Catholic Church. When the scheme was ineffective, Viliam Siroky, at a Central Committee meeting in June 1949, proposed the assignment of government overseers to each diocesan chancery and the conversion of priests into state employees. These proposals were passed into law in autumn 1949, and a Slovak Office of Church Affairs was created. Soon state officials were monitoring activities in diocesan offices, screening visitors, and 'proofreading' all incoming and outgoing mail. The bishops were effectively isolated in their chanceries and subjected to enormous psychological pressures. (Frantisek Vnuk, *Vladni zmocnenci v biskupskych uradoch v rokoch 1949–1951* [Governmental Overseers in Diocesan Chanceries in 1949–1951]. Martin: Matica Slovenska, 1999.)

The Communist assault on the Church escalated in 1950 with the forcible closure of monasteries and convents, and the liquidation of Byzantine Rite Catholic churches through integration into the Orthodox Church. The three bishops mentioned by Spiesz resisted Communist pressures and underwent trial for High Treason, while some bishops chose accommodation to pressure as the lesser evil. Undefeated, the Church went underground, becoming a 'Church of Silence'. This situation lasted until 1968, when the Dubcek government recalled the chancery overseers and restored some dignity to church-state relations. (Cardinal Jan Chryzostom Korec, S.J. *The Night of the Barbarians: Memoirs of the Communist Persecution of the Slovak Cardinal*. Wauconda, IL: Bolchazy-Carducci Publishers, Inc., 2002.)

Chapter 14.

Summary: In this final chapter Spiesz summarizes the thirty years that preceded the 1989 overthrow of Communism in Czechoslovakia. He stresses the simple failure of Communism to compete with the West, since its principles were in conflict with human nature itself. Instead of building Socialism, it planted the seeds of its own destruction, in both ideology and practice. Because he believes that a historian needs at least thirty years remove from events to gain perspective, Spiesz does not elaborate on how the system failed.

The one positive aspect of the Communist period that Spiesz recognizes is the revival of Slovak self-awareness after the purges of the 1950s. Rehabilitation of the Slovak 'bourgeois nationalists' stimulated party reform. In the 1960s Alexander Dubcek and other Slovak leaders teamed up with Czech reformers to oust the Czech Antonin Novotny from party leadership. Spiesz gives only a brief summary of the 1960s experiment labeled 'Socialism with a Human Face'. Despite insisting that the Communist Party retain its commanding role in government, Dubcek became a popular national figure. The August 1968 invasion by Warsaw Pact troops brought an end to any hopes of enduring reform.

A note of pessimism intrudes into this concluding chapter. As Spiesz was completing his manuscript, the Communists still controlled many important posts in the country. Though a new era had begun, vestiges of forty years of totalitarian rule still abounded. Nevertheless, a new chance to build democracy was at hand.

[1] A National Party Conference in Prague approved a new constitution in July 1960, which haughtily proclaimed 'the completion of socialization' in Czecho-Slovakia. Of course, its ultimate goal was Communism, with power concentrated in the Party. (Suda, *Ibid.* pp. 287–289.)

[2] For a discussion of the issue of Slovak Nationalism during the reform era see Robert W. Dean, *Nationalism and Political Change in Eastern Europe: the Slovak Question and the Czechoslovak Reform Movement.* Denver: East European Monographs, 1973.

[3] One might describe Novotny as a man mired in mud. Afraid of change, he strove to preserve the Communist system and the privileges which it conferred on him and his cronies. Furthermore, he was hostile to Slovak needs and displayed his crass attitude by suggesting the archives of Matica Slovenska be moved to Prague. (S. J. Kirschbaum, *History of Slovakia,* p. 314, note 29.)

[4] Dubcek's autobiography has been published posthumously: Alexander Dubcek, *Hope Dies Last: Autobiography of Alexander Dubcek.* New York: Kodanska International, 1993.

[5] Dubcek was literally conceived in the United States. His mother was preg-

nant with him when his parents left Chicago after World War I and returned to Slovakia. For a biography of Alexander Dubcek up to the time of the Velvet Revolution see William Shawcross, *Dubcek*. New York: Simon and Schuster, Inc., 1990.

6   Dubcek lost his brother, a partisan, in the war. This loss strengthened his determination to make Socialism work after the war.

7   Perhaps it would be better to state that Dubcek agreed with the changes made by the Communists during the 1950s. It was a time of laying foundations for Communist rule, and 'true believers', like Dubcek, accepted the necessity of eliminating enemies of socialism for the good of society. They hardly realized that these tactics were to become a way of life. Dubcek was a true believer in Marxian socialism, but he wanted to inject gentler and more humane features. His approach achieved immense popularity, both in Slovakia and the Czech lands. He kept the faith until his death, in an auto accident, in 1992.

8   For a survey of the reform movement see Galia Golan, *Czechoslovak Reform movement: Communism in Crises 1962–1968*. Cambridge: Cambridge University Press, 1971. For a masterful presentation of the reform movement see H. Gordon Skilling, *Czechoslovakia's Interrupted Revolution*. Princeton: Princeton University Press, 1976.

9   For details of Dubcek's ordeal in Moscow and near nervous breakdown there, see Zdenek Mlynar, *Nightfrost in Prague*. London: 1980.

10 Expelled party members could no longer occupy plush jobs: many were forced into manual labor. For a summary of post-1968 'normalization' see Vladimir Kusin, *From Dubcek to Charter 77: Study of Normalization in Czechoslovakia 1968–1978*. Edinburgh: Q Press, 1978.

11 Charter 77 had little support in Slovakia; nearly all its signatories were Czechs. Of the three Slovaks who did sign, two lived in Prague. A better measure of Slovak opposition was the Bratislava prayer demonstration on Good Friday, in March 1988, which the regime brutally suppressed with water cannon and vicious dogs.

Afterword

1   These 'ethnogenesis' theories are re-examined by F. Curta, 'Making an Early Medieval *Ethnie:* Case of the Early Slavs, Sixth to Seventh Century A.D.' (Dissertation, 2 vols.), Western Michigan University, 1989.

2   Saint Gorazd (835–?) was a priest from a famous family in the area of Nitra who had originally studied in Bavaria at a Latin school before the time of Cyril and Methodius. Upon the arrival of the two missionary brothers, he adopted the Slavic liturgy and probably accompanied them on their journey to Rome. The German authorities detained Methodius on his return trip and held him in Bavaria. Methodius appears to have considered Gorazd to be

his successor and was among his five closest followers. See *Slovakia and the Slovaks*: p. 222.

3 Caplovic has used the word 'genocide', which is too strong a word for what happened. The Habsburgs attempted to quell any possibility of future rebellion by ridding the Protestants of their leaders. Protestants could still worship, but under strict limitations and severe restrictions.

4 Here again Caplovic has used the word 'genocide', which evokes images of people being slaughtered en masse. The Hungarian nationalists were more interested in wiping out traces of Slovak ethnic self-awareness than in killing people. See #6, below.

5 James Ward, a graduate student in 2002, examined only available records and states that no more than 1,000 Jews received presidential dispensations during 1942. See 'People Who Deserve It: Jozef Tiso and the Presidential Exemption', *Nationalities Papers* 30/4 (2002), pp. 571-602.

6 While it is true, as Caplovic states, that Pope Pius XII remained quiet and exercised restraint in publicly criticizing Nazi genocide, to add that he 'enabled the genocide of the Jews' is a controversial statement.

The historian, Rev. Dermot Fenlon, contends that public statements from the Vatican might have worsened conditions for prisoners. A former Dachau inmate, Monsignor Jean Bernard, who later became Bishop of Luxembourg, related that papal statements "generally led to worse treatment of the clergy and had little effect on the behavior of the Nazi incarcerators."

"The detained priests trembled every time news reached us of some protest by a religious authority, but particularly by the Vatican. We all had the impression that our warders made us atone heavily for the fury these protests evoked ... whenever the way we were treated became more brutal, the Protestant pastors among the prisoners used to vent their indignation on the Catholic priests: 'Again your big naive Pope and those simpletons, your bishops, are shooting their mouths off ... why don't they get the idea once and for all, and shut up. They play the heroes and we have to pay the bill'."

Writing in 1963, Albrecht von Kessel, a former German Embassy official who had served at the Vatican during the World War II, provided the following assessment:

"We were convinced that a fiery protest by Pius XII against the persecution of the Jews ... would certainly not have saved the life of a single Jew. Hitler, like a trapped beast, would react to any menace that he felt directed at him, with cruel violence".

Those defending papal policy say that one should look at how the Vatican acted, rather than what it stated or did not say publicly. Vatican policy approached the Jewish question on a country-by-country basis and coordinated efforts to help Jews at the local level. In Rome itself, it is estimated that as many as 7,000 Jews were saved due to actions of the Vatican. See Joseph L. Lichten, 'A Question of Judgment: Pius XII & the Jews' (http://www.jewishvirtuallibrary.org/jsource/anti-semitism/piusdef2.html).

This position is maintained by two recent authors, who extol the work of the Pope and the Vatican in fighting Nazism and saving Jews. See David G. Dalin, *The Myth of Hitler's Pope: How Pius XII Rescued Jews from the Nazis.* Washington, DC: Regnery Publishing, 2005. Also see Tatiana Tonsmeyer, *Das Dritte Reich und die Slowakei 1939–1945: Politischer Alltag zwischen Kooperation und Eigensinn.* Paderborn: Ferdinand Schoningh, 2003.

On the other hand, historians such as Michael Phayer strongly disagree with those defending Vatican reticence. (Michael Phayer, *The Catholic Church and the Holocaust 1930–1965.* Bloomington: Indiana University Press, 2000. Also see the website http://iupress.indiana.edu/textnet/0-253-33725-9/0253108349.htm)

[7] Milan Durica would sharply disagree with Caplovic's statement about Tiso being loyal to Nazi Germany to the end. In his book about the Catholic Church in Slovakia during World War II, Durica wrote that Tiso was keenly aware of the probable defeat of Nazi Germany. Because of his beliefs in honoring treaties signed in good faith, Tiso always observed all Slovak obligations, but in the last couple years of the war, he began expressing his gratitude and loyalty toward the German nation, rather than Adolf Hitler. Thus in examining German documents, Durica found that German embassy officials noticed a shift in Tiso's language and emphasis. Tiso knew that the German nation would survive the war, even if Hitler and Nazism were obliterated. I quote a personal letter from Professor Durica (June 18, 2005):

"As it became more certain that the war would not end well for Hitler, it became clearer that Tiso distanced himself from the Reich. I can testify that when I was a student at the Salesian preparatory school in Sastin, the local economist and priest Anton Mihalik (1907-1982) in strict confidence between the two of them asked Tiso in the spring of 1943 whether Germany would win this war. Tiso answered him: 'May God protect us!'

"As the head of state he strictly observed obligations stemming from the Treaty of Protection, because his honor as a statesman and his Christian conscience dictated that he adhere to the long-established principle of international law, *pacta sunt servanda* – agreements must be kept.

"However, that proved to him that he had to voice even more emphatically that the top priority of Slovak politics must be the vital interests of the Slovak nation and its statehood.

"He had publicly stated this innumerable times in his public speeches from the original start of Slovak independence. And when forced, more than once by the direct request of the German envoy, to remember the German help in the establishment and protection of the Slovak state, Tiso mentioned not Hitler, but the German nation:

"'**Whoever recognized the right to freedom, the right to have one's own independent state, that person is my friend. Whoever does not recognize this right, or wants to rob me of it, is my enemy. The German nation not only recognized right of Slovaks to free and independent state, but it also helped us to make it a reality**'.

"He declared this, for instance, in his public speech **in October 1944,** which gave his positions regarding Benes' Czechoslovakism and the imminent threat of occupation of Slovakia by Stalin's Red Army.

"Tiso was not so naive as to believe in Hitler's 'thousand-year Reich'. But he knew that the German nation would always be one of the strongest and most influential factors in international politics. For this reason, he always emphasized the relationship of the Slovak Republic to the German nation. He knew that Hitler would lose the war, but the German nation and its state would remain. Therefore, in line with Christian morals, he respected even Hitler, whom the Germans had legally elected as their head. When Admiral Karl Donitz, who belonged to no party, succeeded Hitler as the head of the German Reich, Tiso expressed his greetings in a telegram in line with the protocols of international rules. He did this mainly to show that the Slovak Republic, which was tied to Germany by a Treaty of Protection lasting 25 years, honored this agreement and expected that the new leaders of Germany would likewise honor it and protect the Slovak Republic against its enemies, including in the upcoming peace conference. To attribute this telegram as proof of 'Tiso's loyalty toward Hitler's Nazism' is neither logical nor fair.

"As a matter of fact, way back when the German Secret Service from Vienna announced to Berlin in August 1943 that on the occasion of the Pribina celebration in Nitra Tiso had spoken these exact words: 'If Italy deserts and becomes neutral or defects to the enemy, Romania and Hungary will follow suit. The Slovaks will then find it impossible to remain behind'. The agent then added, that Tiso's speech 'for the first time indicated that Slovakia presented itself as a fully independent state with its own capability of decision-making and national unity. Not a word referred to the Reich or the Fuhrer. **Tiso's attitude toward the Reich was so unprecedented, that in its report, the embassy spoke about this to the Foreign Ministry, noting that this was a first and that Tiso's attitude in this speech, while not directly hostile toward the Reich, communicated, in fact, a strong effort to distance himself from it**'. [the emphasis is Professor Durica's] – Secret document: Bundesarchiv, R70, Slowakia 181".

8   The Milovy Agreement was a compromise on division of state power, negotiated between 3 and 8 February, 1992. It proposed creation of three government entities – one in Slovakia, one in the Czech lands, and a common one in Prague. The vote by the Slovak National Council was deadlocked with 10 pro, and 10 con. With this deadlock the last attempt at compromise failed. The matter then rested with the general elections of June 1992. Vladimir Meciar's Movement for a Democratic Slovakia, which had campaigned for creation of a confederation, was victorious in Slovakia. However, confederation was unacceptable to Czechs. A new stalemate resulted. Meciar then met with Vaclav Klaus, the Czech leader, with a resultant decision to dissolve the Czecho-Slovak Federative Republic. The dissolution was subsequently ratified by both the Slovak National Council and the Czecho-Slovak Parliament. The Czecho-Slovak Federative Republic thus ceased to exist. D. Kovac, *Dejiny Slovenska*. Praha: 1998, p. 320.

Central Europe, 9th Century

Spheres of influence

- ▓ Bulgarian Empire, 889
- ▓ Papal States after 814
- ▓ Moravian Empire, 836
- ▓ Frankish Kingdom and the Duchy of Benevento, 843
- ▓ Byzantine Empire, ca. 890
- ▓ Kievan Rus', 912

- Farthest extent of Greater Moravia, ca. 894
- Bulgarian Empire, 927
- ◄ Arrival of the Magyars
- ◄ Magyar raids
- ◄ Arab raids
- SERBS Slavic peoples
- VLACHS Romance peoples
- KURS Baltic peoples
- **MAGYARS** Finno-Ugric peoples
- ● Major concentrations of Magyar tribes, 10th century

0   150 miles
0   150 kilometers
Scale 1:8 890 000

Central Europe, 1918–1923

International boundaries, 1914
Hungarian Kingdom, 1914
International boundaries, 1923
Soviet republic boundaries, 1923
Temporary boundaries, 1918-23
Curzon line
Plebiscite area
Demilitarized 'Zone of the Straits'

Allied-Hungarian demarcation line, November 1918
Farthest advance of Hungarian communist troops, June 1919
Farthest advance of Polish troops, June 1920
Farthest advance of Soviet troops, August 1920
Internationalized rivers

0   150 miles
0   150 kilometers
Scale 1:8 890 000

Slovakia in the 20th Century

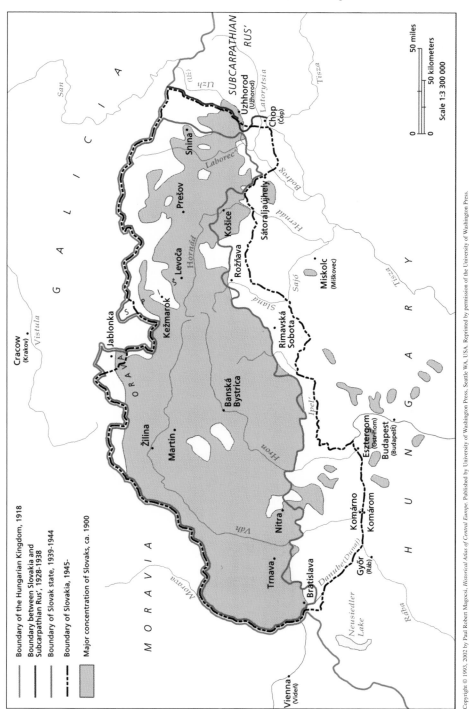

Boundary of the Hungarian Kingdom, 1918

Boundary between Slovakia and
Subcarpathian Rus', 1928-1938

Boundary of Slovak state, 1939-1944

Boundary of Slovakia, 1945-

Major concentration of Slovaks, ca. 1900

Central Europe, ca. 1930

1 LIPPE
2 BRUNSWICK
3 ANHALT
4 THURINGIA

⊙	State capitals
⊙	Capitals of kingdoms, duchies, principalities, and socialist republics
•	Provincial capitals
○	District or county centers
ZETA	Names of provinces and administrative subdivisions other than their capitals or centers

- - - - International boundaries, 1930

———— Boundaries of kingdoms, duchies, principalities, free cities and Soviet republics

– – – – Boundaries of provinces and autonomous republics

·········· Boundaries of districts and counties

0   150 miles

0   150 kilometers

Scale 1:8 890 000

Central Europe, ca. 1930

Districts and counties, ca. 1930
(Seat indicated in parentheses if different from district or county name)

Hungary
1. Sopron
2. Györ-Moson-Pozsony (Györ)
3. Komárom-Esztergom (Esztergom)
4. Nógrád-Hont (Balassagyarmat)
5. Heves (Eger)
6. Borsod-Gömör-Kishont (Miskolc)
7. Abaúj-Torna (Szikszo)
8. Zemplén (Sátoraljaújhely)
9. Szabolcs-Ung (Nyíregyháza)
10. Szatmár-Bereg-Ugocsa (Máteszalka)
11. Vas (Szombathely)
12. Veszprém
13. Fejér (Székesfehérvár)
14. Pest-Pilis-Solt-Kiskun (Budapest)
15. Jász-Nagy-Kun-Szolnok (Szolnok)
16. Hajdú (Debrecen)
17. Bihar (Berettyóújfalu)
18. Zala (Zalaegerszeg)
19. Somogy (Kaposvár)
20. Tolna (Szekszárd)
21. Baranya (Pécs)
22. Bács-Bodrog (Baja)
23. Csongrád (Szentes)
24. Békés (Gyula)
25. Csanád-Arad-Torontál (Makó)

Romania
1. Satu-Mare
2. Maramureş (Sighet)
3. Rădăuţi
4. Storojineţ
5. Cernăuţi (Chernivtsi)
6. Hotin (Khotyn)
7. Soroca
8. Sălaj (Zalău)
9. Someş (Dej)
10. Năsăud (Bistriţa)
11. Cîmpulung (Cîmpulung Moldovenesc)
12. Suceava
13. Dorohoi
14. Botoşani
15. Bălţi
16. Orhei
17. Bihor (Oradea)
18. Cluj
19. Mureş (Tîrgu Mureş)
20. Neamţ (Piatra Neamţ)
21. Fălticeni
22. Roman
23. Iaşi
24. Vaslui
25. Fălciu (Huşi)
26. Lăpuşna (Chişinău)
27. Tighina (Bendery/Tighina)
28. Arad
29. Turda
30. Alba (Alba Iulia)
31. Tîrnava Mica (Blaj)
32. Tîrnava Mare (Sighişoara)
33. Odorhei
34. Ciuc (Miercurea Ciuc)
35. Trei Scaune (Sft. Gheorghe)
36. Putna (Focşani)
37. Bacău
38. Tecuci
39. Tutova (Bîrlad)
40. Covurlui (Galaţi)
41. Cahul
42. Ismail (Izmaïl)
43. Cetatea Albă (Bilhorod)
44. Timiş-Torontal (Timişoara)
45. Caraş (Oraviţa)
46. Severin (Lugoj)
47. Hunedoara (Deva)
48. Sibiu
49. Făgăraş
50. Braşov
51. Mehedinţi (Drobeta-Turnu Severin)
52. Gorj (Tîrgu Jiu)
53. Vîlcea (Rîmnicu Vîlcea)
54. Argeş (Piteşti)
55. Muscel (Cîmpulung)
56. Dîmboviţa (Tîrgovişte)
57. Prahova (Ploieşti)
58. Buzău
59. Rîmnicu Sărat
60. Brăila
61. Tulcea
62. Dolj (Craiova)
63. Romanaţi (Caracal)
64. Olt (Slatina)
65. Teleorman (Turnu Măgurele)
66. Vlaşca (Giurgiu)
67. Ilfov (Bucharest)
68. Ialomiţa (Călăraşi)
69. Durostor (Silistra)
70. Constanţa
71. Caliacra (Balchik)

Bulgaria
1. Vidin
2. Vratsa
3. Pleven
4. Tŭrnovo
5. Ruse
6. Shumen
7. Varna
8. Kyustendil
9. Sofia
10. Plovdiv
11. Stara Zagora (Nova Zagora)
12. Burgas
13. Petrich
14. Pashmakli (Smolyan)
15. Khaskovo
16. Mustanli (Momchilgrad)

Albania
1. Shkodër
2. Kosovë (Kukës)
3. Dibër (Peshkopi)
4. Durrës
5. Tiranë
6. Elbasan
7. Berat
8. Korçë
9. Vlorë
10. Gjirokastër

Greece
1. Florina
2. Pella
3. Kilkis
4. Serrai
5. Drama
6. Kavalla
7. Rhodope (Komotiní)
8. Évros (Alexandroúpolis)
9. Kozánē
10. Thessalonike (Salonika)
11. Chalcidice (Polygyros)
12. Mount Athos (Karyai)
13. Corfu/Kérkira
14. Ioannina
15. Trikkala
16. Larissa
17. Lesbos (Mytilene)
18. Préveza
19. Arta
20. Aetolia and Acarnania (Mesolóngion)
21. Phthiotis and Phocis (Amphissa)
22. Euboea/Évvoia (Chalcis)
23. Cephalonia/Kefallinia (Argostolion)
24. Zante/Zákinthos
25. Elis (Pyrgos)
26. Achaea (Patras)
27. Corinth/Kórinthos and Argolis (Corinth)
28. Attica and Boeotia (Athens)
29. Chios/Khíos
30. Arcadia (Tripolis)
31. Messenia/Messíní (Kalamata)
32. Laconia/Lakonikós (Sparta)
33. Cyclades/Kikládhes (Hermoupolis)
34. Samos (Vathy)
35. Canea/Khaniá
36. Rethýmnē (Rethymnon)
37. Hērákleion (Candia)
38. Lasithion (Hagios Nikólaos)

Central Europe, 2000

State capitals
Capitals of federal republics
and German states
Capitals of autonomous regions
Province, district, county, or oblast centers

- - - · - - - International boundaries, 2000
- - - - Boundaries of federal republics
and German states
- - - - - Boundaries of autonomous regions
· · · · · · · · · Boundaries of provinces, districts,
counties, and oblasts

KOSOVO Names of autonomous regions
and other administrative subdivisions
other than their capitals or centers

0   150 miles
0   150 kilometers
Scale 1:8 890 000

Central Europe, 2000

Districts, counties, regions, and provinces, 2000 (Seat indicated in parentheses if different from district or county name)

Austria
1. Upper Austria (Linz)
2. Lower Austria (St. Pölten)
3. Vorarlberg (Bregenz)
4. Tyrol (Innsbruck)
5. Salzburg (Salzburg)
6. Styria (Graz)
7. Burgenland (Eisenstadt)
8. Carinthia (Klagenfurt)
9. Vienna

Hungary
1. Györ-Moson-Sopron (Györ)
2. Komárom-Esztergom (Tatabánya)
3. Nógrád (Sálgótarján)
4. Heves (Eger)
5. Borsod-Abaúj-Zemplén (Miskolc)
6. Szabolcs-Szatmár-Bereg (Nyíregyháza)
7. Vas (Szombathely)
8. Veszprém
9. Fejér (Székesfehérvár)
10. Pest (Budapest)
11. Jász-Nagykun-Szolnok
12. Hajdú-Bíhar (Debrecen)

13. Zala (Zalaegerszeg)
14. Somogy (Kaposvár)
15. Baranya (Pécs)
16. Tolna (Szekszárd)
11. Bács-Kiskun (Kecskemét)
18. Csongrád (Szeged)
19. Békés (Békéscsaba)
20. Budapest

Romania
1. Satu-Mare
2. Maramureş (Baia Mare)
3. Suceava
4. Botoşani
5. Bihor (Oradea)
6. Sălaj (Zalău)
7. Cluj (Cluj-Napoca)
8. Bistriţa-Năsăud (Bistriţa)
9. Mureş (Tirgu Mureş)
10. Harghita (Miercurea Ciuc)
11. Neamţ (Piatra Neamţ)
12. Iaşi
13. Bacău
14. Vaslui
15. Arad
16. Timiş (Timişoara)
17. Hunedoara (Deva)
18. Alba (Alba Iulia)
19. Sibiu

20. Braşov
21. Covasna (Sfintu Gheorghe)
22. Vrancea (Focşani)
23. Galaţi
24. Caraş-Severín (Resita)
25. Gorj (Tîrgu Jiu)
26. Vîlcea (Rîmnicu Vîlcea)
27. Argeş (Piteşti)
28. Dîmboviţa (Tirgovişte)
29. Prahova (Ploieşti)
30. Buzău
31. Brăila
32. Tulcea
33. Mehedinţi (Drobeta-Turnu Severin)
34. Dolj (Craiova)
35. Olt (Slatina)
36. Teleorman (Alexandria)
37. Giurgiu
38. Ialomiţa (Slobozia)
39. Călăraşi
40. Constanţa
41. Bucharest

Bibliography

BOOKS

Abrahám, Samuel. 'The Rise and Fall of Illiberal Democracy in Slovakia, 1989-1998: An Analysis of Transformation in a Post-Communist Society' (Dissertation). Carleton University, 2001.

Ash, T. G. *The Magic Lantern: The Revolution of 1989.* New York: Random House, 1990.

Axworthy, Mark W. *Axis Slovakia: Hitler's Slavic Wedge, 1938-1945.* Bayside, NY: Axis Europa Books, 2002.

Bakker, E. *Minority Conflicts in Slovakia and Hungary.* Capelle and Ijssel: Labyrinth Publication, 1997.

Balawyder, A. (Ed.), *Cooperative Movements in Eastern Europe.* Santa Fe, NM: Pro Libertate Publishing, 1989.

Banac, I. (Ed.), *Eastern Europe in the 1990's.* Ithaca, NY: Cornell University Press, 1991.

Baumgarten, V. 'Slovakia in the Revolution of 1848' (Dissertation). University of Florida, 1982.

Benes, E. *Mnichovske dny*: *Pameti* (Memoirs of Munich). Praha: Svoboda, 1968.

__, *Sest let exilu a druhe svetove valky* (Six Years of Exile and World War II). Praha: Orbis, 1946.

Berend, I. T. and Ranki, G. *Economic Development in East-Central Europe in the 19th and 20th Centuries.* New York and London: 1974.

__, *Hungary: A Century of Economic Development.* New York: Barnes and Noble, 1974.

Bielik, F. (Ed.), *Slovaci vo svete II* (Slovaks in the World II). Martin: Matica Slovenska, 1980.

Bloomfield, J. *Passive Revolution: Politics and the Czechoslovak Working Class 1945–1948.* London: Allison and Busby, 1979.

Bloss, E. *Labor Legislation in Czechoslovakia with Special Reference to the Standards of the International Labor Organization.* New York: Columbia University Press, 1939.

Bogdan, H. *From Warsaw to Sophia: A History of Eastern Europe.* Sante Fe, NM: Pro Libertate Publishing, 1989.

Boker, H. *The Rural Exodus in Czechoslovakia.* Geneva International Labor Organization Report, 1935.

The Cividal Gospel

372

Bokes, F. *Slovenska vlastiveda: Dejiny Slovakov a Slovenska od najstarsich cias az po pritomnost* (Slovak History and Geography: A History of the Slovaks from the Earliest Times to the Present). Bratislava: SAV, 1946.

Borovicka, J. *Ten Years of Czechoslovak Politics.* Prague: Orbis, 1929.

Bosl, K. (Ed.), *Die demokratisch-parlamentarische Struktur der ersten tschechoslowakischen Republik* (The Democratic-Parliamentary Structure of the First Czechoslovak Republic). Munich: 1975.

__, *Die erste tschechoslowakische Republik als multinationaler Partienstaat* (The First Czechoslovak Republic as a Multinational State). Munchen-Wien: 1979.

__, *Handbuch der Geschichte der bohmischen Lander: Die bohmischen Lander in Habsburgerreich 1848–1919;* and *Der tschechoslowakische Staat in Zeitalter der modernen Massendemokratie und Diktatur,* 4 vols. (A Handbook of the History of the Czech Lands: The Czech Lands in the Habsburg Monarchy 1848–1919; and The Czechoslovak State in the Age of Modern Popular Democracy and Dictatorship, 4 Vols.). Stuttgart: 1968–1970.

__, *Die Slowakei als mitteleuropaische Problem in Geschichte und Gegenwart* (Slovakia as a Central European Problem in History and in the Present). Munchen: Verlag Robert Lerche, 1965.

Bradley, J.F.N. *Czechoslovakia: a Short History.* Edinburgh: 1971.

__, *Czechoslovakia's Velvet Revolution: A Political Analysis.* Boulder: East European Monographs, 1992.

Brisch, H. and Volgyes, I. (Eds.), *Czechoslovakia: The Heritage of Ages Past.* Boulder: East European Quarterly, 1979.

Brock, P. *The Slovak National Awakening.* Toronto: University of Toronto Press, 1976.

Brown, J. F. *Eastern Europe and Communist Rule.* Durham, NC: Duke University Press, 1988.

__, *Surge to Freedom: The End of Communist Rule in Eastern Europe.* Durham, NC: Duke University Press, 1994

Broz, A. *The First Year of the Czecho-Slovak Republic.* London: 1920.

Buchvalek, M. et al. *Dejiny Ceskoslovenska v datech* (Dates in Czechoslovak History). Praha: 1968.

Butora, M. and Huncik, P. (Eds.), *Global Report on Slovakia: Comprehensive Analyses from 1995 and Trends from 1996.* Bratislava: Sandor Marai Foundation, 1997.

Butora, M.; Meseznikov, G.; Butorova, Z.; and Fisher, S. (Eds.), *The 1998 Parliamentary Elections and Democratic Rebirth in Slovakia.* Bratislava:

*Old Slavonic
Order of Confession*

Institute for Public Affairs, 1999.

Butora, Z. (Ed.), *Democracy and Discontent in Slovakia: A Public Opinion Profile of a Country in Transition.* Bratislava: Institute for Public Affairs, 1998.

Butora, Z. and Butora, M. *Slovensko rok po: cesty a krizovatky noveho statu ocami jeho obyvatelov* (Slovakia a Year After: the Roads and Crossroads of a New State in the Eyes of its Inhabitants). Praha: SLON, 1994.

Butora, Z. et al. *Aktualne problemy Slovenska na prelome rokov 1995–1996* (Pressing Problems of Slovakia 1995–1996). Bratislava: FOCUS, 1996.

Butvin, J. *Slovenske narodnozjednocovacie hnutie 1780–1848* (Slovak National Unification Movement 1780–1848). Bratislava: SAV, 1965.

Butvin, J. et al. *Dejiny Slovenska slovom i obrazom* II (History of Slovakia in Words and Pictures II). Bratislava: Osveta, 1982.

Butvin, J. and Havranek, J. *Dejiny Ceskoslovenska* (History of Czechoslovakia), 3 vols. Praha: SNPL, 1968.

Cada, V. *Strategia a taktika KSC v rokoch 1921–1938* (Strategy and Tactics of the Czechoslovak Communist Party, 1921–1938). Bratislava: Pravda, 1982.

Cambel, S. (Ed.), *Dejiny Slovenska: 1918–1945* (History of Slovakia V: 1918–1945). Bratislava: SAV, 1985.

Capek, M. and Hruby, K. (Eds.), *T. G. Masaryk in Perspective: Comments and Criticism.* [S.I.]: SVU Press, 1981.

Capek, T. *The Slovaks of Hungary.* New York: Fleming H. Revel Co., 1915.

Carsten, F. L. *Revolution in Central Europe, 1918–1919.* London: 1972.

Cervinka, F. *Prehled dejin Ceskoslovenska v epose kapitalismu* (Survey of Czechoslovak History in the Era of Capitalism). Praha: Statni pedagogicke nakladatelství, 1963.

Ceskoslovenska vlastiveda: Dejiny II (Czechoslovak History and Geography: History II). Praha: Horizont, 1969.

Chaloupecky, V. *Zapas o Slovensko 1918* (Struggle for Slovakia in 1918). Praha: 1930.

Cierna-Lantayova, D. *Podoby cesko-slovensko-madarskeho vztahu 1938–1949* (The Nature of Czech-Slovak-Hungarian Relations 1938–1949). Bratislava: VEDA, 1992.

Chirot, D. (Ed.), *Origins of Backwardness in Eastern Europe: Economics and Politics from the Middle Ages until the Early Twentieth Century.* Berkley: University of California Press, 1989.

Chmelar, J. *Political Parties in Czechoslovakia.* Prague: Orbis, 1926.

Chovanec, J. *Path to Sovereignty of the Slovak Republic.* Bratislava: Slovak Information Agency, 1996.

Cohen, S. J. *Politics without a Past: Absence of History in Postcommunist Nationalism.* Durham: Duke University Press, 1999.

Crane, J.O. and S. *Czechoslovakia: Anvil of the Cold War.* New York: Praeger, 1991.

Cross, S. H. *Slavic Civilization through the Ages.* New York: Russel & Russel, 1963.

Crowe, D. and Koltsi, J. (Eds.). *Gypsies in Eastern Europe.* Armonk, NY: M.E. Sharpe, 1991.

Curta, F. 'Making an Early Medieval *Ethnie:* Case of the Early Slavs, Sixth to Seventh Century A.D.' (Dissertation, 2 vols.). Michigan: Western Michigan University, 1998.

Czech and Slovak Experience: Selected Papers from the Fourth World Congress for Soviet and European Studies. Harrogate: 1990.

Czechoslovakia: Crossroads and Crises 1918–1988. New York: St. Martin's Press, 1989.

Dalin, D. G. *The Myth of Hitler's Pope: How Pope Pius XII Rescued Jews from the Nazis.* Washington, DC: Regnery Publishing, 2005.

Deak, I. *The Lawful Revolution: Louis Kossuth and the Hungarians 1848–1849.* New York: Columbia University Press, 1979.

Deak, L. *Hungary's Game for Slovakia: Slovakia in Hungarian Politics in the Years 1933–1939.* Bratislava: 1996.

Dean, R. W. *Nationalism and Political Change in Eastern Europe: the Slovak Question and Czechoslovak Reform Movement.* Denver: Denver University, 1973.

Derer, I. *The Unity of the Czechs and Slovaks.* Prague: Orbis, 1938.

Doellinger, David Paul. 'From Prayers to Protests: The Impact of Religious-Based Dissent on the Emergence of Civil Society in Slovakia and the GDR' (Dissertation). University of Pittsburgh, 2002.

Domarus, M. *Hitler: Speeches and Proclamations 1932–1945* (4 vols.). Wauconda, IL: Bolchazy-Carducci Publishers, 1990–2004. (*Hitler. Reden und Proklamationen 1932–1945: Kommentiert von einem deutschen Zeitgenossen.* Leonberg, Germany: Pamminger & Partner Verlagsgesellschaft mbH, 1973, revised 1988.)

Doob, L. W. *Patriotism and Nationalism: Their Psychological Foundations.* New Haven: Yale University Press, 1964.

Dubcek, A. *Hope Dies Last: Autobiography of Alexander Dubcek.* New York: Kodanska International, 1993.

Duchacek, I. *Strategy of Communist Infiltration: The Case of Czechoslovakia.* New Haven: Yale University Press, 1949.

Durica, M. S. *Cultural Relations between Slovakia and Italy in Modern Times.* Padova: CESE–Liviana Editrice, 1983.

__. *Katolicka cirkev na Slovensku 1938–1945 v hodnoteni nemeckych diplomatov a tajnych agentov* (The Catholic Church in Slovakia 1938–1945 in the Evaluation of German Diplomats and Secret Agents). Trnava: SSV, 2001.

__. *Dr. Jozef Tiso: Slovensky knaz a statnik 1887–1939* (Tiso: A Slovak Priest and Stateman 1887–1939). Matica Slovenska: 1992.

__. *Dejiny Slovenska a Slovakov* (History of Slovakia and the Slovaks). Bratislava: 1996, revised 2003.

Dvornik, F. *Making of Central and Eastern Europe.* Golf Breeze, FL: Academic International Press, 1974.

__. *The Slavs: Their Early History and Civilization.* Boston: American Academy of Arts and Sciences, 1956.

Eidlin, F. H. *The Logic of 'Normalization': The Soviet Intervention in Czechoslovakia of 21 August 1968 and the Czechoslovak Response.* New York: Columbia University Press, 1980.

El Mallakh, D. H. *The Slovak Autonomy Movement 1935–1939.* Boulder: East European Monographs, 1979.

Encyklopedia Slovenska (vols. I–IV). Bratislava: SAV, 1977–1982.

Entlerova, L. *The October Revolution and Czechoslovakia.* Prague: Orbis, 1977.

Faltan, S. *Slovenska otazka v Ceskoslovensku* (The Slovak Question in Czechoslovakia). Bratislava: 1968.

Faltus, J. *Povojnova hospodarska kriza v Ceskoslovensku v rokoch 1921–1923* (The Post-War Economic Crisis in Czechoslovakia in 1921–1923). Bratislava: 1966.

Faltus, J. and Prucha, V. *Prehlad hospodarskeho vyvoja na Slovensku v rokoch 1918–1945* (Survey of Economic Development in Slovakia between 1918 – 1945). Bratislava: Vydavatelstvo politickej literatury, 1969.

Felak, J. R. *'At the Price of the Republic': Hlinka's Slovak People's Party, 1929–1938.* Pittsburgh: 1994.

Focus. *Aktualne problemy Slovenska po rozpade CSFR Oktober 1993* (Pressing Problems of Slovakia after the Break-up of the Czecho-Slovak Federative Republic 1993). Bratislava: 1993.

Fredegarii Chronicorum Liber Quartus cum Continuationibus ('Fourth Book of the Chronicles of Fredegar and Sequels', translated from the Latin with introduction and notes by J. M. Wallace-Hadrill.) London: Thomas Nelson and Sons Ltd., 1960.

Fric, P. et al. *Madarska mensina na Slovensku* (The Hungarian Minority in Slovakia). Praha: Hic et Nunc, 1993.

Frydman, R. et al. *Capitalism with a Comrade's Face*. Budapest: Central European University Press, 1998.

Fugedi, E. *Castles and Society in Medieval Hungary 1000–1437*. Budapest: Akademiai Kiado, 1986.

__. *Kings, Bishops, Nobles and Burghers in Medieval Hungary*. London: Variorum Reprints, 1986.

Gajda, V. *Modern Austria: Her Racial and Social Problems*. New York: Dodd, Mead and Co., 1915.

Gati, C. *The Bloc that Failed: Soviet-East European Relations in Transition*. Bloomington: Indiana University Press, 1990.

Gellner, E. *Nations and Nationalism*. Ithaca: Cornell University Press, 1983.

Gesta Hungarorum (The Deeds of the Hungarians [Magyars]), translated from the Latin by L. Veszpremy, et. al. Budapest: Central European University Press, 1999.

Glaser, K. *Czechoslovakia: a Critical History*. Cardwell, Idaho: The Caxton Printers, 1961.

Glettler, M. *Pittsburgh–Wien–Budapest: Programm und Praxis der National-itatenpolitik bei der Auswanderung der Ungarischen Slowaken nach America um 1900* (Pittsburgh–Vienna–Budapest: Nationality Politics and Practice Affecting the Emigration of Hungarian Slovaks to America around 1900). Vienna: Osterreichische Akademie der Wissenschaften, 1980.

Golan, G. *The Czechoslovak Reform Movement: Communism in Crisis, 1962–1968*. Cambridge: Cambridge University Press, 1971.

__. *Reform Rule in Czechoslovakia: the Dubcek Era 1968–1969*. Cambridge: Cambridge University Press, 1973.

Golan, K. et al. *Ceskoslovenske dejiny* (Czechoslovak History). Bratislava: Osveta, 1961.

Goldman, M. F. *Slovakia Since Independence: A Struggle for Democracy*. Westport: Greenwood Publishing, 1999.

Gruber, J. (Ed.), *Czechoslovakia: a Survey of Economic and Social Conditions*. New York: 1924.

Hajda, J. (Ed.), *Czechoslovakia*. New Haven: Human Relations Area Files, Inc. 1955.

Hajdu, Tibor. *The Hungarian Soviet Republic*. Budapest: Akademiai Kiado, 1979.

Hammond, T. (Ed.), *The Anatomy of Communist Takeovers*. New Haven: Yale University Press, 1975.

Harris, Erika. *Nationalism and Democratization: Politics of Slovakia and Slovenia.* Burlington, Vt.: Ashgate, 2002.

Havel, V. *Disturbing the Peace: a Conversation with Karel Hvizdala.* New York: Alfred A. Knopf, 1990.

Henderson, Karen. *Slovakia: The Escape from Invisibility.* New York: Routledge, 2002.

Hermann, A. H. *A History of the Czechs.* London: Allen Lane, 1975.

Hoensch, Jörg K. *A History of Modern Hungary 1867-1994.* New York: Longman, 1995.

Hoch, C. *The Political Parties of Czechoslovakia.* Prague: Orbis, 1936.

Hodza, M. *Federation in Central Europe.* London: Jarrolds Publishers, Ltd. 1942.

Hoensch, J. K. *Die Slowakei und Hitlers Ostpolitik* (Slovakia and Hitler's Policies for Eastern Europe). Koln: Bohlau Verlag, 1965.

___. *Dokumenten zur Autonomiepolitik des Slowakischen Volkspartei Hlinkas* (Documents of the Policies of Hlinka's Slovak People's Party on Autonomy). Munchen: Oldenbourg Verlag, 1984.

___. *Geschichte der Tschechoslowakischen Republik 1918 bis 1965* (History of the Czechoslovak Republic from 1918 to 1965). Stuttgart: W. Kohlhammer Verlag, 1966.

___. *A History of Modern Hungary 1867–1986.* New York: 1988.

Hoffman, Eva. *Exit into History: A Journey through the New Eastern Europe.* New York: Viking, 1993.

Hrabovec, E. *Der Heilige Stuhl und die Slowakei 1918–1922 im Kontext internationaler.* Frankfurt am Main: Peter Lang, 2002.

Hruby, P. *Fools and Heroes: The Changing Role of Communist Intellectuals in Czechoslovakia.* Oxford: Pergamon Press, 1980.

Hrusovsky, F. *This is Slovakia.* Cambridge, ON: Friends of Good Books, 1978.

Hungarians in Slovakia. Information Centre of the Hungarian Coalition in Slovakia. Bratislava: 1997.

Husak, G. *Speeches and Writings.* New York: 1986.

___. *Svedectvo o Slovenskom narodnom povstani* (Reports on the Slovak National Uprising). Bratislava: Vydavatelstvo politickej literatury, 1964.

Ihnat, J. Editor/Translator, et al. *General Milan R. Stefanik.* New York: Gross Bros. Printing Co., 1981.

Immer, I. 'Struggle for Slovakia 1780–1918' (Dissertation). Rice University, 1979.

Innes, A. *Czechoslovakia: the Short Goodbye.* New Haven: Yale University

Press, 2001.

Jahn, E. *Die Deutschen in der Slowakei 1918–1929: Ein Beitrag zur Natio-nalitatenproblematik* (Germans in Slovakia 1918–1929: An Essay on Problems of Ethnicity). Munchen-Wein: 1971.

Janos, A. C. *The Politics of Backwardness in Hungary 1825–1945.* Princeton: 1982.

Jaszi, O. *Dissolution of the Habsburg Monarchy.* Chicago: University of Chicago Press, 1971 (orig. 1927).

Jelinek, Y. A. *The Lust for Power: Nationalism, Slovakia, and the Communists 1918–1948.* Boulder: East European Monographs, 1983.

___. *The Parish Republic: Hlinka's Slovak People's Party 1939–1945.* Denver: 1976.

Johnson, O. *Slovakia 1918–1938: Education and the Making of the Nation.* New York: Columbia University Press, 1985.

Josko, A. 'Slovak Resistant Movement', *History of the Czecho-Slovak republic 1918–1948.*

Juricek, J. *Milan Rastislav Stefanik.* Elmhurst, NY: Nase snahy, 1980.

Kabos, E. and Zsilak, A. (Eds.), *Studies in the History of the Hungarian Trade Union Movement.* Budapest: 1977.

Kalvoda, J. *Czechoslovakia's Role in Soviet Strategy.* Washington: University Press of America, 1978.

___. *Genesis of Czechoslovakia.* Boulder: East European Monographs, 1986.

Kann, R. A. *The Multinational Empire: Nationalism and National Reform in the Habsburg Monarchy 1849–1918* (2 vols.). New York: Columbia University Press, 1950.

___. *The Habsburg Monarchy 1804–1918.* Princeton: D. Van Nostrand Co., 1961.

Kaplan, K. *The Communist Party in Power: A Profile of Party Politics in Czechoslovakia* (Translated and edited by Fred Eidlen). Boulder: Westview Press, 1987.

___. *The Short March: The Communist Takeover in Czechoslovakia 1945–1948.* New York: 1987.

Kerner, R. J. *Czechoslovakia: Twenty Years of Independence.* Berkley: University of California Press, 1940.

Kirschbaum, J. M. *Slovakia: Nation at the Crossroads of Central Europe.* New York: Robert Speller & Sons, 1960.

___. (Ed.), *Slovak Culture through the Centuries.* Toronto: Slovak World Congress, 1978.

___. (Ed.), *Slovakia in the 19th and 20th Centuries* (2nd ed.). Toronto: Slovak World Congress, 1978.

Kirschbaum, S. J. (Ed.), *East-European History.* Columbus: Slavica Publishers, 1988.

___. *History of Slovakia: A Struggle for Survival.* New York: St Martin's Press, 1995.

___. *Historical Dictionary of Slovakia.* Lanham, MD: Scarecrow Press, 1998.

___. (Ed.), *Slovak Politics: Essays on Slovak History in Honor of Joseph M. Kirschbaum.* Cleveland: Slovak Institute, 1983.

Kirschbaum, S. J. and Roman, A. C. R. (Eds.). 'Reflections on Slovak History'. Toronto: Slovak World Congress, 1987.

Komlos, J. *The Habsburg Monarchy as a Customs Union.* Princeton: Princeton University Press, 1983.

Kopanic, M. J., Jr. 'Industrial Trade Unions in Slovakia, 1918–1929' (Doctoral Dissertation). University of Pittsburgh, 1986.

Korbel, J. *Communist Subversion of Czechoslovakia, 1938–1948.* Princeton: Princeton University Press, 1959.

___. *Twentieth Century Czechoslovakia: The Meaning of its History.* New York: Columbia University Press, 1977.

Korec, J. Ch. *The Night of the Barbarians: Memoirs of the Communist Persecution of the Slovak Cardinal.* Wauconda, IL: Bolchazy-Carducci Publishers, Inc., 2002.

Kovac, D. *Dejiny Slovenska* (History of Slovakia). Praha: Nakladatelstvi Lidove noviny, 1998.

___. *Slovaci – Cesi – Dejiny* (The Slovaks – The Czechs – A History). Bratislava: AEP, 1997.

Kovtun, G. J. *The Czechoslovak Declaration of Independence: A History of the Document.* Washington: Library of Congress, 1985.

Kramoris, I. J. *A Chronological Outline of Slovak Literature and History from the Sixth Century to 1939.* Passaic: Slovak Catholic Sokol, 1936.

Krejci, J. *Ethnic and Political Nations in Europe.* New York: St. Martin's Press, 1981.

___. *Social Change and Stratification in Post-War Czechoslovakia.* New York: Columbia University Press, 1972.

Krejci, J. and Machonin, P. *Social Change and Stratification in Post-War Czechoslovakia 1918–1992: A Laboratory for Change.* Basingstoke: Macmillan, 1996.

Krivy, V; Feglova, V.; and Daniel, B. *Slovensko a jeho regiony: Sociokulturne suvislosti volebneho spravania* (Slovakian Regions: Socio-Cultural Relationships Affecting Voting Patterns). Bratislava: Nadacia Media, 1996.

Krofta, K. *A Short History of Czechoslovakia.* New York: 1934.

Kusin, V. V. *The Intellectual Origins of the Prague Spring: The Development of Reformist Ideas in Czechoslovakia 1956–1967.* Cambridge: Cambridge University Press, 1971.

___. *From Dubcek to Charter 77: A Study of 'Normalization' in Czechoslovakia, 1968–1978.* New York: St. Martin's Press, 1978.

Leff, C. S. *The Czech and Slovak Republics: Nation versus State.* Boulder: Westview Press, 1997.

___. *National Conflict in Czechoslovakia: The Making and Remaking of a State 1918–1987.* Princeton: Princeton University Press, 1988.

Lengyel, E. *1000 years of Hungary.* New York: The John Day Co., 1958.

Lesko, M. *Meciar a meciarizmus* (Meciar and Meciarism). Bratislava: VMW, 1996.

Lettrich, J. *History of Modern Slovakia.* New York: Praeger, 1953.

Lipscher, L. *Zidia v Slovenskom state 1939–1945* (Jews in the Slovak State 1939–1945). Banska Bystrica: Print Servis, 1992.

___. *K vyvinu politickej spravy na Slovensku 1918–1938* (Development of Political Administration in Slovakia 1918–1938). Bratislava: 1966.

___. *Ludacka autonomia – Iluzie a skutocnost* (Ludak Autonomy – Illusions and Reality). Bratislava: SVPL, 1957.

Liptak, L. *Slovensko v 20. storoci* (Slovakia in the 20th Century). Bratislava: Kalligram, 2000.

Luza, R. *The Transfer of the Sudeten Germans: A Study of German-Czech Relations, 1933–1962.* New York: New York University Press, 1964.

Macartney, C. A. *The Habsburg Empire 1790–1918.* New York: Macmillan, 1969.

___. *Hungary and Her Successors: The Treaty of Trianon and its Consequences 1919–1937.* London: 1937.

Macartney, C. A. and Palmer, A. W. *Independent Eastern Europe.* London: Macmillan, 1966.

Magocsi, R. M. *Historical Atlas of Central Europe.* Washington: University of Washington Press, 2002.

Mamatey, V. S. *The United States and East Central Europe 1914–1918: A Study in Wilsonian Diplomacy and Propaganda.* Princeton: Princeton University Press, 1957.

Mamatey, V., Luza, R. (Eds.), *History of the Czecho-Slovak Republic 1918–1948.* Princeton: Princeton University Press, 1973.

Mannova, E. (Ed.), *Concise History of Slovakia* (Trans. by Martin C. Styan and David P. Daniel). Bratislava: Historicky ustav SAV, 2000.

Markus, J. *Zaujem o planovanie a zaujmy v planovani* (Interest in Planning and Planning Interests). Bratislava: Nakladatelstvo Pravda, 1988.

Marsina, R. et al. *Slovenske dejiny* (Slovak History). Martin: Matica Slovenska, 1992.

___. *Dejiny Slovenska* (A History of Slovakia, 4 Vols.). Bratislava: Veda, 1986–1988.

Masaryk, T. G. *The Making of a State: Memories and Observations 1914–1918* (An English version, arranged and prepared with an introduction by Henry Wickham Steed). New York: Frederick A. Stokes Co., 1927.

May, A. J. *The Habsburg Monarchy 1867–1914*. Cambridge: Harvard University Press, 1951.

Maxwell, Alexander Mark. 'Choosing Slovakia 1795-1914: Slavic Hungary, the Czech Language, and Slovak Nationalism' (Dissertation). Madison: University of Wisconsin, 2003.

Meseznikov, G.; Ivantysyn, M.; and Nicholson, T. (Eds.). *Slovakia 1998–1999: A Global Report on the State of Society*. Bratislava: Institute for Public Affairs, 1999.

Meseznikov, G.; Kollar, M.; and Nicholson, T. (Eds.). *Slovakia 2000: A Global Report on the State of Society*. Bratislava: Institute for Public Affairs, 2001.

Miklosko, F. *Nebudete ich moct rozvratit: Z osudov katolickej cirkvi na Slovensku v rokoch 1943–1989* (You Will Not Be Able to Destroy Them: Trials of the Catholic Church in Slovakia 1943 to 1989). Bratislava: Vydavatelstvo Archa, 1991.

Mikus, J. A. *Slovakia: A Political History 1918–1950*. Milwaukee: Marquette University Press, 1963.

___. *Slovakia: A Misunderstood History*. Hamilton: The Battlefield Press, 1977.

___. *Slovakia and the Slovaks*. Toronto: Three Continents Press, 1977.

Mlynar, Z. *Nightfrost in Prague: The End of Humane Socialism* (Translated by Paul Wilson). New York: Karz Publishers, 1980.

Mlynarik, J. *Nezamestnanost na Slovensku 1918–1938* (Unemployment in Slovakia 1918–1938). Bratislava: Osveta, 1964.

Mommsen, H. *Die Sozialdemokratie und die Nationalitatenfrage in Habsburgischer Vielvolkerstaat* (Social Democracy and the Nationalities Question in the Multinational Habsburg Monarchy). Wien: 1963.

Murin, C. *Spomienky a svedectvo* (Remembrances and Testimony). Montreal: RealTime, 1992.

Musil, J. (Ed.), *End of Czechoslovakia*. Budapest: Central European University Press, 1995.

Myant, M. R. *Socialism and Democracy in Czechoslovakia 1945–1948*. Cambridge, MA: 1981.

Navratil, J. and Kural, V. *The Prague Spring '68*. Budapest: Central European University Press, 1998.

Navratil, J. et al. (Compiled and Edited). *The Prague Spring 1968*. Budapest: Central European University Press, 1998.

Nurmi, Ismo. Slovakia – *A Playground for Nationalism and National Identity: Manifestations of the National Identity of the Slovaks 1918-1920*. Helsinki: Suomen Historiallinen Seura, 1999.

Oddo, G. *Slovakia and Its People*. New York: R. Speller & Sons, Inc., 1960.

Olivova, V. *The Doomed Democracy: Czechoslovakia in a Disrupted Europe, 1914–1938*. London: 1972.

Ondruchova, M. *Organizacia politickych stran a hnuti na Slovensku* (The Organization of Political Parties and Movements in Slovakia). Bratislava: Institut pre verejne otazky, 2000.

Opocensky, J. *The Collapse of the Austro-Hungarian Monarchy and the Rise of the Czechoslovak State*. Prague: Orbis, 1928.

Osusky, S. *Benes and Slovakia*. Middletown, PA: Jednota Press, 1943.

Palickar, S. J. *Slovakian Culture in the Light of History*. Cambridge, MA: The Hampshire Press, Inc., 1954.

Pamlenyi, E. et al. *A History of Hungary* (Translated by Laszlo Boros, Istvan Farkas, Gyula Gulyas and Eva Rona). Collet's, 1975.

Paul, D. *The Cultural Limits of Revolutionary Politics: Change and Continuity in Socialist Czechoslovakia*. Boulder: East European Quarterly, 1979.

Pauliny, E. *Dejiny spisovnej slovenciny od zaciatkov po sucasnost* (History of Literary Slovak from Its Beginnings to the Present). Bratislava: Slovenske pedagogicke nakladatelstvo, 1983.

__. *Slovesnost a kulturny jazyk Velkej Moravy* (Literature and the Cultural Language of Great Moravia). Bratislava: Slovenske vydavatelstvo krasnej literatury, 1964.

__. *Zivot a dielo Metoda, prvoucitela naroda slovienskeho* (Life and Work of Methodius, First Teacher of the 'Slovene' Nation). Bratislava: Tatran, 1985.

Pech, S. Z. *The Czech Revolution of 1848*. Chapel Hill, NC: University of North Carolina Press, 1969.

Pelikan, J. (Ed.), *The Czechoslovak Political Trials 1950–1954: The Suppressed Report of the Dubcek Government's Commission of Inquiry 1968*. Stanford: Stanford University Press, 1971.

Perman, D. *The Shaping of the Czechoslovak State: A Diplomatic History of the Boundaries of Czechoslovakia 1914–1920*. Leeds: F. J. Brill, 1962.

Pielalkiewicz, J. *Public Opinion in Czechoslovakia 1968–1969: Results and Analysis of Surveys Conducted During the Dubcek Era.* New York: Praeger Publishers, 1972.

Peroutka, F. *Budovani statu* (The Building of the State). Perth Amboy, NJ: Universum Sokol Publ., 1974, 1980, 1981.

Petro, P. *History of Slovak Literature.* Montreal: McGill-Queens University Press, 1995.

Plevza, V. (Ed.), *Prehlad dejin KSC na Slovensku* (Survey of the History of the Czechoslovak Communist Party in Slovakia). Bratislava: Pravda, 1971.

Plevza, V. *Slovakia in Socialist Czechoslovakia.* Prague: Orbis, 1981.

Polak, Suzanne Therese. 'In the Spirit of Democratic Unity: The Slovak Democratic Party and the National Front of Czechs and Slovaks 1945-1948' (Dissertation). Bloomington: Indiana University, 1999.

Pynsent, R. B. *Questions of Identity: Czech and Slovak Ideas of Nationality and Personality.* Budapest: Central European University Press, 1994.

Ramet, S. P. *Social Currents in Eastern Europe: The Sources and Meaning of the Great Transformation.* Durham, NC: Duke University Press, 1991.

Ratkos, P. (Ed.), *Velkomoravske legendy a povesti* (Great Moravian Legends and Tales). Bratislava: Tatran, 1990.

Rechcigl, M. (Ed.), *Czechoslovakia: Past and Present.* The Hague and Paris: 1964.

Reimann, P. *Dejiny Komunisticke strany Ceskoslovenska* (History of the Communist Party of Czechoslovakia). Praha: 1931.

Reimann, P. et al. *Dejiny KSC* (History of the Czechoslovak Communist Party). Bratislava: SVPL, 1961.

Reitlinger, G. *The Final Solution: The Attempt to Exterminate the Jews of Europe 1939–1945* (2nd revised and augmented edition). London: Vallentine, Mitchell, 1968.

Reitzner, A. *Alexander Dubcek: Manner und Machte in der Tschechoslowakei* (Alexander Dubcek: Leaders and Power Wielders in Czechoslovakia). Munchen: Verlag Die Brucke, 1968.

Renner, H. and Samso, I. *Dejiny Cesko-Slovenska po roku 1945* (History of Czecho-Slovakia after 1945). Bratislava: Slovak Academic Press, 1993.

Riha, O. and Mesaros, J. *Prehled ceskoslovenskych dejin* (Survey of Czechoslovak History). Praha: 1960.

Ripka, H. *Czechoslovakia Enslaved: The Story of the Communist Coup d'etat.* London: Victor Gollanz Ltd., 1950.

Robertson, P. *Revolutions of 1848: A Social History.* Princeton: Princeton University Press, 1967.

Rothschild, J. *East Central Europe between the Two World Wars.* Seattle: University of Washington Press, 1974.

Rupnik, J. *Histoire du Parti Communiste Tchecoslovaque: Des Origines a la Prise du Puvoir* (History of the Czechoslovak Communist Party: From Origin to Seizure of Power.) Paris: 1981.

Rychlik, J. *Cesi a Slovaci ve 20. stoleti: Cesko-slovenske vztahy 1914–1945* (The Czechs and Slovaks in the 20th Century: Czech-Slovak relations from 1914 to 1945). Bratislava: Academic Electronic Press; Praha: Ustav T. G. Masaryka, 1977.

__. *Cesi a Slovaci ve 20. stoleti 1945–1992* (The Czechs and Slovaks in the 20th Century 1945–1992). Bratislava: Academic Electronic Press; Praha: Ustav T. G. Masaryka, 1998.

Rydlo, J. M. (Ed.), *Slovensko v retrospective dejin* (Slovakia in Historical Perspective). Lausanne: Liber, 1976.

Sandorfi, E. *Slovo ku krestanskym robotnikom* (A Word to Christian Workers). Budapest: 1904.

Sandorfi, R. *History of Slovakia (A Survey).* Toronto-Bratislava: Zahranicna Matica Slovenska, 1996.

Schmid, K. *Die Slowakische Republik 1939–1945. Eine staats und volkerreichliche Betrachtung* (The Slovak Republic 1939–1945. A Treatise on the State and its Inhabitants, 2 vols.). Berlin: Berlin Verlag, 1982.

Schwartz, K. P. *Cesi a Slovaci: Dlha cesta k mierovemu rozchodu* (The Czechs and Slovaks: The Long Road to their Peaceful Parting. Translated by Karl Gronsky.) Bratislava: Odkaz, 1993.

Scotus Viator (R. W. Seton-Watson). *Racial Problems in Hungary.* London: Archibald Constable, 1908.

Sedliakova, A. *Historiografia na Slovensku 1990–1994* (Historiography in Slovakia 1990–1994). Bratislava: Historicky ustav Slovenskej akademie vied, 1995.

Seton-Watson, H. *Eastern Europe between the Wars.* Hamden, CT: Archon Books, 1962.

__. *The Eastern European Revolution.* New York: F. E. Praeger, 1951.

__. *Nations and States: An Inquiry into the Origins of Nations and the Politics of Nationalism.* London: Methuen, 1977.

Seton-Watson, R. W. *Documents (Dokumenty) 1906–1951,* 2 vols. Rychlik, J.; Marzik, T; and Bielik, M., (Eds.). Matica Slovenska, 1996.

Seton-Watson, R. W. *A History of the Czechs and Slovaks.* Hamden, CT: Archon Books, 1965 (Reprint of 1943 edition).

__. *Masaryk in England.* Cambridge: Cambridge University Press, 1943.

__. *The New Slovakia.* Prague: Fr. Borovy, 1924.

__. *Racial Problems in Hungary.* New York: Howard Fertig, 1972.

__. (Ed.), *Slovakia Then and Now.* London: George Allen & Unwin Ltd., 1931.

Shawcross, W. *Dubcek.* New York: Simon & Schuster, Inc., 1990.

Shepherd, R. *Czechoslovakia: The Velvet Revolution and Beyond.* New York: Palgrave MacMillan, 2000.

Sidor, K. *Andrej Hlinka 1864–1926.* Bratislava: Knihtlaciarne Sv. Andreja, 1934.

__. *Slovenska politika na pode prazskeho snemu* (Slovak Politics on the Floor of the Prague Parliament, 2 vols.). Bratislava: Knihtlaciarne sv. Andreja, 1943.

Silin, M. *A Critique of Masarykism.* Moscow: Progress Publishers, 1975.

Simmons, G. (Ed.), *Nationalism in the USSR and Eastern Europe in the Era of Brezhnev and Kosygin.* Detroit: University of Detroit Press, 1977.

Simonis de Keza Chronicon Hungaricum, 2nd ed., rev. Buda: Landerer, 1782. (Simonis de Keza: The Deeds of the Hungarians, ed. and tr. Laszlo Veszpremy and Frnak Schaer). Budapest, Hungary: 1999.

Skilling, H. G. *Charter 77 and Human Rights in Czechoslovakia.* London: George Allen & Unwin, 1981.

__. *Czechoslovakia's Interrupted Revolution.* Princeton: Princeton University Press, 1976.

__. *T. G. Masaryk: Against the Current 1882–1914.* University Park, PA: Pennsylvania State University, 1994.

__. (Ed.), *Czechoslovakia 1918–1988.* London: MacMillan, 1991.

Skultety, J. *Sketches from Slovak History.* (Translated from the Slovak by O. D. Koref.) Middletown, PA: First Catholic Slovak Union, 1930.

Slovak History: Chronology and Lexicon. Bratislava: SPN; and Wauconda, IL: Bolchazy-Carducci Publishers, Inc., 2002.

Slovakia and the Slovaks: A Concise Encyclopedia. (Compiled and edited by Milan Strhan, translated by David P. Daniel) Bratislava: SAV, 1994. (Unedited version.)

Slovak Biographical Dictionary. Martin: Matica Slovenska; Wauconda, IL: Bolchazy-Carducci Publishers, Inc., 2002.

Solle, Z. and Gajanova, A. *Po stope dejin: Cesi a Slovaci v letech 1848–1938* (Tracking History: The Czechs and Slovaks from 1848 to 1938). Praha: 1969.

Spiesz, A. *Dejiny Slovenska: Na ceste k sebauvedomeniu.* (A History of Slovakia: On the Road to Self-Awareness). Bratislava: Vydavatelstvo Perfekt, 1992.

Srobar, V. *Politicke problemy Slovenska* (The Political Problems of Slovakia).

Praha: 1926.

Stasko, J. (Ed.), *Shaping of Modern Slovakia.* Cambridge, Ont.: Friends of Good Books, 1982.

Stefanik, A. *Slovenska vlastiveda III: Zaklady sociografie Slovenska.* (History and Geography of Slovakia III: Fundamentals of Slovak Sociology.) Bratislava: SAV, 1944.

Stefanek, M. 'Activities of the United States in the Establishment of the Czechoslovak Republic 1914–1919'. (Master's Thesis). Kent State University.

Steiner, E. *The Slovak Dilemma.* Cambridge: University Press, 1973.

Stevcek, P. (Ed.), *Slovaks and Magyars: Slovak-Magyar Relations in Central Europe.* Bratislava: Sprava kulturnych zariadeni MK SR, 1995.

Stolarik, M. M. *The Slovak Republic: A Decade of Independence 1993 – 2002.* Wauconda, IL: Bolchazy-Carducci Publishers, 2004.

Street, C. J. C. *Slovakia Past and Present.* London: P. S. King & Sons, 1928.

Strhan, M. *Kriza priemyslu na Slovensku v rokoch 1921–1923* (Crisis of Industry in Slovakia 1921–1923). Bratislava: SAV, 1960.

Suda, Z. *The Czechoslovak Socialist Republic.* Baltimore: Johns Hopkins Press, 1969.

___. *Zealots and Rebels: History of the Communist Party of Czechoslovakia.* Stanford: Hoover Institution Press, 1980.

Sugar, P.; Hanak, P.; and Frank, T. *A History of Hungary.* Bloomington: Indiana University Press, 1990.

Suhaj, S. *Madarska mensina na Slovensku v rokoch 1945–1948* (Magyar Minority in Slovakia 1945–1948). Bratislava: SAV, 1993.

Sumberova, L. *Antonin Zapotocky 1884–1957.* Praha: Prace, 1984.

Sutherland, A. X. *Dr. Jozef Tiso and Modern Slovakia.* Cleveland: First Catholic Slovak Union, 1978.

Szentpetery, E. *Scriptores Rerum Hungaricarum* (Writers of Hungarian History, 2 vols.). Budapest: Academia Litter. Hungarica, 1938.

Taborsky, E. *Czechoslovak Democracy at Work.* London: 1945.

___. *President Eduard Benes: Between East and West 1938–1948.* Stanford, CA: Hoover Institute Press, 1981.

Taylor, A. J. P. *The Habsburg Monarchy 1809–1918.* New York: Penguin Books, 1948.

Teichova, A. *The Czechoslovak Economy 1918–1980.* London: Routledge, 1988.

Temperley, H. W. V. (Ed.), *History of the Peace Conference of Paris, Vol. V.* London: Henry Frowde and Hodder & Stoughton, 1921.

Thomson, H. S. *Czechoslovakia in European History.* Princeton: Princeton University Press, 1953.

Tiso, J. *Dr. Jozef Tiso o sebe* (Dr. Jozef Tiso about Himself). Passaic, NJ: Slovensky Katolicky Sokol, 1952.

Tobolka, Z. *Politicke dejiny ceskoslovenskeho naroda od r. 1848 az do dnesni doby* (Political History of the Czechoslovak Nation from 1848 to Present, 4 Vols.). Praha: 1932–37.

Tokes, R. *Bela Kun and the Hungarian Soviet Republic.* New York: Praeger, 1967.

Toma, P. A. and Kovac, D. *Slovakia from Samo to Dzurinda.* Stanford: Hoover Institute Press, 2001. (D. Kovac has retracted affiliation with this publication because of changes in his text made without his approval or editing.)

Tonsmeyer, T. *Das Dritte Reich und die Slowakei 1939–1945: Politischer Alltag zwischen Kooperation und Eigensinn.* Paderborn: Ferdinand Schoningh, 2003.

Toth, D. et al. 'Tragedy of the Slovak Jews: Proceedings of the International Symposium at Banska Bystrica'. Banska Bystrica: 1992.

Turnock, D. *Eastern Europe: A Historical Geography 1815–1945.* London: Routledge, 1989.

___. *Making of Eastern Europe from the Earliest Times to 1815.* London: Routledge, 1988.

Ulicny, F. *Dejiny osidlenia zemplinskej zupy* (Development of the Zemplin County, History of). Michalovce, Slovakia: Zemplinska spolocnost, 2001.

Varsik, B. *Husitske revolucne hnutie a Slovensko* (The Hussite Revolutionary Movement and Slovakia). Bratislava: Veda, 1965.

Vatikan a Slovenska republika 1939–1945: Dokumenty. (The Vatican and the Slovak Republic 1939–1945: Documents.) Bratislava: Slovak Academic Press, 1992.

Venor, W. *Aufstand in der Tatra: der Kampf um die Slovakei 1939–1944* (Uprising in the Tatra's: The Battle for Slovakia 1939–1944). Konigstein: Athenaum, 1979.

Veteska, T. *Velkoslovenska risa* (The Great Slovak Kingdom). Hamilton, ON: MSA-ZMS, 1987.

Vnuk, F. *Dedicstvo otcov: Eseje na historicke temy.* (Heritage of Our Fathers: Essays on Historical Themes). Toronto-Bratislava: Kruh priatelov boja za samostatnost Slovenska, 1991.

___. *Kapitoly z dejin Komunistickej strany Slovenska* (Chapters from the History of the Communist Party in Slovakia). Middletown, PA: Slovak v Amerike, 1968.

__. *Mat svoj stat znamena zivot ... Politicka biografia Alexandra Macha.* (Having one's Own State Means Life Itself ... A Political Biography of Alexander Mach). Cleveland, OH: Slovensky ustav, 1987.

__. *Sedemnast neurodnych rokov: Nacrt dejin slovenskej literatury v rokoch 1945–1962* (Seventeen Lean Years: A Sketch of the History of Slovak Literature from 1945–1962). Middletown, PA: Slovak v Amerike, 1965.

__. *Stopatdesiat rokov v zivote naroda: Slovensko v rokoch 1843–1993* (150 years in the Life of a Nation: Slovakia in 1843–1993). Bratislava: LUC, 2004.

__. *Vladni zmocnenci v biskupskych uradoch v rokoch 1949–1951* (Government Commissioners of Episcopal Functions 1949–1951). Martin: Matica Slovenska, 1999.

Volgyes, I. (Ed.), *Hungary in Revolution 1918–1919.* Lincoln: University of Nebraska Press, 1971.

Vondracek, F. J. *The Foreign Policy of Czechoslovakia 1918–1935.* New York: Columbia University Press, 1937.

Wallace, W. W. *Czechoslovakia.* London: 1976.

Weber, N. *Women and the Slovakian National Movement: Gender and Class as Components of National Efforts in Slovakia 1848–1990.* International Scholars Publications, 1999.

Wheaton, B. and Kavan, Z. *The Velvet Revolution: Czechoslovakia 1988–1991.* Boulder: Westview Press, 1992.

Whittle, A. *Neolithic Europe: A Survey.* Cambridge: Cambridge University Press, 1985.

Williams, K. *The Prague Spring and its Aftermath.* Cambridge: Cambridge University Press, 1997.

Williams, K. and Deletant, D. *Security Intelligence Services in New Democracies: The Czech Republic, Slovakia and Romania.* Basingstoke: Palgrave, 2000.

Wojtasek, C. *From Trianon to the First Vienna Arbitral Award: The Hungarian Minority in the First Czechoslovak Republic 1918–1938.* Montreal: Institute of Comparative Civilizations, 1981.

Wolcik, S. L. *Czechoslovakia in Transition: Politics, Economics and Society.* London: Pinter Publishers, 1991.

Wymer, J. *The Paleolithic Age.* New York: St. Martin's Press, 1982.

Young, E. P. *Czechoslovakia: Keystone of Peace and Democracy.* London: 1938.

Yurchak, P. P. *The Slovaks.* Whiting, IN: Rev. John J. Lach, 1946.

Zatkuliak, J. *November 1989 a Slovensko: chronologia a dokumenty 1985–1990*

(November 1989 and Slovakia: Chronology and Documents 1985–1990). Bratislava: Historicky ustav SAV, 1999.

Zbornik o Slovenskom narodnom povstani (A Festschrift on the Slovak National Uprising, 2 Vols.). Toronto: Nase snahy, 1976–1980.

Zeman, Z. A. *The Break-up of the Habsburg Empire 1914–1915: A Study in National and Social Revolution.* London: 1961.

Zeman, Z. *The Masaryks: The Making of Czechoslovakia.* London: 1976.

Zinner, P. E. *Communist Strategy and Tactics in Czechoslovakia 1918–1948.* Westport, CT: Greenwood Press, 1963 (1975 Reprint).

Zudel, J. *Stolice na Slovensku* (Counties in Slovakia). Bratislava: Obzor, 1984.

SELECTED ARTICLES

Abrams, B. 'The Politics of Retribution: the Trial of Jozef Tiso'. *East European Politics and Society,* V. 10. No. 2 (1996).

Agnew, Hugh LeCaine. 'New States, Old Identities? The Czech Republic, Slovakia, and Historical Understandings of Statehood'. *Nationalities Papers* 28. No. 4 (2000): 619-650.

Alexander, M. 'Leistungen, Belastungen und Gefahrdungen der Demokratie in der Ersten Tschechoslowakischen Republik'. (Accomplishments, Encumbrances and Pitfalls: Democracy in the First Czechoslovak Republic). *Bohemia,* 27. No. 1 (1986): 72–87.

Anderle, J. et al. 'Uncharted Areas for Research on the History of Slovakia and the Slovaks'. *East Central Europe/L'Europe du Centre-Est,* 7. No. 1 (1980): 48–88.

Balaz, O. 'Vyvoj polnohospodarstva na Slovensku v rokoch 1949–1960'. (Agricultural Development in Slovakia 1949–1960). *Historicky casopis,* 9. No. 1 (1961): 3–28.

Benes, E. 'Czechoslovak Policy for Victory and Peace'. In *Czechoslovak Documents and Sources,* No. 10, London: Czechoslovak Ministry of Foreign Affairs, Information Service, 1944.

__. 'Discours aux Slovaques sur le present at l'avenir do notre nation'. (Discourse to the Slovaks on the Present and Future of our Nation). *Le Monde slave*, February (1934): 1–72.

Bohmerova, A. 'The Camaldolese Dictionary'. Paper read at the 1993 National Convention of the American Association for the Advancement of Slavic Studies. Honolulu: HA, 22 November 1993.

Bosak, E. 'Czech-Slovak Relations from the 1840's to 1914'. *Slovakia,* 35

(1991–1992): 63–77.

___. 'Intellectual Currents among the Slovak Intelligentsia during the Nineteenth Century'. Paper read at the Fourth World Congress for Soviet and East European Studies. Harrogate: England, July 21–26, 1990.

Bubrin, V. 'Prince Pribina and the Pre-Cyrillomethodian Political and Missionary Activities in Great Moravia and Pannonia'. *Slovak Studies,* 12 (1972): 135–147.

Carnogursky, J. 'Politicke procesy'. *Pohlady,* 6 (1988): 62–122.

Carpenter, Michael. 'Slovakia and the Triumph of National Populism'. *Communist and Post-Communist Studies,* 30. No. 2 (1997): 205–219.

Chorváthová, Lubica. 'On the Dynamics of Changes in Social and National Identity in Slovakia in the 19th and 20th Centuries'. *Human Affairs,* 11. 2 (2001): 130-133.

Conway, J. S. 'The Churches, the Slovak State, and the Jews, 1939–1945'. *Slavonic and East European Review* 52:126 (January 1974): 85–112.

Daniel, D. P. 'Hungary'. Pettegree, A. (Ed.), *The Early Reformation in Europe.* Cambridge: Cambridge University Press, (1992): 49–69.

___. 'The Impact of the Protestant Reformation on Education in Slovakia'. *Slovakia,* 34 (1989–1990): 9–27.

___. 'No Mere Impact: Features of the Reformation in the Lands of the Austrian Habsburgs'. *Archiv fur Reformationsgeschichte.* Sonderband (1993).

___. 'The Protestant Reformation and Slovak Ethnic Consciousness'. *Slovakia,* 28 (1978–1979): 49–65.

___. 'The Reformation and Eastern Slovakia'. *Human Affairs,* 1. No. 2 (1991): 172–186.

Durica, M. S. 'Der slowakische Anteil in der Tragodie der europaischen Juden'. (Slovak Participation in the Tragedy of the European Jews.) *Slowakei,* 27 (1984): 109–148.

Evans, G. and Whitfield, S. 'The Structuring of Political Cleavages in Post-Communist Societies: The Case of the Czech Republic and Slovakia'. *Political Studies,* 46. No. 1 (1998): 115–139.

Evanson, R. K. 'Regime and Working Class in Czechoslovakia 1948–1968'. *Soviet Studies,* 37 (April 1985): 248–268.

Felak, James. 'Catholics and Communists in Post-War Slovakia'. *REECAS Newsletter,* University of Washington Russian, East European and Central Asian Studies Center, pp. 13-15. http://depts.washington.edu/reecas/newsletter/SprSum02/reecas_spring_2002.pdf.

___. 'The Slovak Question in the Inter-War 1918–1938 and Post-War 1945–1948 Czechoslovak Republics'. *Slovakia,* 37 (2003): 7–27.

Grebert, A. 'Die Slowaken und das Grossmarische Reich: Beitrag zum ethnischen Charakter Grossmahrens'. (Slovaks and the Great Moravian Kingdom: a Contribution to the Ethnic Characterization of Great Moravia.) *Slovak Studies,* 3 (1963): 126–134.

Haughton, T. 'HZDS: the Ideology, Organization and Support Base of Slovakia's Most Successful Party'. *Europe-Asia Studies,* 53. No. 5. (2001): 745–769.

Henderson, K. 'Minorities and Politics in the Slovak Republic'. In: S. Trifunovska (Ed.), *Minorities in Europe: Croatia, Estonia and Slovakia.* The Hague: T.M.C. Asser Press (1999): 143–173.

Hilde, Paal Sigurd. 'Slovak Nationalism and the Break-up of Czechoslovakia'. *Europe-Asia Studies,* 51. 4 (1999): 647-665.

Hrusovsky, F. 'The Relations of the Rulers of Great Moravia with Rome'. *Slovak Studies,* 3 (1963): 21–77.

Innes, Abby. 'The Breakup of Czechoslovakia: The Impact of Party Development on the Separation of the State'. *East European Politics and Societies,* 11. 3 (1997): 393-435.

Jansak, S. 'The Land Question in Slovakia'. *Slavonic and East European Review 8,* No. 24 (March 1930): 612–626; and Part 2, 9, No. 25 (June 1930): 177–186.

Kamenec, I. 'Snem Slovenskej republiky a jeho postoj k problemu zidovskeho obyvatelstva na Slovensku v rokoch 1939–1945'. (The Slovak Parliament and its Attitude towards the Jewish population of Slovakia, 1939–1945.) *Historicky casopis,* 17. No. 3 (1969): 329–362.

Kirschbaum, J. M. 'The Role of the Cyrilo-Methodian Tradition in Slovak National and Political Life'. *Slovak Studies,* 3 (1963): 153–172.

___. 'Slovakia in the de-Stalinization and Federalization Process of Czechoslovakia'. *Canadian Slavonic Papers/Revue canadienne des Slavistes,* 10. No. 4 (1968): 522–556.

Kirschbaum S. J. 'An Act of Faith and Integrity. Bishop Korec's Letter to Czechoslovak Television'. *Slovakia,* 34. Nos. 62–63 (1989–90): 61–126.

___. 'Andrej Hlinka ako politik v prvej CSR'. (Andrej Hlinka as a Politician in the First Czechoslovak Republic). *Historicky casopis,* 40. No. 6 (1992): 694–706.

___. 'Czechoslovakia: The Creation, Federalization and Dissolution of a Nation-State'. *Regional Politics & Policy,* 3, No. 1 (1993): 69–95.

___. 'The Czech Question in Slovakia in the Post-War Years'. *Slovakia,* 35. Nos. 64–65 (1991–1992): 97–108.

___. 'Die Entwicklung des Foderalismus in der Tschechoslowakei'. (The Development of Federalism in Czechoslovakia'. *Zeitschrift fur Ostforschung,* 24. No. 2 (1975): 272–287.

__. 'Federalism in Slovak Communist Politics'. *Canadian Slavonic Papers,* 19. No. 4 (1977): 444–467.

__. 'The First Slovak Republic 1939-1945: Some Thoughts on its meaning in Slovak History'. *Österreichische Osthefte,* 41. 3-4 (1999): 405-425.

__. 'The Martinovics Conspiracy and the Slovaks'. *Österreichische Osthefte,* 43. 1-2 (2001): 45-55.

__. 'National Opposition under Communism: The Slovaks in Czechoslovakia'. *Slovak Studies,* 19 (1979): 5–19.

__. 'Nationalism in Eastern Europe: Disease and Cure'. *Slovak Studies,* 26–27 (1986–1987): 125–136.

__. 'L'Opposition en regimes communists: le cas des intellectuals slovaques'. (The Opposition in Communist Regimes: The Case of Slovak Intellectuals). *Canadian Slavonic Papers/Revue canadienne des Slavistes,* 17. No. 1 (1975): 1–43.

__. 'Slovak Nationalism in the First Czechoslovak Republic 1918–1938'. *Canadian Review of Studies in Nationalism,* 16. Nos. 1–2 (1989): 169–187.

__. 'Slovak Nationalism in Socialist Czechoslovakia'. *Canadian Slavonic Papers/Revue canadienne des Slavistes,* 22. No. 2 (1980): 220–246.

__. 'The Slovak Republic and the Slovaks'. *Slovakia,* 29. Nos. 53–54 (1980–1981): 11–38.

__. 'The Slovak Republic, Britain, France and the Principle of Self-Determination'. *Slovak Studies,* 23 (1983): 149–170.

__. 'Slovakia: Whose History, What History?' *Canadian Slavonic Papers,* 45. 3-4 (2003): 459-467.

__. 'Turciansky Svaty Martin and the Formation of the Slovak Nation'. *Slovak Review,* 2. No. 1 (1993): 113–123.

Kopanic, Michael J., Jr. 'The Czech and Slovak Federative Republic'. *European Labor Unions,* ed. Joan Campbell (Greenwood, 1992): 67-86.

__. 'From Slovak Steal to US Steel: Salvaging the Eastern Slovak Iron Works'. *Národny Kalendár NSS,* CX. (2002): 87-100.

__. 'Hungarian-Slovak Relations in Austria-Hungary'. *Národny Kalendár NSS,* C. (1992): 66-70.

__. 'Labor Unions in Interwar Slovakia: The Case of Slovakia'. *East Central Europe,* 19. 1 (1992): 26-44.

__. 'Meciar Battles Back'. *Národny Kalendár NSS,* CIII. (1995): 105-114.

__. 'The Recent Elections in Slovakia'. *Analysis of Current Events* (Monthly

Publication of the Assn. for the Study of Nationalities of the CIS and Eastern Europe), VI, 9 (May 1995).

__. 'Slovak-Magyar Relations in Cleveland, 1880-1930'. *Western Reserve Studies Symposium* (1989): 1-24.

__. 'The Slovaks'. *Identity, Conflict, and Cooperation: Central Europeans in Cleveland 1850-1930* (Cleveland: Western Reserve Historical Society, 2003): 249-306.

__. 'The Slovak Community of Cleveland: Historiography and Sources'. *Ethnic Forum,* 10. 1-2 (1990): 83-97.

__. 'Slovakia's First 1,000 Days: An Assessment'. *Národny Kalendár NSS,* CIV. (1996): 92-96.

__. 'Slovaks in Cleveland 1870-1930'. *Czechoslovak and Central European Journal,* 9, 1-2 (1990): 117-33.

__. 'Stealing the Eastern Slovak Steelworks'. *Central Europe Review,* 2. 2-3 (10 and 17 January 2000), http://www.ce-review.org .

__. 'The Unification of the Social Democratic Trade Unions in Slovakia 1918-20'. *Premeny,* 24. 4 (October 1987): 84-92.

__. 'Victory in Round Three: Meciar's 1994 Electoral Triumph'. *Kosmas: Journal of Czechoslovak and Central European Affairs,* 12. 2 (Fall 1997): 156-191.

Kowalska, E. 'Kontroverzna tolerancia: Protestanti a skolske reformy osvietenskeho obdobia'. (Controversial Tolerance: Protestants and the School Reforms of the Enlightenment Period.) *Historicke Studie,* 34. (1993): 55–76.

__. 'Learning and Education in Slovakia during the Late 17th and 18th Centuries'. *Slovakia,* 34. Nos. 63–64 (1989–1990): 28–49.

Kovác, Dusan. 'The Twentieth Century Transformation of Slovak Society'. *Human Affairs,* 6. 2 (1996): 142-153.

Kraus, D. 'Czechoslovakia in the 1980's'. *Current History,* 84. (November 1985): 372–376, 383.

Kraus, M. 'The Kremlin and the Slovak National Uprising of August–October 1944'. *Slovakia,* 34. Nos. 62–63 (1989–1990): 50–60.

Krause, K. 'The Political Party System and Democracy in the Slovak Republic'. University of Notre Dame (Master's Thesis) (date unavailable). (http://www.nd.edu/~kkrause/papers/ma.htm).

__. 'Public Opinion and Party Choice in Slovakia and the Czech Republic'. *Party Politics,* 6. No. 1 (2000): 23–46.

Kusin, V. V. 'Challenge to Normalcy: Political Opposition in Czechoslovakia, 1968–1978'. *Opposition in Eastern Europe.* Ed. Rudolf Tokes. London:

Macmillan, 1979.

___. 'Reform and Dissidence in Czechoslovakia'. *Current History*, 86. (November 1987): 361–364, 383.

Lacko, M. 'The Cyrilomethodian Mission and Slovakia'. *Slovak Studies*, 1. (1961): 23–49.

___. 'The Union of Uzhorod'. *Slovak Studies*, 6 (1966): 7–190.

Liptak, L. 'Slovensky stat a protifasisticke hnutie v rokoch 1939–1943'. (The Slovak State and the Anti-Fascist Movement, 1939–1943). *Historicky casopis*, 14. No. 2 (1966): 161–218.

Lukacka, J. 'Uloha slachty slovanskeho povodu pri stabilizacii uhorskeho vcasnofeudalneho state' (The Role of Nobility of Slavic Origin in the Stabilization of Medieval Hungary). In: *Typologie ranofeudalnich slovanskych statu*. Praha: Ustav ceskoslovenskych a svetovych dejin CSAV, (1987): 191–200.

Marsina, R. 'Slovenska historiografia 1945–1990'. *Historicky casopis*, 39. Nos. 4–5 (1991): 370–379.

Matula, V. 'The Conception and Development of Slovak National Culture in the Period of National Revival'. *Studia Historica Slovaca*, 17. (1990): 150–189.

Mikula, S. 'Relations between Slovaks and Czechs in the First Czechoslovak Republic'. *Slovakia*, 35. Nos. 64–65 (1991–1992): 78–96.

Papin, J. 'Christian Inroads into the Territory of Present-Day Slovakia Prior to the Cyrillo-Methodian Era'. *Slovak Studies*, 3. (1963): 9–20.

Ramet, S. P. 'Catholic Church in Czechoslovakia 1848–1991'. *Studies in Comparative Communism*, 24. No. 4 (1991): 377–393.

Rothkirchen, Livia. 'The Slovak Enigma: A Reassessment of the Halt to the Deportations'. *East Central Europe*, 10. 1-2 (1983): 3-13.

Sobell, V. 'Legacy of Normalization'. *East European Politics and Society*, 2:1 (Winter 1998): 36–69.

Stolárik, M. Mark. 'The Painful Birth of Slovak Historiography in the 20th Century'. *Zeitschrift für Ostmitteleuropa-Forschung*, 50. 2 (2001): 161-187.

___. 'The Role of American Slovaks in the Creation of Czechoslovakia'. *Slovak Studies*, 8 (1968): 7–82.

___. 'Slovak Historiography since the Downfall of Communism 1989'. *Canadian Review of Studies in Nationalism*, 29. 1-2 (2002): 67-82.

___. 'Slovaks in the Old World and the New to 1914'. *Slovak Studies*, 8. Cleveland-Rome: Slovak Institute, 1968.

___. 'The Struggle with Slovak History Continues'. *Canadian Review of Studies in Nationalism*, 30. 1-2 (2003): 147-149.

Sutherland, A. X. 'The Fathers of the Slovak Nation: From Juraj Tranovsky to Karol Salva, or from the Reformation to the Rise of the Populists (1500's–1890's)'. *Slovak Studies,* 21 (1981): 5–187.

Teich, Mikulás. 'The Meaning of History: Czechs and Slovaks'. *Historical Journal,* 39. 2 (1996): 553-562.

Vnuk, F. 'Slovakia and the western allies'. In: J. M. Rydlo (Ed.), *Studi in onore di Milan S. Durica.* Bratislava (1995): 717–726.

Vnuk, F. 'Slovakia's Six Eventful Months (October 1938–March 1939)'. *Slovak Studies,* 4 (1964): 7–164.

Ward, James Mace. 'People Who Deserve It: Josef Tiso and the Presidential Exemption'. *Nationalities Papers,* 30. 4 (2002): 571-602.

Wightmann, G. 'The Collapse of Communist Rule in Czechoslovakia and the June 1990 Parliamentary Elections'. *Parliamentary Affairs,* 44. No. 1 (1991): 94–113.

Williams, K. 'The Magyar Minority in Slovakia'. *Regional and Federal Studies,* 6. No. 1 (1996).

Wolchik, S. 'The Politics of Ethnicity in Post-Communist Czechoslovakia'. *East European Politics and Society,* 8. No. 1 (Winter 1994): 167–186.

__. 'Regional Inequalities in Czechoslovakia'. In: D. Nelson (Ed.), *Communism and the Politics of Inequalities.* Lexington Mass: Lexington Books, (1983): 249–270.

List of the Rulers and Presidents

List of the rulers and presidents on the territory of Slovakia and their time in office

1. Samo
   623/4-658/9
2. Pribina
   beginning of 9th century -833
3. Mojmir I
   833-846
4. Rastislav (Rastic)
   846-870, 871-894
5. Svatopluk
   870-871
6. Slavomir
   871
7. Mojmir II
   894-907
8. Svatopluk II
   end of 9th cent. –
   beg. of 10th century
9. Gaza (Gejza)
   940-997
10. Stephen I
    997-1038
11. Peter
    1038-1041
    1044-1046
12. Samuel Aba
    1041-1044
13. Andrew I (Ondrej)
    1046-1060
14. Bela I (Belo)
    1060-1063
15. Solomon (Salamun)
    1063-1074
16. Geza I (Gejza)
    1074-1077
17. Ladislav I
    1077-1095
18. Coloman (Koloman)
    1095-1116
19. Stephen II
    1116-113
20. Bela II the Blind
    1131-1141
21. Geza II (Gejza)
    1141-1162
22. Stephen III
    1162-1172
23. Ladislav II
    1162-1163 rival king
24. Stephen IV
    1163-1165 rival king
25. Bela III (Belo)
    1173-1196

26. Imre (Imrich)
    1196-1204
27. Ladislav III
    1204-1205
28. Andrew II (Ondrej)
    1205-1235
29. Bela IV (Belo)
    1235-1270
30. Stephen V
    1270-1272
31. Ladislav IV Cuman (Kumansky)
    1272-1290
32. Andrew III (Ondrej)
    1290-1301
33. Wenceslas (Ladislas, Vaclav)
    1301-1305
34. Otto
    1305-1307
35. Charles Robert (Karol Robert)
    1308-1342
36. Louis the Great (Ludovit the Great)
    1342-1382
37. Maria
    1382-1395
38. Charles the Small (Karol the Small)
    1385-1386
39. Sigismund (Zigmund)
    1387-1437
40. Albrecht
    1438-1439
41. Vladislav I
    1440-1444
42. Ladislav V
    1453-1457
43. Mattias Corvinus (Matej Korvin)
    1458-1490
44. Vladislav II
    1490-1516
45. Louis II (Ludovit)
    1516-1526
46. John Zapolya (Jan Zapolsky)
    1526-1540
47. Ferdinand I
    1527-1564
48. Maximilian I
    1564-1576
49. Rudolf I
    1576-1608
50. Mattias II (Matej)
    1608-1619
51. Ferdinand II
    1619-1637

52. Ferdinand III
    1637-1657
53. Leopold I
    1657-1705
54. Joseph I (Jozef)
    1705-1711
55. Charles III (Karol)
    1711-1740
56. Maria Theresa
    1740-1780
57. Joseph II (Jozef)
    1780-1790
58. Leopold II
    1790-1792
59. Francis I (Frantisek)
    1792-1835
60. Ferdinand V
    1835-1848
61. Francis Joseph I
    (Frantisek Jozef)
    1848-1916
62. Charles IV (Karol)
    1916-1918
63. Tomas G. Masaryk
    1918-1935
64. Edvard Benes
    1935-1938
65. Emil Hacha
    1938-1939
66. Jozef Tiso
    1939-1945
    Edvard Benes
    1945-1948
67. Klement Gottwald
    1948-1953
68. Antonin Zapotocky
    1953-1957
69. Antonin Novotny
    1957-1968
70. Ludvik Svoboda
    1968-1975
71. Gustav Husak
    1975-1989
72. Vaclav Havel
    1989-1992
73. Michal Kovac
    1993-1998
74. Rudolf Schuster
    1999-2004
75. Ivan Gasparovic
    2004-

Index

Aba, Omodej 51
Aba, Palatine Samuel 315
Abrahamaides, Lutheran Superintendent 81
Academia Istropolitana 60
Action B, eviction campaign 294
Action Committees 249
Adalram, Archbishop of Salzburg 20, 271
Admonition to Rulers, An 272
Agrarian Party 200, 201, 206, 218, 227, 235, 239, 246, 288, 336, 339, 341
National Committee of 197
Agrarians, Czech 164
Agrarians, German 204
Agreement of Friendship, Mutual Assistance and Post-War Cooperation 226, 238, 247, 194, 195, 244, 251, 255, 356
Agriculture, capitalism evolution in 173
Agriculture, emigration of seasonal workers 202
Agriculture, forestry 251
Agriculture, great drought of 1947 245, 354
Agriculture, growth of 254, 255
Agriculture, jutros 47, 173
Agriculture, ministry of 339
Agriculture, sessios 47
Agriculture, upland tracts 82
Albert of Saxony-Cieszyn, viceroy 85
Albrecht of Austria, Grand Duke 54, 125
Ales, Mikulas; *Mikuláš Aleš* 151
Alexander Dubcek Square 302
Alexander Leopold, Palatine 92
Alfred, King of England 273
Allied Forces (Second World War) 228
Allies (First World War) 190
Amadeus family 277
(see also Omodejov family)
American Civil War 158
American Slovak League; *Slovenská liga v Amerike* 167
American Slovak, The 159
(see also *Americký Slovák*)
American Slovaks 158, 168, 169, 331, 333, 335, 353
Americký Slovák 159
(see also *American Slovak, The*)
Andrassy family; *Andrássy, Andrássyovci* 174
Andrassy, Count Gyula;

Július Andrássy 143, 144, 185
Andrew I, King; *Ondrej I* 31, 275, 315
Andrew II, King; *Ondrej II* 32, 36, 316
Andrew III, King; *Ondrej III* 50, 276
Anonymous Chronicle 279
Antiquity period 269
anti-Semitism 147, 216, 220, 291, 331, 349
anti-Trinitarian Church 77
Apológia Slovákov 279
(see also *Apology for Slovaks, An*)
Apology for Slovaks, An 279
(see also *Apológia Slovákov*)
Apponyi Laws 284
Apponyi, Albert 153, 163, 168, 335
Aragonese Estates 64
Argentina, Slovak emigration to 202
Arnulf 24, 25
Arpad 314
Arpad Dynasty; *Arpád, Arpádovci* 29, 30, 50, 275, 277, 313, 314
art 351
art, primitive 267, 307
Association of Gemer Ironworkers 141
Association of Lutheran Pastors 218
Association of Slovak Journalists 298
Attila the Hun 15
Augustinian monks 60
Auschwitz 217, 221, 231
(see also Oswiecim)
Austerlitz, Battle of 93
(see also Slavkov, Battle of)
Austrian armed forces 119
Austrian Empire 71, 123, 139
Austrian industry 139
Austro-Hungarian Compromise 139, 143–145, 147, 175, 179, 284, 328, 330, 331
(see also Equalization)
Austro-Hungarian Empire 139, 143, 144, 166, 169, 185, 189, 286
Austro-Hungarian Empire, capitulation of 171
Austro-Slavism 107, 326
Auxiliary Technical Brigades 294
Avar Kingdom 271
Avar tribes 15, 17–19, 270, 274, 309, 311
Avar-Slavic burial sites 18
Babenberger Dynasty 32
Bacilek, Karol; *Karel Bacílek* 227, 236,

252, 255, 257
Bach absolutism 136
Bach hussars 125
Bach regime 130, 283, 328
Bach system 131
Bach, Alexander 125, 283, 328
Bala family 66
Balas, Melicher 68
Balkan linen markets 87
Balkans: civil war in 299
Banffy, Dezso; *Bánffy Dezsö* 153, 155, 162
Banska Bystrica, German occupation of;
  Banská Bystrica 230
Banska Bystrica, mining district of;
  Banská Bystrica 277
Banska Sloboda; Banská sloboda 45
  (see also *Mining Freedoms*)
Banska Stiavnica, massacre at;
  Banská Štavnica 229
Banska Stiavnica, Mining Academy of;
  Banská Štiavnica 280
Banska Stiavnica, mining district of;
  Banská Štiavnica 276
Baroque style 74, 75, 318
Baroque style, Dutch 75
Bartolomeides, Ladislav 81
Baso, Matej; *Matej Bašo* 68
Batthany, Count Jan; *Ján Batthyányi,*
Batáni 125, 144
Batthany, Count Lajos;
  Ľudovít Batáni 105
Batu, Khan; *Batu, chán* 33, 34
Bavarian armed forces 273
Bednar, Stefan; *Štefan Bednár* 225
Bel, Matej 280
Bela I, King; *Belo I.* 315
Bela III, King; *Belo III.* 30, 315
Bela IV, King; *Belo IV.* 30, 31, 32, 33,
  275, 276, 314, 315
Belgium, Slovak emigration to 202
Bella, M. M. 162
Bella, Stefan Vladimir; 224
Belobrd culture 273
Benderovci 247, 248
  (see also partisans, Ukrainian)
Benes' Czecho-Slovak government-in-exile
  (see also Czecho-Slovak government-in-exile)
  197, 214, 220, 226, 232, 240, 342, 344
Benes, Edvard; *Edvard Beneš* 167, 193,
  197, 198, 201, 203, 204, 206, 214, 219,
  226, 227, 230, 232, 235–238, 243, 246,
  248, 249, 250, 286, 331, 339-342,
  351–352, 354, 355, 357, 358, 364
Benes, Edvard, death of;

Edvard Beneš 249
Benes, Edvard, resignation of;
  Edvard Beneš 341
Benicky, Ludovit; *Ľudovít Benický* 117, 120
Benka, Martin 225
Berlin, German seat of power 95, 145, 207
Bernolak, Anton;
  Anton Bernolák 82, 90, 91, 98–100,
  126, 128, 281, 282, 323
Berzevici family 50
Bethlen, Gabriel 70, 71
Biatec coin 12, 267
Biela Hora, Battle of 64, 70, 81, 317, 318
  (see also White Mountain, Battle of)
Bielik, Anton 155, 168
Biely Potok, massacre at 229
Bilak, Vasil; *Vasil Biľak* 258, 260
bi-ritualism 265
Bismarck, Otto von 144
Bjornson, Bjornstjerne;
  Björnstjerne Björnson 162, 165
Black Death 42
Blaho, Pavol 157, 158, 162, 164, 165,
  190, 191, 196, 285
Blazko of Borotin; *Blažko* 53
Bloudek, Bedrich; *Bedřich Bloudek* 114,
  115, 119, 120, 121
Bobula, Jan; *Ján Bobula* 146
Bocskay, Prince Stephen of
Transylvania; *Štefan Bočkaj* 67
Bogat-Radvan family 275
Bohemia 189
Boii tribe 11
Boleslav I, Duke 29
Boleslav the Brave, King;
  Boleslav Chrabrý 29
Bolshevik regime 170, 198, 224, 294, 295
Bolshevik revolution 167
Bolshevization 201, 250, 260
Borova, primitive fort at 264
Bosak, Michal; *Michal Bosák* 168
Bosnian vassalage 30
Bourgeois Nationalism, Slovak 232, 250,
  252, 255, 257, 294, 358, 360
Bratislava 273, 308, 326
  (see also Brezalauspurc; *Prešporok*;
  Pressburg; Pozsony)
Bratislava castle 52, 75, 85, 271, 276, 306
  (see also Bratislavský hrad)
Bratislava News 90
  (see also *Presburské noviny*)
Bratislava, announcement of first
  independent Slovakia 207
Bratislava, capital of Hungary 321

Bratislava, Commenius University 194, 224
Bratislava, Congress of Slovak
  Communist Party at 252
Bratislava, financial market/exchange 301
Bratislava, International
  Danube Fair at 225
Bratislava, Lutheran lyceum at 101, 281
Bratislava, papal visit 302
Bratislava, royal charter granted to 276
Bratislava, seat of Czecho-Slovak
  power 239
Bratislava, signing of federative
  restructure 295
Bratislava, signing of peace treaty
  with France 93
Bratislava, Slovak National
  Museum at 307
Bratislava, Soviet embassy founded 220
Bratislava, St. Martin's Cathedral 74, 331
Bratislava, Statue of Blessed Virgin at 75
Bratislava, statue of St. George at 75
Bratislava, summit at 306
Bratislava, synagogue at 331
Bratislava, Technical University 224, 351
Bratislava, Velvet Revolution
  demonstrations 261, 296
Bratislavský hrad 52, 75, 85, 271, 276, 306
  (see also Bratislava castle)
Bratstvo (see also Brotherhood) 200
Brethren 55
Brezalauspurc 273, 308, 326
  (see also Bratislava; *Prešporok;* Pressburg;
  Pozsony)
Brezhnev, Leonid 258–260
Brezova, public rally at; *Brezová* 112
Bronze Age 8, 9, 265
Bronze Age artifacts 265
Bronze Age jewelry 265, 266
Bronze Age man 266
Bronze Age, Late 9
Bronze Age, Middle 9
Brotherhood (see also Bratstvo) 200
Brothers of Mercy, Order of 72
Bubek family; *Bubekovci* 49
Bubek, Frantisek; *František Bubek* 68
Bucany, primitive fort at; *Bučany* 264
Budapest Intelligencer, The 132, 135, 146
Bugar, Milos; *Miloš Bugár* 247, 293
Bulcsu; *Bölcs* 314
Bulgaria 305
Bulgaria, vassalage of 30
Bulgars, liberation of 150
Burebista, King 11
burial mound culture 265–267

Bush, George W. 306
Buzalka, Bishop 253, 294
Bytca, residence of Palatine; *Bytča* 74
Byzantine 23, 29
Byzantine Empire 17, 19, 22, 55, 270, 310
Byzantium 22, 27, 32
Cak, Mattias; *Matúš Čák Trenčiansky*
  50, 51, 277, 317
  (see also Csak, Mate; Trenciansky)
Calvinism 65, 278, 319
Calvinist Church 72, 77, 105
Calvinist Protestants 80, 103, 210, 280,
  321, 326
Calvinist Protestants, Magyar 69
Calvinist regions 144
Canada, NATO member 305
Canada, Slovak emigration to 202
capitalism 151, 160, 175, 183, 252, 257,
  261, 330
Caplovic, Dusan; *Dušan Čaplovič*
  xii, 2, 263–293, 361–364
Capuchin religious order 72
Carnuntum *(Hainburg)* 14
Carpathian burial mounds 9
Carpathian-German Party 203
  (see also Karpatendeutsche Partei)
Carpatho-Rusyn ethnic people 41, 68, 145,
  154, 155, 196, 210, 215, 277, 284, 316,
  332, 333
  (see also Carpatho-Ruthenians; Rusyns;Ruthenians)
Carpatho-Rusyn language 174
Carpatho-Ruthenian ethnic people 41, 68,
  145, 154, 155, 196, 210,
  215, 277, 284, 316, 332, 333
  (see also Carpatho-Rusyns; Rusyns; Ruthenians)
Carpatho-Ukraine, autonomy of 206
Carpatho-Ukraine, Magyar annexing of 212
Cassius Dio 13
Castle hill; *Hradny vrch* 302
Catholic Action 359
Catholic Church 41, 60, 63, 66, 69, 78,
  79, 80, 98, 100, 150, 153, 163,
  209, 210, 253, 280, 336, 355
Catholic church schools 128, 148, 284
Catholic Church, Byzantine Rite 41, 79,
  144, 175, 210, 332, 336, 359
Catholic Church, Byzantine Rite,
  abolishment of 253
Catholic Church, Byzantine Rite,
  churches of 359
Catholic Church, clergy 78, 284
Catholic Church, estates of 71
Catholic Church, Magyar 65, 77, 210
Catholic Church, Moravian 137

Catholic Church, opposition to
Jewish transport 220
Catholic Church, repression of 359
Catholic Church, Slovak 137
Catholic News, The 126, 127, 148, 151,
155, 158
Catholic People's Party 235
Catholic regions 89, 144, 152
Catholicism, anti- 98, 106, 196
Catholicization, re- 66, 69, 70, 72, 80, 278,
280, 320
Catlos, General Ferdinand 218, 227–229,
232, 236
Cech, Peter 49
Celts 10–14, 267, 268, 308
Central Association of
Slovak Industries 227
Central Bank 177
Central Cooperative for Agriculture
and Business 177
Central Slovak Mining District 129
Central Slovak National Committee 162
ceramics, early modeling of 265, 267
Cernan, Eugene 1
Cernova, massacre at; *Černová* 164, 285
Cerveny Kamen Hrad; hrad *Červený*
Kameň 58
Cesko, Morava, Sliezko ; Česko 164
(column in *National News*)
Československá Jednota 157, 164, 166, 333
(see also Czecho-Slovak Unity)
Charlemagne 19, 271, 311, 315
Charles I, Emperor; *Karol I.* 190
Charles III, King of Hungary;
Karol III. 84, 320
(see also Charles VI, Emperor)
Charles IV, Holy Roman Emperor;
Karol IV. 52
Charles of Lorraine, Prince; *Karol* 319
Charles Robert of Anjou, King;
Karol Róbert z Anjou 45, 50, 51,
277, 316
Charles the Fat, Caroligian Emperor;
Karol III. 24
Charles V, Emperor; *Karol V.* 63, 64
Charles VI, Emperor 84, 320
(see also Charles III, King of Hungary)
Charles VII, Elector of Bavaria and
Emperor and King of Czech lands 84
Charter 77 261, 295, 297, 361
cholera epidemic 97, 175, 324
Cholera Uprising 97, 324
Chrastek, Michal; *Michal Chrástek* 126
Christian Democratic Movement 298

Christian Farmers' Association 200, 201
Christian Church, First Slavic 20
Christian Socialist Party 183, 187
Christian Socialist Party, Magyar 348
Christian Socialist Trade
Union Association 351
Christian Socialist Unions 183, 187
Christianity 18, 19, 22, 24, 29, 78, 144,
269, 271, 291, 292, 311, 314
Christianization 22, 29
Christmas Pact 292
Chrobak, Dobroslav;
Dobroslav Chrobák 225
Churchill, Winston 226
Cicero, Marcus Tullius 263
Cikker, Jan; *Ján Cikker* 225
Cisleithania 113, 121, 123, 143, 165,
190, 327, 332
Citizens' Block 235, 239, 243, 246–249,
293, 294, 353, 355
(see also Democratic Party, Slovak)
Citizen's Democratic Party, Czech 298
Citizen's Forum 296, 297
Clementis, Vladimir;
Vladimír Clementis 206, 226, 252, 258,
290, 294
Clementis, Vladimir, execution of;
Vladimír Clementis 252
Cleveland Pact 168, 171, 286, 335
Coburg family; *Coburgovci* 174
Comenius University 224
Command of the Ground Army 230
Committee for the Defense of the
Homeland 106
Commodus, Emperor 268
communism 80, 209, 250, 252, 253, 257,
295, 296, 332, 334, 336, 344, 355,
357, 360
communism, collapse of 237, 261, 337, 360
Communist Central, Moscow 237
communist collectivization 251, 253
communist coup 241, 242, 250,
251, 354–355
communist internement camps 219, 241,
294
Communist Party 200, 201, 203, 206,
219, 227, 230, 232, 233, 236, 293, 294,
297, 356–359
Communist Party, Czech 235, 257, 296, 356
Communist Party, Czecho-Slovak 200,
237, 238-240, 242, 244-246, 248, 251,
252, 257, 258, 260, 261, 340, 356, 359
Communist Party, Czecho-Slovak, Central
Committee of 251, 255, 257, 258, 356

Communist Party, Czecho-Slovak,
Congress of   245, 252
Communist Party, German   203
Communist Party, Slovak   235, 239, 240,
242, 244, 247, 250, 251, 257,
258, 296, 339, 354, 356
Communist Party, Slovak, Central
Committee of   248, 252, 255, 258,
259, 359
Communist Party, Twentieth
Congress of (Moscow)   254
communist propaganda   224, 230, 253
communists   130, 198, 215, 241, 246,
292, 352, 353, 354, 355
Compacts of Prague   319
Concerning the Administration of the
Empire   274
(see also De administro imperio)
Confessio Heptapolitana   66
Confessio Pentapolitana   66
Confessio Scepusiana   66
Congress of Slovak Intelligentsia   298
Conrad II, King of Germany;
Konrád II.   30
Constantine; Konštantín   22, 23, 137, 272,
309, 312, 361
(see also Cyril)
Constantine VII Porphyrogenitus,
Emperor; Konštantín VII. Porfirogenet
274, 311
Constantine, Life of; Konštantín   272
Constantinople, Byzantine seat of power 17,
44, 54
Constitutional Court   304
Consumer Bank   177
Consumers' Party   206
Corpus Juris Hungarici   67, 146
(see also Hungarian Legal Code)
Cotini tribe   11, 267
Council of Europe   301
Counties   36, 143
credit unions   176
Crimean War   130, 328
Croat ethnic people   277, 284
Croatia, component of Magyar state   146
Croatian constitution   113
Croatian Diet   113, 327
Croatian National Assembly   327
Croatian subjugation by Hungary   32
Crusades   32
Csak, Mate   50, 51, 277, 317
(see also Čák, Mattias; Trenčiansky)
Csemadok   251
(see also Cultural Association of Magyar Workers

in Czecho-Slovakia)
Culen, Martin; Martin Čulen   129, 136
Cultural Association of Magyar Workers in
Czecho-Slovakia   251
(see also Csemadok)
Cuman tribe   315
Currents (see also Prúdy)   165, 201
Curta, Florin   309, 361
Cvincek, Canon; Cvinček   240
Cyprus   305
Cyril   22, 23, 137, 272, 309, 312, 361
(see also Constantine)
Cyril and Methodius   126, 127
Cyril-Methodian traditions   151
Czech Agrarian Bank   177
Czech culture   196
Czech ethnic people, deportation of   352
Czech chauvinism   204
Czech Kingdom   89, 105, 123
Czech language   113, 126, 149, 151, 203,
260
Czech language, Biblical 98, 99, 126, 129,
196, 284
Czech language, Slovakized   47, 58
Czech literature   196
Czech National Association   167, 168
Czech National Committee   192
Czech National Council   167, 298
Czech National Movement   107
Czech National Museum   100
Czech national revival   99, 100, 126, 324
Czech Parliament   237
Czech People's Party   246, 249
Czech Republic   299, 305
Czech schools   196
Czech Social Democratic Party   187
Czech Youth (see also Omladina)   157
Czechization   330
Czech-Moravian industry   139
Czecho-Slovak armed forces 197, 198, 204
205
Czecho-Slovak Business Company   177
Czecho-Slovak Government   247
Czecho-Slovak government-in-exile   197,
214, 220, 226, 232, 240, 342, 344
(see also Benes' Czecho-Slovak government-in-
exile)
Czecho-Slovak Legion   227, 335
Czecho-Slovak nation   162, 165, 170, 192,
220
Czecho-Slovak National Committee   189,
190
Czecho-Slovak National Council   167, 171
Czecho-Slovak People's Party   240

Czecho-Slovak reciprocity   100, 156, 166, 282, 285

Czecho-Slovak Republic   236, 244, 250, 257, 259, 261, 264, 295, 297, 298, 299, 355–357, 360

Czecho-Slovak Republic, dissolution of   364

Czecho-Slovak Republic, First   191, 193–197, 201, 203–207, 209, 222, 230, 235, 286–289, 290, 292, 293, 324, 330, 331, 335–340, 352

Czecho-Slovak Republic, First, armed forces   167, 223, 229, 233

Czecho-Slovak Republic, First, dissolution of   236, 290

Czecho-Slovak Republic, First, formation of   171, 189

Czecho-Slovak Social Democrats   243

Czecho-Slovak Socialism   238

Czecho-Slovak Socialist Republic   255

Czecho-Slovak Trade Union Association   200, 340

Czecho-Slovak Unity   157, 164, 166, 333
  (see also *Československá Jednota*)

Czecho-Slovak Workers' Party   159

Czechoslovakism 157, 158, 163, 189, 201, 230, 235, 239, 243, 336, 363

Czech-Slovak Grammar   81

Dacian tribe   11,14, 268, 308

Dagobert I, Frankish ruler   310

Dalmatia, component of Hungarian state146

Danubian Gate   18

Danubian nations   197

Daxner, Dr. Igor   246, 357

Daxner, Ivan   286

Daxner, Stefan Marko; *Štefan Marko Daxner*   133, 134, 136

De administrando imperio   274
  (see also *About Managing an Empire*)

De Bohemis Kishontensibus   81, 82
  (see also *Of the Czechs in Malohont County*)

Deak, Ferenc; *Ferenc Deák*   143, 144

Declaration of Slovak Independence   299

Declaration of the Slovak Nation 191, 192, 287, 337, 338
  (see also Martin Declaration)

Demands of the Slovak Nationality   112

Democrat Board of Commissioners   246

Democratic Party, Slovak   235, 239, 243, 246–249, 293, 294, 353, 354, 355
  (see also Citizens' Block)

Derer, Ivan; *Ivan Dérer* 201, 243, 288, 341

Detvaner   151, 156, 332

Deutsch-Bohemis, independent state of 193

Deutsche Bank   223

Deutsche Partei   215, 343

Devin, church schools at; *Devín*   272

Devin, royal fortress at; *Devín*   276

Die Wahrheit   186

Diet Reporter, The   106

Dilong, Rudolf   226

Dissertatio Philologico-Critica de Literis Slavorum (Philologico-Critical Dissertation on the Slovak Language) 91

Divin Stronghold; *Divín*   65, 66

Dobriansky, Adolph   138

Dobrovsky, Josef; *Josef Dobrodský* 99, 100

Dolezal, Pavol; *Pavol Deležal*   81

Domarus, Max   341, 342

Dominican monks   60

Donitz, Admiral Karl; *Karl Dönitz*   364

Donoval, Jan; *Ján Donoval*   158
  (see also Milkin, Tichomir)

Doza, Juraj; *Juraj Dóža*   56

Dresdner Bank   223

Dubcek, Alexander; *Alexander Dubček*   58–260, 295, 297, 359–361

Dudcky, Jan   305

Dula, Matus; *Matúš Dula*   157, 166, 190, 191, 285

Durcansky, Ferdinand; *Ferdinand Ďurčanský*   211, 218, 246, 290, 347, 348

Durica, Milan S.; *Milan S. Ďurica*   339, 344, 345, 346, 347, 348, 349, 350, 351, 352, 353, 363–364

Duris, Julius; *Július Ďuriš*   252

Dusik, Gejza; *Gejza Dusík*   225

Dzurinda, Mikulas; *Mikuláš Dzurinda*   303–305, 306

Eastern Front   223, 226, 230, 232, 343

Eastern Church   22

Eastern Orthodox Church   175, 210

economy   222, 223, 337

Edict of 1861   131

education   255

Eger, Bishop of   38

Eichmann, Adolf   220, 221

Elan; *Elán*   225

Elizabeth, dowager Queen; *Alžbeta*   54

Emory, Prince   275

Engels, Friedrich   183

Engelschalk, Duke   21

Enlightenment   90, 98, 280, 321–323

Equality; *Rovnost'*   159, 333
  (see also Rovnost)

Equalization 139, 143–145, 147, 175, 179, 284, 328, 330, 331

(see also Austro-Hungarian Compromise)
Erdody family; *Erdödyovci*   174
Esterhazi, Palatine Mikulas; *Mikuláš*
    Esterházy   69
Esztergom, Archbishopric of; *Ostrihom* 37
Eszterhazy, Janos; Ján *Eszterházy* 215, 289,
                                    348
Estonia   305
Etrucsan, culture   267
Etymologia Vocabulorum Slavicorum 91
    (see also *An Etymology of Slovak Words*)
European Parliament   301, 303
European Union (EU)   302, 305
Fandly, Juraj; *Juraj Fándly*   99, 281
Farmers' Association   109
Farmers' League   241
fascism 203, 209, 229, 232, 233, 239, 290,
                        292, 343, 345
fascism, clerico-   209, 343
Fascist Party   206
Federal Assembly   297, 299
Federal Republic of Germany   250
Federation of Slovak Rail Workers 200
Fejervari, Gejza; *Gejza Fejerváry* 161
Felvidek; Felvidék   150
    (see also *The Uplands*)
FEMKE   150
    (see also Upper-Hungarian Educational Association)
Ferdinand I, King   64, 65
Ferdinand II, Emperor   318
Ferdinand V   119
feudalism   44, 48, 96, 171, 275, 325
Fierlinger, Zdenek; *Zdeněk Fierlinger* 237,
                        249, 358
Figuli, Margita   225
Filakovo Stronghold; *Fiľakovo* 65, 66, 73
Finnland, annexation of
    by Soviet Union   347
First Catholic Slovak Ladies Union 333
First Catholic Slovak Union   159
First Hungarian Self-help and Advisory
    Association of Railroad Employess 185
First International   184, 186
First World War 148, 164, 166, 175, 177,
        209, 227, 284, 285, 330, 331, 332, 333,
                    334, 336, 338, 341, 361
    (see also World War I)
Flora; *Flóra*   227
Forgac family; *Forgáč*   49
Forgac, Anton; *Anton Forgáč*   131
Forgac, Archbishop Frantisek; *František*
    Forgáč   69
Forward (see also Vpred)   185, 186
Fourth Estate   44, 67, 78, 79, 279

(see also free royal towns)
France, Slovak emigration to   202
Francis II Rakoczi, Emperor; *František II.*
    Rákoci   92, 93, 95, 98, 279
    (see also Rakoczi, Francis II)
Franciscan friar   93
Franciscan churches   75
Franciscans religious order   72
Francisci, Janko   121, 133–135, 147
Frank, Karl Herman   213
Frankel, Leo   186
Frankish army   309
Frankish Empire   270
Frankish Kingdom, East 19, 22, 24, 27, 309
Frankish missionaries   271
Frankish society   271
Franks   17, 18, 21, 22, 270, 271
Franz Ferdinand, Crown Prince and Arch-
    duke; *František Ferdinand*   164, 165
Franz Joseph I, Emperor;
    *František Jozef I.*119, 125, 131, 132, 143,
                                    325
Fraternal Fund   181
Frederick the Great, King of Prussia 84
    (see also Friedrich II)
free royal towns   44, 67, 78, 79, 279
    (see also Fourth Estate)
Freedom Party   243
French Revolution   93, 95, 103, 281, 318,
                        322, 323, 324
Friedrich II, King of Prussia   84
    (see also Frederick the Great)
Friend of School and Literature 127
Fuggers of Augsburg   45, 58
Fugger-Thurzo Company   45, 46
Fulla, Ludovit; *Ľudovít Fulla*   225
Furdek, Stefan; *Štefan Furdek* 159, 168
Gabcik, Jozef; *Jozef Gabčík*   350
Gaboltov, pilgrimage site of   80
Galicia   32, 79, 96, 119, 313, 315, 347
Gardista   213
Gasparovic, Ivan;
    Ivan Gašparovič   1, 2, 302, 305
Gejza, Prince (Geza)   29, 274, 275
Gepids   269
Geringer, Baron   122
German armed forces   205, 209, 224, 228,
                        229, 241
German Army Group Center   228
German Command   224
German Democratic Republic   250, 261
German Empire, First 19, 32, 72, 114, 123,
                    144, 310, 314, 315
    (see also Holy Roman Empire)

German Empire, Second   144
German ethnic people   154, 186, 196, 210, 214–215, 238–239, 274, 276–278, 284, 287, 316, 319, 322, 326, 336–337, 339, 341, 344–345, 348, 363
German ethnic people, deportation of   241, 250, 354, 357
German Federal Republic   250, 257
German Führer   203–207, 209, 211–213, 216, 218, 233, 290, 292, 337, 341, 342, 343, 347, 348, 357, 362–364
   (see also Hitler, Adolf)
German language   86, 91, 107, 151, 174, 346
German language, literary   68, 127
German language, offical administration language   129, 322, 328
German National Assembly   114
German National Socialism   212, 213
German occupation of Slovakia   233, 291, 344, 352
German Reich   203, 205, 211–213, 215, 216, 222, 223, 232, 343, 347, 350, 363–364
German Reich, Chancery of   207, 211, 341
German Security Police   213
   (see also Sicherheitsdienst)
German schools   194, 336
German Wermacht   223
Germanic nations   19, 151, 309
Germanic tribes   268
Germanization   129, 283
German-Magyar, schools   194
German-Slovak Volunteer Guard   220, 293
   (see also Schutzstaffel; SS)
Germany, dividing of   250
Germany, Greater   114, 118
Germany, national unification movement 94
Germany, Nazi   288, 290, 292, 342, 344, 363
Germany, unification   123, 156
Geza II, King; *Gejza II.*   276
Ghent system   340
Gisela, Queen; *Gizela*   29
glasnost   296
Gojdic, Bishop;
   Pavol Peter Gojdič   253, 294
Golden Bull of King Andrew II;
   Ondrej II.   36, 37, 41, 52, 83, 276, 316
Golian, Jan; *Ján Golian*   230, 292
Good Friday 1988   296, 361
Gorbachev (Gorbacov), Mikhail;
   Michail Gorbačev   261, 296
Gorgei family; *Görgey*   50
Gorgei, commander of Magyar forces;
   Görgey   120, 125

Gothic style   58, 108
Goths   15, 269
Gottwald, Klement   201, 237–240, 244, 247–251, 260
Gottwald, Klement, death of   253, 258
Gottwald, Klement,
   Magna Carta speech   244, 250
Grammatica Slavica   91
Grassalkovich Palace   303
Great Moravia; *Veľká Morava*   18, 20, 21, 22, 24, 25, 137, 151, 271–275, 309, 310, 311, 312, 313, 324, 327
   (see also Magna Moravia)
Great Moravian Legal Procedures   272
Great Pannonian revolt   14
Great-Moravian Legal Code   272
Greeks   9, 10, 61
Grunwald, Bela; *Béla Grünwald*   148, 150
guilds   43, 68
guilds, abolition of   178, 183
Gutenberg, Johannes   61
Habsburg absolutism   77, 125, 329
Habsburg dynasty   63–67, 70, 73, 74, 278, 317–320, 362
Habsburg Empire   83, 84, 93, 94, 96, 103, 106, 111, 114, 123, 164, 190, 195, 320, 322, 331, 325, 326
Habsburg estates   71, 327
Habsburg monarchy   94, 121, 125, 127, 167, 278, 279, 280, 325–327, 334, 338
Habsburg, Ferdinand   63
Hadik, Count   190
Hadrian II, Pope; *Hadrián II.*   23
Hacha, Emil; *Emil Hácha*   207, 290
Hajnoci, execution of; *Hajnóci*   281
Hallstatt Age   10, 308
Hanzlicek, Karol; *Karol Hanzlíček*   186
Hassik, Stefan; *Štefan Haššík*   204, 232
Hattala, Martin   126, 128, 282
Havel, Vaclav; *Václav Havel*   297
Havlicek, Fratinsek; *František Havlíček*   326
Haynau, Baron   122, 328
Hazding tribe   268
Hellenic civilization   267
Helsinki Conference on Human Rights   295
Helsinki, Summit   304
Henry II, Emperor; *Henrich II.*   29, 30
Henry III, Emperor; *Henrich III.*   31, 32
Henry V, German Ruler; *Henrich V.*   32
Heruli tribe   15, 269
Heydrich, Reinhard   220, 350
Heyduk, Adolf   151
High Tatras   302
Himmler, Heinrich   231

Historia Mundi (History of the World) 273
History of Slovak Literature 151
Hitler, Adolf 197, 202–207, 209, 211–213,
   216, 218, 233, 290, 292, 337, 341–343,
         347–348, 357, 362–364
  (see also German Führer)
Hitler: Speeches and Proclamations
         263, 342
Hitlerjugend (Hitler Youth) 215
Hittite peoples 9, 265
Hlas 157, 158, 165, 285
  (see also *Voice, The*)
Hlasists 158, 162, 285, 346
Hlinka Guard 206, 209, 213, 214, 220, 226,
     232, 290, 291, 293, 343, 347
Hlinka Guard Emergency Force 232
Hlinka Youth 213, 214
Hlinka, Andrej 150, 155, 161–164, 166,
   171, 189–191, 196, 200, 201, 203, 210,
   211, 213, 243, 284, 285, 287–290, 331,
     336, 338, 340, 341, 346, 350
Hlinka's Slovak People's Party 196, 203,
   204, 206, 209, 210, 218, 219, 225, 226,
   232, 235, 236, 247, 288, 290, 292, 331,
   336, 337, 338, 341, 347, 349, 350, 351,
         352, 355
Hloznik, Vincent; *Vincent Hložník* 225
Hodonin, public demonstration at (1905);
  Hodonín 161
Hodza, Fedor; *Fedor Hodža* 240
Hodza, Michal Miloslav; *Michal Miloslav*
  Hodža 101, 107, 112, 114, 115, 126,
       149, 158, 282
Hodza, Milan; *Milan Hodža* 160–165, 171,
   189, 190, 196, 197, 205, 206, 226, 285,
     288, 290, 336, 339, 341, 346
Hohenlohe, Prince 174
Holly, Jan; *Ján Hollý* 100, 101, 126–128,
       282, 324
Holocaust 362
Holy Alliance 94
Holy Roman Empire 19, 32, 72, 114, 123,
      144, 310, 314, 315
  (see also German Empire, First)
Homola, General 207
Horvath, Jozef 119, 327
House of Bourbon 94
Hradcany Castle, seat of President;
  Hradčany 297
Hradec Kralove, Battle of;
  Hradec Králové 139
  (see also Konigsgratz, Battle of)
Hronec, Jur 224
Hronsky, Jozef Ciger;

Jozef Cíger Hronský 225
Humanism 61
Hunady, Jan; *Ján Huňady* 54, 55
Hungarian Constitution 131, 143
Hungarian Constitution, Article XII 143
Hungarian Diet 41, 44, 50, 54, 58, 64, 65,
   67, 84, 91, 92, 97, 105, 106, 110, 111,
   115, 121, 131, 133, 135, 138, 139, 144,
       146, 160, 168
Hungarian Diet (1608–09) 68, 69
Hungarian Diet (1620) 70
Hungarian Diet (1646–47) 319
Hungarian Diet (1687) 83
Hungarian Diet (1796) 93
Hungarian Diet (1811–12) 95
Hungarian Diet (1825) 95
Hungarian Diet (1830) 95
Hungarian Diet (1832–36) 95
Hungarian Diet (1839–40) 95
Hungarian Diet (1843–44) 95
Hungarian Diet (1847–48) 103, 115
Hungarian Diet (1867–68) 143, 145
Hungarian Diet (1918) 190
Hungarian Diet, dissolution of 118, 125
Hungarian Diet,
  National Committee of the 134, 135
Hungarian Estates 54, 64, 91, 95
Hungarian Governorship 136
Hungarian Legal Code 67, 146
  (see also *Corpus Juris Hungarici*)
Hungarian National Directory 329
Hungarian nationalists 362
Hungarian Parliament 186
Hungarian Revolution 122, 125, 129, 130,
      325, 326, 328
  (see also Magyar Revolution)
Hungarian Royal Chancery 136
Hungarian Workers' Party 186
Hungarianism, anti- 134
Hungary, EU Membership 305
Hungary, German occupation of 221
Hungary, Greater 289
Hungary, Kingdom of 131, 163, 194, 274,
   276, 280, 279, 313, 314, 316–317
Hungary, Old 29, 58, 68, 77, 98, 103,
       174, 243
Huns 15, 269, 274, 308
Hunt-Poznan family 275
Hurban, Anna; *Anna Hurbanová* 333
Hurban, Jozef Miloslav 101, 108,
   112–117, 121, 122, 126, 132, 134, 149,
     150, 158, 282, 327, 330
Hus, Jan 195, 317
Husak, Gustav; *Gustáv Husák* 236, 237,

244, 246, 247, 249, 250, 252, 255, 260,
    261, 292, 294, 353, 357, 358
Husak, Gustav, imprisonment of;
  Gustáv Husák   252, 358
Husak, Gustav, release of;
  Gustáv Husák   258
Husak, Gustav, resignation of;
  Gustáv Husák   261, 297
Hussites   52–56, 68, 100, 317
Hviezdoslav   150, 332
  (see also *Országh, Pavol*)
HZDS   298, 299, 301–305, 364
  (see Movement for Democratic Slovakia)
Ilava, concentration camp at   219
Ileshazi, Stephen; *Štefan Ilešházi*   67
Illyrian peoples   10, 268, 308
Imperial armed forces   117, 123
Imperial Constitution   113, 121
Imperial Council   131, 136, 329
Imperial Court 67, 97, 113, 115, 121, 149,
    282, 283
Imperial Diet   113, 118, 119, 131
Imperial Chancery   136
Imperial Parliament   165
Independent Association of
  Economists in Slovakia   298
Independent Party   148
Independent Socialists Party   165
Indo-Europeans   10, 308, 309, 358
industrialization   245, 252, 331, 336
industrialization, de-   338
industry   195, 244, 251, 322, 329
industry, Apollo (munitions) Refinery   223
industry, banking   168, 173, 176, 244
industry, brewing   141
industry, building   180
industry, cellulose   177, 180
industry, cement/lime   177
industry, clothing and footwear   180, 181
industry, construction   251
industry, copper   68
industry, Czech film   224
industry, distilleries   141
industry, Dynait-Nobel Chemical Works
  (munitions)   223
industry, early coin-minting   267
industry, early copper forging   44
industry, early copper mining   46, 68, 265
industry, early gold mining   44, 277
industry, early iron forging   44
industry, early silver mining   39
industry, finishing mills   141
industry, flour mills   141, 179
industry, food-processing   141, 180

industry, furniture   141
industry, general strike   198, 261
industry, German film   224
industry, glass working   177, 179
industry, gold   179, 181
industry, grain   97, 141
industry, growth of   329
industry, increase of productivity   254
industry, iron forging   139, 178, 180, 181,
    185, 202
industry, leather   141, 180, 185
industry, machinery manufacture   141, 179
industry, mining   178, 180, 182, 223, 276
industry, modernization of Slovak   181
industry, paper   180
industry, productivity slump   202
industry, Protectorate film   224
industry, rail   181, 182, 185, 200
industry, sawmills   141, 179
industry, silver mining   179, 181, 277
industry, steel   223
industry, sugar   141, 179, 181, 185
industry, textile   179–181, 200
industry, tobacco   141, 181
industry, trade unions   160, 185, 186, 200,
    334, 340
industry, woodworking   179
industry, wool   97
Interhelp   258
International Agrarian Bureau   197
Irish, missionaries   271
Iron Age   10, 266
Iron Age, Early   267
Iron Age, Late   267, 308
Ismaelites   37, 316
Italian Front   224
Italian master masons   276
Italian missionaries   271
Italy, national unification movement   94
Jacobins, Hungarian   281
Jager fortress (today Eger)   66
Jagiellonian kings   41
Jakes, resignation of; *Jakeš*   261
Jan of Podebrady   56, 317
  (see also *Jiří z Poděbrad*)
Janosik, Juraj; *Juraj Jánošík*   321
Janousek, Antonin; *Antonín Janošek*   198
Jaszi, Oskar; *Dr. Oskar Jászi*   165, 334
Jazygos tribes   268
Jehlicka, F.; *F. Jehlička*   161, 162, 201
Jednota (see also *Unity*)   159
Jelacic, Josip; *Josip Jelačič* 113, 115, 116,
    118, 119
Jesensky, Janko; *Janko Jesenský* 225, 289

Jesuit churches   75, 78
Jesuit Order   80, 98, 278
Jesuit universities   72, 278
Jesuits   69, 72, 318
Jewish business, aryanization of   216, 221,
                                   223, 343, 349
Jewish business, coin-minting controllers 37
Jewish business, lenders   97, 155, 216
Jewish business, tavern keepers   97, 155,
                                   216, 324, 331
Jewish Code   213, 215–217, 219, 221,
                                   291, 349
Jewish Council, Bratislava   221
Jewish shadow government (Bratislava) 221
Jews, deportation of   214, 217, 218,
                     220–222, 231, 233, 291, 350
Jews, extermination of   231, 232
Jews, labor camps for   216, 221, 231, 291,
                                   344, 350
Jews, Slovak   89, 147, 174, 179, 201,
                                   210, 239
Jiri of Podebrady; *Jiří z Poděbrad* 56, 317
   (see also Jan of Podebrady)
Jiskra the Hungarian Baron, Jan   54, 55
John 'Lackland', King of England   36
John Paul II, Pope; *Ján Pavol II.* 297, 302
John VIII, Pope; *Ján VIII.*   24
Joseph I, Emperor; *Jozef I.*   84, 320
Joseph II, Emperor; *Jozef II.*   89– 91, 280,
                                   281, 321–323
Joseph, Palatine; *Jozef*   92
Josko, Matej   227, 292
Judaism   292
Juriga, Ferdinand   161, 162, 165, 166,
                     189–191, 201, 285, 287
Jurkovic, Samuel; *Samuel Jurkovič*   109
Just, Jozef   133
Kandrac, Pavel; *Pavel Kandráč*   304
Karlman, East Frankish ruler   21
Karmasin, Franz   204, 215
Karoly family   174
Karolyi, M.   190, 198
Karpatendeutsche Partei   203
   (see also Carpathian-German Party)
Kellner-Hostinsky, Peter;
   Peter Kellner-Hostinský   109
Kempny, Jan; *Ján Kempný*   247, 293
Khagan Bayan   17
Khuen-Hedervary, Karol   165
Kievan Rus   312
   (see also Old Rus, state of)
Kimerian tribe   10, 267
Kirchburg   301
Klaus, Vaclav; *Václav Klaus*   364

Klempa, Stefan; *Štefan Klempa*   126
Klimo, Dusan   305
Kmet, Andrej;
   Andrej Kmeť   152, 161, 284
Kmetko, Bishop;
   Dr. Karol Kmeťko   196, 347
Kocúr   214, 348
   (see also *Tomcat, The*)
Kolisek, Dr. Alois; *Dr. Alois Kolísek*   152
Kollar, Adam Frantisek;
   Adam František Kollár   281
Kollar, Jan; *Ján Kollár*   100, 126, 129,
                                   136, 282
Kollar, Martin; *Martin Kollár* 152, 158, 159,
                                   161, 162
Koloman, King   30, 32
Komarno fortress; *Komárno*   75
Komsomol (see also Soviet Youth)   258
Koniarik, Jan; *Ján Koniarik*   225
Königgrätz, Battle of   139
   (see also *Hradec Králové*, Battle of)
Koppanyi, King   275
Korec, Jan Cardinal   304, 359
Korean War   250
Kormendy, Ekes   289
Kosice Agreement; *Košice*   237, 238, 244,
                                   250, 356
Kosice Government Program; *Košice*   293
Kosice, Jesuit university of; *Košice*   278
Kosovo, Battle of   52
Kossuth, Louis; *Ľudovít Košút*   96, 103,
         104–106, 110, 111, 121–123, 129, 139,
                144, 204, 323, 325, 326, 329
   (also known as Kossuth, Lajos)
Kostka family   66
Kostka, Jozef   225
Kovac, Michal; *Michal Kováč*   298,
                                   301–303
Kozacek, Jozef; *Jozef Kozáček*   129
Kral, Janko; *Janko Kráľ*   111, 129, 149
Kramar, Karel; *Karel Kramář*   193
Kremnica, founding of royal mint at   277
Krman, Daniel   81, 281, 321
Kromeriz, Diet of; *Kroměříž*   121
Krushchev, Nikita   254, 258
Kubac, Frantisek; *František Kubač*   252
Kubala, Otomar   232
Kucera, Matus; *Matúš Kučera*   271, 310
Kufoldy, Victor   186
Kurutzi (Rakoczi's uprising army)   73, 84
Kusin, Vladimir   260, 361
Kusy, M; *M. Kusý*   296
Kuzmany, Karol   136, 138, 284
Kvetko, Dr. Martin   353

La Tene era 10, 308
Labor News, The 166, 187
Ladislas I, King; *Ladislav I.* 30, 314
Ladislas IV the Cuman, King;
  Ladislav IV. 33, 34
Ladislav V, King; *Ladislas V.* 49, 50, 317
Lake Blatno; *Blatenské jazero* 20
Lamberg, Count 117, 118
Land Register 85, 86, 139, 280
  (see also Urbar)
Langsfeld, Juraj 120
Lasallists 185
Lassalle, Ferdinand 183
Latin 68, 90, 91, 96
Latin, Esperanto 277
Latin, language of teaching 59
Latin, liturgical 58, 312
Latin, official language 47, 68, 103, 314
Latin, study of 61
Latour (see also Letour) 118, 327
Latvia 305
Lausman, Bohumil;
  Bohumil Laušman 249, 358
League of Slovak Partisans 241
Legal Landbook, The 127
Lehocky, Emanuel; *Emanuel Lehocký* 187,
     190, 191, 285
Lechfeld, Battle of 28, 273, 313
Lechnica, Carthusian monastery at 53
Lenin, Vladimir 201, 257
Leninism 250, 260
Leo IX, Pope; *Lev IX.* 32
Leopold I, Emperor 72, 73, 77, 78, 83,
     84, 320
Leopold II, King and Emperor 91, 92, 323
Leopoldov fortress 75, 83
Lessons in the Slovak Language 101
Letopis (scientific Annals) 149
Letour (see also Latour) 118, 327
Lettrich, Jozef 227, 235, 238, 239, 243,
     292, 293, 355
Lev printery 163
Levoca, Master Paul of;
  Majster Pavol z Levoče 58
Levoca, conferences at 303
Levoca, papal visit 302
Levoca, pilgrimage site of; *Levoča* 80
Lewartovsky, Major 122
Liberal Party, Hungarian 144, 153, 161
Lichard, Daniel 109, 126, 136, 147
Likava Fortress 53
Limes Romanus 13, 15, 268, 269
Linz, Peace of 71, 319
Lipany, Battle of 53

Liptovsky Svaty Mikulas, Mayday
  demonstration at;
  Liptovský Svätý Mikuláš 189, 190
Lithuania 305
Little Entente 203, 341
Little Orphans 53
  (see also *Sirotkovia*)
Lombard people 15, 17, 269, 270
Lotrinsky, Frantisek Stefan;
  Štefan František Lotrinský 87
Louis I The Great, King; *Ľudovít I.* 41, 46,
     49, 51, 277, 316
Louis II, King; *Ľudovít II.* 47, 54, 57
Louis the German; *Ľudovít Nemec* 20, 21,
     312
Louis V the Posthumous, King;
  Ľudovít V. 54, 55
Louis XIV, King of France;
  Ľudovít XIV. 319
Lower Saxony 39
LS-HZDS 298, 299, 301–305, 364
  (see Movement for Democratic Slovakia)
Ludaci 187, 189, 225, 235, 240, 247,
     338, 341
  (see also Populists; Hlinka's Slovak People's Party)
Lukac, Emil Boleslav;
  Emil Boleslav Lukáč 225
Lusatian culture 308
Luther, Martin 317
Lutheran 72
Lutheran Church 68, 77, 116, 132, 150,
     209, 220, 253
Lutheran churches 72, 75
Lutheran intelligensia 99
Lutheran person 163
Lutheran preachers 65
Lutheran regions 144, 228
Lutheran religion 66
Lutheran schools 109, 128, 136
Lutheran, Augsburg confession 278
Lutheranism 278, 318
Lutherans 80, 81, 166, 210, 235, 239, 280,
     319, 320, 356
Lutherans, Slovak 68, 81, 82, 98, 100, 103,
     148, 196, 278, 285
Mach, Alexander 214, 218, 221, 222, 246,
     290, 291
Madarovce culture; *Maďarovce* 8
Magin, Jan Baltazar;
  Ján Baltazár Magin 279, 281
Magna Moravia; *Veľká Morava* 18, 20, 21,
  22, 24, 25, 137, 151, 271–275, 309, 310,
     311, 312, 313, 324, 327
  (see also Great Moravia)

Magyar Academy of Sciences 96
Magyar administration, liquidation of 125
Magyar armed forces 115, 116
Magyar armed forces,
    capitulation of 122, 125
Magyar culture 96, 98, 281
Magyar ethnic people 25, 27, 28, 29, 30,
    50, 95, 96, 186, 196, 210, 215, 216, 238,
    239, 251, 273, 274, 277, 279, 287, 290,
        309, 312–315, 326, 327, 336
Magyar ethnic people, deportation of 241,
        242, 348, 354, 357
Magyar Honved
    (Magyar Home Guard) 120, 121, 325
Magyar language 68, 86, 91, 96, 98, 103,
    105, 111, 131, 150, 153, 174, 210, 242,
        281, 285, 356
Magyar Liberal Party 161
Magyar nation 84, 96, 125
Magyar National Council 190
Magyar national revival 103
Magyar nationalism 123, 322
Magyar official language 158
Magyar oppression of nationalities 162, 165
Magyar People's Party 161
Magyar property rights 47
Magyar regime 106, 116
Magyar Republic (see also Hungary) 305
Magyar Revolution 122, 125, 129, 130,
        325, 326, 328
    (see also Hungarian Revolution)
Magyar science 281
Magyar United Party 203
Magyarization 91, 96, 100, 101, 103, 111,
    121, 147, 148, 150, 154, 157, 163, 174,
    175, 204, 242, 284, 285, 325, 330–332,
        349, 357
Magyarones 117, 119, 121, 327, 346–347
Magyarorszag 313
Majernik, Cyprian; Cyprián Majerník 225
Major, Stefan; Štefan Major 239, 356
Malar, Jan, General;
    Ján Malár 227, 229, 352
Malta 305
Mamatej, Albert 168
Mandl company 185
Marcomani tribes 13–15, 268
Marcus Aurelius, Emperor 14, 268
Marcus Vinius 11
Marchfeld, Battle of 33
    (see also Moravske Pole, Battle of)
Maria Theresa, Queen of Hungary;
    Mária Terézia 79, 84, 85, 89, 139, 280,
        320–321, 323

Marianka, pilgrimage site of; Mariánka 80
Mark, Karl 183
Markovic, Ivan; Ivan Markovič 201
Marobuduus, King 13, 268
Marshall Plan 246, 250, 357
martial law 112, 166, 207
Martin Center 156, 158, 189
    (see also Slovak National Center)
Martin Declaration 191, 192, 287, 337–338
    (see also Declaration of the Slovak Nation)
Martincek, Stefan;
    Štefan Martinček 159, 333
Martinovic, Ignac; Ignác Martinovič 93, 281
Martin's Knoll, Nitra 25
Marx, Karl 186
Marxism 161, 163, 187, 237, 246, 250,
        257, 346
Marxist Leftist Party 200
Masaryk, Jan 237, 243
Masaryk, Tomas Garrigue;
    Tomáš Garrigue Masaryk 157, 158, 163,
    167, 171, 193, 203, 249, 285, 286, 289,
        324, 331, 335, 339, 352
Masonic lodges 92, 196
Matejka, Peter 225
Matica Ceska; Matice česká 151
Matica Slovenska;
    Matica slovenská 135–138, 149–151,
        203, 284, 299, 310, 328, 330-331,
        332, 360
Matica slovenská v Amerike 159
    (see also Slovak Cultural Institute of America)
Matica slovenská, Annals of 138
Mattias Corvinus, King; Matej Korvín
        46, 49, 55, 56, 58, 60, 316
Mazak, Jan Judge 304
Meciar, Vladimir;
    Vladimír Mečiar 301–305, 364
Medieval Ages 36, 41–43, 46-48, 58, 59,
        61, 68, 83, 90, 105, 277, 314, 316
Meditations 14, 268
Medvecky, K. A.; K. A. Medvecký 158, 191
Megyeri tribe 273, 274, 313
mechanization, agricultural 139, 194
Memorandum of Slovak Demands 132
Memorandum of the Slovak
    Nationality, A 133, 134, 135, 137, 146,
        147, 151, 283
Men of October 287
Merovingian realm 270
Mesolithic Period 264, 307
    (see also Stone Age, Middle)
Metalworkers' Union 356
Methodius; Metod 22, 23, 24, 27, 137, 272,

273, 308, 312, 361
Methodius, Life of; *Metod* 272
Metternich of Austria,
  Count von 94, 281, 325
Middle Ages 35, 269, 313, 316, 321,
  326, 331
Michael III, Emperor; *Michal III.* 22
Michael, Emperor of Byzantine Empire;
  Michal 309
Michalovce 59, 167
Migas, Jozef 303
Mikulov, Peace of 70
Mikulas Resolution; *Mikuláš* 189, 286
Miletic, Svetozar;
  Svetozár Miletič 139, 148–150
Milkin, Tichomir; Tichomír Milkin 158
  (see also Donoval, Jan)
Milovy Agreement; *Mílovy* 364
Miners' Bureau, The 181
Mining Freedoms 45
  (see also *Banská Sloboda*)
Mocsary, Lajos 148
Modry Kamen Stronghold;
  Modrý Kameň 65, 66
Mohac, Battle of;
  Moháč 57, 61, 63, 65, 277, 317–319
Mojmir dynasty; *Mojmír* 271
Mojmir I, King;
  Mojmír I. 20, 25, 271, 272, 309
Morava river, battle at 32
Moravcik, Jozef; *Jozef Moravčík* 299, 302
Moravia 117, 121, 189
Moravian Principality 20, 271
Moravian Uprising 21
Moravske Pole, Battle of 33
  (see also Marchfeld, Battle of)
Moscow, venue of Twentieth Congress of
  Communist Party 254
Movement for a Democratic
  Slovakia (HZDS) 298, 299, 301–305, 364
Moyses, Stefan; *Štefan Moyzes* 126, 129,
  135, 137, 138, 149, 284
Moyzes, Alexander 225
Mudroch, Jan; *Ján Mudroch* 225
Mudron, Michal; *Michal Mudroň* 149, 332
Mudron, Pavol;
  Pavol Mudroň 149, 154, 166, 332
Munich Pact 197, 205, 207, 209, 226, 290,
  337, 351, 354
Muran Stronghold; *Muráň* 68
Muran Union; *Muráň* 140,141
Muran, battle at; *Muráň* 121
Murgac, Jozef 1
Murin, Dr, Karol; *Dr. Karol Murín* 214

Mussolini, Benito 202, 203
Mycenean civilization 9, 265, 308
Myjava Bank 177
Napoleon Bonaparte 93–95, 326
Napoleon III 130, 329
Napoleonic Wars 93–95, 97, 281, 324
Národniari (see also Nationalists) 147
Narodnie noviny 333
Naše Slovensko (see also *Our Slovakia*) 164
Nastup film company; *Nástup* 224
National Assembly, Prague 251, 289, 297
National Bank 301
National Council of the Slovak Republic
  (NRSR or NR SR) 115, 117–119, 159, 166,
  189–192, 197, 227, 236–239 243, 252,
  255, 283, 287, 292, 298, 301–305, 325,
  356, 364
  (see also Slovak National Council)
National Front 237, 238, 243, 245, 247,
  249, 251, 293, 294
National News, The 147, 155, 164, 166
National Party 153, 162, 218, 227
National Revolutionary Committees 233
National Slovak Fraternal Society 159
National Slovak Society 333, 358
National Socialism 291
National Socialist German
  Workers' Party 204, 207, 213, 215, 217,
  221, 337, 357
  (see also Nazi Party)
National Socialist Party 206
National Socialist, Czech 357
National Socialists 246, 249
Nationalists, Slovak 147
  (see also *Národniari*)
Nationalities Act of 1868 162, 165, 284
nationalization 244, 354
Nationalization Day 238
NATO 250, 304, 305
  (see also North Atlantic Treaty Organization)
Naum 272
Naum, Life of 272
Nazi concentration camps 219, 362
Nazi defeat 226
Nazi Party 204, 207, 213, 215, 217, 221,
  337, 357
  (see also National Socialist German Workers' Party)
Nazi techniques 232, 291
Nazism 290, 292, 357, 363–364
Neanderthal Man 264
Neapolitan Kingdom 63
Nejedly, Zdenek; *Zdeněk Nejedlý* 237
Nemec; *B. Němec* 341
Neolithic Period, Lower 8

Neolithic Period, Upper   8
Neo-Utraquists   66, 319
Neppart   154, 155
   (see also Zichy People's Party)
New Era, The (see also *Nova Doba*)   333
New School (political wing)   146, 147
Nicholas I, Czar; *Mikuláš I.*   121, 127
Nitra   101
Nitra, Bishopric of   37, 275
Nitra, castle   271, 275
Nitra, coat-of-arms   275
Nitra, fortified town of   271
Nitra, church of St. Emeram   274
Nitra, church schools at   272
Nitra, papal visit   302
Nitran Slovenes/Slovaks   274
Nitranian Principality   20, 271, 273, 275, 276
NKVD   233
Nogaj, Khan; *Nogaj, chán*   34
Nomenklatura   295, 296
Nonnus coin   12
Norbertine canons   316
   (see also Premonstratensian canons)
Noricum, Roman province of   13, 268
normalization   357, 361
North Atlantic Treaty Organization   250
   (see also NATO)
Notes on Letters by the Monk Chrabr   272
Nová Doba   333
   (see also New Era, The)
Nove Zamky, fortress; *Nové Zámky*   71, 83
Novohrad, trade route   270
Novomesky, Laco;
   Laco Novomeský 225, 252, 258, 292, 294
Novotny, Antonin; *Antonín Novotný*   258, 260, 360
NRSR   115, 117, 118, 119, 159, 166, 189–192, 197, 227, 236,–239, 243, 252, 255, 283, 287, 292, 298, 301–305, 325, 356, 364
   (see also NR SR or Slovak National Council)
Obrenovic, Prince Michal of Serbia;
   Michal Obrenovič   327
October Diploma   131, 132, 328
October revolt of 1956   254
Of the Czechs in Malohont Country   81, 82
   (see also *De Bohemis Kishontensibus*)
Olah, Archbishop Mikulas;
   Mikuláš Oláh   66
Old Czech faction   332
Old Rus state (see also Kievan Rus)   312
Old Rus, language   23
Olmutz (Olomouc); *Olomúc*   121

Omladina (see also Czech Youth)   157
Omodej family; *Omodejovci*   277
   (see also Amadeus family)
Ongri tribe   273, 274
   (see also Uhri; Ungari)
Oravsky Hrad (Orava Fortress);
   Oravský hrad   73
Order of Confession, The   272
Orosius   273
Orsag, Jan; *Ján Országh*   138
Orszagh, Pavol; *Pavol Országh*   150, 332
   (see also Hviezdoslav)
Osusky, Stefan; *Štefan Osuský*   290
Osvald, F. R.   161
Oswiecim (see also Auschwitz)   217, 221, 231
Otoman culture   9, 308
Otto I the Great, King; *Oto I.*   28, 273
Ottoman Empire   54, 278, 279, 308
Ottoman Turkish occupation   278, 318
Ottoman Turks   73, 317, 319
Ottonian dynasty   274
Our Slovakia (see also *Nase Slovensko*)   164
Palacky, Frantisek;
   František Palacký   205, 326
Palarik, Jan; *Ján Palárik*
     126, 128, 132–134, 146, 149
Palatine   36
Paleolithic Period, Early   7
Paleolithic Period, Late   7, 264
Paleolithic Period, Middle   7
Paleolithic Period, Upper   307
Palffy family; *Pálffyovci*   174
Palffy, Moric; *Móric Pálffy*   131
Palkovic, Juraj; *Juraj Palkovič*   100, 281
Paloci family   49
Pan-Magyarism   281, 283, 284, 286
Pannonia, Roman province of   13, 15, 27, 268, 269
Pannonian Sabaria   269
Pan-Slavism   112, 122, 130, 150, 155, 187, 210, 330, 346
Paris Commune   185, 186
Paris, peace conference at (1919)   201
partisan guerillas   228, 229, 231, 232, 292, 344, 352
partisans, Ukrainian   247, 248
   (see also Benderovci)
Partisans, Union of   354
partisans, Yugoslav   228
Party of Independence   144
Party of Revival   249
Party of Slovak National Unity   348
Party of the Democratic Left   299
Passau, Bishop of   23

Paul VI, Pope; *Pavol VI.* 295
Pauliny-Toth, Viliam;
  Viliam Pauliny-Tóth 147, 149, 176
Paulist church 75
Paulist religious order 72
Pazmaneum University 127, 163, 210
Pazmany, Peter;
  Peter Pázmaň 69, 70, 77, 319
Pecheneg incursions 30, 312, 315
People's bank 163
People's Democracy 238, 239
People's Militia 249, 253, 258, 261,
  354, 355
People's News, The 155, 162, 165
People's Party 191, 206, 339, 341, 345
Pereni family; *Peréniovci* 49, 66
perestroika 261, 296
Pest, University of 133
Pesti Hirlap 103, 105
Peter of Bardejov (printer) 61
Peter, King 31, 315
Philologico-Critical Dissertation on the
  Slovak Language (Dissertatio Philologico-
  Critica de Literis Slavorum) 91
Piarist religious order 72
Piast Dynasty 29
Piava, Austro-Hungarian defeat at 171
Piedmont-Sardinia, Kingdom of 130
Pietor, Ambro 159, 333
Pika Uprising 278
Pika, Gaspar; *Gašpar Pika* 73, 319
Pittsburgh Pact 170, 171, 286, 288, 335
Pius XII, Pope 218, 221, 292, 362, 363
Plavci people 314
Plavecsky Hrad; *Plavečský hrad* 55
Pobedim, fortress at 271
Podbrezova, ironworks at; *Podbrezová* 139
Podmanicky, Jan; *Ján Podmanický* 68
Podmanicky, Rafael; *Rafael Podmanický* 68
Podmanicky family; *Podmanickovci* 49
Pohornad Ironworks 177
Pokorny, Rudolf; *Rudolf Pokorný* 151
Polabian Slavs 19
Poland 305
Polish ethnic people 196
Polish Uprising 94, 95
Polovci people 27, 314
Pomerania, german control of 156
Pongrac family; *Pongrácovci* 49, 50
Ponrad 7
Poor Man's Truth, The 200
  (see also *Pravda Chudoby*)
Populists 187, 189, 225, 235, 240, 247,
  338, 341

  (see also Ludaci; Hlinka's Slovak People's Party)
Pozsony 308, 326
  (see also Bratislava; Brezalauspurc; *Prešporok*;
  Pressburg)
Prago-Centrism 294
Prague Congress 327
Prague Spring 261, 295, 296
Prague, seat of First Czecho-Slovak
  Republic 189, 250
Pravda Chudoby 200
  (see also *Poor Man's Truth, The*)
Premonstratensian canons 38, 60, 316
  (see also Norbertine canons)
Premysl dynasty; *Přemyslovci* 274
Premysl Otakar II, King;
  Přemysl Otakar II. 32, 33, 276
Presburske noviny 90
  (see also *Bratislava News*)
Presov, butchery of; *Prešov* 278
Presov, Lutheran lyceum at; *Prešov* 278
Presporok; *Prešporok* 308, 326
  (see also Bratislava; Brezalauspurc; Pressburg;
  Pozsony)
press censorship, abolition of 104
Pressburg 308, 326
  (see also Bratislava; Brezalauspurc;
  Prešporok; Pozsony)
Pressburg News 104
  (see also *Pressburger Zeitung*)
Pressburg, Treaty of 93
Pressburger Zeitung 104
  (see also *Pressburg News*)
Pribina, Prince 20, 271, 309, 311
Pribis, Rudolf; *Rudolf Pribiš* 225
Procopius of Caesarea 269
Proglas; Prologue 23
Prologue, A; Proglas 272
Protectorate of Bohemian and
  Moravia 221–223, 235, 350, 351
Protestant confessions 66
Protestant Estates 71, 72
Protestant nobility 67
Protestant regions 89
Protestant religiosity 80
Protestant schools 278
Protestantism 65, 77, 318, 323
Provisional Government of Russia 167
Prudy; Prúdy 165, 201
  (see also *Currents*)
Prussia, german control of 156
Prussian armed forces 139
Prussian Empire 93, 94, 144
Public Against Violence 296–298
Puchov culture 14, 308
Pusty Hrad, royal fortress; *Pustý hrad* 276

Putin, Vladimir 306
Quadi (see also Swabians) 13–15, 268, 307
Rab fortress; (today Györ) 66
Radicalization 203
Radlinsky, Andrej; *Andrej Radlinský*
126–128, 132, 136, 137, 148, 152
Radvansky family; *Radvanský* 66
rail networks 139, 176
Rakoczi uprising 81, 279, 320
Rakoczi, Francis II;
František II. Rákoci 83
(see also Francis II Rakoczi, Emperor)
Rakoczi, Prince George I of Transylvania;
Juraj Rákoci I. 71
Rastislav, King 20–22, 271, 272, 309, 312
Razus, Martin; *Martin Rázus* 289
Red Army 227, 228, 231, 233, 235–237,
354, 356, 364
(see also Soviet armed forces)
Reformation, Catholic Counter- 69, 318
Reformation, Protestant 61, 63, 65, 66,
103, 278, 317–318
Religious Effusions 128
Renaissance ideas 60, 61
Renaissance style 58, 74, 75, 318
Republican Employment Center 200
Republican Party of Agriculture, the
and Small Farmers 197
Revai, Baron; *Révaj* 132
Revais family; *Révajovci* 66
Revolutionary Trade Union Movement 241
Ribbentrop,
German Foreign Minister 223, 347
Rieger, Fratisek Ladislav 149, 332
Rimamuran Iron Company 141, 178
Rimamuran-Salgotariany Ironworks 177
Rimava Coalition 139
Roman 11, 13–15, 308
Roman army 268
Roman Empire 17, 269, 309, 310
Romance nations 151, 309
Romanesque style 38
Romania 305
Romanian ethnic people 145, 165, 186, 277,
284, 322
Romanian Orthodox Church 132
Romanov dynasty 193
Romany ethnic people 68, 305
Rotarides, Jan; *Ján Rotarides* 111
Rovnianek, Peter Vitazoslav;
Peter Víťazoslav Rovnianek 158, 168
Rovnost (see also Equality) 159, 333
Rozgon family; *Rozgoňovci* 49
Rozhanovce, Battle of (1312) 51, 277

Rudnai, Cardinal Alexander; *kardinál*
Alexander Rudnay 99, 281
Rudolf of Habsburg,
Holy Roman Emperor 33, 315
Rugi tribe 15
Russia, allies 93
Russia, invasion of 94
Russian armed forces 121, 167
Russian ethnicity 175
Russian Orthodox Church 332–333,
336, 355
Russo-Finnish War 347
Russo-French Pact 145
Russo-Turkish war 150
Rusyn ethnic people; *Rusíni, Rusniaci* 41,
68, 145, 154, 155, 196, 210, 215, 277,
284, 316, 332, 333
(see also Carpatho-Rusyns; Carpatho-Ruthenians;
Ruthenians)
Rusyn language 175
Ruthenia 308, 327, 356
Ruthenian ethnic people;
Rusíni, Rusniaci 41, 68, 145, 154, 155,
196, 210, 215, 277, 284, 316, 332, 333
(see also Carpatho-Ruthenians; Carpatho-Rusyns;
Rusyns)
Ruzomberok Cellulose and Paperworks;
Ružomberok 177
Rybay, Juraj 99
Sacred Scriptures 90, 100
Safarik, Pavol Jozef;
Pavol Jozef Šafárik 100, 114, 158, 282
Sagun, Bishop 132
Salgotariany Iron-Ore Refinery 178
Salonica, Byzantine 272, 312
Salva, Karol 157, 225
Samizdat literature 296
Samo 17, 270, 309–311
Sanjaks (districts) 64, 318–319
Sarajevo, assassination in 166
Saris dialect; *Šariš* 151
Sarmatian peoples 268
Sasinek, Frantisek; *František Sasinek* 138
Sastin, pilgrimage site at; *Šaštín* 80
Sastin, papal visit 302
Schlaraffenland 223
Schulze-Delitzsch, Franz Hermann 183
Schutzstaffel 215, 220, 231, 293
(see also German-Slovak Volunteer Guard; SS)
Schuster, Rudolf 304, 305
Scientific Socialism 184
Scitovsky, Archbishop of Esztergom Jan;
Ján Krstiteľ Scitovský 129, 137
Scottish, missionaries 271

Scotus Viator 165, 334
(see also Seton-Watson, R. W.)
Scythian tribes 10, 267
Second International 160, 186, 334
Second World War 203, 212, 216, 230,
292, 342–343, 348, 351–353, 336
(see also World War II)
Self-Study Association of
Trade Union Youth 184
Serb-Croatian alliance 113
Serbian ethnic people 145, 147, 154, 155,
165, 186, 284, 322
Serbian vassalage 30, 52
Serbs of Vojvodina, uprising of 113
serfdom, abolition of 89, 107, 111, 139,
280, 282, 328
Sessie 47
Seton-Watson, R. W. 165, 334
(see also Scotus Viator)
Severini, Jan; *Ján Severíni* 281
seven Magyar chieftains 314
Short Grammar of the Slovak
Language 282
Sidor, Karol 207, 218, 235, 290, 342, 350
Sisigmund (Sigmund) of Luxembourg,
King 44, 49, 52, 54, 56, 316
Sigynnian tribe 267
Sicherheitsdienst 213
(see also German Security Police)
Silesia 156, 189
Singing and Songs 127
Siroky, Viliam;
Viliam Široký 236, 237, 239, 250,
257, 356, 359
Sirotkovia (see also Little Orphans) 53
Sixty-one Steps to Slovak Identity 298
Sklene, massacre at 229
Skultety, Augustin Horislav;
August Horislav Škultéty 136
Skultety, Jozef; *Jozef Škultéty* 281
Skycak, Frantisek; *František Skyčák* 161,
162, 165, 166, 190
Slav ethnic people 17, 18, 19, 107, 127,
151, 269, 270, 279, 309, 311, 312,
324–326, 332, 346
(see also Slavic peoples)
Slavdom, idea of 193
Slavic Congress, Prague 112, 114, 115, 325
Slavic ethnogenesis 17, 269, 361
Slavic languages 28
Slavic peoples 17, 18, 19, 107, 127, 151,
269, 270, 279, 309, 311, 312, 324–326,
332, 346
(see also Slav ethnic people)

Slavic reciprocity 100
Slavic society 271
Slavic state 19
Slavistics 100
Slavkov, Battle of 93
(see also Austerlitz, Battle of)
Slavomir; *Slavomír* 21
Slavonia, component of Hungarian state 146
Slavonic alphabet 22, 272
Slavonic language/literature
Old Church 23, 24, 272, 273, 312
Slavonic Rite 23
Slavonic, church schools 273
Slavs and the World of the Future 127
Slavs Austro-Hungarian 112
Slavs, Danubian 17, 19
Slavs, East 35, 309
Slavs, South 35, 68, 113, 115, 309, 312
Slezak, Johan 2
Slavs, West 271, 309, 312
Slota, Juraj 126, 129
Slovacka Bouda 164
(see also Slovak Booth)
Slovak Academy of Arts and Sciences 224
Slovak armed forces 209, 224, 228, 229,
230, 232
Slovak art 225, 255
Slovak autonomy 196, 200, 205–207, 210,
211, 213, 282, 290, 295, 299, 337
Slovak Booth (see also Slovacka Bouda) 164
Slovak Catholic People's Party 161, 164
Slovak Center for State Security 219
Slovak Crown; *Slovenska Koruna* 301
Slovak Communist Party 226, 235, 237, 241
Slovak Cultural Institute of America 159
(see also Matica Slovenska v Amerike)
Slovak culture 149, 255
Slovak Daily News, The 159
(see also *Slovensky Dennik*)
Slovak Democratic Party 246, 249, 250
Slovak Dialect or the Need to Write
in Slovak, The 101
Slovak ethnic people 186, 210, 274, 275,
277, 279, 284, 290, 323, 337, 353, 359,
363
Slovak Christian Democratic Movement 298
Slovak Gas Works 304
Slovak independence 363–364
Slovak Labor News 186
Slovak language 58, 86, 90, 91, 100, 101,
107, 110, 111, 121, 133, 158, 163, 174,
187, 282, 321, 322–323, 346
Slovak language, Bernolak codification
of 99, 126, 323, 322

Slovak language, cultural Western 101, 323
Slovak language, East   101
Slovak language, instruction in   128, 282,
                                          330
Slovak language, official   136
Slovak language,
   Stur codification of Central   100, 101,
      126, 127, 132, 281, 282, 323, 324, 328
Slovak language, Western cultural 58, 126,
                                          129
Slovak League of America   159, 168, 286,
                                          358
Slovak Learned Fellowship   99, 281
Slovak Learned Society   224
Slovak Letters   157
Slovak literature   225, 255
Slovak Movement   149, 150
Slovak Museum Association   152
Slovak music   225
Slovak national assembly   116
Slovak National Bank   222
Slovak National Center   156, 158, 189
   (see also Martin Center)
Slovak National Council 115, 117, 118, 119,
      159, 166, 189–192, 197, 227, 236–239,
         243, 252, 255, 283, 287, 292, 298,
            301–305, 325, 356, 364
Slovak National Council Board of
   Commissioners (Trustees)   239, 244,
      248, 249, 250, 252, 255, 293, 294, 356
Slovak National Council Board of
   Commissioners, formation of   238
Slovak National Home   152
Slovak National Movement   108, 109
Slovak National Museum   307
Slovak National News, The;
   Slovenskje Narudaje Novin: 108, 109,
                                          159
Slovak National Party   155, 161, 162,
   164–166, 189, 191, 206, 285, 288, 298,
                                     299, 341
Slovak National Revival   280, 281
Slovak National Socialism   213
Slovak National Theater   194
Slovak National Uprising   116, 117, 118,
      213, 215, 225, 229, 230, 231, 232, 237,
         239, 255, 283, 292, 344, 353–354
Slovak National Uprising,
   suppression of   293, 352, 353
Slovak News, The   126, 146
Slovak Office of Church Affairs   359
Slovak Ore Mountains   8, 45, 308
   (see also Slovenske Rudohorie)
Slovak Parliament   207, 215, 216

Slovak Party   162
Slovak People's News, The   165, 166, 189
Slovak People's Party   161, 162, 165, 166,
      171, 196, 200, 285, 288, 331, 350–352
Slovak Petition to the Throne   101
Slovak populist and Catholic movement 155
Slovak Precincts (*'okolia', Region*)   284
Slovak Region *(Precints)*   133, 136, 284
Slovak Republic   299, 301
Slovak Republic, First   207, 209–212, 218,
      219, 222, 224–226, 232, 235, 239, 290,
            292, 342–345, 350, 351, 364
Slovak science   255
Slovak scuplture   225
Slovak separatism   134
Slovak schools   148
Slovak Socialist Party   333
Slovak Society   156
   (see also Slovensky Spolok)
Slovak Soviet Republic   198, 292
Slovak State Council   219
Slovak Unity   348
   (see also Slovenska Jednota)
Slovak Views on the Sciences,
   Arts and Literature   108, 126
Slovak Volunteer Corps 108, 114, 117–119,
                         121–123, 283, 325
Slovak Weekly News, The   160, 189
Slovak World Congress   348
Slovak Youth   148
   (see also Slovenska Omladina)
Slovak, property rights   47
Slovak-Czech-Latin-German-Magyar
   Dictionary   91, 99
Slovakization, re-   242
Slovakophile movement   151
Slovaktown, Arkansas   159
Slovenia   305
Slovenska Jednota   348
   (see also Slovak Unity)
Slovenska Omladina   148
   (see also Slovak Youth)
Slovenske Rudohorie   8, 45, 308
   (see also Slovak Ore Mountains)
Slovensky Dennik   159
   (see also *Slovak Daily News, The*)
Slovensky Spolok   156
   (see also Slovak Society, The)
Smidke, Karol; *Karol Šmidke* 227, 236, 238,
               239, 241, 244, 252, 292, 351
Smigovsky, Major J.;
   major Ján Šmigovský   230
Smolnik, copper mines at; *Smolník*   45
Smrek, Jan   225

Sobieski, Jan 83
Social Democratic Party of
  Upper Hungary 187
Social Democratic Party, Hungarian 153,
  161, 166, 186, 187
Social Democratic Party, Slovak 187,
  189–191, 198, 200, 204, 206, 227, 235,
  237, 241, 243, 257, 288, 330, 334, 340,
  343, 354, 357, 358
socialism 185, 248, 255, 257, 258, 259,
  261, 295, 360, 361
socialism, Christian 330
Socialist Workers' 333
Societas excolendae linguae Slavicae
  (Society for the Cultivation of the Slovak
  Language) 91
Society of Slovak Writers 298
socio-economic growth, Slovak 255
Sokol, Koloman 226, 351
Solferino, Battle of 130, 329
Solidarity (see also Svornost) 148
Soloman, (King Andrew I's son) 32
Sopron Compromise; Šoproň 320
Sopron, Diet of; Šoproň 73, 77, 78
Soviet Academy of Sciences 224
Soviet armed forces 224, 227, 228, 231,
  233, 235–237, 354, 356, 364
  (see also Red Army)
Soviet Army 254, 259
Soviet occupation of East Germany 250
Soviet occupation of Slovakia 233, 235,
  241, 295
Soviet POWs 228
Soviet Union 203, 209, 212, 216, 219,
  236, 238, 247, 249, 258–261, 292–296,
  347, 351, 352, 354, 356–358, 363
Soviet Union, Benes' alliance with 203, 351
Soviet Youth (see also Komsomol) 258
Soviet-German Pact (1939) 220
Sovietization 293
Spis Stronghold; Spišský hrad 54
  (see also Spissky Hrad)
Spissky Hrad; Spišský hrad 54
  (see also Spis stronghold)
Srobar, Vavro; Vavro Šrobár 157, 158, 165,
  170, 189–191, 197, 227, 235, 243, 285,
  286, 288
SS 215, 220, 231, 293
  (see also Schutzstaffel; German-Slovak
  Volunteer Guard)
St. Adalbert 274
St. Adalbert Pilgrim, The 148
St. Adalbert, feast of 42
St. Adalbert, Society of 127, 148, 152, 159,

203, 331
St. George, feast of 41
St. Gorazd 272, 273, 361
St. John the Baptist Cathedral 75
St. Martin's Cathedral 74, 331
St. Martin of Tours 269
St. Petersburg,
  capital of Russian Empire 95
St. Stephen 29, 30, 274, 275, 313, 315
  (see also Stephen I, King; Vajk)
St. Stephen, Society of 127
Stadion, Count 121
Stalin, Joseph 233, 244, 247, 250, 253, 258,
  340, 351, 354, 356
Stalin, Joseph, death of 253
Stalinism 254, 258
Stano, Vladimir 2
Stara Tura, torching of; Stará Turá 117
Starai family; Stáraiovci 50
Stare Hory, pilgrimage site of;
  Staré Hory 80
State Council 220, 350
State Security 226
Stefanek, Anton; Anton Štefánek 162, 164
Stefanik, Milan Rastislav;
  Milan Rastislav Štefánik 167, 286, 331,
  335, 339, 346
Stefanik, Milan Rastislav, death of;
  Milan Rastislav Štefánik 197, 198, 286
Stefanovic, Samuel; Samuel Štefanovič 149
Stefunko, Frano; Fraňo Štefunko 225
Stephen I, King; Štefan I. 29, 30, 274,
  275, 313, 315
  (see also St. Stephen; Vajk)
Stephen II, King; Štefan II. 276
Stephen V, King; Štefan V. 32–34, 36
Stetina, Mikulas Bakalar;
  Mikuláš Bakalár Štetina 61
Stibor II 49
Stibors of Stiborice 49
Stodola, Emil 189
Stone Age man 307
Stone Age, Early 7
Stone Age, Early New 7
Stone Age, Late New 8
Stone Age, Middle 265, 307
  (see also Mesolithic Period)
Strank, Michael 1
Strechaj, Rudolf 252
Strossmayer, Bishop 132
Students' Day, demonstration 261
Stur, Karol; Karol Štúr 127
Stur, Ludovit; Ľudovít Štúr 107–110, 112,
  114, 115, 120–123, 126, 127, 158, 281,

323, 324, 327–329, 335
Sub-Carpathia 175
Sudeten Germans, ethnic people 195, 197,
203, 204, 241, 249, 339
Sudeten Germans, ethnic people,
deportation of 357
Sudetenland 205, 241, 342, 357
Suetonius 13
Suchon, Eugen; *Eugen Suchoň* 225
Suleiman, Sultan 57
Summa Legum Raimundi 58
Svantner, Frantisek;
František Švantner 225
Svatojansky, Baron; *Svätojánsky* 132
Svatopluk I, ruler of Great Moravia;
Svätopluk I. 21, 24, 25, 271, 272, 273,
312, 313
Svatopluk II, Prince; *Svätopluk II.* 25, 273
Svehla, Anton; *Anton Švehla* 339
Svehla, Jan; *Ján Švehla* 55
Sverma, Jan; *Ján Šverma* 240
Svoboda, Ludvik;
Ludvík Svoboda 237, 259, 295
Svodin, primitive fort at; *Svodín* 264
Svornost; Svornosť 148
(see also *Solidarity*)
Swabians (see also Quadi) 13
Sylvester II, Pope; *Silvester II.* 274
Szapari, Count Gyula 153
Szechenyi, Count Istvan;
Štefan Sečéni 96, 103, 105, 323
Szeklers, language and customs 27, 314
Szell, Kalman (Koloman) 153
Szentivanyi, M. 289
Tablic, Bohuslav 281
Taborites (splinter group of Hussites) 53
Tacitus 13
Tatar (Tartar) 30, 33, 34, 39, 83, 276, 315
Tatarka, Dominik 345
Tatra Eagle, The 108
Tatrabanka 152, 176, 179
Tatraner (Tatran) 156
Tatrin cultural society 107, 127
Tauriscans 11
Thesalonike (Thessalonica), *Solún* 23, 312
Thokoli, Imrich; Imrich Tököli 72, 73, 83,
278
Third International 201
Thirty Years War 71
Thracians 10, 267
Thurzo family 66
Thurzo, Francis, Bishop of Nitra 66
Thurzo, Jan 45
Thurzo, Palatine George 67, 74

Tiberius, Emperor 13
Timon, Samuel 280
Tiso, Jozef 221, 229, 290,
292, 342, 343, 345–348,
358, 363, 364
Tiso, Jozef, 1939 meeting with Hitler
207, 211, 342
Tiso, Jozef, public statements
213, 229, 363, 364
Tiso, Jozef, relationship with Benes
341, 357, 358, 363
(see also Benes, Edvard)
Tiso, Jozef, relationship with
Catholic clergy 214, 344, 347, 350
Tiso, Jozef, relationship with
Communism 241, 346, 355
Tiso, Jozef, relationship with Donitz 364
(see also Donitz, Admiral Karl)
Tiso, Josef, relationship with Hitler
207, 211, 342, 363, 364
(see also Hitler, Adolf)
Tiso, Jozef, relationship with Hlinka
204, 210, 213
(see also Hlinka, Andrej)
Tiso, Jozef, relationship with Jews 213,
217–218, 221, 231, 343–345, 349, 350
(see also Jews)
Tiso, Jozef, relationship with Mach
222, 290, 291
(see also Mach, Alexander)
Tiso, Jozef, relationship with
Nazi leaders 213, 231, 344, 347, 348,
363, 364
Tiso, Jozef, relationship with Stalin 363
(see also Stalin, Joseph)
Tiso, Jozef, relationship with Tuka
211, 213, 222, 290, 293, 348
(see also Tuka, Vojtech)
Tiso, Jozef, relationship with the Vatican
210, 218, 344, 350
Tiso, Jozef, role in National Uprising
231, 232, 293, 354
(see also Slovak National Uprising)
Tiso, Jozef, trial and execution of
245, 246, 357, 358
Tiso, Stefan; *Štefan Tiso* 231, 353
Tisovec Credit Cooperative
and Savings Bank 177
Tisza, Count Istvan 161
Tisza, Count Koloman 135, 149, 153,
161, 284
Tisza, Koloman 284
Tito, Josip Broz 250
Titoists 294

Toleration Edict 78, 82
Toleration Patent 89, 91, 98, 280, 321, 323
Tomcat, The (see also *Kocúr*) 214, 348
Tranoscius (Lutheran publishing house) 148
Trans-Danubia 105, 115
Transleithania 327
Treasures of the Art of Preaching 127
Treaty of Protection 347, 363–364
Trenciansky;
  Matúš Čák Trenčiansky 50, 51, 277
  (see also Cák, Matus)
Trencin, royal fortress; *Trenčín* 276
Tridentine Council 66
Tripartium 58
Trnava, university of 278
Tuka, Vojtech 201, 211, 213, 219–223,
  232, 290, 291, 342, 343, 347, 348
Tuka, Vojtech, execution of 246
Turciansky Svaty Martin meeting;
  Turčiansky Svätý Martin 337
Turciansky Svaty Martin, issuing of Martin
  Declaration; *Turčiansky Svätý Martin* 191
Turciansky Svaty Martin, massacre at;
  Turčiansky Svätý Martin 228, 229, 352
Turciansky Svaty Martin, Slovak rally at;
  Turčiansky Svätý Martin 132
Turdus 13
Turkish defeat 278
Turkish Empire 44, 327
Turkish Front 71
Turkish occupation 64, 98
Turkish Porte 64, 71, 72
Turks, expulsion of 144, 279
Ughetai, Khan 34
Ugric tribes 308, 313
Uhri tribe 273
  (see also Ongri; Ungari)
Ukrainian partisans (nationalists) 247, 248
  (see also Benderovci)
UNESCO 301
Unetice culture 8
Ungari tribe 273, 274
  (see also Ongri; Uhri)
Union of Slovak Youth 109
United Nations 242, 299, 301
United States Census Bureau 159
United States, NATO member 305
United States, Rusyn emigration to 333
United States, Slovak emigration to 158,
  159, 285, 329, 340
United States, presidential visits to 302
Unity (see also *Jednota*) 159
Universal German Workers' Association 183
Universal Workers' Party 186

Uplands; Horné Uhorsko, the; 150
  (see also *Felvidek*)
Upper-Hungarian Educational
  Association 150
  (see also FEMKE)
Urban, Milo 213
Urbar; *urbár* 85, 86, 139, 280
  (see also Land Register)
Urbarial Edict (1853) 139
Urbarial legal cases 149
Ursiny, Jan; *Ján Ursíny* 227, 235, 237, 239,
  247, 292, 293
Ursuline religious order 72
US, emigration to 202
USSR 203, 209, 212, 216, 219, 236,
  238, 247, 249, 258–261, 292–296, 347,
  351, 352, 354, 356, 358
  (see also Soviet Union)
Utraquists 319
Uzhorod Union; *Užhorod* 78
Vajansky, Svetozar Hurban; *Svetozár
  Hurban Vajanský* 150, 151, 157, 330, 335
Vajk 29, 30, 274, 275, 313, 315
  (see also Stephen I, King; St. Stephen)
Valentian I, Emperor 269
Vandals, people 269
Vannius, Kingdom of 14, 268
Vata, tribal chief 315
Velicko, Lt. Peter;
  Piotr Alexejevič Veličko 352
Velvet Revolution 261, 346, 349, 361
Veneti 10
Venus of Moravany figurine;
  moravianska venuša 7, 307
Vercik, Julius; *Július Verčík* 201
Versailles Peace Conference 337, 340
Versailles, Treaty 209
Veseleni, Palatine; *Vešeléni* 71
Veselovsky, F.; *František Veselovský* 159
Vesely, Frantisek Kristof;
  František Krištof Veselý 225
Vesin, Jaroslav; *Jaroslav Věšín* 151
Vienna Resolution 206
Vienna, Imperial capital 317
Vienna, Imperial Council 167
Vienna, Imperial Court of 80, 94–96, 118,
  123, 125, 126, 130, 138, 139, 145, 150
Vienna, regime of 129, 130
Vienna, Treaty of 67
Viest, General R 230, 292
Vilagos, capitulation at; *Világoš* 125
Visegrad four 302
Vislany, Slavic tribe 312
Vladislas II Jagiello, King;

Vladislav Jagelovský   56, 57, 63, 317
Vlcek, Jaroslav; *Jaroslav Vlček*   151
Voice, The   157, 158, 165, 285
  (see also *Hlas*)
Vojtassak, Jan;
  Ján Vojtaššák   196, 218, 253, 294, 350
Vojtassak, Jan, execution of;
  Ján Vojtaššák   350
Volunteer Guard Unit   215
  (see also Freiwillige Schutz-staffel)
Vpred (see also Forward)   185, 186
Vyhne, massacre by partisans   229
Wach, (Lombard) King   269
Walker, General Walton H.   350
Wallachian vassalage   30
Wannsee Conference   349
Warsaw Pact   259, 260
Warsaw Pact invasion   259, 295, 345, 357,
    360
WASA   305
  (see World Association of Slovaks Abroad)
Weismandel, Rabbi   221
Wekerle, Alexander   153, 163, 190
Wenceslaus II, King   50
Werboci, Stephen   58
Werke, Hermann Gohring   223
Wesselenyi, F.   71, 72
Western Church   22
White Mountain, Battle of   64, 70, 81, 318
  (see also Biela Hora, Battle of)
Wiching, Bishop of Nitra   24, 272, 273
Wilhelm, Duke   21
Wilson, President Woodrow   169, 189
Wilson, President Woodrow, Fourteen
  Points of   189, 190
Windischgratz, Prince   118, 119
Wittemburg University   65
Wladislas I, King   317
  (see also Wladyslaw III Jagiello, King of Poland)
Wladyslaw III Jagiello, King of Poland;
  Vladislav Jagelovský   317
  (see also Wladislas I, King)
Women's League   241

Workers' Party   243
World Association of Slovaks Abroad   305
  (see also WASA)
World War I   148, 164, 166, 175, 177, 209,
    227, 284, 285, 330, 331, 332, 333, 334,
    336, 338, 341, 361
  (see also First World War)
World War II   203, 212, 216, 230, 292,
    342–343, 348, 351–353, 363
  (see also Second World War)
Wycliffe, John   317
Young People's League   241
Zabojsky, Bishop;
  Ladislav Zábojský   136, 137
Zach, Frantisek;
  František Zach   114, 115, 120
Zapolsky, Jan; *Ján Zápoľský*   63, 64
Zatko, Peter; *Peter Zaťko*   227, 292
Zavodnik, Stefan; *Štefan Závodník*   126
Zay, Count Karol   103, 116, 326
Zechenter, Gustav; *Gustáv Kazimír*
  Zechenter-Laskomerský   129
Zelibsky, Jan; *Ján Želibský*   225
Zemplin   49, 55, 79, 106, 267, 269, 271,
    319, 324, 326
Zichy People's Party   154, 155
  (see also Neppart)
Zichy, Count Ferdinand   154
Zilina Agreement; *Žilina*   227, 235
Zilina Financial Aid Association;
  Žilina   177
Zilina, citadel at; *Žilina*   271
Zilina, Synod of; *Žilina*   66
Zingor, Viliam; *Viliam Žingor*   226, 241
Zionists   294
Zivena women's association;
  Živena   148, 152, 333
Zivena women's association, US;
  Živena   159
Zlkovce, primitive fort at; *Žlkovce*   264
Zmeskal, Zoltan; *Zoltán Zmeškal*   161
Zrinsky family; *Zrínsky*   72
Zvolen fortress   54